Roxanne Louiselle Parrott
Celeste Michelle Condit

editors

EVALUATING WOMEN'S HEALTH MESSAGES

A Resource Book

SAGE Publications
International Educational and Professional Publisher
Thousand Oaks   London   New Delhi

For information address:

SAGE Publications, Inc.
2455 Teller Road
Thousand Oaks, California 91320
E-mail: order@sagepub.com

SAGE Publications Ltd.
6 Bonhill Street
London EC2A 4PU
United Kingdom

SAGE Publications India Pvt. Ltd.
M-32 Market
Greater Kailash I
New Delhi 110 048 India

Printed in the United States of America

Library of Congress Cataloging-in-Publication Data

Main entry under title:

Evaluating women's health messages: A resourcebook / editors,
    Roxanne Louiselle Parrott and Celeste Michelle Condit.
        p.   cm.
    Includes bibliographical references and index.
    ISBN 0-7619-0056-X (cloth: acid-free paper).   —   ISBN 0-7619-0057-8
    (pbk.: acid-free paper)
        1. Generative organs, Female—Diseases—Research.   2. Sexism in
medicine.   3. Women—Health and hygiene—Sociological aspects.
4. Women—Health and hygiene—Research.   5. Health education of
women.   6. Mass media in health education.   7. Women's health
services—Social aspects.   I. Parrott, Roxanne.   II. Condit,
Celeste Michelle, 1956-   .
RG103.E93   1996
618—dc20   95-32514

This book is printed on acid-free paper.

96 97 98 99 10 9 8 7 6 5 4 3 2 1

Sage Production Editor: Astrid Virding

We dedicate this book to
Betty Jean Simmons Louiselle
and
Beatrice May Spencer Condit,
our Moms . . .

Contents

Preface

"Because now is the only time there ever is to do a thing in," said Miss Ophelia. "Come, now, here's paper, pen, and ink; just write a paper."
Harriet Beecher Stowe, *Uncle Tom's Cabin*[1]

Because medical research has not kept pace with technology and drug therapy in assessing outcomes for women, women's health demands our attention. Moreover, the messages communicated to women *and* men about women's health obscure this simple fact. This book provides the only existing collection that overviews the pattern of gaps among media, campaigns, and medical and social scientific information about women's reproductive health. For scholars, this volume offers the first systematic attempt to examine the medical, social scientific, and public messages about women's health care—juxtaposing them with one another to identify consistencies and inconsistencies, and highlighting gaps in the research and our understanding.

Two chapters have been devoted to each topic in this volume. The first chapter of each pair provides a critical summary of medical and/or social scientific research on the topic. These chapters describe the state of the research and reveal some of the problems with it. Social scientific research is included because of our commitment to a wholistic health care model, instead of a narrower medical care model. The second chapter in each pair provides a description and critical analysis of mass mediated messages women have been receiving in recent years about this medical research. Messages that are mediated by journalists receive most of the attention in these chapters, but messages that are part of popular books, television shows, and/or movies are described and analyzed where the authors thought them important.

This volume has been divided into six parts in relation to agendas and women's reproductive health: political, historical, campaign, fetal and maternal health, social support, and contemporary priorities. Within each of these arenas a number of specific topics are addressed, each with the presentation of two chapters. Discussions under the section that examines a political agenda include abortion and illicit drug use by pregnant women. The part of the book devoted to a historical agenda reviews birth control and childbirth. The section of the book devoted to a campaign agenda reviews prenatal care and cervical, ovarian, and uterine cancers. The fetal and maternal health agenda analyzes women and smoking, and women and alcohol use. The social support section of this volume considers research and messages associated with breast cancer and with menstruation and menopause. The closing part of the book evaluates reproductive health in terms of women and reproductive technologies, hysterectomy, and HIV/AIDS.

The authors of chapters that provide summaries and analyses of the "Medical and Social Scientific" discourse employed searches of indexes such as *Medline* and *Psychlit* to review both the available information and the key contentious issues over the past decade. These are followed by chapters that provide summaries and analyses of the public discourse, offering a far more systematic set of studies of such messages than is common in this area. Typically, critical descriptions of messages are done on an impressionistic basis. Those critical insights are, of course, valuable, but most of the chapters in this book ground the critical analyses in carefully designed surveys of texts. Authors have selected texts using random samples or full text sets from public indexes for the 3 to 5 years (approximately 1989-1993) surrounding the women's health initiative at the national policy level (this is discussed in more detail in Chapter 1). This helps the surveys to be more comprehensive and less prone to idiosyncratic selection biases than are other critical descriptions in the area.

The latter should not be taken to mean, however, that there is a rote-like uniformity to the studies presented in this volume. Different topics require somewhat different treatments, and the authors have brought their own perspectives and methodological strengths to these chapters—and sometimes they disagree with each other. Some of the authors who examine public messages have highlighted newspapers; others have focused on magazines. Some chapters concentrate on the medical literature; others spend more time on the social scientific studies. Each topic area itself deserves an entire book, and in many cases numerous books have been written about the topic. It is the differences and similarities among the chapters, however, that usefully reveal the broad range of needs that remain both in women's health care research and in the presentation of the messages that allow women to use the medical knowledge and technologies with informed decisions.

Many of you reading this volume will be wrestling with questions and decisions about your own reproduction. Many readers of this volume will have their own children and be wondering how to discuss human reproduction with them, especially at this time when nearly every day brings to light another moral or ethical question about such matters. In relation to the transmission of HIV, for example, information about condom use as a barrier may be viewed as unwarranted and even broaching immorality if individuals' religious principles promote sexual relations only between a married man and woman. Issues of reproductive technology include debate about the use of the eggs of an aborted fetus, the implantation of the egg from a woman of one race into the womb of a woman of another race, and whether or not menopausal women should be eligible to receive fertilized embryos. And for some, prenatal care programs, like access to health care generally, are deemed a benefit to be earned rather than a right that should be afforded.

Debate about human reproduction, we believe, is good and demonstrates fundamental principles upon which this nation is founded. To be actively involved in the debate, however, most of us turn to sources, both interpersonal and mediated, to help bridge our knowledge gaps. Physicians, themselves under significant time constraints and deluged with new medical and technological information published in their scientific journals, may sometimes be a source of information. Often, they provide pamphlets and other reading materials to patients who seek health information. National organizations such as the American Cancer Society and the March of Dimes also disseminate thousands of pieces of printed material to help us understand human reproduction. Newspapers, magazines, radio, and television provide additional grist for the mill. And, whatever we read, hear, or experience we are likely to share with the people closest to us, our family and friends, and vice versa. In the process of moving from scientific research to daily life, health messages change, sometimes without great deliberation and forethought. Significant details are lost, distorted, or added. Patterns in these shifts are the focus of this book.

The contents of this volume are aimed at nonacademicians and academicians alike. For individuals who are interested in reviewing what is presently known about matters relating to women's reproductive health alongside the public messages available in this area, the book's division into chapters addressing particular topics allows the reader to select the ones of most interest and supplement those with others at leisure. We hope that this book is well suited as a primary text in advanced courses in public health campaigns, health communication, and health or media message design or theory, as well as women's studies classes that address reproductive health issues. The book would also provide a supplementary text in similar courses or in a persuasive campaigns class. For health practitioners, the book provides a tool to use in understanding health-seeking behavior and patients' need for more personalized information, including specific guidelines about how to do and to attain behavioral recommendations. Most of the chapters that review bodies of research were reviewed by one or more physicians and/or epidemiologists to ensure that our own "translation" process is valid.

We appreciate the help of some very talented and dedicated doctoral students at the University of Georgia. Sally Caudill, Adrienne Fry, Michele Kilgore, Kim Kline, Raka

Shome, Stuart A. Ainsworth, Darci Slayten, Donald R. Turk, Tricia D. Stuart, and Melanie Williams provided many hours of time and effort to ensure that the countless references and citations used by the authors in this volume were complete and to proofread the galleys. We also thank Kris Bergstad for her excellent work copyediting a difficult manuscript. The contributors exceeded our expectations in providing the materials for this collection. In nearly every case, we have had to make editing choices to cut material from chapters to conform to our page limits. So, if a particular chapter warrants it, please contact the primary author, who may very well have an earlier, more extensive version of the work and/or an expanded reference list. Finally, we wish to thank Renée Piernot for her editorial assistance and Sophy Craze for the superior editorial work that allowed this book to move forward with alacrity after it had been stalled too long in the bureaucratic swamps of academic publishing. She deserves extraordinary thanks.

We enjoyed editing this volume and have learned a great deal from its contents. We hope that you will learn something as well and that the materials will generate debate.

—ROXANNE LOUISELLE PARROTT
—CELESTE MICHELLE CONDIT

Note

1. H. B. Stowe, *Uncle Tom's Cabin or Life Among the Lowly* (Garden City, NY: Nelson Doubleday, n.d.), p. 328. (Original work published 1852)

1

Introduction

Priorities and Agendas in Communicating About Women's Reproductive Health

Roxanne Louiselle Parrott
Celeste Michelle Condit

Each of us has the right and the responsibility to assess the roads which lie ahead.

Maya Angelou, *Wouldn't Take Nothing for My Journey Now,* p. 24[1]

Each human being lives by means of a vital but delicate interaction among thousands of hormones, nutrients, electrical pathways, genetic codes, and chemical structures. The sum of that elaborate biochemical dance constitutes our physical health. It is most precious to each of us. There is, however, a paradox about health for half of us in the United States, for even though women make up the primary patient load for health care professionals and are the major target of health care messages, men have been the primary subjects of medical research.[2]

Several explanations have been offered for the biological sex inequity in U.S. health care research. First, scientific research has traditionally been a male cultural experience, with men conducting the research and choosing to conduct it in relation to other men. Second, the predominant scientific method, which involves the testing of hypotheses about the relationships among two to four variables, attempts to control for differences. Women's lives include obvious and continuous biologic transitions, leading scientists to prefer to use men as research subjects, even when the medications and techniques being tested are designed for women.[3] Third, and the most often cited reason to exclude women from medical research study populations, is the potential for pregnancy. The possibility of causing harm to a fetus deters research for both moral and financial reasons. Fourth, funds for health care research are scarce, creating intense competition among all researchers, which brings the discussion full circle. Men have been primarily responsible for selecting the individuals who conduct the research and have granted preference to other men conducting research about men.[4]

When researchers do examine the effects of medical interventions on different groups of people, varied outcomes are found. Valium, for example, has been found to metabolize slower in older as compared to younger or middle-aged people; Asian Americans need less than half as much of one type of drug prescribed to control high blood pressure as do their Caucasian American counterparts.[5] Cardiovascular disease in females has been found to be responsive to even modest changes in lifestyle and diet; men have to work much harder for the same benefits.[6] Thus, differences *do* make a difference. Yet even with 49% of the more than 750,000 people who die each year of heart disease in this nation being women, almost no major clinical trials of drugs such as beta-blockers or surgeries such as angioplasty have been carried out on women.[7]

That women must be systematically included rather than excluded from medical research is a fundamental thesis of the women's health movement. Two priorities should guide efforts to achieve this aim: (a) Identify gaps in research about women's health; and (b) identify gaps in messages about women's health. This book seeks to contribute to these goals by presenting matched pairs of chapters on key women's health issues related to reproductive concerns. The book examines issues such as pregnancy, childbirth, abortion, AIDS, cancers, reproductive technologies, and chemical substance usage. In each case, the first chapter provides a survey of the available medical and social scientific research on the health topic and the second chapter then provides an analysis of the messages women receive about that health topic. There are many important gaps that become evident from these juxtapositions.

Gaps in Research About Women's Health

Since the birth of the contemporary women's movement, groups of feminist activists have been working to expand attention and information about health care for women. As a result, the National Institutes of Health formed an Office of Research on Women's Health, and Congress has begun to fund its projects.[8] A Women's Health Caucus formed in Congress and a woman-oriented political task force created in the Public Health Service (spearheaded by Representatives Patricia Shroeder and Olympia Snowe and Senator Barbara Mikulski)[9] published a report on women's health issues. Five criteria were identified to be used in categorizing a health condition or disease as a woman's issue for funding purposes:

1. unique to women or some subgroup of women;
2. more prevalent in women or some subgroup of women;
3. more serious in women or some subgroup of women;
4. one for which risk factors are different for women or some subgroup of women; and/or
5. one for which interventions are different for women or some subgroup of women.[10]

This book is consistent with these criteria. The first gap that should be noticed, however, is one created by these criteria themselves. These criteria peremptorily emphasize women's reproductive health, the most apparent area where women differ from men. This is a good start, for surely, reproductive health issues are important to women, and this book is focused at this beginning point. These, however, are not the only health focuses that demand our attention with regard to women. Moreover, as various chapters in this book reveal, this focus can also create problems for women. It may perpetuate the tendency to treat women as distinctive and important only because of their reproductive capacities. As the chapters on drugs, AIDS, alcohol, and tobacco in this volume reveal, a focus on reproduction tends to place the woman as a vessel who should provide a safe haven for the fetus, rather than to treat the woman as important in her own right. These chapters demonstrate that reproductive health research and health messages tend to focus on fetal health rather than on the health of the woman herself.

These chapters also reveal another potential problem with the focus on reproductive health. The flurry of research about women's reproductive health breeds the following paradox: men have babies, too, and the focus on women's reproductive health in relation to fetal health ignores the interaction of effects on the fetus owing to the father's behavior. Thus, even as great strides and significant accomplishments mount in relation to women's health, deficits in understanding and in the direction of research may perpetuate knowledge gaps if only research identified as uniquely relevant to women qualifies for study.

The chapters herein suggest a variety of other concerns about the conduct of medical and social scientific research into women's reproductive health. Many of these concerns are unique to specific topics. However, another pattern that cuts across chapters is the tendency of medical research and practice to focus exclusively on technology. There are insufficient clinical trials of non-technologically intensive practices, such as using nurse midwives to provide prenatal care, having in-home births, or performing breast self-examination. Instead, the clinical trials that are funded and performed focus primarily on the safety and effectiveness of technological aids (e.g., chorionic villus sampling—CVS; mammography). As a consequence, the utility of non-technological health care approaches remains "unproven." The classification as "unproven" becomes equated with "unsafe," and such approaches are, therefore, not applied, whether or not they are safer than other approaches.

Clinical trials of non-technological approaches to health need to be funded and pursued with rigor equal to that for high-technology medicine. Then, medical personnel and campaign practitioners need to adhere to the research results, or at least to present them clearly and plainly to women, so that women can make their own choices. Our chapters suggest that this is not happening. Even where research indicates that medical interventions and/or high-technology approaches are not superior, there may still be a tendency for doctors to feel more comfortable using them. As Nelson's chapter suggests, for example, physicians continue to rely on episiotomy, even though the research does not support its efficacy. Doctors generally do not even give women the chance for an informed choice on its use. Prenatal care includes weighing the woman at every checkup, although this practice, too, may cause more harm than good.

In addition to these broad gaps, individual chapters address specific gaps in our understanding of specific health conditions. We hope that identifying these gaps helps to spur research in these areas. It must be recognized, however, that even if medical research were perfect, women's health care might be grievously problematic if women receive faulty messages about their health.

Identifying Gaps in Messages About Women's Health

Although the problems in medical research on women have received substantial media attention of late, and have even already fostered a backlash,[11] far less public attention has been directed at the quality of the messages women receive about their health. These messages, however, are crucial. Medical care is not something that can be "provided" to women, because each woman must care for her own body. Not only must women act on doctors' orders, but they also must coordinate their health care, decide when to seek out a doctor, monitor their own nutrition, and exercise their body.

As a nation, we struggle to move away from a hospital-based model of acute medical care in which authority figures deliver services to sick persons, toward a wholistic model of health care in which people use their own judgment, along with technical advice from a range of experts, to make decisions about their health as an integral component of their lives. This move is made necessary not only in view of the broad range of research indicating the interrelation of all the factors in one's life upon one's health, but in view of limited societal resources to provide services and care. Having learned that occupational stress, exercise, nutrition, and environment all influence health, along with genetics and microbes, health care is no longer a service to be delivered like auto repair, and health messages must reflect this fact.

Medical science discovers generalities and probabilities, describes risks and trade-offs, and may make advice and techniques accessible, but it cannot make the value decisions necessary to choose among these techniques. The health care messages women receive contain important value messages, and these are sometimes problematic. The health campaigns that address breast cancer, for example, have been plagued with mixed messages, leading to confusion and perpetuating the notion that cancer is a death sentence rather than a chronic disease that may be treated and monitored while the patient continues to live. The debate about breast cancer detection methods—in terms of how often and when to begin this practice—often leaves women confused about whether or not to seek a mammogram, and how often to seek screening (see Part V in this volume).

In other instances, health messages are simply designed to increase audience awareness about prevention and detection of illness and disease. Social scientific research has firmly established the need to provide more than preachments about proper behavior.[12] Successful campaigns need behavioral components that show women *how* to achieve the desired goals within a framework of their own experiences. When people feel they can take part in decisions and do something to ameliorate problems, it gives them a feeling of autonomy.[13]

Mass media can be effective in conveying such messages, which may contribute to physical and mental well-being.[14] To attain these goals, however, messages must focus on women and their perceptions of self-efficacy in specific situations, encompassing the experiences of women that the messages aim to address. Health care messages often ignore women or are inappropriately focused in a variety of ways. Juxtaposing medical and social scientific literature with popular messages allows one to assess the "translation" process that is going on with regard to women's health care, pointing to three patterns that contribute to discontinuities: (a) Health care *is* contested; (b) health care providers (still mostly men) are identified as right, putting women in the often unwarranted position of being wrong; and (c) not all messages are created equal.

HEALTH CARE *IS* CONTESTED: RESIST ABSOLUTISM

Anyone who attempts to stay informed and to keep abreast of developments in women's reproductive health is probably a bit bewildered and vexed. There are multiple approaches to any issue, and women's health care does not escape this diversity of perspectives. "Health care" is often assumed to be a science. Sciences are supposed to offer certain knowledge and clear answers. As the majority of the topics in the area of women's reproductive health make clear, however, this is a false impression. Many health care studies, and particularly those regarding women's health, are controversial. Various subject populations, assumptions, and operationalizations produce different results.

When faced with conflicting results, health care providers may judge the validity and reliability of the research for themselves and take a position (presenting it to women as absolute information or the only option); present alternative findings to women for discussion and consideration; or ignore the research altogether while waiting until the contested grounds appear to be more settled. Providers may also simply be unaware of various viewpoints. The fact is that we know practically nothing about what health care providers do in this regard because too little research has been done in the area of examining conversations providers have with patients about making health care decisions, or asking providers how they decide to present more or less information to patients.

What these chapters do reveal about the effects of the fact that health care is contested is that sources providing the media coverage about these issues often depend upon experts to assist in the presentation of information to the general public. Thus, one filter through which messages about women's health pass is the filter of particular experts' own points of view; the limits of their knowledge limit the presentation. Some women in particular will be affected by this, as women who are already more disenfranchised—poor, illiterate, nonwhite, noncitizen—are less likely to share the provider's worldview and also less likely to question the provider's recommendation.

Women must consider how diagnosis and treatment plans are presented to them and resist the urge to seek absolute statements about causes and effects. Women should understand that such decisions are dependent upon a whole host of factors and accept such uncertainty, while at the same time attempting to understand both the settled grounds—such as the fact that both men's and women's behavior prior to conception affects fetal health outcomes—and the unsettled grounds. As a result, there should be less likelihood of either accepting or promoting a pattern all too common in the messages about women's health—one that suggests physicians are right and women are wrong, in their behavior, attitudes, or understanding.

MEDICAL MEN AND WRONGFUL WOMEN

Subtle cultural values play key roles in the general treatment of women and doctors. As a rule, health care messages portray doctors—who are generally represented as being male—favorably, whereas women are often blamed for their behaviors and predicaments, or are ignored. Stories about women's health that appear in newspapers, for example, inform readers about research findings and ongoing programs, including who funds them, eligibility requirements, program costs, and outcomes for both women and the general public. To tell these tales, newspapers select particular sources and content.

One review of the way that newspapers report about prenatal care programs in the United States found that the projected users of such programs—pregnant women themselves—are seldom quoted, yet the administrators of such programs and the physicians providing the services are frequently quoted.[15] The physicians are often depicted as benevolent caregivers, volunteering their time in the face of already being overworked. Women, when they appear at all in the first person in these stories, are depicted as dependent, helpless, and even hopeless. The institutions providing the care could be cast in those very same terms, for they depend upon a certain caseload of women to sustain their existence, are helpless in the face of budget cuts, and may even be described as hopeless in terms of the bureaucracy enacted as part of the delivery of services.

In those few cases where blame might be cast on doctors, physicians may attempt to treat errors as though they were the fault of individual "bad" doctors, rather than considering whether institutional forces or professional norms provided causes, as in the use of reproductive technology (see C. Condit, Chapter 23, this volume) or AIDS research (see Cline & McKenzie, Chapter 26, this volume). Moreover, organizations such as the American Cancer Society "routinely discredit doctors who study 'unproven' causes of cancer—such as environmental carcinogens."[16]

In contrast to the way that physicians often represent themselves and their knowledge, women who seek health care and are found to have health care problems are sometimes, although not uniformly, treated as incompetent, emotional, or immoral. For example, reports about infertility (see C. Condit, Chapter 23, this volume) and hysterectomy (see Sefcovic, Chapter 25, this volume) reveal cases in which women were portrayed as emotionally unbalanced. Reports about hysterectomy also reveal treatment of women as though they were immoral. When women are not being blamed for their health problems, they may simply be ignored—a powerful message in and of itself, as previously discussed in terms of the design and implementation of medical research and campaign messages. In response, women should adopt a critical lens when evaluating health messages and consider what the underlying intentions associated with particular presentations might be—the maintenance of status and authority, or the maintenance of the woman's own good health.

ALL HEALTH MESSAGES ARE NOT CREATED EQUAL

Locating the repeated biases in modes of delivering messages may assist media consumers in becoming media literate, granting the skills necessary to "read" health care messages in a critical and productive fashion.[17] Each media form has strengths and weaknesses. Each should be supplemented with others, depending upon the user's goals, as these sources act as useful "translators" for women, but in every translation process decisions are made about what is important and what is not; what evidence is credible and what is not; what women might value and what they might disregard.

In every translation process, moreover, some meaning is lost due to the inequivalence of expression; some words may simply have no equivalent expression in the lay language to which a technical scientific message is converted. Newspapers react quickly to breaking developments. That makes them useful for "keeping current." They are also among the least reliable sources, however, often providing conflicting reports based on the same information (see Daniels & Parrott, Chapter 15, this volume). Newspapers operate for profit, and they have their own "news values" (see Kilgore, Chapter 17, this volume). These values are not designed to convey maximally valid and reliable information to health care consumers.

Because newspapers are interested in what is new, exciting, and controversial, they do not provide coverage over a sustained period. The press tired easily and early of covering the interaction of pregnancy and smoking (see D. Condit, Chapter 11, this volume) and the overreliance on hysterectomy (see Sefcovic, Chapter 25, this volume). These are messages that women need to hear continuously, but in the press, the messages are here today and gone tomorrow. The focus on "breaking developments" leads newspapers to *telescope findings*. They often present the results of a single study as though it summarized all knowledge in a field of research. Medical knowledge is not equivalent to single studies. It takes an accumulation of studies, pursuing different angles, populations, and conditions, to explain health phenomena and to locate effective treatments. In their effort to hype the importance of the studies they report, newspapers may mislead readers into concluding that a single study "proves" that a certain treatment is desirable. Readers should not rely on singular press accounts to decide whether or not to favor a particular course of treatment or prevention.

For related reasons, the newspaper media routinely display a *pro-technology bias*. An examination of news messages about cancers of the womb show the media portraying technological developments as wonderful magic (see Kilgore, Chapter 17, this volume). The same trend is evident in reproductive technologies (see C. Condit, Chapter 23, this volume) and hysterectomy coverage (see Sefcovic, Chapter 25, this volume). News values may drive reporters to overrate and overhype "high-tech" solutions. Careful screening for such "technoboosterism" by readers, planning by campaigners to account for it, and avoidance by responsible reporters should reduce belief in and reliance on such reports.

Hype and interest are best generated through *dramatization*, and newspapers tend to dramatize events in ways that may misrepresent the medical findings. An examination of birth technologies shows that the use of singular dramatic stories constructs midwives as unusual and undesirable (see Sterk, Chapter 9, this volume). An examination of reproductive technologies shows that the use of one-sided dramas constructs IVF (in vitro fertilization) as though it were a happy and successful technique for most women (see C. Condit, Chapter 23, this volume). This can even extend to blaming women, as stories about drug use and pregnancy suggest (see Kline, Chapter 5, this volume) or about women and AIDS (see Cline & McKenzie, Chapter 26, this volume).

In many ways, magazines are similar to newspapers in terms of their strengths and weaknesses as a source of health information. Magazines are interested in making a profit and therefore need to be dramatic and timely, but tend to be more balanced and informative than newspapers. Even better than magazines in this regard, however, are books. Any woman making a serious health decision should locate and read books on the subject. Books have the space to provide more thorough and balanced information. Still, not all books are created equal. Therefore, readers must remember the injunction to "get both sides of the story." Locate books that are written by traditional providers and researchers, plus books that are written by respectable critics of the tradition. Campaign designers might consider incorporating references and access to books as a component in campaigns, but only if target audiences are likely to be readers. Newspaper reporters, too, could rely more on books to provide relatively condensed backgrounds about health issues, which might reduce misleading "telescoping." Book reviews are useful resources for locating books that represent multiple views on a topic. One disadvantage of books, however, is that they are quickly outdated, although the computer age has greatly enhanced the turnaround time for publications.

Pamphlets provide an interesting halfway house between books and newspapers. They are generally constructed by well-informed groups that have concentrated on a single issue. They may be issued by physicians' groups such as dermatologists, by nonprofit health groups such as the March of Dimes, or by government agencies such as the National Cancer Institute. Pamphlets are especially useful for providing referrals on major and immediate health issues (such as a decision to have a hysterectomy or how to treat cancer) and for providing information on less immediately pressing health issues (such as the effects of alcohol or smoking). All the same, there are problems with pamphlets, too. These include failure to deliver to target audiences the existence of biases in the source that prepares them, and the failure to generate adequate pamphlets on a host of subjects.

Entertainment media and advertising are sources that carry particularly subtle value messages. They reinforce the sense that menstruation should be treated as an embarrassing secret (see Part V) and that the only safe place for childbirth is a hospital (see Part II). Health campaigners, reporters, and women must take these social messages into account when making health choices. When health information is presented on television news stories, the emphasis is on the visual quality, with drama and action, together with an abbreviation of themes influencing the construction of the report. Researchers have shown that in order to receive extensive television coverage, a social issue must be contrasted with the status quo to indicate a shift, be consequential for a large number of people, be defined as affecting at least 10% of the population, show victims, and provide a place to put blame.[18] A metaphor such as a wave will be used to give the issue symbolic meaning, whereas prior crises of a similar nature will be ignored.[19]

In general, then, three considerations should be held foremost in an analysis of gaps in the messages about women's health. First, health care is contested, so messages that appear to contradict one another may actually be based on the findings of medical research. Women should not insist upon absolute answers to health questions, as psychologically uncomfortable as such uncertainty may be. Insisting that a health care provider mandate solutions or regimens reinforces an all-too-prevalent situation, physicians as incontrovertible authorities and women as dependent upon their medical wisdom, a second consideration in the analysis of health care messages. Third, in a world as media dependent as ours, becoming media literate—gaining the ability to understand and locate the strengths and weaknesses of various delivery modes—constitutes an important responsibility, enabling and empowering the user to gain the most from an information-rich age.

Conclusion

Considering the medical and social scientific literature alongside media messages about health available to the general public serves several purposes. First, a description of the state of the medical and social scientific knowledge about key reproductive health care issues provides women with insights about the status of such research, a basis from which to ask questions, form opinions, and make decisions. Second, a comparison of the relationships between the current state of medical discourse, and the medical "findings" and evaluations thereof, demonstrates the importance of women actively and critically evaluating the information received about their reproductive health. The comparison highlights systematic translation biases that occur between the two areas.

Each woman must decide for herself what set of trade-offs she wishes to make in relation to her health, and which sources she believes to be most accurate and honest in helping her to be informed to make these decisions. The ability to decipher health information is not a simple one to attain, as disparity runs to the very basics of medical research design. Health research is done on people who are relatively healthy. Medical subjects must be well-fed, sheltered, and free of secondary diseases, despite the fact that the recipients of the medical care certified by these procedures are not necessarily well-fed, sheltered, and free of secondary diseases. The impact of the medicines and technologies on many people is bound to be different from the effects observed in research subjects.

Problems of targeting health messages to nonmainstream groups and of providing health care itself are similar manifestations of a focus on a hypothetical individual patient instead of the social conditions of health care in use. Hence, the messages aimed at the treatment of individual health should be placed in larger social contexts more rigorously and more regularly. It is always important to ask oneself what "the other side" of the story may be.

On the other hand, conflict for conflict's sake can be taken too far. As the messages on breast cancer hint, the mass media love a good conflict, sometimes at the expense of getting to the substance of the debate. By emphasizing the conflict about the age at which women should begin to get regular mammography, medical professionals and the media may discourage women from getting a health screening that might save their life. There is a continual struggle in health care research to define what the settled grounds are and which grounds are contested.

Perhaps most promising is the simple fact that there presently exists a lively public discussion about the nature and treatment of women in medical research and health care that quite simply was unavailable not so long ago. The priorities for this debate should be considered within a framework of the agendas, both public and "hidden," that affect present circumstances. These agendas reflect political and historical interests, social action and commercial campaign foci, fetal and maternal health hypotheses, social support considerations, and contemporary research questions—each competing for the direction that women's health research will take, as the content of the chapters in this book illustrate.

Readers, campaigners, and researchers should take neither conflict nor the absence of conflict for granted. Discovering what the best information available is always requires contact with more than one opinion. Fortunately, a wide variety of media and interpersonal sources are available to facilitate one's search. In the final analysis, communicating about women's reproductive health depends upon an individual information seeker's willingness to examine the priorities that led to the information and whose agenda such priorities served. Through such analysis, individuals will be better able to achieve "their right to know."

Notes

1. M. Angelou, *Wouldn't Take Nothing for My Journey Now* (New York: Random House, 1993): 24.

2. National Women's Health Network (NWHN), *Research to Improve Women's Health: An Agenda for Equity* (Washington, DC: Author, 1991).

3. See, for example, J. S. Gavaler, "Effects of Alcohol on Female Endocrine Function," *Alcohol Health & Research World* 15 (1991): 104-108.

4. NWHN, *Research to Improve Women's Health.*

5. P. Cotton, "Is There Still Too Much Extrapolation From Data on Middle-Aged White Men?" *Journal of the American Medical Association* 263 (1991): 1050.

6. J. Sachs, "Heart-Healthy Relaxation," *Savvy* (November 1991): 128.

7. B. J. Culliton, "NIH Push for Women's Health," *Nature* 353 (1991): 383.

8. L. R. Monroe, "Women's Health Gains Priority: Pressure in Congress Pays Off in Major New Research Funding," *Atlanta Journal & Constitution,* May 10, 1992, p. D10.

9. NWHN, *Research to Improve Women's Health,* 13.

10. U.S. DHHS PHS, *Women's Health: Report of the PHS Task Force on Women's Health Issues* 2 (1985): 58.

11. A. G. Kadar, M.D., "The Sex-Bias Myth in Medicine," *Atlantic Monthly* (August 1994): 66-70.

12. See, for example, E. Maibach, J. Flora, & C. Nass, "Changes in Self Efficacy and Health Behavior in Response to a Minimal Contact Community Health Campaign," *Health Communication* 3 (1991): 1-16.

13. K. Whitehorn, "The Use of the Media in the Promotion of Mental Health," *International Journal of Mental Health* 18 (1990): 40-46.

14. Whitehorn, "The Use of the Media," 45.

15. R. Parrott & M. Daniels, "Prenatal Policies and Practices: Organizing Care for Women or Women to Receive Care?" (manuscript submitted for publication, 1995).

16. S. S. Epstein, *The Politics of Cancer* (San Francisco: Sierra Club Books, 1978): 82.

17. H. Karl, "Media Literacy: The Right to Know," *English Journal* 63 (October 1974): 7-9.

18. D. L. Altheide, "The Impact of Television News Formats on Social Policy," *Journal of Broadcasting & Electronic Media* 35 (Winter 1991): 3-21.

19. Altheide, "The Impact," 17.

PART I

Political Agendas and Women's Reproductive Health Messages

For it is precisely because certain groups have no representation in a number of recognized political structures that their position tends to be so stable, their oppression so continuous.

Kate Millett, *Sexual Politics*, p. 24[1]

The first part of this book acknowledges the role that politics plays in the process of constructing the messages that women receive about reproductive health. That role is at least twofold, with these effects being interdependent and interwoven with other agendas driving health research and messages about the same. First, politics determines what topics will be formally discussed, debated, and included in (as well as what will be excluded from) the public record. Second, politics determines who and what will be funded with the taxpayers' monies. It is no accident that the attention that women's health has received in terms of funding and messages parallels an increase in the election of women to Congress. These outcomes highlight the need to be circumspect about what decision makers rule out by ruling in particular political agendas in lieu of others.

The issues brought to the representative bodies governing this nation impact our lives in many untold ways, and one goal of this book, as represented by the chapters in this opening section, is to provoke thought and conversation about this truth in relation to women's health and the care that we receive. No better illustration of the validity of the statement that politics affects the conduct of medical research and women's health can be found than the topic of abortion. When a candidate announces the decision to seek the office of President of the United States, a position on abortion will be one of the first statements capturing the waves of televised sound bites. Nominees for the U.S. Supreme Court and the Surgeon General must also make public declarations about their views on abortion. Candidates for these offices have managed to sidestep several other value-laden issues, such as extra-marital affairs and sexual harassment, but beliefs about abortion—or, at least, a public statement about these beliefs—are mandated.

Miller deftly reviews the competing voices in the political debate about abortion. She highlights the impact that political authority has, not only on whether or not research on women and abortion gets done in the first place, but whether or not such research is considered to be "scientifically sound." Small sample sizes and a host of differences between and among women characterize much of the work done in the abortion arena, making the charge that we know nothing far too easy to support within a framework of usual criteria for judging these matters. Yet if the usual foundational claim that what is known must be representative of all women evolves to an assumption that to know something about some women, and another thing about other women is more "scientifically sound" anyway, then we have a whole other kind of science going on. For, as Miller reviews, we have gained important insights about women's health (although, certainly, gaps remain in our understanding) based on the research that has been done relating to abortion.

The messages available to women about abortion clearly emphasize the superior status afforded fetal health as compared to maternal health, with the discourse barely and only rarely mentioning women's health in relation to abortion. The messages generally available to women represent abortion as a decision in which the primary consideration is a comparison and contrast of choice versus no choice. The messages often construct choice narrowly and negatively. According to such messages, affective considerations or cognitive decisions about a woman's personal health history appear to have no place in guiding a woman's behavior. These messages offer little or no discussion about the health impacts of abortion for women, except in reference to back-alley butchers, limiting discussion of physical and/or mental consequences of abortion to extreme negative outcomes and further reinforcing a maternal focus rather than a woman-centered approach.

More recent than the abortion issue, research and reporting about drug use and pregnant women in many ways parallels the effects of politics on women's health demonstrated in the abortion arena. Disputes over access define these issues. Access consists minimally of both availability and eligibility. To argue that a rural area needs a hospital is an access issue in terms of availability. To argue that rural citizens' lower socioeconomic status decreases the likelihood that they will have health insurance to cover preventive exams such as mammograms is an eligibility issue. Usually, both parts of the equation must be satisfied if an environment is actually to support the receipt of health care.

As Lemieux points out in the chapter about drug use and the pregnant woman, more dollars must be allocated and more support given to providing *access* to drug cessation and treatment programs for pregnant women to promote the health and well-being of both the woman and the fetus. Placing emphasis on the woman's *access* to illicit drugs interrupts the process at a different point in the causal chain, but may also deter the woman who is already pregnant and drug dependent from seeking prenatal care. It also creates the impression that these women are not deserving and, therefore, should not be *eligible* for public support. These latter effects are particularly likely if a woman views or reads televised or newspaper stories about pregnancy and illegal drug use, as Kline points out.

Ironically, the very emphasis being given to pregnancy and drug use originated with a political hearing before the Select Committee on Children, Youth, and Families of the 99th Congressional House of Representatives during the second session, at which time Chasnoff, a professor of Pediatrics and Psychiatry at Northwestern University Medical School in Chicago, asserted that, "It is erroneously believed by many women that the placenta acts as a barrier protecting the fetus from various toxic substances taken by the mother during pregnancy."[2] Rather than leading to a focus on informing women about their bodies, such information engineered efforts to adopt policies and pass laws to restrain and restrict pregnant women. These actions do little or nothing to increase our understanding of women's health, to promote women's health, or—for that matter—to promote fetal health. They appear generally to be mostly a matter of political posturing and should be recognized as such. They certainly do not increase a woman's access to health care and health information, or support the skills necessary to adopt or change behavior.

Thus, this opening section suggests a call to political action for all women who seek greater understanding about reproductive health. Two case studies—abortion and drug use during pregnancy—offer illustrations of how political agendas affect the focus of the questions undertaken in medical research, which in turn offers the content for reports in the media, which can in turn focus the priorities of elected representatives. A single picture of a writhing baby born drug dependent captures the hearts and minds of countless Americans who are moved to tell their elected officials to prevent such tragedies.

What can be done to counter the influence of political agendas on medical research and women's health care? At a minimum, register to vote . . . and vote. Also, consider the influence that politics has on medical research and media messages to which you are exposed. The nonprofit organization, National Women's Health Network, based in Washington, D.C., provides another avenue to keep track of what women's health issues are being debated and which elected representatives to contact in order to be heard. Quite simply, we are a nation founded on knowledge built out of such action.

Notes

1. K. Millett, *Sexual Politics* (Garden City, NY: Doubleday, 1970): 24.
2. I. Chasnoff. Statement. (Hearing before the Select Committee on Children, Youth, and Families; House of Representatives, 99th Congress, 2nd session, 1986): 12-20.

2

Medical and Psychological Consequences of Legal Abortion in the United States

Diane Helene Miller

On July 30, 1987, at a briefing for Right-to-Life leaders, President Ronald Reagan asked Surgeon General C. Everett Koop to initiate a study on the medical and psychological consequences of legal abortion in the United States. Reagan claimed that he was concerned about women's lack of access to health information regarding this very commonly performed surgery. He therefore asked Koop to review existing studies and meet with scientific, medical, psychological, and public health experts, as well as representatives of pro-choice and pro-life organizations, about the issue of abortion's health risks. As Koop himself later reports, the idea for the study had been suggested to the President by conservative aide Dinesh D'Souza, like Reagan a strong opponent of legalized abortion. Koop himself was an outspoken opponent of abortion, and so D'Souza believed that the evidence Koop would report would be so damaging as to permit overturning *Roe v. Wade,* which had been defended in part based on issues of women's health.[1]

Two years and $200,000 later, Koop sent a letter to President Reagan in which he declined to issue his report. In the letter, he told the President that all of the 250 studies he had reviewed were methodologically flawed, and none could be considered reliable enough to produce any scientifically defensible conclusions. Koop determined that, "the available scientific evidence about the psychological sequelae of abortion simply cannot support either the preconceived beliefs of those pro-life or of those pro-choice." Koop later complained that the first press release by a wire service "completely misinterpreted my letter to the President. The release implied that there was no evidence of health effects post-abortion, rather than saying there was insufficient scientific and statistical evidence on which to base an unimpeachable report."[2]

In lieu of his report, Koop offered advice: The President should authorize a scientifically sound government study on the consequences of abortion, ideally to be conducted over a period of 5 years at a cost of $100 million. Failing that, Koop suggested that a lesser but still satisfactory study could be produced over the same period with the more reasonable price tag of $10 million. To date, such a governmental study has not been attempted, although other organizations have produced smaller, less costly studies. In addition, later that same year the report that Koop and his staff had prepared but declined to release was released to Congress (at the demand of Representative Ted Weiss, Chair of the Human Resources and Intergovernmental Relations Subcommittee of the House Committee on Government Operations), and a hearing was held on the contents of the report.

The Surgeon General's report had been long awaited, no doubt with some eagerness on the part of pro-life forces and equal trepidation by pro-choice advocates. The story behind this incident and the reception of the Surgeon General's letter offers an unusually vivid example of the ways in which the two sides of this debate adjusted quickly to make the facts fit their political views. Pro-choice forces interpreted the lack of evidence to indicate a lack of problems from abortion. Conversely, pro-life forces felt that the report validated their suspicions that the most common post-abortion reaction is deep and lasting denial. In their interpretation, the absence of evidence in these studies (all of which looked only at post-abortion effects in the short term, generally within 1 year after abortion) confirmed their belief that the experience of abortion is so traumatic and the "real" psychological effects of abortion are so powerful that they are often suppressed until years or even decades later. The government's assertion that medical studies provided no unassailable answers was accepted by both sides as an invitation to shift the medical debate to the public forum, where both sides seemed to feel it could better be resolved, or at least where they could maintain a greater degree of control over what sort of information would reach the public.

The issue of control over the "facts" lay at the heart of the debate from its inception. The administration's interest in the issue arose, ostensibly, from a concern for women's health. The President's stated intent was to provide women with information so that they could make better choices about their health. Barely masked (because the directive for the report was issued in a Right-to-Life briefing) was the politically motivated attempt to use women's health as a smoke screen for pursuing the ends of a pro-life administration.

The visibility of political interests is only one of several ways that abortion differs from most women's health issues. Abortion is not heavily dependent upon hospitals in the way that many other women's health care procedures are, because only 13% of all abortions are performed in hospitals.[3] In addition, there has been no independent social action campaign aimed at changing the attitudes or behaviors of women as health care consumers. Information about the health aspects of abortion is often presented to the public only in conjunction with particular political agendas, and even claims made by the medical community are often suspected of being politically motivated.

In this context, it is admittedly difficult to distinguish politics from medicine. Nevertheless, published medical studies of the physical and psychological effects of abortion in the years following Koop's report evidence a perhaps surprising degree of agreement and consistency, surprising because of the continuing volatility of the debate in the public forum and the continuing reluctance of many doctors to perform abortions. This chapter will present an overview of current scientific perspectives on both the most visible issues of abortion as a women's health issue and on those aspects of the issue that remain nearly invisible to the public eye. It will supplement this information with critiques from outside the medical community that present women's health care concerns related to abortion that have been overlooked or ignored in medical research. In order to understand the evolution of discussion on these issues, however, it is first necessary to examine the influence of the legal arena on the medical issues.

THE LEGAL CONTEXT OF ABORTION

On January 22, 1973, the Supreme Court's landmark *Roe v. Wade* decision affirmed women's legal right to choose abortion. In the years since the Supreme Court enacted *Roe v. Wade,* subsequent decisions have modified that ruling. The Hyde Amendment of 1977 weakened the assertion of women's right to choose by allowing Congress to prohibit federal Medicaid funding for abortions. In *Belotti v. Baird* in 1979, the Court affirmed that parental notification or consent laws were constitutional, provided that an alternative—usually a hearing before a judge—was available.

In what was considered by many to be the most damaging case against abortion rights, the Court's 1989 *Webster v. Reproductive Health Services* decision extended the state's right to restrict abortion in the interest of the fetus throughout a woman's pregnancy, rather than only at the point of viability. In their decision, a majority of justices argued that the interest of the state did not "come into existence only at the point of viability. . . . The State's interest, if compelling after viability, is equally compelling before viability."[4] By failing to strike down a Missouri abortion statute, the Court affirmed the state's right to prohibit abortions in public facilities or in private hospitals receiving public funds, as well as discarding the trimester system established in *Roe v. Wade*. Perhaps most detrimental to *Roe* was that the Court refused to speak against "the legislative finding that 'life begins at conception.' "[5] This decision suggested that the Court might legalize restrictions on abortion that it had previously struck down, including spousal notification or consent laws, waiting periods for women requesting abortions, requiring physicians to give women unrequested information about the developing fetus, or requiring that all abortions after the first trimester be performed in hospitals even in the absence of a medical reason for doing so.

Throughout the late 1980s and into the early 1990s, those who wished to see the *Roe* decision reversed appeared to be gaining ground. In *Rust v. Sullivan,* the Supreme Court upheld a policy written by the Reagan administration that enacted a "gag rule," preventing physicians or counselors in publicly funded clinics from providing any information about abortion even if women specifically requested it. Other proposed laws have attempted to prevent publicly funded hospitals from providing abortions, effectively prohibiting abortions for women whose risk of complications would necessitate the medical facilities only a hospital could offer, as well as for those women on public aid whose health plans would only pay for procedures performed in a public hospital. Because Medicaid funding for abortion has been restricted in all but 13 states, many poor women are simply unable to afford legal abortions.[6] To understand the medical ramifications of these legal decisions, one must first understand the various procedures used to perform abortions, and how the risks involved in abortion vary at different stages in a woman's pregnancy.

ABORTION PROCEDURES

The method used to perform an abortion is dependent largely on the stage of the pregnancy, as measured from the first day of the last normal menstrual period. In the United States, more than half of all abortions take place in the first 8 weeks of pregnancy, and 91% of all abortions are considered "early" abortions, performed in the first trimester of pregnancy (within the first 12 weeks). More than 96% of all abortions take place during the first 15 weeks of pregnancy. Most of these abortions are performed by a method known as vacuum aspiration, which involves dilating the cervix, inserting a tube (known as a cannula) into the uterus, and using suction to draw out the contents of the uterus through the tube. This procedure lasts only 5 minutes and can be performed up to 14 weeks of pregnancy. It is usually done with a local anesthetic, although it can also be done with a general anesthetic at the patient's request. Vacuum aspiration is usually performed in an abortion clinic or a doctor's office, and occasionally in a hospital.

Abortions performed in the second or third trimester are rare; only one half of 1% take place past 20 weeks, and 0.01% take place after 24 weeks. Such abortions require more difficult procedures involving an increased risk of complications, and so are more often performed in hospitals. Dilation (also called dilatation) and Evacuation (D&E) is the method most commonly used in second-trimester abortions. A D&E requires dilating the cervix over a period of several hours, or sometimes overnight. The physician then uses a suction machine and, if necessary, forceps to ensure that all contents of the uterus are removed. Once the cervix is dilated, the D&E takes 10 minutes or less. Ninety-five percent of abortions in the United States are performed using either the vacuum aspiration or D&E method.

Many of the remaining abortions that take place late in the second trimester are performed by the induction method. In this procedure, an abortion-causing liquid (originally saline, more recently a class of drugs called prostaglandins) is injected through the abdomen into the amniotic sac around the fetus. The liquid induces contractions that cause the cervix to dilate, and the woman expels the fetus and placenta. The contractions are painful and can last several hours. This method must be performed in a hospital, usually with a combination of local anesthesia and painkillers. Although this list of procedures does not exhaust the options for abortion, these are the most frequently discussed options in the medical literature.

Medical Consequences

The health aspects of abortion fall into two broad categories, both of which can be considered in terms of both short- and long-term effects. *Physical sequelae* refer to medical risks up to and including death, whereas *psychological sequelae* encompass the emotional and psychological effects of abortion on women who undergo the procedure (although the term is often extended to refer to purported effects on the woman's boyfriend, husband, or other family members).

PHYSICAL SEQUELAE

By far the largest body of research on physical sequelae to abortion refers to studies of women undergoing first-trimester abortion. In fact, there is little dispute among the published studies that first-trimester abortions are not only safe, but are in fact safer for the woman than carrying her pregnancy to term. During Congressional testimony, a representative of the Centers for Disease Control (CDC) concurred with a 1987 article in the *American Journal of Public Health* that put the risk of death at 25 times greater for childbirth than for abortion.[7] The risk of death from abortion was estimated as less than 1 death per 100,000 procedures, or "less than the risk of death from an injection of penicillin."[8]

The Centers for Disease Control's Abortion Surveillance report of September 4, 1992, noted 10 deaths in 1986 and six deaths in 1987 attributed to legal induced abortions, or case-fatality rates of 0.8/100,000 and 0.4/100,000 respectively. The 1987 rate represents the lowest rate of maternal death since the CDC began its surveillance of legal abortion in 1972.[9] A 1990 Fact Sheet from the National Abortion Federation (NAF) estimates that only 1 in 200,000 women die from legal abortions each year.[10] Causes of death from legal abortion may include infection, embolism, anesthesia reactions, and hemorrhage, or, more rarely, death from a preexisting heart condition.[11] Although any deaths may seem like too many, as medical researchers Cates and Grimes note, "Once pregnant, a woman encounters an increased risk of death, no matter what her choice of outcomes."[12]

Medical researchers have largely dismissed the suggestion that a single first-trimester abortion can lead to other deleterious health effects. In studies comparing outcomes of a first pregnancy following an abortion with outcomes of the first pregnancy of women who have never had an abortion, the CDC concludes that first-trimester abortions performed by vacuum aspiration pose "no additional risk regarding the outcome of the pregnancies in terms of miscarriage, ectopic pregnancy, preterm delivery or low birthweight." According to medical research, "abortion does not affect subsequent fertility . . . vacuum aspiration abortion has no significant impact on women's health or subsequent pregnancies."[13]

These data, it should be noted, are based largely if not exclusively on studies of women who have had a *single* vacuum aspiration abortion. A report in the *Journal of the American Medical Association* (*JAMA*) cautioned that although "Most women who have a single abortion with vacuum aspiration experience few if any subsequent problems getting pregnant or having healthy children," much less "is known about the effects of multiple abortions on future fecundity."[14] In one of the few studies available on multiple induced abortions, the authors, "were unable to detect a significant linear trend in risk with an increasing number of prior induced abortions," noting that, "we found very little, if any, increased risk associated with multiple induced abortions." The authors, however, qualify these findings by noting that, "These results apply only to white women delivering their first child and to the risk of only one adverse pregnancy outcome."[15] More research is needed before conclusions can be drawn with regard to other adverse outcomes or with regard to the effects of multiple induced abortions on women of color.[16]

Complications in First-Trimester Abortions. Complications from induced abortion are difficult to track in the United States for two reasons. An article in the *JAMA* explains, "definitions of what constitutes a complication vary widely," and to make matters more difficult, "in the United States there are no national surveillance data on abortion-related morbidity."[17]

Post-abortion complications include the possibility of incomplete abortion; continued pregnancy; uterine infection; excessive bleeding; perforation of the uterus, bowel, or adjacent organs; reaction to medication or anesthetic; and uterine tear or laceration. An NAF Fact Sheet estimates that among women obtaining abortions during the first 13 weeks of pregnancy, "97% have no complications or any post-abortion complaints; 2 ½% have minor complications that can be handled at the physician's office or abortion facility; and less than ½ of 1% require some additional surgical procedure and/or hospitalization."[18] The Fact Sheet cites physician skills, the kind of anesthesia used, the woman's health, and the abortion method used as four factors that influence the possibility of complications. Doctors and researchers agree that the risk of complications and mortality are most strongly correlated with the stage of the pregnancy at which the abortion is performed, and on the choice of the abortion procedure—largely contingent on the stage of the pregnancy.

Complications in Late Abortions. The NAF Fact Sheet on the safety of abortion offers a simple guideline for evaluating the relative safety of abortion: "After 6 weeks LMP [after the last menstrual period] the earlier the abortion, the safer it is."[19] This is one of the few claims within the abortion debate that seems to be uncontested. Cates and Grimes estimate that the relative risk of death from an abortion doubles for every 2 weeks the abortion is delayed after 8 weeks' gestation.[20]

Complications of late abortion are similar to those of early abortion. They include infection, perforation of the uterus or other organs, injury to the cervix, bleeding severe enough to require transfusion, and incomplete abortion. Late abortions more often involve the use of general anesthetic, posing other hazards. Dr. Warren Hern, in his book *Abortion Practice,* notes, "The principal complications experienced with D&E occur during the procedure itself. Delayed complications, such as retained tissue, which are relatively common with first-trimester procedures, are infrequent following midtrimester D&E."[21]

Long-Term Risks. The evaluation of long-term risks following abortion remains the most elusive data in the discussion of physical sequelae.[22] Specific examples of adverse effects on later fertility and pregnancy that have been hypothesized include the risk of Rh immunization, menstrual disorders, secondary infertility, subsequent spontaneous abortions, subsequent premature births, ectopic pregnancies, and various complications in the third trimester of later pregnancies.[23] No strong support exists for the claim that abortion contributes to any of these outcomes, however, and medical claims remain at best "contradictory." As one researcher emphasizes, "there is no type of pregnancy outcome, spontaneous or induced, which could not cause similar late somatic sequelae," and he advises that, "All publications . . . should take this fact into account."[24] Though no clear conclusions may be drawn from available studies, physicians do agree that avoiding immediate complications can reduce the risk of long-term complications, because, "Any problems with future childbearing that come about because of abortion are the result of damage to the reproductive organs or infection."[25]

EFFECTS OF LEGAL RESTRICTIONS ON PHYSICAL CONSEQUENCES

Among the often incomplete and sometimes contested assertions surrounding the health aspects of induced abortion, one principle seems to be universally acknowledged—abortion is safest when performed early, and delaying an abortion results in increased risks of morbidity and mortality. Because of this finding, many researchers warn that greater health risks will be posed for women who are subject to laws that mandate waiting periods or impose other delays by limiting women's access to abortion, such as parental and spousal notification laws and laws restricting public Medicaid funding that impose financial hardships on poor women. In addition, decreasing numbers of physicians and facilities willing to provide abortion services cause delays for those who must travel, often great distances, to have an abortion.[26] In particular, legal decisions that restrict or prohibit public funding for abortions "will have a disproportionate impact on poor Black, Latina, Native American, and Asian-Pacific American women, who often cannot afford private medical care."[27] In fact, women of color experience a number of additional circumstances that make them often disproportionately disadvantaged by the imposition of laws restricting abortion.

The differential health effects of abortion on women of color went unmentioned in the Surgeon General's report, as they have been in the vast majority of medical studies on abortion. A report issued by the Alan Guttmacher Institute does note that, "Perhaps because of differences in income and overall health status in our population, women who are black or are members of other minority groups face a greater risk than do white women,"[28] but it does not pursue this observation. Women of color face an additional health risk as a result of restrictive abortion legislation in at least two ways. First, restrictive abortion laws may disproportionately bar them from obtaining abortions in the early stages of pregnancy, or may prevent them from obtaining a legal abortion at all. Second, pregnancy itself may present greater health risks for women of color, so that denied abortion places an extra burden on their health.

Because "the majority of women seeking services from public hospitals are women of color," restricting public funds for abortion will disadvantage women of color as a group far more than white women.[29] The lack of access to abortion exposes poor women and women of color to a threat that has historically been directed disproportionately against them: the threat of sterilization abuse.[30] Even though federally funded abortions ceased in 1977, the federal government has continued to pay 90% of the cost of sterilizations.[31] Women who cannot afford abortions are often left with the alternative of sterilization to terminate an unwanted pregnancy. In states that will not provide public funds for abortion, the effect has been marked.[32]

The relative safety of induced abortion in terms of a woman's physical health has been well documented before and since the issuing of Koop's report, and although certain questions—particularly those surrounding the differential effects on women of color—remain to be addressed, concerns about physical health have moved largely out of the abortion spotlight. Instead, public debate and a significant proportion of medical interest have turned toward the psychological consequences of abortion.

PSYCHOLOGICAL SEQUELAE

Although the Surgeon General's report was expected to settle the question of the psychological effects on women, Koop's refusal to draw any conclusions instead inflamed controversy. His assertion that no methodologically sound studies on the question existed provoked a response from such institutions as the American Psychological Association, whose representatives were invited to speak at the Congressional hearing.

Koop cited three reasons for the inconclusiveness of existing studies on the question of psychological effects: the lack of consensus on what variables should be identified and investigated, the problem of controlling for psychological symptoms resulting from life events experienced before or after the abortion, and the difficulty of establishing appropriate control and study groups. He thus declined to draw any conclusions, offering only his opinion that "it appears likely that certain factors combine to make deciding to have an abortion and coping with its aftermath more difficult for some women than for others."[33] In his testimony at the Congressional hearing, however,

Koop conceded that "from a public health perspective," the psychological problems caused by abortion are "minuscule."[34]

The broad divergence of experience among women who undergo abortion points to the need to understand abortion as it is situated in various social and psychological contexts, rather than perceiving it as an isolated event, somehow separable from other influences in women's lives. Some process of grief following an abortion may occur as a normal and *healthy,* rather than pathological, response to an unquestionably stressful event.[35] Studies of other stressors judged to be similar to abortion suggest that, "women who do not experience severe negative responses within a few months after the event are unlikely to develop future significant psychological problems related to the event."[36]

Some researchers see positive developmental outcomes resulting from the decision to have an abortion.

> There is . . . evidence to suggest that like other major life events, pregnancy and abortion contain the potential for maturation and personal growth. The very process of making a difficult life decision like that about abortion can have positive effects on a woman's self-esteem and sense of autonomy.[37]

Although "Many women experience sadness as well as a sense of loss," women also "may feel new strength in having made and carried out an important, often difficult decision."[38] These writers note that negative feelings may result not from the abortion itself but rather from the social and economic circumstances that made the abortion necessary.[39] Anger can also result from the personal circumstances that precipitated the abortion. "If your birth control method failed, if you didn't use birth control, if you were pressured into having intercourse when you didn't really want to or if you were raped, you may feel angry about the abortion."[40] Although medical researchers have failed to take such factors into account in discussions of psychological sequelae, these factors may be central to women's experiences of abortion.

Effects of Ethnicity on Psychological Outcomes. Although differences in psychological reactions among women of various ethnic groups are rarely addressed in the medical literature on abortion, several nonmedical sources have noted the importance of this variable.[41] In particular, what Bland terms "racial and ethnic value-laden issues," or group values surrounding such issues as fear of genocide or attitudes toward adoption, as well as religion and level of education, are strong predictors of attitudes toward abortion, and thus may influence post-abortion adaptation.[42] Bland emphasizes that even when women of various ethnic groups make the same final choice about abortion, the psychological influences on that decision may differ greatly based on group history and ethnic value-laden issues.

Post-Abortion Syndrome. In his report to the President, the Surgeon General summarized the views of the National Right-to-Life Committee and others who believe abortion causes negative psychological consequences. These organizations have identified a specific "post-abortion syndrome" (PAS) that may manifest itself in any of three forms: acute (appearing within 30 days after an abortion); chronic (appearing 6 months or longer after the procedure); or delayed (appearing 5 to 10 years, or more, after the abortion). Symptoms include "reexperiencing of the abortion death," "reduced responsiveness toward one's environment," and other reactions such as "sleep disorders, depression, secondary substance abuse, intense hostility, and guilt."[43]

A representative of the National Right-to-Life Committee told the Congressional Committee that the effects of abortion resemble the Post Traumatic Stress Disorder that afflicted many Vietnam veterans, and described severe emotional trauma characterizing women's post-abortion experience.[44] Despite claims of supporting "clinical experience" for this trauma,[45] however, medical research does not support the existence of such a syndrome. On the contrary, even though anecdotal evidence from those involved in the pro-life movement has been widely quoted in the media, studies have repeatedly failed to find any scientific evidence for such claims.[46]

ABORTION LEGISLATION: THE PSYCHOLOGICAL
EFFECTS OF LIMITED OR DENIED ACCESS

In his report, Koop summarized the beliefs of those who attribute some psychological benefits to abortion, noting that unwanted births pose a risk of postpartum depression and psychosis, presenting a greater threat to the mother than would a legal abortion.[47] When laws are enacted restricting access to abortion, women may be forced to delay abortion or to carry to term an unwanted pregnancy. Henshaw cites a study of the effects of eliminating public funds for abortion, which found that "about 20 percent of women who would have had a Medicaid-funded abortion carried their pregnancies to term when funding was cut off."[48] In another study reported by various sources, researchers discovered that "the time needed to acquire enough money for an abortion is a common cause of delay that leads to abortions performed at later gestations,"[49] and that, "About half of women who have an abortion after 15 weeks of pregnancy are delayed by financial problems."[50]

Despite the findings that abortion itself does not lead to negative psychological consequences, the amount of stress a woman experiences may be greatly increased by difficulties or delays in obtaining an abortion.[51] Later abortions may also contribute to stress by involving greater surgical intervention and/or hospitalization, which "adds to the other stresses of abortion, thereby increasing the emotional risk of the experience."[52] As with most abortion legislation, negative effects are unequally distributed, affecting most directly women with fewer resources and thus fewer alternatives for obtaining legal abortions, a group that includes adolescents.

ADOLESCENT ABORTION

In the United States, teenage women obtain one quarter of all abortions. In 1988 alone, the number of women aged 17 or younger who had abortions reached 172,000.[53] A small number of studies have focused specifically on the population of adolescent women who undergo abortion. A study that reviews the research findings on adolescent abortion offers evidence that the safety of abortion relative to childbearing is even greater for teenagers than for women of other ages. "The medical consequences of childbearing are more adverse than those of abortion at all stages of gestation" for adolescent women, and moreover, "the evidence seems increasingly clear that no negative psychological sequelae exist."[54]

Many states have laws requiring consent or notification of one parent, and other states require consent or notification of both parents. One review of such laws concluded that they "have adverse consequences for pregnant adolescents such as heightened stress and potentially health-jeopardizing delays in seeking pregnancy termination."[55] The Council on Ethical and Judicial Affairs of the American Medical Association asserts that some minors may "be physically or emotionally harmed if they are required to involve their parents in the decision to have an abortion." For adolescents from abusive homes, disclosing a pregnancy could lead to violent treatment from parents. Minors who fear violence may resort to self-induced or back-alley abortions in order to avoid disclosing the pregnancy to parents. As the Council's report explains, "The desire to maintain secrecy has been one of the leading reasons for illegal abortion deaths" since abortion became legal in 1973.[56]

RU-486: An Alternative to Surgical Abortion

In 1980, a group of scientists employed by a French company named Roussel Uclaf (the *RU* in the drug's name) were working on a drug that could be used as medication to block the action of certain steroid hormones. Unexpectedly, they discovered that the drug also blocked the steroid hormone progesterone, which is necessary for maintaining pregnancy. A consultant for the company, Dr. Etienne-Emile Baulieu, recognized that the drug had potential as an abortifacient and pursued its uses for ending pregnancy. He discovered that on its own RU-486 induced abortion about 80% of the time, and when used in combination with a follow-up injection of prostaglandin (PG), RU-486 could be used to induce abortion with 96% effectiveness, similar to the success rate of surgical and suction abortions.

Baulieu discovered that RU-486 blocks gestation by serving as a progesterone "impostor," attaching itself to progesterone receptors but not acting as progesterone would. An *American Health* article explains, "It's rather like a key that fits a lock but won't turn it—and keeps the real key from working."[57] When RU-486 is administered at an early stage of pregnancy, the egg is dislodged, the uterine lining breaks down, and the lining and egg are expelled. Baulieu terms the drug a *contragestive* (from *contragestation*), because it blocks gestation.

MEDICAL SAFETY

RU-486 is only effective if taken when a woman is less than 7 weeks pregnant. In France, a woman is required to make four visits to a medical facility in order to receive the treatment: one for a pregnancy test and to declare her intention to have an abortion, a second to take the RU-486 pills, a third for the follow-up prostaglandin injection and abortion, and the final visit as a follow-up. Although some women will experience a miscarriage after taking RU-486 alone, most women will miscarry within 4 hours following the prostaglandin injection. In the remaining cases, the abortion may be incomplete and medical or surgical intervention required to remove the remaining tissue. Baulieu estimates that 3% to 4% of women who undergo the RU-486/PG treatment will have incomplete abortions requiring surgical intervention, and in a few additional cases the procedure is entirely unsuccessful and pregnancy continues.[58]

The safety of RU-486 continues to be a highly contested issue in the medical community, even (or perhaps, especially) among those who support a woman's right to choose abortion. Clinical trials of RU-486 note several common side effects, usually blamed not on the drug itself but on the prostaglandin administered subsequently. These side effects include nausea and vomiting, abdominal pain, headaches and dizziness, diarrhea, and prolonged bleeding. Researchers note that, "excessive bleeding should be considered as the major hazard even if it occurs rarely."[59] Baulieu and others have been testing the use of safer prostaglandins that will cause fewer side effects and reduce the risk of serious disturbances in heart function. Baulieu himself believes that RU-486 is both physically and psychologically advantageous for women relative to surgical abortions.[60]

PSYCHOLOGICAL IMPLICATIONS

The question of whether the experience of RU-486 abortion benefits or harms women psychologically, as compared to surgical abortion, is unresolved among medical professionals. Researchers recognize that some women prefer surgical abortions, "because of the depressingly solitary process of taking the pill."[61] The "intensely solitary" nature of the act has also led some women to *prefer* RU-486 to surgical abortion, however, because as one French woman expressed it, "You do it yourself. It is entirely your responsibility."[62]

Whether or not RU-486 is proven safe and becomes available in the United States, these articles provide evidence of a movement among U.S. women to take greater control over the process of abortion, control they are also demanding in many other arenas of women's health care. In response to a growing dissatisfaction with the health care system's treatment of women, a self-help movement that first emerged in the early 1970s has experienced a recent resurgence in the feminist community.

Menstrual Extraction
and the Women's Self-Help Movement

Menstrual extraction was first developed in the early 1970s as a means of alleviating the discomfort of menstrual periods and of helping women learn about menstruation and basic health care skills. It was performed by women in advanced self-help groups who worked together and came to know one another over a long period of time. These women would practice on one another in order to develop safe instruments and techniques. Because menstrual extraction removes the contents of the uterus, it can be used to remove an early pregnancy of up to 8 weeks.

The resurgence of interest in menstrual extraction has been a controversial issue even among feminists and pro-choice supporters, many of whom fear that attention to this method will divert energies from the important work of protecting a woman's right to legal abortion. Some feminists are disturbed because the method recalls the days of back-alley abortions. Women involved in education on menstrual extraction, however, believe that this is a precaution that must be taken to ensure that with increasingly restrictive abortion laws and the possibility that *Roe v. Wade* might be overturned, women will never again have to put themselves in the hands of back-alley abortionists.[63]

MEDICAL CLAIMS

There has been virtually no medical research on the safety of menstrual extraction, yet the practice has been widely condemned by the medical community.[64] Noting that more than 20,000 abortions have been performed through menstrual extraction over the past 20 years, advocates of the method claim that menstrual extraction "is an almost inherently safe procedure."[65] They contend that the use of flexible instruments makes it nearly impossible to perforate the uterus and that the ability to perform the procedure without delays brought about by the inconvenience and expense of surgical abortion means that women can have earlier and safer abortions.

Although at-home practitioners argue that menstrual extraction is safer for women than surgical abortion, they also acknowledge its experimental status. The authors of *The New Our Bodies, Ourselves* caution, "We need to do more research before we can know whether frequent extraction of the uterine lining creates any long-term or delayed health problems, although there is no evidence of any so far."[66]

PSYCHOLOGICAL SEQUELAE

The strongest arguments presented by the self-help groups are for the psychological advantages for women. Just as the degree of care and personal attention these groups give to women will enhance the medical safety of the procedure, the groups also argue that by affirming a woman's decision and her well-being, they create a supportive atmosphere that is healthier psychologically.[67] The financial advantages of menstrual extraction decrease stress about the procedure, allowing access to abortion to women who could not otherwise afford it.

Conclusion

Investigating what is known by the medical community about the health aspects of abortion requires identifying, in addition, those issues that scientific research has neglected. In attempting to go beyond a review of existing medical research and inquire into what health consequences have been overlooked, one omission seems to present itself most urgently. In their efforts to find answers to the question of whether abortion has any negative physical and/or psychological sequelae, researchers have largely ignored the differences among women and the variance in personal and social contexts that may affect the occurrence of such sequelae. These might include racial and ethnic differences, differences in levels of nutrition and health, socioeconomic variables, and circumstances related to the cause of the unwanted pregnancy.

Finally, too little research has recognized the possibility that what have been termed "negative" psychological sequelae may be part of a healthy process of grieving that leads to successful resolution of the experience of unwanted pregnancy, a process that may foster personal growth. For women who have felt trapped by circumstances that make them unable to afford a child, anger may be a healthy response to an oppressive situation and may spur them to activism in helping other women or working for social change. This is not to deny evidence of women, presented in some of the medical literature, who *do* experience ongoing negative feelings without being able to resolve them. A perspective that affirmed differences among women would recognize the legitimacy of these women's experiences and seek explanations for their responses. Too often, medical research homogenizes diverse experiences by attempting to discover clear, unambiguous answers. An issue as complex as abortion, which affects so many women, can have no such answers . . . nor should it.

Notes

1. Committee on Government Operations, "The Federal Role in Determining the Medical and Psychological Impact of Abortion on Women," Washington, D.C., December 11, 1989, hereafter referred to as "Committee Report."

2. Hearing Before the Human Resources and Intergovernmental Relations Subcommittee, "Medical and Psychological Impact of Abortion," March 16, 1989, hereafter referred to as "Hearing." In his letter, Koop did not mention medical risks. When asked about this omission at the Hearing, he explained that "obstetricians and gynecologists had long since concluded that the physical sequelae of abortion were no different than those found in women who carried pregnancy to term or who had never been pregnant."

3. The remaining 87% are performed in physicians' offices or freestanding clinics. See R. Benson Gold, *Abortion and Women's Health: A Turning Point for America?* (New York: Alan Guttmacher Institute, 1990): 24.

4. L. T. Shepler, "The Law of Abortion and Contraception—Past and Present," in N. L. Stotland (Ed.), *Psychiatric Aspects of Abortion* (Washington, DC: American Psychiatric Press, 1991): 51-73.

5. Shepler, "The Law of Abortion," p. 61.

6. A. Thompson Cook, "Fact Sheet: Economics of Abortion" (Washington, DC: National Abortion Federation, 1991). Only 13 states pay for abortions in all or most circumstances. Although all states will fund an abortion if the pregnancy endangers the woman's life, only 19 states will fund abortions for women who become pregnant by rape or incest, and only 16 states will pay for an abortion when the fetus has severe defects.

7. Committee Report, p. 6.

8. Committee Report, testimony of David Grimes, M.D., pp. 5-6.

9. L. M. Koonin, J. C. Smith, M. Ramick, & H. W. Lawson, "Abortion Surveillance—United States, 1989," *Centers for Disease Control Morbidity and Mortality Weekly Report* 41 (Atlanta: U.S. Department of Health and Human Services, September 4, 1992): 1-33.

10. A. Thompson Cook, *Fact Sheet: Safety of Abortion* (Washington, DC: National Abortion Federation, 1990). Quoted material used by permission.

11. W. Cates, Jr., & D. A. Grimes, "Morbidity and Mortality of Abortion in the United States," in J. E. Hodgson (Ed.), *Abortion and Sterilization: Medical and Social Aspects* (London: Academic Press, 1981): 155-180. See also Council on Scientific Affairs, American Medical Association, "Induced Termination of Pregnancy Before and After *Roe v. Wade:* Trends in the Mortality and Morbidity of Women," *Journal of the American Medical Association* 268 (December 9, 1992): 3231-3239.

12. Cates & Grimes, "Morbidity and Mortality," p. 170.

13. Committee Report, p. 6.

14. Council on Scientific Affairs, American Medical Association, "Induced Termination," p. 3231.

15. M. T. Mandelson, C. B. Maden, & J. R. Daling, "Low Birth Weight in Relation to Multiple Induced Abortions," *American Journal of Public Health* 82 (March 1992): 391-394.

16. Recent writing by women of color suggests that variables such as race and class, which have been largely ignored in medical studies to date, are important influences on the health consequences of abortion and require further study. See S. Jenkins, "Abortion Rights, Poor Women, and Religious Diversity," and D. Dixon, L. Ross, B. Avery, & S. Jenkins, "The Reproductive Health of Black Women and Other Women of Color," both in M. Gerber Fried (Ed.), *From Abortion to Reproductive Freedom: Transforming a Movement* (Boston: South End, 1990): 151-156 and 157-159, respectively; and I. J. Bland, "Racial and Ethnic Influences: The Black Woman and Abortion," in N. L. Stotland (Ed.), *Psychiatric Aspects of Abortion* (Washington, DC: American Psychiatric Press, 1991): 171-185.

17. Council on Scientific Affairs, American Medical Association, "Induced Termination," p. 3235. Some rare but possible complications that can occur during the procedure itself include allergic reaction to local anesthesia, asthma attack, seizures, shock, and cardiopulmonary arrest.

18. Cook, *Fact Sheet: Safety of Abortion.*

19. Cook, *Fact Sheet: Safety of Abortion.*

20. Cates & Grimes, "Morbidity and Mortality," p. 171. See also Hearing, p. 221.

21. W. M. Hern, *Abortion Practice* (Philadelphia: J. B. Lippincott, 1984): 194.

22. Hern, *Abortion Practice,* p. 276.

23. B. M. Berić, "Late Somatic Sequelae: The Delayed Complications of Induced Abortion," in J. E. Hodgson (Ed.), *Abortion and Sterilization: Medical and Social Aspects* (London: Academic Press, 1981): 379-389.

24. Berić, "Late Somatic Sequelae," p. 389.

25. M. K. Denney, *A Matter of Choice: An Essential Guide to Every Aspect of Abortion* (New York: Simon & Schuster, 1983): 82.

26. Council on Scientific Affairs, American Medical Association, "Induced Termination," p. 3238.

27. L. Ross, S. Ifill, & S. Jenkins, "Emergency Memorandum to Women of Color," in M. Gerber Fried (Ed.), *From Abortion to Reproductive Freedom: Transforming a Movement* (Boston: South End, 1990): 147-150.

28. Gold, *Abortion and Women's Health,* p. 32.

29. Ross et al., "Emergency Memorandum," p. 148.

30. For further discussion of sterilization abuse, see The Boston Women's Health Book Collective, *The New Our Bodies, Ourselves: Updated and Expanded for the '90s* (New York: Simon & Schuster, 1992): 301-302, 377; and The Committee for Abortion Rights and Against Sterilization Abuse, *Women Under Attack: Victories, Backlash, and the Fight for Reproductive Freedom* (S. E. David, Ed.) (Boston: South End, 1988): 15-30.

31. "Abortion and Sterilization in the Third World," in M. Gerber Fried (Ed.), *From Abortion to Reproductive Freedom: Transforming a Movement* (Boston: South End, 1990): 63-64.

32. The Boston Women's Health Book Collective, *The New Our Bodies, Ourselves: A Book by and for Women* (New York: Simon & Schuster, 1984): 312.

33. Hearing, p. 221.

34. Hearing, p. 241.

35. N. L. Stotland, "The Myth of the Abortion Trauma Syndrome," *Journal of the American Medical Association* 268 (October 21, 1992): 2078-2079. See also "No Regrets," *The Lancet* 335 (May 19, 1990): 1188-1189; R. S. Good, R. P. Lederman, H. J. Osofsky, & D. D. Youngs, "Birth-Related Reactions as Sources of Stress," in J. D. Noshpitz & R. D. Coddington (Eds.), *Stressors and the Adjustment Disorders* (New York: John Wiley, 1990): 176-188.

36. N. E. Adler, H. P. David, B. N. Major, S. H. Roth, N. F. Russo, & G. E. Wyatt, "Psychological Responses After Abortion," *Science* 248 (April 6, 1990): 41-44.

37. S. L. Minden & M. T. Notman, "Psychotherapeutic Issues Related to Abortion," in N. L. Stotland (Ed.), *Psychiatric Aspects of Abortion* (Washington, DC: American Psychiatric Press, 1991): 119-133.

38. Boston Women's Health Book Collective, *The New Our Bodies, Ourselves* (1984 ed.), p. 306.

39. Boston Women's Health Book Collective, *The New Our Bodies, Ourselves* (1984 ed.), pp. 307-308. See also The Committee for Abortion Rights and Against Sterilization Abuse, *Women Under Attack,* pp. 68-71, for further discussion of the social conditions that may force a woman to choose abortion.

40. Boston Women's Health Book Collective, *The New Our Bodies, Ourselves* (1984 ed.), p. 308.

41. Bland, "Racial and Ethnic Influences," p. 172.

42. Bland, "Racial and Ethnic Influences," pp. 180-182.

43. Hearing, p. 221.

44. Hearing, pp. 114-115.

45. Hearing, p. 116.

46. Stotland, "The Myth of the Abortion Trauma Syndrome," p. 2079.

47. Hearing, p. 221.

48. Stanley K. Henshaw, "The Accessibility of Abortion Services in the United States," *Family Planning Perspectives* 23 (November/December 1991): 246-252.

49. Henshaw, "The Accessibility," p. 246.

50. Council on Scientific Affairs, American Medical Association, "Induced Termination," p. 3238.

51. Adler et al., "Psychological Responses," p. 42.

52. Good et al., "Birth-Related Reactions," pp. 176-188.

53. S. K. Henshaw & K. Kost, "Parental Involvement in Minors' Abortion Decisions," *Family Planning Perspectives* 24 (September/October 1992): 196-213.

54. L. Schwab Zabin & V. Sedivy, "Abortion Among Adolescents: Research Findings and the Current Debate," *Journal of School Health* 62 (September 1992): 319-324.

55. M. D. Resnick, "Adolescent Pregnancy Options," *Journal of School Health* 62 (September 1992): 298-303.

56. Council on Ethical and Judicial Affairs, American Medical Association, "Mandatory Parental Consent to Abortion," *Journal of the American Medical Association* (January 6, 1993): 82-86.

57. J. Gooding & R. Williams, "RU-486: The Fuss, the Fears and the Facts," *American Health* (December 1991): 65-68. Quoted material used by permission of American Health © 1991 by Goodring & Williams.

58. E. E. Baulieu, "Contragestion and Other Clinical Applications of RU-486, an Antiprogesterone at the Receptor," *Science* 245 (September 22, 1989): 1351-1357.

59. W. Shangchun, G. Ji, W. Yuming, W. Muzhen, F. Huimin, Y. Guangzhen, Z. Shurong, W. Ping, D. Mingkun, H. Zirong, H. Juxiang, Z. Ge, L. Zhenwu, C. Xiaoqin, P. Dunren, S. Lijuan, W. Xirui, H. Sha, X. Jingzhong, & Z. Jianguo, "Clinical Trial on Termination of Early Pregnancy With RU-486 in Combination With Prostaglandin," *Contraception* 46 (1992): 203-210.

60. Baulieu, "Contragestion and Other," 1355-1356.

61. Gooding & Williams, "RU-486: The Fuss, the Fears," p. 67.

62. Gooding & Williams, "RU-486: The Fuss, the Fears," p. 67.

63. S. Buttenweiser & R. Levine, "Breaking Silences: A Post-Abortion Support Model," in M. Gerber Fried (Ed.), *From Abortion to Reproductive Freedom: Transforming a Movement* (Boston: South End, 1990): 121-128.

64. A search of *Medline* from January 1989 through March 1993 found no articles under the subject heading "menstrual extraction."

65. L. Punnett, "The Politics of Menstrual Extraction," in M. Gerber Fried (Ed.), *From Abortion to Reproductive Freedom: Transforming a Movement* (Boston: South End, 1990): 101-111.

66. The Boston Women's Health Book Collective, *The New Our Bodies, Ourselves* (1984 ed.), p. 295.

67. Punnett, "The Politics," p. 101.

3

A Matter of Consequence

Abortion Rhetoric and Media Messages

Diane Helene Miller

The rhetoric of abortion has largely been aimed at voters, and its overtly political intent is not to inform women about health issues but rather to change the legal status of abortion. In fact, the health issues of abortion, as I will argue, are not widely discussed in the media, and where they are addressed, the health of women is portrayed as largely peripheral to the central focus of the legal debate. Terms of women's health are invoked only when their use is politically expedient, creating a fragmented, incomplete, and often misleading picture of abortion's health issues. As a result, reports of medical findings are often reframed by activists on both sides, and consequently by the media, in terms of their legal ramifications.

Methodology

I collected articles available from *NewsBank* for the years 1986 through 1992, from *Infotrac* for the years 1989 through September 1992, and from the *Readers' Guide to Periodical Literature* for the years 1988 through 1992. The scarcity of articles indexed under health-related headings is itself revealing. For example, *Infotrac* listed only eight articles under the category "abortion—health aspects," compared to 699 articles under "political aspects" and 797 under "laws, regulations, etc." The heading "abortion complications" contained only three entries, and "physiological aspects" likewise added three entries—and one of these was about the possibility that the drug RU-486 could be used as a treatment for a rare tumor. Even the more controversial topic of "psychological aspects" offered only nine listings.

In the *Readers' Guide,* 13 articles were listed under the heading of "abortion—psychological aspects." This list included 5 articles focusing solely on male reactions to abortion, 1 story about the fate of children born to mothers who were denied abortions, and 2 that discussed the need for support groups for couples whose prenatal tests showed evidence of a deformed fetus. In a listing of articles from *NewsBank,* of the 4,108 articles under the general heading of "abortion," 24 were listed under the subheading "psychological aspects" and 16 under the subheading "post-abortion syndrome." There were no subheadings for either "medical aspects" or "health aspects," although the subheading "abortion and safety" yielded two entries. As a result, my article collecting involved piecing together from various subheadings articles that bore some relation—sometimes remote—to the health issues related to abortion.[1]

PHYSICAL CONSEQUENCES

The medical issues surrounding legal abortion remain for the most part uncontested and, as a result, largely unmentioned in media coverage. Many of the media articles note that abortion is today the most commonly performed surgery in the United States, with approximately 1.5 million abortions performed every year. The risk of death from legal abortion is approximately 1 in 100,000, less than the number of people who die annually from penicillin shots.[2] Any more extended discussion of mortality centers around testimony, usually in the form of personal narratives in support of a pro-choice position, from women who know others who died or who themselves nearly died from illegal abortion and who recount the dangers and horrors of pre-*Roe* abortion.[3]

The existing media coverage of abortion's physical risks focuses largely on morbidity rather than mortality, and even that discussion is infrequent. Only 35 media articles mentioned the physical effects of abortion at all, and only 13 differentiated between the effects of early and late abortion, although this appears to be one of the most important indicators of the likelihood of medical complications. The articles that discuss physical risks fell into two broad categories. The substance of one group of articles claimed the essential safety of the procedure, often with the qualification that restrictive abortion laws delay abortions, thus posing greater threats to women's health by postponing abortion into the later trimesters.

The remainder of the articles that discussed physical consequences were skeptical of claims that abortion is safe, suggesting that the procedure is fraught with as-yet-unrecognized or unacknowledged medical risks. Most of these articles also noted then-Surgeon General C. Everett Koop's equivocation on the issue of whether medical problems that may occur after abortion can ever be attributed causally to abortion. One article typical of these reports notes that,

> after an abortion women were sometimes infertile, suffered a damaged cervix or subsequently had a miscarriage, gave premature birth or gave birth to underweight babies. But [Koop] said that when those problems arose, it was often difficult to attribute them to an abortion.[4]

Koop's unwillingness to take a stand effectively defused the potential political power of the issue, and so the media has given it scant attention.

As a result, the information women need as health care consumers appears nowhere in these articles. Though some of the articles on physical risks make ominous reference to the increased danger of abortion in the second and third trimesters of pregnancy, none of the articles discusses what these possible dangers are and how much more risk is actually involved. Although all surgical procedures involve some possibility of complications, only one article notes what those complications are for early abortions. None of the articles discusses factors that influence the possibility of complications, such as the physician's skill, the kind of anesthesia used, the abortion method used, and the woman's health prior to the abortion.

In addition, none of the articles that talk about physical consequences address the differences in risk between white women and women of color, although a report released by the Alan Guttmacher Institute suggests that, "Perhaps because of differences in income and overall health status in our population, women who are black or are members of other minority groups face a greater risk than do white women."[5] Because they do not identify risks, the articles fail to offer women any practical information about how to seek a safe abortion or how to choose an abortion provider, tending to obscure the issue of differences in the quality of care available. Women who seek an understanding of the procedure and its risks are thus left with many questions regarding how to ensure their own safety and how to be knowledgeable health care consumers.

PSYCHOLOGICAL CONSEQUENCES

By far the most controversial aspect of the risks of abortion, in the media and among medical and nonmedical observers alike, is the question of the existence and nature of negative psychological consequences resulting from the abortion procedure. As Koop explained in an interview with the *Los Angeles Times,* "The thing that was important [to document] was the psychological problems. . . . There was no point to concentrating on a medical report when it's been proven that abortions are medically safe."[6] When the Surgeon General refused to issue his report (see Chapter 2 in this volume), he opened the door to widespread speculation that could proceed through testimonial claims unhindered by scientific evidence. His assertion that the studies he reviewed would not support the claims of either side was widely quoted and (mis)interpreted by the press.

Koop's finding that the scientific studies provided "insufficient scientific and statistical evidence"[7] about the "health effects of abortion on women" was summarized in one article with the statement that "there's no scientific evidence proving the existence of such a [post-abortion] syndrome."[8] Another article, although accurately quoting Koop's statement that "no scientific basis existed to draw any conclusions," has a headline announcing, "Effect of Abortion on Women Is Discounted" and a large subtitle reading, "Koop says there is no evidence of psychological problems."

These examples are a case study of how slight alterations in wording permit significant misinterpretation. Koop's original statement refers only to the quality or reliability of scientific studies and acknowledges an ignorance of abortion's health effects. The rephrased statement, however, is equally amenable to (at least) two interpretations. Pro-choice activists read "no evidence" as synonymous with "no negative effects." Pro-life activists, however, read this statement as a message that there was a problem with the available evidence, not with their belief that abortion causes harm. They believed the evidence was simply incomplete and more studies were necessary in order to conclusively confirm their belief. The response of pro-life advocates was to formulate a more focused argument around the experience of their most powerful and persuasive spokespeople: regretful post-abortion women.

Post-Abortion Syndrome: Pro-Life Claims

The pro-life presence in the media is dominated by representatives from the National Right-to-Life Committee and various therapists, primarily affiliated with Christian Counseling Centers. The recent rhetoric of these groups has focused on proving that there is a trauma reaction to abortion termed "post-abortion syndrome" (PAS), as described in the previous chapter. As portrayed in the media, the symptoms of PAS are wide-ranging, almost limitless, including "depression, anxiety, shame, helplessness, lowered self-esteem, flash-backs of the abortion, uncontrollable crying, alcohol or drug dependency and eating disorders."[9] Articles reporting on the post-abortion syndrome warn that these symptoms may strike victims at any time, because post-traumatic reactions are often "submerged within the person and it may take six months or fifteen years for something to trigger the event and emerge it."[10] One article summarizes therapists' claims about the disease's effects as encompassing "everything from alcoholism to unsatisfying personal relationships."[11]

The evidence presented in support of PAS is entirely anecdotal. It is comprised of observations from therapists and personal narratives from women who claim to suffer from the syndrome. Half of the articles that focus on PAS begin with a story about a particular woman's experience with the syndrome. About two thirds of the articles (13 of 21) present both sides of the controversy, but the remaining articles present PAS as though its existence is undisputed. Estimates of how many women are affected by the syndrome vary widely, ranging from few or none, to 1 in 5, to 8 out of 10, to assertions that all women who undergo abortions suffer from at least some PAS symptoms.[12] The articles on PAS, taken as a group, share at least three common strategies.

VICTIMIZATION

The personal testimony of PAS sufferers is framed by a rhetoric of victimization, in which individual women are shown to have suffered either from being forced into having abortions they didn't want, or from being misled by abortion providers or pro-choice rhetoric into believing that the procedure would be simple and have no aftereffects. The support organizations for PAS explicitly adopt the portrayal of women as innocent victims, calling themselves by such names as "American Victims of Abortion," "Victims of Choice," and "Women Exploited by Abortion."[13] Within this terminology, women who suffer from PAS are considered "survivors of abortion."

The articles report that women who suffer from PAS feel "victimized by the medical system and family members who had 'failed' them."[14] Terry Selby, a counselor widely quoted in the media for his role in treating PAS sufferers, considers "a sense of victimization" one of the characteristics that defines the experience of PAS.[15] Another therapist, who claims that 80%-90% of women who have had abortions suffer emotionally, explains that these women "feel bitter toward professional people, they feel bitter toward whoever told them everything was going to be fine."[16] Even more forcefully, another article argues that, "most of the women studied felt they were deceived and even abused by the medical system." It quotes a letter written (though never sent) by a woman as part of her therapy. "Dear Doctor, You killed my baby and violated me. How would you like your child torn apart piece by piece?"[17]

The portrayal of women as victims invokes a belief in the moral incapacity of women that has specific implications for pro-life arguments. On the one hand, this move denies women's rational capacities and places culpability for the act of abortion squarely on the shoulders of the medical establishment, portraying doctors as rational and therefore capable of misleading or mistreating their (less rational or irrational) female patients. By emphasizing women's inability to make choices in their own best interest, pro-life advocates redefine maternal health as an interest of the state, rather than the individual, and so justify restricting abortion as a necessary measure for the woman's "own good." Invalidating women as decision makers in this way permits the introduction of laws that remove the locus of choice from women, in the name of their own protection.[18]

The media also portray women as children, another group considered unable to make choices for themselves and so "protected" by law from having to do so. The treatment of women as children is particularly evident both in parental consent laws required in many states for pregnant minors, and in waiting periods required in some states for women of all ages.[19] An abortion opponent featured in one article believes "freedom of choice is the big lie" and cites the results of a study in which, "Forty to 70 percent of women interviewed after an abortion reported feeling forced into the choice by circumstances, family, society or their boyfriends."[20] Personal narratives also support this position. One woman, whose husband "insisted" that she have an abortion, later admits, "I blamed my husband" and tells of putting pictures of fetuses up on the walls of their bedroom "so he could see what he made me do."[21] Selby accuses abortion providers themselves of bullying women. "The minute you walk into an abortion clinic selling services and talk to a counselor paid by a clinic, that's not counseling. That's cheerleading."[22] A nurse who once helped with abortions, but has since ceased to do so, believes, "Doctors and nurses are accomplices to murder."[23]

The rhetorical context of victimization, by placing responsibility on the doctors who perform abortion, nevertheless also blames the woman for her unwanted pregnancy. In the terms of the pro-life argument, women's sexuality must be controlled, restricted to its "natural" function of childbearing, and any resistance to this role can only be seen as further evidence of women's need for guidance. In this way, the woman is denied agency and culpability, recast as the innocent victim of suffering, and so made an excellent candidate for redemption.

REDEMPTION: GUILT, SUFFERING, AND FORGIVENESS

Post-abortion women who display symptoms of PAS are viewed by the articles as having undergone an awakening, akin to a conversion experience.[24] In reaching this new awareness, the woman emerges from a period of denial, realizes that she has made a terrible mistake, and renounces her past actions. An article relates one woman's story:

> She spent the next two months [following her abortion] in a cocaine- and alcohol-induced stupor with her boyfriend until finally one day she heard a voice ask her, " 'Dottie, where's your baby?' It was God . . . He told me, 'Dottie, your baby's blood cries to me from the ground.' " From there [she] says she "was lead to a church" where she met others who had had similar experiences.[25]

Other women's experiences of guilt and forgiveness are expressed in similarly religious terms. One woman said she was able to accept her decision to have two abortions only after "I named my children and gave them to the Lord."[26] Another woman said, "It was difficult for me to forgive myself. But after acknowledging my actions and grieving for my loss, I realized God had forgiven me and I should forgive myself."[27] A psychologist explains that the healing process cannot begin until sufferers "forgive themselves and everyone involved."[28]

Women's dual status as victims and perpetrators is reinforced by a metaphor that pervades the discussion of PAS: the understanding of abortion as the "woman's Vietnam" and PAS as a form of the post-traumatic stress disorder experienced by Vietnam veterans.[29] The metaphor seems to have originated with Selby, who claims he was working through his own "survivor's guilt" from Vietnam when he recognized the similarities with women's post-abortion trauma. The Vietnam metaphor suggests that like the soldiers, the women committed an act of violence that had not been their choice to commit. The metaphor is useful to a pro-life stance because it invokes images of war and terror, of needless maiming and death that elicit feelings of deep regret. Perhaps more important, it reminds us that as a nation we have made grievous and tragic errors in judgment and policy before and thus associates abortion with a sense of national disgrace and shame. The metaphor makes clear, then, that not only the individual survivors but the nation as a whole must experience an awakening, a redemption, in which we will renounce our past wrongs, recognize our national error, and "redeem" ourselves by making abortion illegal and so putting an end to the "killing." In describing this pattern of change, pro-life advocates construct a rhetoric of guilt, suffering, and forgiveness that provides a context for women to denounce abortion while still viewing themselves as helpless victims rather than evil agents. The positioning of post-abortion women as victims who are redeemed through their suffering serves a double function. On the one hand, it permits these women to join forces with the largely Christian organizations on the side of goodness without the appearance of hypocrisy. On the other hand, the pro-life activists position themselves as the only group truly committed to empowering women by giving them a voice in the controversy.

WOMEN'S VOICES: THE USES OF FEMINISM

The call for validation of personal narratives of women "victimized" by abortion represents a new twist on an old argument: the issue of women's silencing by institutions and the refusal of the medical profession to validate women's experiences of their own bodies. The Surgeon General's report is viewed as further evidence of this problem. One article on PAS calls the report an "ivory tower approach to the issue." It quotes a psychologist with a Christian counseling practice as saying, "I have a lot of respect for Dr. Koop, but quite frankly, he's not out in the clinic."[30] Women and their counselors tell horrific stories of pain and suffering they attribute to abortion, whereas doctors and other "experts" respond with claims that women experience no significant negative psychological effects from abortion. In what is perhaps the most blatant appropriation of feminist rhetoric, an article describes the view of one psychotherapist that, "it's demeaning and unfair to say that if a woman has emotional problems after an abortion it's just because she had problems before." He argues, "It's just like blaming a rape victim for what happened to her."[31]

This rhetoric is particularly effective because feminists have argued for years that women are too often taken advantage of by medical practitioners and institutions, and that they are often prevented by the medical establishment, their families, and the men with whom they are involved from making their own choices or acting in their own best interest. Personal narratives, arising from feminist consciousness-raising groups, have frequently been invoked by feminists to show connections between the personal and political and to encourage women to "find their own voices" and speak out against their own oppression. Pro-life rhetoric co-opts this approach to place pro-choice advocates, along with the medical institutions that support their claims, in the position of oppressors, whereas the counselors who treat post-abortion syndrome sufferers are framed as the "true" advocates of victimized women. Abortion is seen as a case in point of women being coerced (this time, ironically, by feminists) into making a choice they don't want to make. *Choice* itself is given a new context; the choice *not* to have an abortion is, they argue, the true issue of choice for women.

Post-Abortion Syndrome:
The Pro-Choice Response

Just as pro-life supporters are portrayed as entirely in agreement about the existence of post-abortion syndrome, those who favor choice are characterized by a general skepticism about its existence. One abortion clinic director says, "I think the post-abortion syndrome . . . is really a figment of somebody's fertile imagination."[32] The administrator of a woman's health organization puts it more succinctly: "It's baloney."[33] Pro-choice advocates argue that, "Psychological problems never happen because of one event in a person's life."[34] At most, some pro-choice advocates concede that for women who have existing psychological problems, or for those whose religious or social beliefs conflict with the idea of abortion, some problems may emerge after abortion that were not apparent prior to the procedure. In general, the pro-choice voices report that the dominant emotion women feel after an abortion is relief that they are no longer pregnant.

This model of psychological response is notable in its absolute stance; it positions women as making rational choices unconflicted by emotional responses, in direct opposition to the position taken by pro-life advocates that women are unable to make rational decisions. For adolescents faced with an unwanted pregnancy, similarly the articles cite studies revealing that those who choose abortions are at least as satisfied with their choice, if not more so, than those who carry their pregnancies to term.[35] The pro-choice discussion of the health consequences of abortion share at least three common characteristics and strategies.

NEGATION OF FEELINGS OF CONFLICT OR SADNESS

The case against PAS is premised at times on the available medical evidence and at times on a lack of it. In the first case, medical organizations such as the American Psychological Association and other independent organizations have studied the possibility of a post-abortion syndrome, and have overwhelmingly concluded that it does not exist. One article, noting that, "Some women experience some negative psychological reactions . . . but the effect may be due to other things besides abortion," quotes a therapist who explains that "[t]he central question in this debate is not whether women who have abortions suffer emotionally, but whether the abortion causes that suffering."[36]

Pro-choice arguments are designed with one general intention: to keep abortion safe, legal, and accessible to women. Pro-choice activists Buttenweiser and Levine write,

> While the pro-choice movement has been on the defensive, it has felt the need to minimize the emotional aspects of abortion for women while emphasizing the incredible importance of legal abortion for women's lives and health . . . there has been little room for addressing the pain that may accompany the experience.[37]

Pro-choice rhetoric must avoid too much complexity or equivocation to match the hard line of its opponents. Acknowledging the validity of any of the pro-life supporters' claims could be perceived as a weakening of belief in the necessity of legal abortion.

ANGER AND THE POLITICS OF CHOICE

Pro-choice arguments, in their insistence on the absolute safety of abortion, have overlooked the possibility that women who have had abortions may have very good reasons to have mixed or negative feelings, ranging from anger to depression to a variety of emotional problems. Among minority women this is a particular problem, as minority women have argued that a true right-to-choose campaign should include protection against sterilization abuse, an option that has in the past been used to control the bodies of women of color.[38] Sterilizations are federally funded and are available on demand to poor women.[39] Because federal funds for abortion were eliminated by the Hyde Amendment in 1977, sterilization has become the only alternative for many poor women. This issue, and the health consequences of chosen or enforced sterilization, were not discussed in any of the articles addressing abortion's health issues.

The pro-choice discussion likewise avoids the issue of birth control failure, a problem that accounts for an estimated 43% of all unintended pregnancies in the United States, and fails to question why medical science has been unable to produce a birth control method that is safe, easy to use, and highly effective.[40] These issues, along with many I have not raised here, could lead to legitimate anger that might be channeled toward demanding social change. Pro-choice advocates, like their pro-life counterparts, seem unable or unwilling to address these complexities. By adopting an oppositional stance, they permit blame for an unwanted pregnancy to fall on the individual, diverting attention from other blameworthy forces.

ABORTION AS A DEVELOPMENTAL EVENT

The unwillingness of the pro-choice movement to address directly women's stories of post-abortion suffering, or to entertain the possibility that women do experience negative feelings post-abortion, implicitly endorses an assumption of the pro-life movement: that if women have negative or conflicting feelings about abortion, abortion must be inherently bad for women. Continued association of conflict with guilt implies that unwanted pregnancy does have easy choices, if only the woman will make them. It fails to pose such alternative possibilities as the notion that the grief results from another kind of loss, such as the loss of one's youth or sexual freedom.[41]

In denying the possibility of conflict in the choice or experience of abortion, pro-choice rhetoric obscures the possibility that abortion may serve as a stage of growth for women, a developmental event that can have both positive and negative connotations.[42] This view tends to isolate women from one another, denying them the support they might find in the company of other women, many of whom have had the same experience. "One of the biggest obstacles to having power and control is isolation—not sharing information and not feeling comfortable enough to open up and talk."[43] Pro-choice advocates prevent efforts to disperse information to women about how to cope with emotional responses, information that would adopt a different perspective from the pro-life stance that focuses on guilt and forgiveness.[44] By leaving the task of post-abortion counseling to pro-life groups, pro-choice advocates sacrifice the opportunity to help define this part of the experience for women.

Opposition and Agreement

Despite the polar opposition of the positions of pro-choice and pro-life articles, they have in common three characteristics: an insistence upon universalizing conclusions for all women; the need to define issues of safety narrowly, in terms of the event of abortion, without examining the larger social considerations that may lead to negative psychological responses; and a tendency to assume that negative emotions are a sign of having made the wrong decision. As a result, the media coverage of both perspectives denies post-abortion women the right to acknowledge conflicting feelings and still affirm the choice they made. By posing the issue of emotional response in terms of absolutes, both sides deny women the right to feel sadness while still believing they have made the right decision.

In addition, the articles on both sides tend to restrict their focus to issues of white, middle-class women and ignore the differences that may exist for poor women and women of color. Abortion is not a color-blind issue, though the media would make it appear so. Ross, Ifill, and Jenkins argue that legal restrictions on abortion, particularly those that restrict public funding for abortions, "have a disproportionate impact on poor Black, Latina, Native American, and Asian-Pacific American women, who often cannot afford private medical care."[45] In addition, they note that "women of color already suffer disproportionately from a variety of serious health conditions which may be exacerbated by pregnancy," including high blood pressure, hypertension, diabetes, cervical cancer, and AIDS.[46] Only one article, in the black publication *Jet,* mentioned this differential health effect.[47] Only three articles note the special problems of abortion for women with AIDS, including the double bind many may experience by being at once discouraged from carrying their pregnancy to term and encountering the unwillingness of some abortion clinics to perform abortions on them.[48]

None of the articles that discussed PAS mentioned the influence of socioeconomic status as a factor, although clearly the women meeting the high costs of therapy from the private therapists interviewed are middle- to upper-class.[49] Very few articles examined the incidence of repeat abortions, or how having two or more abortions might affect women's mental or reproductive health. Yet according to the Surgeon General's report, "approximately five percent of abortions [are] to women who had had three or more abortions."[50] The complexity and differences of the situations involved begin to give us a glimpse of why the media and the medical community cannot seem to present the public with any firm conclusions.

There are in fact two questions that both sides should address if they are truly concerned with women's health—if they are willing to pose questions to which they have not already constructed answers. The first of these is: Do women who have had abortions suffer more than women with unwanted pregnancies who choose other options (adoption, or bearing and raising the child themselves)? However researchers answer this question, they must also ask: Do women who experience suffering after abortion feel that they have been forced—by individuals, social circumstances, or by the abortion industry itself—to do something they did not truly want to do? As a *Glamour* magazine article points out, even among pro-life advocates, "Fascination with the fetus has not led to a commitment to provide each woman with what she needs to have a safe, wanted pregnancy and each child with the basic decencies of life."[51] Because of the problematic nature of abortion rights and social attitudes, alternatives to surgical abortion have been hailed by some feminists as introducing a new age for women's reproductive rights.

RU-486 and Menstrual Extraction

Media reports of the safety of RU-486 have varied significantly, with reactions generally, though not always, divided along pro-choice and pro-life lines. Some newspaper and magazine reports on trials in France and the United States show that RU-486 has few or no side effects, and generally take a positive approach to describing the benefits of the drug for women.[52]

Of 84 articles reviewed, 38 evaluated RU-486 as safe and as producing only mild side effects. The most optimistic of these foresaw a new era in women's reproductive freedom, evident in headlines proclaiming, "Hassle-free Abortion," and "Abortions Will Be Moot Soon." A smaller number of articles saw the drug in a more negative light; the headlines of this group varied from the mildly negative "The Trouble With RU-486," to the emphatic "The Human Pesticide," to the provocative and damaging "Female Scientists Slam Safety of Abortion Pill." The remaining articles deferred judgment, mirroring the uncertainty of many Americans and reflecting the embattled nature of the pill: "RU-486: A Hope or a Threat?" and "RU-486: Liberation or Nightmare?" illustrate headlines typical of this wait-and-see attitude.

Although media coverage of RU-486 overall presents a wide range of evaluations of the drug, articles that presented the stories of American women involved in trials of RU-486 expressed overwhelming approval of the drug's safety and effectiveness.[53] One reason for their preference is the differential degree of pain experienced in the two procedures.[54] The studies also indicate that the stress involved in making the decision is minimized by the time restrictions involved in using the pill.[55]

A smaller number of articles (12 out of 84) present the view that RU-486 may have mild to devastating effects on the physical and emotional health of women. Many of these critiques come, not surprisingly, from pro-life advocates, but others come from a more unexpected source: a group of feminist scientists. These women, scientists at MIT's Institute on Women and Technology, question the use of RU-486 and dispute the wisdom of devoting so much feminist energy toward getting it into general use.[56] In concluding that RU-486 is not as safe as many believe, the Institute recommends that instead of pursuing further research on the pill, resources should be directed to providing women greater access to conventional abortions. Dr. Janice Raymond advises, "Don't focus on an unproven drug. . . . Push for less medical control over the whole abortion procedure."[57]

Reporting on RU-486 brings out two issues related to surgical abortion that the articles on abortion did not themselves discuss. The first of these issues, mentioned earlier, is that of pain. Only one article on surgical abortion mentioned pain as a factor in surgical abortion, and then the pain was characterized as "nothing worse than the pain of regular menstrual cramps."[58] Yet seven of the articles on RU-486 specifically mentioned the pain of surgical abortion and how much less painful RU-486 is in contrast. One doctor notes, "Nobody talks about the fact that [surgical] abortions are painful. . . I stay with women during the procedures and hold their hands, and I know it can hurt a lot. RU-486 is so much easier."[59] Yet another article counters this view by noting, "RU-486 may hurt almost as much . . . [as] surgical abortion."[60]

The second issue involves the psychological consequences of abortion. Though pro-choice articles on surgical abortion consistently deny the existence of any negative consequences, pro-choice articles on RU-486 nevertheless note the tremendous psychological advantages for women of the RU-486 method over any surgical procedure. In a position paper printed in the National Women's Health *Network Newsletter,* the MIT scientists note,

> It is interesting that in pre-RU-486 times conventional abortion procedures were called safe and efficient by women's health advocates. It is only *now,* in the promotion of RU-486, that conventional abortion has suddenly become unsafe and is referred to as "surgical." This description bears little resemblance to low-tech (manual) vacuum aspiration.[61]

Pro-life concerns over RU-486, as expressed in media coverage, note three general concerns with regard to women's health. First, pro-life advocates argue that abortion by RU-486 will necessitate the woman "seeing" the fetus expelled and will cause greater psychological distress. Second, by accepting greater responsibility for the procedure, the woman will experience her later regret even more deeply. Finally, RU-486 will have long-term effects on women's reproductive health that have not yet appeared in tests, because the drug has been in use for too short a period of time to ascertain its long-term consequences.[62]

One concern that is shared by both sides and conveyed in media stories is the possibility that a black market for the pill will develop in the United States, as the pill becomes available in many other countries and the demand in this country increases. Doctors warn that use of the pill without medical supervision is dangerous because of the possibility that complications may arise and women will not have ready access to medical help.[63]

The interest in RU-486 coincides with a movement among American women to gain greater control over their own medical decisions and to take a more active role in providing for their own health care needs. As a sudden spate of media coverage attests, the reemergence of a self-help movement and a woman-performed technique of abortion called "menstrual extraction" introduces a host of new issues and concerns in the field of women's health care. The competing claims of doctors and of women who perform menstrual extraction are well documented by media coverage, and two thirds of the articles presented the views of both sides. Doctors in the articles unanimously claim that the procedure is dangerous and an unnecessary risk because abortion is legal and (they argue) generally accessible. Even Planned Parenthood and the American College of Obstetricians and Gynecologists evidence concern over the procedure, fearful that it "heightens the risk of incomplete abortions, uterine perforations, infection, sterility, and even death from an undetected ectopic pregnancy that ruptures."[64]

Yet self-help group participants argue that the medical care a woman would get in a clinic or even from her own doctor cannot compare with the kind of caring and personal attention that the women in her group will give her.[65] Others assert that the method "has to be better than needles and Drano douches and coat hangers."[66] These women concede, however, that there is no data on side effects or long-term effects of this procedure, and they admit that "the procedure could be deadly in the hands of the inexperienced."[67]

The pro-life stance is represented in only one third of the articles on this topic, and it generally presents a reiteration of the pro-life position on surgical abortion, with little additional comment on women's health issues. John Willke, former leader of the National Right-to-Life Committee and frequently quoted as a representative of the pro-life movement, believes that, "there isn't a single responsible physician who has a good thing to say about this," and that therefore "it's hypocritical of feminists to endorse a method that will 'kill women' after arguing for twenty years that doctors should do abortions."[68] Perhaps the only common ground is the concession by all sides that abortion by menstrual extraction, though illegal, will no doubt persist and that it will be very difficult if not impossible to police or prevent the efforts of determined women.[69]

Abortion in Context: Reproductive Control

What this study makes apparent is the way in which the media make so many of women's concerns subservient to political concerns, so that women themselves are often marginalized by the terms of the debate. Not only are women unable to find in these articles the information they need to become knowledgeable health care consumers, but the media may exert a negative influence by limiting the "acceptable" range of post-abortion responses in terms of political positions and defining reactions outside those boundaries as unacceptable or deviant.

At the same time, these articles maintain a rigidly narrow focus that obscures larger issues and constructs choice in an especially limited manner. The goal for social change that empowers women must reflect a commitment to rejecting

> all efforts to coerce or otherwise influence women *to* have abortions at the same time that we resist attempts to prevent women from having abortions. Creating the conditions that enable women to have the children they want to have is a long-term goal of reproductive rights activists.[70]

This goal requires expanding the debate to include issues related to all women, not only women of a particular race or class. "Thus far, the abortion debate has largely been between white men and white women," insists one pro-choice activist.[71]

Empowerment requires recognizing the interconnections among issues as well as among individual women. Questions regarding the consequences of abortion invite not only our analysis, but our intervention. Alongside efforts to keep abortion safe and legal, pro-choice activists must commit themselves to redefining and reshaping women's experience of abortion, for the millions of women who have had abortions, and for all those yet to come.

Notes

1. In all, I found 121 articles on surgical abortion that were related to its health consequences. The majority of these, however, cannot accurately be classified as articles "about" abortion's health aspects, nor do they address a common group of issues. As a result, the samples supporting each of my individual conclusions are noticeably small, my generalizations drawn from what may appear to be insufficient evidence. Yet the scarcity of such articles in itself communicates a message, and so my analysis is faithful to the reality that the information available to women is both partial and scattered. In addition, the paucity of these articles draws attention to the kind of information that has been omitted from public discussions of abortion, and it is this issue that I will address in my concluding discussion.

2. Committee on Government Operations, "The Federal Role in Determining the Medical and Psychological Impact of Abortion on Women," Washington, D.C., December 11, 1989, testimony of Dr. David Grimes, pp. 5-6. Death from illegal abortion today is rarely mentioned in the articles except in cases of unlicensed practitioners, but reproductive rights advocates have documented the case of the first woman who died as the result of an illegal abortion in Mexico shortly after Texas stopped providing government-funded abortions. See A. Davis, "Racism, Birth Control, and Reproductive Rights," in M. Gerber Fried (Ed.), *From Abortion to Reproductive Freedom: Transforming a Movement* (Boston: South End, 1990): 15-26.

3. In addition, a modern version of these horror stories appears in articles on abortion providers who are sued for malpractice or for performing abortions illegally (i.e., without a license, or later in a pregnancy than is permitted by law). Such cases are seemingly rare; only five, one of these in Canada, were documented by the media during the years I surveyed. These cases have remained largely outside the central debate.

4. M. Tolchin, "Koop's Stand on Abortion's Effect Surprises Friends and Foes Alike," *New York Times,* June 11, 1989, p. 20. Copyright © 1989 by The New York Times Company. Reprinted by permission.

5. R. Benson Gold, *Abortion and Women's Health: A Turning Point for America?* (New York: Alan Guttmacher Institute, 1990): 32.

6. M. Cimons, "House Panel Accuses Koop of Ignoring Medical Evidence on Safety of Abortion," *Los Angeles Times,* December 11, 1989, p. A22.

7. Hearing Before the Human Resources and Intergovernmental Relations Subcommittee, "Medical and Psychological Impact of Abortion," March 16, 1989, hereafter referred to as "Hearing."

8. "Debate: Is Post-Abortion Syndrome an Emotional Disorder or Political Tool?" *Detroit News,* January 27, 1989, pp. B3-B4. (Quoted material used by permission.) See also M. Specter, "Koop Won't Issue Report on Abortion," *Washington Post,* January 10, 1989, pp. A1-A5.

9. B. Conley, "Catholics Offer Post-Abortion Counseling," *Argus Leader,* February 20, 1988, p. A6. Quoted material used by permission.

10. K. Audia, "Post-Abortion Syndrome Surfaces Years Later," *Dominion Post,* April 24, 1988, HEA 44: pp. B12-B14. Quoted material used by permission.

11. "Debate: Is Post-Abortion Syndrome an Emotional Disorder or Political Tool?," p. B3.

12. J. Weintraub, "Review Disputes Abortion Trauma," *Milwaukee Journal,* April 6, 1990, p. A5; C. Lyons, "After Abortion," *New York Daily News,* March 11, 1991, p. D11 (© New York Daily News, L. P., used with permission); H. Smith, "Scope of PAS a Matter of Hot Debate," *Colorado Springs Gazette Telegraph,* June 26, 1988, pp. B10-B11.

13. "Women Exploited by Abortion" has changed its name to "Miami Valley Aborted Women." See W. Hundley, "Post-Abortion Syndrome," *Dayton Daily News/Journal Herald,* February 13, 1989, pp. A6-A7. Quoted material used by permission.

14. P. Laws, "Post-Abortion Syndrome," *Virginian-Pilot,* May 28, 1986, pp. E5-E7. Quoted material used by permission.

15. A. Kuebelbeck, "These Women Grieve for Empty Wombs," *Grand Forks Herald,* September 11, 1988, pp. C11-C13. Quoted material used by permission of the Grand Forks Herald.

16. Hundley, "Post-Abortion," p. A6.

17. Laws, "Post-Abortion," p. E6.

18. See R. J. Branham, "The Role of the Convert in *Eclipse of Reason* and *The Silent Scream,*" *Quarterly Journal of Speech* 77 (November 1991): 407-426.

19. See A. Thompson Cook, "Fact Sheet: Abortion After Twelve Weeks" (Washington, DC: National Abortion Federation, 1992); and A. Thompson Cook, "Fact Sheet: Teenage Women, Abortion, and the Law" (Washington, DC: National Abortion Federation, 1992).

20. M. Powers, "Abortion Foe: Study Points to Adverse Effects in Women," *Commercial Appeal,* September 12, 1992, p. C6. The reporter does note, however, that these conclusions "are not universally accepted." (Quoted material used by permission. Copyright 1992, *The Commercial Appeal.*)

21. M. Barrineau, "After Abortion," *Dallas Times Herald,* March 5, 1989, pp. E3-E5. Reprinted with permission of the Dallas Morning News.

22. Kuebelbeck, "These Women," p. C12.

23. Audia, "Post-Abortion," p. B14.

24. See Branham, "The Role of the Convert," pp. 407-426.

25. "Debate: Is Post-Abortion Syndrome an Emotional Disorder or Political Tool?" p. B3.

26. Audia, "Post-Abortion," p. B13.

27. Audia, "Post-Abortion," p. B13.

28. Lyons, "After Abortion," p. D11.

29. H. Smith, "Abortion's Unforeseen Consequences Take Their Toll," *Colorado Springs Gazette Telegraph,* June 26, 1988, pp. B12-B14.

30. Hundley, "Post-Abortion," p. A6.

31. Barrineau, "After Abortion," p. E4.

32. J. Grelen, "Post-Abortion Distress Divides the Experts," *Denver Post,* March 25, 1990, HEA 25, pp. B5-B7. Quoted material used by permission.

33. Kuebelbeck, "These Women," p. C12.

34. L. M. Terman, "Post-Abortion Syndrome Stirs Debate Beyond the Medical World," *Washington Times,* January 22, 1987, pp. B1-B2. Quoted material used by permission from The Washington Times.

35. N. E. Adler, H. P. David, B. N. Major, S. H. Roth, N. F. Russo, & G. E. Wyatt, "Psychological Responses After Abortion," *Science* 248 (April 6, 1990): 41-44.

36. Hundley, "Post-Abortion," p. A7.

37. S. Buttenweiser & R. Levine, "Breaking Silences: A Post-Abortion Support Model," in M. Gerber Fried (Ed.), *From Abortion to Reproductive Freedom: Transforming a Movement* (Boston: South End, 1990): 121-128.

38. Davis, "Racism, Birth Control," pp. 20-25.

39. Davis, "Racism, Birth Control," p. 24. See also The Boston Women's Health Book Collective, *The New Our Bodies, Ourselves: Updated and Expanded for the '90s* (New York: Simon & Schuster, 1992): 301-302, 377.

40. As with abortion, birth control technology is a highly charged political issue, and the health issues surrounding the need for safe and effective birth control are often eclipsed by political interests that block birth control research. For a comprehensive discussion of the political dimensions of birth control, see L. Gordon, *Woman's Body, Woman's Right: Birth Control in America* (New York: Penguin, 1990).

41. Buttenweiser & Levine, "Breaking Silences," p. 126.

42. K. M. Lodl, A. McGettigan, & J. Bucy, "Women's Responses to Abortion: Implications for Post-Abortion Support Groups," in M. R. Walsh (Ed.), *The Psychology of Women: Ongoing Debates* (New Haven, CT: Yale University Press, 1987): 396-408.

43. B. Avery, "A Question of Survival/A Conspiracy of Silence: Abortion and Black Women's Health," in M. Gerber Fried (Ed.), *From Abortion to Reproductive Freedom: Transforming a Movement* (Boston: South End, 1990): 75-81.

44. Lodl et al., "Women's Responses," p. 406.

45. L. Ross, S. Ifill, & S. Jenkins, "Emergency Memorandum to Women of Color," in M. Gerber Fried (Ed.), *From Abortion to Reproductive Freedom: Transforming a Movement* (Boston: South End, 1990): 147-150.

46. Ross et al., "Emergency Memorandum," 148.

47. "Black Women's Plight Cited at Pro-Choice Rally in D.C.," *Jet* 76 (April 24, 1989): 13.

48. For an overview of the problems of abortion and AIDS, see R. J. Welch Cline & N. J. McKenzie, "Women and AIDS: The Lost Population," Chapter 26 in this volume.

49. The counseling center most frequently mentioned in the articles as a provider of post-abortion counseling was listed in a 1988 article as charging $1,000 a week for a program lasting 2 to 4 weeks. The article notes that, "most major medical and health insurance plans will cover most of the costs of the program . . . but inpatients must also pay their transportation, lodging and food costs." H. Smith, "Psychodrama Helps Patient Heal the Wound," *Colorado Springs Gazette Telegraph,* June 26, 1988, pp. B4-B5.

50. Hearing, p. 205.

51. K. Pollitt, "Why Do We Romanticize the Fetus?" *Glamour* (October 1992): 260-298.

52. None of the articles on RU-486 mentions race as a factor in determining the safety of the drug. Yet Judy Norsigian, a Board member of the National Women's Health Network and coauthor of *Our Bodies, Ourselves,* notes that clinical trials of the drug have been done mostly with white women, and emphasizes the need for additional testing on women of different racial and socioeconomic backgrounds as well as women with particular medical conditions. For example, she asks, "Would malnutrition play an unforeseen role in outcomes with RU-486?" J. Norsigian, "RU-486," in M. Gerber Fried (Ed.), *From Abortion to Reproductive Freedom: Transforming a Movement* (Boston: South End, 1990): 197-203.

53. L. Fraser, "486: The 'Abortion Pill,' " *Glamour* (September 1990): 317-360.

54. Fraser, "486," p. 356.

55. Fraser, "486," pp. 356-357.

56. S. Brink, "Female Scientists Slam Safety of Abortion Pill," *Boston Herald,* September 12, 1991, pp. A1-A2.

57. S. Ince, "The Trouble With RU-486," *Vogue* (July 1991): 88-90. Quoted material used by permission.

58. V. Frankel & E. Tien, "How to Tell if You're Pregnant (and What You Can Do if You Are)," *Mademoiselle* (November 1991): 106-110.

59. Fraser, "486," p. 356.

60. D. Alvarado, "RU-486: What the Abortion Would Be Like," *San Jose Mercury News,* July 22, 1992, pp. A6-A7. Quoted material used by permission from the San Jose Mercury News.

61. R. Klein, L. Dumble, & J. Raymond, "RU-486: A Dialogue—Against," *National Women's Health Network News* (September/October 1992): 1-8. Quoted material used by permission.

62. B. Armstrong, "RU-486: The Abortion Pill," *San Jose Mercury News,* February 20, 1990, pp. A2-A3.

63. Brink, "Female Scientists," p. A1; Ince, "The Trouble," p. 88.

64. J. Gehorsam, "In the Hands of Women," *Atlanta Journal,* January 7, 1992, pp. A1-A4. Reprinted with permission from The Atlanta Journal and The Atlanta Constitution.

65. D. Alvarado, "The Abortion Kit," *San Jose Mercury News,* September 11, 1991, pp. A3-A4.

66. T. Vercellotti, "At-Home Abortion Procedure Is Revived," *Pittsburgh Press,* August 27, 1989, pp. C1-C2.

67. K. Newcomer, "Do-It-Yourself Abortion Video Shown at Local NOW Meeting," *Rocky Mountain News,* October 30, 1989, pp. A4-A5.

68. Gehorsam, "In the Hands," p. A3.

69. For a comprehensive discussion of the history and practice of menstrual extraction, see R. Chalker & C. Downer, *A Woman's Book of Choices: Abortion, Menstrual Extraction, RU-486* (New York: Four Walls Eight Windows, 1992).

70. The Boston Women's Health Book Collective, *The New Our Bodies, Ourselves,* p. 377.

71. L. Ross, "Raising Our Voices," in M. Gerber Fried (Ed.), *From Abortion to Reproductive Freedom: Transforming a Movement* (Boston: South End, 1990): 139-143.

4

Illicit Drug Use and the Pregnant Woman

Prevalence, Social Impact, Effects, and Legislative Action

Robert Lemieux

There was a time when a drug such as cocaine was in everything from Coca-Cola to hay fever remedies.[1] In fact, it was not until President Woodrow Wilson signed the Harrison Act into law, in 1914, that cocaine became obtainable only through a doctor's prescription. The law, coupled with new-found awareness concerning the drug's habitual effects, helped limit its use such that by the start of World War II, cocaine use was relatively uncommon and by 1960 virtually nonexistent.[2] Times have changed since then, and as of this writing the drug is unquestionably one of America's biggest social problems. As Chavkin and Kandall note, "Our national budget is being rewritten, our foreign policy is being revised, and a national drug czar has been appointed, evidence that Americans consider drug abuse the most serious problem facing our society."[3]

AUTHOR'S NOTE: A tip of the hat to Ms. Debra Pomerleau for her valuable comments on a previous draft.

One increasingly significant aspect of this social problem is its use, or rather misuse, by pregnant women.[4] And unfortunately it is a problem that has become much more prevalent. It should be understood, however, that although cocaine is the predominant drug associated with drug-related pregnancies, it is not a solo act. There are a variety of other licit and illicit drugs that impact pregnancies.

Alcohol and tobacco are of equal concern for women's reproductive health and are addressed in other chapters in this volume; the illicit drugs under discussion in this chapter include cocaine, marijuana, and methadone/heroin. The rationale for selecting these is that they seemingly receive the majority of attention in the research literature.

An estimated 30 million Americans have used cocaine, and more than 5 million use it regularly.[5] Although the vast majority of cocaine users are professional males with a higher than average income,[6] the use among females has increased across all socioeconomic levels.[7] More to the point, cocaine use by women is most prevalent during their childbearing years.[8] More than 5 million women of childbearing age (15-44) currently use illicit drugs. Of these, 1 million use cocaine and 3.8 million use marijuana.[9] In 1990, the President's National Drug Abuse Strategy report estimated that 100,000 cocaine exposed babies were born in the United States.[10] Other government agencies indicate there may be as many as 375,000 drug exposed infants.[11]

Cocaine can be ingested by snorting, injection, orally, vaginally, rectally, and it can be smoked.[12] Much of the reason for its increased use is based upon the false assumption that it is harmless and nonaddictive.[13] This type of ignorance concerning the drug's affects is not solely attributable to the general population. As recently as 1982, a major obstetric textbook indicated that, "Cocaine is not known to have direct deleterious effects on the fetus."[14]

Throughout the literature, the study of cocaine and pregnancy is approached from three angles. The first approach involves animal studies and the generalization of the results to the human population.[15] The second approach focuses on the drug's impact upon the mother; the third approach on the neonate or infant. The literature appears evenly split in regard to the amount of research and discussion devoted to each approach.

Much of the research involving the mother focuses on (a) the reported prevalence of cocaine use during pregnancy and (b) the physiological affects. The general approach to measuring cocaine use during pregnancy is via urine test and/or an interview. In most instances, there is at least one prenatal interview and one immediate postpartum interview. As a whole, most of the findings within the literature report consistently disturbing results.

In one study of 679 pregnant women, 17% used cocaine during pregnancy. Of these, 61% reported using cocaine only during a single trimester, whereas 18% used the drug throughout all three trimesters. Perhaps more astonishing is that 33% of the users reported using the drug within 7 days of delivery or had postpartum urine samples that tested positive.[16] Chasnoff found that 60% of the subjects using cocaine continued to use it throughout the pregnancy.[17] Little, Snell, Klein, and Gisltrap found that 77% of their cocaine using subjects ($n = 53$) continued using the drug throughout the pregnancy, and 85% reported intravenous injection of the drug.[18]

In New York City, anonymous toxicological surveys at municipal hospitals indicated that 10% to 20% of delivering mothers tested positive for illicit substances, usually cocaine.[19] In a survey of 36 hospitals nationwide, the average overall incidence of substance abuse was 11%, with the highest rate at any one hospital being 27%.[20] When one considers that not every means possible is employed to detect drug use, it becomes apparent that the figures, and the problem's magnitude, are almost certainly underestimated.[21]

It is not unusual for cocaine to be used in combination with other illicit drugs. One of the primary additional drugs is marijuana—apparently used as often as cocaine.[22] Richardson et al. found that in the first trimester, approximately 3-4 joints per week are smoked by users of the drug. Furthermore, approximately 40% of the 373 pregnant women in their sample indulged in the drug. During the second and third trimesters, both the amount smoked and the number of smokers decreased by one half (1-2 joints per week, 20% of sample used the drug).[23] The decrease is obviously a positive sign; however, the drug's impact has already been registered during the initial fetal development of the first trimester.

The use of marijuana in conjunction with cocaine also seems relatively prevalent. Frank et al. reported that 72% of cocaine using subjects indulged in marijuana at some point during pregnancy.[24] Similarly, Richardson and Day reported that 71% of their cocaine using subjects used marijuana.[25]

The final drug under discussion is actually two drugs—heroin and methadone. Heroin is a powerfully addictive opiate and methadone is a synthetically derived version of heroin. Ironically, methadone was created for medicinal purposes with the intent of helping heroin addicts break their addiction. Although it is less rapidly habit forming, it carries many of the same negative implications. An estimated 10,000 births per year involve women using heroin, methadone, or other lethal opiates.[26] Use of both drugs is particularly noticeable among lower-income females of metropolitan areas. Frank et al. found that 14% of their cocaine using subjects used opiates during pregnancy.[27]

Although cocaine, marijuana, and heroin/methadone are the primary drugs cited within the research, there are a number of other illicit drugs that draw attention. Drugs such as amphetamines, barbiturates, and hallucinogens are also part of the overall picture. They comprise a smaller percentage of drugs used, but that does not diminish their presence and effects.

In addition, attention should be given to the potential for abuse of licit or prescription drugs. There are a large number of prescription drugs that if taken in excess can be as dangerous as many illicit drugs. Many of these drugs, even when taken as medically directed, have unknown effects on pregnancy. Considering both the vast number of prescriptions filled annually in the United States and the black market for such drugs, the opportunities for easy access to the drugs makes them viable candidates for abuse by drug users.

Social Forces and Other Variables

One of the main criticisms of illicit drug research is that the samples are skewed or unrepresentative—specifically, that they are drawn from largely minority, indigent populations. In addressing such criticisms, Clayton notes that drug use is also prevalent among other classes of women and may be associated with different risk factors than in less impoverished samples.[28] Similarly, Chasnoff, Landroff, and Barrett found comparable prevalence of drug use at both public and private hospitals, rich or poor, black or white (total number of subjects in public hospitals was 380, total in private hospitals was 335).[29] Similarly, Marques and McKnight compared their adolescent sample with an older adult sample. The results indicate the social contacts of both groups used similar drugs in similar frequencies. The adult sample, however, discussed drugs more with their friends; reported drug use during pregnancy was generally the same for both groups.[30]

As a possible answer to the differing research findings, both Boyd and Hickner and colleagues indicate that the increase or decrease in drug use may be affected by the amount of health information received during pregnancy or by the pregnancy experience itself.[31] Furthermore, there may be specific characteristics of the sample that determine whether drug use increases or decreases and whether health information is received. Or, perhaps there are other variables that influence the decision to use drugs during pregnancy, such as the environment in which a woman lives.

Marques and McKnight found that subjects considered as high-risk but infrequent users reported approximately 33% of their closest reference groups used cocaine and/or marijuana. Subjects categorized as abusers with frequent use indicated that 70% of their closest reference groups used these same drugs. In a further breakdown, the same study found that for the high-risk group, more than 50% of the drug using reference group consisted of friends and significant others (remaining percentage comprised of parents, siblings, and extended family). For the abuser group, more than 70% of the drug using reference group consisted of friends and significant others with 50% being strictly significant others.[32] In sum, the social and family networks can have a strong impact on the continued use of drugs during pregnancy.

In a study with adolescent subjects, Gilchrist, Gilmore, and Lohr found that 51% of subjects' boyfriends and 36% of subjects' best friends used marijuana.[33] Frank et al. found that among mothers who used cocaine, 52% of babies' fathers also used the drug.[34] In somewhat of a reverse approach, Yamaguchi and Kandel found that illicit drug use had a strong impact on the occurrence of premarital pregnancy, especially among African Americans. After analyzing a number of factors (e.g., age, cohabitation, peer activity, etc.) that might influence the occurrence of a premarital pregnancy, two of their significant findings included current use of illicit drugs and former use of illicit drugs. Current use of illicit drugs also increases the likelihood of abortion.[35]

Of further interest is that Gilchrist et al. noted, "the earlier the age of sexual initiation, the greater the frequency of prepregnancy drug use."[36] Although the percentages of boyfriends and best friends who used the drug were high, only prepregnancy use remained significantly associated with subjects' use during pregnancy.[37] In other words, "When prepregnancy drug use was taken into account, neither boyfriends' use nor best friends' use contributed to the explained variance in subjects' use of these drugs."[38] Regardless of the findings concerning boyfriends and best friends, the authors assert that, "boyfriends may be influencing prepregnancy use and thereby indirectly influencing subjects' use of drugs during pregnancy."[39]

Upon closer inspection, the Gilchrist et al. and Yamaguchi and Kandel findings present a pattern of behavior that seemingly pinpoints women who would be prime candidates for drug use during pregnancy. If one were to merge the results of these two studies, a chain of related events would become evident. The chain begins with earlier-than-normal sexual experiences, which increases the likelihood of illicit drug use as noted by Gilchrist.[40] The combination of these two events increases the likelihood of premarital pregnancy, as noted by Yamaguchi and Kandel.[41] Finally, the combination of all three events (earlier sexual experiences, illicit drug use, and/or premarital pregnancy) increases the likelihood of continued drug use during pregnancy.

It is as if the events build upon one another such that if a woman has experienced all three events, it seems highly probable she will abuse drugs during the pregnancy. If this chain of events is plausible, perhaps the focus of prevention programs and campaigns should be to identify and educate those women who are at greater risk. In other words, catching them before they fall into the final stage of a drug abusing pregnancy. To date, however, no campaign has segmented the audience in this fashion, by considering the women's experiences.

Effects of Illicit Drugs

The effects of cocaine and other illicit drugs are observable in two ways. First are the effects on the mother and second the effects on the newborn. Among the effects upon the mother, abruptio placentae (premature detachment of a normally implanted placenta) is perhaps the most heavily documented.[42] Additional complications include premature labor, precipitous labor, spontaneous abortion, pregnancy induced hypertension, vaginal bleeding, hepatitis, and a higher rate of infectious disease complications.[43] Much of the research indicates that the risk of maternal complication after delivery is 3 to 8 times greater among drug users than non-drug users.[44]

Effects upon the newborn are heavily documented. Consistent findings include lower weight, shorter length, and a smaller head circumference.[45] Additional complications include abnormal sleep patterns, poor feeding, tremors,[46] dying or dead cerebral tissue (cerebral infarction), meconium staining, cardiac anomalies, and withdrawal symptoms.[47] The findings are based on an acceptable number of subjects and indicate the chance of complication is 2 to 6 times greater for drug exposed infants.

Of course, the most serious side effect is infant mortality. In a 1986 review of birth certificates by the New York City Department of Health Division of Biostatistics, the mortality rate for narcotic babies was 2.5 times higher than the overall rate.[48] In the District of Columbia, after witnessing a decline in infant mortality from 1986 to 1987, officials reported a sharp rise in 1988 and 1989, attributed mainly to substance abuse.[49] Obviously, one cannot generalize New York City and the District of Columbia to other cities or geographical regions. The statistics are nonetheless alarming.

Perhaps one of the more intriguing areas of research is the possible link between substance use and sudden infant death syndrome (SIDS). Kandall and Gaines have presented a good review of the literature regarding SIDS and various types of drugs.

As they noted in their conclusion, there is "somewhat [of an] association between maternal opiate use and SIDS . . . the relationship of cocaine use during pregnancy to SIDS is not clear."[50] They reported that summated data from various studies suggest that exposure to opiates during pregnancy increases the risk of SIDS about tenfold. They noted, however, that no study has yet separated the effects of opiates per se from the many intervening variables associated with a drug using lifestyle.

Legislative Action

> The pregnant woman needs prenatal care in order to avoid a host of obstetrical complications which may occur if she does not have this care. If she is drug dependent, she needs medical care because her drug dependency adds to a host of other problems.[51]

The problems of illicit drug abuse by pregnant women has not gone unnoticed by the various government social agencies and legislative committees. In February 1980, the Select Committee on Narcotics Abuse and Control of the 96th Congress heard testimony from various medical doctors on the emerging problem of drug abuse among pregnant women. Much of what was discussed in that hearing, and in subsequent hearings throughout the 1980s, became the impetus for the current programs that address maternal and child health issues.

In 1981, Congress combined 10 federal grant programs for alcohol, drug abuse, and mental health services into the Alcohol, Drug, and Mental Services (ADMS) Block Grant. The Department of Health and Human Services was tasked with addressing the issues relevant to drug abuse among pregnant women (Maternal and Child Health Services also address such issues, but from a limited perspective). The impetus of the block grant was for the federal government to provide the necessary funding to improve the health of all mothers and children and for the states to oversee the appropriation and spending. In a sense, this was a decentralization or partnership between the two entities.

During the 1984 reauthorization of this block grant, the women's set-aside was created. This required states to use at least 5% of the total block grant to provide or initiate new or expanded women's drug abuse and alcohol services. A subsequent reauthorization in 1988, keyed in part by the realization of the health, financial, and social costs related to the impact of maternal drug use, increased the set-aside from 5% to not less than 10% for services and programs designed for women. In terms of actual dollars, the 1988 set-aside for women was $24.4 million. Due to an increased appropriation to the ADMS Block Grant in 1990, that amount had increased to $119.3 million.[52]

Unfortunately, the grant does not specifically define those services designed for drug abusing pregnant women nor does it require that a program or service be strictly for these women. Thus, there exists the possibility that the total amount of the set-aside is not being used as it was perhaps originally intended. In an attempt to ascertain whether the monies were being used as intended, legislation (The Anti-Drug Abuse Act of 1988) was implemented in 1989 that redefined the mission and required states to collect data regarding the use of various services. This step was meant to make the states more accountable for the types of programs offered and their accessibility. To what degree has this change been effective?

The findings of a 1991 U.S. General Accounting Office (GAO) Report on the ADMS Block Grant indicate that,

> the women's set-aside does not assure that funds will be used to provide appropriate treatment services to drug-abusing pregnant women and mothers with young children. This is because the women's set-aside encourages, but does not require, states to fund treatment specifically designed for these women.[53]

In fact, of the 4 million women needing drug treatment in 1990, only an estimated 14% received such treatment.[54]

The above-mentioned GAO report further indicated that despite monetary increases in the women's set-aside, Congress still lacks the information to determine whether the set-aside has been effective in addressing the problems associated with drug abuse and pregnant women. The report places the blame on the Department of Health and Human Services—as administrator of the ADMS block grant—indicating that the agency has not specified to the states what must be provided. Thus, although funds are available, there is still no clear direction as to how they should be used. Consequently, no systematic campaign has been planned, implemented, or evaluated.

At the center of the report are what the GAO identifies as eight "critical barriers" to drug treatment for pregnant women. The barriers are a reflection of the lack of direction within the women's set-aside. Either separately or in combination, the barriers constrain or prevent pregnant women from seeking and receiving drug treatment. Furthermore, the eight barriers seemingly represent an open criticism of the lack of attention and seriousness that the issue requires and deserves. Perhaps more specifically, it is a criticism of how the problem has been inappropriately addressed. Whatever the case, the eight barriers provide excellent insight into the needs that should be considered if the problem of drug using mothers is to be curbed.

First and foremost is the lack of available treatment. The demand for drug treatment exceeds the availability. When there is availability, patients have reported having to wait weeks between appointments or having to put their names on waiting lists and often not receiving return calls from the program.[55] The greater the amount of time between appointments, the greater the chance for relapse or dropout. As a response to this criticism, some drug treatment providers indicated that their reluctance to treat pregnant women was based on the fear of lawsuits or increased insurance costs associated with treating pregnant women for drug abuse. The GAO, in discussion with some state officials, believes this to be an excuse of providers who are unequipped for or uninterested in treating these women.

The second barrier is the lack of appropriate programs. A number of states do not provide specially designed treatment services for pregnant women. The set-aside funds are used for treating women in general. A drug treatment survey in New York City indicated that 50% of the programs excluded pregnant women, 67% refused pregnant

Medicaid patients, and 87% excluded crack-abusing women receiving Medicaid.[56] As one woman noted, "you keep [using drugs] then you go for an appointment and they tell you you're a bad mom for doing drugs and you don't want to go back."[57]

There may also be more programs for certain types of drug abuse than others. For example, women in some of the larger metropolitan cities claim it is easier to get help for heroin than for crack cocaine.[58] In some cases, women are falsely indicating they use heroin just to get into a program! Considering the percentage of pregnant women who use cocaine (as opposed to heroin), it appears that a number of women, who are not deceptive enough, are turned away from drug treatment.

To complicate matters, there are some programs that are short-lived due to funding under smaller grants. Although the intentions are good, it becomes a situation of programs opening and closing without having fully achieved their goal. Thus, the women are forced to look for yet another program. Lack of program continuity results in high dropout and avoidance rates.[59]

The third barrier is a result of the political problems and public outcry that accompany the placing and building of new facilities. The "not in my backyard" syndrome makes it difficult to place treatment centers in locations that are away from drug infested areas. For those programs situated outside the drug infested areas, the issue of transportation becomes a problem. This represents the fourth barrier cited in the GAO report.

The transportation issue focuses on the lack of public transportation (subway or bus service) to the program site, which is generally a problem in the smaller communities, or the difficulty of riding the public transportation for extended periods of time, especially in the larger metropolitan areas. As an example, the report notes a Los Angeles woman's $2\frac{1}{2}$-hour bus ride to get to a program that would accept her. This barrier, coupled with the "not in my backyard" syndrome noted above, can be formidable, resulting in geographically inaccessible programs.

Health care professionals are also a barrier to effective treatment. Cited as the fifth critical barrier are the attitudes and behaviors of health care providers. A large number of drug addicted women reported negative encounters with their health care providers. These encounters represent one of the most formidable barriers in obtaining drug treatment or prenatal care: "They treat me like I'm nothing, like I'm dirt, like I'm scum of the earth, the bottom of the barrel. I feel like a throw-away, a cast-off."[60] There are reports of doctors ignoring obvious symptoms of addiction or failing to inquire about possible drug use. One mother tells of her difficulties in finding a concerned physician:

> The first one—I got up my nerve and told him right out I was an addict. It didn't seem to affect his plans for me or my baby one bit. It was like he just did not want to hear me—he ignored what I said. So I went to another doctor. He never even asked and I didn't tell him.[61]

The issue of Medicaid can also be a problem. There are health care providers who are unwilling to accept drug abusing mothers who lack Medicaid or have yet to be accepted for it. Some of the patient referrals for prenatal treatment are based on whether providers accept Medicaid. For a woman lacking Medicaid, this can complicate the referral process, resulting in a greater distance to go to seek treatment or abandonment of treatment.[62]

A woman's inadequate knowledge of drugs and their effects on the neonate and her denial of pregnancy is what is termed a personal barrier and represents the sixth critical barrier. Feedback from focus groups indicates that a number of women continue using drugs in an attempt to forget their pregnancy and other related worries.[63] Obviously, this type of behavior and denial can be a major deterrent for women seeking treatment. In addition, personal barriers can develop from bad experiences related to some of the other barriers (e.g., negative experiences with health care providers, lack of transportation).

In terms of education about prenatal care, most of these women lack the knowledge and understanding to realize the harm the drug is committing. The report identifies one anonymous woman who indicated she would "eat a lot of white bread, y'know like Wonder Bread," before smoking crack: "I figured all that bread would stop up the passage through the umbilical cord so the crack wouldn't get through to the baby."[64] This statement reflects the misguided beliefs that can result in continued drug use.

Within the past few years, there has been a movement toward criminalizing the pregnant addict—send her to jail instead of the hospital.[65] Despite (a) two Supreme Court decisions that viewed addiction as an illness instead of willful criminal behavior, (b) the American Medical Association's endorsement of medical as opposed to punitive approaches to addiction, and (c) the categorizing of drug dependency as a psychiatric condition, there is an obvious movement toward criminalizing drug use during pregnancy.[66] Consequently, the fear of being prosecuted has kept a certain percentage of pregnant women from seeking treatment, and this represents barrier number seven.

As of 1990, there were 17 states that had cases pending against drug addicted women.[67] There are four states (Florida, Illinois, Oklahoma, Rhode Island) that now include drug use during pregnancy as child abuse. Minnesota considers prenatal exposure to drugs as criminal child neglect. Finally, three states (Minnesota, Oklahoma, Utah) require doctors to report positive urine toxicology tests to the state.[68] In terms of actual prosecutions, Florida has had two child abuse prosecutions of women who gave birth to drug addicted babies. Although such prosecutions are rare, women in need of treatment are aware of the possible legal consequences. Needless to say, this poses a major barrier to their seeking treatment.

The eighth and final critical barrier mentioned in the GAO report refers to the need for outreach and referral services for women seeking treatment. Because the personal and social barriers described above can make it difficult for women to receive treatment, it is important that such services are available. Finding a program that treats drug abusing, pregnant women can be difficult. Many times, the women are unaware of the programs' locations and how to contact them. Hospitals and health care agencies may not always be able to refer women to appropriate places. Communities with limited outreach or referral programs make it difficult for the women to receive treatment.

Conclusion

As previously mentioned, the GAO report was a blistering criticism on the state of affairs for available assistance to pregnant drug abusers. In view of the prevalence of illicit drug use and its physiological and social effects, it becomes apparent that such criticisms should not fall on deaf ears.

There are a few states (most notably California, Washington, and Florida) that provide extensive services for pregnant women. As of 1991, however, none of the 50 states had determined the number of pregnant drug abusers needing treatment. None of the 721 programs available under the ADMS block grant in Texas are designed for pregnant women. Of the 56 programs available in South Carolina, none are designed specifically for pregnant women.[69] In short, there is great disparity among the states' individual approaches to helping pregnant drug abusers.

The problem has been recognized and defined. Funds have been made available to help diminish the problem and its effects. There is no question that treatment and prenatal care can make a difference. Yet a large gap still remains between the number of women who could benefit from such treatment and the treatment's availability. Until systematic campaign efforts are made to target pregnant drug abusers specifically, the effects of the gap will continue to be evident in the delivery rooms throughout America's hospitals.

Notes

1. D. Musto, "Evolution of American Attitudes Toward Substance Abuse," in D. Hutchings (Ed.), *Prenatal Abuse of Licit and Illicit Drugs* (New York: New York Academy of Sciences, 1989): 3-7.

2. Musto, "Evolution of American," pp. 3-7.

3. W. Chavkin & S. Kandall, "Between a Rock and a Hard Place: Perinatal Drug Abuse," *Pediatrics* 85 (1990): 224.

4. U.S. Government Accounting Office, *ADMS Block Grant: Women's Set-aside Does Not Assure Drug Treatment for Pregnant Women* (May 1990).

5. H. Abelson & J. Miller, "A Decade of Trends in Cocaine Use in the Household Population," *National Institute on Drug Abuse Research* 61 (1985): 35-49.

6. R. Mittleman & C. Wetli, "Death Caused by Recreational Cocaine Use: An Update," *Journal of the American Medical Association* 252 (1984): 1889-1893; L. Cregler & H. Mark, "Medical Complications of Cocaine Abuse," *The New England Journal of Medicine* 315 (1986): 1495-1499.

7. F. Gawin & E. Ellinwood, "Cocaine and Other Stimulants: Actions, Abuse, and Treatment," *The New England Journal of Medicine* 318 (1988): 1173-1182; M. Gold, A. Washton, & C. Dackis, "Cocaine Abuse: Neurochemistry, Phenomenology, and Treatment," *National Institute on Drug Abuse Research* 61 (1985): 130-150.

8. R. Clayton, "Cocaine Use in the United States: In a Blizzard or Just Being Snowed?" *National Institute on Drug Abuse Research* 61 (1985): 8-34.

9. Hearing Before the Select Committee on Children, Youth, and Families, House of Representatives, "Beyond the Stereotypes: Women, Addiction, and Perinatal Substance Abuse," 101st Congress (April 30, 1990): 1-99.

10. National Drug Control Strategy, The White House, January 1990 (Washington, DC: Government Printing Office, April 19, 1990): 32.

11. Hearing Before the Select Committee on Children, Youth, and Families, House of Representatives, "Beyond the Stereotypes," pp. 1-99.

12. R. Siegel, "Cocaine Smoking," *Journal of Psychoactive Drugs* 14 (1982): 271-343.

13. Cregler & Mark, "Medical Complications," pp. 1495-1499.

14. R. Lee, "Drug Abuse," in G. Burrow & T. Ferris (Eds.), *Medical Complications During Pregnancy* (Philadelphia: W. B. Saunders, 1982): 38.

15. J. Woods, M. Plessinger, K. Scott, & R. Miller, "Prenatal Cocaine Exposure to the Fetus: A Sheep Model For Cardiovascular Evaluation," in D. Hutchings (Ed.), *Prenatal Abuse of Licit and Illicit Drugs* (New York: New York Academy of Sciences, 1989): 267-279; T. Moore, J. Sorg, L. Miller, T. Key, & R. Resnik, "Hemodynamic Effects of Intravenous Cocaine on the Pregnant Ewe and Fetus," *American Journal of Obstetrics and Gynecology* 155 (1986): 883-888; D. Dow-Edwards, "Long-Term Neurochemical and Neuro-behavioral Consequences of Cocaine Use During Pregnancy," in D. Hutchings (Ed.), *Prenatal Abuse of Licit and Illicit Drugs* (New York: New York Academy of Sciences, 1989): 280-289; L. Spear, C. Kirstein, J. Bell, R. Greenbaum, J. O'Shea, V. Yoottanasumpun, H. Hoffman, & N. Spear, "Effects of Prenatal Cocaine on Behavior During the Early Postnatal Period in Rats," *Teratology* 35 (1987): 8B; R. McGivern, W. Raim, R. Sokil, & P. Peterson, "Long-Term Effects of Prenatal Cocaine Exposure on Scent Marking and the HPG Axis in Male Rats," *Teratology* 37 (1988): 518.

16. D. Frank, B. Zucherman, H. Amaro, K. Aboagye, H. Bauchner, H. Cabral, L. Fried, R. Hingson, H. Kayne, S. Levenson, S. Parker, H. Reece, & R. Vince, "Cocaine Use During Pregnancy: Prevalence and Correlates," *Pediatrics* 82 (1988): 888-895.

17. I. Chasnoff, "Drug Use and Women: Establishing a Standard of Care," in D. Hutchings (Ed.), *Prenatal Abuse of Licit and Illicit Drugs* (New York: New York Academy of Sciences, 1989): 208-210.

18. B. Little, L. Snell, V. Klein, & L. Gisltrap, "Cocaine Abuse During Pregnancy: Maternal and Fetal Implications," *Obstetrics and Gynecology* 73 (1989): 157-160.

19. Chavkin & Kandall, "Between a Rock and a Hard Place," pp. 223-225.

20. Chasnoff, "Drug Use and Women," pp. 208-210.

21. Chavkin & Kandall, "Between a Rock and a Hard Place," pp. 223-225.

22. P. Fried, B. Watkinson, & A. Willan, "Marijuana Use During Pregnancy and Decreased Length of Gestation," *American Journal of Obstetrics and Gynecology* 150 (1984): 23-27; H. Abelson & J. Miller, "A Decade of Trends in Cocaine Use in the Household Population," *National Institute on Drug Abuse Research* 61 (1985): 35-49; Frank et al., "Cocaine Use During Pregnancy," pp. 888-895; G. Richardson, N. Day, & P. Taylor, "The Effect of Prenatal Alcohol, Marijuana, and Tobacco Exposure on Neonatal Behavior," *Infant Behavior and Development* 12 (1989): 199-209.

23. Richardson et al., "The Effect of Prenatal Alcohol, Marijuana, and Tobacco Exposure on Neonatal Behavior," pp. 199-209.

24. Frank et al., "Cocaine Use During Pregnancy," pp. 888-895.

25. G. Richardson & N. Day, "Maternal and Neonatal Effects of Moderate Cocaine Use During Pregnancy," *Teratology* 13 (1991): 455-460.

26. S. Hans, "Developmental Consequences of Prenatal Exposure to Methadone," in D. Hutchings (Ed.), *Prenatal Abuse of Licit and Illicit Drugs* (New York: New York Academy of Sciences, 1989): 195-207.

27. Frank et al., "Cocaine Use During Pregnancy," pp. 888-895.

28. Clayton, "Cocaine Use in the United States," pp. 8-34.

29. I. Chasnoff, H. Landress, & M. Barrett, "Prevalence of Illicit Drug and Alcohol Use in Pinellas County, Florida," *The New England Journal of Medicine* 322 (1990): 1202-1206.

30. P. Marques & A. McKnight, "Drug Abuse Risk Among Pregnant Adolescents Attending Public Health Clinics," *American Journal of Drug and Alcohol Abuse* 17 (1991): 399-413.

31. M. Boyd, "Patient Motivation During Pregnancy," *Maryland Medical Journal* 10 (1985): 977-981; J. Hickner, C. Westenber, & M. Dittenbir, "Effect of Pregnancy on Smoking Behavior: A Baseline Study," *Journal of Family Practice* 18 (1984): 241-244.

32. Marques & McKnight, "Drug Abuse Risk," pp. 399-413.

33. L. Gilchrist, M. Gillmore, & M. Lohr, "Drug Use Among Pregnant Adolescents," *Journal of Consulting and Clinical Psychology* 58 (1990): 402-407.

34. Frank et al., "Cocaine Use During Pregnancy," pp. 888-895.

35. K. Yamaguchi & D. Kandel, "Drug Use and Other Determinants of Premarital Pregnancy and Its Outcome: A Dynamic Analysis of Competing Life Events," *Journal of Marriage and the Family* 49 (1987): 257-270.

36. Gilchrist et al., "Drug Use Among Pregnant Adolescents," p. 405.

37. Gilchrist et al., "Drug Use Among Pregnant Adolescents," pp. 402-407.

38. Gilchrist et al., "Drug Use Among Pregnant Adolescents," p. 405.

39. Gilchrist et al., "Drug Use Among Pregnant Adolescents," p. 406.

40. Gilchrist et al., "Drug Use Among Pregnant Adolescents," pp. 402-407.

41. Yamaguchi & Kandel, "Drug Use and Other Determinants," pp. 257-270.

42. Chasnoff, "Drug Use and Women," pp. 208-210; Cregler & Mark, "Medical Complications of Cocaine Abuse," pp. 1495-1499; Chasnoff et al., "Prevalence of Illicit Drug and Alcohol Use," pp. 1202-1206.

43. Little et al., "Cocaine Abuse During Pregnancy," pp. 157-160; Chasnoff, "Drug Use and Women," pp. 208-210; D. Acker, B. Sachs, K. Tracey, & W. Wise, "Abruptio Placentae Associated With Cocaine Use," *American Journal of Obstetrics and Gynecology* 146 (1983): 220-221; Chasnoff et al., "Prevalence of Illicit Drug and Alcohol Use," pp. 1202-1206; Cregler & Mark, "Medical Complications of Cocaine Abuse," pp. 1495-1499.

44. Chasnoff et al., "Prevalence of Illicit Drug and Alcohol Use," pp. 1202-1206.

45. Little et al., "Cocaine Abuse During Pregnancy," pp. 157-160; Chasnoff, "Drug Use and Women," pp. 208-210; Acker et al., "Abruptio Placentae," pp. 220-221; Chasnoff et al., "Prevalence of Illicit Drug and Alcohol Use," pp. 1202-1206; Cregler & Mark, "Medical Complications of Cocaine Abuse," pp. 1495-1499.

46. A. Oro & S. Dixon, "Perinatal Cocaine and Methamphetamine Exposure: Maternal and Neonatal Correlates," *Journal of Pediatrics* (1987): 571-574.

47. Chasnoff, "Drug Use and Women," pp. 208-210; Little et al., "Cocaine Abuse During Pregnancy," pp. 157-160.

48. H. Risenberg, "Fetal Neglect and Abuse," *New York State Journal of Medicine* (1989): 148-151.

49. Hearing Before the Subcommittee on Health and the Environment of the Committee on Energy and Commerce, House of Representatives, "Drug Treatment Issues," 101st Congress (April 30, 1990): 1-275.

50. S. Kandall & J. Gaines, "Maternal Substance Use and Subsequent Sudden Infant Death Syndrome (SIDS) in Offspring," *Neurotoxicology and Teratology* 1 (1991): 25-240.

51. Hearing Before the Select Committee on Narcotics Abuse and Control, House of Representatives, "The Use of Drugs During Pregnancy," 96th Congress (February 6, 1980): 1-99.

52. U.S. Government Accounting Office, *ADMS Block Grant: Women's Set-Aside Does Not Assure Drug Treatment for Pregnant Women* (May 1991): 1-20.

53. U.S. Government Accounting Office, "ADMS Block Grant," p. 2.

54. Directors, *Directors' Survey of State Alcohol and Drug Agency Use of Fiscal Year 1989 Federal and State Funds* (Rockville, MD: National Association of State Alcohol and Drug Abuse Directors, 1990).

55. D. Pittman, W. Staudenmeier, & A. Kaplan, "Alcohol and Other Drugs: The Response of the Political and Medical Institutions," *British Journal of Addiction* 86 (1991): 967-975.

56. Chavkin & Kandall, "Between a Rock and a Hard Place," pp. 223-225.

57. U.S. Government Accounting Office, "ADMS Block Grant," p. 17.

58. U.S. Government Accounting Office, "ADMS Block Grant," pp. 1-20.

59. Nancy White, Office of Maternal and Child Health, Georgia State Government, personal communication (March 3, 1993).

60. U.S. Government Accounting Office, "ADMS Block Grant," p. 4.

61. U.S. Government Accounting Office, "ADMS Block Grant," p. 19.

62. Nancy White, Office of Maternal and Child Health, Georgia State Government, personal communication (March 3, 1993).

63. U.S. Government Accounting Office, "ADMS Block Grant," pp. 1-20.

64. U.S. Government Accounting Office, "ADMS Block Grant," p. 19.

65. Pittman, "Alcohol and Other Drugs," pp. 967-975.

66. Chavkin & Kandall, "Between a Rock and a Hard Place," pp. 223-225.

67. Hearing Before the Subcommittee on Health and the Environment of the Committee on Energy and Commerce, "Drug Treatment Issues," pp. 1-275.

68. Hearing Before the Subcommittee on Health and the Environment of the Committee on Energy and Commerce, "Drug Treatment Issues," pp. 1-275.

69. U.S. Government Accounting Office, "ADMS Block Grant," pp. 1-20.

5

The Drama of in Utero Drug Exposure

Fetus Takes First Billing

Kimberly N. Kline

In 1985, an article titled "Cocaine Use in Pregnancy" by Chasnoff and colleagues provided the spark that ignited the issue of in utero drug exposure.[1] Although the media had shown some concern in the past about the use of drugs such as cigarettes and alcohol by pregnant women, Chasnoff et al.'s 1985 study set off a media blitz regarding illicit drug use during pregnancy that continues today. This media blitz includes messages from a number of different media. In Los Angeles a billboard depicts a "newborn boy with life-support tubes connected to his tiny neck and nostrils, struggling to survive" with a caption that reads, "He couldn't take the hit. If you're pregnant, don't take drugs."[2] In New York City, a subway placard "imaged a womb, unattached to any female body, with a foetus inside; just outside the cervical entry to the womb hung a drug addict's needle."[3] An Atlanta television station recently aired a commercial that portrayed a woman berating herself for using drugs during her pregnancy. It concludes with her assertion that, "It's too late for my baby but not for yours." These illustrations

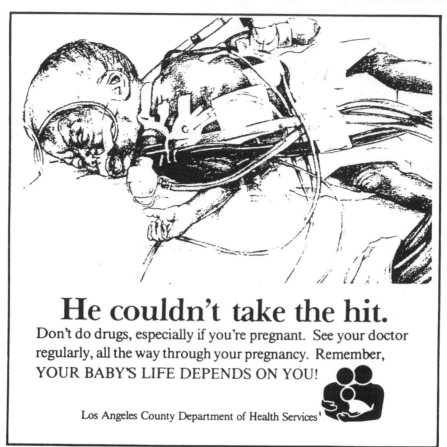

He couldn't take the hit.

Don't do drugs, especially if you're pregnant. See your doctor
regularly, all the way through your pregnancy. Remember,
YOUR BABY'S LIFE DEPENDS ON YOU!

Los Angeles County Department of Health Services¹

Figure 5.1.
SOURCE: Great Beginnings for Black Babies, Los Angeles.

exemplify how this media blitz regarding illicit drug use during pregnancy both
dramatized the situation and emphasized concern for the fetus/child over concern for
the health interests of the woman.

This media blitz was supported and/or driven by medical, legal, and political interest.
As Murray Edelman explains in *Constructing the Political Spectacle,* there is a
reciprocal relationship between media and politics. "The spectacle constituted by news
reporting continuously constructs and reconstructs social problems."[4] Whereas medical, legal, and political activities provide the material from which media accounts are
generated, at the same time medical researchers, lawyers, and politicians pursue those
areas of interest reported by the media.

Thus, the first of many congressional hearings to address the issue of drug use during
pregnancy was held in 1986.[5] The first of many prosecutions against women who
"endangered" their fetus by using drugs during their pregnancy was also reported by
media writers around the time of the 1985 study.[6] The following account reflects that
interdependency. First, it examines the way the media set the scope of the problem.
Second, it analyzes the way in which a "medical drama" centered on the fetus rather

than on the woman is depicted. Third, it notes the way in which this "medical drama" sets the stage for a "political drama" and how the "political drama" in turn sets the stage for the coverage of a "legal drama."

SCOPE OF THE PROBLEM

The amount of media attention given to the results of the 1985 study was only a beginning. A search of articles from newspapers and magazines revealed 28 articles between 1985 and 1988 that addressed drug use during pregnancy.[7] By 1988, however, there was an explosion of interest spawning 89 articles in that year, and 47, 51, and 23 in 1990, 1991, and 1992, respectively. The significant increase in media attention coincides with the release of information from a study by Chasnoff in September 1988.[8] It was around this time that reporting of medical research in relation to illicit drug use during pregnancy took on dramatic overtones.

Chasnoff's 1988 study was probably more exciting for media producers because it provided an opportunity to address the problem's scope. The statistic most often cited by media, 375,000 incidents of illicit drug use during pregnancy, was an extrapolation of the findings from this 1988 study. Chasnoff indicated in his study that "the overall incidence of substance abuse in pregnancy . . . in the 36 hospitals was 11%." A publication of the U.S. Department of Health and Human Services states that, "based on the live birth rate of 3.8 million in the United States, the investigator estimated that there may be as many as 375,000 babies being born each year that may be exposed to one or more illicit drugs prenatally."[9]

Based on Chasnoff's study, this statistic should refer to the number of women using illicit drugs during pregnancy. Media representations, however, conflate this interpretation with the number of infants born exposed, thus shifting the emphasis from the woman to the fetus. When the media refer to this statistic, it is *not* 375,000 women suffering from drug use during pregnancy. They refer to babies that "faced the possibility of health damage from their mother's drug abuse,"[10] babies "born every year to mothers who used illegal drugs during pregnancy,"[11] "babies born addicted,"[12] "drug-exposed"[13] babies, and "affected babies."[14] I rarely found an article that referred to the original meaning (incidence of substance use by pregnant women) of the statistic or that indicated that the 375,000 number was an extrapolation. Because the majority of media accounts focus on crack/cocaine (the others refer to drug addiction in general), this number is probably associated by the reader with crack addiction. It is likely that the readers of these media accounts come to believe that 375,000 is the number of babies born addicted to crack each year.

Although the scope of this problem justified the media's attention to it, the emphasis on the babies helped to lend the dramatic element generally sought by media producers. The drama was bolstered by the media's emphasis on crack/cocaine. The consequences of crack/cocaine use during pregnancy appear to be more dramatic than those of other illicit drugs, as shown by the "38-year-old woman [who] recently arrived at D.C. General having seizures and nearly comatose but still clinging to a piece of crack."[15] Cocaine also affects the child more dramatically. Other drugs like marijuana may have effects on the child, but they may not be as dramatic or as visible (at least, according to media accounts). Babies born to women who have used cocaine during their pregnancies provide more dramatic stories. For example:

> Guillermo, a newborn . . . has spent his whole short life crying. He is jittery and goes into spasms when he is touched. His eyes don't focus. He can't stick out his tongue, or suck. Born a week ago to a cocaine addict, Guillermo is described by his doctors as an addict himself.[16]

This same article also describes another baby, Paul, who

> lies motionless in an incubator, feeding tubes riddling his tiny body. He needs a respirator to breathe and a daily spinal tap to relieve fluid buildup on his brain. Only one month old, he has already suffered two strokes.[17]

Furthermore, as many media writers are quick to note, pregnant women (I'd add nonpregnant women, too) *die* from using crack. Their babies *die* from exposure to crack. As Dr. Michael Weitzman, director of maternal and child health at Boston City Hospital, points out, cocaine use is "bigger than all the other 'don'ts' of cigarettes, alcohol and marijuana. . . . Using it just once can potentially kill the child and the mother."[18] Media writers seem to justify the emphasis on crack/cocaine because its use has risen significantly over the past few years.

Medical Drama:
Fetus/Child in the Spotlight

Having set the scope of the problem as widespread and serious, the stage was set for a medical drama that spotlighted the effects of in utero drug exposure on the fetus. These medically focused stories dramatized the situation in such a way as to promote sympathy for the child while discouraging empathy for the woman, because there are no balancing depictions of the woman's medical status.

"IMMEDIATE EFFECTS" AND "LONG-TERM EFFECTS"

This lack of sympathy in the depiction of the woman is manifest in the reports on cocaine's affect on the pregnancy itself. In these reports, the concern with the effects on the mother's *body* are only significant in as much as they affect the fetus. Crack/cocaine affects the mother's body by inhibiting blood flow (it constricts blood vessels) and, therefore, reducing flow of oxygen to the fetus. This can result in physical and neurological damage to the fetus. A *Time* author, referring to one infant whose mother had used crack-cocaine during her pregnancy, states that, "Every so often she shakes uncontrollably for a few moments—a legacy of the nerve-system damage that occurred when she suffered a shortfall of blood and oxygen just before birth."[19] In her description of this child, Toufexis also illustrates the drama of premature birth that is frequently referred to in reports on cocaine's affect on pregnancy. The girl was born "three months early, weighing less than 3 lbs. Her tiny body is entangled in a maze of wires and tubes that monitor her vital signs and bring her food and medicine."[20]

The prevailing focus of media writers in terms of medical implications is on the effects of actual exposure to the drug on the fetus/unborn child. In almost every article there are descriptions of the pathological and emotional effects on the fetus. Physical effects include "prenatal strokes and lasting brain damage, seizures after birth . . . retarded fetal growth, breathing lapses, absence of part of the gut and structural abnormalities in genital and urinary organs."[21] Cocaine exposed babies have more physical, respiratory, and neurological defects at birth. Frequent mention is made of withdrawal symptoms. And one writer points out that though not every baby exposed to cocaine goes through withdrawal, "those who do face a special torment."[22] Similar depictions of the effects of crack on women were lacking.

Media depictions of the long-term consequences of in utero drug exposure to the child are also very dramatic because they describe children that are the antithesis of how most people view children. Coryl Jones, a research psychologist at the National Institute on Drug Abuse, asserts that crack/cocaine "interfer[es] with the central core of *what it is to be human*" (my emphasis).[23] This view of the situation is most probably linked with the fundamental problem these children experience in their interactions with both toys and people: They seem emotionless. "When playing with toys, if they did play with an object, they would walk away from it long before most children would, their faces dispassionate, joyless."[24] The interaction of these children with caregivers focuses on their lack of emotion. "Most of the drug babies did not show any strong feelings—pleasure, anger or distress."[25] On the other hand, drug-exposed infants suffer from overstimulation when adults try to interact with them as they would with other infants. When adults try to cuddle them or "coo" at them, these babies cry and pull away.

The lack of emotion may reverse as the child grows older. Later articles, those that refer to the problems children face as they start to attend school, tend to emphasize the moodiness and impulsiveness of the older child. "[T]hey can be very aggressive with the other children so that they are hard to stop."[26] Most articles that address the issue of how in utero drug exposure will affect the children as they grow older, however, also frequently add a disclaimer to the effect that there just is not enough evidence yet to make any generalized claims.

These accounts seem to be a good reflection of the medical studies available. These accounts are nevertheless problematic because they imply that all babies born to mothers who use crack will be physically and emotionally handicapped because of exposure to the drug. Yet this may not be the case. "The real danger of cocaine use is the risk of having a premature birth rather than having an 'addicted baby,' " a *Newsweek* writer quotes Dr. Ivan Frank of the New England Medical Center in Boston.[27] Even so, women who use crack or other drugs during pregnancy may be treated as if their child is already malformed before the child is even born. These women may be blamed for potentialities rather than realities. Rita Esposito Watson of the Yale Department of Psychiatry says, "[i]f a man is a substance abuser and he goes into a program, they don't say 'Has your substance abuse affected your children and family?' But if a woman is a substance abuser they assume it's already affected her children and family and she's already stigmatized."[28]

One further aspect of the medical drama is that media writers tend to emphasize the supporting role of medical professionals. Not only do these articles note the extensive professional efforts of these people, but also the personal agony they experience in trying to care for the children. A feature article about the head nurse at Boston City Hospital reported that because she found "the stress of dealing with such problems to be withering," she almost changed careers.[29] Her crisis passed, however, and now "she is a tireless advocate for dependent infants."[30] These types of statements stress the activities of medical professionals, glorifying medical personnel and removing consideration of the actions of women who struggle to overcome their addictions and other problems.

Political Drama: Public and Government in the Spotlight

Though the medical drama presented by the media features the children and their medical champions in the lead roles, the political drama presented by the media places the public and governmental representatives center stage. In this aspect of the drama, the public must assume the costs, both financial and societal, of women who use drugs during pregnancy. Thus, the public is no longer a casual observer of the drama, it is now situated within the drama.

When reporting on the political implications of women using drugs during pregnancy, the media typically note the financial burden to society. The medical expenses that are associated with the problem focus on the cost of caring for a baby that is born drug exposed/addicted.[31] As one article asserts, "Jane Doe can buy a 'hit' of crack cocaine for $10. If she uses it while she is pregnant, society could pay up to $100,000 to care for her child during the first three months of its life."[32] Another estimates $100,000 or more a year.[33] Still another figures the cost to be $750,000 in medical care for the first 18 years of life.[34] Richard Durbin, a member of Congress, stated that "cocaine exposed babies cost the country more than $500 million a year for delivery and care alone."[35] Although the media tend to emphasize cost, one neonatologist probably hits at the heart of the issue, stating that, "With multi-thousands [of dollars] [sic] for each infant, crack babies are not profitable."[36]

Medical expenses are not the only expenses associated with drug-exposed children. If these children survive the intensive medical care required to get them through the first months of life, there are the child-welfare expenses associated with placing these children in "appropriate" homes and the cost of caring for them until such homes can be found. Media accounts frequently referred to the numbers of drug-exposed children that are abandoned at birth. While waiting for child-welfare services to find adoptive or foster homes, these "boarder babies" live at the hospital they were born in or taken to at birth.[37] These accounts do not generally refer to dollar amounts as in the case of medical costs but, rather, indirectly indicate that the cost is just too high.

Not only are the costs exorbitant in the case of babies that remain in the hospital they were born in, but the costs to the welfare system are high as well. The Department of Human Services in Washington, D.C., stated that the city's child welfare protection and foster parent system was "under great strain, and is not able to discharge its duties well."[38] Many other articles note the rising numbers of children that need to be placed in foster homes. This is not only due to the abandonment of the children, but the fact that many cities are taking custody of the children at birth if they show any signs of drug exposure. "About 30% of drug exposed infants are removed from their parents at birth," one *Atlanta Journal* writer points out.[39] And a *Time* writer stated that "the two U.S. cities with the biggest crack problems have backed away from their initial seize-the-kids approach."[40] He goes on to cite Gerhard Moland, a children's service administrator in Los Angeles County as saying, "If we took away every child who came out with a positive tox screen . . . it would overwhelm the system."[41]

There are also the more recent financial concerns with the cost of schooling for children who are emotionally and physically handicapped. A few articles tried to indicate just what the costs associated with educating drug-exposed children might be. One article cites the Georgia Department of Labor as stating that the "immediate cost of meeting the special educational needs of each of these 'crack kids' probably will be between $3,000 and $5,000 a year—more than twice the current per-student allocation."[42] Another notes that "[a] Los Angeles pilot education project costs taxpayers $15,000 a year *per pupil*."[43] Most of the articles indicate that there is no way to know at this point just what kind of educational programs will need to be developed for the children or at what cost. There seems to be widespread agreement, based on the emotional and physical handicaps that the children suffer from now, that there will be additional costs.

Although it is clear that there is widespread concern about the costs of attending to the medical and educational needs of the children, it is implied that these costs will be borne in order to aid these children. In striking contrast to this attention to fetal needs is a lack of attention to the medical and educational costs for helping women addicts. Women who are addicted to illicit drugs require treatment—treatment that, as Lemieux argues in the previous chapter and as is frequently mentioned in these media articles, is not available. Thus, the only aspect of this rhetoric to deal directly with women's health issues sends a clear message—*help for female addicts is just not available*.

The net effect of articles that refer to these social costs is threefold. First, the public is informed of their forced obligations to care for the women who use drugs during pregnancy and their children. Second, the mothers are inherently blamed for causing these costs. And third, in the process of blaming the mother, the articles applaud the people and organizations who provide assistance for the children.[44]

Legal Drama: Activists in the Spotlight

The rise in litigation against women who use illicit drugs during pregnancy coincided with the increased media reports about this issue. In a hearing before the

Committee on Finance, it was reported that by 1990 there were at least 26 court cases against women who were alleged to have harmed their unborn child through the use of drugs (this doesn't include the numerous arrests made).[45] Although another article notes that there are about 50 cases,[46] an article in the *Atlanta Constitution* states, "More than 87 women have been charged with similar offenses here [Atlanta] and in Charleston."[47]

There have been few convictions of women involved in these cases, not only because many women submit to enforced treatment rather than face charges, but also because most states do not have legal provisions for prosecuting a woman for her actions regarding her fetus. A 1991 article in *Time,* however, notes that 19 states now have provisions for fetal abuse charges to be pressed against a woman who gives birth to a child that tests positive for illegal drugs upon birth.[48] Moreover, the media reports feature increased proposals for legislation that would allow for such prosecutions. A Georgia representative is cited as suggesting that a woman who does not seek help after giving birth to one crack baby should go to jail if she gives birth to other crack babies.[49] In Illinois, a representative proposes that it should be a felony for a woman "who knowingly and intentionally took illegal drugs to deliver a newborn with traces of the drug in its blood or urine."[50] Similarly, a Kansas representative is reported as urging that it be mandatory for convicted female addicts to accept Norplant birth control inserts.[51]

Media representations of the legal debate focused on how or whether the law should regulate the management of a woman during her pregnancy to facilitate the best environment for the fetus. Specifically, the issue has been whether women can or should be punished or whether they can or should be forced into involuntary "assistance" situations. Articles that addressed this issue were generally hard news reports, recounting the prosecution or conviction of a woman who had used illicit drugs during her pregnancy. Although most of these articles also acknowledged the debate regarding maternal rights versus fetal rights, they did not provide counterbalancing depictions of the women. Rather, they noted the views of those opposing and advocating punishment.

Proponents' Views of Punishment

The proponents of punishing a woman for using illicit drugs during pregnancy are portrayed as taking the hard-line approach that fetal rights clearly outweigh the rights of the mother. "When you consider that her actions caused the death of another human being, that of a child who had absolutely no chance to live, in our view, the balance tips in favor of the child, and not in treatment of the mother."[52] In a similar vein, Judge Peter H. Wolf asked, "Obviously you want to protect society from a dangerous armed robber who is going to rob again. Is not an unborn baby equally entitled to protection from a mother who cannot stay away from cocaine?"[53] Even when the child showed no effects from exposure to illicit drugs, the argument was the same. "It's the same as if a mother gave a child a pack of razor blades to play with in the crib. The child might drop the blades out of the crib and not get hurt, but the exposure to danger is the same."[54]

Many advocates of punishment are depicted as believing that just the threat of punishment may be beneficial in halting the spread of illicit drug use during pregnancy. "People get it wrong when they think that criminal prosecution means go . . . directly to jail. This is not Monopoly," points out one fetal rights activist.[55] Rather, they believe that the threat of legal action can "encourage" drug-using pregnant women to seek treatment. Regardless of how making such punishment legal will work in effect, the views of proponents of punishment are summed up by one writer who states, "Drug dependency may be an illness, but drug users are nonetheless responsible for their actions."[56]

Opponents' Views of Punishment

One of the most often mentioned flaws of punishing women for illicit drug use during pregnancy (even by the staunchest supporters of fetal rights) was that women who are threatened with punishment might avoid seeking prenatal care. "If I were a woman about to have a baby, and if I knew that if the baby had drugs in the urine I could be prosecuted, I would probably have my baby in a back alley," argued one doctor.[57] Chasnoff, the doctor whose medical studies initiated the interest in this issue, is often cited in opposition to punishment of women. Even some of those who considered punishment acceptable were shown as recognizing that it might be counterproductive.[58]

Another concern of the opponents of punishment that receives wide coverage is the bias of this solution against sociodemographically disadvantaged women, particularly black women. A *New York Times* writer notes that about 70% of the women prosecuted are black.[59] Other writers note a study that indicates that black women are 10 times more likely to be reported to health authorities than are white women.[60] A number of articles point out that one factor in this bias may be the fact that the poor women who do seek prenatal care are more likely to use government agencies and public hospitals as providers of that care, and these are the agencies most likely to engage in screening practices. Private care physicians (used by middle- to upper-class women) may be less inclined to report or even screen their patients because of their financial interest or perhaps because they assume that drug abuse could not be a problem for *these* women. Because lack of prenatal care frequently precipitates drug testing and because "only half of black American women get adequate prenatal care" compared to the 72.6% of whites, poor women of color are more likely to be subjected to drug testing.[61] In these instances, poor women "are more likely to be reported to government authorities because of discriminatory hospital screening practices and the stereotyped assumptions of health-care professionals."[62] But Chasnoff's question hits at the heart of the issue— "If these were white middle-class women, wouldn't they be talking about Betty Ford treatment programs rather than jail?"[63]

Other women besides sociodemographically repressed women use crack/cocaine. In fact, many articles refer to the fact that crack/cocaine cuts across class and race lines (probably because Chasnoff's 1988 article indicated that this was the case). The media presentation of this substance abuse, however, is such that the public may not *perceive* the use to be across racial and class lines. Articles might include *statements* that say drug use cuts across class and race lines, but the pervasive *descriptions* of the women, or when individual women are mentioned, did not indicate that this is actually the case. "Many crack mothers such as Ms. Newell and Cynthia Woods . . . are low-income, inner city residents, but crack also . . . has cut across social and economic lines."[64] One of the rare times when a mother was quoted, the writer purposely preserved her dialect, "Sometimes when I hit and it don't move, I be, like, 'Oh, my God.' "[65] Here the women we visualize are the poor women, the others that cut across those lines are just nameless and faceless "others."

   Having noted the problems inherent in the punishment solution, opponents go on to express concerns over potential dilemmas regarding women's rights during pregnancy. Specifically, the concern is that the emphasis on fetal rights necessary for such laws to be passed will affect abortion rights and will extend to control of the pregnant woman in other aspects of pregnancy. Frequently mentioned was the concern that laws establishing fetal rights could chip away at the *Roe v. Wade* decision. That is, those who raise the issue of abortion are concerned that allowing unborn life legal protection could eventually nudge abortion out of the picture.[66] Others note that *Roe v. Wade* allows state regulation after the first trimester and, therefore, legal action regarding the second and third trimesters could be constitutional.[67] Also, there are states that have statutes that protect the fetus from assaults from those other than the mother. But these types of assertions sidestep the concerns of those concerned with women's rights: The initial application of fetal rights laws may not apply to abortion, but in the future, who knows?

   Concern is also expressed that allowing punishment of the woman for her actions during pregnancy could affect other aspects of control during pregnancy.[68] This concern has been dubbed the "slippery slope." "If you can arrest a woman for endangering a baby with crack," says Lynn Paltrow of the American Civil Liberties Union, "why not someone who is drinking, smoking or just on her feet too much?"[69] As Katha Pollitt, a writer for *The Nation* points out,

> The "save the babies" mentality may look like a necessary, if troubling, approach when it's a matter of keeping a drug addict away from a substance that is, after all, illegal . . . [but what if] the list of things women are put on legal notice to avoid expands to . . . dangers . . . posed by junk food, salt, aspirin, air travel and cigarettes.[70]

For some, this may seem like an absurd suggestion. "It is difficult to imagine a public, a jury, a prosecutor or a judge too unenlightened to make such distinctions," argues one writer, between "a cocaine mother and baby . . . from a pregnant woman who eats too much salt or fat."[71] Yet one of the charges against Pamela Rae Stewart was having sex with her husband against her doctors orders.[72] In other words, as the *Christian Science Monitor* questions, could such laws "indict women who, for instance, elect methods of prenatal care that differ from those prescribed by most doctors?"[73] Considering the power that the medical establishment already wields,[74] this concern may not be unfounded.[75]

   These three aspects, medical, political and legal, can be viewed as three parts of the drama. Part 1, the medical aspect, provides the pathos of the drama. The "innocent victims" are introduced along with their champions, the medical professionals. In this part, the public (audience members) is placed in the position of feeling morally obligated to side with the fetus/child. In Part 2, the political aspect, the public is drawn into the drama as the costs to society are presented. With the introduction of this aspect, the audience members are no longer bystanders to the drama, they are participants poised to side with the fetus/child and against the woman. In Part 3, the legal aspect, the fetal rights and maternal rights activists prod the involved public to make a stand on legal issues that stem from the moral questions involving the rights of the fetus and mother. With these three aspects of the drama explored, the key actors in the drama have been identified. They are the doctors and caregivers, the politicians, the attorneys, and the fetal rights and maternal/women's rights activists. At the heart of the drama are the children. The question remains, then, where do the mothers (and the fathers) fit into this drama?

In reference to the fathers of these children, the answer is clear: They are simply not part of the drama. Mentions of the father are very rare. Articles occasionally note that the father was also using drugs, or that the father is no longer in residence with the mother, but little else is said. It is not only by omission that fathers are written out of this drama; in one case it was explicitly stated. In the case of Pamela Rae Stewart, a woman charged with, among other things, having sex with her husband against her doctor's orders, "Police decided not to bring any charges against [her] husband."[76] Katha Pollitt noted in her article for *The Nation* that Stewart's husband also beat her. And Pollitt, the only writer in the articles reviewed to ask about the father, asks the question, "What about dad?"[77]

> It's his kid too, after all. His drug and alcohol use, his prescription medications, his workplace exposure and general habits of health not only play a part in determining the quality of his sperm but affect the course of pregnancy as well. Cocaine dust and smoke from crack, marijuana, and tobacco present dangers to others who breathe them; his alcoholism often bolsters hers.[78]

Pollitt also points out that physical violence against women by their male partners increases during pregnancy. But issues such as those that she raises are significantly absent from any other media reports. One article, however, does suggest the possible future involvement of fathers in this issue: as the initiators of the prosecutions against the mothers of their children. In Maryland, a father requested that a restraining order be brought against his estranged wife ordering her to refrain from drinking alcohol and taking illicit drugs during her pregnancy.[79] If, as this man's attorney argues, "It's all about men's rights as fathers—trying to get men treated equally,"[80] then these men should also bear the brunt of the punishments leveled against the mothers of their children.

Conclusion

An analysis of the media representations about illicit drug use during pregnancy points to a number of deficiencies in reference to this issue. First, because these representations indicate that this is a problem that predominately affects sociodemographically disadvantaged women, a large population of women may get the impression that this is not a health concern for them. Not only is there some indication that illicit drug use during pregnancy is not bounded by sociodemographic status, the questions that are emerging in relation to the issue (abortion, slippery slope, etc.) are health issues affecting all women.

A second deficiency is that the information in regard to *women's* health, not just fetal health, is clearly lacking. Although the media accounts seem to be a good reflection of the medical research available about this issue (albeit an overdramatized reflection), these accounts reflect the serious shortage of medical research on psychological and physiological effects of illicit drug use during pregnancy on the woman herself.

Finally, these media representations indicate that the historical dilemma of who takes precedence, the mother or the child, is still a matter of debate today. What these media representations seem to ignore is that both the mother and the child could (and should) receive equal emphasis without negating the significance of the problem. Representations that reflect this shift in thinking will be problematic, at best, until all those involved in this issue (medical researchers, attorneys, politicians, activists, etc.) come to recognize that pregnancy affects both the mother and the child.

Notes

1. Chasnoff et al.'s study indicated that the 23 cocaine-using women in his study had a higher incidence of spontaneous abortion and early onset of labor than the 15 methadone-using women and the 15 drug-free women. I. J. Chasnoff, W. J. Burns, S. H. Schnoll, & K. A. Burns, "Cocaine Use in Pregnancy," *The New England Journal of Medicine* 313 (September 1985): 666-669.

2. J. L. Mitchell, "Billboard's Message Is Graphically Anti-Drug," *Los Angeles Times,* March 30, 1991, pp. B1, B6.

3. A. Kaplan, *Motherhood and Representation: The Mother in Popular Culture and Melodrama* (New York: Routledge & Kegan Paul, 1992): 192.

4. M. Edelman, *Constructing the Political Spectacle* (Chicago: University of Chicago Press, 1988): 1.

5. Before 1986, there was one Congressional hearing that addressed the use of drugs during pregnancy. From 1980 to 1986 there were no further Congressional hearings on this matter, whereas from 1986 to 1990 there were approximately nine such hearings (list provided upon request: Kimberly N. Kline, Purdue University, Department of Communication, West Lafayette, IN).

6. Both the American Civil Liberties Union and an *ABA Journal* writer note that these types of prosecutions began in earnest around the mid-1980s. See Mark Hansen, "Courts Side With Moms in Drug Cases," *ABA Journal* (November 1992): 18; and Statement of the American Civil Liberties Union, "Infant Victims of Drug Abuse: Hearing Before the Committee on Finance, United States" (June 28, 1990): 233-253. Also, the first conviction to be upheld in an appellate court for delivery of a controlled substance to a minor through the umbilical cord was in 1991. See Julia Elizabeth Jones, "State Intervention in Pregnancy," *Louisiana Law Review* 52 (1992): 1159-1181.

7. I collected articles from *Infotrac* (1989-September 1992), *Newspaper Abstracts* (January 1985-October 1992), and the *Readers' Guide to Periodical Literature* (1986-1992). From the two databases that provided newspaper articles, I found 239 articles. From this set of articles I used all samples from 1985 (4 articles) and 1987 (2 articles). I took a random sample of approximately 40% from the other years, leaving me with the following: 4 articles from 1986, 4 from 1988, 36 from 1989, 19 from 1990, 20 from 1991, and 9 from 1992. The total sample size from newspaper articles was 99. From the *Readers' Guide* I found 42 magazine articles (chosen from those magazines that circulate on average newsstands). I used all of these articles for this analysis.

8. I. Chasnoff, "Drug Use and Women: Establishing a Standard of Care," in D. Hutchings (Ed.), *Prenatal Abuse of Licit and Illicit Drugs* (New York: New York Academy of Sciences, 1989): 208-210.

9. U.S. Department of Health and Human Services, *Maternal Drug Abuse and Drug Exposed Children: Understanding the Problem* (Washington, DC: Government Printing Office, 1992): 12.

10. J. E. Brody, "Widespread Abuse of Drugs by Pregnant Women Is Found," *New York Times,* August 30, 1988, pp. A1, C13. Copyright © 1988 by The New York Times Company. Reprinted by permission.

11. J. Beck, "Mothers' Drug Use Causes an Epidemic of Damaged Babies," *Chicago Tribune,* September 5, 1988, sec. 1, p. 15. (Copyrighted Chicago Tribune Company. All rights reserved. Used with permission.) See also Hansen, "Southerners Back Penalties," p. A1; and L. Matchan, "More Middle-Class Drug Use in Pregnancy Seen," *Boston Globe,* November 11, 1990, p. 1.

12. J. Kennedy, "Cloudy Future After Infant Cocaine Case," *Boston Globe,* August 23, 1989, pp. 1, 22. Quoted material used by permission.

13. "How to Protect Babies From Crack," *New York Times,* May 15, 1991, p. A14; see also W. Plummer & S. A. Brown, "Children in Peril," *People Weekly* (April 16, 1990): 82-85. Quoted material used by permission.

14. Durbin, "Pregnant Addicts," *Chicago Tribune,* November 10, 1991, sec. 4, p. 2. Copyrighted Chicago Tribune Company. All rights reserved. Used with permission.

15. C. Trost, "Born to Lose: Babies of Crack Users Crowd Hospitals, Break Everybody's Heart," *Wall Street Journal,* June 18, 1989, pp. A1, A6. Reprinted by permission of *The Wall Street Journal,* © 1989 Dow Jones & Company, Inc. All rights reserved worldwide.

16. B. Barol, L. R. Prout, K. Fitzgerald, S. Katz, & P. King, "Cocaine Babies: Hooked at Birth," *Newsweek* (July 28, 1986): 56-57.

17. Barol et al., "Cocaine Babies," p. 56.

18. L. Tye, "Alarm Raised on Cocaine, Pregnancy," *Boston Globe,* July 1, 1986, p. 21. Quoted material used by permission.

19. A. Toufexis, "Innocent Victims," *Time* (May 13, 1991): 56-60.

20. Toufexis, "Innocent Victims," p. 59.

21. Brody, "Widespread Abuse," p. C13.

22. Trost, "Born to Lose," p. A1.

23. S. Blakeslee, "Crack's Toll Among Babies: A Joyless View, Even of Toys," *New York Times,* September 17, 1989, pp. 1, 26. Copyright © 1988 by The New York Times Company. Reprinted by permission.

24. Blakeslee, "Crack's Toll," p. 26.

25. Blakeslee, "Crack's Toll," p. 26.

26. Toufexis, "Innocent Victims," p. 60.

27. Barol et al., "Cocaine Babies," p. 57.

28. J. Mann, "Cure an Addict, Save a Child," *Washington Post,* April 5, 1991, p. C3. Quoted material used by permission.

29. Plummer & Brown, "Children in Peril," p. 85.

30. Plummer & Brown, "Children in Peril," p. 85.

31. Although some media accounts indicate that not all fetuses exposed to drugs are born addicted, they typically do not explicate a distinction. The distinction seems to be whether a baby actually suffers from withdrawal (drug-addicted) or not (drug-exposed). This distinction is generally summarily dismissed as unimportant, however—the baby suffers regardless.

32. C. Sullivan, "US Health-Care Crisis in the Making," *Christian Science Monitor,* February 15, 1989, pp. 1, 2. Quoted material used by permission.

33. M. Abramowitz, "Help Urged for Pregnant Drug Users," *Washington Post,* June 25, 1989, p. D10. Quoted material used by permission.

34. L. Uzych, "The Problem of Drug Babies," *Christian Science Monitor,* December 10, 1990, p. 18.

35. Durbin, "Pregnant Addicts," sec. 4, p. 2.

36. Sullivan, "U.S. Health-Care Crisis," p. 2.

37. Very likely the dollar amounts estimated for medical expenses include costs associated with housing a child rather than providing medical care for the child. Considering the cost of one day's stay in an infant room (when my daughter was born in 1990 her cost was $850.00 a day), this has interesting implications for how money is being allocated in this situation.

38. Abramowitz, "Help Urged," p. D10.

39. A. Peterson, "Helping Crack Babies," *Atlanta Journal,* February 16, 1991, p. A19.

40. J. Willwerth, "Should We Take Away Their Kids?" *Time* (May 13, 1991): 62-63.

41. J. Willwerth, "Should We Take," p. 63.

42. F. Schwartzkopff, "Schools Brace for First Classes of 'Crack Kids,' " *Atlanta Constitution,* April 11, 1990, pp. A1, A6. Quoted material used by permission.

43. M. Dorris, "A Desperate Crack Legacy," *Newsweek* (June 25, 1990): 8.

44. "Crack Mothers, Crack Babies and Hope," *New York Times,* December 31, 1989, sec. 4, p. 10.

45. Hearing Before the Committee on Finance, "Infant Victims of Drug Abuse," June 28, 1990, 244-248.

46. Mann, "Cure an Addict," p. C3.

47. E. Coady, "S. Carolina Prosecutors Force Mothers to Seek Treatment," *Atlanta Constitution,* June 5, 1991, p. A10. Quoted material used by permission.

48. Willwerth, "Should We Take," p. 62.

49. M. Curriden, "Legislator Urges Help for Pregnant Addicts," *Atlanta Constitution,* June 7, 1991, p. E3.

50. R. Pearson, "Cocaine-Baby Debate Legislature-Bound," *Chicago Tribune,* November 23, 1989, sec. 1, p. 8. Copyrighted Chicago Tribune Company. All rights reserved. Used with permission.

51. Willwerth, "Should We Take," p. 62.

52. "Woman Charged in Her Baby's Drug-Linked Death," *Chicago Tribune,* August 22, 1987, sec. 1, p. 8.

53. J. Davidson, "Pregnant Addicts: Drug Babies Push Issue of Fetal Rights," *Los Angeles Times,* April 25, 1989, pp. 1, 3, 19. Copyright 1989, Los Angeles Times; reprinted with permission.

54. "Cocaine Use in Pregnancy Amounts to Child Abuse, a Judge Rules," *New York Times,* May 4, 1989, p. 22. Copyright © 1989 by The New York Times Company. Reprinted by permission.

55. Coady, "S. Carolina Prosecutors," p. A10.

56. E. J. Delattre, "Should Criminal Laws Be Applied to Pregnant Drug Users? Yes-Sanctions Can Be Incentive for Treatment," *Atlanta Journal,* July 30, 1989, p. B8. Quoted material used by permission of the author.

57. "Cocaine Babies: The Littlest Victims," *Newsweek* (October 2, 1989): 55.

58. As Clarence Page of the *Chicago Tribune* maintains, "[i]f jailing mothers was a good remedy for low-birthweight and other fetal problems, it would make sense to prosecute and jail every woman who engages in behavior harmful to the fetus, including . . . an unbalanced diet of soda pop and cheese snacks." He concludes, however, that, "It doesn't make sense, so we don't do it." C. Page, "Women and Crack," *Chicago Tribune,* May 21, 1989, p. 1. Copyrighted Chicago Tribune Company. All rights reserved. Used with permission.

59. D. Roberts, "The Bias in Drug Arrests of Pregnant Women," *New York Times,* August 11, 1990, p. A25. Copyright © 1990 by The New York Times Company. Reprinted by permission.

60. Coady, "S. Carolina Prosecutors," p. A10; S. Sternberg, "Pregnant Blacks Feeling Brunt of Fla. Drug Law," *Atlanta Constitution,* April 26, 1990, p. E3.

61. Roberts, "The Bias In Drug Arrests," p. A25.

62. Roberts, "The Bias In Drug Arrests," p. A25.

63. "Punishing Pregnant Addicts: Debate, Dismay, No Solution," *New York Times,* September 10, 1989, sec. 4, p. 5. Copyright © 1989 by The New York Times Company.

64. Schwartzkopff, "Schools Brace," p. A6.

65. L. Duke, "For Pregnant Addict, Crack Comes First," *Washington Post,* December 18, 1989, pp. A1, A10. Quoted material used by permission.

66. Davidson, "Pregnant Addicts," p. 19.

67. Davidson, "Pregnant Addicts," p. 19.

68. See R. Hubbard, *The Politics of Women's Biology* (New Brunswick, NJ: Rutgers University Press): 172.

69. T. Gest, "The Pregnancy Police on Patrol," *U.S. News & World Report* (February 6, 1989): 50. Quoted material used by permission.

70. K. Pollitt, "A New Assault on Feminism," *The Nation* (March 26, 1990): 409-418. Quoted material used by permission.

71. Delattre, "Should Criminal Laws," p. B8.

72. Davidson, "Pregnant Addicts," p. 19.

73. "Jail for Crack Moms," *Christian Science Monitor,* October 25, 1989, p. 20. Quoted material used by permission.

74. In one notorious case, a woman with cancer was forced to undergo a cesarean section even though doctors knew it might shorten her life—both she and the baby died.

75. Since the time when male physicians replaced female midwives in providing prenatal care and delivery assistance, women have been "controlled" during their pregnancies. They are told (ordered) to eat certain

foods, take certain drugs, submit to certain procedures, and engage in or abstain from certain activities during their pregnancy.

76. M. I. LaGanga, "Of Drugs and Death: Prosecutors Raise the Ante," *Los Angeles Times,* October 1, 1986, pp. Il1, Il6. Copyright 1986, Los Angeles Times; reprinted with permission.

77. Pollitt, "A New Assault," p. 416.

78. Pollitt, "A New Assault," p. 416.

79. C. Mitchell, "Woman Is Told to Stay Sober While Pregnant," *Atlanta Constitution,* January 11, 1990, pp. A1, A6. Quoted material used by permission.

80. Mitchell, "Woman Is Told," p. 6.

PART II

Historical Issues in Communicating About Women's Reproductive Health

---

History provides us with numerous examples of the difficulty that innovative views . . . have in finding a place.

Brenda Dervin,
"The Sense-Making Approach," p. 71[1]

The second part of this handbook acknowledges the role that history plays in guiding the design of questions asked and answers rendered about women's health. Three functions are fulfilled by a historical agenda:

- History guides the development of norms and expectations.
- History underlies the origin of rules within organizations to satisfy clients' expectations—reinforcing and reifying normative practices.
- History suggests appropriate government interventions and policies—emphasizing the interaction between political and historical agendas.

Thus history helps to define what is right and what is wrong; what is good and what is bad. When these definitions relate to such matters as how a woman in labor will be admitted to the hospital, they may appear to be simple matters, standard operating procedures for the personnel involved. Yet as Nelson and Sterk examine these practices, more subtle outcomes emerge. Such rules contribute to myths about the significance of performing some actions in lieu of others in relation to maternal and fetal health and well-being. Standard operating procedures also muffle the voices of innovators both inside and outside of health care delivery systems.

The two areas selected to illustrate the impact of history on women's health—birth control and childbirth—demonstrate how a historical agenda in women's health too often leads to debate about, or reflection on, morality. Once someone defines something as good or bad, right or wrong, the next step in judging behavior as moral or immoral has precedence. Solomon Watson, Trasciatti, and King provide evidence to support the observation that messages about birth control methods and use, rather than addressing the response efficacy of methods and the self-efficacy of users, too frequently have direct as well as indirect messages about the morality of users. These messages are so ingrained and so intertwined with the use of condoms, for example, that they affect individuals' willingness to use condoms for disease control, as Owen and Caudill reveal.

The chapters included in this section of the book also show how a historical agenda serves the function of defining what is an acceptable standard and, therefore, what is unacceptable as well. During this century, women have seen an evolution in child-birth practices that has practically come full circle. At the turn of the century, women attending women during the labor and birth of one another's babies constituted the primary means and circumstance of this event, with the techniques used to direct the process being those that had worked for the women attending or for their mothers and grandmothers. Hospitals were synonymous with pesthouses—a place for those too poor and/or too isolated from family and friends to receive care. They were often filthy, and patrons frequently contracted illnesses and diseases that they did not have to start with. As medical training and technology (research focusing on new knowledge in engineering) evolved, a system for delivering the use of services associated with both the professionals and their tools more than kept pace. The norm for childbirth became hospital delivery. Now, women, asserting their desires to maintain more personal control and involvement with childbirth and to share the process with life partners and family, seek situations where certified nurse midwives may assist in childbirth, and those in attendance are not strangers.

Some parallels can be drawn in the history of birth control methods and use in this nation. At the turn of the century, women shared—in secretive and closeted fashion—their means of preventing pregnancy. Again, with the tides of research (this time, in relation to drugs and their short-term effects on conception) and specialties focusing on women's reproductive health, new methods of birth control were heralded. Women who began using oral contraception at the time of the Federal Drug Administration's approval in 1960 had no information about potentially harmful effects for their health. It took nearly a decade and the publication of Barbara Seaman's book, *The Doctors' Case Against the Pill,* to "ignite the fire which began the modern women's health movement"[2] and to bring some of the research and messages about birth control methods to a focus on women's experiences and long-term health. Since that time, the inter-relationships among political and historical agendas have become apparent, with ample evidence of how history and politics become so intertwined that the agendas frequently work hand in hand, and history repeats itself.

One method of knowing is tradition—largely equivalent to history and the agenda associated with the past—and so it should not be at all surprising to find the epis-temological assumptions ascribed to this method of gaining knowledge characterizing at least some of what we know about women's health. One linchpin of this method of knowing focuses on how to answer the question "why" in relation to the performance of an action. The answer within this epistemological domain is some version of "that's how it's always been done." Quite simply, it is not enough to know that it's always been done this way in relation to the conduct of research about women's health, or the design and delivery of health care to women, or the messages about both.

Notes

1. B. Dervin, "The Sense-Making Approach," in R. E. Rice & C. K. Atkin (Eds.), *Public Communication Campaigns,* 2nd ed. (Newbury Park, CA: Sage, 1989): 70.

2. See A. S. Bloom & P. E. Parsons, "25th Anniversary of *The Doctors' Case Against the Pill,*" in *The Network News* (Washington, DC: National Women's Health Network, November/December 1994): 1, 3.

6

Contraception and Clinical Science

The Place of Women in Reproductive Technology

Susan A. Owen
Sally A. Caudill

Feminine management of sexuality has been fraught with paradox and contradiction. Male arousal, for example, has been attributed to the female—simply by virtue of being female ("she" cannot be otherwise), women "cause" male sexual desire. Paradoxically, women (and not men) have borne the responsibility for the consequences of sexual thought or behavior on the part of the male. Women also have borne the primary responsibility for contraception.

One primary and obvious reason for women's responsibility for contraception is pregnancy and its effects on a woman's body and life. The historic role of contraception in women's struggle for equality is also notably important. Historically, contraception was advocated as a means for women to develop reproductive and sexual autonomy. Margaret Sanger, recognized as a great emancipator of reproductive rights for women, dedicated her life to the fight for contraception for women. She was committed to the idea that, "access to a safe and reliable means of preventing pregnancy is a necessary condition of women's liberation and, in turn, of human progress."[1] Women's responsibility for contraception is not only a means to control pregnancy, but a source of personal and political empowerment.

Although the struggle for safe and reliable contraception for women is nearly a century old,[2] many questions and problems still exist. Recent scholarship focuses on some of these issues while identifying research that still needs to be conducted. The purpose of this chapter is to explore recently published academic literature (medical and social scientific) on contraception. We begin by briefly identifying and explaining the types of contraception available in three categories: barrier methods, oral contraception, and recent contraceptive technologies. Although this discussion of types of contraception is quite simple, it is important, because it provides the essential framework for identifying three primary concerns in women's reproductive health care. We discuss these concerns at length and examine how current research and contraceptive methods address these issues. Finally, we briefly look at sociocultural and psychological factors that influence contraceptive choices.

Types of Contraception

BARRIER METHODS

Barrier contraceptives are the oldest type of fertility control measure and play an important role in our discussion of primary concerns in women's health care. The types of barrier contraceptives include: mechanical (condoms, cervical caps, diaphragms, and intrauterine devices), chemical (spermicides in the form of suppositories, foams, creams or jellies, and films), or a combination, such as the contraceptive sponge. Mechanical barriers have a higher degree of disease and fertility control when used with spermicides. Douching is also a form of barrier contraceptive, although associated with increased risk of pelvic inflammatory disease and with low efficacy for fertility control.[3]

Barrier contraceptives have broad histories. Sheaths for the penis and occlusion of the cervix can be documented in preliterate cultures.[4] An early version of what we know as the cervical cap was invented in the 19th century; the diaphragm followed shortly thereafter. Obviously, recent advances in substance and design of barrier methods have resulted in higher efficacy and fewer health complications. The intact latex condom, for example, has no microscopic holes and is therefore effective both for fertility control and for protection from nearly all "sexually transmissible organisms."[5] Recent design modifications in the cervical cap reduced the risk of cervical abrasions that can increase risk for toxic shock.[6]

Cervical Cap. This device is a physical barrier placed over the cervix; it is designed to be used with spermicides. The cervical cap began to be used less during the 1960s because of the pill and the IUD (intrauterine device). It was reintroduced in the 1970s by Lamberts (Dalston) Ltd. of London. In 1977, the Food and Drug Administration (FDA) banned the device because of increased risk of toxic shock. In July 1988, The Prentif Cavity Rim cervical cup was approved by the FDA.[7] This device can be "fitted" by lay health care workers under the supervision of licensed health professionals. This method is considered the most effective barrier method both for controlling disease and fertility. Observational studies show a 50%-100% reduction of sexually transmitted diseases (STDs) and a 82%-98% efficacy with control of pregnancy.[8] The advantages of the device are safety, convenience, and comfort of user. The disadvantages are perceived to be insertion-removal, odor, and partner discomfort. This is a female-controlled device.[9]

Diaphragm. This device is a physical barrier for use in the interior vagina; it is designed for use with spermicides. A diaphragm can be fitted by lay health care workers under the supervision of licensed health professionals. "Use of the diaphragm is associated with a significant increase in candidiasis (when compared with the use of condoms)."[10] Observational studies show that the diaphragm controls STDs better than the condom, especially gonorrhea and trichomoniases.[11] Observational studies show a 50%-100% reduction of STDs with this method, and 82%-92% efficacy with pregnancy.[12] The approximate cost for initial fit and spermicide is $50-$100.[13] The advantages of the device are perceived to be safety, convenience, and comfort of user. The disadvantages include insertion-removal and upkeep of device.

Spermicide. Spermicides are chemical barriers that provide protection against bacterial infection of the cervix, and against gonorrhea and chlamydia.[14] They are available over the counter, and can be used with or without mechanical barriers. Clinical trials suggest that spermicides "effectively kill a variety of STD pathogens, including HIV."[15] Some researchers argue, however, that spermicides could increase the risk for HIV infection through irritation of vaginal tissues, which would then "act as a pathway for HIV acquisition."[16] Other researchers assert that the connection between HIV and spermicides is "inconclusive," and that the benefits outweigh potential risks.[17] In addition, there is disagreement about whether spermicides decrease the risk of cervical cancer.[18] Candidiasis, any variety of infection caused by fungi, may be elevated with continuous spermicide use. Studies show a 50% efficacy with disease control and 79%-99% with pregnancy control.[19]

Contraceptive Sponge. This device provides both a physical and a chemical barrier for the cervix. The sponge "absorbs ejaculate" and contains spermicide that is released over a period of time. This method was made available in the United States in July 1983. This device is available over the counter, and is a female-controlled device. Like the diaphragm, the sponge reduces gonorrhea and trichomoniasis, and, to a lesser degree, chlamydia. The sponge is related to increased incidence of candidiasis compared to the condom, but less than the diaphragm. Clinical trials show a 25%-40% reduction in chlamydia with use of the sponge; 10%-69% reduction in gonorrhea; and a 79%-99% efficacy with fertility control.[20] The perceived advantages of the method are safety, availability, 24-hour protection, and ease of use. Disadvantages include insertion-removal.[21]

Condoms. Probably the most widely recognized of the barrier methods, the condom is a male-controlled device that provides protection from viral and bacterial infections, vaginally and cervically.[22] This device is available over the counter. Observational studies show that correct use of intact latex condoms reduces STDs by 30%-60%; condoms are 88%-98% effective in controlling fertility.[23] Advantages include availability, cost, and safety, but the disadvantages of condoms are misuse and partner cooperation.

Intra-Vaginal Pouch or Female Condom. This new mechanical barrier was approved by the FDA in August 1993. The polyurethane device works much like a condom, only it is female controlled. The female condom allows women to use just one method to respond to anxieties about both AIDS and pregnancy, and it is expected to provide greater comfort for men than the male condom. One of the primary benefits of this type of condom is that there is no reliance on male arousal. Wider use will provide more information about women's reactions to this condom.

ORAL CONTRACEPTIVES

The pill is a daily contraceptive made of synthetic estrogen that raises a woman's natural estrogen level just enough to keep an egg from developing and maturing in the ovary. It was approved for use by the FDA in 1960. During a month on the pill, a woman's ovaries remain inactive. As a result, there is no egg that can be fertilized by sperm. If a woman forgets to take a pill for 2 or more days, pregnancy may occur. The pill is 98% effective for preventing unwanted pregnancy but offers no protection from STDs. The advantages of the pill include: almost complete protection against pregnancy, regularity of menstrual cycles, lighter flow during periods, relief from premenstrual tension, fewer menstrual cramps, and no intrusion in lovemaking. It is a female-controlled form of contraception.

There are several possible disadvantages to pill use. Primarily, researchers are still uncertain about the long-term effects of use. Women who have used the pill have a higher risk of heart attack, stroke, high blood pressure, and clotting disorders, a risk expected to increase the longer a woman takes the pill. Researchers still disagree about linking the pill to cancer. Other side effects include: headaches, diabetes, depression, change in sexual desire, nausea, fatigue, vaginal discharge, urinary tract infection, changes in menstrual flow, bleeding, breast changes, skin problems, gum inflammation, liver and gallbladder disease, epilepsy and asthma, virus infection, and cervical dysplasia. Most women who use the pill do not suffer from all these side effects, and some experience none. Women should decide to continue or discontinue use by being aware of and discussing side effects with a physician.[24]

OTHER CONTRACEPTIVE TECHNOLOGIES

Several other contraceptive developments have received medical attention. These developments have played integral roles in helping researchers identify the primary concerns in women's contraceptive health care.

Norplant. Norplant, approved by the FDA in December 1990, is the first new prescription contraceptive method introduced since the mid-1960s.[25] The use of Norplant as a contraceptive device involves the placement of rods or capsules under the skin of the upper arm; these release a pregnancy preventing hormone over a 5-year period.[26] It is controlled by a health care provider and cost, including placement, ranges from $300 to $750.[27] Although studies are incomplete, Norplant appears to be quite effective and has several advantages over other methods, with few side effects. Thus far, Norplant has been 99% effective over the 5-year period that the capsules are in place. Some of the advantages include reversibility, low dose, sustained level of hormone infusion, no estrogen, and its nonintrusiveness to sexual intercourse. The biggest disadvantage is that there is no disease control with this method. The documented side effects include irregularities in menstrual bleeding, contraindications for certain preexisting diseases and health conditions (e.g., diabetes), infection of implant site, removal problems, and a still unknown effect on lactating women. Though no causal links are proven, associated potential problems include headaches, dizziness, weight gain, and weight loss.[28] Research addressing the possibilities for "compulsory contraception," as well as advantages and disadvantages, still needs to be conducted.

Depo Provera (DMPA). This method is an "injectable contraceptive" that lasts for 3 months.[29] It is controlled by a health care provider. DMPA was approved by the U.S. Food and Drug Administration in October 1993.[30] The estimated cost is $120. As with Norplant, much research is inconclusive, although DMPA has serious documented disadvantages. The perceived advantages parallel Norplant in that DMPA is easily administered, nonvisible, and nonintrusive in sexual intercourse. The documented disadvantages of DMPA include the nonreversible nature of the method, menstrual disturbances such as irregular and heavy bleeding, infection risk with the injection (hepatitis), and iron depletion for women. The method has been linked to reproductive cancers in lab animals. Other problems include adverse effects on lactating women, absence of disease control, and that it may be misused as a drug or device for inducing abortion.

Contraceptive Vaccine. Like DMPA, this method is an "injectable contraceptive" controlled by health care providers. It generates antibodies to HCG (human chorionic gonadotropin), which are associated with the early stages of pregnancy. This vaccine blocks development of fertilized eggs and initiates onset of menstrual flow. As with Norplant and DMPA, there is no disease control with this method. Its purpose is interference with implantation of a fertilized egg. Like Depo Provera, this method may be misused as an abortifacient.[31] Its expected advantage is that it will have fewer side effects than DMPA.[32]

Primary Concerns in Women's Reproductive Health Care

An interesting dialogue on women's contraceptive/reproductive health care needs exists in the medical and social scientific literature. Three primary concerns emerge addressing (implicitly) the consequences of the historical double bind women have faced regarding their own reproductive and sexual lives.

CONTRACEPTION AND DISEASE CONTROL

One of the most urgent needs in women's reproductive health care is the integration of contraceptive methods with the prevention of sexually transmitted diseases (STDs). Currently, condom use is the only method that is marketed as both a contraceptive and a means of disease control. As one pair of researchers commented, "there is an inverse relationship between the degree of protection afforded against pregnancy and that afforded against sexually transmitted diseases."[33]

As explained earlier, women are primarily responsible for birth control and, by extension, disease control; yet remarkably little public education is directed specifically to them. Further, the spread of sexually transmitted diseases, especially to women, has increased dramatically since 1980. In particular, the threat of HIV has elevated disease control to a level of urgency comparable to or surpassing fertility control. Importantly, the male-controlled condom is widely recommended as the "first line of defense" against HIV infections, further complicating women's control of their contraceptive/reproductive health care choices.

Researchers investigating barrier methods remark that, "STD prevention efforts have emphasized condoms to the virtual exclusion of other barrier methods, [therefore] there is a need to identify methods that women can use independently of their partners."[34] It is important to note that barrier methods are presently the only types of contraception that allow for prevention of *both* pregnancy and STDs. Thus, *women's ability to control pregnancy and disease transmission have become largely dependent on male partners, and messages reflect this fact.*

Barrier methods went out of style in the United States with the marketing of oral contraceptives in the 1960s. Women's health advocates, however, continued to promote barrier methods because of health risks associated with early high-dose progestin "pills." The recently renewed interest in barrier methods has everything to do with protection from sexually transmitted diseases. This means that many of the researchers studying barrier contraceptives stress the potential risks of using *only* oral, hormonal, injectable, or implanted contraception. Two researchers put it this way: "Women should be informed that these methods of birth control offer no protection against sexually transmitted diseases, and they should be advised to use one or more additional methods for disease prevention."[35]

Notably, writers stress an alarming disparity between the rise in rates of sexually transmitted diseases and the move to combine contraceptive practices with disease control. *The New England Journal of Medicine* published an article that concludes that "there has been little change in sexual practices in response to new and serious epidemics of sexually transmitted diseases, with the exception of an increase in the use of condoms (which still does not reach 50 percent)."[36] Further, there is evidence that the medical profession may be uncomfortable combining reproductive and disease-control protocols. "Uneasiness may exist with the idea of combining contraception (*health*) and sexually transmitted disease/HIV (*disease*) prevention messages," two authors comment, as they encourage and admonish health care professionals to "achieve a better balance between these two needs of sexually active [women]."[37]

Available statistics verify the "urgent need" for balance of "contraceptive-related STD prophylaxis."[38] The *American Journal of Public Health* reports that in 1988, "12 million new cases of sexually transmitted diseases occurred in the United States."[39] Further, in 1989, there were 500,000 visits to medical offices for pelvic inflammatory disease (PID), resulting in 180,000 hospitalizations for serious complications from that disease.[40] These figures have special significance for women, because: (a) "STDs can be transmitted more easily from men to women than vice versa"; and (b) "women experience more frequent and [more] serious complications" from these diseases.[41] The consequences of complications from chlamydia, trichomoniasis, gonorrhea—to name a few of the STDs—are pelvic inflammatory disease, increased risk for ectopic pregnancies, and infertility.

Research needs to be conducted to help us formulate criteria for evaluating the relative efficacy (fertility *and* disease control) of barrier contraceptives, because of their dual role in the prevention of conception and in disease control. Research examining the effectiveness of barrier methods when used in conjunction with oral or hormonal forms of contraception will strengthen the criteria and evaluation of methods. Very little research exists that identifies the effectiveness of using combined methods. This research must be conducted with the two remaining concerns in women's reproductive health care needs as guiding factors in order truly to meet the needs of women.

RESEARCH AND CLINICAL STUDIES

The second primary concern in women's contraceptive/reproductive health care needs is that contraceptive research, development, policy making, and marketing are inadequately integrated with women's everyday lives. Researchers discuss how women might be given more control over their reproductive health and more options for birth and disease control. This entails identifying how pharmaceutical companies, research protocols, and policy-making procedures ignore or neglect the needs and interests of women. One particular problem is the recognition and discussion of the limitations of clinical studies.

One researcher articulated the problem with clinical trials this way:

> Pharmaceutical and clinical researchers, and authorities in charge of drug regulation, need to be more aware of the enormous discrepancy between conditions in clinical trials and conditions commonly found in developing countries.[42]

Such cautionary advice also is warranted in consideration of contraception needs in *developed* countries as well.

As we identified, there are a number of problems with each method, which are compounded for unhealthy women and women in developing countries. For example, clinical trials for contraceptive development are based on research populations that generally are unrepresentative in a variety of ways: The women are healthy, the women have an interest in participating in the studies, the setting of the study is carefully controlled, the women are not lactating, and the women generally are not already pregnant. Another limitation is that clinical trials make recommendations based on the study of short-term effects. Little is known about the cumulative long-term effects of these methods with regard to women's health.[43]

In a related vein, "acceptability studies" of contraceptive methods are criticized for being "marketing" methods rather than sincere efforts to accommodate women's needs.[44] Critics argue that these studies are designed to overcome rather than understand resistance. In other words, there is a feeling that these studies are more a matter of public relations management than viable "research." As one critic put it, "Family planning studies tend to be reactive, accepting without question whatever contraceptive technology emerges from the laboratory."[45]

The history of contraception technology and the FDA's approval of methods with little conclusive research bears testimony that substantial risks have been taken with the health and well-being of women.[46] Further, the technological control of fertility has been valued above and sometimes to the exclusion of the socially complicated matters of reproductive practices and health concerns for women. Clinical trials do not fully incorporate women's reproductive health care needs. For example, with the methods described in this chapter, we see that menstrual disorders may be considered "nonthreatening" and/or "minor." One critic of this minimization of menstrual intrusion expresses her frustration like this: "It is *remarkable* that so little has been written about the consequences of menstrual disturbances for the day to day life of . . . users."[47] Not only is irregular and heavy bleeding problematic for most women, but it may have special cultural and religious significance (e.g., women may be excluded from important rituals or sexual intimacy because of the bleeding). We have already noted that the preexisting health conditions of women are not taken into account in clinical trials. Thus, what we know about the side effects of various methods is not always applicable. Certain health problems such as obesity, malnutrition, kidney disease, and high blood pressure would make the use of some methods dangerous or impossible.

Researchers critical of current approaches explain that clinical trials "are conducted to define a 'gold standard' for how well a drug or device works under optimal circumstances, including correct usage [every time]. Observational studies . . . measure the effectiveness of devices under circumstances of everyday life, including intermittent or improper use."[48] Clearly, the practical usefulness of clinical trials can be amplified through observational study of how women view their bodies, sexuality, reproduction, and health care—in a variety of cultural contexts. Discovering how contraception and disease control methods work in the everyday lives of a wide range of women requires integrated research. In short, *women's experiences should inform research, development, and marketing and the design of health messages, rather than the former placing constraints on the latter.*

USER IMPLEMENTATION

A third concern in women's reproductive health care is that methods of fertility and disease control are only as good as user implementation. Use of contraceptive methods may be constrained by inadequate information, interpersonal dynamics, and awkwardness regarding the human body and sexuality. Researchers interested in this dynamic explain that "those at highest risk for STDs . . . often young or socio-economically disadvantaged, may lack the interpersonal skills necessary to negotiate the use of condoms."[49] In addition, selection of method is constrained by cost, over-the-counter availability, and health care provider-client relationship. In practice, "user" error can include nonuse, sporadic use, or incorrect use. Factors such as health care settings, gender differences, and youth populations all affect user implementation.

The development of contraceptive technology may overlook practical problems in implementation. For example, with the contraceptive technologies discussed in this chapter, we can see that many contraceptive choices require women to increase their dependence on medical professionals. Yet medical infrastructures in both developing and developed countries may be inadequate, already economically overburdened, or inaccessible to some women. Further, the costs of supervision and training for implementation of these technologies of contraception may be overwhelming to current programs. The cost of the method and the attendant health care may be prohibitive for many women. Perhaps most urgent, there is no guarantee that hygienic health facilities will be available. This is a substantial problem; for example, in each of the three recent contraceptive technologies, the risks of infection and complication increase dramatically if sanitary conditions are not maintained; if use of hypodermics and needles is not strictly regulated; and if follow-up care is not available.

Health care settings and health care provider-client relationships are important to successful management of contraception. One study suggests that the interpersonal dimension of this relationship receives little attention from researchers and medical training curricula alike.[50] This research team found that,

1. Nonphysician health care professionals provided the most information about effectiveness, safety, and use of contraceptive devices.
2. Female practitioners were more likely than males to recommend the diaphragm to their clients.
3. Female practitioners (both physician and nonphysician) spent more time with clients and were rated higher on "affective" factors such as friendliness, interest, and nonjudgmental attitude.

4. Client satisfaction was highest with female health care providers.

5. Poor clients were less likely than socially well-positioned clients to receive detailed information and support.[51]

Women and *not* men tend to be the focus of most research in health care provider-patient relationships and in contraception in general. Researchers have learned that women are more likely to accept responsibility for fertility management, tend to know more about contraception, and are most likely to choose the fertility method to be used in sexual relationships.[52] One study suggests that the most important features are effectiveness and safety; the least important features are convenience and lack of interference. This study also suggests that women choose contraception based on the characteristics of the method. So, for example, the sponge often is chosen because of what is most valued for the user: no physician contact is necessary, no fitting is necessary, and the method is reasonably affordable. On the other hand, users of the pill and the diaphragm may choose these methods because they are recommended by "traditional" sources, like physicians, and because the methods are well tested. Users of the pill may choose the hormonal method because they prefer an "invisible" fertility control. Conversely, in some cultural settings, women would *avoid* the pill because they associate taking pills with being ill.[53] Thus, contraceptive methods are chosen by women for a vast variety of reasons.

In youth populations, the psychology of decision making that results in increased risk for exposure to STDs is based in contradiction, rejection of authority, logical fallacy, and denial: "It won't happen to me"; "It hasn't happened yet, so it probably won't happen"; "They just don't want us to do it"; and "I don't want to talk about it." Researchers interested in the psychology of risk management (and this certainly extends to adult populations) are interested in these expressions of unique invulnerability.[54] One researcher in particular studies how youth populations make decisions about protecting themselves from STDs, particularly HIV. Those choosing unprotected sex believed that they could "tell by looking" whether potential partners were free of disease. Further, if potential partners were well known to a circle of friends, they were perceived to be "OK."[55] The gambler's fallacy confuses avoidance of pregnancy with avoidance of infection. Because fertility is possible only certain days of the month, unprotected sex may not result in pregnancy. This, however, is not the case with sexually transmitted diseases.[56]

Campaigns and Future Research

One campaign conducted in South Carolina addressed the needs of women in relation to contraception in youth populations, and its results have been evaluated and published. Its goal was the reduction of unintended adolescent pregnancy. This campaign was informed by using social learning theory and the health belief model. It incorporated the adolescents' self-esteem, relationship with parents, religious views, peer influences, and knowledge about sexuality and contraception to guide the design and diffusion of innovations within the targeted community. The communities that received the intervention demonstrated a decrease by more than half in pregnancy rates for teens compared with teens not exposed to the intervention.[57]

The South Carolina campaign serves as an excellent example of the type of study that needs to be developed in regard to contraception and its role in women's reproductive health care needs. This campaign incorporated experiences, education level, age, and other factors in order to help adolescent women determine the types of contraception that were most appropriate for their personal use. Future campaigns must rely on information affecting user implementation as the South Carolina study did and incorporate information on STDs and useful clinical trials. Before this can occur, however, research that specifically addresses women's reproductive needs must be conducted. Extensive research identifying the effectiveness of contraceptives for prevention of pregnancy and STDs must be completed. Research must consist of more thorough clinical trials that include women with a wide variety of health concerns, and messages to recruit these women must be designed with their experiences in mind.

Conclusion

Future development in contraceptive technologies must not only identify how well a method controls fertility—in a strictly technical sense; we must also know how well contraceptive methods will be integrated with a diversity of cultural perspectives and practices. With such knowledge, messages to increase perceptions of self-efficacy in relation to use can be developed. In this chapter, we have reviewed many problems with current contraception: new contraceptive technologies are "user unfriendly"; methods do not fit needs; methods create health risks; methods are expensive and require the services of a health care professional; and menstrual disorders created by the methods are minimized. Most important, however, the newest advances in fertility control do not protect users from sexually transmitted diseases. Our review of barrier methods illustrates problems with cost, availability, effectiveness, and proper use. We have also seen a lack of institutional support for women's reproductive health needs.

It is disturbingly clear that public health messages about disease control are not achieving the desired changes in "safer sex" practices. Research in social psychology suggests that this may be due, in part, to "differences in cultural, familial, or educational backgrounds."[58] Family planning research has not focused on the culturally diverse manner in which people make sense of sexuality itself, human relationships, and information about fertility and disease control.

A review of academic literature clearly suggests that clinical science knows too little about the conditions of women's daily lives and about women's ways of knowing. Further, institutional and pharmaceutical practices often place women's health and well-being second to profit making, population control, and professional management of fertility and disease control. It is hoped that these issues, as well as lesbian health care, will be integrated into research on contraception and sexually transmitted diseases. Currently, the research on STDs is focused exclusively on heterosexual intercourse.

The good news is that this critique comes from within these established professions, signaling self-reflexivity and a willingness to be educated about women's contraceptive health care needs. So far, there is not much exchange between and among medical researchers and the field of social psychology.[59] More interdisciplinary work will strengthen research and development of contraceptive technology.

Notes

1. E. Chesler, *Woman of Valor: Margaret Sanger and the Birth Control Movement in America* (New York: Simon & Schuster, 1992): 11.

2. For example, Chesler identifies Sanger's involvement in contraception rights as beginning before 1910.

3. M. J. Rosenberg & E. L. Gollub, "Commentary: Methods Women Can Use That May Prevent Sexually Transmitted Disease, Including HIV," *American Journal of Public Health* 82 (1992): 1477; M. J. Rosenberg, A. J. Davidson, J. H. Chen, F. N. Judson, & J. M. Douglas, "Barrier Contraceptives and Sexually Transmitted Diseases in Women: A Comparison of Female-Dependent Methods and Condoms," *American Journal of Public Health* 82 (1992): 673.

4. See, for example, J. Peel & M. Potts, *Textbook of Contraceptive Practice* (New York: University Printing House, 1969). Cited in J. A. Zimmet & P. A. Reagan, "An Historical Look at a Contemporary Question: The Cervical Cap," *Health Education* (1986): 53-57.

5. Rosenberg & Gollub, "Commentary," 1473. These researchers cite a study where 33% of condoms tested leaked particles the size of HIV virus.

6. See, for example, Zimmet & Reagan, "An Historical Look"; D. M. Gallagher & A. Richwald, "Feminism and Regulation Collide: The Food and Drug Administration's Approval of the Cervical Cap," *Women and Health* 15 (1989): 87-97.

7. Zimmet & Reagan, "An Historical Look"; Gallagher & Richwald, "Feminism and Regulation Collide."

8. Rosenberg & Gollub, "Commentary," p. 1474; Rosenberg et al., "Barrier Contraceptives," p. 669.

9. Zimmet & Reagan, "An Historical Look," p. 55.

10. Rosenberg et al., "Barrier Contraceptives," p. 671.

11. Rosenberg & Gollub, "Commentary," p. 1475; Rosenberg et al., "Barrier Contraceptives," pp. 669-670.

12. Rosenberg & Gollub, "Commentary," p. 1476.

13. Rosenberg & Gollub, "Commentary," p. 1480.

14. W. Cates, F. H. Stewart, & J. Trussell, "Commentary: The Quest for Women's Prophylactic Methods— Hopes vs. Science," *American Journal of Public Health* 82 (1992): 1480.

15. Rosenberg et al., "Barrier Contraceptives," p. 669.

16. Cates et al., "Commentary," p. 1480.

17. Rosenberg & Gollub, "Commentary," p. 1474; see also Z. A. Stein, "Editorial: The Double Bind in Science Policy and the Protection of Women From HIV Infection," *American Journal of Public Health* 82 (1992): 1471-1472.

18. Rosenberg & Gollub, "Commentary," disagree with Cates et al., "Commentary."

19. Rosenberg & Gollub, "Commentary," p. 1476.

20. Rosenberg & Gollub, "Commentary," p. 1474; Rosenberg et al., "Barrier Contraceptives," pp. 669-770.

21. Rosenberg & Gollub, "Commentary," p. 1476.

22. Cates et al., "Commentary," p. 1480.

23. Rosenberg & Gollub, "Commentary," p. 1473.

24. The Boston Women's Health Collective, *The New Our Bodies, Ourselves: A Book by and for Women* (New York: Simon & Schuster, 1984): 238-246.

25. M. J. Rosenberg & E. L. Gollub, "Compulsory Contraception," *The Economist,* June 1991, pp. 2, 22. See also S. Platt, "Fertility Control," *New Statesman and Society* (June 28, 1991): II.

26. We rely heavily in this chapter on an excellent article written by a female researcher who clearly speaks on behalf of women's interests: A. Hardon, "The Needs of Women Versus the Interests of Family Planning Personnel, Policy-Makers and Researchers: Conflicting Views on Safety and Acceptability of Contraceptives," *Social Science and Medicine* 35 (1992): 753-766. See also The Population Council, *Norplant Contraceptive Subdermal Implants: Manual for Clinicians* (New York: Population Council, 1990); Rosenberg & Gollub, "Commentary."

27. Rosenberg & Gollub, "Compulsory Contraception," pp. 2, 22.

28. Hardon, "The Needs of Women," pp. 753-766.

29. Hardon, "The Needs of Women," pp. 755-756; P. Bunkle, "Calling the Shots? International Politics of Depoprovera," in R. Arditti, R. Duelli-Klein, & S. Minden (Eds.), *Test Tube Women: What Future for Motherhood* (Boston: Pandora, 1984): 165-188.

30. "Upjohn Begins Marketing New Contraceptive," *New York Times,* January 13, 1993, p. D4; "3-month Contraceptive Shot Approved by FDA," *Los Angeles Times,* October 30, 1992, p. A1.

31. A. LeGrand, "The Abortion Pill: A Solution for Unsafe Abortions in Developing Countries?" *Social Science and Medicine* 35 (1992): 772-773.

32. "Unit Enters Licensing Pact for Contraceptive Vaccine," *Wall Street Journal,* January 21, 1992, p. C21; "Health Agency Backs 2 New Contraceptives," *New York Times,* June 6, 1993, p. 20L.

33. Rosenberg & Gollub, "Commentary," p. 1477.

34. Rosenberg et al., "Barrier Contraceptives," p. 673.

35. Rosenberg & Gollub, "Commentary," p. 1475.

36. B. A. DeBuono, S. H. Zinner, M. Daamen, & W. M. McCormack, "Sexual Behavior of College Women in 1975, 1986, and 1989," *The New England Journal of Medicine* 322 (1990): 821-825.

37. Rosenberg & Gollub, "Commentary," p. 1477.

38. See Z. A. Stein, "Editorial: The Double Bind," pp. 1471-1472.

39. Rosenberg et al., "Barrier Contraceptives," p. 669; Division of Sexually Transmitted Diseases, *Annual Report, 1989* (Atlanta, GA: Centers for Disease Control, 1990).

40. Rosenberg et al., "Barrier Contraceptives," p. 673.

41. Rosenberg et al., "Barrier Contraceptives," p. 673.

42. LeGrand, "The Abortion Pill," pp. 772-773.

43. Hardon, "The Needs of Women," pp. 753-766; LeGrand, "The Abortion Pill."

44. Hardon, "The Needs of Women"; Office of Technology Assessment, "Strategies for Medical Technology Assessment," (Washington, DC: Government Printing Office, 1982).

45. J. F. Marshall, "Acceptability of Fertility Regulating Methods: Designing Technology to Fit People," *Preventive Medicine* 6 (1977): 65-73. Cited by Hardon, "The Needs of Women," p. 763, who says Marshall's view, "Seems to be the case at present."

46. See, for example, B. Seaman & G. Seaman, *Women and the Crisis in Sex Hormones* (New York: Bantam, 1977).

47. Hardon, "The Needs of Women," 761, emphasis ours.

48. Rosenberg & Gollub, "Commentary," p. 1473.

49. Rosenberg et al., "Barrier Contraceptives," p. 673.

50. S. M. Harvey, L. J. Beckman, & J. Murray, "Health Care Provider and Contraceptive Care Setting: The Relationship to Contraceptive Behavior," *Contraception* 40 (1989): 715-729.

51. Harvey et al., "Health Care Provider," pp. 715-729.

52. M. Gerrard, C. Breda, & F. X. Gibbons, "Gender Effects in Couples' Sexual Decision Making and Contraceptive Use," *Journal of Applied Social Psychology* 20 (1990): 449-464; S. M. Harvey & S.C.M. Scrimshaw, "Coitus-Dependent Contraceptives: Factors Associated With Effective Use," *The Journal of Sex Research* 25 (1988): 364-378.

53. Harvey & Scrimshaw, "Coitus-Dependent Contraceptives," p. 774.

54. H. Shaklee & B. Fischoff, "The Psychology of Contraceptive Surprises: Cumulative Risk and Contraceptive Effectiveness," *Journal of Applied Social Psychology* 20 (1990): 385-403; V. Green, S. Johnson, & D. Kaplan, "Predictors of Adolescent Female Decision Making Regarding Contraceptive Usage," *Adolescence* 27 (1992): 613-632; J. M. Burger & L. Burns, "The Illusion of Unique Invulnerability and the Use of Effective Contraception," *Personality and Social Psychology Bulletin* 14 (1988): 264-270.

55. E. Maticka-Tyndale, "Sexual Scripts and AIDS Prevention: Variations in Adherence to Safer Sex Guidelines by Heterosexual Adolescents," *Journal of Sex Research* 28 (1992): 62-63.

56. Shaklee & Fischhoff, "The Psychology of Contraceptive Surprises," pp. 386-387.

57. U.S. Department of Health and Human Services, "Reducing Unintended Adolescent Pregnancy Through School/Community Educational Interventions: A South Carolina Case Study" (Columbia, SC: Department of Health Promotion and Education, 1988).

58. R. J. McDermott & R. S. Gold, "Racial Differences in the Perception of Contraception Option Attributes," *Health Education* (December 1986/January 1987): 9.

59. We arrived at this conclusion by cross-referencing citations.

7

Our Bodies, Our Risk

Dilemmas in Contraceptive Information

Martha Solomon Watson
Mary Anne Trasciatti
Cynthia P. King

In her autobiography, birth control pioneer Margaret Sanger traces her slow, uncertain drift toward a lifelong commitment to informing women about their reproductive lives. One significant event in that progress was Sanger's first experience with official censorship. At the request of her socialist friends, she wrote a series of general women's health articles, titled "What Every Mother Should Know," to run in their organization's journal, *Call*. Those were so successful that a second series, "What Every Girl Should Know," was commissioned. Much to Sanger's surprise, after three or four issues, the Post Office Department censored the material, replacing the article under her title, "What Every Girl Should Know," with a two-column-wide box, containing the government's proposed answer: "NOTHING!"[1]

During her long career as a public advocate for freely available birth control, Margaret Sanger made remarkable progress in changing both the government's and the public's attitudes toward contraceptive information. Today, articles reminiscent of Sanger's pioneering efforts appear frequently in magazines targeted to various ages of women explaining contraceptive options in detail. For example, a chatty article titled "Birth Control Etiquette" (written by a man) in *Glamour* magazine indicated how much has changed since Sanger's time:

> Birth control is a Sensitive Social Topic. We all know a lot of technical stuff about it, but that's not the problem. . . . Once you decide to have sex, a major question of etiquette lies ahead: What is the proper way to decide which contraception or chemical will be used, and whose orifice or appendage will it be used in or on?[2]

In the same spirit, *Mademoiselle* offered specific guidance to women in picking the best condom, urging, "Pick the best-protecting condoms—then don't love him without them."[3] Clearly, birth control has become an openly discussed topic in American life. Even a cursory glance at popular magazines targeted toward women suggests that a wide variety of information is available. But the large number of abortions performed in this country each year as a form of backup contraception and the sky-rocketing rates of teenage pregnancy raise questions about how effectively birth control information is being disseminated in our society. A closer look at available contraceptive messages seems warranted.

For our chapter, we reviewed pamphlets published after 1980 and distributed by Planned Parenthood, various pharmaceutical companies, and the offices of private physicians. Consultation of the *Readers' Guide to Periodical Literature* from 1985 to 1992 directed us to articles on contraception in popular, religious, and women's magazines. The *New York Times* and *Washington Post* indices for 1992 and 1993 were also examined.

Accessibility of Information

A PLETHORA AND DEARTH OF INFORMATION

The development of the birth control pill and the advent of the modern women's movement ushered in an era of refreshingly candid and public discussions of reproductive options. Some termed the time a "revolution" in contraception. Another glance reveals, however, that women's access to birth control information and to new methods is far from unhampered. A survey of the media reveals an odd pattern, with some women receiving a plethora of information and other women facing a drought.

Some women are inundated with information about birth control in all its varieties. Women's magazines run regular updates on contraceptive choices and developments. Often these are, as we shall see, quite detailed. Other kinds of magazines also flood the public with information. For example, *Parents* in October 1986 ran "Birth Control: What You Need to Know,"[4] a complete discussion of contraceptive options, describing them and featuring pros/cons and contraindications. In addition to general advice about condom usage, *Ms.* offered "Condom-mania: A Buyer's Guide," giving brand names and brief physical descriptions.[5] Citing the high rate of teenage pregnancy (more than one million were projected for 1987) and noting that the majority of teenagers who are sexually active do not generally use birth control (an amazing 27% reported never using contraception), the April 1987 issue of *Seventeen* provided "honest answers to your questions," including discussions about how to obtain contraceptives without parental knowledge, even if the young persons were not old enough to drive.[6]

News magazines regularly follow contraceptive developments in their science and medical sections. Newspapers also report on the latest contraceptive developments. For example, a recent issue of the *Washington Post* not only reported on the research on the female condom, it also included a picture of the device with an inset illustration of it correctly in place.[7] In November 1992, the *New York Times* listed the three options for hormonal birth control (the pill, the new implant, and long lasting injections) with their relative effectiveness rates in an article detailing the political issues surrounding the possibility that the implant would be forced on welfare mothers.[8] General interest periodicals like *Jet* and *People* have run columns or brief reports on the subject.

The various print media are only one source of contraceptive information. Physicians supply patients with information provided by drug companies, family planning clinics offer brochures to clients, and a host of public and private agencies provide materials in many formats to women of all ages. Planned Parenthood, for example, has available a wealth of pamphlets, from those explaining individual methods (e.g., *Vaginal Contraceptive Sponge* and *Why Are Rubbers So Popular?*) to those that survey methods (e.g., *Facts About Birth Control*—also available in Spanish) to those targeted toward less experienced persons (e.g., *Making Responsible Choices About Sex*). The U.S. Department of Health and Human Services offers a pamphlet, titled *Many Teens Are Saying 'No,'* that provides guidance for teenagers by providing answers to seven key questions: "What should I know about my body? What should I know about my feelings? What should I know about making up my mind? What should I know if I decide not to have sex? What should I know about pressure? What should I know about boy/girl relationships? Where can I get information that will help me?"[9] The dramatic differences in the style and format of these various materials will be discussed below.

Even the electronic media offer some assistance to women. Although contraceptive ads per se do not appear on television, public service announcements about AIDS prevention mention condoms. Perhaps as part of both the AIDS prevention and "Just Say No" campaigns, at least one recent PSA declared: "Virgin is not a dirty word!" PBS broadcast a special hosted by Linda Ellerbee, "Contraception: The Stalled Revolution,"[10] that provided a broad survey of both contraceptive options and the dissemination of information about them. The program included a lengthy segment on natural conception through planned abstinence, an alternative not frequently treated in written materials.

The wide range of sources of information might suggest that all women have access both to information and even to supplies. Unfortunately, such is not the case. In some communities, public pressure has kept birth control information out of the schools. In

1991, only 13 states had mandatory sex education classes, with or without contraceptive information. Ads for condoms, sponges, and other contraceptive technologies do not appear on the electronic media, although condoms are now advertised as a means of "safe sex." In an age of rising teenage pregnancy rates and MTV, the media most used by teenagers do not feature contraceptive information. Non-English-speaking women have far less information available to them in printed form. In areas that have large, ethnically diverse populations, virtually no information on contraception in languages other than English is available. Birth control information is generally targeted to English-speaking, literate, middle-class women. Indeed, the higher one's socio-economic status, *the greater one's access not only to the technologies but to information as well*.

When Margaret Sanger began her crusade to provide birth control information she was prompted in part by a concern for the plight of poor women, whose physical, emotional, and financial resources were drained by too frequent childbearing. Even in her day, she insisted that only women of means had access to information about and methods of contraception. In our own time, though more information is available, the situation that Sanger perceived prevails. Access to information too often follows socioeconomic and ethnic lines. The nature of the information that is available also privileges some types of women.

What Every Woman Should Know

One significant change since Sanger's time is the array of types of contraception that are available. These range from simple abstinence to such physically invasive and medically complicated procedures as IUDs (intrauterine devices) and the new Norplant contraceptive patch. Although a choice of contraception is obviously desirable, each option requires a different explanation, sometimes rather technical, and each has advantages and disadvantages. Because information is so widely available through various media, the number of messages about birth control is almost dizzying. The nature of the varied messages merits scrutiny.

COMMUNICATING A TECHNOLOGY

The nature of the contraceptive method or methods under consideration largely determines the complexity of the information provided. Simple methods, including abstinence and "barriers" (i.e., condoms), require relatively little technical discussion. Thus, abstinence is defined as "saying 'no' to sex."[11] A condom is described as something that "covers [the] penis and stops sperm from going into [the] vagina."[12] Periodic abstinence ("natural family planning" or the rhythm method) involves refraining from sexual intercourse during ovulation. But this "simple" method requires women to be sensitive to subtle body changes and usually involves counseling from a health care professional. A 1982 pamphlet produced by the U.S. Department of Health, Education and Welfare suggests the complexity of periodic abstinence: "Techniques [for natural family planning] include maintaining chart of basal body temperature, checking vaginal secretions, and keeping calendar of menstrual periods, all of which can help predict when you are most likely to release an egg."[13] This "natural" method requires strong motivation and demands careful monitoring.

Barrier contraceptives, which prevent contact between sperm and egg (see Chapter 4 in this volume), vary in their technological sophistication and in the messages about their use. A Planned Parenthood brochure succinctly declares that a condom is a "latex rubber sheath, unrolled onto penis to catch sperm when [a] man ejaculates (comes)."[14] In contrast, messages about the vaginal sponge, a more complex method, contain more information and sophisticated terminology:

> It is made of a special polyurethane, a synthetic spongy polymer with tiny open cells. These tiny cells are filled with a spermicide called monoxynol-9. . . . It continuously releases a spermicide . . . which stops sperm. . . . It absorbs sperm so they are trapped and lessens the chance that they may get past the cervix.[15]

Similarly, the technical nature of chemical contraceptives, such as birth control pills and contraceptive implants, as well as the IUD, results in messages that are sometimes complex and detailed. A pamphlet distributed by Wyeth-Ayerst Laboratories, developer of the Norplant System, describes the product as a "unique subdermal contraceptive system" containing "a synthetic hormone, levonorgestrel (a progestin), that is also one of the active ingredients in many oral contraceptives used in the U.S. today."[16]

Messages about the pill identify women who should not take it as well as its possible side effects. This information, too, is couched in technical language. For example, in addition to "moodiness,"[17] the May 1990 issue of *Essence* magazine identified "decreased libido" as a side effect of the pill. In sum, messages about contraceptive methods vary widely in the nature of the language and the quantity of information needed to describe and explain them. The simplest methods are described in technical language with relatively little information; barrier methods require more detailed explanations with sophisticated technical terminology. Messages about the most technologically advanced chemical contraceptives are sometimes detailed and quite complicated, requiring at least a rudimentary familiarity with medical/technical terminology.

CHOICE IN CONTRACEPTION

Because various methods are available, each woman must make a choice about which is suitable in her case. The titles of contraceptive literature reflect this dimension: "Choices in Birth Control," "Contraception: The Choice Is Yours," and "Contraception Choices: For Now, For Later." Making an informed choice means weighing the potential health risks and benefits of available contraceptives against a desire to avoid pregnancy. For this reason, three elements impinge on the issue of choice: safety, reliability, and convenience. A tension exists among these elements that must be resolved by women choosing a contraceptive. For some women, balancing serious health problems with their desire to avoid pregnancy is the central concern; the tension is between safety and reliability. For other women, the most immediate concern is balancing frequent, spontaneous sexual activity with a desire to avoid pregnancy; for them the primary tension is between reliability and convenience.

Even the simplest pamphlets offer a discussion, however limited, of health concerns, and even the simplest forms of contraception are not portrayed as risk free. The safety of a method often has two dimensions: health risks and protection. The first is more commonly discussed. Thus, for example, a pamphlet distributed by Planned Parenthood Alameda/San Francisco (1991) identifies health concerns associated with Norplant implants as: "bleeding patterns may change, especially in the first year. Must be inserted and removed by a clinician, no protection against STDs."[18]

In another pamphlet, the IUD is described as raising one relatively benign concern: "Small chance of increased infection *(chance increases with multiple partners)"* (emphasis in original), and health concerns of the sponge, an arguably safer method, are listed as, "Possible allergic reaction to spermicide" and "Chance of Toxic Shock Syndrome."[19] In the absence of further explanation, potential dangers from the sponge may seem equal to the dangers from the IUD, but in reality the IUD is probably more dangerous. Thus, small doses of information about various methods of contraception do not always guarantee a satisfactory and balanced account.

Medical reports, a source of information that can overwhelm an audience with facts, have sometimes offered conflicting information about the health risks associated with a particular form of birth control. Information about the pill and cancer was so conflicting that the Alan Guttmacher Institute, a research organization that studies reproductive issues, published an extensive report in 1991, attempting to correct some of the misconceptions about the safety of the pill. The report concluded that, "women who have ever used the pill will experience 150 fewer cancer deaths per 100,000 women than those who have never used the pill."[20]

Safety discussed in terms of how a method offers protection from problems other than pregnancy is generally addressed in a discussion of a method's advantages or disadvantages. A pamphlet about the vaginal contraceptive sponge avers: "The presence of the spermicide [in the sponge] is thought to provide some protection against gonorrhea and some other sexually transmissible diseases."[21] Diaphragms and cervical caps are also said to "offer some protection against certain STDs, including HIV."[22] Similarly, a *Vogue* article of October 1991, recognizing the health advantages offered by the pill, indicates that, "Pill users are half as likely to develop PID (pelvic inflammatory disease)" and "women who have ever used the pill have a 40 percent lower risk of developing ovarian cancer and endometrial cancer than women who have never used it."[23]

Because preventing pregnancy is the primary aim of contraception, reliability or effectiveness may be the pivotal element in choice. A major criticism of contraceptives, however, is that women are forced to compromise on the issue of reliability as well as safety. A *Mademoiselle* article of August 1986 voices this criticism, declaring,

"Does it work? Is it safe?" Women have a right to birth control that qualifies on both counts, yet too often they are forced to settle for an unsatisfactory compromise: The contraceptive that is most effective may have suspicious side effects, while a more benign variety may be much less successful at preventing pregnancy.[24]

Using statistics, information about reliability takes one of two forms: effectiveness ("how well it works"), or failure rates ("chances of becoming pregnant"). A popular woman's magazine rated the effectiveness of natural family planning, the IUD, and the vaginal sponge as "84 percent," "94 percent," and "82 percent,"[25] respectively; *Ladies Home Journal* expressed the reliability of the same methods in terms of failure rate: "10 to 24 percent," "5 percent," "17-24 percent,"[26] respectively. A pamphlet distributed by Planned Parenthood Medical of Maryland (1988) provided a statistic that considered effectiveness when used "correctly every time," and " 'typical' use"; thus, the diaphragm, when used "correctly every time" has a 97% effectiveness rate; however, the "typical" use yields an 82% effectiveness rate.

Although reliability messages are necessarily replete with statistical information, they generally do not disclose information about the circumstances under which these statistics were obtained. Information about the number of couples studied, their demographic background, and the length of the study is usually omitted. Because most media have time and space constraints, including all of the above would be difficult. But women should know that these factors can affect the results of research and that they often account for conflicting statistics.

Discussions of convenience generally consider accommodation of spontaneous lovemaking and ease of use. A Planned Parenthood brochure, "A Guide to Birth Control Methods" (1988), explained the advantages and disadvantages of a diaphragm; for the former it notes: "Can be inserted before sexual intercourse, encourages partner involvement"; disadvantages include: "requires planning; requires prescription." In an explanation of the contraceptive suppository, *Ladies Home Journal* notes its disadvantage as, "Heat may soften suppositories—hold under cold water to harden before insertion."[27]

In messages of choice, the standard elements of safety, reliability, and convenience must be negotiated within the context of a woman's physical makeup and her lifestyle. "Negotiation" is an especially appropriate concept for the process of choosing a contraception; choice involves reviewing messages associated with each of the elements and "trading-off" certain benefits of one element for certain of others.

One element frequently absent in birth control literature is a discussion of cost. Though technical information on contraception is readily available, information on the specific cost of each method is generally not included in most printed information, especially in pamphlets. One *Ms.* article provided the estimated cost associated with the IUD, "about $200," and the diaphragm, "estimated cost is $140."[28] Similarly, an article in the *Washington Post* reported the predicted cost of the female condom is "between $2.25 and $2.50."[29] That discussions of cost in contraception literature are infrequent implies that cost is often perceived as unessential information in making a contraceptive choice. Clearly, this is not the case for all women, especially those who are uninsured and/or do not have access to the services of a birth control clinic where free contraceptives are supplied.

ADAPTING TO AN AUDIENCE

One of the most noticeable things about birth control information is how different it looks when targeted to different audiences. Information aimed at well-educated, highly literate groups, though not unattractive, is generally not designed to be visually striking. Most often, a substantial amount of text is printed in a standard typeface with a relatively small point size; if graphics are included, they illustrate the method or methods under consideration and/or provide visual instructions for proper use. These physical attributes reflect an awareness on the part of publishers and distributors that individuals who regularly consult print media are likely to be attracted to an article or pamphlet because of its content; also, if a piece is interesting but somewhat lengthy, a reader has the luxury of putting it down and picking it up again later.

Information designed to appeal to individuals who are not inclined to read or who are more accustomed to television and other nonprint media must be visually striking. Consequently, birth control literature intended for teenagers and those without extensive formal education is usually printed in bright colors, with a minimal amount of text in relatively large typefaces that vary from the standard forms and combinations. Several graphics are included, not only to illustrate birth control methods and the proper way to use them, but also to capture the eye of the reader and visually depict the text, thereby reinforcing the message. Channing L. Bete, a company that distributes numerous pamphlets utilizing a combination of text and graphics in a visually stimulating and appealing format, advertises this format, known as scriptography, as an effective means to "present your messages quickly and simply."[30]

As with visual elements, the level of complexity of the text of birth control messages varies with the nature of the intended audience. The strategies by which messages are targeted to different audiences are clear in information about the male condom. A *Ms.* article from September 1987, titled "Condoms: A Straight Girl's Best Friend," offered the following advice:

Condom should be put on an erect or semi-erect penis. Be sure to leave about a half inch of slack at the end and pinch to make sure there is no air bubble. . . . The condom should be put on before the penis can have any contact with the vulva, vagina, mouth or anus. Seminal fluid released prior to ejaculation could deposit sperm close enough to the vagina to allow conception or infection. . . . Be sure to use a spermicide containing monoxynol-9, as it has been demonstrated to kill the AIDS virus.[31]

"Why Are Rubbers so Popular?," a pamphlet prepared and distributed by Planned Parenthood of North Central Florida, tackled a similar issue:

If rubbers are used right, and if birth control foam is used at the same time, there is very little chance of pregnancy. . . . You must put on a rubber before there is any sex contact. When the penis has become hard, unroll the rubber onto it. First, leave a little space at the end of the rubber to catch the sperm. . . . The penis should be withdrawn from the vagina shortly after the sperm is released. You must hold onto the ring as you withdraw the penis. This is to be sure that all the sperm stays in the rubber.[32]

Obviously, the Planned Parenthood pamphlet is written more simply and contains less jargon than the *Ms.* article. Terms such as *condom, seminal fluid,* and *spermicide* are replaced by *rubber, sperm,* and *birth control foam,* respectively. Moreover, because it aims for simplicity, the pamphlet does not intertwine the issues of pregnancy prevention and AIDS. Providers of information are aware of the tension between adapting to an audience and providing "full" information in a particular context. Thus, messages from pharmaceutical companies are usually complex.[33]

Information distributed by government and community agencies contains the least amount of technical complexity and medical jargon. Because they produce and distribute brochures for a broad cross-section of the population, these organizations must use a language and format that is accessible to women of all ages, levels of education, and socioeconomic status. Such literature often omits important information in the name of simplicity, however. This places the burden of filling this informational gap on professionals at counseling, health, and family planning centers. Yet as "The Stalled Revolution" vividly demonstrated, the success of instructional conversations between counselors or health care professionals and their patients is anything but certain. The PBS documentary featured a real-life instance in which a patient at a family planning clinic serving low-income women was offered one-on-one instruction on how to use the pill and the condom, respectively. Yet when asked a few basic questions about the instructions she had just received, the woman was unable to answer them correctly. Thus, even the simplest birth control messages are problematic for some audiences.

Adapting to an audience is not always a simple matter. An important question arises about whether the need for simplicity should override the obligation to make full information about health concerns equally accessible to all women. Surely anyone who comes to a Planned Parenthood clinic for birth control counseling could benefit from information on AIDS prevention. Unless she specifically requests such information, however, a woman might learn all about condoms as a form of contraception without learning the potentially life-saving fact that condoms reduce the risk of contracting AIDS. At issue is whether women whose information comes from simplistic pamphlets such as those cited are learning all that they need to know about issues that are vital to their health and well-being.

Contraceptive Information in a Communication Environment

THE PUBLIC ARENA

Many women are faced with a plethora of information, from simple to complex, about methods that range from basic to technologically sophisticated. Other women have little or inadequate information. But messages about contraception do not occur in a vacuum; rather, women are besieged by information not only about the methods themselves, but also about issues of morality and about the social as well as political implications of their personal choices. A brief look at the moral discourse on contraception related to theology and population issues suggests the complexity of the situation.

No area of concern has generated more heated discussion than the question of the morality both of particular methods as well as of contraception as a whole. The public debate includes expressions of concern about the impact on their sexual morality of supplying birth control information to unmarried women.[34] The Catholic Church, a perennial opponent of the use of "artificial" birth control, suggests that the use of any method by married couples is deeply immoral, and the mass media convey these sentiments to women. For example, Bishop Flavin, in the November 7, 1991, issue of *Origins,* warned that, "Catholics who practice artificial birth control and those who cooperate with them in their immoral actions may not receive holy communion without committing sacrilege."[35]

Such objections do not go unanswered. An editorial in the March 13, 1992, issue of *Commonweal* responds to this view, arguing,

> When he [Bishop Flavin] states that those using contraception commit a sacrilege when they receive Communion, when he urges them to discontinue the "sinful practice" that is contraception and when he calls physicians' cooperation "gravely sinful," he is making judgments about the consciousness and hearts of Catholic people that are . . . unjust . . . and is not consistent with Humane vitae, and deviates from long-standing Catholic moral and pastoral tradition.[36]

This debate, often perceived as limited to Catholics, now occurs within the Evangelical Christian community as well. A collection of essays in a special issue of *Christianity Today* debated the question, "Is Birth Control Christian?" Some Protestant leaders, like their Catholic counterparts, categorically reject birth control as a violation of the biblical "command" of God to "be fruitful and multiply, and fill the earth." This religious discourse also defines birth control as "planned barrenhood." Dissenting Protestant voices get media attention as well, and contraception is thus presented to women as a controversial practice.[37]

Although the details of this controversy may not be salient for some women, theological and moral issues do impinge on public discussions about contraception. Furthermore, sometimes religious and moral opinions may influence legal limitations on contraceptive discourses, as was the case with the imposition of the gag rule on abortion.[38] Even when they do not legally constrain women, such issues may perplex and disturb women who feel torn between their personal needs and the voices of theologians and moralists. This tension is especially acute with two of the most reliable forms of birth control, the pill and the IUD. Widely circulated and well-documented arguments by credible sources that reveal that these methods are, in fact, often abortifacients rather than contraceptives makes women's search for a highly reliable yet life-protecting method far more complicated.[39]

A second public discourse that may impinge on women concerns population issues. Individuals and organizations concerned about population control urge women to have smaller families as a means of protecting "human welfare," which is threatened by "congestion" and "over population." Introducing these issues moves birth control decisions from the personal to the global arena. Women's choice, far from being unfettered, is constrained by the need to be responsible to the larger community, because, as Negative Population Growth (NPG) avers, "freedom is never unlimited."[40]

Efforts to control population do not always assume a lofty, global perspective and may, in fact, raise concerns about social engineering in regard to particular groups. For example, Governor William Schaefer of Maryland recently proposed a highly controversial program "mandating Norplant and vasectomies for welfare recipients who have had several children out of wedlock."[41] Because young black women would form the majority of those receiving Norplant, Schaefer's plan and a similar albeit noncoercive one proposed in Virginia were criticized as both racist and paternalistic by prominent figures within the African American community. Much of the criticism that appeared in the media echoed the sentiments of Susan Bell, who asserted that,

> Since the 1950s, the population control establishment [the U.S. government and private groups such as Planned Parenthood and the Association for Voluntary Sterilization] has dominated the development and distribution of contraceptives. These organizations typically have been more interested in limiting the size of certain groups (especially poor and minority populations) than in helping individual women control their fertility.[42]

At a Baltimore public hearing on the proposal, a local leader of the nation of Islam, Jamil Muhammad, made this point quite graphically: "I'm not going to sit by and let my sisters and my children be destroyed by Norplant."[43]

Programs that link family planning to receipt of social services, such as those proposed by NPG, Governor Schaefer, and the Virginia Assembly, send a distinct message to women, especially minority women, that they may have to sacrifice the right to control their own bodies, allegedly to serve the interests of the state or the global community.

ON THE PRIVATE FRONT

Although moral and social issues can impinge on women as they consider contraceptive options, perhaps the most daunting task for some women is negotiating the use of a method with a partner. Materials addressed to teenagers offer the simple, direct alternative of saying no, using one of the following approaches: "I like you a lot, but I'm just not ready to have sex"; " I don't believe in having sex before marriage, I want to wait"; or "I enjoy being with you, but I don't think I'm old enough to have sex."[44] Some discussions, though not suggesting that a person be totally insensitive to the partner's feelings, argue that self-protection should take precedence over relational issues. A 1987 *Vogue* article, about responding to a man's refusal to wear a condom, is illustrative:

> Women have to learn to resist . . . emotional blackmail. If a man is going to be impotent in a condom, he will be impotent with almost anything. And if his pleasure is so dependent on direct stimulation of the nerve endings in the glans penis, then he is not likely to be sensitive to other zones of pleasure, including those in his partner.[45]

Such an assertive attitude, however, may not be within the grasp of many women, particularly those who are economically dependent on their mates.

Information for those in long-term continuing relationships sometimes addresses the larger issues of mutual respect and the need to accommodate and compromise. "Talking With Your Partner About Birth Control" offers rather simplistic advice for this sensitive task:

> Picking the right moment to bring up the subject is important. Don't wait until you've started to have sex. . . . Don't accuse or blame your partner. It's hard to talk when one person is upset. . . . Tell your partner what you know about birth control and how you feel about using it. Remember to listen. Let him/her express his/her point of view.[46]

Although this advice seems sound, it assumes a certain interpersonal healthiness that does not exist in every relationship. Not all partners are cooperative and supportive; moreover, relational problems like mental, physical, and sexual abuse may supersede concerns for the niceties of interpersonal communication. None of the literature surveyed addressed these volatile issues. Thus, women receive little helpful guidance on how to implement their contraceptive choices.

Conclusion

When Sanger began her crusade for birth control, her vision was that all women would know their contraceptive options and have access to reliable methods. Certainly, much progress has been made. Women have much more information about contraceptive methods than in Sanger's day. But, unfortunately, birth control information is still not fully available to many of the women Sanger most wished to help. Nonaffluent, non-English-speaking women must often rely on underfunded, understaffed public service agencies to help them make contraceptive choices.

Ironically, although medical research has produced highly effective, medically complex methods, the very sophistication of the methods may make it difficult to communicate about them clearly and fully. In addition, some women lack the knowledge and experience necessary to ask probing questions or to understand fully the physical implications of their choices.

On another level, many women receive virtually no help in negotiating the use of methods that are invasive to their interpersonal relationships. The lack of sex education classes in schools and the dearth of educational programs related directly to contraception, both in terms of choice and of implementation, force many young women to remain uninformed about their options. External pressures and conflicting messages from the medical community, theologians, and groups with specific social agendas further complicate the situation facing women. In comparison to Sanger's era, contemporary women may be bombarded by too many disparate messages about their contraceptive choices.

Perhaps the most distressing fact is that contraception remains largely the province of women. The choices, the risks, the problems fall almost entirely on their shoulders. Since Sanger's day women have achieved greater contraceptive choice, but the burden and responsibility of contraception, the conflict and the confusion, continue to constrain their lives.

Notes

1. M. Sanger, *Margaret Sanger: An Autobiography* (New York: Norton, 1938): 77.

2. D. Barry, "Birth Control Etiquette," *Glamour* (October 1986): 196.

3. C. Hacinli, "All Condoms Are Not the Same," *Mademoiselle* (November 1988): 133-134.

4. D. Edmondson, "Birth Control: What You Need to Know," *Parents* (October 1986): 156-158, 161-162.

5. P. Hendricks, "Condoms: A Straight Girl's Best Friend," *Ms.* (September 1987): 98, 100, 102. Quoted material used by permission.

6. K. McCoy, "The Practical Facts About Birth Control," *Seventeen* (April 1987): 56.

7. S. Rovner, "Sex, Pregnancy, and Condoms (for Women)," *Washington Post,* December 22, 1992, p. WH14. Quoted material used by permission.

8. F. Barringer, "Making Birth Control Easier Raises Touchy Political Issues," *New York Times,* November 8, 1992, p. 6E.

9. U.S. Department of Health and Human Services, *Many Teens Are Saying "No"* (Washington, DC: Office of Public Affairs, 1989).

10. Maryland Public Television aired this program several times in 1992.

11. Channing L. Bete, Inc., *Abstinence—Saying "No" to Sex* (South Deerfield, MA: Author, 1992).

12. Planned Parenthood Alameda/San Francisco, *The Methods of Birth Control* (Alameda/San Francisco: Planned Parenthood Alameda/San Francisco, 1991).

13. U.S. Department of Health Education and Welfare, *Family Planning Methods of Contraception* (Rockville, MD: U.S. Department of Health Education and Welfare, 1982).

14. Planned Parenthood Medical Centers, *A Guide to Birth Control Methods* (Baltimore, MD: Planned Parenthood Medical Centers, 1988).

15. Planned Parenthood Federation of America, Inc., *Vaginal Contraceptive Sponge* (New York: Planned Parenthood Federation of America 1985).

16. Wyeth-Ayerst, Inc., *Norplant System: Levonorgestrel Implants* (Philadelphia, PA: Author, 1991).

17. M. Kort, "Making Choices," *Essence* (March 1990): 57-58.

18. Planned Parenthood, *The Methods of Birth Control.*

19. Planned Parenthood, *A Guide to Birth Control Methods.*

20. P. Kaufman, "The Good News About Contraception," *Vogue* (October 1991): 202, 204.

21. Planned Parenthood, *Vaginal Contraceptive Sponge.*

22. Planned Parenthood Federation of America, *Facts About Birth Control* (New York: Planned Parenthood Federation of America, 1992).

23. Kaufman, "The Good News About Contraception," 202.

24. G. Blair, "The Pill: What's Right With It," *Mademoiselle* (August 1986): 196, 199.

25. Kort, "Making Choices," p. 58.

26. "How Women Really Feel About Birth Control," *Ladies Home Journal* (August 1986): 55-56.

27. "How Women Really Feel About Birth Control," p. 56.

28. E. Sweet, "A Failed Revolution," *Ms.* (March 1988): 76.

29. Rovner, "Sex, Pregnancy, and Condoms (for Women)," p. WH14.

30. Channing L. Bete, Inc., *Scriptographic Booklets for Health Promotion & Education Programs* (Deerfield, MA: Author, 1991).

31. Hendricks, "Condoms: A Straight Girl's Best Friend," p. 102.

32. Planned Parenthood of North Central Florida, Inc., *Why Are Rubbers so Popular?* (Gainsville: Planned Parenthood of North Central Florida, n.d.).

33. Ortho Pharmaceutical Corporation, *A Guide to the Methods of Contraception* (Raritan, NJ: Author, 1983).

34. D. Evans, "The Price of the Pill," *Christianity Today* 11 (November 1992): 39-40.

35. "Artificial Contraception Called Ban to Receiving Communion," *Origins* 7 (November 1991): 359.

36. R. B. Connors, "Contraception & Communion, the Church's Teaching: Bishop Flavin Has It Wrong," *Commonweal* (March 1992): 7-8.

37. R. C. Van Leeuwen, "Breeding Stocks or Lords of Creation," *Christianity Today* 11 (November 1992): 37.

38. J. Seligmann, D. L. Gonzalez, & B. Cohn, "A Challenge to School Clinics," *Newsweek* (August 10, 1987): 54.

39. D. Sterns, G. Sterns, & P. Yaksich, *The Birth Control Game: Gambling With Life* (Stafford, VA: American Life League, 1990).

40. A. Smith, *The Greatest Mercy* (pamphlet, no place of publication) (May 1987), published and distributed by Negative Population Growth.

41. P. W. Valentine, "Baltimore Eyes Study of Norplant," *Washington Post,* January 26, 1993, p. D1. Quoted material used by permission.

42. Susan Bell, in The Boston Women's Health Book Collective (Ed.), *The New Our Bodies Ourselves* (New York: Touchstone, 1992): 259.

43. Valentine, "Baltimore Eyes Study of Norplant," p. D1.

44. U.S. Department of Health and Human Services, *Many Teens Are Saying "No."*

45. H. Drummond, "Condoms: The Offer You Can't Refuse," *Vogue* (June 1987): 293.

46. ETR Associates, *Talking With Your Partner About Birth Control* (Santa Cruz, CA: Author, 1984). Adapted with permission from ETR Associates, Santa Cruz. For information about other related materials, call 1-800-321-4407.

8

The American Experience of Childbirth

Toward a Range of Safe Choices

Elizabeth Jean Nelson

The diary of Martha Ballard, an early 18th-century midwife in Maine, recounts a time when childbirth took place in the woman's home.[1] Women commenced labor as directed by their bodies, and when the time was right, sent for the midwife. Husbands and male relatives might be present, but women attended to the needs of the laboring woman. The skills a midwife brought to the laboring woman were those she learned in tutelage within a community of women. Physicians were not routinely involved in the birthing process.[2]

Of course, many women and many babies died. Poor nutrition and overwork rendered some women's bodies incapable of surviving childbirth.[3] The natural occurrence of an umbilical cord wrapped around the baby's neck might suffocate the baby during birth (although an experienced midwife could often prevent such a tragedy). The development of placenta previa (the location of the placenta directly over the birth canal) might result in the death of both mother and baby. Without the benefit of modern knowledge and technology, women had to do the best they could.

By 1940, 50% of women gave birth in hospitals.[4] Current estimates hold hospital births at 97%-99%.[5] As a result, the practice of women in labor being attended by midwives and female relatives has virtually disappeared. The shift in childbirth from the natural setting of the home to the sterile setting of hospitals has occurred within a larger cultural and economic context. This chapter examines the physical and emotional health outcomes that result from a range of birth settings including hospitals, homes, and birth centers. The goal is a better understanding of the wide range of "safe" choices women may make as they approach their experience of delivering their young.

Health Outcomes Related to Childbirth Settings

Among women rated as "low risk," delivering in selected American hospitals, rates for intrapartum death (deaths occurring during delivery) and neonatal deaths (soon after delivery) ranged between 1 and 4.3 per thousand.[6] These compare very favorably to the numbers on infant mortality nationwide (which include all high-risk and nonhospital births). In 1982, there were 13 infant deaths per thousand live births in the United States.[7] By 1986, that number had fallen to 11.5 per thousand.[8] These figures mask the contradictory advantages and disadvantages of hospital birth. Hospitals offer the security of knowing that emergency care is close at hand in the event of a medical crisis. On the other hand, they also add risks, including maternal and infant infection[9] and the problems associated with the "cascade of intervention"[10] described below. There are also psychological problems associated with hospital birth. Dissatisfaction with hospital birth stems from expectations that are not met, such as the unexpected difficulty in managing pain, the unanticipated episiotomy, the decision to deliver by cesarean section that might not have been "medically necessary."[11]

HOME BIRTH

A few women are opting for home births, and that number appears to be growing.[12] Studies considering the safety and health outcomes of home delivery observe the difficulty in establishing a controlled study on a practice deemed to be dangerous. They acknowledge that using data gathered for other purposes poses methodological problems for scientific inquiry.[13] Still, these studies offer numbers that enlighten our discussion.

Studies evaluating health outcomes in home birth distinguish between "planned" and "unplanned" home births, though definitions of "planned" vary. Most studies characterized a "planned" delivery as one in which a woman secured the services of a nurse-midwife or other "trained" health care professional in advance and in which some provision was made for emergency hospital care.[14] Women who planned home births generally had at least a high school education, attended prenatal classes, and received routine prenatal exams.

Women opting for home birth reported a variety of motives, including a bad previous hospital experience, the desire to avoid unnecessary interventions in the birth process,[15] and, significantly, the inability to afford a hospital or birth-center birth. Including the cost of a midwife's services, the cost for a home birth is significantly less than the cost of a hospital delivery.[16] For women with no health insurance, this difference was a significant factor in opting for birth at home, although some women with full insurance that would have covered a hospital delivery opted for home birth anyway.[17] Although home births overall reflect higher rates of neonatal mortality, women in the "planned" home delivery group experienced infant death rates no higher than for those delivering in hospitals.[18]

One study of home births in Calgary, Canada, between 1984 and 1987, considered 90 home births.[19] The low number in this study is accounted for in terms of laws prohibiting physicians from participating in home births, combined with the absence of licensure for midwives. Birth outcomes in the Calgary study were similar between the "planned" and "unplanned" groups. Both groups reported labors lasting more than 24 hours. Planned and unplanned home birth babies breathed spontaneously within 5 minutes (a Canadian measure similar to the U.S. Apgar score).[20]

Studies on U.S. populations show more disparity in health outcomes between "planned" and "unplanned" groups. In one study of women in North Carolina, unplanned home deliveries experienced a neonatal mortality rate 20 times that in the "planned" group. In summary, the researcher stated, "Planning, prenatal screening, and adequate training of birth attendants emerged as the most important variables in differentiating the risk of neonatal mortality in North Carolina."[21]

Statistical measures of outcomes suggest that a woman at low risk has as great, if not greater, likelihood for good outcome at home as she might expect in a U.S. hospital, provided she seeks prenatal care and secures the services of a trained midwife or other health professional trained in the delivery of babies. Moreover, women report a fairly high degree of psychological satisfaction with the outcomes of their decision to deliver at home. In one study of women choosing home deliveries in the San Francisco Bay Area, 95% reported either "extremely positive" or "positive" satisfaction with the home birth experience; only 3% reported a "negative" reaction.[22] Despite such findings, no campaigns promote home birth as an option for women delivering a child in the United States.

FREESTANDING BIRTH CENTER (FSBC)

Many women elect to deliver in a birth center, which is a facility dedicated to the process of childbirth. Birth centers generally have admission privileges at a nearby hospital to facilitate emergency care, and services are covered by most insurance policies.[23] Birth centers have grown in number in the past several decades. The first in-hospital birth center came into existence in 1964 as a "compromise" in a Connecticut hospital. Freestanding birth centers (FSBCs) emerged shortly after that experiment.[24] By 1982, there were 130 FSBCs in the United States.[25] By 1987, that number had risen to 240, although some have subsequently closed in response to the "liability insurance crisis."[26] The increased number of centers suggests the success of *commercial* messages to promote the centers' use.

The largest study of birth centers concludes that birth center births may be a reasonable, safe choice for those women who wish to avoid a hospital setting and who prefer the security of knowing emergency care is nearby. This study screened patients for levels of risk according to measures accepted within obstetric practice. Compared to all U.S. women birthing in 1986, women birthing in birth centers were "less likely to smoke, drink alcohol, or be black, unmarried, poorly educated, or under 18 years of age."[27] These women also averaged 11.3 prenatal exams by health care professionals.

The health outcomes among women delivering in birth centers were impressive. These women had fewer premature or low birth weight babies than U.S. women overall. Of course, it is important to recall that most women delivering in a birth center are screened regularly, and any signs of trouble warrant immediate referral to a hospital, so "potential risks" are removed from the study at any point in the process.[28] Compared with home births, birth center births are more "medicalized," but women delivering in birth centers experienced far less intervention than women in hospitals.[29]

Women polled after delivering in birth centers were quite happy with their experiences. Rooks et al. report that among women who delivered in the birth center, 98.8% indicated they would recommend the birthing center to friends, and 94% said they would use the services of the birthing center again for another pregnancy.[30] Eakins's study reported equally high satisfaction among women delivering in birth centers, with 87% saying the experience was "extremely positive" or "positive," and only 5% indicating that the experience was "extremely negative."[31]

In response to the study by Rooks et al., Lieberman and Ryan argued that further study is needed to evaluate the safety of FSBCs.[32]

HOSPITAL BIRTHING ROOMS

Many U.S. hospitals still divide labor rooms from delivery rooms; but many also offer birthing rooms, assigned on a first come, first served basis. Some hospitals have enough such rooms that the mother and baby may remain in the room even after the birth of the baby. Such arrangements appeal to one aspect of women's rejection of hospital birth, namely, misgivings about delivering in a sterile environment. But women expressed the desire for control over, or at least active participation in, the birth process, which hospital birthing rooms do not necessarily "allow."

In sum, the studies available do not suggest that hospitals are in and of themselves *un*safe; but rather, that other options, home and birth center births, can be equally safe *for low-risk women who follow a routine of prenatal care and regular screening.* In addition, studies show that home and birth center births are cost-effective among women who plan their birthing experience. The satisfaction rate is also high among women who planned to deliver at home or in a birth center. This is not a call for all women to abandon hospital births in favor of home or birth center delivery, but for medical personnel to broaden their measurement of "good outcomes" and acknowledge women's role in the satisfaction they experience in their birthing experiences.[33]

Health Issues Related to Midwives and Other Attendants

The presence of any nonmedical personnel in the labor and delivery room is a fairly recent phenomenon in the United States. A study reported in the *Journal of the American Medical Association* in May 1991 suggests that the continuous presence of a trained *female* companion can significantly improve birth outcomes in some populations. This study was conducted at Jefferson Davis Hospital, a public institution that serves many of the indigent women in Houston, Texas. The study was prompted by two studies of women in Guatemala, which suggested that the presence of a companion (called a *doula,* a Greek word meaning "experienced mother") during labor and delivery shortened labor and reduced the need for cesarean sections and other interventions.[34] The *doula* parallels the traditional role that female relatives play in many cultures.[35] Midwives, more skilled than *doulas,* also have a long history in relation to childbirth.

MIDWIVES AND HEALTH OUTCOMES

Many women who deliver at home or in a birth center do so with the aid of a midwife. So, just as both of these "alternative birth" choices have risen in the past decade, so too have the number of midwife-attended births grown, from 0.9% of all births in 1975 to 3.4% in 1988. This growth was predominantly among midwives practicing within hospitals, where populations served by midwives differ from those served outside hospitals.[36] Midwives in hospitals serve women who are younger than average, less well educated than average, and are more likely to be unmarried than their out-of-hospital counterparts. Midwife-attended women delivering outside of hospitals are older than average, more likely to be white and have had three children already, and better educated than those who have midwife-assisted hospital deliveries.

That mothers benefit emotionally from the presence of a midwife is clear from the reports of women.[37] Even when the baby's father has been trained in a Lamaze-type course, the presence of a midwife or *doula* provides emotional support. "One study suggests that childbirth education does not sufficiently prepare men for the sights and sounds of childbirth, and indicates that men express enthusiasm for the additional emotional support of a midwife or doula."[38]

Beyond the emotional benefits associated with the presence of a midwife, midwife-assisted birth appears to hold good health outcomes for the mothers. Certified nurse midwives working at the Maternity Center in Bethesda, Maryland, attended 25 home births per month from 1975 to 1982 and then began attending birth center births as well. In all that time, not a single mother has died; any infant deaths were due to congenital problems that would have caused death in the hospital.[39] Women delivering with a midwife, inside and outside the hospital, are half as likely as the overall population to have a low birth weight baby. Among babies born to midwife-assisted mothers outside hospitals, 58.5% have a 1-minute Apgar score of 9 or 10, compared to 45% of babies born to midwife-assisted women in hospitals and to 42.1% of babies born in all categories.[40] The statistics do not prove a *causal* relationship between midwives and improved outcomes for babies but may reflect midwives' efficiency in referring higher-risk patients to physicians.[41]

Economic considerations in the practice of midwifery in the United States are connected to the issue of women's health outcomes at both the individual and system levels. In the Netherlands, which boasts the world's lowest infant mortality rate, midwives care for nearly all pregnant women. Indeed, the Dutch government subsidizes health care for roughly 70% of the population and will cover the costs of a physician's involvement in childbirth *only* if it is demonstrated that the mother has a complication requiring medical intervention. Thus, costs remain low and outcomes remain good.[42]

Health Issues Related to Hospital Intervention in Childbirth

Those who choose hospital birth face a variety of procedures that have become standard in hospital births. Some of these may benefit some women, but most are not necessary for all women.[43] Evaluation of and choice among procedures might improve hospital birth.

THE PREPARATION PROCEDURES

Upon arrival at the hospital, many pregnant women are settled into a wheelchair, wheeled off to the labor room, and "prepped"—which usually means donning a hospital "gown," receiving a vaginal exam, and sometimes getting an enema and a pubic shave.[44] To transport women in a wheelchair is "policy" in most hospitals and results from concern for legal suits that could be brought against a hospital in the rare chance a woman falls during a walk to the labor room.[45]

The rationale for routine use of enemas is that clearing the bowel will make more room for the baby's head to descend into the birth canal, which will in turn stimulate contractions and thus shorten labor. It is suggested that reducing the likelihood of mother's elimination during delivery will reduce the risk of infection rates for mother and baby.[46] Studies questioning the utility of the enema have suggested that the enema has little impact on elimination during the first stage of labor. During the second stage of labor, women who have had an enema were less likely than women in the control group to "soil," but cleanup was more difficult with women in the enema group. There appeared to be no impact on the length of labor or on the incidence of infection. Some women in this study had requested an enema and were pleased to have had one; others were either indifferent or had negative feelings associated with the enema.[47]

Routine shaving of a woman's pubic hair is generally justified in terms of improved visibility for physicians,[48] the reduction of risks of infection,[49] and anticipation of possible surgery.[50] Serious testing has not been done to determine the legitimacy of this routine practice, though as early as 1922, "a controlled trial provided evidence that challenged these assumptions."[51] Many women express no particular objection to the pubic shave, whereas others acknowledge notable discomfort in the weeks after delivery during which the hair grows back.

MONITORING THE BABY'S HEART RATE

Fetal heart rate monitoring is routine in hospitals. There are two types of monitoring: auscultation, and electronic monitoring. Auscultation involves listening to fetal heart-beat at regular intervals, usually immediately following a contraction. Both stethoscope and Doppler ultrasound devices may be used for auscultation. Electronic monitoring occurs throughout the labor and may be external or internal. External electronic monitors are strapped to the mother's body, one receiver measuring the strength of contractions, the other measuring the baby's heart beat. Internal monitoring, employed only after the amniotic sac is broken, involves the application of an electrode to the baby's scalp.[52] Both internal and external electronic monitoring relay information about the baby and the mother to a machine that prints out a record of the mother's contractions and the baby's reactions to contractions. Electronic monitoring is preferred in most hospitals, because the information is continuous and printed out for study. Internal monitoring is generally the norm in a labor involving any degree of risk.[53]

Although physicians prefer the amount of information offered via electronic fetal heart monitoring, many women find this uncomfortable. The monitors strapped to the woman's belly in external electronic monitoring are binding and need to be frequently reapplied, as the mother's movement easily displaces the monitors. Internal electronic monitoring is even more confining because once applied, the woman is almost completely bedbound, which may hinder the progress of labor.[54]

Intensive monitoring of mothers does not necessarily yield improved outcomes for babies. The incidence of low Apgar scores and the rates of admissions to special-care nurseries did not decrease among babies whose heart rates were monitored intensively.[55] In addition, one study found "no significant differences in stillbirths or fetal health between the universally monitored and selectively monitored women. Even among premature births, no benefits were found to result from electronic fetal monitoring."[56]

CONFINING THE LABORING WOMAN TO BED

Confining a laboring mother to bed is routine in many hospitals, especially when the woman is in active labor or is attached to the internal electronic fetal monitor. For many women, this poses no problems: They would prefer to labor in the comfort of a bed. Other women prefer the freedom to walk about between contractions, use the bathroom as they need, and assume positions during contractions that are not possible in a bed.

Studies evaluating the position of women during labor and delivery suggest that lying on her back compromises a woman's uterine blood flow during labor, threatening the progress of labor and reducing oxygen flow to the fetus. Changing position frequently during labor may help avoid some negative effects of the reclining position.

When a woman rests in a reclining position, or lies flat on her back, contraction intensity is reduced, although frequency is increased.[57] A slightly higher incidence of maternal hemorrhage is associated with those women who labor in a standing position.[58]

Numerous studies have been initiated to evaluate the use of birthing chairs as an implement to aid women in assuming a comfortable position during labor. One researcher observes that, "in controlled trials this method has failed to show any clinical advantages over conventional recumbent positions. . . . In fact, there is now substantial evidence that birth chairs have drawbacks such as a higher rate of post-partum haemorrhage and severe vulvar oedema."[59]

Based on the observation that throughout history women in many cultures have adopted a squatting position during second-stage labor (the phase during which the woman bears down and pushes the baby out), studies have been conducted evaluating the use of the birth cushion as an alternative to reclining in bed or sitting in a birth chair. Developed by a hospital equipment company in England, the birth cushion is lightweight, portable, and can be installed in any hospital bed.[60] An extended study of the birth cushion's use among women in England delivering their first baby reported that among the "squatters" there was a 91.3% rate of spontaneous vaginal delivery, compared to 82.8% in the control group. Related to that number is the 8.7% rate of forceps delivery among squatters compared to 16.3% among the controls.[61]

INDUCTION AND AUGMENTATION OF LABOR

Physicians agree that length of gestation varies significantly woman to woman; 37 to 42 weeks is the norm. Beyond that, the woman is diagnosed as "post-term," with risks to the developing baby seen to rise and physicians often opting for the induction of labor. Allowing a woman 42 weeks is based on a historical measure of gestation that dates back to ancient Rome. Studies conducted by the Harvard School of Public Health of middle-class white women determined that the delivery date for first babies was, on average, 8 days past the traditionally established due date.[62]

There are a variety of methods for inducing labor. Stripping the membranes has been proven to be a relatively safe and effective means for producing the onset of labor, although it is quite a slow method. This method is mildly invasive and requires that the woman see her physician daily for several days prior to the anticipated labor. Because the amniotic sac remains intact, infection is not a particular concern.[63]

The amniotomy (breaking the amniotic sac) is a second, popular method for inducing and augmenting the progression of labor. Used alone, this method is effective in some women, but can take some time. With the sac broken, infection is a risk, so amniotomy starts the clock on a woman's labor. Physicians vary in risk assessment; for many, 24 hours is the time within which a woman ought to deliver after her amniotic sac breaks. Amniotomy is associated with events that suggest or demand cesarean section, including decelerations in the fetal heart rate, prolapsed umbilical cord, and bleeding from the cervix.[64]

Oxytocic drugs (most usually oxytocin and pitocin) are drugs that bring on uterine contractions and are often used for both induction and augmentation of labor. Applied intravenously, this form of labor management can be effective when carefully monitored. More frequently, oxytocic drugs can cause excessive uterine contractility, which compromises the blood flow to the baby[65] and increases the likelihood of cesarean section.

MEDICATION FOR PAIN

There are non-pharmacological methods for the reduction of pain during labor, many of which are featured in Lamaze-type classes. These methods include maternal movement and position changes (providing the woman is free to move about); techniques that activate other senses such as heat therapy, hydrotherapy, and massage; and techniques that distract and relax the laboring woman, such as focusing on and counting breathing. These can help reduce pain or help the laboring mother cope with pain, and present no particular risk to an otherwise low-risk delivery.[66]

Although some women make it through labor without the benefit of medication, one study suggests that 86% of all women who deliver in a hospital receive pain medication.[67] The medical means for easing a laboring woman's discomfort divide into two general categories. Analgesic medicines relieve pain without a total loss of sensation. Analgesics can be effective in removing pain, but there can be some risk to the baby, because analgesics cross the placenta and enter the baby's bloodstream.

Anesthesia involves the total loss of sensation and includes such procedures as the epidural. The benefit of this form of anesthesia is that the mother loses all sense of pain but remains awake and aware. The epidural has increased in popularity for both cesarean section and vaginal delivery. One study reports that as many as 24% of women delivering in larger maternity hospitals in England use epidurals.[68] Another study suggests that up to 40% of the women opt for epidural pain relief, and of those, 80% experience total analgesia.[69] That the epidural is effective in cutting pain is clear. What is not clear is whether the complete removal of pain warrants such outcomes as extreme shivering, nausea, headache, and backache. Perhaps more significantly, the epidural may prolong the second stage of labor and is associated with an increased likelihood of delivery by forceps or cesarean section.[70]

THE EPISIOTOMY

The episiotomy is a widespread obstetrical practice that has undergone increased scrutiny in recent years. The rationale for the episiotomy has been that a surgically created cut will facilitate the delivery of the baby's head and shoulders, thus shortening the second stage of labor and reducing risks of reduced oxygen to the baby. Further, it is argued that a surgical incision is easier to repair (suture) than random tears and prevents the tearing of muscle tissue that has implications for urinary and bowel control and for muscles of the pelvic floor. One British study claims that the practice is becoming less routine,[71] although the same trend may not be occurring in the United States.[72] A text produced by the American College of Obstetrics and Gynecology claims that 50% to 90% of first-time mothers will have an episiotomy in U.S. hospitals.[73] One researcher, evaluating all the available data regarding use and outcomes of episiotomy, concluded that, "A substantial review of the literature was unable to uncover any evidence to support these postulated benefits of liberal use of episiotomy."[74]

The episiotomy fails to solve the problems as promised and is associated with significant risks, including maternal blood loss, infection, and possible incontinence and "loss of rectal tone."[75] A study of 241 first-time hospital births reports that "the proportion of deep perineal lacerations was lowest (0.9%) in women without episiotomy who were not confined to the lithotomy position; it was greatest (27.9%) in women delivered in stirrups with an episiotomy."[76]

VAGINAL EXAMINATIONS

Vaginal exams during labor can be quite uncomfortable, and potential problems arise with vaginal examination, especially among women whose amniotic sac has broken. Increased risk of infection is associated with women having more than three vaginal exams over the course of their labor.[77] Another study suggests that there is significant variance among midwives and obstetricians in the accuracy of assessments rendered through vaginal or cervical exam, with the greatest errors in the assessment of dilation between 5 and 7 centimeters.[78]

INSTRUMENTAL VAGINAL DELIVERY

The conditions under which instrumental delivery are justified are "when the fetal heartbeat slows or becomes irregular, when the baby's position makes delivery difficult, or when the mother is too tired to push."[79] Instrumental vaginal delivery comprises 11% of deliveries in hospitals in the United States.[80] To be achieved, the mother's cervix must be fully dilated, and the appropriate pain medication must be established.

Women delivering with forceps report a significantly higher incidence of pain than women delivering with vacuum extraction and are more likely to receive an injury to the genital tract. Apgar scores of infants delivered by forceps tend to be lower than infants born through vacuum extraction, and forceps babies are more likely to receive scalp and facial injuries. Babies delivered by vacuum extraction experience more bruising of the scalp and signs of neonatal jaundice.[81]

In sum, although each of the birthing routines discussed is distinct, they also interrelate. For regardless of how routine it might be, one act paves the way for subsequent interventions. Findings support the conclusion that the more "medicine" applied in childbirth, the more medicine may subsequently be needed.[82]

Health Outcomes Related
to Cesarean Section

Cesarean section is the surgical removal of the baby from the mother's body through abdominal incision. Cesarean section probably derives its name from the Latin *lex caesarea,* a Roman law requiring physicians to cut a woman open in a last-ditch effort to save the baby of a woman dying in childbirth.[83] Not until the development of antiseptic techniques and sufficient anesthesia late in the 19th century did cesarean section become a feasible solution to demands for emergency delivery.[84]

In 1970, the cesarean section rate in the United States was 5.5%; by 1988 that rate had risen to 24.4%. Some hospitals report rates ranging between 40% and 50%, twice the national average.[85] This gives the United States the third highest cesarean section rate internationally, following Brazil (31.6%) and Puerto Rico (28.8%).[86] That cesarean section offers a relatively safe surgical procedure in a true emergency is a benefit of modern medicine. Emergencies that absolutely warrant cesarean section include placenta previa, a condition in which the placenta rests directly over the birth canal.[87] Cesarean section is also indicated in a situation where the umbilical cord is prolapsed or is preceding the baby into the birth canal.[88]

Cesarean section carries risks that must be considered, especially in light of charges that many cesarean sections currently performed are not truly necessary.[89] Cesarean section is major surgery: All the risks of surgery in general associate with cesarean section. Among women delivering vaginally, the mortality rate is 10 per 100,000 births; among women delivering by cesarean section, the rate is 40 per 100,000. The researcher offering these numbers is quick to observe that some of these women die from the condition that warranted the cesarean section in the first place. With that caveat, the estimate is that mortality among women delivering via cesarean is between 2 and 4 times that among women delivering vaginally.[90]

Morbidity—medical problems caused by the birth process—is higher among women delivering by cesarean section than those delivering vaginally. A woman delivering by cesarean section is more likely to experience problems with her urinary tract and bowels. All the risks associated with anesthesia apply to the women having a cesarean. Between 20% and 40% of women delivering via cesarean section develop infection that produces fever. Such infection is readily treated with antibiotics but prolongs the mother's hospital stay.[91] The woman delivering vaginally is generally able to resume daily routines—altered of course by the presence of a new baby—within a week or two, but a woman delivering by cesarean section can expect to take many weeks, or even months, to get her strength and stamina back.[92]

Delivering by cesarean section also poses specific risks to the babies, who have a higher risk of respiratory distress syndrome than babies born vaginally at the same gestational age. Respiratory problems also result from preterm birth based on a miscalculation of due dates.[93] One researcher concludes that in situations where the indication for cesarean section is more or less absolute (e.g., prolapsed cord), cesarean section is safer for the baby than vaginal delivery. In most cases, however, "the cesarean has not proved itself safer for the infant."[94]

A practice intended to minimize risk in fact increases risk in terms of maternal death and in terms of maternal morbidity. In addition, cesarean section poses a great financial burden, both to individual women and to society as a whole. By 1989, it was estimated that unnecessary cesarean sections cost $728 million annually.[95] Some hospitals have tried to curb and to reduce the rate of cesarean section, with varying methods and varying rates of success.[96]

Conclusion

Hospital childbirth, and all the technology that attends it, does not necessarily lead to "harm," defined as mortality among women and babies. Likewise, the medical literature suggests that options such as trained midwife care and medical support for home birth—practices not generally affirmed by U.S. obstetricians—are not necessarily any more hazardous than hospital birth. In some cases, these alternate birthing situations have been shown to have better outcomes than their hospital counterparts. Such practices pose far less drain on U.S. health care resources than the status quo, and information about these options should be offered to women through commercial and social action campaigns.

Women's experience in labor and delivery is part of women's experience in U.S. health care more generally. In considering the relationship between health care and health costs, one physician wrote, "the outcomes of many decisions can affect patients profoundly; and the ultimate responsibility for these decisions, from both an ethical and a legal perspective, rests with the physician, not the payer or policymaker."[97] Where labor and delivery are concerned, I reject this perspective in favor of decision making by women.

For those who prefer a high-tech birth, hospitals and technology are there. Women who would prefer less technology within a hospital, or who would prefer to deliver outside of a hospital, should have their options and these should be presented as options in campaigns designed to inform Americans about childbirth. By considering these options intelligently, we can experience safe childbirth, reclaim a significant degree of power over our bodies, and broaden the range of childbirth options for women in the future.

Notes

1. L. T. Ulrich, *A Midwife's Tale: The Life of Martha Ballard, Based on Her Diary, 1785-1812* (New York: Knopf, 1990). See also L. T. Ulrich, " 'The Living Mother of a Living Child': Midwifery and Mortality in Post-Revolutionary New England," *William and Mary Quarterly* 46 (1989): 27-48.

2. P. Armstrong & S. Feldman, *A Wise Birth* (New York: William Morrow, 1990): 72-73.

3. Armstrong & Feldman, *A Wise Birth,* pp. 71-72.

4. Committee on Assessing Alternative Birth Settings, *Research Issues in the Assessment of Birth Settings* (Washington, DC: National Academy Press, 1982): 2-3.

5. E. Lieberman & K. J. Ryan, "Birth Day Choices," *The New England Journal of Medicine* 321 (December 1989): 1824-1825.

6. J. P. Rooks, N. L. Weatherby, E.K.M. Ernst, S. Stapleton, D. Rosen, & A. Rosenfeld, "Outcomes of Care in Birth Centers: The National Birth Center Study," *The New England Journal of Medicine,* 321 (December 1989): 1804-1811.

7. P. S. Eakins, "Out-of-Hospital Birth," in P. S. Eakins (Ed.), *The American Way of Birth* (Philadelphia: Temple University Press, 1986): 242.

8. A. Stoline & J. P. Weiner, *The New Medical Marketplace: A Physician's Guide to the Health Care Revolution* (Baltimore, MD: Johns Hopkins University Press, 1988): 42.

9. C. Jones, *Alternative Birth: The Complete Guide* (New York: Tarcher, 1991): 161.

10. S. Inch, *Birthrights: What Every Parent Should Know About Childbirth in Hospitals* (New York: Pantheon, 1984): 1-18.

11. Jones, *Alternative Birth,* pp. 27-28.

12. N. Clarke & A. B. Bennets, "Vital Statistics and Nonhospital Births: A Mortality Study of Infants Born Out of Hospitals in Oregon," *Research Issues,* pp. 171-181.

13. Committee on Assessing Alternative Birth Settings, *Research Issues,* pp. 2-9. See also T. J. Abernathy & D. M. Lentjes, "Planned and Unplanned Home Births and Hospital Births in Calgary, Alberta, 1984-87," *Public Health Reports* 104 (July-August 1989): 373-377.

14. Abernathy & Lentjes, "Planned and Unplanned Home Births," pp. 373-374. See also Eakins, "Out-of-Hospital Birth," pp. 238-242.

15. Abernathy & Lentjes, "Planned and Unplanned Home Births," p. 375.

16. D. C. Wertz & P. S. Eakins, "A Note on the Future of American Birth," in P. S. Eakins (Ed.), *The American Way of Birth* (Philadelphia: Temple University Press, 1986): 331-337, observe that in 1986 the average hospital vaginal birth cost $3,500, and that new technologies are rapidly making birth even more expensive. In contrast, the cost in Vermont for prenatal, delivery, and postnatal midwife care was only $450, according to R. L. Teasley, "Nurse and Lay Midwifery in Vermont," in *The American Way of Birth,* pp. 246-272. Costs for midwives' services vary from state to state. See E. Becker, M. Long, V. Stamler, & P. Sallomi (Eds.), *Midwifery and the Law* (Santa Fe, NM: Mothering, 1990).

17. Eakins, "Out-of-Hospital Birth," pp. 226-230. The Abernathy study was performed on a population of women in Canada, where there is national health insurance for all women; cost was not listed as a reason for home birth in that study.

18. The Oregon study reflected a high home birth death rate between 1970 and 1974 (26.1 per thousand), but between 1975 and 1979 the neonatal death rate dropped to 7.5 per thousand, compared to 10.1 per thousand for all U.S. births. The Abernathy study compared outcomes in terms of baby's breathing patterns; none of the babies in that study died, planned home delivery or not. Eakins's research showed the difference between planned and unplanned was most pronounced among poor, rural women residing in the Southern United States.

19. Abernathy & Lentjes, "Planned and Unplanned Home Birth."

20. The Apgar score assigns a value of 0, 1, or 2 in five categories that measure a baby's health within 1 minute of birth and at regular intervals. An Agar score of 7 at 5 minutes appears to be the number physicians use in determining that a baby is "healthy"; see Inch, *Birthrights,* pp. 49-50.

21. Eakins, "Out-of-Hospital Birth," p. 239.

22. Eakins, "Out-of-Hospital Birth," p. 232.

23. Rooks et al., "Outcomes of Care," p. 1804.

24. Eakins, "Out-of-Hospital Birth," p. 214.

25. Clark & Bennets, "Vital Statistics," p. 91.

26. Rooks et al., "Outcomes of Care," p. 1804.

27. Rooks et al., "Outcomes of Care," p. 1805.

28. As a corrective to this self-regulation that might artificially inflate birth center outcomes, the Oregon study recommends that extensive studies be performed to compare birth center outcomes to the overall population, and to low-risk hospital births among women demographically similar to women who deliver at birth centers.

29. Rooks et al., "Outcomes of Care," p. 1806.

30. Rooks et al., "Outcomes of Care," p. 1808.

31. Eakins, "Out-of-Hospital Birth," p. 232.

32. Lieberman & Ryan, "Birth Day Choices," p. 1824.

33. J. Kennell, M. Klaus, S. McGrath, S. Robertson, & C. Hinkley, "Continuous Emotional Support During Labor in a U.S. Hospital," *Journal of the American Medical Association* 265 (1991): 2197-2201. This article is summarized in B. Bower, "Emotional Aid Delivers Labor-Saving Result," *Science News* 13 (1991): 277.

34. J. Kennell et al., "Continuous Emotional Support," pp. 2197-2201.

35. Bower, "Emotional Aid," 277. See also A. Gilgoff, *Home Birth: An Invitation and a Guide* (Granby, MA: Bergin & Garvey, 1989).

36. E. R. Declercq, "The Transformation of American Midwifery: 1975-1988," *American Journal of Public Health* 82 (May 1992): 680-684.

37. H. M. Sterk & K. Sterk, "Birthing: Women Owning Their Stories," in C. Berryman-Fink & D. Ballard Reisch (Eds.), *Communication and Sex Role Socialization* (New York: Garland, 1993). Sterk and Sterk argue that the stories of childbirth have tended to be offered from a male-medical perspective and seek to remedy that situation by offering birth stories in the women's own words.

38. Bower, "Emotional Aid," p. 277.

39. Jones, *Alternative Birth,* pp. 96-97; P. Armstrong & S. Feldman, "Midwives: Tapping Every Woman's Strength," *American Heart* (January 1989): 75, report a far lower rate of cesarean sections and episiotomies for midwife-assisted deliveries.

40. Declercq, "The Transformation of American Midwifery," p. 681.

41. Declercq, "The Transformation of American Midwifery," p. 683.

42. Jones, *Alternative Birth,* pp. 95-96.

43. M. Enkin, M.J.N.C. Keirse, & I. Chalmers, *A Guide to Effective Care in Pregnancy and Childbirth* (Oxford, UK: Oxford University Press, 1989): 179.

44. *Planning for Pregnancy, Birth, and Beyond* (New York: E. P. Dutton, 1992): 178. This is a publication of the American College of Obstetricians and Gynecologists.

45. R. E. Davis-Floyd, *Birth as an American Rite of Passage* (Berkeley: University of California Press, 1992): 76.

46. Enkin et al., *A Guide to Effective Care,* p. 181.

47. Enkin et al., *A Guide to Effective Care,* pp. 181-182.

48. Davis-Floyd, *Birth as an American Rite of Passage,* p. 83.

49. Enkin et al., *A Guide to Effective Care,* p. 182.

50. B. L. Flamm, *Birth After Cesarean: The Medical Facts* (New York: Simon & Schuster, 1992).

51. Enkin et al., *A Guide to Effective Care,* p. 182.

52. The electrode is a tiny coil that is literally screwed into the baby's scalp.

53. *Planning for Pregnancy,* pp. 178-181.

54. Enkin et al., *A Guide to Effective Care,* p. 192.

55. Enkin et al., *A Guide to Effective Care,* pp. 192-193.

56. Davis-Floyd, *Birth as an American Rite of Passage,* p. 106.

57. Enkin et al., *A Guide to Effective Care,* pp. 187-188.

58. "Stand and Deliver," *The Lancet* 353 (March 1990): 761.

59. J. Gardosi, N. Hutson, & C. B. Lynch, "Randomised, Controlled Trial of Squatting in the Second Stage of Labour," *The Lancet* 8 (July 1989): 74.

60. P. Scherer, "Supported Squatting Enhances the Second Stage of Labor," *American Journal of Nursing* 89 (October 1989): 1266.

61. Gardosi et al., "Randomised Controlled Trial," p. 74.

62. W. Stolzenburg, "Expectant Moms Take Longer Than Expected," *Science News* 137 (June 1990): 372.

63. Davis-Floyd, *Birth as an American Rite of Passage,* p. 275.

64. Davis-Floyd, *Birth as an American Rite of Passage,* p. 276.

65. Davis-Floyd, *Birth as an American Rite of Passage,* p. 278.

66. Enkin et al., *A Guide to Effective Care,* pp. 212-218.

67. Davis-Floyd, *Birth as an American Rite of Passage,* p. 99.

68. "Stand and Deliver," p. 761.

69. "Pain Relief in Labour: Old Drugs, New Route," *The Lancet* 337 (June 1991): 1446.

70. Enkin et al., *A Guide to Effective Care,* pp. 221-222.

71. D. Gibb, *A Practical Guide to Labour Management* (Oxford, UK: Blackwell Scientific Publications, 1988): 74.

72. Davis-Floyd, *Birth as an American Rite of Passage,* p. 112, claims that U.S. medical schools do not even train obstetricians how to deliver babies without an episiotomy.

73. *Planning for Pregnancy,* p. 188.

74. Enkin et al., *A Guide to Effective Care,* p. 231.

75. Enkin et al., *A Guide to Effective Care,* p. 230.

76. Reported in Davis-Floyd, *Birth as an American Rite of Passage,* pp. 128-129.

77. D. K. James & G. M. Stirrat, *Pregnancy and Risk: The Basis for Rational Management* (New York: John Wiley, 1988): 128.

78. D. J. Tuffnell, F. Bryce, N. Johnson, & R. J. Lilford, "Simulation of Cervical Changes in Labour: Reproducibility of Expert Assessment," *The Lancet* (November 1989): 1089.

79. *Planning for Pregnancy,* p. 189.

80. F. C. Notzon, "International Differences in the Use of Obstetric Interventions," *Journal of the American Medical Association* 263 (June 1990): 3290.

81. Enkin et al., *A Guide to Effective Care,* pp. 244-246.

82. P. G. Greene, A. Zeichner, N. L. Roberts, E. J. Callahan, & J. L. Granados, "Preparation for Cesarean Delivery: A Multicomponent Analysis of Treatment Outcome," *Journal of Consulting and Clinical Psychology* 57 (989): 484.

83. C. Norwood, *How to Avoid a Cesarean Section* (New York: Simon & Schuster, 1984): 21.

84. M. Rosen & L. Thomas, *The Cesarean Myth: Choosing the Best Way to Have Your Baby* (New York: Penguin, 1989): 14.

85. S. Lutz, "Providers Forced to Defend C-Section Rates," *Modern Healthcare* 19 (February 1989): 66.

86. Notzon, "International Differences," pp. 3286-3287.

87. Enkin et al., *A Guide to Effective Care,* p. 256.

88. Rosen & Thomas, *The Cesarean Myth,* p. 48.

89. Stoline & Weiner, *New Medical Marketplace,* p. 149.

90. Enkin et al., *A Guide to Effective Care,* p. 249.

91. Rosen & Thomas, *The Cesarean Myth,* pp. 64-65.

92. F. G. Cunningham, P. C. MacDonald, & N. F. Gant, *Williams Obstetrics,* 18th ed. (Norwalk, CT: Appleton & Lange, 1989): 254-255.

93. C. Jones, *Alternate Birth,* pp. 9-12.

94. Rosen & Thomas, *The Cesarean Myth,* p. 64.

95. Lutz, "Providers Forced," p. 66.

96. P. Scherer, "Cutting the C-Section Rate With Strict Review," *American Journal of Nursing* (May 1989): 641.

97. Stoline & Weiner, *New Medical Marketplace,* p. 126.

9

Contemporary Birthing Practices

Technology Over Humanity?

Helen M. Sterk

Since Lucy produced "Little Ricky," birth has been a part of U.S. popular culture. Mary Tyler Moore as Laura on *The Dick Van Dyke Show,* Rhea Perlman on *Cheers,* Meredith Baxter-Birney on *Family Ties,* Joanna Kerns on *Growing Pains,* Marilu Henner on *Evening Shade,* and Markie Post on *Night Court* (among others) have all shared their birth experiences with the United States.[1] These portrayals of childbirth have tended to communicate clear norms about where babies should be born, who should decide what should be done during labor and delivery, and the appropriate use of medical interventions. Murphy Brown may have been a single mom, but she did not hire a midwife and have her baby at home. She attended Lamaze classes, asked a close male friend to be her labor coach, and gave birth in the hospital. Popular magazines, books on birthing by obstetricians, and other mass media all portray a woman giving birth as a patient, not as an agent who might participate in the decision of what may be best for her and her baby.

124

In order to determine what the mass media have been saying about birth, I surveyed 25 mass market books available in popular book stores such as Waldenbooks and B. Dalton's in 1993, 37 mass market magazine articles published between 1987 and 1993, 80 newspaper articles published in the *New York Times* and *Chicago Tribune* between 1980 and 1992, 18 television shows airing between 1991 and 1993, and seven movies shown in the late 1980s and early 1990s. I tried to select the media that anyone could happen upon, as well as media that pregnant women themselves might seek out to guide their thinking (such as *Parents* magazine and readily available books). The survey showed a marked preference for doctor managed, hospital births, with a weak strain of arguments designed to help women enter into decisions about how to give birth.

The American Way of Giving Birth

As the previous chapter has demonstrated, the vast majority of women give birth in hospitals. Why do U.S. women so overwhelmingly choose hospitals over homes or birthing centers? Several reasons come to mind, such as convenience and available insurance coverage, but the strongest reasons may be these three: the control of the American Medical Association over licensing and over practicing midwives,[2] U.S. faith in the "expert," and women's desire to do what they are told is right for their babies. The latter two items are strongly influenced by mass media portrayals, the majority of which present birth in a hospital, place doctors as the primary attendants, and manage birth through drugs and technology.

Locating Birth in Hospitals

Telling the story of an emergency home birth, a *Parents* magazine article proclaimed that babies belong in hospitals, not on bathroom floors.[3] That magazine, as did almost all the other media surveyed, assumed birth would take place in a hospital unless the birth was so rushed that the woman could not get to the hospital in time. In fact, 73% of the magazine articles (27 out of 37), 83% of the television shows (15 out of 18), and 72% of the books (18 out of 25) took hospital birth for granted. The only exception could be found in newspapers. Of the 33 articles in the *New York Times* dealing with birthplaces, fully 29 (88%) promoted birthing centers or home births. Given their focus on what is *newsworthy,* this exception proves to be only apparent, rather than real. Hospitals were still assumed to be the norm.

Most media messages about home birth were negative. Not a single one of the doctor-authored sources surveyed spoke positively about home birth. Dr. Barry Herman's argument in the 1992 book, *The Twelve-Month Pregnancy,* was typical. Drawing his conclusion from a single case, he told the story of "Barbara." Barbara gave birth at home and her baby died. Citing no evidence beyond the single instance, Dr. Herman warned of the dire consequences that could befall babies born at home, including brain damage and, possibly, death.[4] This kind of tactic also was employed in a *Newsweek* advertisement run by the American Medical Association. It pictured a young couple; the woman pregnant. The ad copy raised fears that the birth would be difficult because the closest obstetrician was in a far-away town.[5] No mention was made of other options.

Another strategy used was to belittle other options. *USA Today* presented a doctor speaking disparagingly about more "homelike" labor, delivery, and recovery rooms in hospitals. Parents, he said, have become enamored of fads and trends—such as soft lighting, personally chosen music, and video cameras—which do not affect the health of the child at all.[6] This comment places the authority of doctors, "science," and the "well- being of the baby" above the well-being of the woman in labor.

Another strategy manipulated the structure of information given in the argument. For example, in virtually every description of the range of options open to a laboring woman, the authors of *What to Expect When You're Expecting* first gave information based on hospital policies and then encouraged women to do what worked best for the individual mother.[7] *Priority* implies *importance*—hospital policies matter more than women's preferences.

A further issue associated with argument is how conclusions are reached. What reasons do the arguers give to support their conclusions? In several books and articles taking the doctors' perspective, only one reason was given for why women might seek out birthing centers (freestanding birthplaces associated with hospitals, yet run by mid-wives): lower cost. One doctor admitted the low cost issue but immediately implied birthing centers also offer lower quality, saying that some physicians fear complica-tions for the birthing pair at midwifery centers.[8] This argument employed a very low level of evidence, one that relied for its force solely on the phrase *some physicians,* but it is not clear that this argumentative weakness would undermine its persuasiveness given the social status of doctors.

Finally, magazines, television, and film, the mass media most easily available to consumers, all stressed the normalcy of hospital birth by the way they presented the alternatives. Most typically, the alternatives were given in the form of a single story that was characterized as anomalous. For example, Opal gave birth at home during a snowstorm on *All My Children,* while Palmer was coached over the telephone by Dr. Martin. The woman whose emergency home birth was featured in *Parents* provides another example. The assumption underlying media treatments of home or birthing center births is that such choices are singular and therefore remarkable, but certainly not intended to be seen as reasonable or normal choices.

In contrast, the few sources that spoke from the perspective of women who had successfully borne children at home stressed the sense of security they experienced. *Good Housekeeping* featured a story of home birth in which a woman chose to have her third and fourth babies at home. In the hospital, she felt something had been taken from her because hospital personnel kept her baby away from her for 12 hours after birth.[9] Yet even in this story, the organizational pattern reinforced the perception of hospitals as the normal place to give birth, because her story followed stories of three, more "typical," hospital births.

The sources that encouraged home birth pointed to statistically significant studies (unlike the doctor who cited the experience of one woman) based on home births in

Europe showing home birth to be as safe as, if not safer than, hospital birth.[10] Home birth advocates cited dangers to women and babies found in hospitals—such as increased exposure to disease and problems with the establishment of breast-feeding. The major danger they cited, however, lay in hospital personnel's inevitable use of technology to monitor and manage a natural process.

Birthing centers were suggested in some sources as viable alternatives to either hospital or home birth. These centers were described as freestanding, yet close enough to a hospital so a woman could be transferred if need be. Staffed by certified nurse-midwives, birthing centers were portrayed as offering the best of both worlds. The media that spoke about birthing centers argued that they were safe. *U.S. News & World Report* cited *The New England Journal of Medicine's* findings that a survey of almost 12,000 women found birth centers equaled hospitals in nonproblematic deliveries.[11] Furthermore, some media presented birthing centers as reassuring environments for laboring women. One woman wrote of her experience in *Parents* magazine, saying that she appreciated being in a place where her delivery was seen as natural, rather than as a potential medical crisis. Her baby was born in a dimly lit room and placed on her belly as soon as he was born, with the midwife quietly caring for the newborn's physical needs.[12]

Who Will Attend the Birth?

The sources surveyed showed that once a woman was inside the hospital, her labor and delivery would be managed by a doctor. Statements in books and by journalists routinely put the doctor in control. For example: Doctors are presented as controlling the amount of sedation a woman will get[13] and the sort of care that will be given—implying that a woman is foolish if she resists any of the doctor's orders.[14] It is clearly doctors as an institutional group who are in control here.

In contrast, the few media messages on midwifery tended to focus on individual midwives rather than midwifery as an institution and a practice with standards. One such example was the story of Onnie Logan, a lay midwife. In 1989, Onnie Logan retired from midwifery after 28 years, with a record of only two stillbirths and no deaths of mothers or babies. Her story was featured in magazines such as *Life* and *American Medical News.* The only other media that gave detailed information about midwives were newspapers.

Messages on midwifery displayed midwives' focus on the needs and concerns of laboring women rather than on caregivers. An interview with Shirley Moore, a certified nurse-midwife, reported in the *Chicago Tribune,* revealed what proved to be typical routines for midwives: prenatal care that included not only examinations but conversations about all aspects of the woman's health—including her sexuality and relationships; consistent personal care throughout the entire labor and delivery; and individual attention and decision making.[15] Moore's approach—to watch, to guide, to listen, rather than to intervene—was portrayed as typical of other midwives.

In those cases where the media presented both options—doctors and midwives—strategies of language and argument generally supported the choice of doctors over midwives. Language used by those favoring traditional medicine figured the midwife as an unattractive option—not safe and not as able as a physician to know what needed to be done in an emergency. Particularly instructive of this point was a 1987 *McCall's* article. In it, *McCall's* said that the best thing a midwife could do for her clients was to decide when to call the doctor.[16] Calling this their most important duty discounted the considerable training and human skills midwives bring to birthing and positioned them as observers of birth whose most crucial job is deciding when to call in a doctor.

Furthermore, as was the case in the media presentations of alternatives to hospitals, the articles depicting midwife-assisted births told singular stories—such as those of Onnie Logan and Shirley Moore—rather than explaining the institution, practices, and standards of midwifery. That individual focus implied that midwifery was eccentric and anomalous. Further, Onnie Logan was shown as quaint, picturesque, and from a bygone era, not as an example of midwives currently at work. The articles on Logan highlighted her dialect-marked speech, not so subtly underscoring the "primitive" nature of midwife-assisted births.

These uses of language and argument positioned birthing women as in ever-present danger and unconscious of the threats to their own and their babies' safety. As a result, the women were presented as in need of doctors to tell them what to do.

How Will the Labor Be Managed?

The phrasing of the question—How will labor be managed?—implies that labor cannot be allowed to happen in its own time and in its own way, but that it must be controlled. The mass media surveyed did not question the need for control. The first issue of control was the induction of labor. The mass media articles recognized that very soon after the due date passes, both women and their caregivers start to consider ways to encourage labor to start. Although there are many ways to stimulate labor, a clear separation of perspectives appeared in the mass-mediated texts. Of those few that dealt with inducing labor, only four, all books, described in useful detail how a woman could try to start her own labor.[17] The rest, including not only books but also television, film, and print media, assumed induction would be managed by the doctor—either through rupturing the amniotic sac or by administering a drug such as pitocin. The only medium that offered instruction to women on self-induction were books that took the view that women should exercise control over their own birth experience. Techniques suggested included lovemaking, walking, acupuncture, massaging the cervix, bowel stimulation, nipple stimulation, herbal teas, and prostaglandin suppositories. Some of these were presented as softening the cervix, each having the effects of encouraging the uterus to start contracting.

The media addressed another issue of controlling labor with drugs and that was through pain management. Most media recognized that it hurts to deliver a baby. Doctor-authored texts described pain as something that must be eliminated. One denigrated use of Lamaze methods because they reduced pain by only 30%—implying the need for 100% reduction. When Lamaze training was endorsed by doctor-authored media, descriptions of its benefits included praise for its role in making women familiar with hospital routines. In contrast to the Lamaze ideal of woman-controlled pain, doctor-authored texts assumed medication would be used; the only question was whether it would be a tranquilizer, analgesic, epidural, or some combination.

Mainstream media messages downplayed the possibility of negative effects of drugs on fetuses. Doctors used two strategies to reduce the perception of the impact of drug crossover: First, they stated authoritatively that spinal, caudal, and epidural drugs do not pass significant quantities of drugs to the fetus, so the drugs can be used throughout labor as well as during delivery. Second, doctors suggested any negative effects on the baby could be countered quickly after birth by carrying out resuscitation procedures or administering more drugs.

In sharp contrast, media sources that acted to empower women urged great care in deciding if and how to use drugs. The reasons given by these sources considered both child and mother. For example, several sources noted that drugs may slow down a fetus' intake of oxygen in the womb and its ability to breathe once it is born. In terms of the laboring women, several sources argued that drugs could slow down labor.

In addition to labor induction and pain medication, a third issue of birthing management was how to monitor the progress of labor. The mass media surveyed assumed *all* labor would be monitored. The issue was *how* would that be done—by fetal stethoscope or by some sort of electronic fetal monitoring device (EFM)? When the media discussed the use of an EFM, they either endorsed it for its value to doctors or condemned it for the danger it presented to mothers and babies. Doctor-authored sources tended to see EFMs as good, even necessary, whereas sources favoring midwives preferred the more intermittent and less invasive use of a fetal stethoscope.[18]

TERMS OF ADDRESS

Throughout media coverage, differences in style of argument characterized physician-centered and patient-centered discourse. Doctor-authored media tended to speak in absolute terms, through authoritative statements, when discussing decisions on drug use rather than to give good reasons why the drugs should be used or to explain the effects of the drugs. For example, one doctor asserted that spinal, caudal, and epidural drugs "do not pass significant quantities of drugs into the fetus. They can, therefore, be used during labor as well as delivery."[19] Several sources argued that drugs were not so bad for a fetus. If it seemed sluggish and drugged after birth, other drugs could be administered to resuscitate the baby. No evidence was given for these claims.

In contrast, media sources that took the position that the laboring woman was a kind of consumer who deserved to make her own well-informed decisions, tended to give both the positive and negative potential outcomes of drug and technology use. They tended to describe, for example, how EFM was administered and explored the effects EFM could have on a woman—that is, keeping her immobile on a bed—giving her information that may have seemed much more precise than it actually was, perhaps causing unnecessary fear if she saw jumps on the monitor graph that she was unable to decipher. These sources invited women to participate in creating the meaning of medical messages, rather than placing them in the position of receivers of authoritative, one-way messages.

How Will Birth Be Facilitated?

The mass media surveyed made it clear that they recognize giving birth as a momentous experience for women. The intensity of that experience was shown in many different ways. Some women, like Murphy Brown, screamed at the people around her. Some swore at their partners. Most experienced time distortion, where their sense of passing time was either compressed or expanded. Several sources compared women's emotional responses to the experience of transition (from labor to delivery) with sexual responses. Given that this is the moment when decisions need to be made about what, if any, procedures to facilitate birth will be used, sources indicated that women are most dependent upon the judgment of their caregivers and partners and least able to assert their own wishes.

Options presented for facilitating procedures ranged from the nontechnological (using upright birthing positions and giving directions on when and how to push) to the technological (forceps and suction, as well as episiotomies). The electronic, visual mass media by and large avoided presenting any procedures for facilitating birth except the caregiver directing the woman to push, such as in *Nova's* "The Miracle of Life." In contrast, the print media had a lot to say on the issue of intervention, much of it critical of invasive interventions, such as cutting women open. Unlike the other labor and delivery options discussed earlier in this chapter, interventions were not endorsed wholeheartedly, even by the mainstream mass media. Even some doctors publicly expressed reservations about routinely intervening in the delivery process.

The main controversy over intervention techniques presented in the media centered on whether the episiotomy should be routine. Some doctors maintained its value, arguing that by cutting the perineum, they preserve the tone of the muscles. One described episiotomies as good because they ease delivery and cause little pain. Yes, he said, women often do not know that they are being given an episiotomy.[20] Virtually every source cautioned that episiotomies might be unnecessary at best and harmful at worst. The majority view in the media surveyed was that episiotomies benefit neither women nor babies. Even though episiotomies once were considered necessary, research findings reported in most of the birthing books indicated perceived benefits far outweigh real good.

Most of the media that discussed episiotomies offered suggestions on how to avoid episiotomies. First, they recommended making a birth plan in which the mother specifies her desires for treatment. Second, they encouraged mothers or their partners to prepare the perineum by massaging it as the date of birth nears. Third, they suggested finding a midwife, because midwives use their hands on women's bodies to help babies come into the world. Midwives' stated preferences were for hot tubs, hot towels, a little oil and massage. There seemed to be growing recognition that stretched muscles can be exercised back into shape quite readily.

The magazine articles surveyed addressed all issues on procedures to facilitate birth *except* those under the control of women themselves, such as birthing positions and how to push. Advice on these issues is found only in the books that sought to empower women. Their authors recommended that women should pay attention to their bodies' signals. For instance, Balaskas encouraged women to "let go" rather than to push.[21] Authors who take the attitude that women should listen to their bodies on pushing also said women should decide for themselves how to sit or stand in order to deliver. They not only described upright postures but also pictured them and encouraged women to use them.

Those advocating a nontechnological approach to birth argued that delivery interventions could be lessened if drug use during labor was reduced. Drugs such as epidurals "can affect the bearing-down reflex, and even though you want to push the baby out yourself, you end up with a forceps or vacuum-extraction delivery."[22] From this perspective, use of intervention technology becomes necessary because other medical technologies have already been used.

What About Cesarean-Section Deliveries?

There was a wealth of information in the mass media about cesarean deliveries in the late 1980s and early 1990s, most of it unfavorable. For example, over a 12-year period, the *New York Times* devoted 22 articles to issues surrounding cesarean surgeries. Of the 22, 15 criticized the surgery and advocated reducing its occurrence, 3 endorsed vaginal birth after cesarean (VBAC), and only 4 reported neutrally on caesareans in general. An often-repeated statistic in all media sources was that, in the late 1980s and early 1990s, 1 in 4 American births ended in a cesarean delivery. And, consumers of the mass media were told, as *Consumer Reports* noted that cesarean deliveries are necessary less than 15% of the time.[23] The media audience was informed that about half of the caesareans performed in the United States may have been unnecessary. The case of cesareans was one where the medical and technological means of delivery were questioned, if not condemned.

In particular, a women-directed anti-cesarean movement caught the attention of the mass media. The movement's goal was to make vaginal birth after cesarean (VBAC) part of normal hospital routine. Mass-mediated reports, picking up on the movement's concerns, argued that the practices of the medical establishment overrode any real benefits of cesarean surgery. For example, *Ms.* magazine noted that half of the hospitals in the United States did not *allow* attempts at vaginal birth if a woman had had a cesarean delivery before. The article argued that greater harm comes from cesarean surgeries than from VBAC, finding that roughly 500 women die from complications stemming from cesarean deliveries each year, but no one is known to have died from VBAC.[24] *Time* magazine reported that even the American College of Obstetricians and Gynecologists recommended that doctors support women in their efforts for VBAC delivery unless there is a presenting medical need for cesarean delivery.[25] Women who were exposed to media such as these heard strong messages countering any arguments that pregnant women should submit quietly to doctors' recommendations for cesarean delivery, even if earlier births were by that method.

Media such as magazines that can be picked up in the grocery checkout line featured cesarean stories that pitted one woman against the medical establishment. *Redbook* magazine carried a vivid story about a woman who wanted to deliver her second baby vaginally. In all of Tampa, she could find only two groups of doctors that would allow her to try a VBAC. So, she chose one and hired a *doula* (a trained female assistant who herself had given birth) to help her. When her labor started, she called the *doula* and stayed home until she was just 2 centimeters shy of full dilation, a condition that usually indicates birth is near. When she was checked at the hospital, however, the dilation had regressed to 5 centimeters. When the doctor wanted to break her amniotic sac, she refused. According to the woman, the doctor became incensed at her questioning his judgment.[26] After being in the hospital 12 hours with little progress toward delivery, the woman checked out against her doctor's wishes. She went home, ate, took a bath, and labored with the assistance of her *doula*. In the morning, she returned to the hospital. A new doctor took care of her—one whom she called "terse and angry" at her impertinence.[27] After about two pushes, her baby was born. Such stories held up models for action.

There is something quite different about mass media messages on cesarean-section deliveries. The overt media messages questioned the medical establishment and the presumption that the technological birth intervention of cesarean delivery should be exercised at a doctor's discretion. The very media that endorsed doctors over midwives, hospitals over homes, and drugs and technology over wholistic methods of labor management, called the medical establishment to task for its high incidence of surgical deliveries. The language used in the media, as well as media arguments, carried the presumption that this was one area where women should question doctors' authority. Language such as "too many cesareans" and "unnecessary" surgeries and arguments such as those that give evidence that more women die from cesarean deliveries than from VBAC granted power to consumers. They encouraged women to recognize that perhaps doctors do not always know best, and that women may well have good reasons to question doctors' recommendations for cesarean surgeries.

All the same, the media also carried some strong doctors' voices defending these older practices. Moreover, the covert messages embedded in media coverage of cesarean deliveries carried the strong suggestion that women exercise agency at their own peril. Stories such as the one quoted above from *Redbook* may give some women a sense of their own agency, but they may well silence others who may read this as a horror story. That woman had to fight hard against doctors who did not support her successful attempt at VBAC. Stories of solitary, unsupported struggle may inspire quiescence rather than argument.

Conclusion

If the only media a pregnant woman consulted were those that are most readily available, such as television, film, women's magazines, and newspapers, she would receive mainly information that encouraged her silence. She would learn little about midwives, birthing centers, or standing or squatting while delivering, but she would learn a lot about hospital routines and how she should adapt to them. If she were a lesbian, she would hear nothing about how her and her partner's needs might be accommodated. If she miscarried or labored over a stillborn child, she would find virtually nothing to help her through her grief. If she bore a child with birth defects, she would find no information to guide her. If she were single, she would find no advice on how to make it through labor and delivery.

Women's needs for useful, empowering information on birthing are met best by the medium of books. As noted earlier, the electronic media surveyed were mute on issues such as EFM, induction, drugs, and episiotomies. Perhaps the intimacy of such visualizations limited the picturing of their use. Popular print media such as magazines and newspapers did not offer significantly more information. If a pregnant woman wants to know what the U.S. system of birth is like and how she can negotiate her way through it to a satisfactory birth experience, she will have to read books.

For purposes of comparison, a woman facing birth should read one of the doctor-authored books that presents the standard U.S. medical institutional line, such as Curtis's *Your Pregnancy Week-by-Week* or Cherry's *Understanding Pregnancy and Childbirth*. Then, compare and contrast the doctor-authored book to a book such as Kitzinger's *The Complete Book of Pregnancy and Childbirth,* Samuels and Samuels's *The Well Pregnancy Book,* or Balaskas's *Active Birth*. These three books are examples of published media that will explain hospital procedures in a way that helps women to know what is most likely going to be the case for them, while also preparing them to negotiate with caregivers. Books such as these may even encourage a woman to seek out a midwife for herself, to demand her local hospital grant privileges to midwives so the safety concerns can be met, and to petition her insurance company to cover noninstitutional labor and delivery care. Finally, these books reassure women that they matter just as much as their babies, and that birth *is* a natural process that can be not only endured but enjoyed.

Notes

1. For a fuller listing of television babies up to 1991, see B. Bruns, "TV's Baby Formula," *TV Guide* (April 20, 1991): 2-5.

2. E. Becker, M. Long, V. Stamler, & P. Sallomi, *Midwifery and the Law* (Santa Fe, NM: Mothering, 1990).

3. B. Friedland, "Our Emergency Home Birth," *Parents* (September 1991): 216.

4. B. Herman & S. Perry, *The Twelve-Month Pregnancy* (Los Angeles: Lowell, 1992): 189.

5. American Medical Association, "Imagine Having Your Baby in a Town Without a Doctor," *Newsweek* (March 8, 1993): 50-51.

6. "Birth Environments: Just a Fad?" *U.S.A. Today* (July 1992): 7.

7. A. Eisenberg, H. Murkoff, & S. Hathaway, *What to Expect When You're Expecting* (New York: Workman Publishing, 1991): 330.

8. S. Cherry, *Understanding Pregnancy and Childbirth,* 3rd ed. (New York: Collier, 1992): 176.

9. G. Edelman, "Childbirth: How It Was for Me," *Good Housekeeping* (September 1987): 88.

10. F. Lunzer Kritz with J. Silberner & J. Shapleigh, "Deciding Where to Have the Baby," *U.S. News & World Report* (January 8, 1990): 67; E. Ubell, "Are Births as Safe as They Could Be?" *Parade* (February 7,

1993): 9-11; D. Pinckney, "Onnie's Children," *American Medical News* (April 20, 1990): 25, 28-29; D. Korte & R. Scaer, *A Good Birth, a Safe Birth,* 3rd ed. (Boston: Harvard Common Press, 1992).

11. A December 28, 1989, study cited in Lunzer Kritz, Silberner, & Shapleigh, "Deciding Where to Have the Baby," p. 67.

12. D. Heiligman, "The Birthing-Center Experience," *Parents* (October 1990): 79, 81.

13. A. Gross & D. Ito, "All About Anesthesia," *Parents* (April 1990): 220.

14. G. Curtis, *Your Pregnancy Week-by-Week* (Tucson, AZ: Fisher Books, 1989). 378.

15. K. Schwartz, "Nurse-Midwife: 'I've Gotten Used to Being Awakened in the Middle of the Night,' " *Chicago Tribune,* August 9, 1992, Magazine section, p. 37.

16. S. Fibich & T. Yulsman, "Modern Midwifery: New Childbirth Options," *McCall's* (September 1987): 92.

17. These four include S. Kitzinger's *The Complete Book of Pregnancy and Childbirth* (New York: Knopf, 1989); J. Balaskas's *Active Birth* (Boston: Harvard Common Press, 1992); P. Simkin, J. Whalley, & A. Keppler's *Pregnancy, Childbirth, and the Newborn* (Deephaven, MN: Meadowbrook, 1991); and S. McCutcheon-Rosegg & P. Rosegg's *Natural Childbirth the Bradley Way* (New York: Penguin, 1984).

18. N. Lauerson, *Childbirth With Love* (New York: Berkley, 1983): 463; Curtis, *Your Pregnancy Week-By-Week,* 344; "Too Many Caesareans," *Consumer Reports* (February 1991): 123.

19. Lauerson, *Childbirth With Love,* p. 167.

20. S. Cherry, "What Is Labor Really Like?" *Parents* (October 1991): 156.

21. Balaskas, *Active Birth,* p. 146.

22. McCutcheon-Rosegg & Rosegg, *Natural Childbirth the Bradley Way,* p. 168.

23. "Too Many Caesareans," p. 126.

24. H. Nakdime, "Cesarean Myths," *Ms.* (May 1988): 22.

25. D. Thompson, "Safer Births the Second Time," *Time* (November 7, 1988): 103.

26. J. Zaritt, "I Refused to Have a Second Cesarean," *Redbook* (May 1988): 54.

27. Zaritt, "I Refused," p. 54.

PART III

A Fetal and Maternal Health Approach
to Communicating About Women's Reproductive Health

Starting in the late '70s and accelerating in the '80s, at least fifteen of the nation's largest corporations, from DuPont to Dow to General Motors, began drafting "fetal protection policies" that limited or barred women from traditionally "male" higher-paying jobs that involved exposure to chemicals or radiation—exposure that the companies said might cause birth defects.

[T]he corporate desire to guard female fertility vanished mysteriously for women who worked outside the high-paid circle of the "male" workplace. Working women were exposed to proven reproductive risks and many of the same chemicals and radiation in garment sweatshops, hospitals, dental offices, dry cleaners, and beauty parlors, but no one was calling for their protection.

Susan Faludi, *Backlash: The Undeclared War*
Against American Women, pp. 437-438[1]

Part III of this volume examines a fetal and maternal health approach to communicating about *women's* reproductive health. This agenda—a focus reified through tradition and supported by politics—treats *women's* reproductive health as synonymous with maternal and fetal health. Such an emphasis obscures two basic and significant facts about women's health:

1. Reproductive capacity and function is inherently intertwined with *women's* health, but reproductive health encompasses more than pregnancy; and

   2. we know far less about how pregnancy affects *women's* health than we know about how
      women's health affects fetal health.

In addition, a maternal and fetal health approach to communicating about women's
reproductive health obscures the basic fact that fetal health *and* reproductive safety are
not the exclusive domain of women but must be shared with men, who father children
and whose exposure to proven reproductive risks affects paternal and fetal health.

   A maternal and fetal health approach to women's reproductive health defines a
woman in terms of her ability to conceive, to carry, and to deliver a fetus. Medical research
findings get highlighted in relation to outcomes for the fetus, with such study often
bypassing opportunities even to attempt to assess outcomes for the pregnant woman.
The two cases used to illustrate a fetal and maternal health approach to communicating
about women's health provide ample evidence of the limits associated with such a
focus. Pfau, Nelson, and Moster thoroughly review the voluminous research available
about the effects of tobacco consumption on women's health.[2] Kraft does the same in
relation to a woman's alcohol consumption and fetal health. In juxtaposing these two
chapters, two quite different pictures emerge.

   From Pfau et al.'s review, we are able to discern patterns of effects that tobacco
consumption has uniquely on a woman. These effects are not due to pregnancy. Rather,
a woman's complex reproductive system interacts with tobacco consumption to cause
outcomes that differ from what happens when a man consumes tobacco. Yet as Pfau et
al. reveal, communication about these effects is too seldom available to women—in
media campaigns or in treatment such as smoking cessation programs. Women need
to understand the "benefits" that they may be deriving from tobacco use, including
perceptions of enhanced motor skills, anxiety reduction, control over eating, and
coping with depression. Awareness of these demonstrated relationships between smoking and living can provide an additional incentive to develop new skills. At an
organizational level, cessation counselors should provide strategies to cope with and
replace the loss of these "benefits" of smoking.

   Findings from medical research have also demonstrated that a woman's tobacco
consumption affects fetal health. These effects have become the primary focus for
communicating about pregnant women's tobacco use. Interpersonal sources, including
physicians, and media accounts emphasize and dramatize the most negative outcomes.
We know practically nothing about the interaction of pregnancy and tobacco use on
women's health generally or their reproductive health specifically. This occurs despite
the fact that at the same time data about the effects of a woman's use on fetal health is
being collected, data about the woman's own health could be systematically documented.

   From Kraft's chapter, effects of a woman's alcohol consumption on fetal health
emerge, suggesting a continuum of negative outcomes from bad to worse. Kraft's
chapter shows striking parallels between the research on tobacco and alcohol consumption by women in terms of the thorough and carefully drawn scientific protocols
relating to fetal health, side by side with the almost absent efforts aimed toward understanding the combined effects of pregnancy and alcohol use on women, their general
health, and even their reproductive health—apart from a current pregnancy.

In reviewing the public messages about women and smoking, D. Condit provides an apt metaphor for the situation women face in relation to smoking (and equally in the realm of drinking): a tug of war. Competing interests and concerns place women in the middle. The pregnant woman—faced with loss of control in so many arenas regarding her body—must mightily exert control over both her body's addiction to nicotine and/or alcohol *and* the suasory influence of commercial messages. The non-pregnant woman (and men, as well) will find even less support for stopping use but no fewer images promoting use.

In view of history and in view of politics, a maternal and fetal health focus in communicating about women's reproductive health simply follows the most predictable trajectory. But as has sometimes been shown in the past, it is the counterintuitive hypothesis that proves to be most interesting and that affords the greatest understanding and insights. To derive such a prediction requires a reexamination of the data to consider how to communicate about women as reproductive beings when pregnancy is neither a condition nor a goal, and how to communicate about women's health when women are pregnant—only a temporary state, at best.

Notes

1. S. Faludi, *Backlash: The Undeclared War Against American Women* (New York: Crown, 1991): 437-438.
2. M. Pfau has a substantially longer version of this work, available to authors upon request.

10

Women and Smoking

Consequences and Solutions

Michael Pfau
Margot L. Nelson
Mary Moster

Historically, women have enjoyed a gender advantage in life expectancy; as a group, they have had longer and healthier lives than men. In recent years that advantage has eroded, largely because of increased cigarette smoking among women. Smoking has become an "equal-opportunity tragedy."[1] Although problematic for both men and women, unique addictive effects have been found in women because of differences in male and female physiology.[2]

Impact of Smoking on Women's Health

Women appear to be at risk for the same health problems men encounter as a result of smoking. Women also have some gender-specific risks to themselves and their children, born and unborn.

139

CIGARETTE SMOKING AND CANCER

Smoking has been identified as a definite cause of many cancers. As expected, those organs in direct contact with inhaled smoke (the mouth, throat, and lungs) are at greatest risk. Lung cancer was the primary cause of cancer-related deaths in both men and women in 1992, with most of these cancer deaths (87%) attributable to cigarette smoking. Exposure to tobacco combustion and exhaled smoke from other smokers (passive smoking) is an additional significant causative factor.[3] Women who smoke have a 12 times greater likelihood of developing lung cancer than nonsmoking women, with the death rate from lung cancer in women having increased by 425% in the past 30 years, compared to only 121% in men.[4] Although more diagnoses are made of breast cancer than lung cancer in women (180,000 new cases of breast cancer in 1992 compared to 66,000 new cases of lung cancer), the death rate for lung cancer is higher (53,000 deaths from lung cancer vs. 46,000 deaths from breast cancer in 1992).[5]

CIGARETTE SMOKING
AND RESPIRATORY CONDITIONS

Research findings indicate that smoking interferes with both the structure and function of the lungs. Compared to nonsmokers, smokers have a higher death rate from pneumonia, influenza, and COPD (chronic obstructive pulmonary disease), a condition of permanent airflow obstruction.[6] COPD encompasses the diseases of emphysema and chronic bronchitis and is characterized by a loss of lung elasticity, necessary for adequate exhalation of air. Smoking is the most important risk factor for COPD in both men and women, accounting for an estimated 82% of deaths.[7]

CIGARETTE SMOKING
AND CARDIOVASCULAR DISEASES

Even in individuals with other significant risk factors, cigarette smoking contributes significantly to the development of heart disease.[8] For those who smoke 25 or more cigarettes per day, fatal and nonfatal coronary events occur 5 times as frequently as in nonsmokers. The risk for such events is more than double in light smokers (1-4 cigarettes per day) as compared to nonsmokers; but the risk in former smokers is not significantly elevated above nonsmokers.[9] Although use of low tar and low nicotine cigarettes may reduce the lung cancer risk, it does not appear to lower the risk of heart disease.[10]

Women who smoke are from 2 to 6 times more likely to suffer a heart attack than nonsmoking women, with the risk increasing with the number of cigarettes smoked per day; women's heart attacks are more likely to be fatal than men's.[11] Additional factors specific to women, such as menopause, interact with smoking to further increase the risk of heart disease.[12]

HORMONE-RELATED CONSEQUENCES

Research indicates that the effects of nicotine may vary by gender and across the menstrual cycle in women. Women achieve comparable blood nicotine levels to men after smoking fewer cigarettes.[13] Findings of animal studies suggest that females may be more sensitive to the effects of nicotine on body weight and feeding.[14] The interaction of nicotine with female hormones may influence smoking behavior in women, as most female subjects smoke more during menstruation[15] and the premenstrual period.[16]

Both cigarette smoking and nicotine administration improve motor performance in women, decrease the preference for and consumption of sweet-tasting food, decrease total food consumption, alleviate anxiety, and decrease pain.[17] Smokers are more likely to have a history of depression, leading to the suggestion that smoking may be used as self-medication for depressive symptoms, particularly in women.[18] Medications used to treat smoking addiction may affect women differently than men. Clonidine promotes cessation of smoking in women but not men[19]; nicotine polacrilex is more effective in men than women.[20]

Research findings also suggest that women who smoke may have reduced fertility. In a 1985 study, 38% of nonsmoking women became pregnant in their first cycle after stopping birth control pills compared to 28% of smoking women, whereas smokers were 3.4 times more likely than nonsmokers to have taken more than a year to conceive.[21] Similar effects on fertility have been documented in men.[22] Smoking also lowers rates of estrogen production,[23] with women who smoke reaching menopause an average of 1.74 years earlier than nonsmoking women[24] and having an increased incidence of osteoporosis, which is associated with decreased estrogen levels characteristic of menopause.[25]

CONSEQUENCES OF SMOKING
DURING PREGNANCY

Current research does not directly address the interaction between pregnancy and smoking upon women's health. Given the increased demands placed on a woman's body during pregnancy, however, one might expect pregnancy to accentuate the harmful effects of smoking on women's health. Smoking during pregnancy increases a woman's risk of miscarriage, preterm delivery, low birth weight babies, fetal death, and infant death.[26] It has been suggested that if all pregnant women stopped smoking, the number of fetal and infant deaths would be reduced by approximately 10%. In the United States, this would result in approximately 4,000 fewer infant deaths each year.[27]

Maternal smoking has a significant dose-related effect on infant birth weight, a predictor of infant survival and development.[28] Women who reported smoking cigarettes during pregnancy delivered infants who weighed an average of 141.8 grams less than infants of nonsmoking mothers. Smoking also interacts with the effect of alcohol consumption on infant birth weight. A weekly alcohol consumption of 120 grams or more is associated with a greater reduction in the average birth weight of babies born to smoking mothers than to nonsmoking mothers.[29]

The risk of sudden infant death syndrome (SIDS) is also increased by maternal smoking. In a study of normal birth weight infants, those who died of SIDS were more likely to have had mothers who smoked.[30] The underlying explanation for the relationship between maternal smoking and effects on the fetus and newborn is insufficient oxygen delivery to the fetus.[31]

EFFECTS OF PASSIVE SMOKING
ON WOMEN AND CHILDREN

There is substantial evidence that passive smoking (exposure to the exhaled smoke of another person who smokes) is harmful to the health of both nonsmoking adults and children. The American Cancer Society reports that environmental tobacco smoke causes an estimated 53,000 deaths annually in the United States, about two thirds from heart disease and about 4,000 from lung cancer.[32] Findings of a 14-year Japanese study of 90,000 married women showed a significantly higher risk of death from lung cancer if the spouse smoked. The relative risk was as high as 4.6 in younger agricultural families, representing approximately one half to one third the risk of direct smoking.[33] These findings were similar to those of a more recent autopsy-based study in which lung specimens from adults who had died of causes other than respiratory disease and cancer were examined for the presence of epithelial precancerous lesions (EPPL). The EPPL values were significantly higher among smokers and nonsmoking women married to smokers as compared to nonsmokers.[34] Children exposed to passive smoke have a higher incidence of respiratory symptoms and illnesses,[35] persistent wheeze,[36] bronchitis,[37] and reduced expiratory air flow.[38] Also, children whose parents smoke are twice as likely to become smokers themselves.[39]

The Nature and Impact
of Cessation Efforts

Although it is encouraging to note the increasing percentage of smokers who have successfully quit, cessation rates for women lag behind men's.[40] The problem for most smokers is not just quitting, but successfully abstaining. These are two quite different processes with important implications for women and for health campaigners who promote smoking cessation. Messages aimed at pregnant women who smoke should address the following.

CESSATION APPROACHES

The 1980 Report of the Surgeon General on Women's Health and Smoking finds that although men and women make a similar number of attempts to quit smoking, men are more likely than women to remain successful abstainers.[41] Orlandi suggests that, although women had a lower probability of quit attempts and successful cessation than men, the gender difference has since narrowed, becoming insignificant except involving adolescents.[42] Others find evidence of gender differences in long-term but not initial cessation rates.[43] Smoking cessation programs found to be the most effective are multicomponent programs that address both physiological and psychological dependence on nicotine.[44]

Pharmacological interventions have been useful in alleviating nicotine withdrawal symptoms associated with physiological dependence. These approaches generally involve various nicotine replacement strategies (chewing gum, transdermal patch), because nicotine is the critical dependence-producing component in tobacco. If women are more dependent on nicotine and have more severe withdrawal symptoms, this could explain why they might be more likely to relapse. This is supported by Gunn who reported that intensity of withdrawal symptoms predicted relapse for women but not men.[45] Another study indicated that menstrual cycle phase when quitting smoking influences severity of withdrawal symptoms.[46] Several studies found that women do not differ from men in severity of withdrawal symptoms, but women report more symptoms associated with nicotine withdrawal.[47]

Gender differences in nicotine intake or its effects could also influence smoking cessation rates. Smoking higher nicotine cigarettes before cessation and experiencing more craving after cessation were predictors for relapse in women but not men.[48] If these studies indicate that women are more sensitive than men to the physiological effects of nicotine, then nicotine replacement therapy may help women maintain long-term abstinence from smoking. Gender differences in effectiveness of nicotine gum are ambiguous, however. One study found no gender difference,[49] whereas another found nicotine chewing gum more effective for men than women,[50] contrary to expectation. Nicotine replacement therapy helps relieve some withdrawal symptoms, but may have little effect on craving.[51] Over a longer period, craving may be a more potent factor in relapse than the severity of withdrawal symptoms.

Most smokers, both women and men, report they would like to stop smoking. Some studies find no gender difference in intentions to quit or in quit attempts.[52] Sorensen and Pechacke report that more men than women smokers intended to quit completely, but more women than men intended to cut down on number of cigarettes smoked.[53] Although men were not more likely than women to have tried to quit, men have higher confidence in their ability to quit. Smokers with high confidence in their ability to quit smoking are more likely to stop smoking initially, to reestablish abstinence following a slip, and to maintain long-term abstinence successfully.[54] One study, however, reported that although men may have somewhat greater confidence in their ability to quit than women, the differences in success rates fell short of statistical significance.[55]

Stress is a predictor for relapse in men *and* women. High levels of stress can trigger a smoking episode in ex-smokers, often leading to full-blown relapse. Women are more likely than men to smoke to reduce stress. They admit it may be difficult to stop smoking without finding ways to cope with tension and pressure.[56] Identifying alternative ways of coping with stress, especially job-related stress, may help to maintain abstinence. Relaxation training provides another means for smokers to cope with stress. By itself it is not as effective as when part of multicomponent behavioral skills training programs.[57]

Psychological distress (i.e., depression, anxiety, tension, nervousness) also may account for higher relapse rates in women.[58] Depression is more common in women than in men.[59] Depressed individuals find it harder to quit smoking and are more likely to relapse.[60] Women are more likely than men to smoke in order to reduce negative affect[61] and to drop out of smoking cessation programs for reasons related to depression.[62] Although smoking to reduce psychological distress may not affect initial smoking cessation, it is likely to increase susceptibility for relapse, because these individuals experience not only the loss of cigarettes but of an important coping mechanism as well.

Weight gain is another concern for smokers because women and men tend to gain weight after quitting, an effect that is more pronounced among those who smoke more.[63] These gains begin soon after cessation, but reverse upon resuming smoking behavior.[64] Women are more concerned than men about this weight gain and more likely to consider smoking as a weight control strategy.[65]

Social support is another factor that may affect women and men differently as they attempt to stop smoking. Partner support may be especially important in maintaining abstinence. Spousal support "appears to function by promoting and rewarding the behavior changes required for successful abstinence, avoiding domination or pressure, facilitating personal problem solving, and providing an effective stress buffer."[66] Although social support can help prevent relapse by encouraging ex-smokers to remain abstinent, socializing or living with a smoker can provide the stimulus for a smoking relapse.[67] Social support is an important factor to consider in smoking cessation programs, especially for women, who seem to benefit more than men do from treatments where support is provided.[68]

The vast majority of successful quitters stop on their own without the help of smoking cessation programs, but only about 10% are able to maintain abstinence for 1 year.[69] The best multicomponent programs incorporating pharmacological, behavioral, and cognitive strategies report almost universal initial cessation and close to 50% longer-term abstinence.[70] Only a small proportion of the smoking population participates in smoking cessation programs, however, limiting their effectiveness in reducing overall smoking prevalence.[71] Because these programs require greater resources, they may not be perceived to be cost-effective unless considered together with the cost of health care to treat conditions that may arise due to smoking.

CESSATION AND PREGNANCY

One subgroup of the smoking population that it is critical to reach with smoking cessation programs due to the effects smoking has on both the pregnant woman and the fetus is pregnant women. About one third of all pregnant women are smokers.[72] Although most women are aware that smoking during pregnancy is harmful to them and to their baby, 65% to 85% of pregnant women continue to smoke during pregnancy.[73] This has become a national health concern, as documented previously.

Though pregnant women are more likely to quit smoking than nonpregnant women,[74] smoking cessation rates are still low. Women most likely to continue smoking are young, single, white, unemployed, with less than a high school education, who lack strong beliefs about the dangers of smoking and did not plan on becoming pregnant.[75] When pregnant, smoking rates in women drop from 29% to 23%, with the heaviest smokers being least likely to quit but most likely to reduce consumption.[76] Quitting or reducing tobacco use lessens the health risk of having a low birth weight baby. Women who smoked previous to pregnancy but not during pregnancy were not at increased risk; those stopping during the first trimester had risk similar to nonsmokers; mothers who smoked throughout pregnancy were at greater risk; reducing consumption or smoking intermittently during pregnancy lessened the risk somewhat.[77] The strongest health benefits accrue to smoking cessation early in pregnancy, but reducing consumption is also beneficial in lessening the risk of having a low birth weight baby.

Pregnancy provides an ideal opportunity for health care professionals to advise and reinforce nonsmoking behavior in women. Early in pregnancy, the mother is receptive to information and instructions about her health and the baby.[78] Encouragement and follow-up of nonsmoking behavior can be continued during prenatal visits. Because most pregnant women who quit do so early in pregnancy, they have several months of abstinence. This takes them beyond the initial experience of withdrawal from nicotine and the first weeks and months where relapse rates are greatest. Although most women who quit smoking during pregnancy did not plan to resume smoking after delivery, 70% relapsed within 1 year of delivery. Of those who relapsed, 67% did so within 3 months of delivery, and 93% relapsed within 6 months.[79] The value of pregnancy as an intervention point in smoking behavior is somewhat lost in this high relapse rate. Concern about losing weight, less social pressure or encouragement to abstain after delivery, and living with or socializing with other smokers are factors influencing postpartum relapse rates.[80]

Smoking cessation programs have been designed that use several ways to meet the national health objective of a 10% or less smoking prevalence rate for pregnant women. Strategies include physicians' advice to quit; general health information about the effects of smoking; programs and self-help information on how to quit smoking; and programs geared for pregnant women, giving information during prenatal visits about the importance of smoking cessation for prenatal and postnatal development. Advice and information is not as effective as multicomponent programs emphasizing skills and specific smoking cessation techniques.[81]

The most effective programs to help pregnant smokers quit and successfully maintain abstinence offer strong advice to quit, provide readable risk information, and continue reinforcement from a health care professional.[82] After delivery, there should be follow-up on women who quit smoking during pregnancy to reduce the high postpartum smoking relapse rate. The cost-benefit of smoking cessation programs for pregnant women is quickly evident when weighed against the cost of caring for low birth weight infants and the increased infant mortality rates. One cost-benefit analysis of a health education program found ratios of 1 : 6 (low estimate) and 1 : 17 (high estimate), strongly supporting the benefit of helping pregnant smokers quit smoking.[83] There is an immediacy about smoking cessation during pregnancy to reduce health risks to mother and baby, but the ultimate objective should be long-term smoking cessation.

The Nature and Impact
of Antismoking Communication

Estimates indicate that between 1964 and 1985 approximately 750,000 smoking-related deaths were avoided or postponed by an average of two decades due to individual decisions to quit smoking or not to start.[84]

CESSATION CAMPAIGNS

Systematic communication to discourage smoking originated during the 1950s. In 1951, the national news media disseminated the first reports of research linking cigarette smoking and lung cancer.[85] This coverage resulted in a temporary 10% decline in per capita cigarette consumption between 1953 and 1954.[86] Rates of consumption soon resumed an upward trend, however, and the most lasting effect of this coverage was to accelerate sharply the movement to filtered cigarettes, which rose from a mere 2.9% of cigarette production in 1953 to 45.3% by 1958.[87] In 1964, following intensive news media coverage of the contents of the Surgeon General's Report on Smoking and Health, per capita cigarette consumption dipped slightly "before resuming a gradual upward climb."[88]

Public communication campaigns against smoking intensified in the late 1960s, following a ruling that the Fairness Doctrine required equal time for antismoking and prosmoking messages. The ruling resulted in approximately $200-million of free television and radio airtime, much of it in the most desirable time slots, for the broadcast of antismoking messages from 1967 to 1970, until the cigarette industry voluntarily pulled its television advertising in lieu of pending federal legislation that banned it.[89] These antismoking messages were "relatively amateurish,"[90] but were highly visible.

The decision to curtail cigarette television advertising produced two side effects. First, it freed up the industry's resources for more emphasis on advertising and promotional campaigns that targeted women, and following this action, cigarette advertising in women's magazines increased sharply. Second, most antismoking television messages were moved from prime time to less desirable time slots.[91]

Most early antismoking campaigns relied primarily on public service announcements (PSAs), aired during donated time slots over radio and television, and used fear appeals, attempting to scare smokers into cessation. Fear appeals can be effective, but two steps are required for a fear appeal to succeed.[92] First, the fear appeal must convince receivers that there is a reasonable probability of the negative consequence happening to them, and in the near term.[93] Most of the early antismoking campaigns stressed long-term consequences of cigarette smoking (e.g., lung cancer). As a result, success in promoting cessation was limited primarily to middle-aged male smokers, who were more able to internalize the health effects of smoking.[94] Younger smokers reason that the immediate positive rewards of smoking outweigh potential consequences of remote long-term negative effects.[95] They dismiss "long-term health hazards of smoking because . . . [they] are associated with adulthood and old age."[96] To reach younger smokers, antismoking communication needs to stress immediate physiological and social effects.[97]

A second requisite step for a fear appeal to succeed is that the message must demonstrate potential efficacy by recommending actions that the individual can take to avert the consequence, and "convince individuals that they are psychologically capable of performing the recommended action."[98] Fear appeals employed in early antismoking campaigns stressed the health consequences of smoking, but largely ignored the issue of efficacy.

Research on smoking cessation indicates that the perceived efficacy of recommended action is a prerequisite to behavior change.[99] Research indicates that mass media campaigns of the 1960s and 1970s exerted minimal impact on smokers[100] but did affect nonsmokers.[101] A review of antismoking campaigns in the United States and United Kingdom during the 1960s revealed "negligible long-term effects."[102] The author chided health educators involved in such campaigns for unrealistic assumptions about the rationality of receivers: "For the health educator the solution is as simple as it is obvious: disseminate the facts about the health hazards associated with cigarette smoking and the facts would speak for themselves."[103] These campaigns were characterized as "largely notional and atheoretical, with each one drawing upon a seemingly arbitrarily selected battery of propaganda techniques."[104]

Some subsequent campaigns were theoretically grounded and more carefully constructed. For example, the Stanford Three Community Study sought to inform, persuade, and train audiences in smoking cessation. The investigation employed mass media, mass media plus interpersonal training, and control conditions. The results indicated modest success for the mass media and the mass media plus interpersonal conditions. Additional studies, North Karelia (Finland), Quit for Life (Australia), and the Stanford Five-City Project (United States), also point to modest longitudinal success for smoking cessation campaigns that employ intensive multimedia lifestyle campaigns, representing a vast improvement over the earlier PSA-based efforts.[105]

What antismoking campaigns have accomplished is to inform people about the health consequences of smoking. "Today, nearly everyone accepts the fact that heavy smoking can have serious consequences."[106] More than 90% of adults now acknowledge that smoking increases the risk of heart disease, emphysema, and lung cancer, and "most smokers are persuaded that they should stop smoking."[107] In mobilizing nonsmokers to restrict smoking in public places, antismoking campaigns have been successful in protecting nonsmokers from health risks associated with involuntary smoking and "may have had the side effect of discouraging tobacco use by reducing opportunities to smoke."[108]

PREVENTION CAMPAIGNS

Because cigarette smoking exerts such a "tenacious grip" on regular users, "most health professionals agree that the ultimate conquest of tobacco-related disease can only be achieved through primary prevention."[109] Once a person acquires the smoking habit, it is very difficult to break, especially for women.[110] The issue of prevention is particularly relevant to discussions of smoking and women's health. Two developments are important. First, adolescents are initiating smoking at younger ages among more recent birth cohorts.[111] It is estimated that more than 3,000 American teenagers take up smoking each day,[112] and that most of them smoked their first cigarette before the age of 12.[113] This is particularly alarming because of the evidence indicating that earlier smoking initiation is associated with higher levels of subsequent cigarette consumption[114] and, as a result, with higher morbidity and mortality.[115]

Second, adolescent females are taking up smoking in greater numbers, and at younger ages, than ever before. Prior to the 1970s, adolescent females were less likely to initiate smoking than males, and if they did take up smoking, started later than males.[116] An examination of smoking trends indicate that after 1977 the percentage of 12- to 18-year-old females engaged in both experimental smoking (31% vs. 28%) and regular smoking (21% vs. 18%) surpassed males.[117] Further, an increasing number of females are initiating smoking prior to the age of 12.[118]

The net result of this trend is that the decline in overall smoking rates of women has slowed and now approaches rates for men.[119] Furthermore, similar demographic trends are under way in the United Kingdom and other Western nations.[120] Findings indicate that if preventative strategies are to work, they must target younger adolescents, at or before the transition from elementary to secondary school (e.g., prior to sixth or seventh grades), employing a strategy designed to instill resistance to attitude slippage.[121]

Inoculation is a strategy designed to strengthen existing attitudes against change. In its pure form, inoculation employs two components: threat, which warns of impending challenges to existing attitudes, thus motivating people to bolster attitudes against change; and refutational preemption, which raises and then answers, likely challenges.[122] A number of studies have employed various permutations of inoculation in the attempt to prevent and delay smoking initiation in adolescents. Indeed, a problem with this line of research is that the studies employed such varied strategies under the broad heading of "social inoculation."[123] An examination of the methodologies employed in these studies reveals that some operationalized threat, but most did not.[124] Threat is viewed as an essential element in inoculation because it serves as the motivational catalyst.[125] In addition, these studies relied on an array of message vehicles, including: peer modeling, guest speakers, teacher-led discussions, videos, slide shows, and schoolwide campaigns. Thus, it remains unclear "which of these program components are necessary for program effectiveness or how other components . . . might or might not add to program effectiveness.[126]

In addition, most of the social inoculation studies ignored relevant receiver characteristics, such as self-esteem,[127] and *failed* to *incorporate gender in their designs,* apparently operating on the assumption that the same pretreatments will work equally well with young males and females.[128] Barton and colleagues examined motivators of smoking initiation among adolescents and found that, whereas male adolescent smokers were not perceived positively by either male or female peers, female smokers were rated more attractive and more sociable than nonsmokers by adolescent boys.[129] Other research indicates that young males smoke cigarettes to demonstrate their assertiveness and masculinity, whereas young females smoke to demonstrate their confidence, sophistication, and extroversion.[130] These images, consistent with cigarette industry advertising themes, further bolster the case for gender-specific prevention messages. The results suggest that prevention strategies for adolescent females "should either attack the positive image of the smoker or provide alternative means of self-image improvement."[131]

Research further indicates that adolescent females, as opposed to males, are likely to smoke to relieve tensions[132] and "as a legal and sanctioned means of weight control."[133]

These findings further document the need to tailor smoking prevention approaches to female adolescents, placing much greater emphasis on "social context and social supports."[134] *It seems clear that smoking prevention strategies that target adolescent women should place less emphasis on refusal skills and more emphasis on affect skills, tension reduction, and approaches to weight control that do not involve cigarettes.*[135]

In this vein, prevention strategies designed for, and targeted to, young women must be tested in future research. *Such research holds the greatest promise to curtail pregnant women's smoking, and thereby reduce the harm to themselves, their fetuses, and others who would be passively exposed.*

Notes

1. J. E. Fielding, "Smoking and Women: Tragedy of the Majority," *The New England Journal of Medicine* 317 (1987): 1343-1345.

2. C. S. Pomerleau, O. F. Pomerleau, & A. W. Garcia, "Biobehavioral Research on Nicotine Use in Women," *British Journal of Addiction* 86 (1991): 527-531.

3. National Institutes of Health, "Cigarette Smoking—A Risk Factor for Cardiovascular Disease for Women," *The Search for Health* NIH (1990): 61-HLBI-3/90.

4. American Cancer Society, *Cancer Facts & Figures—1992* (Atlanta, GA: American Cancer Society, 1992).

5. American Cancer Society, *Cancer Facts & Figures.*

6. C. B. Sherman, "The Health Consequences of Cigarette Smoking. Pulmonary Diseases," *Medical Clinics of North America* 76 (1992): 355-375.

7. U.S. DHHS (U.S. Department of Health and Human Services), *Reducing the Health Consequences of Smoking: 25 Years of Progress. A Report of the Surgeon General* U.S. DHHS, PHS, CDC, Center for Chronic Disease Prevention and Health Promotion, Office on Smoking and Health. DHHS Publication No. (CDC) 89-8411, 1989 (Washington, DC: Government Printing Office, 1989).

8. T. A. Miettinen & H. Gylling, "Mortality and Cholesterol Metabolism in Familial Hypercholesterolemia. Long-term Follow-Up of 96 Patients," *Arteriosclerosis* 8 (1988): 163-167.

9. W. C. Willett, A. Green, M. J. Stampfer, F. E. Speizer, G. A. Colditz, B. Rosner, R. R. Monson, W. Stason, & C. H. Hennekens, "Relative and Absolute Excess Risks of Coronary Heart Disease Among Women Who Smoke Cigarettes," *The New England Journal of Medicine* 317 (1987): 1303-1309.

10. National Institutes of Health, "Cigarette Smoking."

11. B. N. Das & V. S. Banka, "Coronary Artery Disease in Women. How It Is—and Isn't—Unique," *Postgraduate Medicine* 91 (1992): 197-200, 203-206.

12. U.S. DHHS, *Reducing the Health Consequence of Smoking.*

13. Pomerleau et al., "Biobehavioral Research."

14. N. E. Grunberg, D. J. Bowen, & S. E. Winders, "Effects of Nicotine on Body Weight and Food Consumption in Female Rats," *Psychopharmacology* 90 (1986): 101-105.

15. N. K. Mello, J. H. Mendelson, & S. I. Palmieri, "Cigarette Smoking by Women: Interactions With Alcohol Use," *Psychopharmacology* 93 (1987): 8-15.

16. Pomerleau et al., "Biobehavioral Research."

17. U.S. DHHS, *The Health Consequences of Smoking: Nicotine Addiction. A Report of the Surgeon General* (U.S. DHHS Publication No. CDC 88-8406), U.S. DHHS, CDC, Center for Health Promotion and Education, Office on Smoking and Health (Washington, DC: Government Printing Office, 1988).

18. A. H. Glassman, F. Steiner, B. T. Walsh, P. S. Raizman, J. L. Fleiss, T. B. Cooper, & L. S. Covey, "Heavy Smokers, Smoking Cessation, and Clonidine," *Journal of the American Medical Association* (1988): 2863-2866.

19. Glassman et al., "Heavy Smokers."

20. J. D. Killen, S. P. Fortmann, B. Newman, & A. Varady, "Evaluation of a Treatment Approach Combining Nicotine Gum With Self-Guided Behavioral Treatments for Smoking Relapse Prevention," *Journal of Consulting and Clinical Psychology* 58 (1990): 85-92.

21. D. D. Baird & A. J. Wilcox, "Cigarette Smoking Associated With Delayed Conception," *Journal of the American Medical Association* 253 (1985): 2979-2983.

22. R. J. Albin, "Cigarette Smoking and Quality of Sperm," *New York State Journal of Medicine* 86 (1986): 108.

23. J. J. Michnovicz, R. J. Herschcope, M. D. Naganuma, H. L. Bardlow, & J. Fishman, "Increased 2-Hydroxylation of Estradiol as a Possible Mechanism for the Anti-Estrogenic Effect of Cigarette Smoking," *The New England Journal of Medicine* 21 (1986): 1305-1309.

24. S. M. McKinlay, N. L. Bifano, & J. B. McKinlay, "Smoking and Age at Menopause in Women," *Annals of Internal Medicine* 103 (1985): 350-356.

25. J. A. Baron, "Smoking and Estrogen-Related Disease," *American Journal of Epidemiology* 119 (1984): 9-22.

26. E. R. Gritz, "Cigarette Smoking by Adolescent Females: Implications for Health and Behavior," *Women & Health* 9 (1984): 103-115; I. D. McIntosh, "Smoking and Pregnancy: Attributable Risks and Public Health Implications," *Canadian Journal of Public Health* 75 (1984): 141-148.

27. M. Bonati & G. Fellin, "Changes in Smoking and Drinking Behavior Before and During Pregnancy in Italian Mothers: Implications for Public Health Intervention," *International Journal of Epidemiology* 20 (1991): 927-932.

28. T. D. Abell, L. C. Baker, & C. N. Ramsey, Jr., "The Effects of Maternal Smoking on Infant Birth Weight," *Family Medicine* 23 (1991): 103-107.

29. J. Olsen, A. daPereira, & S. F. Olsen, "Does Maternal Tobacco Smoking Modify the Effect of Alcohol on Fetal Growth?" *American Journal of Public Health* 81 (1991): 69-73.

30. K. C. Schoendorf & J. L. Kiely, "Relationship of Sudden Infant Death Syndrome to Maternal Smoking During and After Pregnancy," *Pediatrics* 90 (1992): 905-908.

31. D. Rush & P. Cassano, "Relationship of Cigarette Smoking and Social Class and Birth Weight and Perinatal Mortality Among All Births in Britain, April 5-11, 1970," *Journal of Epidemiology and Community Health* 37 (1983): 249-255.

32. American Cancer Society, *Cancer Facts & Figures*.

33. T. Hirayama, "Non-Smoking Wives of Heavy Smokers Have a Higher Risk of Lung Cancer: A Study From Japan," *British Medical Journal* 282 (1981): 183-185.

34. D. Trichopoulos, F. Mollo, L. Tomatis, E. Agapitos, L. Delsedine, X. Zavitsanos, A. Kalandidi, K. Katsouyanni, E. Riboli, & R. Saracci, "Active and Passive Smoking and Pathological Indicators of Lung Cancer Risk in an Autopsy Study," *Journal of the American Medical Association* 268 (1992): 1697-1701.

35. B. H. Azizi & R. L. Henry, "The Effects of Indoor Environmental Factors on Respiratory Illnesses in Primary School Children in Kuala Lumpur," *International Journal of Epidemiology* 20 (1991): 144-150.

36. S. Chinn & R. J. Rona, "Quantifying Health Aspects of Passive Smoking in British Children Aged 5-11 Years," *Journal of Epidemiology and Community Health* 45 (1991): 188-194.

37. A. M. Ugnat, Y. Mao, A. B. Miller, & D. T. Wigle, "Effects of Residential Exposure to Environmental Tobacco Smoke on Canadian Children," *Canadian Journal of Public Health* 81 (1990): 345-349.

38. Azizi & Henry, "The Effects of Indoor Environmental Factors."

39. S. B. Meltzer & E. O. Meltzer, "Harmful Effects of Passive Smoking," *Western Journal of Medicine* 154 (1991): 457-458.

40. U.S. DHHS, *The Health Benefits of Smoking Cessation*.

41. U.S. DHHS, *The Health Benefits of Smoking Cessation*.

42. M. A. Orlandi, "Gender Differences in Smoking Cessation," *Women and Health* 11 (1987): 237-251.

43. L. Hirvonen, "Premises and Results of Smoking Withdrawal," in W. F. Forbes, R. C. Frecker, & D. Nostbakken (Eds.), *Proceedings of the 5th World Conference on Smoking and Health* Vol. 2 (Ottawa: Canadian Council on Smoking and Health, 1983): 215-220; G. Sorensen & T. F. Pechacke, "Attitudes Toward Smoking Cessation Among Men and Women," *Journal of Behavioral Medicine* 10 (1987): 129-137.

44. U.S. DHHS *The Health Consequences of Smoking*.

45. R. C. Gunn, "Reactions to Withdrawal Symptoms and Success in Smoking Cessation Clinics," *Addictive Behaviors* 11 (1986): 49-53.

46. P. O'Hara, S. A. Porster, & B. P. Anderson, "The Influence of Menstrual Cycle Changes on the Tobacco Withdrawal Syndrome in Women," *Addictive Behaviors* 14 (1989): 595-604.

47. J. R. Hughes & D. K. Hatsukami, "Signs and Symptoms of Tobacco Withdrawal," *Archives of General Psychiatry* 43 (1986): 89-294; E. R. Gritz, "Women and Smoking: A Realistic Appraisal," in J. L. Schwartz (Ed.), *International Conference on Smoking Cessation* (New York: American Cancer Society, 1978): 119-141.

48. G. E. Swan, C. E. Denk, S. D. Parker, D. Carmelli, C. T. Furze, & R. H. Rosenwan, "Risk Factors for Late Relapse in Male and Female Ex-Smokers," *Addictive Behaviors* 13 (1988): 253-266.

49. N. G. Schneider, M. E. Jarvik, & A. B. Forsythe, "Nicotine vs. Placebo Gum in Alleviation of Withdrawal During Smoking Cessation," *Addictive Behaviors* 9 (1984): 149-156.

50. Killen et al., "Evaluation of a Treatment Approach," pp. 85-92.

51. U.S. DHHS, *The Health Consequences of Smoking.*

52. H. A. Lando, P. L. Pirie, W. L. Hellerstedt, & P. G. McGovern, "Survey of Smoking Patterns, Attitudes, and Interest Quitting," *American Journal of Preventative Medicine* 7 (1991): 18-23.

53. Sorensen & Pechacke, "Attitudes Toward Smoking Cessation."

54. M. M. Condiotte & E. Lichtenstein, "Self-Efficacy and Relapse in Smoking Cessation Programs," *Journal of Consulting and Clinical Psychology* 49 (1981): 648-658.

55. Sorensen & Pechacke, "Attitudes Toward Smoking Cessation."

56. U.S. DHHS, *The Health Consequences of Smoking for Women;* Sorensen & Pechacke, "Attitudes Toward Smoking Cessation."

57. U.S. DHHS, *The Health Consequences of Smoking.*

58. Hirvonen, "Premises and Results of Smoking Withdrawal."

59. B. P. Dohrenwend & B. S. Dohrenwend, "Sex Differences and Psychiatric Disorders," *American Journal of Sociology* 81 (1976): 1447-1454.

60. A. H. Glassman, J. E. Helzer, L. S. Covey, L. B. Cottler, F. Stetner, J. E. Tipp, & J. Johnson, "Smoking, Smoking Cessation, and Major Depression," *Journal of the American Medical Association* 264 (1990): 1546-1549.

61. F. F. Ikard & S. Tomkins, "The Experience of Affect as a Determinant of Smoking Behavior," *Journal of Abnormal Psychology* 81 (1973): 172-181; Gritz, "Women and Smoking."

62. U.S. DHHS, *The Health Consequences of Smoking for Women.*

63. P. H. Blitzer, A. A. Rimm, & E. E. Giefer, "The Effect of Cessation of Smoking on Body Weight in 57,032 Women: Cross-Sectional and Longitudinal Analyses," *Journal of Chronic Disease* 30 (1977): 415-429.

64. K. A. Perkins, L. H. Epstein, & S. Pastor, "Changes in Energy Balance Following Smoking Cessation and Resumption of Smoking in Women," *Journal of Consulting and Clinical Psychology* 58 (1990): 121-125.

65. U.S. DHHS, *The Health Consequences of Smoking for Women;* Sorensen & Pechacke, "Attitudes Toward Smoking Cessation."

66. H. C. Coppotelli & C. T. Orleans, "Partner Support and Other Determinants of Smoking Cessation Maintenance Among Women," *Journal of Consulting and Clinical Psychology* 53 (1985): 455-460.

67. Hirvonen, "Premises and Results of Smoking Withdrawal."

68. J. S. Tamerin, "The Psychodynamics of Quitting Smoking in a Group," *American Journal of Psychiatry* 129 (1972): 589-595; Gritz, "Women and Smoking."

69. S. Cohen, E. Lichtenstein, & J. Prochaska, "Some Misconceptions About Self-Quitting: Evidence From Ten Prospective Studies of Persons Quitting Smoking by Themselves," *American Psychologist* 44 (1989): 1355-1365.

70. U.S. DHHS, *The Health Consequences of Smoking.*

71. M. C. Fiore, T. E. Novotny, & J. P. Pierce, "Methods Used to Quit Smoking in the United States: Do Cessation Programs Help?" *Journal of the American Medical Association* 263 (1990): 2760-2765.

72. K. Haug, "The Smoking Fetus," *Scandinavian Journal of Primary Health Care* 7 (1989): 187-188.

73. E. R. Gritz & B. A. Berman, "Smoking and Pregnancy," *Journal of the American Medical Women's Association* (1989): 57.

74. D. F. Williamson, M. K. Serdula, J. S. Kendrick, & N. J. Binkin, "Comparing the Prevalence of Smoking in Pregnant and Nonpregnant Women, 1985-1986," *Journal of the American Medical Association* 261 (1989): 70-74.

75. Gritz & Berman, "Smoking and Pregnancy"; R. J. Madeley, P. A. Gillies, F. L. Power, & E. M. Symonds, "Nottingham Mothers Stop Smoking Project—Baseline Survey of Smoking in Pregnancy," *Community Medicine* 11 (1989): 124-130.

76. E. J. Waterson & I. M. Murray-Lyon, "Drinking and Smoking Patterns Amongst Women Attending an Antenatal Clinic—II. During Pregnancy," *Alcohol and Alcoholism* 24 (1989): 163-173.

77. C. MacArthur & E. G. Knox, "Smoking in Pregnancy: Effects of Stopping at Different Stages," *British Journal of Obstetrics and Gynecology* 95 (1988): 551-555.

78. A. E. Hill, "Considerations for Smoking Advice in Pregnancy," *Ulster Medical Journal* 57 (1988): 22-27.

79. L. A. Fingerhut, J. C. Kleinman, & J. S. Kendrick, "Smoking Before, During, and After Pregnancy," *American Journal of Public Health* 80 (1990): 541-544.

80. C. M. McBride & P. L. Pirie, "Postpartum Smoking Relapse," *Addictive Behaviors* 15 (1990): 165-168.

81. R. A. Windsor, "An Application of the PRECEDE Model for Planning and Evaluating Health Education Methods for Pregnant Smokers," *Hygiene* 5 (1986): 38-44.

82. Windsor, "An Application."

83. J. S. Marks, J. P. Kooplan, J. C. Hogue, & M. E. Dalmat, "A Cost-Benefit/Cost-Effectiveness Analysis of Smoking Cessation for Pregnant Women," *American Journal of Preventive Medicine* 6 (1990): 282-289.

84. U.S. DHHS, *The Health Consequence of Smoking.*

85. K. Warner, "The Effects of the Anti-Smoking Campaign on Cigarette Consumption," *American Journal of Public Health* 67 (1977): 645-650.

86. A. McAlister, A. G. Ramirez, C. Galavotti, & K. J. Gallion, "Antismoking Campaigns: Progress in the Application of Social Learning Theory," in R. E. Rice & C. K. Atkin (Eds.), *Public Communication Campaigns* 2nd ed. (Newbury Park, CA: Sage, 1989): 291-307.

87. U.S. DHHS, *The Health Consequences of Smoking for Women.*

88. McAlister et al., "Antismoking Campaigns," p. 293.

89. Warner, "The Effects of the Anti-Smoking Campaign."

90. Warner, "The Effects of the Anti-Smoking Campaign."

91. McAlister et al., "Antismoking Campaigns," p. 293.

92. F. J. Boster & P. Mongeau, "Fear-Arousing Persuasive Messages," in R. N. Bostrom (Ed.), *Communication Yearbook* 8 (Beverly Hills, CA: Sage, 1984): 330-375.

93. E. M. Rogers, "The Diffusion of Innovations Perspective," in N. Weinstein (Ed.), *Taking Care: Why People Take Precautions* (New York: Cambridge University Press, 1987).

94. L. S. Pettegrew & R. Logan, "The Health Care Context," in C. R. Berger & S. H. Chaffee (Eds.), *Handbook of Communication Science* (Newbury Park, CA: Sage, 1987): 675-710.

95. L. S. Harken, "The Prevention of Adolescent Smoking: A Public Health Priority," *Evaluation & the Health Professions* 10 (1987): 373-393; E. M. Rogers & J. D. Storey, "Communication Campaigns," in C. R. Berger & S. H. Chaffee (Eds.), *Handbook of Communication Science* (Newbury Park, CA: Sage, 1987): 817-846.

96. J. Barton, L. Chassin, C. G. Presson, & S. J. Sherman, "Social Image Factors as Motivators of Smoking Initiation in Early and Middle Adolescence," *Child Development* 53 (1982): 1499-1511.

97. U.S. DHEW (U.S. Department of Health, Education, and Welfare), *Smoking in Children and Adolescents* (Washington, DC: U.S. DHEW, PHS, 1979).

98. R. M. Perloff, *The Dynamics of Persuasion* (Hillsdale, NJ: Lawrence Erlbaum, 1993).

99. R. W. Rogers & C. R. Mewborn, "Fear Appeals and Attitude Change: Effects of a Threat's Noxiousness, Probability of Occurrence, and the Efficacy of Coping Responses," *Journal of Personality and Social Psychology* 34 (1976): 54-61.

100. Warner, "The Effects of the Anti-Smoking Campaign."

101. M. T. O'Keefe, "The Anti-Smoking Commercials: A Study of Television's Impact on Behavior," *Public Opinion Quarterly* 35 (1971): 242-248.

102. P. W. Bradshaw, "The Problem of Cigarette Smoking and Its Control," *The International Journal of the Addictions* 8 (1973): 353-371.

103. Bradshaw, "The Problem of Cigarette Smoking," p. 359.

104. Bradshaw, "The Problem of Cigarette Smoking," p. 360.

105. P. Puska & L. Neittaammaki, "Health Professionals as Educators—Experiences From the North Karelia Project," in L. M. Ramstram (Ed.), *The Smoking Epidemic: A Matter of Worldwide Concern* (Stockholm: Almquist & Wiksell, 1980); T. Dwyer, J. Pierce, C. Hannam, N. Burke, & Quit for Life Steering Committee, "Evaluation of Sydney Quit for Life: Part 2. Changes of Smoking Prevalence," *Medical Journal of Australia* 144 (1986): 344-347.

106. McAlister et al., "Antismoking Campaigns," p. 295.

107. McAlister et al., "Antismoking Campaigns," p. 296.

108. U.S. DHHS, *Reducing the Health Consequences of Smoking.*

109. Warner, "The Effects of the Anti-Smoking Campaign," p. 33.

110. H. A. Coppotelli, *Spouse Support in Smoking Cessation by Women* (Unpublished doctoral dissertation, Department of Psychology, Duke University, 1983).

111. U.S. DHHS, *Reducing the Health Consequences of Smoking.*

112. U.S. DHHS, *Reducing the Health Consequences of Smoking*.

113. A. J. Moss, K. F. Allen, G. A. Gioviono, & S. L. Mills, "Recent Trends in Adolescent Smoking, Smoking-Uptake Correlates, and Expectations About the Future," *Advance Data: Vital Health Statistics of the Centers for Disease Control and Prevention/National Center for Health Statistics* 221 (December 1992): 1-28.

114. Moss et al., "Recent Trends in Adolescent Smoking."

115. U.S. DHHS, *Reducing the Health Consequences of Smoking*.

116. U.S. DHHS, *Reducing the Health Consequences of Smoking*.

117. E. R. Gritz, "Which Women Smoke and Why? Cigarette Smoking Is a Women's Issue," *Not Far Enough: Women vs. Smoking: A Workshop for Women's Group and Women's Health Leaders* NIH Publication No. 87-2949, U.S. DHHS, PHS, NIH (Washington, DC: Government Printing Office, 1987).

118. Moss et. al., "Recent Trends in Adolescent Smoking."

119. Sorensen & Pechacke, "Attitudes Toward Smoking Cessation."

120. E. R. Gritz, "Problems Related to the Use of Tobacco by Women," in *Alcohol and Drug Problems in Women: Research Advances in Alcohol and Drug Problems* Vol. 5 (New York: Plenum, 1980): 487-543.

121. For example, see J. P. Elder & R. A. Stern, "The ABCs of Adolescent Smoking Prevention: An Environment and Skills Model," *Health Education Quarterly* 13 (1986): 181-191.

122. M. Pfau, S. Van Bockern, & J. G. Kang, "Use of Inoculation to Promote Resistance to Smoking Initiation Among Adolescents," *Communication Monographs* 59 (1992): 213-230.

123. A. E. Foon, "Smoking Prevention Programs for Adolescents: The Allure of Social Psychological Approaches," *The International Journal of the Addictions* 21 (1986): 1017-1029.

124. Pfau et al., "Use of Inoculation."

125. W. J. McGuire, "Persistence of the Resistance to Persuasion Induced by Various Types of Prior Belief Defenses," *Journal of Abnormal and Social Psychology* 64 (1962): 241-248.

126. B. R. Flay, "Prosocial Approaches to Smoking Prevention: A Review of Findings," *Health Psychology* 4 (1985): 449-488.

127. Flay, "Prosocial Approaches to Smoking Prevention."

128. L. D. Gilchrist, S. P. Schinke, & P. Nurius, "Reducing Onset of Habitual Smoking Among Women," *Preventative Medicine* 18 (1989): 235-248.

129. Barton et al., "Social Image Factors as Motivators."

130. Gritz, "Cigarette Smoking by Adolescent Females"; K. Urbers & R. Robbins, "Perceived Vulnerability in Adolescents to the Health Consequences of Cigarette Smoking," *Preventative Medicine* 13 (1984): 367-376; Gilchrist et al., "Reducing Onset of Habitual Smoking Among Women."

131. Barton et al., "Social Image Factors as Motivators," p. 1499.

132. A. G. Brunswick & P. A. Messeri, "Gender Differences in the Process Leading to Cigarette Smoking," *Journal of Psychosocial Oncology* 2 (1984): 49-69; W. R. Mitic, D. P. McGuire, & B. Newmann, "Perceived Stress and Adolescents' Cigarette Use," *Psychological Reports* (1985): 1043-1048; Gritz, "Cigarette Smoking by Adolescent Females."

133. Gilchrist et al., "Reducing Onset of Habitual Smoking Among Women."

134. Gritz, "Which Women Smoke and Why?"

135. Gilchrist et al., "Reducing Onset of Habitual Smoking Among Women."

11

Tugging at Pregnant Consumers

Competing "Smoke!" "Don't Smoke!" Media Messages and Their Messengers

Deirdre M. Condit

Tobacco use is an ancient feature of human life. Native North American peoples were smoking tobacco at the time of Christopher Columbus's landing.[1] As an industry, tobacco production has historically been a vital source of income in many regions of the U.S. agricultural economy. Tobacco production remains an economic staple for 16 U.S. states, like North Carolina, which produced 40% of the nation's tobacco in 1989.[2] As a whole, the United States produces one sixth of the world's tobacco, or about one million tons annually.[3] In 1989 that equaled a total of $2.4 billion in U.S. agricultural revenues.[4] For much of the country's history, tobacco use, primarily smoking, has enjoyed an honored place in American culture.

AUTHOR'S NOTE: I would like to thank Elizabeth Martin for her help researching the newspaper indexes, and Celeste Michelle Condit for her help researching the ads for stop-smoking products.

154

Smoking initially entered modern U.S. culture as a man's pastime, a mark of masculinity and worldliness. Mark Twain's robust stogies are American cultural icons. The man's world of politics went hand in hand with the legendary "smoke-filled" rooms at the turn of the century. At the cinema, the dangling cigarette and curling smoke of Humphrey Bogart's characters like the gruff-faced Charlie Aulnut of the *African Queen,* or the suave, American Cafe proprietor, Rick, in *Casablanca,* came to represent America's romance with devil-may-care masculinity in the 1930s and 1940s. As television increasingly captured U.S. attention in the early 1950s, smoking by TV characters became the norm as well. With this romance, and supporting it, cigarette advertising reached its peak between the 1950s and 1960s.

Smoking was hacked almost without challenge across various media forums. Only the voices of pastors warning against smoking for religious reasons answered the pervasive "Smoke!" messages of the period. Tobacco companies were not worried about getting people to smoke—people were flocking to do that—they were worried about how to get them to switch brands. As one advertising executive commented, cigarette marketing in that era was "advertising in its purest sense—no product difference, but a perception of difference in the product."[5] Dancing cigarette boxes gaily trooped across televised tobacco advertisements, and country barn sides touted "exciting" new cigarette brands. The United States was blanketed by a "Smoke!" commercial ethos. The powerful effect of this marketing heyday was easily illustrated by significant increases in smoking rates among most segments of the population.

This smoking free-for-all was not to remain unchecked, however. The first reports linking smoking to lung cancer and other ailments began appearing in the early 1950s; and in 1964, the U.S. Surgeon General, Luther Terry, released his summary report about the connection between smoking and lung cancer.[6] These messages about cigarette smoking and other tobacco use came slowly to U.S. consciousness. The reports were few, not well distributed, and the tobacco interests worked hard to negate their public exposure. Nonetheless, like Pandora's box, the lid could not be slammed back to hide the growing evidence that smoking was bad for people's health.

Various governmental and health-related organizations began to confront the tobacco industry head-on in the late 1960s. Cigarette advertisements on television were banned by the FCC (Federal Communications Commission) in 1970, and the first warning label mandated by Congress appeared on a cigarette pack in 1966. Reaction by U.S. smokers was slow, but the rate of new smokers finally began to decline in the late 1960s and early 1970s, and the numbers of people trying and/or successfully kicking the habit began to rise.

This shift in attitude toward smoking has become evident throughout the culture. Watching cigarette smokers is no longer as alluring to moviegoers as it once was, for example. Many contemporary film buffs are well aware that Humphrey Bogart's dangling cigarettes contributed to his premature and horrid death from lung cancer.[7] Though film characters continue to smoke at a rate 3 times that of the real population, according to research done by the University of California at San Francisco, they now do so primarily to represent "bad" characters.[8] Thus, smoking has come to signify outlaws on the big screen.[9]

The number and ethos of smoking characters represented on television have similarly shifted. Today's television characters, like *L.A. Law's* Susan Bloom, now light up as
a sign that they are "obnoxious" or "rebellious," according to many TV producers.[10]
Networks that portray benevolent or positive characters who smoke are frequently
deluged with protest letters from angry viewers and health-oriented organizations.
Burt Reynolds's character, Wood Newton, on NBC's *Evening Shade,* gave up cigars
in response to such viewer ire.[11]

The consequence of this new "Don't Smoke!" response to the tobacco industries'
"Smoke!" communication efforts has been a drop in the numbers of U.S. smokers. The
media reported that by the late 1980s only slightly more than 25% of the total population continued to smoke.[12] According to a Gallup Poll, more than half of all adult
smokers report that they would like to quit smoking.[13] The American Cancer Society
reports that each year about 17 million people try to kick the habit for at least a day.[14]
The number of U.S. smokers continues to decline by between 1 and 1.5 million people
each year.[15]

Women as a Special Prize
in the Tobacco Tug-of-War and
the Rise of a Taboo on Pregnant Smokers

The history of America's early romance with tobacco initially left women out.
Smoking was a "man's" game until the late 1920s. World War II and the first wave of
the feminist movement brought a new independence to women that ushered in equality
of bad habits as well. For women, like the men of this era, smoking began to represent
a new independence and daring sexuality. Mary Astor's portrayal of independent
Sandra Novak in the 1941 film, *The Great Lie,* was starkly marked by her perpetual
draw on her cigarette and her shocking ability to toss back an evening brandy.[16]
Glamour was another characteristic that oozed from beneath the clouds of smoking
actresses: In 1961 Audrey Hepburn's snaky black cigarette holder was her trademark
as Holly Golightly in *Breakfast at Tiffany's.*[17]

Cigarette smoking among women became de rigueur as women television characters
modeled smoking as well. Lucille Ball, for example, whose weekly situation comedy
was sponsored chiefly by tobacco giant Philip Morris, smoked throughout *I Love
Lucy*—as did the stars of many television programs of the era.[18] This normalization
and perpetual exposure of smoking both contributed to and was fostered by the
prodigious marketing efforts of a then-burgeoning tobacco industry.

The rate of women's smoking climbed correspondingly over the period. Once the
tobacco industries realized the virtually untapped market potential for women smokers,
they focused serious attention on inviting women to pick up the habit. The media
messages went from a timid 1920s print ad that showed a man smoking and a woman
coyly beckoning him to "Blow some my way,"[19] to today's brazen Capri, Eve, and other
brands developed specifically to appeal to potential and confirmed women smokers.

The issue of women smoking while pregnant has had an even more peculiar history. Smoking while pregnant was not initially of concern for U.S. women. Film audiences in the 1930s, for example, failed to take issue with the cigarettes that dangled from Sandra Novak's pregnant hand throughout her role in *The Big Lie*. Public discomfort with the idea of women smoking while pregnant finally began to emerge in the early 1950s, however.

In 1952, for example, Lucille Ball's zany character, Lucy Ricardo, suddenly became a nonsmoker once she became "visibly" pregnant on her television series, *I Love Lucy*. The show had come under public attack for its brazen defiance of decency standards with its decision to include Lucy's real-life pregnant form. Executives at Philip Morris, the show's chief sponsor, feared further negative reactions from viewers if a pregnant Lucy continued to puff away.[20] The real-life Lucy smoked incessantly and continued to do so throughout her pregnancy. She had no reason to quit: Research documenting that smoking threatens developing fetuses was fairly sketchy at the time, and what research there was had not been strongly expressed to the public.

The tobacco industries, keeping a critical eye trained on potential threats to their business, had read the early scientific reports and knew what was coming. As a result, despite developing a sophisticated rhetoric of denial about the hazards of smoking, which the industry maintains yet today, not even the tobacco industry was willing to risk the appearance of openly promoting smoking during pregnancy. Justifying their hesitancy was the mounting evidence of the dangers smoking poses to pregnant women.[21]

These facts, combined with the emergence of the more general "Don't Smoke" messages noted earlier, have exerted a particularly strong influence on media representations of pregnant women who smoke. Just as it was once considered obscene to show pregnant women in the cinema and on television, it has now become, in some sense, almost taboo to present media images of pregnant smokers. That is not to say that images of women who smoke while pregnant are completely absent from both film and television, but most images of pregnant smokers have been confined either to historical representations of characters or to documentary-style pieces. In Donna Deitch's 1985 film, *Desert Hearts*, for example, the character Silver announces she is pregnant and smokes throughout the story, but she is not visibly pregnant and the film is set in 1959.

As the remainder of this chapter suggests, the late 1980s and early 1990s reveal a strong tug-of-war between the "Don't Smoke!" advocates and the "Smoke!" industries for the attention of U.S. women. Pregnant women have been carefully targeted by those attempting to communicate the dangers of smoking.

The Messengers and Their
Messages: What the Media Tell Us
About Women, Smoking, and Pregnancy

The opposing sides in this media tug-of-war for the attention of U.S. women have, what on the surface may be, different goals and thus differing strategies. "Don't

Smoke!" interests are concerned with both women who smoke and women who smoke while pregnant as related but distinct categories. Although they anticipate that pregnant women will be exposed to and attend to public messages about the dangers of smoking aimed at women generally, they have also developed programs intended specifically for pregnant smokers.

The tobacco industry, on the other hand, finds it politically impossible to make overt appeals to pregnant women as potential smokers; rather, their strategies aim at the women's market as a whole. This technique works because women spend most of their lives not pregnant. As smoking is physically addictive, most women find it difficult to quit smoking immediately before or during pregnancy. Thus, the industry simply needs to enlist nonpregnant women as smokers to have recruited pregnant ones.

These differing goals and strategies wind up being projected upon the same media playing field. The messages of both sides appear in printed mediums such as newspapers, magazines, and publicly distributed pamphlets and information guides. Both sides use public airwaves to transmit their differing messages. The cinema remains a major battlefield for the two. Both employ direct marketing strategies in public entertainment forums and the workplace. Cigarette advertisers often have bigger budgets to use paid communications media, whereas health campaigns are forced to rely on free commercial media sources.

The "Don't Smoke!" Messengers and Their Messages

On the "Don't Smoke!" side are both general sources of information about the hazards of smoking, like newspapers and news accounts, and materials generated to attempt specifically to communicate such messages. Although "Don't Smoke!" interest groups primarily focus on a more general campaign to encourage everyone to stop or never to start smoking, many have developed materials aimed specifically at pregnant smokers. Some organizations, like the March of Dimes, are chiefly concerned with pregnancy, and their literature is directly aimed at pregnant smokers.

The organizations mobilizing to broadcast antismoking messages include state and federal governmental bodies, health care providers, nonprofit health care organizations, and insurance companies.[22] Several national organizations such as the American Lung Association, the American Heart Association, and the American Cancer Society have taken a serious interest in pregnancy and smoking issues. These organizations work both separately and in a consortium to communicate their antismoking information. They formed an organization, the Coalition On Smoking OR Health (ConSORH), to address lobbying issues in Congress and disseminate their antismoking materials through their state-level affiliates. ConSORH, with another Washington, D.C.-based consortium, ASH (Action on Smoking & Health), were instrumental in defeating a tobacco industry attempt to market a new "smokeless" cigarette in the 1980s.[23]

In conducting the research for this project, messages provided in the "Don't Smoke!" communication environment were found to be fourfold: (a) Smoking is dangerous; (b)

Figure 11.1.

Figure 11.2.

Don't start smoking; (c) Quit if you do smoke; (d) Here's how to quit. These messages are recrafted to apply to pregnant women: (a) Smoking endangers your developing baby;[24] (b) If you are going to get pregnant and don't smoke, don't start; (c) If you do smoke and are going to get pregnant, quit now!; (d) If you are pregnant and smoking, quit now! Four of the various media venues available for communicating these messages were examined for this chapter.

Warning Labels

The first and probably most highly exposed source for the "Smoking Is Dangerous" message is the warning label required on packs of cigarettes and on printed advertisements for cigarettes. The first cigarette warning label, mandated nearly 30 years ago, read "Warning: The Surgeon General Has Determined That Cigarette Smoking Is Dangerous To Your Health." Today, the warning label has been reconfigured into four warnings statements that are to be rotated every 3 months. They read,

> *Quitting Smoking Now Greatly Reduces Serious Risks to Your Health*
> *Cigarette Smoke Contains Carbon Monoxide*
> *Smoking Causes Lung Cancer, Heart Disease, Emphysema and May Complicate Pregnancy*
> *Smoking by Pregnant Women May Result in Fetal Injury, Premature Birth and Low Birth Weight*

Research for this chapter found that over a 15-month period the cigarette warning labels appearing in cigarette advertisements in three magazines, *Cosmopolitan, Ebony,* and *Redbook,* showed some interesting differences in how the new warning labels were displayed. The first finding was that the two labels that specifically mention pregnancy appeared in 61% of all of the ads. This means that pregnant smokers have a greater chance of seeing a label that pertains particularly to their condition. In addition, pregnancy-specific warnings appeared with the image of at least one woman 60% of the time. If women attend more readily to ads portraying women's images, this may increase exposure to warning labels about smoking and pregnancy.

Besides cigarette ads that featured women-only in them, advertisements in both *Ebony* and *Cosmopolitan* had a high percentage of pictures of single-race couples matched with pregnancy-related warning labels as well. These ads suggest heterosexual coupling and dating. The linkage of heterosexual sex (and thus the issue of pregnancy) and smoking makes exposure to the pregnancy-related labels worth noting. Finally, it is intriguing that although the numbers of ads with men-only in them were very small, the number of ads with men-only and the pregnancy labels occurring at the same time was *extremely* low.

This suggests that the 3-month label rotation mandated by FCC regulations is not being met, or it is being strategically deployed. In both *Redbook* and *Cosmopolitan,* for example, the first label was seldom used, occurring 8% of the time in *Redbook* and never occurring in *Cosmopolitan.* On the other hand, it appeared most in *Ebony,* or

32% of the time. Consequently, the ads are warning women about the dangers of smoking to pregnancy more often than about other problems with smoking.

Finally, it should be noted that these warning labels are required on *all* tobacco and cigarette advertisements of any form. Thus, billboard advertisements for cigarettes— the most frequently advertised product on U.S. billboards—are required to have warning labels as well.[25] No systematic examination of billboards was done for this chapter. An unsystematic and random examination of several billboards, however, revealed that regardless of which label was used, the information is presented in labels that are generally small, poorly placed, and—depending upon the location of the billboard (e.g., alongside a busy highway)—practically useless. The "positive" message about the cigarette simply overwhelms the danger warning.

The Print Media:
Newspapers and Popular Magazines

The second primary source for the "Smoking Is Dangerous" part of the "Don't Smoke!" communication, U.S. daily newspapers, was less encouraging. For the most part, smoking and pregnancy is not a topic for newspaper coverage. Stories about smoking and pregnancy that do hit the news are predominantly generated by new research about the harms of smoking to developing fetuses.

According to a search of *ProQuest,* a computerized index of nine major American newspapers, only 34 articles were published on the topic of cigarette smoking and pregnancy from January 1985 through May 1993. Of these, 24 discussed newly released research and 10 addressed other issues such as the rates of smoking and pregnancy among teens or efforts to prosecute pregnant smokers for so-called fetal abuse. Few of the articles made the front page, and most were either in the "Women's" section or in a section about health. A second search of two other newspaper indexes, *GALIN* (1988-1992) and *Newsbank* (1985-1993) showed similar results.

Two indexes to magazine articles, *ProQuest* and *The Readers' Guide,* were examined for titles of articles about smoking and pregnancy. The *ProQuest* search found only 48 articles that included both smoking and pregnancy in their titles. Of these, 83% were in professional or semi-professional health care journals such as the *American Journal of Medicine* and *Public Health,* whereas *only 8* articles were in more popular magazines such as *Glamour* or *Family Circle.* Five of these popular magazine articles were published before December 1988. Over the most recent 4-year period, relevant articles were found almost exclusively in the professional journals. The *Readers' Guide* search was very similar.

A close look at five popular monthly magazines, *Cosmopolitan, Redbook, Seventeen, Ebony,* and *Parents,* revealed the same paucity of discussion about pregnancy and smoking. A survey of the table of contents and a close scan of regular features on health and/or women's bodies in each issue from November 1991 through February 1993 located few articles or even editorial comments concerning women and smoking or smoking and pregnancy. This was true although all of the magazines regularly featured discussions of women's sexual activity, and two of the magazines routinely featured discussions about both pregnancy or parenting. In a total of 80 issues, there were *no* complete articles specifically about smoking and pregnancy, and the number of articles that even referred to smoking and pregnancy was small. Nor were there many articles about tobacco use and women in general. The messages of the few references made about smoking and pregnancy were either: (a) research reconfirms that smoking endangers pregnancy, or (b) everyone knows smoking during pregnancy is a bad idea, so pregnant women should not do it.

Parents and *Redbook* included the subject of pregnancy and smoking in articles about other topics. In *Parents,* there were three such articles and in *Redbook,* six issues mentioned the hazards of smoking, three of which briefly linked the dangers of smoking and pregnancy. One *Redbook* article written by the March of Dimes, titled, "Having Healthy Babies," covered the topic of smoking while pregnant by noting only that, "By eliminating smoking, you reduce the chance of giving birth prematurely to a low birth weight baby."[26] *Seventeen* magazine addressed the dangers of smoking and pregnancy separately in a June 1992 article called, "Sex, Drugs, and Smoking: Why They're Worse for Women,"[27] but no link was made between the two to suggest that smoking and pregnancy might be of particular concern to young women. Finally, there were no articles about women smoking, or smoking and pregnancy in any of the issues of either *Cosmopolitan* or *Ebony*. Both magazines sported monthly sections on "health."

Smoking researcher Larry White attributes the strikingly low media coverage of the dangers of cigarette smoking he found in his research to two factors: first is the strong influence cigarette advertisements play in magazine budgets; second is a general cultural assumption that smoking is old news and that "there is a general impression that smoking is bad for you."[28] This may be true for coverage of issues of smoking and pregnancy as well. White notes an inverse relationship between the amount of cigarette advertising per issue and the amount of smoking coverage per magazine.[29] This relationship held for *Cosmopolitan* and *Ebony,* which had high numbers per issue of advertisements and no coverage of smoking and pregnancy. The results were less conclusive with *Redbook,* however, which had moderate numbers of each. In the cases of *Seventeen* and *Parents,* periodicals without cigarette ads, there was no marked increase in the number of articles about smoking and pregnancy.

In addition to articles about smoking and pregnancy, advertisements for products such as Habitrol and Nicoderm, which are intended to help smokers quit, were counted as well. Within this sample of women's magazines, advertisements for these new products appeared only in *Ebony* magazine and only in the most recent issues. Three of the four advertisements had images of an African American man in them, and one portrayed an African American woman; no ads had white women or men in them.

Time magazine advertisements for stop-smoking products were also examined. Over the period September 7, 1992 through March 1, 1993, there were 17 ads for either Nicoderm or Habitrol in the 21 issues examined. Of those, 11 (65%) had a picture of a woman in them; 7 were of white women and 4 were of black women. White men appeared in 6 of the ads and African American men appeared in none of the ads. That the target audience for *Time* is different from *Ebony* was readily apparent in the differences in advertisements.

Ebony was also unique in that there were two issues that had an advertisement from cigarette manufacturer Philip Morris proclaiming that the cigarette company is opposed to kids smoking. The ad had photographs of two young women, one white and one African American, on either side of a young, Hispanic man. The advertisement promotes a booklet intended for parents who want to help their children avoid peer pressure to smoke. Given that 90% of the tobacco industries' next customers are children and teenagers routinely exposed to the hard sell of tobacco advertising, the focus on peer pressure as the cause of teen smoking may be a displacement of the problem.[30] The Tobacco Institute, a consortium of cigarette manufacturing interests, has sponsored a similar ad campaign noted in spring 1993 issues of *Time* magazine.

The conclusion drawn from this study of 16 months' worth of five major women's magazines and two periodical index searches is that there is relatively little transmission of the "Don't Smoke!" message through the popular print media. The fact that there were so few magazines that addressed smoking and women was startling; that there were even fewer articles about smoking and pregnancy was even more disconcerting.

The Broadcast Media:
Television and Radio

Exposure to the "Don't Smoke!" messages over the airwaves is not dependent on the newsworthiness of the topic for the broadcast mediums, but rather comes as a consequence of public interests that have set about buying time to get their messages out. According to a report on state activities aimed at decreasing smoking, by 1985 the average state was spending about $70,000 per year on antismoking efforts, and 22 state health departments were in the TV and radio antismoking campaign business. They were either producing their own spots or contracting with antismoking groups such as the National Cancer Institute to produce "Don't Smoke!" spots for broadcast.[31] The State of California, for example, initiated an ambitious $28 million antismoking television advertising campaign and began crafting its own commercials for airing during the mid-1990s.[32] Future ads may look like a recently aired television ad sponsored by the New York ConSORH; their ad portrayed a late-teens to early twenties young white woman contemplating inhaling a cigarette, with a voice-over asking, "You want to put what, where?"

The problem with public service announcements (PSAs) is that without regulations about when these spots must be aired, the networks routinely push them back into the late-night hours, thus decreasing the likelihood that they will be seen by consumers. Trying to combat this, the State of California antismoking campaign bought expensive airtime to ensure that their spots will be broadcast during such prime-time television shows as *The Simpsons* and *In Living Color.* The spots target "teenagers, young women and immigrants," using the same kinds of slick ads employed so successfully in campaigns by the tobacco industry.[33]

This kind of direct advertising attack on smoking meets with mixed reactions from the networks. Many ads first drafted for the California campaign were rejected by network affiliates as "unfair" in their representations of smoking.[34] When the topic is pregnancy and smoking, the networks can be even more reluctant to take such challenges to the air. A 1985 American Cancer Society television commercial showing the image of a fetus smoking a cigarette while a woman narrator's voice said, "Would you give a cigarette to your unborn child? You do, every time you smoke when you're pregnant," was rejected for airing by CBS and NBC, who argued that the images were "too graphic" for airing. ABC decided to run the ad, noting that cancer was more disgusting than the image of the fetus.[35] As cigarette companies diversify holdings into other products, including investments in broadcast networks, resistance to advertising that condemns cigarette smoking may increase even more.[36]

Direct Market Materials: Educational Literature

The last information source examined for this chapter was the "Don't Smoke!" written material available in physicians' offices and through direct requests from sponsoring organizations such as the American Lung Association, the American Cancer Society, and the American Heart Association. There is an interesting array of materials that specifically address smoking and pregnancy available through this media source. The "Don't Smoke!" messages are perhaps the most well rounded of any of the media forum examined: They educate, inform, persuade, and provide help for consumers convinced that they should quit. Health-related organizations are concerned that the "Smoking Is Dangerous to You and Your Baby" message be clearly made. In addition, they recognize that many women are smokers when they become pregnant. There is a strong emphasis in this literature on methods designed to encourage and to help expectant smokers to quit. A great deal of information is presented about the harmful effects of smoking. Less information is provided about how to attain that goal.

The dangers of smoking to pregnancy are routinely included in the more general informational pamphlets and booklets distributed by nonprofit organizations. These organizations send complete packets of information about smoking and smoking and pregnancy for distribution to doctors' offices, Planned Parenthood facilities, work facilities, schools, and events like public health fairs. The pamphlets and posters provide contact numbers for consumers seeking help *and* hands-on materials about smoking cessation programs. Most of the materials collected for this project focused on women and smoking generally, though most of them included information about smoking and pregnancy, and some literature specifically addressed smoking and pregnancy.

One pamphlet located in this search was a five-fold piece of literature called, "facts about . . . Smoking and Pregnancy," distributed by the American Lung Association. Its question-and-answer format provided simple, straightforward information in an easily readable format. It covered questions about the dangers of smoking to both the pregnant smoker and her fetus, and it addressed secondhand smoke's effects; it also suggested methods to quit smoking and recommended many resources to help the pregnant smoker.

An American Lung Association pamphlet, titled "Facts About Cigarette Smoking," had a section on women's health that noted, *"Pregnant women who smoke have higher rates of miscarriage, stillbirth, premature birth, and complications of pregnancy. More of their babies die soon after birth from crib death than the newborns of nonsmoking mothers."* A 1987 American Cancer Society pamphlet titled, "Quit Smoking, the lives you save could be theirs," begins with the message, *"It's true! First of all, if a woman smokes while she's pregnant, her baby may be born with low birth weight, birth defects, chronic breathing difficulties and learning disabilities."* Both are easy to understand and a cartoon illustration on the front of the second pamphlet adds humor to its message, making it more accessible for some readers, particularly adolescent girls.

For pinup purposes, the American Heart Association distributes posters like one that reads, "'Give me one good reason to stop smoking.' 'Your baby.'" over a large photograph of a very pregnant Hispanic woman. Seated in a doctor's office, she smokes a cigarette and stares humorlessly into the camera. In the background are two robustly pregnant women, one white and one African American. The message is simple, direct, and clear. As there are no reasons given on the poster for quitting smoking other than "Your baby," however, it might not be clear to a pregnant smoker why that is a sufficient reason for stopping. For this kind of poster, the location of its posting is probably important to how the message is received by pregnant smokers. Someone who is receiving prenatal care would perhaps be encouraged to ask her health professional about the poster.

A poster by the American Heart Association uses a similar theme: This one is captioned, "Some Kinds of Child Abuse Start Early." A silhouetted profile of a pregnant white woman as she stands smoking a cigarette also targets the pregnant smoker directly. This poster has a bottom caption with more in-depth information about the effects of smoking on pregnancy. The small print text reads, *"With each puff, your baby absorbs growth-retarding doses of nicotine, carbon monoxide, benzopyrene, ammonia and hydrogen cyanide. The results could be hard to live with. Quit smoking now."* The bold and dominant face of the main message about smoking as child abuse is meant to be simple and direct. The focus on child abuse, however, may make the poster's message confusing if one is not cued to the act of abuse being the cigarette in the woman's hand. In addition, the language of the bottom script is complex, scientific, and not particularly enlightening for the average reader. It is unclear why absorption of those chemicals (if one knows they are chemicals) "could be hard to live with" and thus, perhaps, the poster loses some of its punch.[37]

Complete packets for quitting smoking, some intended for health care professionals, others intended for pregnant smokers, are also distributed by many organizations. A 1986 American Lung Association packet, called "Freedom From Smoking for You and Your Baby," presents a "10-Day Quitting Smoking Program for Pregnant Women." The packet is appealingly crafted with a pink cover that again shows a smiling, very pregnant young white woman looking down at her hands as they rest on her voluminous

Figure 11.3.

Figure 11.4.

SOURCE: Reproduced with permission. "Some Kinds of Child Abuse Start Early," PSA, 1987. Copyright © American Heart Association.

Figure 11.5.

stomach. The entire packet is designed to appeal to a wide audience: of the 39 photographs of people in the booklet, 23 depict white women in their late twenties to mid-thirties, either alone (18 pictures) or with a white male (3 pictures) or with a white infant (2 pictures). Fifteen of the 39 photographs depict an African American woman, either alone (12) or with an African American man (2) or with an African American infant (1).

The packet itself is very informative but also very complicated. It requires a lot from anyone who decides to use it. Users must be able to read fairly well, to follow instructions, and to be very self-motivated. The program asks users to fill out daily charts, diaries, and progress notes on themselves, following a strong medical or scientific model. The language is technical and the method is rigorous and systematized. One gets the sense that it is targeted at a middle-class audience. Whether it would work for less educated and less self-motivated women is unclear.

A similar type of kit is provided to physicians by the American Lung Association. Although it is not a stop-smoking program, per se, it gives health care providers visual aids and hands-on tools to use with patients to teach them about the dangers of smoking and pregnancy. Unlike the packet above, the illustrations, language, and directions are simple and clear. Research on smoking cessation programs for pregnant women reveals that working with a health care provider increases the likelihood that a pregnant smoker will quit smoking during her pregnancy.[38] Packets such as this could play an important role in helping pregnant smokers kick the habit.

The workplace has also become an important site for helping people to stop smoking. The American Cancer Society has created a program for employers to use with their employees. Their booklet, called "A Decision Maker's Guide to Reducing Smoking at the Worksite," outlines the benefits employers experience from helping their employees to become nonsmokers. It also evaluates types of smoking cessation programs, to enable companies to choose the program most suitable for their worksite.

Thus, the "Don't Smoke!" messages communicated by the media are diverse and widely disseminated. As has been suggested, these messages are having a strong effect upon U.S. perception of smoking. More Americans are quitting than ever before. But the problem is a glass-half-full-or-half-empty one in nature. Many are not picking up the habit, or are giving it up, but nearly a quarter of Americans continue to smoke and to relapse after attempting to quit. This is due largely to the continuing success of the "Smoke!" media messages of the tobacco industries. Caught in the middle are the scores of pregnant women who are urged to light up.

The "Smoke!" Messengers and Their Messages

Cigarette companies have been looking for ways to reclaim access to the broadcast mediums since the ban on televised commercials. Consequently, they have found backdoor ways to press their influence on the television and film industries. Philip Morris owns Miller Brewing Company and Kraft Foods, for example, and RJR Nabisco Holdings has ownership of Nabisco products. In 1991, according to a January 26, 1993, article in the *Wall Street Journal,* Philip Morris spent $1.1 billion on all types of ads and RJR Nabisco spent $285 million.[39] These investments give the parent cigarette companies significant clout when networks contemplate running antismoking advertisements. They also provide a venue for infusing cigarettes into plots and characters during regular television programming.

In addition, cigarette manufacturers ensure that their products and logos appear at the cinema through these indirect marketing techniques. Movies like *Lethal Weapon II, Thelma & Louise,* and *The Last Boy Scout* all featured renegade main characters as smokers. Cigarettes and their logos often appear in films that one would not predict, given the tobacco industries' insistence that they "don't want adolescents and children to smoke." Walt Disney's *Who Framed Roger Rabbit?* and *Honey, I Shrunk the Kids* both feature Camels, for example.

Finally, the tobacco industries have become big sponsors of public entertainment and sporting events. They regularly fund national tennis, golf, and automobile racing events, among many others. The incentive for funding such events is twofold: first, sponsors enjoy wide exposure for their products when television cameras pan across playing fields and arenas. Second, sports are associated with fun, health, and good old-fashioned competition. By associating sports with cigarettes, tobacco companies can override the "Smoking Is Dangerous" messages.

Exposure to the "Smoke!" media messages put out by the tobacco lobbies is important to women as a general class and to pregnant women specifically. The tobacco companies' marketing strategies aimed at women are chameleon-like, changing rapidly to stay abreast of new cultural attitudes about women, allowing the companies to find ways to incorporate smoking into each new female image. The second wave of the feminist movement, originating in the 1960s and 1970s, encouraged women to be independent, to rebel against an oppressive culture that patronized them, and to take control over their own lives. The working woman has become an important feminist icon since the early 1970s, and the sexual revolution of the 1960s has been alleged to have given a new sense of sexual self-possession and confidence to contemporary women. The cigarette companies have been adept at turning those feminist messages to their own advantage. The longtime running theme of Virginia Slims brand cigarettes—"You've come a long way, baby!"—evokes images of women's liberation and independence. Cigarette brands like Eve and Ritz, in softly colored packages, are intended to appeal to a new, more independent but still "feminine" American woman.

To get a sense of what is out there targeted at women today, six popular monthly magazines, *Ebony, Redbook, Parents, Time, Seventeen,* and *Cosmopolitan,* were surveyed to discover the numbers and kinds of cigarette advertisements being targeted to various audiences. The findings show that magazines that include cigarette advertising are pitched specifically to audiences based on their racial identity and age.

The first issue examined was the prevalence of cigarette ads in these popular magazines. Three magazines had several ads in each issue: *Cosmopolitan* averaged five per issue; *Ebony* averaged three per issue; and *Redbook* averaged slightly more than three ads per issue. No cigarette ads appeared in *Seventeen* or *Parents.* An analysis of the gender and race compositions of the ads confirms that each magazine plays to a distinct audience. *Ebony,* for example, appealed to African American women predominantly, with 54% of the cigarette ads showing a single African American woman in them. The second most common image was of an African American couple together in the ads (26%). Sixteen percent of the ads had no person depicted in them, and single African American men appeared in only 4% of the pictures. *Cosmopolitan* featured no persons most often (34%), single white women appeared 26% of the time, and white men 16% of the time. African American faces of either sex were less than 2% of images counted. *Redbook* ads were split between those with no person and with images of single white women, with 48% and 43%, respectively. No African Americans were portrayed in *Redbook* ads. There were almost no mixed-race ads in any of the magazines.

Sex segregation in audience targeting by cigarette advertisers was equally evident. For all of the magazine advertisements, images of at least one woman occurred in roughly 60% of the ads, with women-only occurring 45% of the time. Pictures with at least one man occurred in nearly 22% of the ads, but men-only ads were only 7.5% of the totals. The remaining ads featured no human images. These results indicate that the market for ads in these three magazines, regardless of race, is women.

Messages about race and gender were combined with a general appeal to young women (predominantly) and men. No middle-aged or older people were depicted, and most models looked to be in their very early twenties. The fact that there were few older men and women and so many young ones suggests that the tobacco companies know the demographics of smoking very well: Young people are more likely to start smoking; older people are more likely to quit.

The captions of the ads communicated important messages to readers, as well. Most cigarette advertisements with images of women in them played on the kinds of feminist themes noted earlier. Capri brand cigarettes is fond of ads featuring one word captions such as, "Brilliant!"; "Fresh!"; "Success!"; "Contemporary!"; "Pleasure!"; "Sporty!"; "Flair!"; and "Sleek!" Capri ads in *Ebony* had themes about cost, such as "Economical!" These adjectives communicate that smokers of this brand are 1990s liberated women, in charge of their lives, bodies, and minds.

Not surprisingly, there were no direct appeals to pregnant women to smoke in any of the materials examined, though as was pointed out earlier, there does not need to be in order for there to be a high population of pregnant smokers.

Conclusions: Who Is Winning the Tug-of-War?

The rates for most groups of smokers are on the decline: That seems to suggest that the "Don't Smoke!" messages are winning the tug-of-war for U.S. consumers. A close examination of the groups where smoking is either on the increase or has yet to begin to decline is less reassuring, however. The rates for young women taking up smoking, for example, exceed those of young men in some age brackets. For women overall, the rate of decline of smoking continues to lag behind that of men.

Given the research findings for this project, it can be inferred that the target audiences of young, poorly educated women may not be getting the "Don't Smoke!" messages needed for them to quit. They may have poor access to prenatal care, a key factor in quitting smoking while pregnant, and they many not see themselves represented in the traditional "Don't Smoke!" media messages. Getting those messages may be key to their ability to quit smoking. As noted in the previous chapter, research confirms that women who learn about the dangers of smoking to their pregnancies are more likely to stop smoking during their pregnancy than women who are unaware of the threat posed by cigarette smoke.

On the other hand, the careful marketing by the tobacco industries seems very likely to be reaching those audiences. The long love affair Americans have shared with smoking is gradually dissipating, but some of it still lingers. A touch of the glamour and allure, once the clear mark of smoking, clings yet to the U.S. consciousness. It manifests itself in ways quite likely to reach America's most vulnerable potential pregnant smokers. A Guess jeans ad, for example, sports model Anna Smith smoking a cigarette as she models their jeans. Likewise, Bijan perfume has an ad campaign featuring a woman smoking a cigar. Sneaking tobacco use back into the general culture this way may have a strong influence on consumers most vulnerable to smoking advertisement: young women. Many ads for products like Guess jeans are specifically targeted toward young women. As noted, smoking among young women is on the rise and rates of smoking among young pregnant women are the highest of any age group.

Despite the efforts of the tobacco industry to the contrary, there is a new "smoking is not cool" ethos beginning to develop among young people. A recent study by the National Health Institute on Drug Abuse showed that "teenagers prefer to date a nonsmoker and strongly dislike being around people who smoke." When that feeling begins to be reflected by a real decline in the numbers of young women smokers, and thus young pregnant smokers, then we will know that the "Don't Smoke!" messages have won the media tug-of-war.

Notes

1. "Tobacco," *The Americana Encyclopedia, International Edition* 26 (Danbury, CT: Grolier, 1991): 800.

2. "North Carolina's Maternal Health Campaign Ignores Smoking, Maternal Health Advocates Fume," *Journal of the American Medical Association* 266 (1991): 3399.

3. "Tobacco," p. 802.

4. "State Tobacco Prevention, Control Activities: Results of 1989-1990 Association of State, Territorial Health Officials Survey—Final Report," *Journal of the American Medical Association* 266 (1991): 3105-3106.

5. L. C. White, *Merchants of Death* (New York: Beech Tree Books, 1988): 117.

6. White, *Merchants of Death,* p. 25.

7. White, *Merchants of Death,* p. 15.

8. M. Cimons, "More Smokers in Movies Than in Reality, Study Says," *Los Angeles Times,* November 12, 1992, p. A14.

9. D. S. Seibel, "Smoke Signals in a New Light," *Los Angeles Times,* January 4, 1992, p. F1.

10. Seibel, "Smoke Signals," p. F1.

11. R. Du Brow, " 'Dateline': Will It Crash and Burn?" *Los Angeles Times,* February 16, 1993, p. F1.

12. B. Horovitz, "Smoking in Ads Now Is Smoldering Issue," *Los Angeles Times,* October 20, 1992, p. D6.

13. American Cancer Society, *Cancer Facts and Figures* (Atlanta, GA: Author, 1993).

14. American Cancer Society, *The Most Often Asked Questions About Smoking, Tobacco, and Health, and the Answers* (Atlanta, GA: Author, 1992).

15. J. R. DiFranza, J. W. Richards, Jr., P. M. Paulman, Nancy Wolf-Gillespie, C. Fletcher, R. D. Jaffe, & D. Murray, "RJR Nabisco's Cartoon Camel Promotes Camel Cigarettes to Children," *Journal of the American Medical Association* 266 (1991): 3149; see also, *Facts About Cigarette Smoking* (American Lung Association, 1990).

16. "Prenatal Nightmare," *New York Times,* April 13, 1990, p. A1.

17. Seibel, "Smoke Signals," p. F11.

18. C. Higham, *Lucy: The Life of Lucille Ball* (New York: St. Martin's, 1986): 132.

19. White, *Merchants of Death,* p. 125.

20. Higham, *Lucy,* p. 134.

21. M. Saltus, "Smoke Tied to Child Behavioral Ills," *Boston Globe,* September 4, 1992, p. D12; American Cancer Society, *The Most Often Asked Questions;* D. Shaman, *It Might Have Been a Beautiful Baby* (American Lung Association Bulletin, 1982).

22. The federal and state governments' involvement in the antismoking agenda is striking. It must be cautioned, however, that the federal government and several state governments are also actively involved in price supports for tobacco farmers and provide tax incentives for cigarette manufacturers to encourage them to remain in business. Direct communication to consumers by the government is overwhelmingly antismoking. The pro-smoking lobbying goes on in less public forums, such as the smoke-filled rooms of Congress; an irony that should not be overlooked. See White, *Merchants of Death,* pp. 51-59, and A. L. Fritschler, *Smoking and Politics* (Englewood Cliffs, NJ: Prentice Hall, 1989).

23. See C. M. Condit & D. M. Condit, "Smoking OR Health: Incremental Erosion as a Public Interest Group Strategy," in E. L. Toth & R. L. Heath (Eds.), *Rhetorical and Critical Approaches to Public Relations* (Hillsdale, NJ: Lawrence Erlbaum, 1992): 241-256.

24. When directed at general consumers, most of the language used in the "Don't Smoke!" messages to pregnant women uses the word *baby* for fetus. Use of the word *baby* is an attempt to communicate more directly. Not everyone would agree that the words *fetus* and *baby* are interchangeable. In communication aimed at health care professionals, the word used most often is *fetus.*

25. White, *Merchants of Death,* p. 120.

26. "Having Healthy Babies," *Redbook* (April 1992): 132-142.

27. "Sex, Drugs, and Smoking: Why They're Worse for Women," *Seventeen* (June 1992): 84-85.

28. White, *Merchants of Death,* p. 133.

29. White, *Merchants of Death,* pp. 137-139.

30. DiFranza et al., "RJR Nabisco's Cartoon Camel," p. 3149.

31. "State Tobacco Prevention," pp. 3105-3106.

32. E. Shapiro, "California Plans More Antismoking Ads," *Wall Street Journal,* January 26, 1993, p. B8.

33. Shapiro, "California Plans," p. B8.

34. Shapiro, "California Plans," p. B8.

35. F. Rothenberg, "2 Networks Reject Antismoking Spot," *Boston Globe,* January 18, 1985, p. 3.

36. Shapiro, "California Plans," p. B8.

37. There is another concern ancillary to this chapter generated by this poster. Women increasingly are under legal and political attack for so-called fetal abuse or fetal neglect during pregnancy. The implications of this new attack on women's body autonomy are serious and worth consideration, but are outside the scope of this work.

38. See for example, P. D. Mullen, V. P. Gunn, & D. H. Ershoff, "Maintenance of Nonsmoking Postpartum by Women Who Stopped Smoking During Pregnancy," *American Journal of Public Health* 70 (August 1990): 992-992; or D. H. Ershoff, P. D. Mullen, & V. P. Gunn, "A Randomized Trial of a Serialized Self-Help Smoking Cessation Program for Pregnant Women in an HMO," *American Journal of Public Health* 79 (February 1989): 182-186.

39. Shapiro, "California Plans," p. B8.

12

Prenatal Alcohol Consumption and Outcomes for Children

A Review of the Literature

Joan Marie Kraft

Public health messages routinely warn pregnant women that drinking alcoholic beverages during pregnancy could have severe consequences for children-to-be. This chapter considers the medical research evidence upon which these warnings are based. Although evidence from animal studies is considered, much of the discussion below rests on evidence from human studies, as this provides more meaningful estimates of the effect of the timing and the amount of alcohol consumption on outcomes for children.

The Most Severe Outcomes: Fetal Death and Fetal Alcohol Syndrome

There is broad consensus among researchers and doctors that a range of possible outcomes is associated with prenatal alcohol consumption, and that the most severe outcomes are associated with heavy drinking during pregnancy. In some respects, the most daunting outcome associated with prenatal alcohol exposure is the potential for fetal death. Several studies point to an association between alcohol consumption during pregnancy and the likelihood of miscarriage. Although relatively few women have detectable miscarriages, a study of pregnant women in California found that women who consumed at least one to two drinks a day during pregnancy were more likely than either women who drank less than that or women who abstained from drinking during pregnancy to have miscarried. Further, the risk of miscarriage was higher for the heaviest-drinking women in the sample (defined as 3 or more drinks a day) than it was for moderate drinkers (1 to 2 drinks a day).[1] Some studies, however, suggest that women who have as few as two drinks per week are more likely than women who abstain from drinking to miscarry.[2] Although prenatal alcohol consumption appears to increase the risk of miscarriage, little evidence suggests that drinking during pregnancy causes stillbirths.[3] Still, one important message to convey to pregnant women is that daily alcohol use increases the risk of miscarriage.

For children carried to term, prenatal alcohol consumption might have a number of negative consequences. Those outcomes can be organized along a continuum. At one end of the continuum are children who experience no ill effects as a result of their mothers' alcohol consumption during pregnancy. Somewhere in the middle are children who suffer a few consequences that are mild in severity. Finally, at the other end are children who experience a number of consequences that are moderate to highly severe. Where a child falls on this continuum is most likely a function of how much alcohol its mother drank during pregnancy and when during pregnancy she drank. Children whose mothers were "heavy drinkers" (i.e., defined as 4 or more drinks a day) are more apt to suffer a number of severe consequences. Researchers and clinicians use the term *fetal alcohol syndrome* (FAS) to refer to these outcomes. Conversely, children of women who drank lightly or moderately should experience fewer, less severe consequences (although there is much variation within this category). Researchers and clinicians use the term *possible fetal alcohol syndrome* or *fetal alcohol effects* (FAE) to refer to these outcomes. (To avoid confusion with FAS, this chapter will use FAE to refer to the less severe outcomes).

Studies of children born to alcoholic parents in France[4] and to alcoholic women in the United States[5] identified two sets of physical and one set of behavioral characteristics that set the children in their studies apart from "normal" children. The two sets of physical characteristics are growth deficiencies and facial dysmorphology (i.e., distinctive facial features or abnormalities). Central nervous system (CNS) functioning is implicated in the behavioral characteristics of FAS.

The U.S. study, by Jones and Smith, used a sample of 11 children born to alcoholic women who drank heavily during pregnancy. Jones and Smith coined the term *fetal alcohol syndrome* to describe the complex of physical and behavioral problems observed. Since their findings were published, a number of researchers have studied the 11 children, as well as other children born to women who drank heavily during pregnancy, in order to provide more details about the characteristics of FAS.

CHARACTERISTICS OF FETAL ALCOHOL SYNDROME: CHILDREN BORN TO WOMEN CLASSIFIED AS "HEAVY DRINKERS"

The first set of physical markers that characterize FAS patients are pre- and post-natal growth retardation in weight, length, and head circumference. At birth, babies diagnosed with FAS are typically in the lowest 3% for height, weight, and head circumference (i.e., 97% of infants are longer, weigh more, and have a larger head circumference than infants with FAS).[6] Most evidence suggests that the growth of FAS children lags behind that of "normal" children, and that more than 80% of FAS children are still in the lowest 3% for height and weight.[7] In addition to being small for their age, many FAS children have disproportionately diminished adipose tissue and thus tend to look small and skinny.[8] A follow-up study of the 11 children studied by Jones and Smith, however, suggests that during puberty the girls gained more weight and started to look "stocky" or "chubby."[9] These findings should be replicated in larger samples before being viewed as conclusive.

The second set of physical markers of FAS is notable physical malformations. The most often noted malformations occur in the face (i.e., facial dysmorphology). FAS children commonly have a low nasal bridge; a short or small nose; an indistinct or missing philtrum (the ridge between the nose and mouth); a thin upper lip; short eye slits on widely spaced eyes; and a flat maxillary area (the area under the eyes). In addition to producing unique facial features, heavy prenatal alcohol consumption might produce one or more of the following: (a) joint anomalies; (b) heart defects; (c) congenital eye defects; (d) altered palmar crease patterns (creases in the palm of the hand); (e) minor genital anomalies; and/or (f) malformation of the external ear.[10] A study of the 11 U.S. children with FAS suggests that some of the facial features might not be permanent. During puberty, growth of the nose and chin altered the appearance of several of the adolescents.[11]

The behavioral markers of FAS probably stem from functional deficits or central nervous system (CNS) disorders. These include, but are not limited to: intellectual impairment, attention deficits, sleep disturbances, hyperactivity, reduced clarity of speech, dependency, and/or developmental delays (motor and intellectual). The range of possible CNS disorders is large, and it is unlikely that any one child diagnosed with FAS will exhibit all of the CNS disorders reported in various studies of FAS. Nonetheless, some CNS disorders are found in most children with FAS. Streissguth and her colleagues report that FAS patients tend to be outgoing and oriented toward social interactions at all ages, with fine motor problems in younger children and difficulty sticking with tasks at most ages.[12]

As is the case for normally developing children, many of the behaviors characteristic of FAS change as children mature.[13] During infancy, some of the most common behavioral traits associated with FAS are: weak suck, sleep disruption, failure to tune out repetitive stimulation, low level of persistent focus on environmental stimuli, absence of stranger anxiety, and fearlessness in social situations. During their preschool years, children with FAS are more likely than non-FAS children to be hyperactive, to be fearless and unresponsive to verbal cautions, and to exhibit speech problems and delayed language development. During elementary school, hyperactivity is still a problem, as are slow performance time and fine motor problems. By adolescence and young adulthood, people with FAS tend to display poor social judgment and to lack impulse control. They find it difficult to make decisions and to direct their own behavior.[14]

A second important consideration in assessing the impact of prenatal alcohol consumption on CNS functioning is the variation in the extent or severity of CNS disorders. Mental retardation is one of the most debilitating CNS disorders associated with heavy prenatal drinking. The average IQ score of 20 FAS patients in one study was 65, with the scores ranging from 15 to 105.[15] Some FAS patients will be in the normal range of intelligence, and others will be in borderline or retarded ranges. Overall, the prognosis for children with FAS is not very good. Children with FAS might be able to "catch up" in a few respects. FAS children raised in stable homes might put some of their emotional difficulties behind them. Even when raised in stable homes, however, FAS children are unlikely to catch up in terms of intellectual and social functioning.[16] These findings suggest several directions for public messages, although campaigners should conduct formative research to determine how and to whom these should be communicated. One audience that needs to be informed of these characteristics is physicians.

For several reasons, doctors sometimes find it difficult to diagnose FAS.[17] One potential difficulty concerns other causes of the same characteristics. Although the unique combination of growth retardation, facial dysmorphology, and CNS disorders has been reported only in the children of women who drank heavily during pregnancy, many substances might cause a particular outcome. Because women who drink during pregnancy might also use some of these substances, it is difficult to determine the cause of the outcome. For instance, smokers have smaller babies than nonsmokers, and women who drink during pregnancy are more likely to smoke during pregnancy. For women who smoke and drink, alcohol might act as a passenger variable that cloaks or disguises the effects of cigarettes.[18] Drugs, prenatal nutrition, and home environment are other confounding factors implicated in growth retardation and CNS disorders. Similarly, fetal hydantoin, which occurs among offspring of epileptic women who took an anticonvulsant drug during pregnancy, is characterized by facial abnormalities similar to those that characterize FAS.[19]

The impact of such confounding factors has generated debate about the attribution of the complex of characteristics (i.e., facial dysmorphology, growth retardation, and CNS disorders) to heavy, prenatal alcohol exposure. Some of the most well-known researchers in the field, however, argue that a diagnosis of FAS (i.e., attribution of the child's problems to prenatal alcohol consumption) can be made with a fully defined appearance.[20]

The third reason it is difficult to diagnose FAS has to do with the nature of the characteristics of FAS. Although measuring length, weight, and head circumference is relatively straightforward, it is often difficult to detect the facial dysmorphology characteristic of FAS in the newborn. Without special training, many doctors may not recognize the uniqueness of a child's features. Adequately assessing central nervous system functioning in newborns is also problematic. Some researchers suggest that a head circumference in the lowest 3% (i.e., microcephaly) be classified as one sign of CNS disorders.[21] As important or more important than designing effective programs to inform physicians about characteristics of FAS are efforts to pinpoint causes and incidence of FAS.

CAUSES OF AND INCIDENCE OF FAS

Early speculation centered on the cause of CNS disorders and growth retardation among children of heavy-drinking mothers. Two schools of thought existed. One argued that it was not alcohol per se, but rather an alcoholic woman's inability to care adequately for her child that caused postnatal growth retardation and CNS disorders. The other school argued that prenatal alcohol exposure alters the physical or genetic makeup of children-to-be and thus causes the negative outcomes. Three types of evidence are used to buttress the second argument. First, all documented cases of FAS have occurred to women who drank at alcoholic levels during pregnancy. Second, the inability of many FAS children to catch up in growth and CNS functioning—regardless of home environment—suggest that in utero exposure to alcohol causes the problems. Third, animal studies report changes in weight, behavior, brain formation, and functioning in the offspring of female rats given heavy doses of alcohol during pregnancy.[22]

Although only women who drink heavily during pregnancy have children with FAS, only about one in three of these women will have a child diagnosed with FAS.[23] Many of the two of three children who do not meet the diagnostic criteria for FAS will meet the diagnostic criteria for FAE. Thus, because relatively few pregnant women drink at alcoholic levels during pregnancy, and because 1 in 3 of those women will have a child with FAS, only about 0.13% of all infants (1 in 750) will be diagnosed with FAS.[24]

Presently, research speculates as to why two out of three women who drink heavily during pregnancy give birth to children who do not have FAS. Research has ruled out explanations based on race and type of alcohol consumed, so explanations focusing on environmental and biological factors are being considered. Among the environmental factors examined is the potentially mediating effect of socioeconomic status on nutrition. The hypothesis here is that high socioeconomic status women who drink heavily have better diets, smoke less, and are less apt to use drugs—factors that might contribute to negative outcomes—than heavy-drinking women from lower socio-economic groups. Animal studies indicate that nutrition might be a mediating factor.[25] Campaigners and lawmakers might serve society and lower-class women by assisting with both diet and nutrition through food supplement programs.

Among the biological factors under consideration are physiological changes due to alcoholism and susceptibility to alcohol. Case studies indicate that later-born children of alcoholic women are both more apt to have FAS and to exhibit more severe consequences than their earlier-born siblings.[26] Although it is possible that an alcoholic woman drinks more heavily during later pregnancies, it is also possible that alcoholism, especially over long periods of time, produces physiological changes that affect all of a woman's subsequent children-to-be.[27] Second, just as some women metabolize alcohol more quickly, so to do some children-to-be. Women and children-to-be who metabolize alcohol more quickly might be protected from the most severe consequences associated with prenatal alcohol exposure.[28] Though these speculations shed some light on the processes that link alcohol consumption to consequences for children, more research must be done in this area.

Less Severe Outcomes:
Fetal Alcohol Effects

Although heavy maternal drinking is associated with an increased risk of FAS, researchers and clinicians warn that light and moderate levels of [prenatal] alcohol consumption are thought to be associated with FAE. Three important distinctions are drawn between children with FAS and children with FAE. First, children with FAE do not have the facial features characteristic of FAS. Second, FAE children have less severe growth deficiencies and CNS disorders. Third, doctors and clinicians are less certain that the outcomes or symptoms are caused by prenatal exposure to alcohol than they are with FAS. All three factors may contribute to pregnant women's and physicians' ability to ignore the topic.

Alcohol is widely regarded as a teratogen. That is, gestational exposure to alcohol affects the child-to-be. Teratogenic substances, like alcohol, can have four effects on children-to-be: fetal death, malformation, growth deficiency, and functional effects (i.e., CNS effects).[29] According to Vorhees, a teratogen that can cause all four effects is characterized both by a dose/effect relationship and by a dose/response curve for each of the four outcomes.[30] A dose/effect relationship implies that higher amounts of alcohol are required to produce, in order: death, malformation, growth deficiency, and CNS disorders. Thus, fetal death and facial abnormalities should occur only at relatively high levels of alcohol consumption (or "doses") during pregnancy, but both high and lower levels of alcohol consumption can produce growth deficiencies and CNS disorders.

The dose/response curve for each outcome implies that a higher dose produces more severe consequences than a lower dose. Children of women who drink the most during pregnancy should have lower IQ scores than children of women who drink the least. Several studies report lower IQ scores among patients with more severe cases of FAS than among patients with FAE. One study reports an average IQ of 65 (i.e., in the mildly retarded range) for a group diagnosed with FAS and an average IQ of 83 (i.e., in the dull to normal range) for a group diagnosed with FAE.[31]

A dose/response curve for each outcome makes it difficult to describe the "typical" child with FAE and to generate precise estimates of the incidence of FAE. The number and severity of effects should vary by the amount of alcohol a woman consumed. Thus, one child with FAE might exhibit a few mild effects, whereas another child will have a greater number of more severe consequences. Although there is also variation among children with FAS, the extreme differences between FAS and "normal" children make it easier to talk about the "typical" child with FAS.

A final distinction between FAS and FAE is the extent to which physicians feel confident attributing a child's problem(s) to prenatal exposure to alcohol.[32] A number of factors cause growth deficiencies and CNS disorders (the two characteristics of FAE). Because of confounding effects and a lack of distinct physical anomalies (i.e., facial features), doctors require information about a woman's drinking patterns during pregnancy as well as information about other habits (e.g., nutrition and smoking) in order to make a diagnosis. Even with this information, it is not always clear that alcohol was the causal agent.

Human Research on the Timing of Alcohol Consumption and the Dose/Response Curve for Each Outcome

Although researchers are fairly confident that heavy prenatal alcohol consumption can produce FAS, the distinctions between FAS and FAE make more research on the effects of alcohol consumption critical. In particular, research that addresses the dose/response curve for each outcome and the impact of the timing of alcohol consumption is crucial. Such information will allow doctors to offer more concrete guidelines to pregnant women.

Research to date provides useful clues as to the nature of association between various levels of alcohol consumption and the outcomes for children, but problems inherent in research with humans make it difficult to specify precise dose/response patterns. Experimental conditions under which scientists can precisely control the amount of alcohol consumed (i.e., some women abstain, others drink lightly, and others drink heavily) and other factors (e.g., cigarettes, drugs, home environment, and nutrition) are necessary to produce estimates of how much alcohol produces a specific outcome. Because alcohol might have negative consequences for children-to-be, encouraging women to drink is unconscionable. Thus, research typically relies on women's recollections of how much they drank during pregnancy (or during a particular trimester). After examining the children at birth and often at regular intervals during childhood and adolescence, researchers consider associations among stated levels of alcohol consumption and outcomes.

Two problems can arise in such studies. First, women's reports of their drinking are subject to faulty recall. Women might forget how much they drank at any given time during pregnancy or deliberately "underreport" how much they drank during pregnancy. Second, because most women have heard the messages that encourage them not to drink while pregnant, they might give low estimates of how much they drank during pregnancy to appear in the best possible light. Evidence supports the latter interpretation. A sample of pregnant women were asked how much they drank during pregnancy. Five years later, the same women were asked about their drinking patterns during the specific pregnancy. Many of the women reported higher levels of drinking during the pregnancy in question at the 5-year interview than at the interview that took place during pregnancy.[33]

If either of these forms of underreporting exists, research results will be biased. If all women underestimate the amount they drink during pregnancy, estimates of how much alcohol produces a certain outcome will be low. If only heavier drinkers underestimate what they drink (because they have the most to "lose" by being honest), then the data will indicate that alcohol has no effect on the outcome being studied, even if it does have an effect. This would happen because any differences in outcomes between the children of women who drank heavily (but report drinking lightly) and the women who drank lightly (and reported doing so) cannot be attributed to differences in drinking (because none are reported). Because of the potential for bias, we need to be cautious in our interpretation of the data.

A second problem with many studies is that they often do not account for confounding factors—like smoking, home environment, and prenatal nutrition—that are associated both with alcohol consumption and outcomes for children. If studies do not take account of confounding factors, then consequences due to those factors might be attributed to alcohol consumption. Fortunately, research is beginning to include measures of confounding factors.

GROWTH RETARDATION

Although heavy levels of prenatal alcohol consumption produce severe growth retardation, research suggests that light and moderate drinking during pregnancy have only modest effects on growth. For instance, one study suggests that once gestation, other substance use, family income, nutrition, and mother's height and weight are accounted for, women who consumed more than two drinks a day during pregnancy gave birth to smaller children than women who drank less than that. The researchers report that effects of smoking cigarettes and using marijuana were larger and potentially more consequential for children than were the effects of alcohol.[34] Further, most studies of the effect of light and moderate drinking on postnatal growth report inconsequential effects of prenatal alcohol consumption on postnatal growth.[35]

FACIAL DYSMORPHOLOGY AND ABNORMALITIES

According to Vorhees's description of the dose/effect relationship curve, only at high levels of prenatal alcohol exposure should children exhibit facial dysmorphology. Hanson and colleagues report that children of women who had two or more drinks a day during the time before they realized they were pregnant (i.e., the first month or so of pregnancy) were more likely to exhibit facial dysmorphology and growth deficiency severe enough for a diagnosis of FAS or FAE.[36] Other studies indicate that only women who drink heavily (in one study, 6 or more drinks a day, and 10 or more units of alcohol at a time in another study) were significantly more likely than women who abstained from alcohol to have children with the facial dysmorphology and other abnormalities associated with FAS. In both of these studies, lower levels of alcohol consumption were not significantly associated with the outcomes.[37]

Although the studies appear to provide different information about how much alcohol produces facial dysmorphology, this might not be so. In the first study, the outcome measure included facial dysmorphology and growth deficiencies *and* children who could be diagnosed either with FAS or FAE were considered to have abnormalities. The second and third studies considered only severe cases of dysmorphology and abnormalities. The less severe outcomes considered in the first study (i.e., FAE) might explain the differences in the levels of alcohol that produce the outcomes. Further, in the first study, the children who could be diagnosed with FAS had mothers who drank much more than two drinks a day. Thus, the *most* severe symptoms of facial dysmorphology are probably associated with drinking significantly more than two drinks a day whereas less severe symptoms are associated with more moderate levels of consumption.

Even though the studies disagree, to some extent, on the amount of alcohol that produces dysmorphology, they do agree that the timing of alcohol consumption is important. The studies indicate that heavy drinking prior to recognition of pregnancy has a larger effect on dysmorphology and abnormalities than does drinking later in the pregnancy. This is in accord with the understanding that the first trimester of pregnancy is characterized by the organization of tissue.

CENTRAL NERVOUS SYSTEM FUNCTIONING

Research on the effects of drinking on CNS functioning has considered a number of areas of functioning, with particular attention paid to intellectual functioning and attention deficit problems. Three research groups have provided possibly the most comprehensive data on the effects of various levels of prenatal alcohol exposure on these outcomes. The first research group, from Washington, studies children born to women who drank heavily, who drank at lower levels, and who abstained during pregnancy. The children in the sample are mostly white and middle class. The second research group, located in Cleveland, examines children of women who drank at various levels during pregnancy. Most of the children in this sample are black and poor. The final research group, located in Atlanta, studies three groups of children born to predominately low-income, black women: children of women who abstained during pregnancy; children of women who drank heavily but quit during the second trimester; and children of women who drank heavily throughout pregnancy. All three research groups use age-appropriate, standardized tests to assess the impact of prenatal alcohol exposure on functioning. Major findings of the three groups are reviewed below.

The Washington group compares approximately 250 children of "heavy drinkers" to 250 children of other women. In general, the group reports that alcohol *does* affect CNS functioning. In some cases, alcohol consumption has a threshold effect (i.e., only if women consume more than a specified number of drinks a day do their children exhibit the CNS disorder being studied), and in other cases alcohol consumption has a linear effect (i.e., even women who drank at low levels will have children with some CNS disorder—but the disorder is more severe for children of women who drank more).

Among other things, infants in the Washington study who were exposed to alcohol scored lower on two of the six factors of the Brazelton Neonatal Behavioral Scale, had lower Apgar scores, experienced more tremors, had an inability to habituate (i.e., how quickly the infant stops responding to a series of redundant stimuli), and had weaker sucks than children not exposed to alcohol.[38] Among 8-month-old children, heavy, prenatal alcohol exposure is associated with lower scores on the Bayley scale of mental and motor development. The size of the effect is relatively small, however. At this age, alcohol exposure has a threshold effect. Lower scores are associated with an average of two to four drinks a day and children exposed to less alcohol than that are no different from children of abstainers.[39]

At 4 years of age, fine and gross motor difficulties are associated with prenatal alcohol consumption; a subtle association between prenatal alcohol exposure and IQ scores was noted among the children. A threshold effect is reported; IQ decrements are noted for children of women who had three or more drinks a day during pregnancy.[40] Alcohol exposure is associated with picture completion tasks, block design, mazes on performance scales, and arithmetic.

Based on their examination of the children at ages 7 and 11, the Washington group reports that prenatal alcohol exposure continues to affect children. Among 7-year-olds, prenatal exposure is associated with abstract reasoning, short-term memory, arithmetic and spatial organizational difficulties, and with parents' reports of learning problems.[41] Prenatal alcohol consumption is associated with standardized test scores, teacher ratings of behaviors indicative of learning disabilities, and lower academic achievement at age 11. At this age, even at low levels of alcohol consumption, children are affected by exposure to alcohol, and larger decrements are noted for children of women who drank more.[42]

Unlike the Washington group, the Cleveland group reports few effects of prenatal alcohol exposure on CNS functioning. The Cleveland group reports that average daily alcohol consumption is unassociated with scores on the Bayley scale at 6 months or 1 year old. Nor is prenatal alcohol consumption associated with scores on the Stanford-Binet test among 3-year-olds or the Full Scale IQ of the WPPSI (the same test used by the Washington group) at age 4.[43] Finally, alcohol consumption during pregnancy is not associated with language development at 1, 2, and 3 years old (using the Sequenced Inventory of Communication Development).[44] The Cleveland group's analyses indicate that the home environment is the best predictor of CNS functioning and language development. This is in contrast to the Washington group, which reports that home environment is important but does not totally account for the effect of prenatal alcohol exposure.[45]

As we might expect based on the forgoing discussion, the Washington and Cleveland groups report differences in the effect of prenatal alcohol exposure on attention deficit disorders. The Washington group reports that prenatal alcohol exposure influences whether 4-year-olds have attention deficit problems (as measured by an automated vigilance task).[46] The Cleveland group, on the other hand, finds no effect of alcohol consumption on attention deficit disorders (using a similar test).[47]

The Atlanta group reports that the timing of alcohol exposure is important. All of the heavy-drinking women in their study (i.e., 24 or more drinks per week) were encouraged to quit drinking during their pregnancies. Some of the women were able to quit drinking in the second trimester. Thus, the researchers are able to compare the offspring of abstainers with the offspring of "quitters" and "continued-to-drink" women. In general, they report that benefits do accrue to the children of quitters.

At birth, the children of women who quit and women who abstained were very similar to each other. The children of women who continued to drink, however, scored lower on three scales of the Brazelton Neonatal Behavioral Assessment Scale. By the time the children were 1 month old, the children of the continued-to-drink women still scored lower than other children on two scales of the Brazelton scale (abnormal reflexes and autonomic regulation).[48] By age 5 (on average), children of women who quit and of women who continued to drink scored lower on various measures of functioning than children of women who abstained throughout pregnancy. Children of women who continued to drink had more severe problems than the children of quitters, however. Differences were noted in pre-reading and arithmetic skills (potential indicators of learning difficulties) and short-term memory.[49]

The findings of the Atlanta group suggest that the most severe damage to CNS functioning might occur during the last trimester of pregnancy. This makes sense, because the last trimester of pregnancy is a time of rapid brain growth and neurophysiologic organization. The results are speculative, however, and more studies are necessary before we can rule out CNS damage at other stages of pregnancy.

A quick review of the findings from the three groups suggests uncertainty about the effect of prenatal alcohol consumption on CNS functioning. The Washington and Atlanta groups report effects of alcohol consumption on CNS functioning, whereas the Cleveland group finds no effect of prenatal alcohol consumption on CNS functioning. Early speculation suggested that sample differences accounted for the observed differences (i.e., the effect of alcohol consumption is dependent on socioeconomic status). The Cleveland group and the Atlanta group, however, both use low-income samples and they get very different results. Thus, socioeconomic status does not appear to be a conditioning factor. One factor that might explain the different results is the inclusion of measures of home environment (included in the Cleveland study, not always included in the Washington study, and never included in the Atlanta study) and maternal intelligence (included in the Cleveland study and not in either of the other studies). Prenatal alcohol consumption might not play as large a role in CNS functioning as genetics (i.e., mother's IQ) and current home environment. Further research is needed to understand the effects of prenatal alcohol consumption and environmental factors on CNS functioning.[50]

Concluding Remarks on FAS and FAE

In the past, physicians and public health officials have used the inconsistent findings about the effects of light and moderate prenatal alcohol consumption on children and animal studies to warn women to abstain. Better safe than sorry! Although this seems reasonable, it is probably true that an occasional drink will not produce negative outcomes for children. More specifically, doctors and public health officials will probably continue to warn heavy-drinking women to stop drinking, because some research indicates that there are benefits to quitting. Although many women reduce their alcohol consumption during pregnancy (regardless of a doctor's recommendation), the heaviest-drinking women need special outreach to attain this goal. Research, however, ought not to be used to convince a woman that one or even a few drinks will cause undue harm to her child.

A Note About the Effects
of Alcohol on Women's Health

Little research documents potential health consequences of prenatal alcohol consumption for women. A substantial body of literature, however, documents associations between sustained drinking at alcoholic levels and a number of health-related consequences for adults in general. This literature requires the same cautious approach regarding dose, confounding factors, and causal mechanisms as does the literature on FAS. A further caution stems from the exclusion of women from some studies of the effects of alcohol consumption on health. When women are not included in studies, it is uncertain whether alcohol has similar effects on men's and women's health. The good news is that more and more studies include women.

With these cautions in mind, it is likely that women and men who drink at alcoholic levels run the risk of developing cirrhosis of the liver, acute pancreatitis, inflammation of the esophagus, exacerbation of peptic ulcers, hormonal deficiencies, diabetes, gastrointestinal disorders, liver cancer, and cancers of the head and neck (especially in conjunction with smoking).[51] Increased alcohol intake may also be a factor in cancer of the large bowel and of the stomach.[52] Cardiovascular diseases associated with heavy drinking include cardiomyopathy, cardiac arrhythmias, hypertension, ischemic heart disease, and cerebrovascular disorders.[53] The risk of liver disease, pancreatic disease, and hormonal dysfunction might be higher in alcoholics because they tend to have poor diets and reduced nutrient digestion. Further, immunological problems might link alcoholism to some cancers.[54] Regarding CNS functioning, alcoholics are more likely to experience dementia, seizures, hallucinations, peripheral neuropathy, Wernicke's disease, and Korsakoff's psychosis.[55] Though those who drink at alcoholic levels over a long period of time are most likely to experience these physical and mental health problems, not all alcoholics will develop these problems.

Research of particular importance to women suggests that heavy alcohol consumption is associated with breast cancer and reproductive health. Although some researchers suggest that existing evidence does not support an association between alcohol and breast cancer,[56] others suggest that the preponderance of evidence strongly supports such an association.[57] If alcohol increases the risk of breast cancer, it may do so through increases in estrogen levels or cell division. Research more clearly documents that heavy alcohol consumption is associated with amenorrhea (suppression or absence of menstruation), anovulation (absence of ovulation), dysfunction in the post-ovulation phase of the menstrual cycle, and pathologic ovary changes. Alcohol-induced alterations in hormonal levels might produce these outcomes.

Finally, research on gender differences in the effect of alcohol on some health outcomes indicates that women may be at greater risk than men. For instance, alcoholic women who drink excessively for shorter periods of time and who drink less per day than male alcoholics were *more* likely than men to develop cirrhosis. Differences between men and women in body weight and mass, how alcohol is metabolized, hormonal levels, or immune mechanisms might account for different levels of risk by gender.[58]

The research in this field shows associations between heavy drinking or alcoholism and health outcomes for men and women. Though little research documents the effect of moderate drinking on health, research on cardiovascular disease is beginning to fill this void. The research also highlights particular areas of concern for women's health. More research is needed in this area before we can ascertain whether alcohol causes certain outcomes and at what daily intake over what duration of time negative outcomes become more likely. Again, such information would provide the impetus to construct concrete recommendations for women in relation to their health.

Notes

1. S. Harlap & P. H. Shiono, "Alcohol, Smoking, and Incidence of Spontaneous Abortion in First and Second Trimester," *The Lancet* II (1980): 173-176.

2. J. Kline, P. Shrout, Z. Stein, M. Susser, & B. Werburton, "Drinking During Pregnancy and Spontaneous Abortion," *The Lancet* II (1980): 176-180.

3. E. M. Ouellette, H. L. Rosett, N. P. Rosman, & L. Weiner, "Adverse Effects on Offspring of Maternal Alcohol Use During Pregnancy," *The New England Journal of Medicine* 297 (1977): 528-530.

4. P. Lemoine, H. Harousseau, J.-P. Borteyru, & J.-C. Menuet, "Les Enfants de Parents Alcholiques: Anomalies Observees a Propos de 127 Cas," *Quest Medicale* 25 (1968): 476-482.

5. K. L. Jones & D. W. Smith, "Recognition of the Fetal Alcohol Syndrome in Early Infancy," *The Lancet* II (1973): 999-1001.

6. S. K. Clarren & D. W. Smith, "The Fetal Alcohol Syndrome: A Review of the World Literature," *The New England Journal of Medicine* 298 (1978): 1063-1067.

7. N. L. Golden, R. J. Sokol, B. R. Kuhnert, & S. Bottom, "Maternal Alcohol Use and Infant Development," *Pediatrics* 70 (1982): 931-935.

8. Clarren & Smith, "The Fetal Alcohol Syndrome," pp. 1063-1067.

9. A. P. Streissguth, S. K. Clarren, & K. L. Jones, "Natural History of the Fetal Alcohol Syndrome: A Ten Year Follow Up of 11 Patients," *The Lancet* II (1985): 85-92.

10. Clarren & Smith, "The Fetal Alcohol Syndrome," pp. 1063-1067.

11. Streissguth et al., "Natural History of the Fetal Alcohol Syndrome," pp. 85-92.

12. A. P. Streissguth & R. A. LaDue, "Fetal Alcohol: Teratogenic Causes of Developmental Disabilities," in S. R. Schroeder (Ed.), *Toxic Substances and Mental Retardation: Neurobehaviorial Toxicology and Teratology* (Washington, DC: AAMD Monograph Series, 1987): 1-32.

13. Streissguth & LaDue, "Fetal Alcohol," 1-32.

14. A. P. Streissguth, J. M. Aase, S. K. Clarren, S. P. Randels, R. A. LaDue, & D. W. Smith, "Fetal Alcohol Syndrome in Adolescents and Adults," *Journal of the American Medical Association* 265 (1991): 1961-1967.

15. A. P. Streissguth, C. S. Herman, & D. W. Smith, "Intelligence Behavior and Dysmorphogenesis in the Fetal Alcohol Syndrome: A Report on 20 Patients," *Journal of Pediatrics* 92 (1978): 363-367.

16. A. P. Streissguth, S. P. Randels, & D. W. Smith, "A Test-Retest Study of Intelligence in Patients With Fetal Alcohol Syndrome: Implications for Care," *Journal of the American Academy of Child and Adolescent Psychiatry* 30 (1991): 584-587.

17. The Fetal Alcohol Study Group of the Research Society on Alcoholism recommended that doctors make a diagnosis of FAS if a child had signs in each of the following categories: prenatal and/or postnatal growth retardation, central nervous system involvement, and a characteristic facial dysmorphology. If a child exhibits signs in only one or two of the three broad categories and if the doctor suspects or knows that the mother drank during pregnancy, then the doctor is advised to make a diagnosis of fetal alcohol effects (FAE). See E. A. Abel, "Prenatal Effects of Alcohol," *Drug and Alcohol Dependence* 14 (1984): 1-10; H. L. Rosett, "A Clinical Perspective of the Fetal Alcohol Syndrome," *Alcoholism: Clinical and Experimental Research* 4 (1980): 119-122.

18. Z. Stein & J. Kline, "Smoking, Alcohol, and Reproduction," *American Journal of Public Health* 73 (1883): 1154-1156.

19. H. L. Rosett & L. Weiner, *Alcohol and the Fetus: A Clinical Perspective* (New York: Oxford University Press, 1984).

20. A. P. Streissguth, S. K. Clarren, S. P. Randels, R. A. LaDue, J. M. Aase, & D. F. Smith, "A Letter 'In Reply,' " *Journal of the American Medical Association* 266 (1991): 1077.

21. S. K. Clarren, "Recognition of Fetal Alcohol Syndrome," *Journal of the American Medical Association* 245 (1981): 2436-2439.

22. CIBA Foundation Symposium No. 15, *Mechanisms of Alcohol Damage in Utero* (London: Pitman, 1984); P. A. Meyer & E. P. Riley, "Behavioral Teratology of Alcohol," in E. P. Riley & C. V. Vorhees (Eds.), *Handbook of Behavioral Teratology* (New York: Plenum, 1986): 101-140.

23. K. L. Jones, D. W. Smith, A. P. Streissguth, & N. C. Myrianthopoulis, "Outcomes in Offspring of Chronic Alcoholic Women," *The Lancet* 1 (1974): 1076-1078.

24. Streissguth & LaDue, "Fetal Alcohol," pp. 1-32.

25. Rosett & Weiner, *Alcohol and the Fetus.*

26. S. Iosub, M. Fuchs, N. Bingol, & D. S. Gromisch, "Fetal Alcohol Syndrome Revisited," *Pediatrics* 68 (1981): 475-479.

27. F. Majewski, "Alcohol Embryopathy: Some Facts and Speculations About Pathogenesis," *Neurobehavioral Toxicology and Teratology* 3 (1981): 129-144.

28. G. F. Chernoff, "The Fetal Alcohol Syndrome in Mice: Maternal Variables," *Teratology* 22 (1980): 71-75.

29. J. G. Wilson, "Current Status of Teratology," in J. G. Wilson & F. C. Fraser (Eds.), *Handbook of Teratology: Vol. 1. General Principles and Etiology* (New York: Plenum, 1977): 47-74.

30. C. V. Vorhees, "Principles of Behavioral Teratology," in E. P. Riley & C. V. Vorhees (Eds.), *Handbook of Behavioral Teratology* (New York: Plenum, 1986): 23-48.

31. Streissguth & LaDue, "Fetal Alcohol."

32. C. B. Ernhart, "Clinical Correlations Between Ethanol Intake and Fetal Alcohol Syndrome," in M. Galanter (Ed.), *Recent Developments in Alcoholism: Vol. 9. Children of Alcoholics* (New York: Plenum, 1991): 127-150.

33. C. B. Ernhart, M. Morrow-Tlucak, R. J. Sokol, & S. Martier, "Underreporting of Alcohol Use in Pregnancy," *Alcoholism: Clinical and Experimental Research* 12 (1988): 506-511.

34. P. A. Fried & C. M. O'Connell, "A Comparison of the Effects of Prenatal Exposure to Tobacco, Alcohol, Cannabis, and Caffeine on Birth Size and Subsequent Growth," *Neurotoxicology and Teratology* 9 (1987): 79-85.

35. N. L. Day, N. Robles, G. Richardson, D. Gera, P. Taylor, M. Scher, D. Stoffer, M. Cornelius, & L. Goldschmidt, "The Effects of Prenatal Alcohol Use on the Growth of Children at 3 Years of Age," *Alcoholism: Clinical and Experimental Research* 15 (1991): 67-71.

36. J. W. Hanson, A. P. Streissguth, & D. W. Smith, "The Effects of Moderate Alcohol Consumption During Pregnancy on Fetal Growth and Morphogenesis," *Pediatrics* 92 (1978): 457-460.

37. C. B. Ernhart, R. J. Sokol, S. Martier, P. Moran, D. Nadler, J. W. Ager, & A. Wolf, "Alcohol Teratogenicity in the Human: A Detailed Assessment of Specificity, Critical Period, and Threshold," *American Journal of Obstetrics and Gynecology* 156 (1987): 33-39.

38. C. B. Ernhart et al., "Clinical Correlations," p. 25.

39. A. P. Streissguth, H. M. Barr, D. C. Martin, & D. S. Herman, "Effects of Maternal Alcohol, Nicotine, and Caffeine Use During Pregnancy on Infant Mental and Motor Development at 8 Months," *Alcoholism: Clinical and Experimental Research* 4 (1980): 152-163.

40. A. P. Streissguth, H. M. Barr, P. D., Sampson, B. L. Darby, & D. C. Martin, "I.Q. at Age 4 in Relation to Maternal Alcohol Use and Smoking During Pregnancy," *Developmental Psychology* 25 (1989): 3-11.

41. A. P. Streissguth, H. M. Barr, & P. D. Sampson, "Moderate Prenatal Alcohol Exposure: Effects on Child IQ and Learning Problems at Age 7 and $\frac{1}{2}$," *Alcoholism: Clinical and Experimental Research* 14 (1990): 662-669; A. P. Streissguth, H. M. Barr, P. D. Sampson, F. L. Bookstein, & B. L. Darby, "Neurobehavioral Effects of Prenatal Alcohol, Part I: Research Strategy," *Neurotoxicology and Teratology* 11 (1989): 461-476.

42. H. C. Olson, P. D. Sampson, H. Barr, A. P. Streissguth, & F. L. Bookstein, "Prenatal Exposure to Alcohol and School Problems in Late Childhood: A Longitudinal Prospective Study," *Development and Psychopathology* 4 (1991): 341-359.

43. T. Greene, C. B. Ernhart, J. Ager, R. J. Sokol, S. Martier, & T. Boyd, "Prenatal Alcohol Exposure and Cognitive Development in the Pre-School Years," *Neurotoxicology and Teratology* 13 (1991): 57-68.

44. T. Greene, C. B. Ernhart, S. Martier, P. Sokol, & J. Ager, "Prenatal Alcohol Exposure and Language Development," *Alcoholism: Clinical and Experimental Research* 14 (1990): 937-945.

45. Olson et al., "Prenatal Exposure to Alcohol and School Problems," pp. 341-359.

46. A. P. Streissguth, D. C. Martin, H. M. Barr, B. M. Sandman, G. L. Kircher, & B. L. Darby, "Intrauterine Alcohol and Nicotine Exposure: Attention and Reaction Time in 4 Year Old Children," *Developmental Psychology* 20 (1984): 533-541.

47. T. A. Boyd, C. B. Ernhart, T. H. Greene, R. J. Sokol, & S. Martier, "Prenatal Alcohol Exposure and Sustained Attention in the Preschool Years," *Neurotoxicology and Teratology* 13 (1991): 49-55.

48. C. D. Coles, I. E. Smith, & A. Falek, "Prenatal Alcohol Exposure and Infant Behavior: Immediate Effects and Implications for Later Development," *Advances in Alcohol and Substance Abuse* 6 (1987): 87-104.

49. C. D. Coles, R. T. Brown, I. E. Smith, K. A. Platzman, S. Erickson, & A. Falek, "Effects of Prenatal Alcohol Exposure at School Age: I. Physical and Cognitive Development," *Neurotoxicology and Teratology* 13 (1991): 357-367.

50. This chapter does not address animal studies, but these studies do generate information on the effect of alcohol consumption on particular outcomes. See S. Norton & L. Kotkoskie, "Basic Animal Research," in M. Galanter (Ed.), *Recent Developments in Alcoholism: Vol. 9. Children of Alcoholics* (New York: Plenum, 1991): 95-115, for a review that indicates that the effects of alcohol on growth is dose-related and poor nutrition does not account for the association between alcohol consumption and growth. Further evidence indicates that acute exposure to alcohol produces facial dysmorphology in animals.

51. U.S. Department of Health and Human Services, *Seventh Special Report to the U.S. Congress on Alcohol and Health* (Rockville, MD: Public Health Service, 1990); A. M. Arria & D. H. VanThiel, "The Epidemiology of Alcohol-Related Chronic Disease," *Alcohol Health and Research World* (1992): 209-216.

52. M. P. Longnecker, "Alcohol Consumption in Relation to Risk of Cancers of the Breast and Large Bowel," *Alcohol Health and Research World* (1992): 223-229.

53. A. L. Klatsky, G. D. Friedman, & A. B. Siegelaub, "Alcohol Use and Cardiovascular Disease: The Kaiser-Permanente Experience," *Circulation* 64 (1981): 32-40.

54. U.S. Department of Health and Human Services, *Seventh Special Report on Alcohol and Health*.

55. Arria & VanThiel, "Epidemiology of Alcohol-Related Chronic Disease," pp. 209-216.

56. U.S. Department of Health and Human Services, *Seventh Special Report on Alcohol and Health*.

57. Longnecker, "Alcohol Consumption in Relation to Risk of Cancers," pp. 223-229.

58. A. Prytkowicz, "Female Alcoholism: Impacts on Women and Children," in M. Galanter (Ed.), *Currents in Alcoholism: Recent Advances in Research and Treatment (Vol. 3)* (New York: Grune & Stratton, 1980): 429-434.

13

Knowing When to Say When and Why

Media Messages Aimed at
Preventing Women's Alcohol Consumption

Kathryn J. French
Theresa D. Frasier
C. Jay Frasier

> *You just don't get many messages that say: Hey, take this stuff seriously.*
> *You look at the beer commercials on TV . . . and you just see alcohol as*
> *another way to have a good time . . . never once did it occur to me that I*
> *was overdosing on a drug.*
>
> The Boston Women's Health Book Collective,
> *The New Our Bodies, Ourselves*, p. 55[1]

This quote appears in a popular reference guide about women's health and acknowledges the conflict between most media messages about alcohol consumption and the classification of alcohol as a drug with harmful consequences associated with use. To explore the latter, we examined print brochures, popular health guides and books, and alcohol warning labels to discern what these messages convey to women to prevent alcohol consumption.

Women and Alcohol
Consumption: Changing Norms

Ironically, alcohol prevention messages have become necessary in the wake of changing societal norms that make alcohol more accessible to and acceptable for women. These societal changes, combined with intense commercial campaign efforts directed at women, have been quite successful, as evidenced by the increase in the numbers of women consuming alcohol. During the four decades between 1940 and 1980, women's drinking increased dramatically, as 3 times as many women as men began using alcohol during those decades.[2] In 1978, 66% of women were drinking, as compared to 77% of men; 80% of women now drink and on a greater variety of occasions than they did less than a generation and a half ago.[3]

A Note About Commercial Efforts
to Promote Alcohol to Women

The multibillion-dollar liquor industry makes no pretense about its interest to sell to women. Publications such as *Glamour, Ms.,* and *Woman's Day* are replete with advertisements for liqueurs, wines, vodka, gin, scotch, and bourbon. For nearly two decades, the alcohol industry has provided advertising revenue to women's magazines. In 1976, "*Cosmopolitan* was among the nation's top 15 magazines in alcohol advertisement revenue, and in 1978, *Better Homes and Gardens* was listed by Seagram, the world's largest distiller, as one of its top five magazine targets."[4] This stands in stark contrast to earlier standards. Until 1958, the liquor industry code explicitly forbade the portrayal of a woman in an ad. During the 1960s, ads for liquor targeted at women consisted of occasional ads for sherry.

With women's changing societal roles, alcohol could more successfully be marketed to women, who have also grown in their financial clout. In the late 1960s and into the 1970s, the liquor industry began to focus on female members of the baby boom with new products, such as wine coolers and other sweet-based drinks that are more like soda pop than alcoholic beverages. By the mid-1970s, the women's alcohol market held great promise for the alcohol industry and had a healthy growth potential.

A consequence of the increased numbers of women consuming alcohol is an increased number of women alcoholics. "Conservative estimates place the number of women alcoholics in the United States at about 900,000 or 20% of the total number of alcoholics."[5] Shuckit and Morrissey report that "women use alcohol as a way of increasing their feelings of power, . . . [and also] to decrease the level of anxiety."[6] They also report a stronger and more direct relationship between stress and the onset of alcoholism in women than in men. Both use and abuse of alcohol contribute to numerous health maladies for women and fetuses, as summarized in the previous chapter. To counter these effects, a multitude of media forms disseminate messages that argue against alcohol consumption.

Approaches to Prevention of Alcohol Use

Nirenberg and Miller's history of the prevention of alcohol abuse in the United States advances three societal models that may be used to represent both the messages available to women about alcohol and the tensions that play between the media messages for and against alcohol use.[7] One of these, the distribution-of-consumption model, involves legislative efforts to restrict access and "assumes a direct relationship between per capita consumption and alcohol abuse."[8] The model suggests that if alcohol availability is decreased, alcohol-related problems will be reduced. The days of prohibition illustrate this societal approach to reducing alcohol use. Other more recent approaches to this method of reducing the availability of alcohol include the imposition of a legal drinking age, "blue" laws, and the adoption of policies that lead to "dry" cities and counties. In each case, society attempts to engineer the prohibition of alcohol consumption. These efforts generally apply equally to both men and women, although some attempts have been made to limit pregnant women's access to alcohol more than for other adults.

SOCIOCULTURAL MODEL

A second prevention model, the sociocultural model, asserts that alcohol abuse results from insufficient social norms regarding the safe use of alcohol, and proposes "the establishment of a new morality about drinking to promote safe, responsible drinking."[9] Many print and broadcast media messages relating to the prevention of alcohol consumption adopt this perspective. These messages often employ fear appeals to urge moderation, if not abstinence, with public service announcements about drinking and driving illustrating this approach.

Perhaps the most pervasive example of a message associated with the sociocultural model is the federal government's mandatory warning label that must be included on all alcoholic beverage containers. The U.S. Surgeon General implemented a warning label (which may be posted in sign-fashion near a cash register in restaurants, on the wall of rest rooms in restaurants, and/or near coolers in quick shops, in addition to the printed version on the bottles of beer, wine, and other alcoholic beverages) on alcoholic products in late 1989. The warning label states,

> *Government Warning: (1) According To The Surgeon General, Women Should Not Drink Alcoholic Beverages During Pregnancy Because Of The Risk Of Birth Defects. (2) Consumption Of Alcoholic Beverages Impairs Your Ability To Drive a Car Or Operate Machinery, And May Cause Health Problems.*

This warning must also be displayed in poster form in all establishments that sell liquor. It is simple and straightforward, but aims at women more than men, for only *pregnant* women are explicitly addressed as an audience in this warning. It is clear by the primary position given to the fetal element of the warning that pregnant women are a primary target, despite the fact that men still outnumber women in overall alcohol consumption. The second portion of the warning emphasizes the risk of drinking and operating automobiles or machinery, even though fatalities associated with drinking and driving far outnumber disabilities associated with pregnancy and alcohol consumption. Finally, a brief clause mentions that alcohol may cause health problems. This may easily be overlooked due to ambiguity.

Alcohol warning labels have been evaluated for their impact on changing consumption patterns among Americans. Snyder and Blood found that "female subjects rated the most severe warning labels lowest in perceived usefulness, while male subjects found the warning increasingly more useful as it became more severe."[10] Current use of warning labels has not stopped people from abusing alcohol, however. Indeed, some researchers argue that, for college students, an emphasis on overuse of alcohol or an exaggeration of binge drinking may actually increase the likelihood of binge drinking through a misperception of student norms.[11] If students—both male and female—think that their peers are drinking more heavily than they are, they will, first, overestimate the amount of "normal" drinking, and second, drink more heavily themselves to fit their perception of this norm. The effectiveness of alcohol warning labels also depends upon individuals reading the labels. DeCarlo and Parrott found that the more alcohol an individual reported drinking, the less likely the person was to read alcohol warning labels.[12] Even those who considered themselves to be highly health-conscious could not accurately recall the content of alcohol warning labels, reporting only that the content consisted of the general statement about "alcohol's harmful effects on one's health."

In addition to the use of warning labels, local communities often seek to influence norms about alcohol consumption through the use of media messages. A newspaper advertisement at Southern Illinois University at Carbondale typifies this approach through its stress on the importance of making healthy choices when drinking.[13] The advertisement, which was funded jointly by the Department of Education, the Fund for Improving Post Secondary Education, and other departments at the university, shows a picture of an attractive young woman standing beside an athletic student. The content includes a statistic that "33% of SIUC students surveyed report they would prefer not to have alcohol available at parties they attend . . . 90% of women reported that they would prefer not to date men who drink heavily."[14] The message then states that alcohol affects blood alcohol concentration and can lead to overintoxication, illness, injury, and risk of harm. The information is intended to lead college students to believe that drinking is not as popular among their peers as the students may have thought. These advertisements are in place in some 100 colleges and universities across the United States to emphasize "Power & Choice"—power to choose not to drink—which is represented as a normative option. Such ads are aimed at both males and females.

Promotional efforts have also been undertaken to design messages aimed at members of drinkers' social networks. These efforts have a twofold purpose. First, they are aimed at changing norms of alcohol consumption. Second, they focus on promoting involvement with others' alcohol consumption decision making. An educational pamphlet titled *The Responsibility of Friendship: How to Talk to a Woman Who Has Problems With Alcohol or Other Drugs*[15] was published by Hazelden, a nonprofit organization that provides rehabilitation, education, prevention, and professional services related to chemical dependency. The pamphlet can be read by individuals with a seventh-grade reading level[16] and gives reasons why women should talk to their female friends who have a drinking problem:

> saving the friend's life;
> helping her to get her life together;
> helping her to stop hiding the drinking problem; and
> helping her to stop drinking alcohol.

The pamphlet asserts that female alcoholics have problems with family, friends, career, financial, and legal matters, and gives tips on speaking to the alcoholic to promote self-efficacy. The friend is advised,

> to speak to the problem drinker when the problem drinker is remorseful;
> not to blame or criticize the individual;
> to talk about specific behaviors and events;
> to talk about whatever it is that the drinker cares about the most (e.g., children, appearance, job); and
> to offer to help the alcoholic seek professional help through treatment centers or AA.

The pamphlet suggests that the alcoholic may hesitate to get help because she is "feeling guilty about her drinking, . . . [and] about taking time for herself and spending less time with her children."[17] The friend is told to encourage the female alcoholic to get help because, "by taking a little time to recover, she'll be more available to her family."[18] This was the only example found of a message that systematically addressed how people can become efficacious in situations where it is presently normative to consume alcohol and tolerate others' consumption.

Although our efforts to examine messages to promote alcohol prevention through changing societal norms revealed some messages aimed at women's health, many more print media addressing alcohol use are targeted at *pregnant* women, with an emphasis on fetal outcomes. The March of Dimes Birth Defects Foundation has created at least two such pamphlets. One is titled, *Drugs, Alcohol, Tobacco Abuse During Pregnancy.*[19] This pamphlet gives basic facts on smoking tobacco; drinking alcohol; and taking prescription drugs, illegal drugs, aspirin, antacids, laxatives, vitamins, and caffeine during pregnancy. The effects of these substances on the unborn fetus are discussed, but the means whereby an individual may attain self-efficacy in response to use is left largely unmentioned. A second March of Dimes pamphlet titled *Will My Drinking Hurt My Baby?*[20] states that when a mother drinks, her baby gets a drink. The symptoms and effects of fetal alcohol syndrome (FAS) are described. The pamphlet recommends *total abstention* from drinking during pregnancy but provides *no* guidance about the ways to attain this goal. It tells women that FAS is 100% preventable by the mother and suggests that women should stop drinking before conceiving a child (although it does not make the same argument for the child's father).

The Fetal Alcohol Syndrome Work Group has prepared yet another alcohol consumption prevention pamphlet, funded by the Illinois Department of Mental Health and Developmental Disabilities, Division of Alcoholism. The pamphlet is titled, *For Your Baby's Sake, Don't Drink.*[21] It, too, emphasizes clinical facts over the means to attain self-efficacy, addressing how alcohol harms the fetus (it damages the fetus's organ systems), outcomes of FAS (e.g., mental retardation, hyperactivity, physical abnormalities), and women at risk for having children with FAS (e.g., 70% of children born to women who drink heavily have at least one symptom of FAS). This pamphlet also suggests that women should not drink any alcohol during pregnancy.

A fourth campaign pamphlet on drinking and pregnancy, written by the Illinois Department of Alcoholism and Substance Abuse, titled *Baby!*[22] describes the responsibilities of pregnant women to their babies, their families, and themselves. It tells women to see a doctor as soon as they think they are pregnant and follow the doctor's advice regarding nutrition, exercise, and the use and abuse of drugs. The brochure also tells women to eat nutritiously and avoid drugs (cigarettes, alcohol, caffeine, cocaine, marijuana, and speed). This is the *only* message reviewed that attempts to establish norms in relation to the responsibility of the father of the baby. It states, "It's important for the baby's father to avoid drugs, too . . . scientists now believe that alcohol or other drugs in his system at conception can damage your baby."[23]

The pamphlet continues, "One of the biggest hazards for you and your baby is alcohol and other drug abuse."[24] The brochure then describes the effects of alcohol as leading to premature delivery and FAS, and tells women to stay "straight" during pregnancy, stressing the role of mothers as models in presenting their values to their children. The final statement gives the positive message: "By doing the right things, you can help make a difference for your baby, your family and you."[25]

Print media aimed at promoting the reform of societal norms associated with alcohol consumption also includes messages that discuss alcohol and sexual behavior. At Southern Illinois University at Carbondale, a brochure (reprinted from Brown University, Department of Health Education) titled, *What You Should Know About Sex and Alcohol But Are Afraid to Ask!!!!!!*[26] discusses how drinking affects sexual behavior. The brochure, too, tells students that it is okay to choose not to drink. It claims that most students disapprove of heavy drinking. The brochure informs students that alcohol "does not really help you meet people."[27] Once more, however, the means to overcome current societal norms and pressures in relation to alcohol consumption are not addressed, reducing the likelihood that such messages will be effective.

The brochure also addresses the reproductive effects of drinking for men, such as testicle atrophy and impotence. The pamphlet lists warning signs for alcohol misuse. Included is the question, "Have you suspected you might be pregnant or actually became pregnant because alcohol made you careless about contraception?"[28] The pamphlet ends by asserting that alcohol misuse can rob people of the power to make good decisions about sex, decreasing the enjoyment that should be in sex. The pamphlet is directed at people who read at the college level.

In sum, we found numerous broadcast and print messages that aim to reduce alcohol consumption through changing societal norms associated with use. Most of these messages emphasize individuals' choice to avert the physical harms associated with overuse of alcohol, with effects on the fetus emerging as a prominent theme undoubtedly designed to invoke a sense of personal responsibility. What too few messages have been designed to do is address the specific actions that individuals must take to become personally responsible in situations where alcohol consumption is presently the norm. Without such messages, these efforts to change the norms of drinking have far less chance for success.

SOCIAL-PSYCHOLOGICAL MODEL

The third model that may be used to describe campaign messages in relation to alcohol prevention efforts in the United States, the social-psychological model, proposes that alcohol misuse results from the interaction of personality and social factors. These factors include "peers, family, sociocultural and environmental factors, and personality."[29] This model suggests that attitudes, peer relationships, and parent-child relationships can be modified and improved to result in a reduction of alcohol abuse. Many media messages relating to alcohol consumption and prevention demonstrate this approach as well. Among the attitudes that have been targeted for change are those dealing with the effects of alcohol on our bodies.

In our review of public messages about alcohol consumption, we found that many colleges and universities across the nation attempt to provide information to students about the adverse health effects associated with alcohol consumption. One of these university health guides that we examined summarizes the facts about alcohol and the human body and even includes the role of gender in these effects.[30] If a female college student reads the guide, she will be exposed to technical information about how the body processes alcohol and definitions of blood alcohol level (BAL).

In addition to this basic information, the guide outlines several factors that influence the way in which the BAL changes and how behaviors may be influenced. These factors include body weight, food intake, type of mixer, strength of the drink, temperature of the beverage, and gender.

Although no data are available to indicate whether or not college students, both males and females, read or retain the information about alcohol contained in such health guides, other research about the use of nutritional health brochures has found such media to be bland and of little worth.[31] Still other evaluative research has determined that college students used information about exposure to the sun, time of day exposure occurs, and sunburn to determine when lying in the sun for the least amount of time produced the fastest evident effect—reddened skin, regarded as a precursor to tanning.[32] The latter in particular leads one to consider whether or not college students, if they do read and retain the information, may use the content contained in the college health guide to determine either how to produce the fastest effect or "buzz" (i.e., use carbonated beverages as mixers) or how to be able to consume more alcohol without showing evident effects (i.e., eat high-protein foods first). Neither of these outcomes is associated with the most likely intentions of the brochure's designers and disseminators.

Messages about alcohol consumption's effects on the human body generally are less available than messages designed to shape attitudes about the effects of consumption on a developing fetus. In the late 19th century, researchers systematically began to research and publish data on alcoholics, but most studies were done exclusively with male subjects. One prominent study, used to support the theory that alcoholic women are promiscuous, for example, is based on the case histories of only *three* women.[33] Despite such limitations in the scientific database, there are some messages available about these matters, including the effects of alcohol in inducing malnutrition, calcium loss, the contraction of STDs including HIV, fibroid tumors, menopausal symptoms, sexuality, fertility, and FAS.

As a final example of a print message associated with alcohol's harmful effects, consider "Alcohol and Your Health,"[34] published by the National Council on Alcoholism and Drug Dependence, Inc. The handout lists dietary guidelines for Americans. Moderate drinking for women is defined as, "No more than 1 drink a day"[35] and moderate drinking for men is defined as, "No more than 2 drinks a day."[36] The handout urges pregnant women, or those trying to conceive, to abstain from drinking alcohol. It makes no mention of the need for men to abstain from consuming alcohol when procreating.

Conclusion

Each of the messages reviewed in this chapter seeks to influence women's drinking behavior. Many cast the woman in a maternal, parental role. Some warn women of their vulnerability in situations in which alcohol is being consumed by her and others. Still others advocate safe-sex practices.

Women are heavily targeted to stop drinking before and during pregnancy. Men, on the other hand, are rarely informed about or discouraged from drinking during or after attempted impregnation. Messages encourage men to avoid contracting an STD but do not encourage men to create healthy, life-giving sperm, or even inform men about the role of their drinking behavior on conception or on the formation of a zygote.

As identified in this and the former chapter, alcohol has many adverse effects on women's health. In particular, research has identified these primary health concerns for drinking women: osteoporosis; AIDS; STDs; fertility; birth defects; increased cancer risk; fibroid tumors linked to hysterectomies; heart disease; women's sexuality; and menopausal complications. Of these health concerns, primarily three—AIDS, STDs, and birth maladies (especially FAS)—are generally discussed in public prevention messages. These three concerns are important. They are not always distinguishable as primarily women's issues, however. They are often the concern of both men and women, or are a societal concern.

In addition to the overemphasis on women's responsibility to their unborn fetus is the underemphasis on women's well-being, as women are seldom encouraged to look at long-term health issues related to alcohol consumption. Alcoholism, osteoporosis, cancer, heart disease, fibroid tumors, and menopausal complications are all long term in nature. Women's alcohol consumption choices and subsequent patterns contribute directly to the prevention, onset, and pervasive nature of these conditions. Public messages have focused primarily on drinking practices of young women, ignoring middle-aged and elderly women, some of whom will become alcoholics and most of whom will go through menopause and/or be threatened by osteoporosis. Thus, messages focus on a narrow spectrum of reproductive issues while ignoring the many others cited here. We would encourage the development and implementation of messages that acknowledge the impact of drinking on reproductive issues and health concerns of all women at any age. Knowing when to say when and why are vital components of efforts to promote the prevention of alcohol consumption. Perhaps even more important, however, is knowing *how* to say when. As observed time and again in this analysis of available messages, information is lacking about the ways and means to attain prescribed recommendations.

Further, careful study of present and proposed campaigns and their effectiveness is imperative to the health of women. It is time that women's health issues be directly addressed with as much energy and concern as the alcohol industry puts into promoting consumption.

Notes

1. The Boston Women's Health Collective, *The New Our Bodies, Ourselves: Updated and Expanded for the '90s* (New York: Simon & Schuster, 1992): 55.

2. M. Sandmaier, *The Invisible Alcoholics: Women and Alcohol Abuse in America* (New York: McGraw-Hill, 1980): 63.

3. The Boston Women's Health Collective, *The New Our Bodies, Ourselves,* p. 55.

4. Sandmaier, *The Invisible Alcoholics,* p. 66.

5. I. J. Beckman, *Alcoholism Problems and Women: An Overview* (New York: Grune & Stratton, 1986): 65.

6. M. A. Schuckit & E. R. Morrissey, "Alcoholism in Women: Some Clinical and Social Perspectives With an Emphasis on Possible Subtypes," in M. Greenblatt & M. A. Schuckit (Eds.), *Alcoholism Problems in Women and Children* (New York: Grune & Stratton, 1976): 5-35.

7. T. D. Nirenberg & P. M. Miller, "History and Overview of the Prevention of Alcohol Abuse," in P. M. Miller & T. D. Nirenberg (Eds.), *Prevention and Alcohol Abuse* (New York: Plenum, 1984): 3-14.

8. Nirenberg & Miller, "History and Overview," p. 9.

9. Nirenberg & Miller, "History and Overview," p. 10.

10. L. B. Snyder & D. J. Blood, "Caution: Alcohol Advertising and the Surgeon General's Alcohol Warnings May Have Adverse Effects on Young Adults," *Journal of Applied Communication Research* 20 (1992): 1, 41.

11. M. P. Haines, "Using Media to Change Student Norms and Prevent Alcohol Abuse: A Tested Model," *Oregon Higher Education Alcohol and Drug Coordinating Committee Newsletter* (May 1993): 1.

12. T. DeCarlo & R. Parrott, *Perceptions of the Effectiveness of Alcohol Warnings and Warning Labels,* paper presented to the Applied Division of the Southern States Communication Association conference, April 1991, Tampa, FL.

13. "Power and Choice," *The Daily Egyptian,* February 8, 1993, p. 10.

14. "Power and Choice," *The Daily Egyptian,* February 8, 1993, p. 10.

15. *The Responsibility of Friendship: How to Talk to a Woman Who Has Problems With Alcohol or Other Drugs* (Center City, MN: Hazelden, n.d.).

16. In estimating readability levels, we applied Rudolph Flesch's Readability Score (sometimes referred to as Reading Ease score) as presented in G. M. Broom & D. M. Dozier, *Using Research in Public Relations: Applications to Program Management* (Englewood Cliffs, NJ: Prentice Hall, 1990): 55-58.

17. *The Responsibility of Friendship,* p. 11.

18. *The Responsibility of Friendship,* p. 11.

19. *Drugs, Alcohol, Tobacco Abuse During Pregnancy* (White Plains, NY: March of Dimes Birth Defects Foundation, 1987).

20. *Will My Drinking Hurt My Baby?* (White Plains, NY: March of Dimes Birth Defects Foundation, 1986).

21. *For Your Baby's Sake, Don't Drink* (Chicago: Fetal Alcohol Syndrome Workgroups, 1980).

22. *Baby!* (Springfield: Illinois Department of Alcoholism and Substance Abuse, 1992).

23. *Baby!* p. 7.

24. *Baby!* p. 9.

25. *Baby!* p. 13.

26. *What You Should Know About Sex and Alcohol but Are Afraid to Ask!!!!!!* (Carbondale: Southern Illinois University, 1992).

27. *What You Should Know,* p. 1.

28. *What You Should Know,* p. 3.

29. Nirenberg & Miller, "History and Overview," p. 11.

30. C. L. Otis & R. Goldingay, *Campus Health Guide: The College Student's Handbook for Healthy Living* (New York: The College Boards, 1989): 311.

31. R. K. Manoff, *Social Marketing: New Imperative for Public Health* (New York: Praeger, 1985).

32. R. Parrott, M. Glassman, & M. Burgoon, "Arizona's Public Campaign to Stop Overexposure to the Sun," paper presented to the Interpersonal Communication Division of the International Communication Association Annual Meeting, May 1989, San Francisco.

33. Sandmaier, *Invisible Alcoholics,* p. 59.

34. *Alcohol and Your Health* (New York: National Council on Alcoholism and Drug Dependence, 1990).

35. *Alcohol and Your Health,* p. 1.

36. *Alcohol and Your Health,* p. 1.

PART IV

A Campaign Perspective for Communicating
About Women's Reproductive Health

---

*As a consequence of the general currency of the culture being created by
only certain segments of society, knowledge from other sources is "sense-
less," has no meaning, because what is considered information or knowledge makes sense within the logic of the very system that created it.*
Lana F. Rakow, "Information and Power," p. 167[1]

The fourth part of this book addresses campaign efforts to design and disseminate
messages to women about their reproductive health. Campaigns are a form of systematic communication involving the identification of an audience and a goal, and the
design of messages aimed at the audience to attain the goal. The campaign process
includes three primary components: planning, implementation, and evaluation.[2] Such
undertakings should be considered within the following framework:

> Campaigns determine what information the public will most likely be exposed to and, by
> extension, what they will not be exposed to as well.

A campaign perspective for communicating about women's reproductive health
affords the opportunity to bridge gaps in an audience's understanding. As outlined by
Parrott and Daniels, prenatal care campaigns expose the general public to information
about benefits of prenatal care for yet-to-be-born babies. Such benefits include higher
birth weights and less infant mortality and morbidity for babies born to mothers who
received regular prenatal care as compared to mothers who did not. Prenatal care
campaign messages seldom address the concerns of pregnant women as women,

however, including their nutrition, exercise, and appearance. In this case, the presence of particular campaigns and messages, in lieu of others, reinforces a maternal and fetal health approach to communicating about reproductive health.

Williams discusses medical and social scientific research about cervical, ovarian, and uterine cancers, revealing the settled grounds, such as the use of a Pap test for early detection of cervical cancer, and the unsettled grounds, such as use of testing to detect ovarian cancer. In this case, the absence of particular campaigns and messages—to promote Pap tests to women, for example—reinforces a maternal and fetal health approach to communicating about women's reproductive health.

Savvy campaigners often utilize the press to extend the *reach* of campaign messages—the primary advantage associated with media. Newspaper messages could help to fill the void left by prenatal care campaign messages' failure to give advice to pregnant women about nutrition, exercise, and appearance. Daniels and Parrott find, however, that inconsistent reports of study findings in the press reduce the likelihood that women will find such reports to be helpful. Kilgore's examination of newspaper reports about cancers of the ovary, cervix, and uterus reveals trends in their underlying messages to women that often cast aspersions on the women and on the science surrounding these issues.

A campaign perspective for communicating about women's reproductive health provides a testing ground for communication social scientists. Communication campaign theory and research afford great promise to describe, predict, explain, and—yes—even *control* (the goal of theory associated with influencing outcomes) women's health behavior. Yet this is likely to be the case *only* if behavioral scientists who apply the communication campaign theory take the lead and follow the direction of medical researchers and scientists.

Rigorous protocols are required in order to proceed with recruiting women into *clinical* trials. Similarly rigorous procedures and practices must be identified to prescribe a precise method for testing proposed treatment regimens. Upon identifying a caveat relevant to the success or failure of a particular approach, it is adhered to in order to increase the likelihood that the regimen will achieve positive effects and avoid negative outcomes. In other words, participants are not simply recruited into *cancer* treatment trials. Nor are they likely to be recruited into a particular *type* of cancer trial. Rather, participants will be recruited based on types of tumors that are further specified according to size, for example, in order to identify the population eligible for a study. This increases the difficulty associated with recruiting participants into clinical trials but enhances the validity of findings.

Similarly, behavioral scientists conducting communication campaigns *must* identify the criteria for inclusion within the campaign's target group. The campaign literature is replete with reports of failures to attain goals and objects, failures that may too often be explained by the lack of adopting a rigorous protocol to specify the types of individuals to be affected by the campaign. Campaigners—faced with tough competition for funding dollars—appear more likely to err on the side of a traditional approach in proposing the design of their studies than to risk no funding. The biggest bang for the buck, so to speak, appears to be associated with constructing messages to reach mass audiences and measuring outcomes in relation to large, randomly selected, heterogeneous populations. An advantage associated with campaign communication is the reach of a message: Greater numbers of individuals are exposed to a common message than would be likely through one-to-one contact. A disadvantage associated with campaign communication is that in order to reach so many people with a common message, the content of the message is too seldom personally relevant to any specific individual.

Perhaps the greatest lesson to be learned in reviewing a campaign perspective for communicating about women's reproductive health—besides the dearth of efforts in areas that need formal campaigns undertaken—is that too many messages fail to be properly focused. In facing the information and techniques provided by medicine, each woman must cope with the fact that she is different from all other women. Her body is unique, her economic resources are finite, her social setting is particular, and her culture is influential. Issues of ethnicity, economic class, and education are all critical determinants in health matters; yet there is still, too often, a tendency to focus on abstract audiences as a subject of health care.

Notes

1. L. F. Rakow, "Information and Power," in C. T. Salmon (Ed.), *Information Campaigns: Balancing Social Values and Social Change* (Newbury Park, CA: Sage, 1989): 167.
2. See M. Pfau & R. Parrott, *Persuasive Communication Campaigns* (Boston: Allyn & Bacon, 1993).

14

Promoting Prenatal and Pregnancy Care to Women

Promises, Pitfalls, and Pratfalls

Roxanne Louiselle Parrott
Margaret J. Daniels

Perhaps the most important change in medicine to occur in recent years relates to patients' unwillingness to be passive recipients of health care coupled with their strong desire to be actively involved in their own care.[1] Among the areas of research to confirm this notion, and one with far-reaching implications for women's health, is prenatal and pregnancy care. Many women no longer passively accept physicians' orders to reduce work commitments, change active lifestyles, or avoid travel because they are pregnant.[2] Some women question physicians' neglect to discuss information that relates to more than the health of the fetus but implicates maternal well-being, encompassing the woman's psychological and physical needs.[3] Others ask if physicians are the most appropriate health care providers to prescribe pregnancy and prenatal routines.[4]

Some of the inquisitors in this evolution to promote women's active involvement in prenatal and pregnancy care are female members of the U.S. Congress.[5] Others are obstetricians and gynecologists.[6] Still others are women representing cultural traditions previously ignored in obstetrical practice.[7] Undoubtedly, for each one of them, hundreds of women simply endure the routines that medical tradition associates with pregnancy or avoid interaction with the formal health care system altogether to escape these circumscribed rituals. This chapter examines these routines, summarizing the available medical and social scientific literature that evaluates their effects on women and fetuses.

Prenatal and Pregnancy Care Defined

> In the Third World today, two systems of prenatal care coexist. The official one, run by doctors and trained nurses and midwives, is accessible to only a small section of the population. The indigenous system draws on practical skills women have learned, handed down, and adjusted to that particular environment, and is closely linked with the religion and belief system of the culture. Inevitably, the two conflict.[8]

Whether in the Third World or not, two systems of prenatal care coexist. Failure to recognize both may preclude a full understanding of women's prenatal practice. Neglecting the importance of information handed down from mother to daughter may be responsible for perpetuating such misinformation as the once-believed notion that the placenta acts as a barrier, so that smoking or drinking will not affect the fetus.[9]

By definition, in pregnancy the woman is *pregnant,* whereas the fetus is *prenatal;* the latter term is used to refer to both what occurs and what exists before birth. To label the formal care given to women who are pregnant as "prenatal care" places a preemptory emphasis on the fetus while placing the pregnant woman in the background. This emphasis on fetal routines occurs despite the fact that even the American Medical Association (AMA) defines prenatal care in terms of care to be given to a pregnant woman *and* her fetus during the course of a pregnancy.[10] Other explanations for focusing on the fetus to the exclusion of the pregnant woman in promoting healthy prenatal practices include the belief that routines promoted in the name of the fetus's welfare will be tolerated by the woman for the "other's benefit."[11] Such routines, when prescribed by experts for the health of the fetus, seem to be beyond reproach, highlighting the power of the physician in obstetrical encounters.[12]

The notion of two systems of prenatal care coexisting together further denotes that prenatal care exists both in terms of a physical component that deals with the woman's and fetus's bodily changes and activities during the woman's pregnancy, and a psychosocial component that deals with the woman's need for information and support during pregnancy. One expanded definition, which incorporates recommendations from the American College of Obstetricians and Gynecologists, the American College of Nurse Midwifery, the Academies of Pediatrics and Family Medicine, and numerous federal and state health agencies, states,

> Prenatal care consists of health promotion, risk assessment, and intervention linked to the risks and conditions uncovered. These activities require the cooperative and coordinated

efforts of the woman, her family, her prenatal care providers, and other specialized providers. Prenatal care begins when conception is first considered and continues until labor begins. The objectives of prenatal care for the mother, infant, and family relate to outcomes through the first year following birth.[13]

This expanded definition highlights the range of persons involved in providing prenatal care, which includes the woman and her family acting together with a variety of other providers.

THE TECHNICAL ROUTINE OF PRENATAL CARE

The physical component of prenatal care has been more precisely defined than the psychosocial component of care. Even here, little attention has been given to what actually takes place during prenatal care exams, or the effects and effectiveness associated with specific practices, particularly with regard to the woman. As Rosen, Merkatz, and Hill suggest, "The effectiveness of prenatal care will be improved by additional research on the specific content of prenatal care."[14] No one has considered, for example, the benefit or harm associated with weighing a pregnant woman at each exam. In view of one study's findings in which hundreds of pregnant women used amphetamines to avoid gaining weight during pregnancy, the specific routines, such as weighing a woman at each visit, warrant careful evaluation in terms of their effects.[15]

The technical routine of prenatal care largely consists of specifying what tests and medical procedures trained personnel should conduct on the woman and fetus during the course of a pregnancy. For the fetus, these include the use of an instrument to record or listen to the fetal heart beat, an ultrasound scan, and fetoscopy and fetal blood sampling if family history warrants. For the pregnant woman, procedures include a vaginal exam of a woman's reproductive organs and pelvis to evaluate whether or not they are normal, which reduces the likelihood of problems occurring during delivery. Physicians perform a series of screenings to include blood tests, a Pap smear, urine tests, and blood pressure checks. Blood sugar is monitored due to the increased risk of diabetes during pregnancy, particularly in families with a history of the disease. Blood pressure is monitored because abnormally high pressure—hypertension—may lead to stroke, heart failure, and kidney and eye damage, as well as confusion and seizures. These tests are also used to check for the hepatitis B virus, cancer of the cervix, anemia, proteinuria, diabetes mellitus, hypertension, rubella, syphilis, and HIV.[16]

After the first visit, the AMA prescribes that a pregnant woman be weighed at each visit, and that she receive regular urine tests and blood pressure checks throughout the pregnancy to provide the means consistently to monitor the woman for diabetes and hypertension. The latter demands meticulous supervision and control, and sometimes early admission of the pregnant woman and premature delivery of the infant.[17] Moreover, over the course of repeated testing, "As pregnancy advances, some previously healthy patients develop gestational diabetes mellitus (GDM)."[18] Signs of GDM include a family history of diabetes, particularly in first-degree relatives; glucose in a "second fasting" urine sample; a history of unexplained miscarriages; a history of a large (for gestational age) infant, history of a malformed infant, and gross maternal obesity in excess of 200 pounds.[19]

Some physicians and medical researchers contend that "there seems no reason to believe that haphazard screening for GDM has contributed in any way to the overall reduction in perinatal mortality rates."[20] Some even conclude that "the obsession with BG (or glucose tolerance) has led to a neglect of other factors which may be much more important in determining or predicting fetal survival."[21] Among the conditions that have been neglected, although physicians believe it to have significant ramifications for the health of the woman and fetus, is that of a woman's thyroid. A number of physicians and medical researchers recommend that a woman's thyroid stimulating hormone (TSH) be measured at the first prenatal care visit, and when too high or too low, be followed with diagnostic tests.[22] Thyroid enlargement during pregnancy has been documented since the time of Rubens's paintings, though the etiology remains in question.[23]

Hyperthyroidism occurs in approximately 3% of the pregnant population but is difficult to diagnose during pregnancy because many symptoms, including anxiety, insomnia, palpitations, sweating, and irritability, "may occur normally in pregnancy."[24] Accurate diagnosis is vital because untreated hyperthyroidism is associated with increased miscarriage, premature labor, and intrauterine growth retardation.[25] Yet this is not part of the prescribed technical prenatal care routine.

Contributing to the use of tests and medical procedures to define the technical routine of pregnancy care is the availability of technology, such as ultrasound. It was impossible to prescribe what did not exist in previous generations. Similarly, scientific support for the claim that "the placenta does not act as a barrier to protect the fetus"[26] appears to parallel the upswing in efforts to promote more tests of and restrictions on pregnant women. The knowledge base that confirms that the pregnant woman's behavior affects the fetus spurred efforts to promote awareness of relationships between a pregnant woman's consumption habits (e.g., caffeine, tobacco, alcohol, illicit drugs) and fetal development. Research into these topics in relation to fetal health may be found in subsequent chapters in this volume.

THE NONTECHNICAL ROUTINE OF PRENATAL CARE

> When I go for checkups . . . they never ask me how I am feeling, what I eat, if I get enough exercise, and rest or if I have any questions or problems.[27]

The psychosocial component of prenatal care has not been prescribed to the degree that the physical component of prenatal care has been. Psychological and emotional changes are at least as significant as any physical symptoms of pregnancy in their effects on women. Despite this, "the psychological aspects of childbirth have received surprisingly little study."[28] As one panel of experts who reviewed prenatal care practices concluded, "Prenatal care should add to the traditional medical concerns a new emphasis on the psychosocial dimensions of that care."[29]

Researchers frequently hypothesize that women will have worries about labor and delivery. Studies have demonstrated, however, that women have a lot of fears about pregnancy generally, not just labor and delivery. Despite these findings, we know little about these fears. The available data indicate that ratings of psychological distress or "mood" do not show any specific patterns of change over the course of pregnancy,[30] which may affect physicians' decisions simply to ignore the pregnant woman's emotional state. If there is no specific "mood" state to characterize a particular stage of pregnancy, providers may feel that they have little objective information to give women in this regard. Bodily and hormonal changes cause pregnant women to have sleep disturbances, appetite disorders, and reduced libido, all of which are used as indices in composite scores to assess psychiatric disorders such as depression.[31] Thus, there is a tension between identifying how a woman feels and making appropriate attributions to the cause, as "normal" progression of a "normal" pregnancy produces symptoms that otherwise would be associated with some psychological maladies.

There are many ways in which the psychosocial component of prenatal care might be delivered, and, undoubtedly, every health care provider offers some advice and support to pregnant women. However, there is a wide latitude for assuming that pregnant women know more than they know or have no particular need for information and support. This is an inaccurate assumption, as illustrated by findings that pregnant women seek information about: health behavior such as nutrition, vitamins, and medication; the fetus in terms of deformities, development, and general health; and such miscellaneous issues as childbirth education classes and sexual relations during pregnancy.[32]

Advice about how to care for oneself during pregnancy might be composed of a number of components. One example of how this component of care has been constructed may be found by examining the Rural Alabama Pregnancy and Infant Health Program founded in 1983 to reach high-risk, African American, childbearing women in three of Alabama's poorest counties. This project includes a home visit program that uses *trained lay community workers* to provide outreach, education, and social support.[33]

In the Alabama program, the topics that are addressed during a woman's first trimester include nutrition and pregnancy; drugs, alcohol, and tobacco; fetal development; planning during pregnancy; *common discomforts;* danger signs; cost of pregnancy; and community service agencies. During the second trimester, education focuses on choosing a name for the baby; *body changes during pregnancy; developing a sense of self; sex during pregnancy; prenatal exercise; dental health; weight gain during pregnancy;* breast feeding; and recipe sharing. For the third trimester, topics focus on labor and delivery; *contraception;* preparing the home for the baby; visit to the labor and delivery rooms; baby items and equipment; true and false labor; and rest and relaxation.[34] Our emphasis designates topics that specifically address issues directly relevant to the pregnant woman without direct involvement of the fetus.

One topic that should be routinely included in the information and advice component of prenatal care is discussion of pregnant women's' nutritional needs. Much research has "repeatedly identified poor maternal nutrition to be a primary determinant of poor pregnancy outcomes."[35] The failure of health care providers to give women information about this topic leads pregnant women to rely more on social network members to obtain the information. Such advice is often conflicting and may cause the pregnant woman anxiety. Some network members, for example, have been found to recommend an increase in food intake to gain weight, whereas others recommend a decrease in food intake to gain less than 24 pounds.[36]

Women in our society often face media depictions of body images that glorify thinness, affecting women's self-image.[37] One study of 42,101 pregnant women found 237 regularly using d-amphetamines to control weight gain during pregnancy.[38] Many women battle eating disorders,[39] and health care providers should not assume that these conditions take a 9-month holiday during pregnancy. Rather, it should be assumed that many pregnant women suffer from such disorders. Prenatal care program evaluators should examine the importance of weighing a woman at every prenatal care exam, given that the image associated with weight gain, however intellectually well understood it may be, may well contribute to a woman's depression and/or a loss in self-esteem. Both depression and low self-esteem have been found to reduce the likelihood of seeking prenatal care, as will be further discussed in relation to barriers to seeking care.[40]

Prenatal Care's Effects on Pregnancy Outcomes: The Promise

The AMA asserts that the purpose of prenatal care is to attain the health and well-being of *both* the mother and child at birth.[41] The average cost to care for a mother and child who received no prenatal care is almost 50% greater than the cost for a mother and child who received such care.[42] This cost relates to health effects observed in women and children, depending upon women's attendance at and use of prenatal care routines.

EFFECTS ON WOMEN

Less is known about specific maternal as compared to fetal outcomes related to receipt or failure to receive formal prenatal care, but care is assumed to benefit the woman as well. This appears to be an appropriate conclusion, particularly because the technical routine provides the opportunity to monitor maternal conditions such as diabetes, hypertension, and malnourishment. Scientific literature supports the efficacy of prenatal care interventions in relation to the diabetic woman.[43] The monitoring of this condition increases the likelihood that a woman's health status will be greater at the time of delivery.

Other maternal outcomes that have been measured include "breaking a woman's water" and the induction of labor. The artificial rupture of the woman's membranes increased 281% between 1980 and 1987, whereas the medical induction of labor was up 209% for the same period of time.[44] The use of ultrasound to date a woman's pregnancy may increase the use of both procedures, as the onset of labor may be deemed to be "late." The rupture of the membranes increases risk for infection, and so unnecessary performance of this practice increases health risk for the woman.

The incidence of postpartum fever and hemorrhage has also been examined in relation to maternal health, with comparisons being made between mothers who received adequate prenatal care versus those who did not. No significant differences between women who participated in formal technical routines associated with prenatal care and women who did not were found.[45]

EFFECTS ON THE FETUS

Preterm deliveries have been found to be more likely when a woman receives no prenatal care, although this outcome is most common in a young adolescent mother whether she receives care or not.[46] Preterm birth has been found to be a particularly potent predictor of perinatal mortality in the United States.[47]

In addition to preterm births, low birth weight (LBW) is an outcome used to judge the success or failure of delivery of prenatal care in the United States. Low birth weight is defined as less than 2,500 grams or 5.51 pounds, and approximately 7% of all babies born in the United States are LBW.[48] Mothers who receive little or no prenatal care increase the likelihood of low birth weight by up to 300%.[49] The receipt of nutritional information has been shown to be directly related to a reduction in the incidence of low birth weight,[50] once more illustrating the specific importance of systematic inclusion of this information in prenatal and pregnancy care routines.

Worthy of note is research demonstrating that LBW is less for certified nurse midwife (CNM) as compared to physician-assisted hospital deliveries and physician attended out-of-hospital births.[51] This suggests that nontechnical prenatal care routines, particularly a pregnant woman's understanding of her nutritional needs, contribute more impact to reducing the incidence of LBW than the technical routines such as ultrasound and fetal heart monitoring. One review of 9,014 prenatal charts from nine public health units showed that women who received more comprehensive prenatal care, including nutritional and educational services, had lower rates of LBW infants.[52]

LBW infants are 40 times more likely to die in the first month of life than normal weight children.[53] LBW infants who survive the first month of life are more likely than normal weight infants to develop temperament and behavioral problems, chronic health problems, physical handicaps, and reduced cognitive performance and coordination.[54] Thus, receipt of prenatal care affects outcomes at birth and other infant morbidity, too.

One final outcome to consider when judging the effectiveness of prenatal care in the United States is the infant mortality rate.[55] Infant mortality rate is used as one of the main indicators of a nation's health status. The United States' ranking, behind Sweden, Japan, Finland, Switzerland, France, Australia, Spain, and Canada, generates concern.[56]

Motivators and Barriers
to Receipt of Care: The Pitfalls

"For prenatal care to be effective, it must be available and it must be used."[57]

Women's decision making about whether or not to use available services represents a too-seldom addressed difficulty in campaigns to promote use. It cannot be said too often in relation to prenatal care that the dictum "Build it, and they will come" *does not apply*. Two primary elements promote cooperation with prenatal and pregnancy care routines. First, a woman must be convinced to seek care from a provider trained to perform such procedures. Second, a woman must be convinced to continue care when the tests may be physically uncomfortable, psychologically embarrassing, and financially costly.

MOTIVATORS

A number of variables have been found to be positively related to the likelihood that women will cooperate with prescribed prenatal care routines.

Advice on How to Care for Oneself. Research has demonstrated that among women who have access to prenatal care, receiving advice on how to care for herself increases the likelihood that a woman will seek prenatal care early. Moreover, such advice is directly related to attending often.[58]

Pregnancy Wantedness. Whether or not a woman plans her pregnancy impacts her decision to enter the formal prenatal care system. Women who plan a pregnancy are more likely to seek prenatal care early. This finding has been shown to relate to maternal behavior, regardless of ethnicity.[59]

Social Support. Some studies have shown that a woman's support group may positively affect her decision to obtain prenatal care.[60] This link is complex, however, for some research shows that women who have strong emotional ties to immediate family, with these relatives living near the pregnant woman, underutilize prenatal care.[61] Perhaps this finding relates to women's experience in receiving care from providers who emphasize technical routines.

BARRIERS

More appears to be known about the variables that inhibit rather than motivate a woman to participate with the formal system of prenatal care. Some of these relate to a woman's personality, some to her skill level, and others to the health care system generally.

Failure to Recognize, Denial, Unplanned Pregnancy. Some women report that they failed to receive early prenatal care because they did not recognize that they were pregnant. Others recognize their condition but move through a denial stage, which also inhibits decision making about formal care.[62] In addition, unplanned pregnancy, as asserted earlier in relation to variables that facilitate receipt of care, inhibits the likelihood that a woman will seek care.[63]

Personal Problems. Both depression and low self-esteem have been found to impact negatively the likelihood that a woman will obtain prenatal care. Also, spousal abuse and/or the absence of a stable relationship with a partner to share the responsibilities of a pregnancy decrease the likelihood that a woman will enter the formal system of care.[64]

Communication Incompetence. Of particular significance for communication scholars, a woman's poor communication patterns with parents and/or partners have been found to prohibit her from seeking care.[65] A more positive outcome associated with a skills-based approach to teaching communication may be that individuals will be able to negotiate their way through the health care system later in life.

Other Obstacles. A number of other variables decrease the positive intentions and behaviors of women who are pregnant and might be well served by prenatal care routines. These include the failure to perceive care as a priority.[66] Such perceptions may arise due to the belief that attendance is a personal inconvenience, perhaps due to lack of transportation and/or child care.[67] But for others, prenatal care is not perceived as a priority because they already have a child and their previous experience with prenatal care did not instill the sense that it was important.[68] Women should receive messages that remind them that each pregnancy is a unique experience and having a prior "normal" pregnancy is not a guarantee that a present pregnancy will be. A redefinition of the nontechnical routine of prenatal care to focus more on the benefits for the pregnant woman may enhance perceptions of the priority of such care, reduce perceptions that attendance personally inconveniences the woman, and enhance a woman's experience with care.

Dissatisfaction With Medical Care. Besides variables relating to the woman's level of awareness about pregnancy or to her emotional state of being, general dissatisfaction with the health care system has been found to contribute to the likelihood that a woman will fail to seek prenatal care early.[69] One review found that the most frequently identified barrier to receipt of prenatal care was negative personal characteristics of the provider. Adjectives used to describe these characteristics included *insensitive, judgmental, sexist,* and *patronizing;* providers' inability to teach, counsel, and communicate effectively with patients was specifically implicated.[70]

In sum, the medical research and social scientific literature offer support for a number of guidelines to direct the planning of prenatal care campaigns and programs.

The final section of this chapter examines whether these appear to have had any effect on the design of pregnancy programs and the messages intended to promote use.

Prenatal Care Messages and Messengers: The Pratfalls

The greatest barrier to receipt of prenatal care has nothing whatsoever to do with women's decision making, nor does it relate to the success or failure of the design of particular programs and messages to promote them. Rather, the most significant blunder in efforts to promote prenatal care is the failure to address the lack of availability of traditional providers—generally obstetricians, but also family and general practitioners.[71] This and the failure to reimburse nontraditional providers such as CNMs through public programs such as Medicaid may be more responsible for women not obtaining prenatal care than the decision making of women, who are typically the focus of blame for failing to obtain care.[72] No matter what messages are communicated to a pregnant woman, nor how aware she is of the value of prenatal care, when there is no provider of prenatal services, she cannot use such services.

The provider barrier is both financial and nonfinancial in nature. For women who can afford to pay for care, the reality is a decreasing supply of physicians who are willing to provide care and then only at an increasing cost. Physicians are simply not willing to offer services to childbearing women, primarily due to increases in malpractice insurance costs, which make this specialty less financially lucrative to physicians.[73] Between the years 1982 and 1989, 30% fewer medical students chose to specialize in obstetrics and gynecology.[74] Moreover, 63% of family practitioners dropped obstetrical care during the early 1980s; 45% of general practitioners chose to do likewise.[75] Among those who continue to specialize in OB/GYN services, migration to cities has been observed, owing to the increased availability of the most modern technology in large urban hospitals.[76] Taking just one state as an example, in 1991, 60% of Georgia's counties had no obstetricians, and 26% had no hospital.[77] Consistently, "rural pregnant women and children face greater obstacles to health care than non-rural women and children."[78]

A second pitfall associated with the promotion of prenatal care to women is the underestimation of the number of women in need of subsidized prenatal care. This occurs primarily due to the overuse of two methods to forecast need. One method is to multiply the number of live births in the current year by an estimate of the proportion below the poverty level as determined from census data. The second method for estimating need is to establish the population of women ages 15 to 44 who are below a defined poverty level using either census data or a combination of census and recent population data. These data are multiplied by the current fertility rate to produce the number of births to women in poverty. Both methods consistently underestimate the need for prenatal care, but planners continue to rely on them.[79]

For women who cannot pay for prenatal and obstetric care, the availability of traditional providers is even more problematic.[80] Up to 36% of low-income women of childbearing age have *no* medical insurance, and the federal government has reduced financial support of maternal and child health programs.[81] Of the family and general practitioners who continue to offer obstetrical services, only half are willing to provide care to Medicaid eligible women.[82] In one study that examined 13,011 births, short-term Medicaid recipients were least likely of all women to obtain prenatal care.[83] Efforts to expand Medicaid coverage have had no effects on the receipt of care, largely due to the paperwork involved with obtaining reimbursement, which strongly affects the willingness of providers to accept it.[84] The Bureau of Primary Health Care, which is part of the Health Resources and Services Administration (one of the eight agencies of the Public Health Service, which is located within the Department of Health and Human Services) has attempted to address such needs through a comprehensive perinatal care program. In 1992, the Bureau provided prenatal services to 180,000 women, a 62% increase since 1990.[85] No evaluation data is available to determine what stage of pregnancy women receiving assistance were in or the outcomes associated with care.

Beyond the availability of providers and programs, problems with the promotion of prenatal care include an absence of messages and messengers to inform women why prenatal procedures are important for the welfare of the woman. One ongoing program sponsored by North Carolina, the Governor's Commission on the Reduction of Infant Mortality, the Health Start Foundation, and the March of Dimes exemplifies this failure. The "First Step" Campaign depends primarily on media messages to communicate information that will change behaviors designed to reduce infant mortality and morbidity in North Carolina. An evaluation report written at the end of the first year boasts the following:

- over 300,000 pieces of printed material distributed
- 97 of 100 local health departments have requested copies of the FIRST STEP video, *Families Behind the Numbers*
- hundreds of presentations
- over 500 billboards have been donated for use by the campaign
- 5,000 state owned vehicles bear FIRST STEP bumper stickers[86]

These outcomes relate to message *exposure* at best, the simplest and most basic variable upon which campaign communication depends. There is no evidence to suggest that the targeted audience of pregnant women has in any way attended to these messages, comprehended them, acquired the skills necessary to change behaviors linked to infant mortality, or behaved in accordance with the recommendations.[87]

An examination of the campaign materials further reveals a total neglect to address issues such as pregnancy wantedness or a woman's need for advice about herself in the design of messages. Elaboration of the First Step theme consists of messages such as, "Take the first step for North Carolina's babies . . . " and "Take the first step for your baby." Within the brochure titled with the latter message, the pregnant woman is told to, "Stop smoking," "Don't drink beer, wine, liquor," "Don't use cocaine, crack, or other drugs," "Know your family history."[88] She is not, however, told *how* to attain these goals nor how they relate to her own well-being, but only that these behaviors affect her "baby." Campaigns such as this demand more guidance from social scientists to enhance the chance for success.[89]

Another program, however, illustrates the development and use of lessons learned from research on prenatal care to guide its operation. The Rural Alabama Pregnancy and Infant Health Program's goals include screening all pregnant women to identify high-risk pregnancies and ensuring the receipt of care appropriate to medical and social needs.[90]

From a communication perspective, this program illustrates both success and failure. The program is exemplary in that planners address a number of the barriers to receipt of care previously identified, such as transportation and the need for information and support. Lay persons are identified and trained to provide information and support to pregnant women, overcoming the lack of traditional providers.[91] The primary fault to be found in the implementation of the Alabama program is the absence of reinforcement. Once women have been enrolled and begin to participate in the practices being promoted to them, there is no provision within the plan to promote continued use. This program, one of the few (a) to have been in existence for a decade, (b) to have been evaluated with published reports, and (c) to demonstrate the adoption of many principles learned from literature about pregnant women's needs, is likely to be even more successful if users are inoculated against threats to the program information and recommended behavior.[92]

Beyond specific campaign efforts aimed at high-risk women, there exists the need to design prenatal campaigns and messages for other groups of women. Many women fail to follow through with obtaining prenatal care, even when providers are available and the women make and keep an initial appointment. This suggests that providers must be involved in promotion efforts of prenatal routines to pregnant women who make and keep appointments. To understand why providers fail to motivate women to attend prenatal care exams, one may consider research that examines pediatricians' conduct during well child exams. Pediatricians spend one third to one half of their office time conducting these preventive checkups.[93] OB/GYNs spend a similar if not greater amount of office time conducting prenatal exams, which are second only to the conduct of general preventive exams in occupying physician time.[94] Pressure on pediatricians' time has been found to relate directly to failure to extend opportunities to parents to seek clarification and elaboration of the events that take place during an office exam.[95] Moreover, the providers assume that everyone understands the nature and purpose of such exams.[96] Analogously, competing demands on obstetricians' time may lead to the failure to invite pregnant women to seek clarification and elaboration of what transpires during the course of a prenatal exam. Obstetricians may assume that a pregnant woman understands the importance of activities such as monitoring her blood pressure and checking her urine.

Research that examines the content of interactions during well child exams has found that pediatricians focus on technical routines to the exclusion of nontechnical attempts to guide and support parenting efforts.[97] Yet parents most often report a desire to receive such information.[98] Similarly, as previously summarized, receipt of advice about how to care for oneself during pregnancy is directly related to attendance at prenatal care exams, and women are more likely to decide to attend prenatal care appointments when they receive such information.

Conclusion

An examination of campaign efforts undertaken to promote prenatal care reveals that *none* of these are directed at promoting the practice in terms of benefits for the pregnant *woman*. In fact, few formal systematic campaign or provider efforts are expended toward informing pregnant women about pregnancy and the tests and procedures associated with prenatal care at all, even during the course of receiving that care. This is *not* a new conclusion. A published report of the findings of an expert panel that convened in October 1986 to assess the effectiveness and efficiency of prenatal care based on scientific evidence concluded exactly the same.[99]

Research revealing that too few obstetricians are available to provide care to pregnant women may be juxtaposed with demonstrations that CNMs "have been highly effective in providing sensitive, respectful, empowering, community-oriented services to women who have often been rejected by physicians by virtue of their economic class, race, ethnicity, foreign birth or geographical location."[100] CNMs are noted for combining education, health promotion, social support, and clinical assessment.[101] Although too few traditional providers are available, no broad-scaled efforts are being made to promote the use of CNMs or to facilitate these professionals' presence within the organized system of prenatal care.

In conjunction with the expansion of providers to nontraditional sources and of content to less procedural areas, national campaigns to educate the public, policy makers, and providers are needed to dispel presently held myths and misinformation about pregnancy and prenatal care.[102] Promotion of pregnancy care must encompass more members of a woman's social network; otherwise, too many opportunities exist to threaten a woman's efforts to understand and to make informed decisions in these matters. After all, much of what is known today simply was not known when our mothers were having us.

A model of pregnancy care must include differences among women—adolescents, rural women, high-risk women, and others. Moreover, women should not have to ask where to go to receive pregnancy care, because asking may be perceived as embarrassing. Perhaps a 1-800 hot line is warranted for women who need prenatal care and others who want to help them find that care. The care and attention that women give to making decisions about prenatal care should be worth the effort expended, which is likely only if the pratfalls of too few providers and too little access can be avoided, together with systematically addressing the pitfalls that function as barriers to women's use. Then, prenatal and pregnancy care's promises to women may be fulfilled.

Notes

1. J. H. Sammons, "Preface," in C. B. Clayman (Ed.), *The American Medical Association: Encyclopedia of Medicine* (New York: Random House, 1989).

2. S. Kitzinger, *Your Baby, Your Way: Making Pregnancy Decisions and Birth Plans* (New York: Pantheon, 1987).

3. N.M.P. King, "Maternal-Fetal Conflicts: Ethical and Legal Implications for Nurse-Midwives," *Journal of Nurse-Midwifery* 36 (1991): 361-365.

4. L. Hsia, "Midwives and the Empowerment of Women," *Journal of Nurse-Midwifery* 36 (1991): 85-87.

5. P. E. Parsons, "Research to Improve Women's Health: An Agenda for Equity," *The Network News* 17 (December 1991): 1.

6. V. Hufnagel, *No More Hysterectomies* (New York: New American Library, 1989).

7. Kitzinger, *Your Baby, Your Way,* p. 99.

8. Kitzinger, *Your Baby, Your Way,* pp. 98-99.

9. I. Chasnoff, "Hearing Before the Select Committee on Children, Youth and Families" (House of Representatives 99th Congress: 2nd Session, 1986): 12-20.

10. C. B. Clayman, "Prenatal Care," in *The American Medical Association: Encyclopedia of Medicine* (New York: Random House, 1989): 818-819.

11. See M. J. Cody & M. L. McLaughlin, "The Situation as a Construct in Interpersonal Communication Research," in M. L. Knapp & G. R. Miller (Eds.), *Handbook of Interpersonal Communication* (Beverly Hills, CA: Sage, 1985): 263-312.

12. M. C. Shapiro, J. M. Najman, A. Chang, J. D. Keeping, J. Morrison, & J. S. Western, "Information Control and the Exercise of Power in the Obstetrical Encounter," *Social Science & Medicine* 17 (1983): 139-146.

13. M. G. Rosen, I. R. Merkatz, & J. G. Hill, "Caring for Our Future: A Report by the Expert Panel on the Content of Prenatal Care," *Obstetrics & Gynecology* 77 (May 1991): 782-787.

14. Rosen et al., "Caring for Our Future," p. 783.

15. R. L. Naeye, "Maternal Use of Dextroamphetamine and Growth of the Fetus," *Pharmacology* 26 (1983): 117-120.

16. Clayman, "Prenatal Care," pp. 818-819.

17. M. I. Drury, "Diabetes in Pregnancy: Considerations for the Management of Delivery," in L. Jovanovic (Ed.), *Controversies in Diabetes and Pregnancy* (New York: Springer, 1988): 134-135.

18. Drury, "Diabetes in Pregnancy," p. 130.

19. Drury, "Diabetes in Pregnancy," p. 130.

20. R. J. Jarrett, "Reflections on Gestational Diabetes Mellitus," *The Lancet* 2 (1951): 1220-1221.

21. Jarrett, "Reflections on Gestational," 1220-1222.

22. L. Jovanovic & C. M. Peterson, "Thyroid Disorders in Pregnant Women With Type I Diabetes," in L. Jovanovic (Ed.), *Controversies in Diabetes and Pregnancy* (New York: Springer, 1988): 90-100.

23. Jovanovic & Peterson, "Thyroid Disorders," pp. 90-100.

24. Jovanovic & Peterson, "Thyroid Disorders," pp. 91-92.

25. M. Drury, "Hyperthyroidism in Pregnancy," *Journal of Rural Medicine* 79 (1986): 317-319.

26. C. N. Chiang & C. C. Lee, "Introduction and Overview," *Prenatal Drug Exposure: Kinetics and Dynamics* (Washington, DC: U.S. DHHS, PHS: Alcohol, Drug Abuse, and Mental Health Administration): 1.

27. Boston Women's Health Collective, *The New Our Bodies, Ourselves: A Book by and for Women* (New York: Simon & Schuster, 1984): 335.

28. S. A. Elliott, "Pregnancy and After," in *Contributions to Medical Psychology: Vol. 3* (Elmsford, NY: Pergamon, 1984): 93.

29. Rosen et al., "Caring for Our Future," p. 783.

30. H. Heymans & S. T. Winter, "Fears During Pregnancy: An Interview Study of 200 Postpartum Women," *Israel Journal of Medical Science* 11 (1975): 1102-1105.

31. Elliott, "Pregnancy and After," p. 94.

32. P. A. St. Clair & N. A. Anderson, "Social Network Advice During Pregnancy: Myths, Misinformation, and Sound Counsel," *Birth* 16 (1989): 103-107.

33. M. C. Nagy, J. D. Leeper, S. Hullett, R. Northrup, & W. H. Newell, "The Rural Alabama Pregnancy and Infant Health Program," *Family & Community Health* 11 (1988): 49-56.

34. Nagy et al., "The Rural Alabama Program," p. 52.

35. J. E. Brown, "Improving Pregnancy Outcomes in the United States: The Importance of Preventive Nutrition Services," *Journal of the American Dietetic Association* 89 (1989): 631-633.

36. St. Clair & Anderson, "Social Network Advice," p. 106.

37. N. Wolf, *The Beauty Myth: How Images of Beauty Are Used Against Women* (New York: William Morrow, 1991).

38. Naeye, "Maternal Use of Dextroamphetamine," p. 117.

39. J. J. Brumberg, *Fasting Girls: The History of Anorexia Nervosa* (New York: New American Library, 1989): 222-225.

40. M. A. Curry, "Nonfinancial Barriers to Prenatal Care," *Women and Health* 15 (1989): 85-99; B. Lia-Hoaberg, P. Rode, C. J. Skovholt, C. N. Oberg, C. Berg, S. Mullett, & T. Choi, "Barriers and Motivators to Prenatal Care Among Low Income Women," *Social Science & Medicine* 30 (1990): 487-495.

41. Clayman, "Prenatal Care," pp. 818-819.

42. T. R. Moore, W. Origel, T. C. Key, & R. Resnik, "The Perinatal and Economic Impact of Prenatal Care in a Low-Socioeconomic Population," *American Journal of Obstetrics & Gynecology* 154 (1986): 29-33.

43. L. Jovanovic, *Controversies in Diabetes and Pregnancy* (New York: Springer, 1988).

44. L. J. Kozak, "The Risk in Procedures Associated With Hospital Delivery: 1980-87," paper presented at the American Public Health Association meeting in Chicago, October 1989.

45. Moore et al., "Economic Impact of Prenatal Care," pp. 29-33.

46. R. D. Ketterlinus, S. H. Henderson, & M. E. Lamb, "Maternal Age, Sociodemographics, Prenatal Health and Behavior: Influences on Neonatal Risk Status," *Journal of Adolescent Health Care* 11 (1990): 423-431; Moore et al., "Economic Impact of Prenatal Care," pp. 29-33.

47. M. C. Freda, K. Damus, & I. R. Merkatz, "The Urban Community as the Client in Preterm Birth Prevention: Evaluation of a Program Component," *Social Science & Medicine* 27 (1988): 1439-1446.

48. J. Brooks-Gunn, M. C. McCormick, & M. C. Heagarty, "Preventing Infant Mortality and Morbidity: Developmental Perspectives," *American Journal of Orthopsychiatry* 58 (1988): 288-296.

49. J. L. Murray & M. Bernfield, "The Differential Effect of Prenatal Care on the Incidence of Low Birth Weight Among Blacks and Whites in a Prepaid Health Care Plan," *The New England Journal of Medicine* 319 (1988): 1385-1391.

50. J. E. Brown, "Improving Pregnancy Outcomes," pp. 631-633.

51. E. R. Declercq, "Out-of-Hospital Births, U.S., 1978: Birth Weight and Apgar Scores as Measures of Outcome," *Public Health Reports* 99 (1984): 63-73.

52. D. L. Taren & S. N. Graven, "The Association of Prenatal Nutrition and Educational Services With Low Birth Weight Rates in a Florida Program," *Public Health Reports* 106 (1991): 259-264.

53. L. R. Eisenstein, "Prenatal Health Care: Today's Solution to the Future's Loss," *Florida State Law Review* 18 (1991): 467-487.

54. J. Brooks-Gunn, F. Liaw, & P. K. Klebanov, "Effects of Early Intervention on Cognitive Function of Low Birth Weight Infants," *The Journal of Pediatrics* 120 (1992): 350-359; D. S. Seidman, A. Laor, D. K. Stevenson, S. Mashiach, & Y. L. Danon, "Birth Weight and Intellectual Performance in Late Adolescence," *Obstetrics & Gynecology* 79 (1992): 543-546.

55. W. O. Willis & J. T. Fullerton, "Prevention of Infant Mortality: An Agenda for Nurse-Midwifery." *Journal of Nurse-Midwifery,* 36 (1991): 343-354.

56. J. Dickerson, "In Infant Mortality, Georgia Can Do Better," *Atlanta Journal & Constitution,* May 15, 1992, p. A8.

57. Rosen et al., "A Report by the Expert Panel on the Content of Prenatal Care," pp. 782-787.

58. Lia-Hoaberg et al., "Barriers and Motivators to Prenatal Care," pp. 487-495.

59. T. J. Joyce & M. Grossman, "Pregnancy Wantedness and the Early Initiation of Prenatal Care," *Demography,* 27 (1990): 1-17.

60. Lia-Hoaberg et al., "Barriers and Motivators to Prenatal Care," pp. 487-495.

61. P. A. St. Clair, V. L. Smeriglio, C. S. Alexander, & D. D. Celentano, "Social Network Structure and Prenatal Care Utilization," *Medical Care* 27 (1989): 823-831.

62. D. Petitti, C. Coleman, D. Binsacca, & B. Allen, "Early Prenatal Care in Urban Black and White Women," *Birth* 17 (1990): 1-5.

63. Lia-Hoaberg et al., "Barriers and Motivators to Prenatal Care," pp. 487-495.

64. C. Young, J. E. McMahon, V. Bowman, & D. Thompson, "Maternal Reasons for Delayed Prenatal Care," *Nursing Research* 38 (1989): 242-243; M. C. McCormick, J. Brooks-Gunn, T. Shorter, J. H. Holmes,

C. Y. Wallace, & M. C. Heagarty, "Outreach as a Case Finding: Its Effect on Enrollment in Prenatal Care," *Medical Care* 27 (1989): 103-111.

65. Young et al., "Maternal Reasons for Delayed Prenatal Care," pp. 242-243.

66. M. R. Sable, J. W. Stockbauer, W. F. Schramm, & G. H. Land, "Differentiating the Barriers to Prenatal Care in Missouri, 1987-88," *Public Health Reports* 105 (1990): 549-555; A. Scupholme, E. G. Roberston, & S. Kamons, "Barriers to Prenatal Care in a Multiethnic, Urban Sample," *Journal of Nurse-Midwifery* 36 (1991): 111-116.

67. Curry, "Nonfinancial Barriers to Prenatal Care," pp. 85-99; Lia-Hoaberg et al., "Barriers and Motivators to Prenatal Care," pp. 487-495.

68. St. Clair et al., "Social Network Structure and Prenatal Care," pp. 823-831.

69. Lia-Hoaberg et al., "Barriers and Motivators to Prenatal Care," pp. 549-555; Scupholme et al., "Barriers to Prenatal Care," pp. 111-116.

70. Curry, "Nonfinancial Barriers to Prenatal Care," pp. 85-99.

71. L. Hsia, "Midwives and the Empowerment of Women: An International Perspective," *Journal of Nurse-Midwifery* 36 (1991): 85-87.

72. Hsia, "Midwives and the Empowerment of Women," pp. 85-87.

73. D. Schleuning, G. Rice, & R. A. Rosenblatt, "Addressing Barriers to Perinatal Care: A Case Study of the Access to Maternity Care Committee in Washington State," *Public Health Reports* 106 (1991): 45-52.

74. M. King, "Progress on State's Infant Death Rate Stalls: Poor, Uninsured Women Still Lacking Prenatal Care," *Atlanta Journal & Constitution,* October 6, 1992, p. A1.

75. A. Owens, "Will Defensive Medicine Really Protect You?" *Medical Economics* 65 (1988): 88.

76. Schleuning et al., "Addressing Barriers," pp. 47-52.

77. "Study: Rural Children Facing Crisis of Poverty, Poor Health," *Atlanta Journal & Constitution,* December 17, 1991, p. A1; M. R. Rosenzweig & T. P. Schultz, "Who Receives Medical Care? Income, Implicit Prices, and the Distribution of Medical Services Among Pregnant Women in the United States," *The Journal of Human Resources* 25 (1990): 473-508.

78. L. L. Albers & D. A. Savitz, "Hospital Setting for Birth and Use of Medical Procedures in Low-Risk Women," *Journal of Nurse-Midwifery* 36 (1991): 327-333.

79. P. A. Buescher, M. D. People-Sheps, P. A. Guild, & E. Siegel, "Problems in Estimating the Number of Women in Need of Subsidized Prenatal Care," *Public Health Reports* 106 (1991): 333-338.

80. Eisenstein, "Prenatal Health Care," pp. 467-487; C. N. Oberg, B. Lia-Hoaberg, E. Hodkinson, C. Skovholt, & R. Vanman, "Prenatal Care Comparisons Among Privately Insured, Uninsured, and Medicaid-Enrolled Women," *Public Health Reports* 105 (1990): 533-535.

81. D. Hughes, K. Johnson, S. Rosenbaum, & J. Simons, "The Health of America's Mothers and Children: Trends in Access to Care," *Clearinghouse Review* 20 (1986): 472-480.

82. M. Machala & M. W. Miner, "Piecing Together the Crazy Quilt of Prenatal Care," *Public Health Reports* 106 (1991): 353-360; M. T. Orr & J. D. Forrest, "The Availability of Reproductive Health Services From U.S. Private Physicians," *Family Planning Perspectives* 17 (1985): 63-69.

83. E. M. Howell, E. J. Herz, R. H. Wang, & M. B. Hirsch, "A Comparison of Medicaid and Non-Medicaid Obstetrical Care in California," *Health Care Financing Review* 12 (1991): 1-15.

84. J. M. Piper, W. A. Ray, & M. R. Griffin, "Effects of Medicaid Eligibility Expansion on Prenatal Care and Pregnancy Outcome in Tennessee," *Journal of the American Medical Association* 264 (1990): 2219-2223.

85. BPHC (Bureau of Primary Health Care), "The People We Serve, The People We Are: Facts and Figures," *Department of Health and Human Services* (Washington, DC: Public Health Service, Health Resources Administration).

86. "First Step Campaign," in *FIRST STEP Campaign* (Raleigh, NC: Healthy Start Foundation & March of Dimes, 1992).

87. W. J. McGuire, "Theoretical Foundations of Campaigns," in R. E. Rice & C. K. Atkin (Eds.), *Public Communication Campaigns,* 2nd ed. (Newbury Park, CA: Sage, 1989): 43-66.

88. "Take the First Step for Your Baby," in *FIRST STEP Campaign* (Raleigh, NC: Healthy Start Foundation & March of Dimes, 1990).

89. See W. J. McGuire, "The Effectiveness of Supportive and Refutational Defenses in Immunizing and Restoring Beliefs Against Persuasion," *Sociometry* 24 (1961): 184-197.

90. Nagy et al., "The Rural Alabama Program," p. 50.

91. Nagy et al., "The Rural Alabama Program," pp. 55-56.

92. McGuire, "The Effectiveness of Supportive and Refutational Defenses," pp. 184-197.

93. P. H. Casey & J. K. Whitt, "Effect of the Pediatrician on the Mother-Infant Relationship," *Pediatrics* 65 (1980): 815-820.

94. National Center for Health Statistics, "The National Ambulatory Medical Care Survey, United States, 1975-81 and 1985 Trends" (Hyattsville, MD: U.S. DHHS, PHS, CDC, 1988).

95. R. Parrott, K. Greene, & R. Parker, "Negotiating Child Health Care Routines Through Pediatrician-Parent Conversations," *Journal of Language and Social Psychology* 11 (1992): 35-45.

96. R. Parrott, M. Burgoon, & C. S. Ross, "Parents and Pediatricians Talk: Compliance-Gaining Strategies' Use During Well Child Exams," *Health Communication* 4 (1992): 57-66.

97. Parrott et al., "Parents and Pediatricians," pp. 57-59.

98. Parrott et al., "Parents and Pediatricians," pp. 60-66.

99. Rosen et al., "A Report by the Expert Panel," pp. 782-786.

100. *Childbearing Policy Within a National Health Program: An Evolving Consensus for New Directions,* paper presented at the national conference Forging a Better Way: Protecting Maternal and Child Care Under National Health Programs, sponsored by Boston Women's Health Book Collective, National Black Women's Health Project, National Women's Health Network, and Women's Institute for Childbearing Policy, Washington, D.C. (1990).

101. Boston Women's Health Book Collective et al., *Childbearing Policy,* pp. 10-15.

102. P. A. Buescher & N. I. Ward, "A Comparison of Low Birth Weight Among Medicaid Patients of Public Health Departments and Other Providers of Prenatal Care in North Carolina and Kentucky," *Public Health Reports* 107 (1992): 54-59.

15

Prenatal Care From the Woman's Perspective

A Thematic Analysis of the Newspaper Media

Margaret J. Daniels
Roxanne Louiselle Parrott

Prenatal health care has been defined in a multitude of ways by various institutions. One prenatal care forum, which included physicians and government representatives, defined it as follows:

> Prenatal health care is defined as pregnancy- and infant-related medical support systems provided with the goal of promoting the health and well-being of the pregnant woman, the fetus, and the family up to one year after the infant's birth.[1]

Common to many definitions of prenatal care, the preceding definition presents prenatal care as a medical service that is given to women. In a broader sense, prenatal care consists of *any* changes that a woman makes to her daily routine simply because she is pregnant. Some of these changes and the corresponding behaviors are likely to be covered in depth during routine medical examinations. Others are likely to be only superficially discussed during her medical examinations. In this chapter, we will use the following definition of prenatal care, presented by the Boston Women's Health Book Collective:

> Prenatal care is the care you give yourself, as well as the care you receive from friends and family. We no longer believe that it is enough just to "see the doctor regularly" or "leave it all to the doctor." When you visit your practitioner (midwife or doctor) every month and then every week, s/he is simply monitoring the care you give yourself.[2]

A substantial amount of research has been published in the area of barriers to the receipt of adequate medical prenatal care, but very little research has been conducted to assess women's conversations during pregnancy. Such research would lead to a more woman-centered, comprehensive understanding of prenatal care as defined above, encompassing the care a woman gives herself. Just three studies were found that described women's self-reported pregnancy conversations. Together, these studies described the following *14 pregnancy-related conversational topics:*

1. avoidance/nonavoidance of "harmful" (legal) substances and practices;
2. technology/utilization of medical services;
3. diet/nutrition;
4. labor and delivery;
5. abnormal symptoms/experiences of pregnancy;
6. exercise and weight;
7. emotions/self-esteem;
8. fashion;
9. relationship with her partner during pregnancy;
10. finances;
11. remedies for discomforts during pregnancy;
12. normal symptoms/experiences of pregnancy;
13. sex during pregnancy; and
14. hygiene.[3]

Many of these issues will be discussed to some extent by the woman's health care provider, but she will *not* receive all her information from this one source, relying as well on mother, friends, husband, and others to fill the knowledge gaps.[4] Beyond these personal sources, another potential source of prenatal care information is the mass media. Newspaper accounts dealing with prenatal care provide an easily accessible mode for communicating information to pregnant women. As such, they are likely to be consumed not only by pregnant women but by persons in their social networks who are often eager to share information with women during their pregnancies. Our goal in this chapter was to assess what these stories convey, both implicitly and explicitly, to pregnant women.

Newspaper Media Search

The newspaper search began with an on-line computer database. At the time of the search, the computer system indexed 29 newspapers from the year 1989 through June 1993. The term *prenatal care* was not even recognized by the computer, and the system defaulted to *prenatal development.* "Prenatal development" produced 278 potential articles, 67 of which related to one of the 14 previously identified topic areas; many of the other articles dealt with legislative efforts to protect developing fetuses, or the effects of such behaviors as maternal smoking and alcohol consumption on *fetal outcomes,* topics covered in other chapters in this volume.

The abstracts of the 67 articles were coded into the 14 topics and illustrated reporting that emphasized technology ($n = 35$) and substance avoidance ($n = 14$). Six dealt with exercise and weight management, 6 with relationships, 5 with diet and nutrition, and 1 with normal symptoms. *None* of these 67 abstracts mentioned abnormal symptoms, emotions, fashion, finances, remedies, sex, hygiene, or labor in their discussion of prenatal care.

We next searched using the term *pregnancy.* This search led to 1,993 article titles, 312 with abstracts relating to one of the 14 previously identified prenatal care topic areas. Coding of these abstracts demonstrated an emphasis on reporting about substance avoidance ($n = 104$) and technology ($n = 52$), with a number of previously neglected topics receiving some coverage. This included labor, abnormal symptoms, emotions, fashion, finances, and remedies.[5]

Of the 312 article abstracts reviewed, 146 actual articles were located on microfilm and copies obtained. These articles came from seven widely read newspapers: The *Wall Street Journal, USA Today,* the *Los Angeles Times,* the *New York Times,* the *Washington Post,* the *Chicago Tribune,* and the *Atlanta Constitution.* Thus, two national papers, a southwestern paper, two northeastern papers, a midwestern paper, and a southeastern paper are represented, suggesting that newspaper stories available to women across the nation are described in this chapter. The distribution of topics across the 146 articles corresponds to a similar percentage in relation to each topic as the original 312 articles. These articles provided the database for this analysis and were found to convey the following three primary themes:

1. competing "Do" and "Don't" advice to pregnant women;
2. competing nature versus technology debates; and
3. preeminence of a medical-centered definition of prenatal care.

Competing "Do" and "Don't" Advice

The overarching theme that was found in the newspaper articles was one of competing "Do" versus "Don't" advice to pregnant women. That is to say, the reports purport to tell pregnant women what to do, but a consensus as to what is the best advice was difficult, sometimes impossible, to reach. Table 15.1 summarizes a list of the "Dos"

TABLE 15.1 "Dos" and "Don'ts" During Pregnancy List

DO	DON'T
Take Aspirin	Take Aspirin
Take Vitamins	Take Vitamins
Use Prenatal Technology	Use Prenatal Technology
Fly	Fly
Use VDTs	Use VDTs
Have Stressful Job	Have Stressful Job
Consume Caffeine	Consume Caffeine

and "Don'ts" compiled from the articles. For items in the "Do" list, it was either indicated that a woman *should* partake in some legal substance or practice, or it was suggested that it was *OK* to partake in some substance or practice. In the "Don't" list, it was either suggested that the woman *not* partake in some legal substance or practice, or it was indicated that it is not *necessary* to partake in some substance or practice.

Unfortunately, pregnant women are too often being told to "do" the same thing that they are told "don't" do. These recommendations include contradictory advice for the use of aspirin, vitamins, and prenatal technology, as well as others. Because much reporting was devoted to the use of aspirin and prenatal vitamins, these two recommendations will be brought forth as examples.

USE OF ASPIRIN DURING PREGNANCY

In 1989, according to an article in the *Los Angeles Times,* aspirin use was said to be safe and potentially helpful, in that it could prevent hypertension in *late* pregnancy.[6] That same year, a study was reported in the *Washington Post* stating that aspirin use was safe in the first trimester of pregnancy.[7] Then in 1990 the controversy began. Several articles between April and July 1990 reported the FDA (Food and Drug Administration) mandate to put warning labels on aspirin.[8] One article specifically discussed the recommendation that women avoid aspirin in the last trimester of pregnancy, indicating that use could cause the mother or her fetus to bleed.[9]

To further confuse the issue, however, that same year an article published in the *Wall Street Journal* reinforced the 1989 finding previously mentioned, suggesting that use of aspirin during the last trimester of pregnancy could help to control the rise of blood pressure in pregnant women. Indeed, the article warned that high blood pressure, if left untreated, could lead to serious detrimental health effects, including seizures, coma, and even death.[10]

In 1991, several studies were reported in newspapers that again indicated that aspirin was helpful in special cases. Pregnancy-induced hypertension (PIH) was noted again, citing its incidence in 5% to 15% of women and noting how deleterious it could be to both mother and child.[11] Yet another 1991 piece stated that daily aspirin could help women deliver healthy babies that would otherwise be dangerously small; a cautionary note warned pregnant women to avoid use if they were not at risk to bear low birth weight infants, citing the earlier mentioned bleeding problems attributed to use.[12]

The conclusion to be reached about use of aspirin during pregnancy is that women should not take aspirin, except under special circumstances. The reality is, these "special circumstances" are not so rare. As noted above, up to 15% of women may suffer from PIH. Furthermore, approximately 7% of all births in the United States are low birth weight.[13] So, as many as 22% of all pregnant women are *potential special cases* and, according to the medical research findings reported in the newspapers, *should* be taking aspirin.

USE OF PRENATAL VITAMINS

A second example of contradictory advice that was highly visible in the newspaper media during this time span concerned the use of prenatal vitamins. One article estimated that up to 95% of all pregnant women take some sort of vitamin supplement during pregnancy.[14] Of 11 articles that directly discussed the use of prenatal vitamins, 5 were *pro*-vitamin and 6 said vitamins were of *little to no use.* In the articles that discussed the need for vitamins, the emphasis was on the intake of folic acid, which—it was suggested—decreases the incidence of birth defects. The majority of the pro-folic acid articles stated that the supplemental folic acid could be gained through "taking a daily multivitamin."[15]

On the side of the fence stating that multivitamins during pregnancy are unnecessary, several articles quoted the same nutritional expert who emphasized that for women eating balanced diets, such supplements were unnecessary and even harmful.[16] One of the dissenting articles noted that to take a strong enough multivitamin to gain the recommended dietary allowance of folic acid could lead to an overdose of vitamins A and D, which could be toxic.[17]

The vitamin controversy continued in the newspapers as doctors criticized the new guidelines that came out during this debate. These guidelines suggested that women gain more weight during pregnancy, by eating a well-balanced diet and not worrying about using prenatal vitamins. Some physicians noted the problems women could experience in relation to excess weight gain, including both infection and bleeding.[18] Another risk mentioned in relation to high weight gain was the increased likelihood of having a cesarean section.[19] Furthermore, several reports also considered the psychological repercussions of weight gain.

The more weight a woman puts on during pregnancy, the more weight she will have to take off, with the societal pressure on women to lose the pregnancy weight immediately after childbirth taking a heavy toll on women's self-esteem. One woman observed that failure to lose the weight was taken as an indication that a woman didn't care for herself.[20] This same article goes on to say that women in support groups for weight loss after pregnancy described their husbands as their most persistent critics.

An attempt at quick weight loss can be difficult and even dangerous, especially if a woman has had a cesarean. As noted in a *Washington Post* article, childbirth is associated with fatigue, and recovery time alone can take up to a month or longer, during which doctors recommend *against* vigorous exercise.[21] Thus the message "gain weight/ be thin" is confusing and potentially damaging to a woman's health *and* self-esteem.

Physical and psychological effects of weight gain for women should be considered in defining a weight gain of up to 30 pounds for one fetus as being "normal,"[22] and in making recommendations about the use of vitamin supplements during pregnancy.

In sum, pregnant women have to be extremely vigilant readers of this overlapping and contradictory advice about what to "do" and "don't" do during pregnancy if they wish to make sense of competing messages. Moreover, they need to be wary consumers, as is further evidenced in the second theme to emerge from these newspaper reports, competing nature versus technology discussions.

Competing Nature Versus Technology Debates

A second theme that emerged from the newspaper articles was a struggle between nature and technology. The prominence and leadership of this nation in medical technology was noted in various articles, with U.S. physicians depicted as loving the instruments and tests available to them and using them in a less-than-judicious fashion.[23] Other reports advanced obstetrical malpractice as a motive for use and even seeming overuse of medical testing and diagnostics.[24]

The paradox is that the more that technology is utilized, the less natural pregnancy and childbirth become. One childbirth educator was quoted as observing that women attending her class want to avoid hospitals in order to avoid the high-tech interference with their labors and deliveries.[25]

Among the nature versus technology debates that arose in the newspaper media during this time period, two are again chosen to exemplify the conflicting messages available for pregnant women in this regard: (a) use of certified nurse midwives, and (b) use of genetic testing.

USE OF CERTIFIED NURSE MIDWIVES

As described in the previous chapter, a certified nurse midwife (CNM) is an individual who has fulfilled the requirements of two disciplines—nursing and midwifery—and who possesses certification from the American College of Nurse Midwives.[26] CNMs are certified nurses who are independently responsible for supervising and counseling clients during pregnancy, during labor, and after birth.[27] The basic tenets of CNM care involve: (a) the facilitation of the natural process of birth, using invasive techniques only when deemed necessary; (b) the belief in continuous, comprehensive care; (c) the promotion and implementation of family-centered care; and (d) the belief in teaching patients to participate actively in their care and to make their own informed decisions.[28]

Several newspaper articles clearly portrayed the medical community's struggle over the use of CNMs. On the one hand, it was shown that pregnant women like CNMs. Sentiments published in newspaper accounts include such adjectives as *encouraging* and *helpful* in letting nature take its course; treating pregnancy like a normal part of life.[29] Physicians, it was noted, are less likely to view pregnancy as a natural process, with one physician defining the obstetrician's role as preventing disasters.[30]

A second benefit of CNM use, noted in several articles, is associated with cost. CNMs work primarily with low-risk pregnancies, which make up 80% of all deliveries.[31] CNMs have lower annual incomes, lower liability insurance, are less frequently sued, and have lower fees.[32] All the articles dealing with this issue suggested the same conclusion: CNMs are playing an increased role in obstetrical care and will continue to do so. It is typically up to the expectant couple to decide which practitioner they prefer. Yet because the newspaper articles discussed CNMs most frequently in terms of their assistance to traditionally underserved populations, mainly the poor, this avenue of care may not be perceived as an option for many pregnant women.

USE OF GENETIC TESTING

The use of genetic testing is the second "nature versus technology" debate that arose in the newspaper reports. Genetic testing is used to screen for a variety of disorders such as Down's syndrome and cystic fibrosis. Nine articles were devoted to the discussion of three genetic tests: standard amniocentesis (from 14th to 18th week of pregnancy), early amniocentesis (from 11th to 14th week of pregnancy), and chorionic villus sampling (CVS) (from 9th to 11th weeks).[33] The articles defined amniocentesis, describing the use of a fine needle inserted through a woman's abdomen into her uterus to withdraw fluid from around the fetus to obtain cells shed from the fetus for use in testing for genetic disorders.[34]

Several articles noted that, due to the risks involved, these tests are typically only recommended for women over the age of 35 or for those with a history of genetic disorders. Although each of the three tests can cause miscarriage, the articles usually noted that the earlier tests are associated with higher rates of fetal risk and lower predictive accuracy.[35] Thus, much of the discussion concerning safety was centered on the use of CVS. In comparison to amniocentesis, CVS is a relatively new test, with newspapers hailing its entrance in 1989. The main advantage of the test was said to be its ability to track chromosome abnormalities earlier than amniocentesis.[36] Early diagnosis, it was stated, would allow couples to make a termination decision in the first trimester of pregnancy, with privacy for the couple and reduced psychological trauma cited as advantages of this method.[37] Should a woman decide to keep the child, it was noted that "early diagnosis also can help prepare a family for the special care a mentally retarded or physically disabled child will require."[38]

The newspaper articles also noted several drawbacks to CVS. In 1991, the safety of the test was called seriously into question, as research studies noted up to a 5% higher fetal death rate than amniocentesis.[39] The test was also suggested to cause limb deformities if not properly administered.[40] Furthermore, several articles reported use of early testing as a means of sex selection. Objections both inside and outside of the medical community in relation to aborting pregnancies due to the sex of a fetus were reported.[41] In one trial, however, 7 times as many women had elective abortions based on sex selection in the CVS group than in the amniocentesis group.[42] The ethical implications of aborting because of a quality-of-life decision also entered into the debate, as pregnant women were quoted as saying that they could not give their husbands retarded children.[43]

Ultimately, in the most recent articles, the medical community described CVS as a safe procedure if properly done.[44] Thus, the question becomes how a woman ensures that the procedure will be properly done and how she makes an informed choice. In terms of the decision-making process, one physician was quoted as advising patients to talk to their doctors.[45] Other articles recommended genetic counseling, the goal of which is to provide test options to couples and provide information in a balanced fashion to allow the couple to make an informed decision.[46] In reality, the newspapers demonstrated that couples often have few options and little choice as to whether they should use genetic testing as a form of prediction or let nature take its course. Some reported reasons to explain why choice may be removed from the woman include,

1. by the time testing is suggested, it is too late for early diagnostic tests;
2. women may not seek medical prenatal care until it is too late for early diagnostic tests;
3. some practices may not offer a full range of tests and may not refer high-risk women to centers that do;
4. some physicians favor amniocentesis because the procedure is easier to perform and has been in use for almost 20 years; and
5. a woman's insurance may cover only certain tests.[47]

Newspaper coverage of certified nurse midwives and genetic testing illustrates the tensions that pregnant women encounter in their decision making about pregnancy. Pregnant women undoubtedly desire to satisfy at least two different and sometimes competing goals—keeping pregnancy within the realm of the woman's control, while promoting her own and her unborn fetus's own best health outcomes. The newspaper stories reviewed for this analysis reflect the issues a pregnant woman must wrestle with in the face of the sometimes many options afforded her and the need to seek further information to clarify these options.

A Medical-Centered Definition of Prenatal Care

The final theme that emerged from the 146 newspaper articles was a focus on a more medical- than woman-centered definition of prenatal care, as presented at the beginning of this chapter. This fact is best evidenced through the review of topic areas that received little to no coverage in the newspaper media. Of the 14 previously identified pregnancy topics discussed by women during their pregnancies, 3 had *no* representation in the 146 articles. These topics include,

1. normal symptoms/experiences of pregnancy;
2. hygiene; and
3. sex during pregnancy.

Each of these issues will not necessarily be discussed with a woman's health care practitioner, yet each is likely to *greatly* impact a woman's pregnancy experience.

The lack of discussion about normal symptoms/experiences of pregnancy might at first seem surprising. In fact, in one study, this very same topic accounted for 28.6% of all analyzed pregnancy conversations, which was the *highest* overall frequency of all of the conversation types.[48] Some examples from this same study of conversations that fell into this category included

- heartburn
- sore breasts
- nausea
- tiredness
- complexion changes[49]

The revelation of these conversation types may help explain why this topic was not well represented in the media. Perhaps because *all* pregnant women are likely to experience heartburn, tiredness, and many other normal symptoms of pregnancy, the topic as a whole may lose its "newsworthiness." In other words, it is typically the new and different that sells newspapers. The fact that topics such as *abnormal* symptoms of pregnancy, new technologies, substances to avoid, diet, and labor and delivery techniques received so much coverage reinforces this point. Most of the reported information from these topic areas came from "just published" research studies.

The fact that the hygiene and the sex during pregnancy topics were not represented in the 146 articles is, perhaps, not too surprising, either. Both topics are highly personal and not often overtly discussed in newspapers in general, let alone in the pregnancy context. Perhaps books, magazines, and, as suggested by social scientific studies, the woman's social network provides this information.[50] Yet newspapers columns provide a nonthreatening method to seek answers to such issues.

Three other topic areas that received minimal newspaper coverage, that is, three or fewer articles, total, in more than 4 years, include,

1. the pregnant woman's relationship with her partner during pregnancy;
2. finances; and
3. remedies for morning sickness.

Again, although these issues are not likely to receive in-depth coverage during medical prenatal care, each is a pregnancy-related conversational topic, as reported by pregnant women, and thus should be considered part of woman-centered prenatal care. For example, several research studies, published in professional journals, were found that discussed marital adjustment during the transition to parenthood.[51] These published articles suggest that pregnancy and childbirth affect couples' rates of satisfaction, sacrifice, sexuality, happiness, and depression. But unless implemented as part of plans for systematic design and dissemination of campaign messages, or "picked up" by a media source such as newspapers or magazines, such information will have a limited audience.

Conclusion

Based on the findings of this analysis of newspapers, greater efforts should be made to report information that will be relevant to pregnant women on a daily basis throughout their pregnancies. These stories might be incorporated into a health column featured for pregnant women. In this way, women could be given an opportunity to write and ask questions about information they read in the column. Due to observable (e.g., weight gain) and unobservable (hormonal) physical changes, as well as adjustments in a woman's relationship with her partner, most women go through changing physical and emotional states *throughout* their pregnancies. Newspaper discussion of physical changes focused too narrowly on abnormal rather than normal symptoms. Moreover, the newspaper articles that discussed emotional states tended to emphasize the end of the pregnancy when women are most uncomfortable, and postpartum depression. Articles exploring common feelings, both positive and negative, throughout pregnancy might also be appreciated by pregnant women and the persons involved in their pregnancies.

A second change that newspapers can make to become more women-centered in their pregnancy articles would be to offer some discussion of intimate topics such as sex and hygiene. It is safe to say that the vast majority of pregnant women will have questions and concerns in relation to these topics. Though some might contend that discussion centered on sex and hygiene do not belong in the newspaper media, the prevalence of AIDS has brought debates regarding these same topics, albeit with a different emphasis, to the forefront. Thus, there seems to be room in the newspaper media for sex and hygiene reports.

In terms of the women, the newspaper articles overall offered a mediocre representation of prenatal care from a woman's perspective. Of the 14 topic areas identified by analyzing women's self-reported pregnancy conversations, 6 received very little to no coverage in a more than 4-year span of time. Furthermore, the topics receiving the most coverage had a technical and, taken together, contradictory slant. As a result, the newspaper media's pregnancy coverage provided less useful and more confusing information than they have the potential to provide. Too often, newspaper stories functioned as a springboard for guilt and paranoia, rather than confidence and competence, with the former belying the latter. What information should newspapers print to satisfy the needs of pregnant women? One must ask the women.

Notes

1. Definition of prenatal care found in L. R. Eisenstein, "Prenatal Health Care: Today's Solution to the Future's Loss," *Florida State Law Review* 18 (1991): 467-487.

2. Boston Women's Health Book Collective, *The New Our Bodies, Ourselves: Updated and Expanded for the '90s* (New York: Simon & Schuster, 1992): 401.

3. M. J. Daniels & R. Parrott, "Social Influence During Pregnancy: Whom Women Talk to, What About, and Levels of Social Influence," paper presented at the 1994 Southern Speech Communication Conference, Norfolk, VA (April 1994); F. M. Deutsch, J. Brooks-Gunn, A. Fleming, D. N. Ruble, & C. Stangor,

"Information-Seeking and Maternal Self-Definition During the Transition to Motherhood," *Journal of Personality and Social Psychology* 55 (1988): 420-431; P. A. St. Clair & N. A. Anderson, "Social Network Advice During Pregnancy: Myths, Misinformation, and Sound Counsel," *Birth* 16 (1989): 103-113.

4. Daniels & Parrott, "Social Influence."

5. The number of articles appearing in each category include diet ($n = 36$), labor ($n = 30$), abnormal symptoms ($n = 27$), exercise and weight management ($n = 19$), emotions ($n = 18$), fashion ($n = 14$), normal symptoms ($n = 5$), relationship ($n = 3$), finances ($n = 2$), and remedies ($n = 2$).

6. J. Scott, "2 Studies Find Aspirin Helpful in Pregnancies," *Los Angeles Times,* August 10, 1989, p. I1.

7. Reuter, "Study Discounts Aspirin Danger to Fetus," *Washington Post,* December 14, 1989, p. A13:1.

8. Associated Press, "FDA Warning: Avoid Aspirin in Last 3 months of Pregnancy," *Atlanta Constitution,* July 3, 1990, p. A3; R. C. Paddock, "Aspirin Label to Warn of Danger in Late Pregnancy," *Los Angeles Times,* July 4, 1990, p. A29; Times Wire Services, "Pregnant Women Warned on Aspirin," *Los Angeles Times,* July 4, 1990, p. A20.

9. Paddock, "Aspirin Label," p. 29.

10. M. Waldholz, "Aspirin Could Save Some Mothers-to-Be," *Wall Street Journal,* January 29, 1990, p. B1.

11. M. Gladwell, "Small Daily Aspirin Doses May Protect Health of Pregnant Women and Fetuses," *Washington Post,* July 10, 1991, p. A3.

12. J. Gehorsam & A. Boer, "Daily Aspirin Helps Prevent Dangerously Small Babies," *Atlanta Constitution,* June 14, 1991, p. C3.

13. J. Brooks-Gunn, M. C. McCormick, & M. C. Heagarty, "Preventing Infant Mortality and Morbidity: Developmental Perspectives," *American Journal of Orthopsychiatry* 58 (1988): 288-296.

14. C. Sugarman, "Pigging Out During Pregnancy? New Recommendations About What—and How Much—to Eat," *Washington Post,* July 17, 1990, p. WH18.

15. Associated Press, "Folic Acid Found to Reduce Birth Defects," *Washington Post,* December 24, 1992, p. A14.

16. Associated Press, "Pregnant Women Can Gain More and Skip Vitamins, a Panel Says," *New York Times,* June 7, 1990, p. B8; W. Booth, "Prenatal Nutrition Guidelines Revised," *Washington Post,* June 7, 1990, p. A1.

17. R. Perl & J. Gehorsam, "Daily Doses of Folic Acid Prevent Some Birth Defects," *Atlanta Constitution,* August 2, 1991, p. D3.

18. R. Kotulak, "Doctors Assail New Pregnancy Guidelines," *Chicago Tribune,* June 7, 1990, sec. 1, p. 1.

19. T. Friend, "Higher Weight Guidelines for Moms-to-Be," *USA Today,* August 10, 1989, p. D1.

20. M. Downey, "Weighting Game: New Moms Find Losing Takes Time," *Atlanta Constitution,* October 28, 1991, p. C4.

21. J. L. Salmon, "Getting Back in Shape," *Washington Post,* May 29, 1990, p. WH14.

22. J. E. Brody, "Early Weight Gain Tied to Fetal Health," *New York Times,* November 20, 1991, p. C15.

23. D. Brown, "The Siren Song of a Diagnostic Test," *Washington Post,* May 25, 1993, p. WH1.

24. D. Schleuning, G. Rice, & R. A. Rosenblatt, "Addressing Barriers to Perinatal Care: A Case Study of the Access to Maternity Care in Washington State," *Public Health Reports* 106 (1991): 47-52.

25. E. Wilds, "Cases Against Fetal Monitoring," *Washington Post,* November 12, 1991, p. A20.

26. Definition found in J. A. Carveth, "Conceptual Models of Nurse-Midwifery," *Journal of Nurse-Midwifery* 32 (1987): 22.

27. H. Varney, *Nurse Midwifery* (Boston: Blackwell Scientific Publications, 1987).

28. Varney, *Nurse Midwifery.*

29. R. Perl, "Hospitals Won't Deliver Midwife Care to Moms," *Atlanta Constitution,* August 4, 1989, pp. J1, J3.

30. Perl, "Hospitals Won't Deliver," p. J3.

31. R. McCarthy, "Midwives on Around the Clock for Needy," *Atlanta Constitution,* December 12, 1990, pp. J1, J4.

32. L. Raimondo, "Nurse-Midwives Playing an Increased Role," *New York Times,* June 9, 1991, pp. I1, I12.

33. S. Roan, "Prenatal-Test Possibilities Have Grown From 1 to 3," *Los Angeles Times,* January 15, 1991, pp. E1, E4.

34. Roan, "Prenatal-Test Possibilities," pp. E1, E4.

35. E. Rosenthal, "Technique for Early Prenatal Test Comes Under Question in Studies," *New York Times,* July 10, 1991, p. C11.

36. T. Friend, "New Prenatal Test Detects Problems Early," *USA Today,* March 3, 1989, p. D1.

37. Roan, "Prenatal-Test Possibilities," p. E4.

38. R. Perl, "Prenatal Screening Can Detect Problems," *Atlanta Constitution,* February 8, 1990, p. E4.

39. Rosenthal, "Technique for Early Prenatal Test," p. C11.

40. S. G. Boodman, "Are Reports of Rare Birth Defects a Fluke? Questions About a Popular Prenatal Test," *Washington Post,* November 3, 1992, p. WH10.

41. R. Steinbrook, "Newer Technique for Detection of Birth Defects Called Safe," *Los Angeles Times,* March 9, 1989, sec. 1, p. 3.

42. Steinbrook, "Newer Technique for Detection," p. 3.

43. Boodman, "Are Reports of Rare Birth Defects a Fluke?" p. 13.

44. Boodman, "Are Reports of Rare Birth Defects a Fluke?" p. 12.

45. Rosenthal, "Technique for Early Prenatal Test," p. C11.

46. S. Roan, "Counselors Present Test Options," *Los Angeles Times,* January 15, 1991, p. E2.

47. Roan, "Prenatal-Test Possibilities," p. E1.

48. Daniels & Parrott, "Social Influence During Pregnancy."

49. Daniels & Parrott, "Social Influence During Pregnancy."

50. St. Clair & Anderson, "Social Network Advice During Pregnancy," pp. 103-113; Deutsch et al., "Information-Seeking and Maternal Self-Definition," pp. 420-431.

51. For example, see: W. J. Adams, "Sexuality and Happiness Ratings of Husbands and Wives in Relation to First and Second Pregnancies," *Journal of Family Psychology* 2 (1988): 67-81; M. W. O'Hara, "Depression and Marital Adjustment During Pregnancy and After Delivery," *The American Journal of Family Therapy* 13 (1985): 49-55; D. N. Ruble, L. S. Hackel, A. S. Fleming, & C. Stangor, "Changes in the Marital Relationship During the Transition to First Time Motherhood: Effects of Violated Expectations Concerning Division of Household Labor," *Journal of Personality and Social Psychology* 55 (1988): 78-87; P. J. Wright, S. W. Henggeler, & L. Craig, "Problems in Paradise?: A Longitudinal Examination of the Transition to Parenthood," *Journal of Applied Developmental Psychology* 7 (1986): 277-291.

16

Cervical, Ovarian, and Uterine Cancer

Advancing Awareness, Choices, and Survival

Melanie Ayn Williams

Every year, cervical, uterine, and ovarian cancers take a striking toll on the lives of women in the United States. The American Cancer Society estimated 66,500 new cases and 23,000 deaths from cervical, uterine, and ovarian cancer in 1992.[1] Despite these alarming statistics, relatively little is mentioned to women regarding such an important health issue.[2] This chapter examines the medical and social scientific literature available on these important topics.

Cervical Cancer

INCIDENCE

Cervical cancer remains the most widespread cancer in women worldwide.[3] Prior to the introduction of the Pap smear, cervical cancer was the leading cause of cancer

AUTHOR'S NOTE: The author thanks Gordon Becnel, M.D., for his reading of the preliminary drafts and making suggestions on the cervical and uterine cancer sections of this chapter.

deaths for women in the United States.[4] Despite cervical cancer being considered to be a virtually preventable disease, the American Cancer Society estimated that in 1992, 13,500 new cases of cervical cancer would be diagnosed and 4,400 women would die, an increase from 1991.[5] Most new cases of cervical cancer occur in women who have not regularly undergone Pap testing, whereas when frequent Pap test screening occurs, researchers have observed a decrease in both incidence and mortality.[6]

CAUSES-RISK FACTORS

During the past 20 years, the medical community has gained a better understanding of cervical cancer. Progression of cervical cancer involves a number of cofactors that can contribute to malignant transformation.

Sexual History. The medical literature attributes a woman's sexual history as one important measure of risk for cervical cancer. Risk is generally considered to be inversely related to the age of a woman at first intercourse and directly related to her lifetime number of sexual partners.[7] So much emphasis on this singular cause leaves the implication that women with cervical neoplasia (a potential precursor for cervical cancer) or cervical cancer are somehow to blame, due to the number of sexual partners and early age at which they began to have intercourse.

The sexual history and behaviors of male sexual partners, however, also play a significant role in women's incidence of cervical cancer.[8] One study in which the authors investigated the role of male behavior in cervical cancer among women in India who had one lifetime sexual partner found that premarital and extramarital relationships of husbands pose significant risk factors.[9] When husbands had sexual relationships before and during marriage, their wives' risk of experiencing cervical cancer increased. History of sexually transmitted disease (STD) of the man before or after marriage was also an important risk factor. Sexual abstinence for 40 or more days after a wife's giving birth or having an abortion provided protection; however, sex with uncircumcised men or men circumcised after age 1 year increased the risk of cervical cancer.

The identification of sexual behavior as a risk factor for cervical neoplasia also motivates a search for venereally transmitted causes.[10] Most initial attention focused on herpes simplex virus—(HSV) 2. The medical literature has since moved toward examination of the role of human papillomavirus (HPV) infection and development of cervical neoplasia.[11] In 1987, one form of HPV received recognition as the most commonly diagnosed sexually transmitted viral disease in the United States. Thus, millions of men and women may possess human papillomavirus infection.[12] Yet most Americans have probably never heard of HPV. A campaign needs to occur, placing emphasis on the prevention of further spread of HPV infection.

Seemingly absent from the literature discussing sexual history and risk behaviors for cervical cancer are the concerns of the lesbian woman. If in fact heterosexual intercourse or the male's sexual behavior is so strongly associated with cervical cancer risk, a lesbian lifestyle may possess certain benefits for this group of women. On the other hand, lesbians could potentially engage in other sexual behaviors that place them at increased risk. The medical literature simply does not acknowledge their existence, thereby jeopardizing the health of these women.

Reproductive History. When considering reproductive history, women who have given birth to four or more children were found at increased risk of cervical cancer. The risk for cervical cancer was found to be inversely related to age at first childbirth. Moreover, cervical cancer was directly associated with the number of spontaneous abortions.[13]

HIV Infection. Immunosuppression is also associated with increased risk, thus the recent addition of cervical cancer by the Center for Disease Control as an AIDS-defining diagnosis.[14] Women infected with HIV are at increased risk; and HIV-infected cervical cancer patients have significantly more advanced disease at time of diagnosis than those not infected with the virus.[15]

Oral Contraceptives. A somewhat controversial relationship exists regarding oral contraceptive use and cervical cancer. Conflicting findings arise from researchers, although more recent research asserts that oral contraceptives are not associated with pre-invasive cervical cancer.[16] Furthermore, if oral contraceptive users continue to be regularly screened, their risk of developing the more invasive cancer should be found to be very low.[17]

Smoking. Cigarette smoking is associated with an increased risk of cervical neoplasia and cancer.[18] In San Francisco, a research team designed a study to understand better why smokers are more likely to develop cervical cancer than nonsmokers.[19] Interviews of 697 women between the ages of 18 and 49 revealed that women who smoked compared to nonsmokers were more likely to have engaged in first intercourse before age 16, to have had a greater number of lifetime sexual partners, and to have been pregnant. Controlling for number of sexual partners, smokers reported more history of pelvic inflammatory disease, chlamydia, and/or gonorrhea than did nonsmokers.

DIAGNOSIS

Cervical cancer often produces symptoms while still at an early stage, including postcoital bleeding and intermenstrual and postmenopausal bleeding, all followed by offensive discharge. In the advanced stages of the disease, lower pelvic and leg pain may occur due to the spread of the tumor.[20] Cervical cancer, however, generally involves a long pre-invasive phase (5-10 years or more). This should yield ample time for screening, detection, and treatment of the disease.[21]

The Pap smear is generally evaluated as an effective method for detecting cervical cancer or its precursors.[22] Doctors contend that the cervix is easily and readily accessible to examination. The test is not foolproof, however, due to human error; the false-negative rate ranges between 15% and 40%.[23]

Frequency of Testing. The American Cancer Society recommends a woman's first Pap smear and pelvic examination when she becomes sexually active or reaches age 18; Pap smears are then recommended every year. After three or more consecutive annual examinations with suitable samples and normal results, frequency is left to the prudence of the physician.[24] More problematic, however, is that the medical community has not made any standard recommendation for the frequency of evaluation after treatment of pre-invasive disease of the cervix.[25]

Sampling Technique. Up to 50% of false negative Pap smear results occur due to errors in sampling technique. To obtain an optimal smear, it is necessary to observe several simple guidelines *that are seldom communicated to women*. These simple guidelines involve women not douching or otherwise cleansing the vagina, as well as not having intercourse, for 24 hours before the Pap smear is taken. In addition, the test should not be done during menses, if possible, and the specimen should be obtained early in the examination, prior to the use of any lubricants or stains.[26]

An Abnormal Result. In a national symposium on women's health issues, physicians recommended that further examination of any abnormal Pap smear must be based on the descriptive diagnosis and the woman's risk factors. Colposcopy, which has become the standard procedure for evaluating abnormalities, involves the insertion of a colposcope into the vagina, allowing for a magnified view of the lower genitalia for more thorough examination. The medical literature argues that when performed with directed biopsy, colposcopy should provide enough clinical evidence for an accurate diagnosis of cervical neoplasia. If the colposcopic examination is satisfactory and invasive cancer is not present, measures such as continued observation and future testing may be used.[27]

TREATMENT

The management of patients with advanced or recurrent cancer of the cervix leaves much to be desired, yet most investigators agree that patients with early stages of cervical cancer can be treated effectively with surgery or radiation therapy.[28] The Wertheim-Meigs radical hysterectomy continues to be the main surgical treatment for early invasive cervical cancer in older women.[29] Surgeries such as electrosurgery, laser surgery, and cryosurgery are the preferred treatments in young women, because they allow preservation of ovarian and sexual functions.[30]

For high-risk cervical cancer, medical researchers note that the role of chemotherapy in surgical management has not yet been defined.[31] They suggest that strategies for combining chemotherapy and surgery may result in improved survival rates; combining therapy also appears to decrease recurrence of the disease.[32]

ERRONEOUS BELIEFS

These basic facts about cervical cancer are not widely known by women. In California, for example, researchers found that Vietnamese women, members of the fastest growing Asian population in California, possessed a significant lack of information. More than one third (39%) thought that breast or cervical cancer could be caused by poor hygiene, and about one third (29%) thought that these cancers could be contagious. Furthermore, 39% did not know that abnormal vaginal bleeding could be a sign of cervical cancer, and 74% did not know that multiple sexual partners could be a risk factor for cervical cancer. Most alarming, however, is that out of 92 women aged 18 or younger, 54% had never heard of a Pap test.[33]

Hispanic female migrant workers were found to believe that cervical cancer could be caused by injury such as cuts, bruises, or blows.[34] Another misconception was that the neglect of an illness or a health problem can lead to cancer. Others stated the belief that untreated vaginal infections and sexually transmitted diseases lead to cancer.[35]

PAST CAMPAIGN EFFORTS

Cervical cancer programs have shown that organized screening, coordinated with educational efforts, are effective in reducing the risk of cancer.[36] Cervical cancer remains one of the most curable cancers if treated early.[37]

Targeting Women of Color. In one study, researchers recognized that despite the Pap smear significantly reducing U.S. deaths related to cervical cancer, screening prevalence for the disease is disproportionately low among women of color.[38] The authors outline techniques for outreach and activism through recruiting and training women of color to serve as lay health educators. These women then serve as mediators between women of color and health agencies, establish social networks, and offer social support. When properly recruited and trained, these educators are thought to be able to bridge the gap between health care professionals and the community, as well as help health care professionals to better understand community and individual concerns about cancer.[39]

In an inner-city campaign targeting low-income black women, a breast and cervical cancer education and screening program received high follow-up rates for suspected malignancies of the cervix (70%) in a population sometimes described as less likely to adhere to recommendations for continued care.[40]

Uterine/Endometrial Cancer

INCIDENCE

During the past 20 years, there has been a noticeable decline of cancers of the uterus. Unfortunately, there has been no noticeable improvement of the survival rate during the past four decades.[41] Approximately 5,600 deaths and 32,000 new cases of cancer of the uterus—primarily of the endometrium—were expected in 1992.[42] Given these statistics, endometrial cancer is the most common tumor on the female genital tract.[43] Most tumors are expected to occur in women 50 years or older (75% occur after menopause).[44]

RISK FACTORS

A woman's risk of having endometrial cancer increases if she experiences any of the following: adenomatous hyperplasia, hormone replacement therapy, obesity, pelvic irradiation for benign conditions, old age, no pregnancy, late menopause, breast cancer, dysfunctional uterine bleeding, Stein-Leventhal syndrome, steroid-secreting tumors, chronic liver disease, hypertension, or diabetes.[45] In addition, a group of medical researchers found a strong inverse trend in risk for endometrial cancer was associated with induced abortions.[46]

DIAGNOSIS

Symptoms of the disease include irregular bleeding, enlargement of the uterus, and an abnormal discharge that may be watery. All women 50 years or older who are at increased risk for endometrial cancer should undergo cancer screening.[47] Interpretation of tests are difficult, however, due to blood and/or contamination by endocervical cells. Diagnostic accuracy is low unless cytopathologic expertise is available, and even then, clumsy sampling can be an obstacle.[48]

TREATMENT

Treatment includes irradiation and/or surgery. Medical researchers recommend that women with early detection of endometrial cancer, if considered medically fit, undergo total abdominal hysterectomy and bilateral oophorectomy. Patients who are medically inoperable can be treated by radiation and may be saved with a well-designed treatment program.[49] Uterine papillary serous carcinoma, a highly malignant form of cancer of the endometrium, has been described as clinically understaged in 40%-50% of reported cases. Furthermore, recurrence rates have been as high as 80%.[50]

PAST CAMPAIGN EFFORTS

Uterine/endometrial cancer studies suggest that systematic mass screening may be effective in reducing mortality from uterine cancer[51] Endometrial cancer, however, does not meet the criteria for a screenable disease to the same extent as breast or cervical cancer.[52] Yet with newer techniques for testing, the feasibility is increasing for attempting screening programs in endometrial cancer high-risk populations.[53] The interest in mass screening programs for the early detection of endometrial cancer has grown with the rising incidence of the disease. In relation to cervical cancer, very few routine education and/or mass screening programs for the early detection of endometrial cancer have been organized.[54]

Ovarian Cancer

INCIDENCE

In the medical literature, ovarian cancer is described as a major problem confronting all clinicians who care for women.[55] Ovarian cancer is the fourth leading cause of cancer deaths in women during the past several decades and estimates conclude that 1 of 70 U.S. women will experience ovarian cancer in her lifetime.[56] Ovarian cancer, almost always silent before diagnosis at an advanced stage, kills more U.S. women each year than all other gynecological cancers combined.[57] Moreover, evidence indicates that ovarian cancer incidence has been increasing in industrialized countries.[58]

Cancer of the ovary remains one of the cancers with poor 5-year survival rates. Long-term survival rates have not significantly changed over the years, in that currently less than 30% of women in whom this diagnosis is made are expected to survive 5 years. Patients with early diagnosis of localized disease can expect an 85% 5-year survival rate. However, 75% of women receive the diagnosis of ovarian cancer after the disease has advanced beyond the early stage.[59]

RISK FACTORS

The etiology of ovarian cancer is unknown, but there are some studies that suggest that multiple factors may contribute to the initiation and progression of ovarian cancer.[60] No one is at greater risk than a woman who has a mother, sister, or daughter with ovarian cancer; family history of ovarian cancer (linkage to genes on chromosome 17q) presents a significant increased risk.[61] Those who have had cancer of the colon, breast, or uterus, or who have undergone irradiation to the pelvis, are also identified as being at increased risk.[62] Furthermore, ovarian cancer displays an increasing incidence with advancing age (65 years and older),[63] although a distinctive earlier age onset curve also occurs.[64]

Increased risk is also presented for those who have never borne children.[65] Women whose reproductive life is long without being interrupted experience a higher risk of cancer and, therefore, should be worth screening. Stimulating the ovaries when treating for sterility also must be considered in the relationship to the possibility of provoking cancer of the ovary.[66]

A recent European study identified a relatively unique set of risk factors in young women.[67] Authors used data from a case control study conducted between 1983 and 1992 in Milan, Italy. An elevated relative risk of ovarian cancer was found among women reporting 12 or more years of education and belonging to the highest social class. Higher risk of ovarian cancer was found in women having first or last birth when more than 30 years old, and a significant trend toward an increased risk of ovarian cancer was observed with decreasing time since last birth.

Protective Factors. Because ovarian cancer is the leading cause of death from gynecological cancer, it is important to explore all options for prolonged survival and/or prevention of ovarian cancer. For example, there appears to be a significant inverse relationship with abortion, both spontaneous and induced.[68] In addition, investigators found an improved survival rate in women with more than one abortion.[69]

Protection also increases with duration of use of oral contraceptives, and this protection continues for a lengthy time after treatment has stopped.[70] Women who have taken the oral contraceptive pill for 4 or 5 years decrease the incidence of ovarian cancer by approximately 40%. Estimates are that oral contraception could prevent about 1,500 ovarian cancer deaths per year.[71] Researchers argue that if the ovaries are put functionally at rest, they are somewhat protected from cancer. Means for placing ovaries functionally at rest include pregnancy, oral contraception, premature menopause, or late puberty.[72]

DIAGNOSIS

There are no truly reliable means of screening or early diagnosis for ovarian cancer, and most cases are not diagnosed until after the disease has spread beyond the ovaries. One contributing factor to late detection occurs because ovarian cancer is often times asymptomatic in its early stages. Symptoms typically cited by women consist of vague gastrointestinal discomfort such as abdominal pain, abdominal swelling, bloating, and pelvic pressure, as well as vaginal bleeding and mild constipation.[73] Physical signs include weight loss[74] or a mass or masses detected in the abdomen, pelvis, and/or ovaries.[75]

TREATMENT

Despite the currently accepted treatment for advanced ovarian cancer that includes a combination of aggressive surgical "debulking" (removal of the tumor) and multi-agent chemotherapy, long-term prognosis for women with this malignancy has not significantly improved.[76] Primary surgical treatment of ovarian cancer plays a dominant role in treatment, generally followed with chemotherapy or radiation therapy.[77]

Chemotherapy plays a major role in the treatment of ovarian cancer due to approximately 75% of patients experiencing advanced surgically incurable disease when the tumor is diagnosed. Despite aggressive treatment, approximately 50% of these women have ovarian cancer reported as intrinsically resistant to conventional chemotherapy.[78]

Suboptimal Care. Some medical researchers argue that most women with ovarian cancer receive "suboptimal care." In 1993, data from an Ovarian Cancer Patient Evaluation Study reported that surgical undertreatment in ovarian cancer patients occurred 33%-45% of the time between 1983 and 1988. These statistics are even more disconcerting given that the results are probably skewed in a favorable direction. Women in this survey were treated at hospitals with designated cancer programs where care might be better than for those who are treated at various community hospitals that often do not have such cancer programs.[79]

Absence of Gynecologic Oncologists. Obstetricians and gynecologists play a dominant role in the diagnosis and management of ovarian cancer, assuming the care of up
to 45% of nationally surveyed patients with ovarian cancer. In one study, however, the
researchers found that even though ovarian cancer is well recognized in the medical
community as difficult to treat, more than 75% of patients with ovarian cancer were
cared for by someone other than a gynecologic oncologist.[80]

ERRONEOUS BELIEFS ABOUT ORAL CONTRACEPTIVES

Women possess a significant amount of misinformation regarding the risk assessment of oral contraceptive use.[81] In a survey of 247 educated women (90% had at least
1 year of college), 49% believed there were substantial risks to oral contraceptive use.
Between 80% and 95% were unaware of the following health benefits from the use of
oral contraceptives: decreased risk of ovarian and endometrial cancer, of pelvic
inflammatory disease, of ectopic pregnancy, of anemia, and of benign breast disease.
Increased educational efforts by health care providers should emphasize the benefits
of oral contraceptives and attempt to dispel possible misconceptions.[82]

AN OVARIAN CANCER CAMPAIGN: SEEMINGLY UNTRIED

High late detection rate and lack of gains in treatment to produce dramatic changes
in the mortality rates have prompted physicians to call for an effort to improve early
detection, as well as for an empirical trial of an ovarian cancer screening campaign.[83]
Thus, an outreach campaign consisting of education and screening could serve a
number of important purposes within the realm of ovarian cancer, and women's health
activists should express their support for such activities.

Psychological Consequences

Examining the medical literature associated with cervical, uterine, and ovarian
cancer primarily reveals insight to the physiologic aspects of the illness; however,
analysis of various psychological consequences is also important. As one scholar points
out, a woman facing cervical, uterine, or ovarian cancer faces enormous physical *and*
emotional trials.[84] In each encounter between a woman and her disease, the outcome
depends on her repertoire of both physiologic and psychologic resources.[85]

SOCIAL SUPPORT AND COPING WITH CANCER

The reactions of others can result in serious consequences regarding the cancer
patient's decisions about how to cope.[86] Although the literature examining coping styles
is not specific to cervical, uterine, and ovarian cancers, the general topic of patients'
coping and cancer remains useful. Coping with serious illness and the struggle for
survival takes many forms.[87] The process of coping is influenced by physical, environ-

mental, and emotional factors. Women are strongly influenced by the dramatic changes in bodily condition, personal priorities, and social relations. How a woman responds to these factors influences her likelihood of recovery and quality of life during the remaining time of survival.[88]

EXPERIENCE OF THE WOMAN'S FAMILY

A woman whose family is coping well with the multiple stresses of cancer possesses a greater chance of coping well herself.[89] However, as a woman goes through treatment, scholars note that repeated and often unpredictable crises generally induce great amounts of exhaustion.[90] As time progresses, family members may consciously or unconsciously anticipate and/or hope that she will die. Common responses of the family include withdrawal of support, numbing of emotion, and immersion in outside activities.[91]

SEXUAL IMPLICATIONS

Women with cervical, uterine, or ovarian cancer and who have partners often fear deterioration or termination of their relationships as a result of sexual alterations. In fact, research has documented that sexuality is the life area that undergoes the greatest disruption from gynecologic cancers.[92] Research reports that couples with preexisting relational problems or emotional bonds highly dependent on sex encounter the most difficulties. Furthermore, long-lasting as opposed to short-term relationships appear better at enduring and withstanding the stresses of cancer.[93] Loss of intimate contact can weaken and dishearten a woman with cancer at a time when she is truly in need of support.[94]

DEATH AND DYING

When curative treatment fails, the woman, physician, family, and/or friends must make the transition to planning for her death and mourning. Mismatch between patients' and families' recognition and acceptance of impending death is not uncommon.[95] Considerations voiced by dying patients, however, include fear of pain, dependency, loss of control, isolation, and of becoming repugnant to other people.[96] At the final level of care, pain medications are used as needed and women may prefer moving home or to a hospice setting.[97]

RECOVERY

If a woman receives cure and recovers, she must still cope for the rest of her life with the apprehension of possible recurrence. Although one study reports that the near death by cancer experience often results in net-positive effects, survivors as a group tend to report long-standing decreases in self-confidence and an increase in health worries.[98] This long-standing decrease in self-confidence and increase in health worries may be due to the sometimes irreversible physical changes from surgery, such as alterations in sexual function, as well as sequelae of radiation and chemotherapy.[99]

Future Recommendations

Examination of the medical and social scientific literature associated with cervical, uterine, and ovarian cancers lends a variety of insights. The physiologic and psychologic toll these cancers take on U.S. women remains staggering, yet relatively little attention by the medical and social scientific communities has occurred toward such an important health issue. The American Cancer Society has been advocating educational and screening programs for these cancers for many years, but with the exception of cervical cancer, few if any have been attempted. Funding for cancer screening and education is limited.[100]

The literature reveals that the most significant campaign initiatives are spent on mere availability to cancer screening programs. The solutions, however, do not lie simply in more access to medical screening or in more groups producing a greater diversity of information for these women. Outreach must include communicating cancer risks, teaching women about identifying signs and symptoms, recommending prevention strategies, discussing potential psychological consequences, and referring those involved for medical treatment and social support. This would in turn improve early detection, choices, and quality of life through engaging women, their families, and friends in a collaborative partnership aimed at controlling these cancers. The possibility occurs for women voicing their own needs, concerns, and hope for greater awareness and survival.[101]

Outreach to women with cervical, uterine, and ovarian cancers must consist of a systematic means of listening to women; how they view their situations, construct sense, and make meaning of their circumstances.[102] Focus would then be shifted to what women actually need or want, rather than on what paternalistic others presuppose. If health institutions expect education and screening efforts to be effective and efficient, they must treat communication and outreach as a cooperative endeavor, finding ways to empower women, their families, and friends. As Brenda Dervin points out, "testimony from the arena of risk communication confirms the point again and again . . . people are willing to involve themselves, to listen, be reasonable, and to act, but only if empowered and heard."[103]

Notes

1. C. C. Boring, T. S. Squires, & T. Tong, "Cancer Statistics: 1992," *CA. A Cancer Journal for Clinicians* 42 (1992): 19-38.

2. L. N. White, "An Overview of Screening and Early Detection of Gynecological Malignancies," *Cancer* 71 (1993): 1400-1405.

3. V. A. Marcial & L. V. Marcial, "Radiation Therapy of Cervical Cancer: New Developments," *Cancer* 71 (1993): 1438-1445.

4. W. B. Jones, "New Approaches to High-Risk Cervical Cancer," *Cancer* 71 (1993): 1451-1459.

5. American Cancer Society, *Cancer Facts and Figures* (New York: Author, 1989); Boring et al., "Cancer Statistics," 19-38; Jones, "New Approaches," p. 1451.

6. Boring et al., "Cancer Statistics," pp. 19-38; J. E. Dunn & V. Schweitzer, "The Relationship of Cervical Cytology to the Incidence of Invasive Cervical Cancer and Mortality in Alameda County, California: 1960-1974," *American Journal of Obstetrics and Gynecology* 139 (1981): 868-876.

7. R. K. Peters, D. Thomas, & D. G. Hagan, "Risk Factors for Invasive Cervical Cancer Among Latinas and Non-Latinas in Los Angeles County," *Journal of the National Cancer Institute* 77 (1986): 1063-1077.

8. S. S. Agarwal, A. Sehgal, S. Sardana, A. Kumar, & U. K. Luthra, "Role of Male Behavior in Cervical Carcinogenesis Among Women with One Lifetime Sexual Partner," *Cancer* 72 (1993): 1666-1669.

9. Agarwal et al., "Role of Male Behavior," pp. 1666-1669.

10. J. Fowler, "Screening for Cervical Cancer: Current Terminology, Classification, and Technique," *Postgraduate Medicine* 93 (1993): 57-70.

11. G. G. Kenter, C. J. Cornelisse, N. M. Jiwa, E. J. Aartsen, J. Hermans, W. Mooi, A.P.M. Heintz, & G. J. Fleuren, "Human Papillomavirus Type 16 in Tumor Tissue of Low-Stage Squamous Carcinoma of the Uterine Cervix in Relation to Ploidy Grade and Prognosis," *Cancer* 71 (1993): 397-401; see also Fowler, "Screening for Cervical Cancer," p. 58.

12. R. Reid, "Human Papillomavirus Infection: The Key to Rational Triage of Cervical Neoplasia," *Obstetrics and Gynecology Clinic of North America* 14 (1987): 407-429.

13. C. LaVecchia, E. Negri, S. Franceschi, & F. Parazzini, "Long-Term Impact of Reproductive Factors on Cancer Risk," *International Journal of Cancer* 53 (1993): 215-219.

14. A. J. Levine, "AIDS-Related Malignancies: The Emerging Epidemic," *Journal of the National Cancer Institute* 85 (1993): 1382-1397.

15. M. Maiman, R. G. Fruchter, L. Guy, S. Cuthill, P. Levine, & E. Serur, "Human Immunodeficiency Virus Infection and Invasive Cervical Carcinoma," *Cancer* 71 (1993): 402-406.

16. A. L. Coker, M. F. McCann, B. S. Hulka, & L. A. Walton, "Oral Contraceptive Use and Cervical Intraepithelial Neoplasia," *Journal of Clinical Epidemiology* 45 (1992): 1111-1118.

17. Coker et al. "Oral Contraceptive Use," pp. 1111-1118.

18. M. F. McCann, D. E. Irwin, L. A. Walter, B. S. Hulka, J. L. Morton, & C. M. Axelrad, "Nicotine and Cotinine in the Cervical Mucus of Smokers, Passive Smokers, and Nonsmokers," *Cancer Epidemiology Biomarkers Prevention* 1 (1992): 125-129.

19. E. A. Holly, R. D. Cress, D. K. Ahn, D. A. Aston, J. J. Kristiansen, & J. S. Felton, "Characteristics of Women by Smoking Status in the San Francisco Bay Area," *Cancer Epidemiology Biomarkers and Prevention* 1 (1992): 492-497.

20. H. E. Lambert & P. R. Blake (Eds.), *Gynecological Oncology* (Oxford, UK: Oxford University Press, 1992).

21. Fowler, "Screening for Cervical Cancer," p. 62.

22. L. G. Koss, "Cervical (Pap) Smear," *Cancer* 71 (1993): 1406-1412.

23. Fowler, "Screening for Cervical Cancer," 62; Koss, "Cervical," 1412; F. J. Montz & J. S. Berek, "Screening, Diagnoses, and Monitoring of Gynecological Malignancies," *Current Opinion in Oncology* 1 (1989): 75-81.

24. Fowler, "Screening for Cervical Cancer," p. 62.

25. J. G. Boyce, R. G. Fruchter, L. Romanzi, F. H. Sillman, & M. Maiman, "The Fallacy of the Screening Interval for Cervical Smears," *Obstetrics and Gynecology* 76 (1990): 627-632.

26. Fowler, "Screening for Cervical Cancer," pp. 63-64.

27. Fowler, "Screening for Cervical Cancer," p. 64; and personal communication with Gordon Becnel, M.D. (December 22, 1993).

28. R. C. Park & J. T. Thigpen, "Chemotherapy in Advanced and Recurrent Cervical Cancer: A Review," *Cancer* 71 (1993): 1446-1450.

29. H. E. Averette, H. N. Nguyen, D. M. Donato, M. A. Penalver, B. U. Sevin, R. Estape, & W. A. Little, "Radical Hysterectomy for Invasive Cervical Cancer: A 25-Year Prospective Experience With the Miami Technique," *Cancer* 71 (1993): 1422-1437.

30. Averette et al., "Radical Hysterectomy," p. 1422.

31. Jones, "New Approaches," pp. 1451-1459.

32. C. T. Pham & S. J. McPhee, "Knowledge, Attitudes, and Practices of Breast and Cervical Cancer Screening Among Vietnamese Women," *Journal of Cancer Education* 7 (1992): 305-310.

33. Pham & McPhee, "Knowledge, Attitudes, and Practices," pp. 305-310.

34. P. M. Lantz, L. Dupuis, D. Reding, M. Krauska, & K. Lappe, "Peer Discussion Among Hispanic Migrant Agricultural Workers," *Public Health Reports* (in press).

35. Lantz et al., "Peer Discussion."

36. K. Sigurdsson, "Effect of Organized Screening on the Risk of Cervical Cancer Evaluation of Screening Activity in Iceland, 1964-1991," *International Journal of Cancer* 54 (1993): 563-570.

37. R.C.S. Ho, "The Past, Present, the Future," *Cancer* 71 (1993): 1396-1399.

38. J. N. Brownstein, N. Cheal, S. P. Ackerman, T. L. Bassford, & D. Campos-Outcalt, "Breast and Cervical Cancer Screening in Minority Populations: A Model for Using Lay Health Educators," *Journal of Cancer Education* 7 (1992): 321-326.

39. Brownstein et al., "Breast and Cervical Cancer Screening," pp. 321-326.

40. L. Lacey, J. Whitfield, W. DeWhite, D. Ansell, S. Whitman, E. Chen, & C. Phillips, "Referral Adherence in an Inner City Breast and Cervical Cancer Screening Program," *Cancer* 72 (1993): 950-955.

41. M. Rotman, H. Aziz, J. Halpern, D. Schwartz, C. Sohn, & K. Choi, "Endometrial Carcinoma Influence of Prognostic Factors on Radiation Management," *Cancer* 71 (1993): 1471-1479.

42. Boring et al., "Cancer Statistics," pp. 19-38.

43. Rotman et al., "Endometrial Carcinoma," p. 1471.

44. The University of Texas M. D. Anderson Cancer Center Prevention and Detection Programs Staff, *Cancer Prevention and Detection in the Cancer Screening Clinic* (Houston: University of Texas M. D. Anderson Cancer Center, 1988).

45. See White, "An Overview," 1402; M. Gronroos, T. A. Salmi, M. H. Vuento, E. A. Jalava, J. E. Trykko, J. I. Maatela, A. R. Aromaa, R. Siegberg, E. R. Savolainen, & T. V. Kauraniemi, "Mass Screening for Endometrial Cancer Directed in Risk Groups of Patients With Diabetes and Hypertension," *Cancer* 71 (1993): 1279-1282F.

46. LaVecchia et al., "Long-Term Impact," pp. 215-219.

47. White, "An Overview," p. 1402.

48. Gronroos et al., "Endometrial Cancer," pp. 1279-1282F; White, "An Overview," p. 1402.

49. Rotman et al., "Endometrial Carcinoma," p. 1471.

50. P. Tseng, H. E. Sprance, M. L. Carcangiu, J. T. Chambers, & P. E. Schwartz, "CA 125, NB/70K, and Lipid-Associated Sialic Acid in Monitoring Uterine Papillary Serous Carcinoma," *Obstetrics and Gynecology* 74 (1989): 384-387.

51. C. M. Gao, T. Kuroishi, K. Hirose, K. Tajima, & S. Tominaga, "An Epidemiological Evaluation of the Efficacy of Mass Screening for Uterine Cancer in Japan," *Nippon-Koshu-Eisei-Zasshi* 39 (1992): 784-788.

52. White, "An Overview," p. 1402.

53. White, "An Overview," p. 1402.

54. Gronroos et al., "Mass Screening," p. 1279.

55. H. E. Averette, "Introduction to the Fourth National Conference on Gynecological Cancers of the American Cancer Society," *Cancer* 71 (1993): 1395.

56. Boring et al., "Cancer Statistics," pp. 19-38; S. J. Cutler & J. L. Young (Eds.), *Third National Cancer Survey: Incidence Data* (Bethesda, MD: National Cancer Institute, 1975).

57. S. C. Rubin, "Monoclonal Antibodies in the Management of Ovarian Cancer," *Cancer* 71 (1993): 1602-1612.

58. Boring et al., "Cancer Statistics," pp. 19-38; American Cancer Society, "Cancer Facts," p. 2.

59. Ho, "The Past, Present, the Future," p. 1397; D. H. Oram, J. Jacobs, J. L. Brady, & A. Prys-Davies, "Early Diagnosis of Ovarian Cancer," *British Journal of Hospital Medicine* 44 (1990): 320-324; E. Silverberg, "Cancer Statistics," *CA. A Cancer Journal for Clinicians* 35 (1985): 19-35.

60. A. K. Godwin, J. R. Testa, & T. C. Hamilton, "The Biology of Ovarian Cancer Development," *Cancer* 71 (1993): 530-536.

61. H. T. Lynch, P. Watson, T. A. Conway, J. F. Lynch, S. M. Slominski-Caster, S. A. Nerod, J. Feunteun, & G. Lenoir, "DNA Screening for Breast/Ovarian Cancer Susceptibility Based on Linked Markers: A Family Study," *Archives of Internal Medicine* 153 (1993): 1979-1987.

62. White, "An Overview," p. 1403; also see M. Koch, H. Jenkins, & H. Gaedke, "Risk Factors of Ovarian Cancer of Epithelial Origin," *Cancer Detection and Prevention* 13 (1988): 131-136.

63. R. Yancik, "Ovarian Cancer: Age Contrasts in Incidence, Histology, Disease Stage at Diagnosis, and Mortality," *Cancer* 71 (1993): 517-523.

64. H. T. Lynch, P. Watson, J. F. Lynch, T. A. Conway, & M. Fili, "Hereditary Ovarian Cancer Heterogeneity in Age at Onset," *Cancer* 71 (1993): 573-581.

65. Koch et al., "Risk Factors," pp. 131-136.

66. B. Taurelle, M. P. Laroussinie, & F. Lecuru, "Cancer of the Ovary and the Hormonal Context," *Journal of Gynecology, Obstetrics, Biology, and Reproduction Paris* 22 (1993): 249-253.

67. A. Tavani, E. Negri, S. Franceschi, F. Parazzini, & C. LaVecchia, "Risk Factors for Epithelial Ovarian Cancer in Women Under Age 45," *European Journal of Cancer* 29A (1993): 1297-1301.

68. Tavani et al., "Risk Factors," pp. 1297-1301.

69. B. K. Jacobsen, S. E. Vollset, & G. Kvale, "Reproductive Factors and Survival From Ovarian Cancer," *International Journal of Cancer* 54 (1993): 904-906.

70. Tavani et al., "Risk Factors," pp. 1297-1301; M. Thorogood & L. Villard-Mackintosh, "Combined Oral Contraceptives: Risks and Benefits," *British Medical Bulletin* 49 (1993): 124-139.

71. H. R. Barber, "Prophylaxis in Ovarian Cancer," *Cancer* 71 (1993): 1529-1533.

72. Taurelle et al., "Cancer of the Ovary," pp. 249-253.

73. H. E. Averette, W. Hoskins, H. N. Nguyen, G. Boike, H. C. Flessa, J. S. Chmiel, K. Zuber, L. H. Karnell, & D. P. Winchester, "National Survey of Ovarian Carcinoma I. A Patient Care Evaluation Study of the American College of Surgeons," *Cancer* 71 (1993): 1629-1638; White "An Overview," p. 1403.

74. B. L. Anderson, "Predicting Sexual and Psychologic Morbidity and Improving the Quality of Life for Women With Gynecologic Cancer, *Cancer* 71 (1993): 1678-1690.

75. Averette et al., "National Survey," p. 1631.

76. P. S. Brady & R. R. Kelvecz, "Flow Cytometric Evaluation of Ovarian Cancer," *Cancer* 71 (1993): 1621-1628.

77. H. R. Menck, L. Garfinkel, & G. D. Dodd, "Preliminary Report of the National Cancer Data Base," *CA. A Cancer Journal for Clinicians* 41 (1991): 7-18.

78. R. P. Perez, T. C. Hamilton, R. F. Ozols, & R. C. Young, "Mechanisms and Modulation of Resistance to Chemotherapy in Ovarian Cancer," *Cancer* 71 (1993): 1571-1580; J. T. Thigpen, R. B. Vance, & T. Khansur, "Second-Line Chemotherapy for Recurrent Carcinoma in the Ovary," *Cancer* 71 (1993): 1559-1564.

79. Averette et al., "National Survey," p. 1635.

80. Averette et al., "National Survey," p. 1635.

81. J. F. Peipert & J. Gutmann, "Oral Contraceptive Risk Assessment: A Survey of 247 Educated Women," *Obstetrics and Gynecology* 82 (1993): 112-117.

82. Peipert & Gutmann, "Oral Contraceptive Risk," pp. 112-117.

83. T. H. Bourne, K. Reynolds, & S. Campbell, "Ovarian Cancer Screening," *Current Opinions in Radiology* 3 (1991): 216-224.

84. A. G. Palmer, S. Tucker, R. Warren, & M. Adams, "Understanding Women's Responses to Treatment for Cervical Intra-epithelial Neoplasia," *British Journal of Clinical Psychology* 32 (1993): 101-112.

85. C. F. McCartney & J. J. Knox, "Psychosocial Issues in the Care of Gynecologic Cancer Patients," in S. B. Gusberg, H. M. Shingleton, & G. Deppe (Eds.), *Female Genital Cancer* (New York: Churchill Livingston, 1988): 777-800.

86. C. F. Sullivan & K. K. Reardon, "Social Support Satisfaction and Health Locus of Control: Discriminators of Breast Cancer Patient's Styles of Coping," in M. L. McLaughlin (Ed.), *Communication Yearbook* (Beverly Hills, CA: Sage, 1986): 707-722.

87. K. K. Reardon & R. Buck, "Emotion, Reason, and Communication in Coping With Cancer," *Health Communication* 1 (1989): 41-54.

88. Reardon & Buck, "Emotion, Reason, and Communication," p. 41.

89. B. R. Cassileth, E. J. Lusk, & T. B. Strouse, "A Psychological Analysis of Cancer Patients and Their Next-of-Kin," *Cancer* 55 (1985): 72.

90. McCartney & Knox, "Psychosocial Issues," p. 785.

91. Cassileth et al., "A Psychological Analysis," p. 72; see McCartney & Knox, "Psychosocial Issues," p. 785.

92. Anderson, "Predicting Sexual and Psychologic Morbidity"; H. H. Sewell & D. W. Edwards, "Pelvic Genital Cancer: Body Image and Sexuality," *Front Radiation Therapy and Oncology* 14 (1984): 35.

93. Sewell & Edwards, "Pelvic Genital Cancer," p. 35.

94. McCartney & Knox, "Psychosocial Issues," p. 791.

95. McCartney & Knox, "Psychosocial Issues," p. 786.

96. McCartney & Knox, "Psychosocial Issues," p. 785.

97. McCartney & Knox, "Psychosocial Issues," p. 786.

98. A. H. Schmale, G. R. Morrow, & M. H. Schmitt, "Well-Being of Cancer Survivors," *Psychosomatic Medicine* 45 (1983): 163-175.

99. McCartney & Knox, "Psychosocial Issues," p. 787.

100. B. K. Holland, J. D. Foster, & D. B. Louria, "Cervical Cancer and Health Care Resources in Newark, New Jersey, 1970 to 1988," *American Journal of Public Health* 83 (1993): 45-48.

101. See L. F. Rakow, "Information and Power: Toward a Critical Theory of Information Campaigns," in C. T. Salmon (Ed.), *Information Campaigns: Balancing Social Values and Social Change* (Newbury Park, CA: Sage, 1989): 164-184.

102. See B. Dervin, "Audience as Listener and Learner, Teacher, and Confidante: The Sense-Making Approach," in R. E. Rice & C. K. Atkin (Eds.), *Public Communication Campaigns* (Newbury Park, CA: Sage, 1989): 67-86.

103. Dervin, "Audience as Listener," p. 85.

17

Magic, Moralism, and Marginalization

Media Coverage of Cervical, Ovarian, and Uterine Cancer

Michele Kilgore

Use of the news media as instruments for improved public health through "public health campaigns" or "information campaigns" has been a frequent topic of research for both health professionals and communication theorists. One analysis of this "popularization" model of the news media's role in public health summarizes its tenets as follows:

> Transmitting medical news is viewed as a one-way information flow beginning with refereed medical journals, expert physicians, and public health officials. These experts provide medical information to journalists, who then popularize specialized biomedical knowledge for lay readers and viewers. Increases in public knowledge about medicine are designed to engender these socially desirable effects: decreases in public superstition about health care, more public acceptance for organized medicine's preferred approaches to biomedical treatment, changes in actual public health care behaviors.[1]

Communication research has offered critiques and refinements of the "popularization" model, motivated by the ambivalent results of past public health campaigns.[2] With respect to women's health issues in particular, the "one-way information flow" assumed in the popularization model is targeted in an article on news content analysis that calls on women to demand and supply real two-way communication with the news media.[3]

This chapter examines news reporting on cervical, ovarian, and uterine cancer and on possible implications for the popularization model. Although the three types of cancer have varying etiologies, treatments, and consequences as detailed in the previous chapter, they are subjects of research and public information efforts by the same set of institutions. The female reproductive system is one biological unit, and women tend to consult the same primary health care professionals for initial diagnosis. If newspapers are serving the kind of function contemplated in the popularization model, they should convey information that endows readers with an improved understanding of the prevalence, symptoms, diagnosis, prevention, and treatment of cancer of the female reproductive system (hereinafter CFRS).

One System, Three Messages

The data examined for this analysis consist of 164 newspaper articles about CFRS drawn from two databases:

1. *Newspaper Abstracts Ondisc* from January 1985 through January 1993 at Georgia State University; and
2. the *Expanded Academic Index* (EAI) at the University of Georgia.[4]

Articles were analyzed to determine the primary form of CFRS discussed. Tables were prepared to show distribution of articles in 6-month periods, first by all types of CFRS and then by each individual type. Article distribution is then compared with selected events. Finally, the articles are examined for evidence of news values as defined by the professional journalist-linguist, Allan Bell.[5]

In reviewing the articles to determine the primary form of CFRS discussed, several findings about reportage of CFRS came to light. The presentation of information in the media about these diseases is: (a) unequal, (b) uneven, and (c) fragmented.

UNEQUAL

Of the 164 articles reviewed for this analysis, 69 made primary reference to cervical cancer, 80 to ovarian cancer, and only 15 to uterine cancer. As the cancer statistics in Table 17.1 show,[6] there is no obvious statistical basis for this disproportionate reporting. Although ovarian cancer is the most lethal form of CFRS, uterine cancer is the most prevalent.

TABLE 17.1 Cancer Facts and Figures 1985-1993 (in thousands)

Year	Ovarian		Cervical		Uterine	
	New Cases	Estimated Deaths	New Cases	Estimated Deaths	New Cases	Estimated Deaths
1985	18.5	11.6	15.0	6.8	52.0	9.7
1986	19.0	11.6	14.0	6.8	50.0	9.7
1987	19.0	11.7	12.8	6.8	44.8	9.7
1988	19.0	12.0	12.9	7.0	46.9	10.0
1989	20.0	12.0	13.0	6.0	47.0	10.0
1990	20.5	12.4	13.5	6.0	46.5	10.0
1991	20.7	12.5	13.0	4.5	46.0	10.0
1992	21.0	13.0	13.5	4.4	45.5	10.0
1993	22.0	13.0	13.5	4.4	31.0	10.1

SOURCE: American Cancer Society. Used by permission.

TABLE 17.2 Articles on Cervical, Ovarian, and Uterine Cancer

Year	1985	1986	1987	1988	1989	1990	1991	1992	1993
Total	5	6	11	20	26	27	27	35	—

Primary Focus	Number	Percentage
Cervical	69	42
Ovarian	80	49
Uterine	15	9
Combined	164	100

TABLE 17.3 Articles on Cervical Cancer

Year	1985	1986	1987	1988	1989	1990	1991	1992	1993
Total for year	0	1	10	16	14	13	7	8	—

Total: 69 articles

TABLE 17.4 Articles on Ovarian Cancer

Year	1985	1986	1987	1988	1989	1990	1991	1992	1993
Total for year	1	1	0	2	10	13	20	27	—

Total: 80 articles

UNEVEN

Tables 17.2-17.5 show that the distribution of articles over time was also uneven. Although the total number of articles increases from 1985 until 1992, this trend masks

TABLE 17.5 Articles on Uterine Cancer

Year	1985	1986	1987	1988	1989	1990	1991	1992	1993
Total for year Total: 15 articles	4	4	1	2	2	0	1	0	—

different patterns for coverage of each illness. Stories on uterine cancer peak in 1986, and on cervical cancer in 1988. The concentration of articles on ovarian cancer in 1991 and 1992 creates the appearance of overall higher coverage.

FRAGMENTED

In addition, only 12 articles mentioned more than one type of CFRS. Of those, only 1 made more than a passing reference to a second or third type. Not one purported to supply a general discussion of causes, symptoms, prevention, or treatment of all three. Again, there is but one reproductive system and women generally rely upon one primary care professional for prevention and diagnosis of problems connected with the cervix, the ovaries, and the uterus.

Themes in Messages About Cancers of the Female Reproductive System

Three themes emerged in reporting about CFRS. These approaches were found in stories about each of the three types of cancer examined in relation to women.

MAGIC

Of the 164 articles reviewed, 98 (50 on ovarian cancer, 36 on cervical cancer, 12 on uterine cancer) discuss scientific developments in the diagnosis and treatment of CFRS, including their promulgation in medical journals, their propagation at professional conferences, and their approval by federal regulators. These articles cast medical treatment as a kind of "magic"—an amazing miracle that solves an unsolvable problem.

Scientific "discovery" themes are especially notable in the articles on ovarian cancer, where two relatively new diagnostic methods (ultrasound and blood testing for CA 125) and one new treatment (chemotherapy with the drug Taxol) generated significant coverage. The tone of these articles is strikingly consistent with an analysis of news coverage of scientific developments generally. Such an analysis found frequent usage of the metaphors of alchemy, warfare, and revolution: "These metaphors add up to an image of science as a solution for intractable dilemmas, a means of uncertainty in an uncertain world, a source of legitimacy, an institution we can trust."[7]

A widely published Associated Press story on a single study of a new drug treatment for uterine cancer began with this lead: "A simple drug treatment is virtually 100 per cent effective in curing a form of reproductive cancer that is a major health hazard among women in many parts of the world, new research concludes."[8] Articles on genetic manipulation of ovarian (and breast) cancer patients also displayed a strong messianic quality. "The procedure itself was astonishingly routine and took less than half an hour, but it marked the dawn of a new era in medicine: the age of human gene therapy."[9] Another article suggested a similar concept: the doctor as magician. A genetic researcher "slammed-dunked his way through a combined M.D. and Ph.D. program in five years," and then pioneered breakthroughs in "heady but grueling days."[10]

Even those articles that described a given "discovery" as controversial tended to treat the controversies as a "clash of the titans" among truth-givers struggling to establish the truth for a waiting world of laypersons. The National Institute of Health and the National Women's Health Network conduct a "debate" over the alleged failure to consider the risk of cervical cancer in a national study of tamoxifen, a drug used to treat breast cancer.[11] The American College of Obstetricians and Gynecologists (OB/GYN) and the American Cancer Society reach a public "compromise" on how often women should get Pap smears.

One OB/GYN spokesperson unhappy with giving up his profession's guidelines concluded: "If we did not change it we would have literally had to continue a war with the American Cancer Society."[12] This 1988 compromise recommended "that women have three annual Pap smears starting when they reach the age of 18 or become sexually active. If all three of the tests are negative then, 'at the discretion of their physicians,' the women can have the test less frequently."[13] The 1988 guidelines were still current in 1992.[14] Another controversy illustrative of this approach focused on the "cost-effectiveness" of Pap smears for women over the age of 65.[15]

MORALISM

Among the articles examined, 58 were found (48 on cervical cancer, 5 on ovarian cancer, 5 on uterine cancer) to aim at correcting behaviors deemed as contributory to CFRS. These included inappropriate treatment and diagnosis, but more typically preventive behavior. As with the "magical" conveyance of biomedical advances, these prescriptive articles often bear a tone that goes well beyond cautionary injunctions to preventive action, linking the risk of CFRS to activities that violate conventional moral and religious codes and fashions.

Tentative research findings that established possible links between a genital virus and high risk for cervical cancer drew reporting on CFRS into the mainstream of gloomy writing on AIDS and other sexually transmitted diseases (STDs). One feature (titled "Dangerous Liaison: A Mysterious, Sexually Transmitted Virus Threatens to Trigger a New Epidemic") on these findings focused on a couple whose lives have been irreparably harmed by acquiring the genital virus. The woman is now at high risk for cervical cancer. The article concludes that the primary risk factor in cervical cancer is the number of sexual partners one has had, thus directly linking the disease to promiscuity.[16]

Another article on cervical cancer cites not only the number of sexual partners but also the frequency of sex and the use of oral contraceptives as major risk factors.[17] Still another asserts that "3 of 4 cases of cervical cancer could be prevented if women used barrier contraceptives."[18] What makes these injunctions to less and safer sex most remarkable is the rarely mentioned fact that a direct linkage between the papilloma virus, genital warts, and cervical cancer is far from established in cancer research. Other risk factors appear to be involved.[19] Yet the newspaper data assume in varying degrees that cervical cancer is itself virtually a sexually transmitted disease.

The strong tendency to telescope tentative findings is exhibited in the lead for an article on a single study. "A highly sensitive test has found a virus linked to genital warts and cervical cancer in nearly half of California college women included in a new study."[20] Several articles also mentioned research suggesting a higher risk for cervical cancer among cigarette smokers. One led with a statement that "cigarette smoking has emerged as a powerful influence in the development of cervical cancer as well as distorted cells that are precursors to malignancy."[21] This net of risky behaviors linked to CFRS is sometimes cast very broadly, as in an article that leads with, "Career women, especially those with no children, may fit the highest-risk profile for deadly ovarian cancer."[22] Conversely, "the only group of women who do not seem to get cervical cancer is nuns,"[23] although they do not generally have children either.

Women are not alone in being lashed for irresponsible behavior; physicians are criticized for failure to prescribe sufficient testing or provide adequate samples, especially for Pap smears.[24] On the other hand, data with even more striking negative implications for the quality of primary care for women are conspicuously under-examined: A study that shows black women have enormously higher rates of death from cervical cancer did not lead to any stormy articles or editorials about the consequences of denying access to care.[25]

MARGINALIZATION

A third striking feature of the data collected is the extent to which medical information about CFRS is so embedded in extrinsic material that lay readers may not be able to conduct a successful excavation. Analysis of the data identified at least 43 "side issues"—ranging from religion in a cancer support group to infighting among California legislators—that varied from dominant themes to subtexts in the articles discussing CFRS. There are four especially notable "side issues."

Business Interests. Thirty-three of the articles reviewed concentrated particularly on the application process for Food and Drug Administration (FDA) approval of new tests and drugs. These articles focus in part on the business interests affected by regulatory actions related to CFRS, especially the effect on stock prices of action by FDA.

Environment. Thirty-six of the articles discuss the environmental implications of the discovery that Taxol, a drug derived from the rare yew tree, is effective in treatment of ovarian cancer. One stream of articles derived from an investigative report blames the logging industry for depleting supplies of yew trees.[26] Another article blames environmentalists for inhibiting their harvest.[27] An editorial uses the discovery to defend the Endangered Species Act.[28]

Celebrity Victims. Seventeen articles discuss celebrities suffering from CFRS. These included Cassandra Harris and Gilda Radner (death from ovarian cancer), and Marilyn Quayle (recovery from cervical cancer).

Media Victims. Twelve articles discuss fictional victims of CFRS in television dramatizations, with all but one derived from the series *thirtysomething,* in which a character is diagnosed as suffering from ovarian cancer.

The celebrity and media victims' categories are especially significant, because public health officials often view personalization of health issues in the mass media as a cardinal opportunity for public education.[29] Readers of articles on Gilda Radner, however, must absorb lengthy appreciations of her career in show business[30] and of her surviving celebrity husband's activities[31] before gleaning the medical information on the ovarian cancer that killed her. Readers of articles on the *thirtysomething* series must digest summaries of the show's genesis and impact, not to mention the equation of cancer with the realization of mortality among baby boomers, before learning much of anything about ovarian cancer.[32]

In the midst of the magic, moralizing, and marginalizing, some medical information is undoubtedly conveyed. Careful readers are made aware of significant new treatments for both ovarian and uterine cancer, even if their availability and consequences are not clearly explained. Women are encouraged to get more frequent Pap smears, although that message may have been obscured by negative reports on the reliability of Pap smears. Victims of CFRS are offered solace in the realization that celebrities, real and fictional, are not immune. Indeed, one article spawned by the *thirtysomething* series is unusually informative.[33] In good reportage, readers are made aware that biomedical developments have business and environmental implications. Generally, however, these 164 articles do not suggest that newspapers have served as an efficient medium for transmission of medical information on CFRS.

News Values Emergent in the Themes Found in CFRS Messages

In examining the data collected for this analysis, special emphasis was placed on the news values reflected in reportage of CFRS on grounds that communication theory has not previously paid "sufficient attention to the study of news as discourse in its own right."[34] To the extent that news articles succeed or fail in effectively conveying information on CFRS, an understanding of the news value of various types of biomedical information may provide an important clue to the inherent strengths and weaknesses of news organizations in serving a key function in popularization.

TABLE 17.6 Articles on Cervical Cancer and Key Events

Jan-Jun 1985	0	
July-Dec 1985	0	
Jan-Jun 1986	1	
July-Dec 1986	0	
Jan-Jun 1987	1	
July-Dec 1987	9	*WSJ* report on Pap smear lab
Jan-Jun 1988	11	Pap test guidelines updated
July-Dec 1988	5	AMA Science Writers Conference
Jan-Jun 1989	8	HPV test marketed; *JAMA* report
July-Dec 1989	6	Susan Dey movie; CDC report
Jan-Jun 1990	4	
July-Dec 1990	9	Marilyn Quayle hospitalized
Jan-Jun 1991	5	
July-Dec 1991	2	
Jan-Jun 1992	5	
July-Dec 1992	3	
January 1993	0	

TABLE 17.7 Articles on Ovarian Cancer and Key Events

Jan-Jun 1985	0	
July-Dec 1985	1	
Jan-Jun 1986	0	
July-Dec 1986	1	
Jan-Jun 1987	0	
July-Dec 1987	0	
Jan-Jun 1988	1	
July-Dec 1988	1	
Jan-Jun 1989	7	Death of Gilda Radner
July-Dec 1989	3	
Jan-Jun 1990	10	*thirtysomething* begins storyline
July-Dec 1990	3	
Jan-Jun 1991	9	*thirtysomething* episode
July-Dec 1991	11	National Cancer Institute announces Taxol study
Jan-Jun 1992	8	*NYT* article on yew tree logging
July-Dec 1992	19	FDA approves Taxol
January 1993	6	

Much traditional analysis of news media and information campaigns has suggested that obstacles to effective transmission may be due either to the inherent bias of reporters and their editors and employers, or to the "social control" function of the news media, which limits its manipulation for persuasive means.[35] An alternative approach is to examine the transmission mechanism itself: newspaper text as discourse, with its own rules, structures and priorities, which inevitably affect the content of what is conveyed. "We cannot separate news form and news content. The value of news drives the way in which news is presented. We may account for the way news stories are structured only with reference to the values by which one 'fact' is judged more newsworthy than another."[36]

TABLE 17.8 Articles on Uterine Cancer and Key Events

Jan-Jun 1985	0	
July-Dec 1985	4	*JAMA* report; *NEJM* report
Jan-Jun 1986	0	
July-Dec 1986	4	World Conference
Jan-Jun 1987	1	
July-Dec 1987	0	
Jan-Jun 1988	1	
July-Dec 1988	1	
Jan-Jun 1989	1	
July-Dec 1989	1	
Jan-Jun 1990	0	
July-Dec 1990	0	
Jan-Jun 1991	1	
July-Dec 1991	0	
Jan-Jun 1992	0	
July-Dec 1992	0	
January 1993	1	

The news text in this study was analyzed to determine the news values represented in each article, according to Bell's set of 12 "values in news actors and events." It is important to understand that none of these values operates in isolation; depending on the information involved, 2 or many more may operate synergistically to shape the "story." Tables 17.6-17.8 attempt to relate events and CFRS media coverage.

The first three values help to explain the relatively high number of articles announcing scientific discoveries. *Recency* reflects the priority that news periodicals place on event-specific material that has occurred during the daily, weekly, or monthly news cycle and was evident in 136 of the 164 articles examined. *Facticity* is the most basic "hard news" value: Facts and figures give the article authority. This value was reflected in 127 articles. *Attribution* reinforces that authority by citing institutionally affiliated or otherwise socially validated sources for information, as was done in 121 articles reviewed.

The value of *negativity,* implying not only "bad news" but controversy, affects the coverage of scientific controversies (e.g., the "war" over Pap smear frequency and reliability), and also contributes to the tendency to exaggerate medical risks (e.g., the suggestion of a future epidemic of cervical cancer). This was found to be apparent in 58 of the 164 articles. The fifth value, *superlativeness,* which seeks stories of magnitude and significance, also tends to add weight to the announcement of discoveries, as was revealed in 42 articles. In addition, all of the above values tend to obliterate unreported counter-information, whether it related to a discovery or to efforts to modify high-risk behaviors.

Relevance (closeness to the audience's personal experience) promotes use of information on avoidance of high-risk behaviors by the reader, an important component of changing health behavior, which appeared in only 18 of the articles. The values of *personalization* (depiction in personal terms, as demonstrated in 35 articles) and *eliteness* (e.g., reference to celebrities, as occurred in 29 articles) both contribute to the emphasis on the personal sagas of real and fictional celebrities suffering from CFRS.

Aside from *personalization* and *eliteness,* a variety of values can combine to promote marginalization of information on CFRS. *Negativity* is clearly a factor in reporting of the Taxol/yew tree/environmental controversy, as is *consonance* (compatibility with stereotypes, in this case "Man vs. Nature," a part of the tone reflected in 16 articles).

Proximity (geographical closeness of the news source; an issue in 18 articles as well) can distort information through excessive emphasis on local references, and *unexpectedness* ("Man Bites Dog" type stories, which also framed the content in 18 instances) can skew the information to stress unlikely elements.

Another way to examine the content-shaping influence of news values is to imagine the ideal story conveying information on CFRS, and then consider the elements that would have to be included to ensure coverage. The ideal story *(for the reader)* would be a cumulative, comprehensive summary of consensus medical opinion on the causes, prevention, diagnosis, and treatment of cervical, ovarian, and uterine cancer. The ideal story *(for the reporter)* would reflect sufficient news value to ensure its approval by the editor and its appearance in print.

Recency would demand an event to which this information is linked. *Facticity* would require numbers and *attribution* an unimpeachable source or sources—not easy, given the fragmentation of researchers. *Negativity* would need a touch of controversy or fear, yet *superlativeness* would demand assertion of a breakthrough or watershed. *Relevance* and *personalization* might be served by identifying the story with a real woman, and *eliteness* would search for a celebrity victim, if possible one from the newspaper's circulation area *(proximity)*. *Consonance* and *unexpectedness* would tug in opposite directions. Finally, the ideal story would have to run the risk that another medical story that satisfied a higher number of news values would compete successfully for space.

Implications for Public Health Information

The findings in this analysis of newspaper reporting about CFRS suggest that those who would use newspaper coverage to promote better public understanding of CFRS and other medical issues need to take more seriously the values that shape newspaper text as discourse. Newspaper coverage of cancer of the female reproductive system since 1985 has not conveyed coherent and intelligible information to women in need of practical advice about their reproductive health. Biomedical information has been conveyed, but it has been fragmented and distorted during its translation into news text through news values. Perhaps these values can be influenced over time, but they cannot be circumvented or dismissed as ideological biases that can be overridden by force of public opinion.

The treatment of news as discourse points to a crucial omission in the popularization model outlined in the Introduction. Biomedical information is not immediately "popularized" or "translated" by newspapers in a linear manner. It is channeled through news values into news text, a process that can transform the information even as it is "popularized." This analysis raises the question of whether public health information campaigns may be struggling against competition from other health information sources that are less interested in public awareness but are powerfully attuned to news values.

Announcements of scientific findings, which appeal to a variety of news values, are motivated by factors other than public health information, including prestige and funding. Many researchers, journals, associations, and biomedical businesses can build on extensive experience in obtaining newspaper coverage. Some manufacture the "events" that reporters crave and consolidate the information that generates stories by holding special conferences and briefings for science and medicine writers. Others undoubtedly cultivate individual reporters like expert witnesses cultivate attorneys.

Public health advocates might well reconsider the relative utility of free and paid media. The one article in the data sample that best resembled an "ideal" conveyance of information was in fact a paid supplement to a weekly magazine.[37] The relative inefficiency of newspapers in conveying information on CFRS is not, however, inevitable for all forms of public health information. Given the reliance of newspapers on specific events and individual authorities, the fragmentation of CFRS research into cervical, ovarian, and uterine segments is a crucial factor in the fragmentation of information. Medical issues in which the research and treatment communities are unified are obviously in a superior position to convey comprehensive and cumulative material in a manner more consistent with news values. Although this study draws sobering implications for the popularization model of the news media's role in public health information, it also suggests that public health advocates can more intelligently utilize newspapers if they accept news as a discourse field with its own rules and needs, and if they acknowledge the power of news values in shaping what we read each day.

Notes

1. R. A. Logan, "Popularization Versus Secularization: Media Coverage of Health," in L. Wilkins & P. Patterson (Eds.), *Risky Business: Communicating Issues of Science, Risk, and Public Policy* (Westport, CT: Greenwood, 1991): 44. Reprinted with permission of Greenwood Publishing Group, Inc., Westport, CT. Copyright © 1991.

2. C. K. Atkin & V. Freimuth, "Formulative Evaluation Research in Campaign Design," in R. E. Rice & C. K. Atkin (Eds.), *Public Communication Campaigns* (Newbury Park, CA: Sage, 1989): 131-173.

3. B. F. Luebke, "No More Content Analysis," *Newspaper Research Journal* 13 (1992): 2-9.

4. The *Newspaper Abstract Ondisc* indexed the *New York Times*, the *Wall Street Journal*, the *Washington Post*, the *Atlanta Journal-Constitution*, the *Boston Globe*, the *Los Angeles Times*, the *Chicago Tribune*, the *Christian Science Monitor*, and *USA Today*. No relevant material was found in the *Christian Science Monitor*. Because issues of the *Boston Globe* from 1990 to 1993 were not retrievable, *Globe* articles were excluded. Obituary notices that cited CFRS as a cause of death were excluded from the sample, though news stories following the death of an individual were included. The *Expanded Academic Index* search was limited to *Newsweek* and *Time* from 1985 through 1993. These two magazines were included because their mass circulation makes them a source of news similar to newspapers. Where the term *newspaper* appears, the reference is meant to encompass these mass circulation magazines as well. For both databases the search terms were ovar? or cervi? or uter? cancer.

5. A. Bell, *The Language of News Media* (Cambridge, MA: Basil Blackwell, 1991). Bell has built upon the theoretical base of other linguists. Quoted material used by permission.

6. *Cancer Facts and Figures* (Atlanta, GA: American Cancer Society, 1985-1993).

7. D. Nelkin, "Why Is Science Writing so Uncritical of Science?" in L. Wilkins & P. Patterson (Eds.), *Risky Business: Communicating Issues of Science, Risk, and Public Policy* (Westport, CT: Greenwood, 1991): ix. Reprinted with permission of Greenwood Publishing Group, Inc., Westport, CT. Copyright © 1991.

8. "Drugs Cure Cancer of Uterus," Associated Press Wirestory, *Atlanta Constitution,* October 28, 1986, p. A5; Untitled article, lead: "A Simple Drug . . . ," *Los Angeles Times,* October 28, 1986, p. I(CC)2; "Drug Cure Found for Uterine Cancer," *Chicago Tribune,* October 28, 1986, pp. 1, 14; Untitled article, lead: "Researchers in Boston Said . . . ," *Wall Street Journal,* October 28, 1986, 1, p. ix. Quoted material used by permission.

9. L. Marsa, "One Last Chance," *Los Angeles Times Magazine,* October 20, 1991, pp. 12, 50. Quoted material used by permission of the author.

10. Marsa, "One Last Chance."

11. S. Boodman, "Tamoxifen Trial Triggers Debate Over Risk," *Washington Post,* January 5, 1993, p. WH15.

12. G. Kolata, "Medical Groups Reach Compromise on Frequency of Giving Pap Tests," *New York Times,* January 23, 1988, p. B13. Copyright © 1988 by The New York Times Company. Reprinted by permission.

13. Kolata, "Medical Groups Reach Compromise."

14. *Guidelines for the Cancer-Related Checkups: An Update* (Atlanta, GA: American Cancer Society, 1993): 9.

15. R. Winslow, "Pap Smears for Some Women Over 65 Are Cost-Effective Practice, Study Says," *Wall Street Journal,* September 15, 1992, p. B6.

16. J. Scott, "Dangerous Liaisons: A Mysterious Sexually Transmitted Virus Threatens to Trigger a New Epidemic," *Los Angeles Times Magazine,* March 11, 1990, pp. 10, 37.

17. S. Blakeslee, "An Epidemic of Genital Warts Raises Concern but Not Alarm," *New York Times,* January 22, 1992, p. C3.

18. M. Elias, "Cutting Cervical Cancer," *USA Today,* April 6, 1987, p. D1. Copyright 1987, *USA Today.* Reprinted with permission.

19. "Cervical Cancer and the HPV Link," *HPV News* 2 (Fall 1992): 1, 4-9. This newsletter is published by the American Social Health Association, P.O. Box 13827, Research Triangle Park, NC 27709, which provides information and access to support groups for persons with HPV.

20. K. Painter, "Test Finds Genital Virus Widespread," *USA Today,* January 23, 1991, p. D1. Copyright © 1991, *USA Today.* Reprinted with permission.

21. E. Rosenthal, "Cervical Cancer Linked to Smoking in Study," *New York Times,* October 18, 1990, p. B12. Copyright © 1990 by The New York Times Company. Reprinted by permission.

22. T. Friend, "Career Tied to Women's Cancer Risk," *USA Today,* October 19, 1988, p. A1. Copyright © 1988, *USA Today.* Reprinted with permission.

23. Rosenthal, "Cervical Cancer Linked to Smoking."

24. T. Friend, "Ovarian Cancer Screening Knocked," *USA Today,* July 16, 1992, p. D1; M. King, "Up to Half of Pap Smears Wrong, Experts Say," *Atlanta Constitution,* April 5, 1988, p. A1.

25. S. Sternberg, "Cervical Cancer Deaths in South Among Highest in U.S., Study Finds," *Atlanta Constitution,* September 29, 1989, p. A1; S. Sternberg, "Deaths From Cervical Cancer Fall, but Black Women's Risk Remains High," *Atlanta Constitution,* April 20, 1990, p. A11.

26. T. Egan, "Trees That Yield a Drug for Cancer Are Wasted," *New York Times,* January 29, 1992, p. A1.

27. D. T. Christensen, "Is a Life Worth a Tree?" *Newsweek* (August 5, 1991): 10-11.

28. "Using Nature's Pharmacy," *Atlanta Constitution,* December 30, 1991, p. A8.

29. C. T. Salmon, "Campaigns for Social 'Improvement': An Overview of Values, Rationales, and Impacts," in C. T. Salmon (Ed.), *Information Campaigns: Balancing Social Values and Social Change* (Newbury Park, CA: Sage, 1989): 19-53.

30. M. Collins, "Gilda Radner and Her Parade of Funny Faces," *USA Today,* May 22, 1989, p. D5.

31. J. Stein, "Wilder's Program Completes a Dream," *Los Angeles Times,* July 24, 1991, p. E3.

32. E. Kastor, "The Shock of *thirtysomething,*" *Washington Post,* January 23, 1990, p. C1; P. Kloer, "Cancer Imperils Characters, Actors," *Atlanta Constitution,* January 23, 1990, p. F1.

33. L. R. Monroe, "When TV and Life Part Company," *Los Angeles Times,* February 27, 1990, p. E1.

34. T. A. van Dijk, *News as Discourse* (Hillsdale, NJ: Lawrence Erlbaum, 1988): 3. Quoted material used by permission.

35. Salmon, "Campaigns for Social 'Improvement,' " pp. 19-53.

36. Bell, *The Language of News Media,* p. 155.

37. D. J. Fink, "An Update on Cervical Cancer Detection," *Newsweek* (March 30, 1988): S14; the controversy focused on the "cost effectiveness" of Pap smears for women over the age of 65.

PART V

A Social Support Framework for Communicating
About Women's Reproductive Health

---

*The social context in which individuals are embedded affects their attitudes
and behaviors. This social context is determined by the patterns of relationships that exist in a particular social structure.*

Rosanne L. Hartman & J. David Johnson,
"Social Contagion and Multiplexity," p. 523[1]

Part V of this volume examines a social support framework for communicating about
women's reproductive health. This focus treats women's reproductive health as an
outcome of their social relations. Such an emphasis pushes to the forefront two
propositions about women and their health:

1. Personal care and tasks that make up caregiving have long been identified as part of
   women's traditional role in the family and in this society; and
2. we know little about what happens when women need caregiving.

A social support framework for communicating about women's reproductive health
emphasizes an odd situation for women. Only women can become pregnant, so only
women can receive prenatal care. Only women can give birth to children, and so only
women can be the targets for debate about how, when, and where this will occur. As
mothers, women assume the primary responsibility for attending well child exams to
promote their children's health. As wives and daughters, women assume a primary role
for supporting spouses and parents when they need care.[2] Thus, it appears as though
women have ample opportunity to receive health information and care, supporting their

own health and well-being. Yet each of these health care interactions occurs for the sake of another—someone with whom and for whom a woman has assumed the caretaking role, be it a fetus, a child, a husband, or a parent. As a result, women are left wanting for health care and information for themselves—even in relation to menstruation and menopause, the quintessential topics defining women's reproductive health, as demonstrated by Kalbfleisch and Bonnell's review of the findings in this area.

A social support framework for communicating about women's reproductive health illustrates the critical need to treat a woman's health wholistically, in terms of her body's systems, and the family, community, and societal systems to which a woman belongs. Otherwise, there may be a failure to communicate such health information as the association between a woman's menstrual cycle and outcomes associated with surgery in relation to breast cancer; or the risk factors associated with *both* use *and* nonuse of hormone replacement therapy after a woman reaches the age of menopause. There may also be a failure to recognize the intersection between medical regimens and women's lives. If a treatment might be costly to a woman in terms of her family's budget, her decision to put off or avoid treatment seems likely. If preventive practices may inconvenience her husband, family, or friends, a woman might fail to follow through for herself, when she would vigorously assist a loved one in maintaining the very same regimen.

A social support framework for communicating about women's reproductive health also emphasizes the intersection between public discourse and private lives, illustrating the neglect of this focus in health campaign communication. As reviewed in previous sections of this volume, sometimes members of one's social network *facilitate* the performance of recommended health practices; other times, family, friends, and co-workers *inhibit* performance. These findings appear in the literature relating to prenatal care; to alcohol, tobacco, and drug use; to practicing birth control; and to decisions about abortion and childbirth.

Only too rarely, however, do communication campaigns address members of social support networks, giving them information and/or promoting their roles as caretakers for women. Keeley clearly outlines the contribution to be made by members of a woman's social network in a woman's recovery from and survival of breast cancer. These behaviors are not within the traditional roles of most members of a woman's social network, confirming the need for more efforts to communicate about these matters to both women and their families. To design such messages, however, demands careful preparation to determine what gaps in understanding and access exist, as Kahl discusses in relation to mammography and women's health.

Furthermore, adopting a social support lens to examine communication about women's reproductive health spotlights a finding from the literature on the interface between mediated and interpersonal communication. People report that the media influence others more than themselves, but individuals are more willing to express their opinions publicly when they perceive support for their viewpoint, as reported by media.[3] Thus, silence about women's health in the media perpetuates silence interpersonally, affecting women's health and their relationships. The obvious way that the media can be silent is to report nothing about a woman's health topic, which is often the case in relation to menstruation, as discussed by Kalbfleisch, Bonnell, and Harris. A less obvious way that the media can be silent is to report about a health topic as if it affects *only* women. Breast cancer and menopause both provide examples of the effects of such "silence." For men, too, get breast cancer, and research has shown that men's testosterone hormone levels decline by about a third between the ages of 48 and 70, which may affect their reproductive health.[4] Media seldom discuss these findings, however, and so the image that these conditions are *female ones* continues unabated. As husbands, fathers, and/or other male relatives and friends get older, the media's silence about the changes likely to occur in male hormone levels and about subsequent noticeable and measurable physical and psychological effects in men sets the stage for relational tension and dissatisfaction. Men and women appear likely to look for other causes of the physical and psychological effects that men may experience, and their relationships become one alternative explanation.

In short, women and their relationships are inseparable. To treat a woman's health in isolation from the social context in which she lives and works reduces the efficacy of treatment and a woman's confidence in her ability to control her health and well-being. To treat a woman's health as if it is synonymous with treating the health of members in her social network, however, misses the woman.

Notes

1. R. L. Hartman & J. D. Johnson, "Social Contagion and Multiplexity: Communication Networks as Predictors of Commitment and Role Ambiguity," *Human Communication Research* 15 (1989): 523-548.

2. B. Miller, "Gender Differences in Spouse Caregiver Strain: Socialization and Role Explanations," *Journal of Marriage and the Family* 52 (1990): 311-321.

3. D. C. Mutz, "The Influence of Perceptions of Media Influence: Third Person Effects and the Public Expression of Opinions," *International Journal of Public Opinion Research* 1 (1989): 3-23.

4. A. M. Matsumato, *Male Menopause* (Seattle, WA: Veterans' Affairs Medical Center, 1994): 14.

18

Menarche, Menstruation, and Menopause

The Communication of Information and Social Support

Pamela J. Kalbfleisch
Karen H. Bonnell

Menarche, menstruation, and menopause are not diseases. They are *natural* parts of women's lives, allowing fertility and playing intimate roles in reproductive and bodily health, though they may involve discomfort and pain. Perhaps more than any other component of reproductive health, the psychological dimensions of menstrual life are central. Therefore, this chapter examines the medical and social scientific literature on the physical nature of menstruation and menopause, as well as their psychological effects. It first covers menarche, then menstruation, and then menopause.

The Onset of Menstruation

Menarche can be a positive, affirming experience for a young girl or a time of high anxiety.[1] Cultural rituals may serve to enhance the menarcheal experience, whereas the lack of preparation for her first period may cause the menarche to be perceived as a terrifying, negative life trauma. The first onset of menstruation usually occurs at about age 12. Mothers typically bear the primary responsibility of preparing their daughters for menarche, but studies have indicated that many young women are not receiving adequate or, in some cases, any information about menstruation prior to menarche.[2] In a survey of adolescents about their attitudes toward menarche, McGrory reported 67 of 162 parents contacted refused even to allow their daughters to participate in such a study, often because the research made the mothers feel uncomfortable and embarrassed.[3]

Studies show that different women receive different preparations for menarche, and this affects their perceptions of it. These differences hold across a range of cultures. In a study of 305 women in India, 37% of the respondents revealed that they had not been prepared for menarche and described their menarche as a horrifying experience.[4] Those Indian women who had received information prior to menarche indicated that they had understood menarche was a natural physiological occurrence. These women cited their mothers, teachers, and sisters as their primary sources of information on menarche and menstruation. Similarly, in one survey of 258 Italian adolescents, 47% of the girls felt that menstruation was a negative event, whereas 41% believed it was positive.[5] Positive family attitudes toward menstruation and advance preparation for menarche were associated with positive adolescent evaluations of menarche. Clearly, adolescent girls' interpersonal relationships with family, friends, and culture can impact attitudes about menarche and menstruation.

Even within a single nation, racial differences may affect the way women learn about menstruation and shape their attitudes about their menstrual cycles. In one study of 120 black women, Jackson found differences between black women and white women in the amount of preparation they received prior to menarche. Of the black women in her survey, 67% reported they were inadequately prepared for menarche; 12% said they had received no information about menstruation before their first period.[6] Such findings suggest that parents need guidance about when, what, and how to communicate information about menstruation to their daughters.

The Cyclical Nature of Menstruation and Its Impact on Women's Lives

Menstruation is a cyclical event and its effects have often been studied with attention to this cyclicity. The first component of the cyclicity of menopause relates to the way it ties women together. After menarche, the level of intimacy between mothers and daughters, female friends, and even romantic partners may change. Ulman found that mothers indicated that they felt more comfortable discussing their intimate feelings with their daughters after their daughters began menstruating.[7] Graham and McGrew studied menstrual patterns in a group of 80 nurses living at two hospitals in Scotland and found that pairs of close friends were significantly more likely to have synchronous menstrual cycles than female pairs selected at random.[8] Researchers are not sure what causes this phenomenon nor are they certain whether any causal relationships exist. In romantic relationships, LeFevre and associates found that the menstrual cycle affected women's moods and men's activation.[9]

Menstruation also has strong cultural components. Attitudes about menstruation are affected by a woman's cultural background. Religion may in part perpetuate menstrual taboos, as demonstrated in Rothbaum and Jackson's study of the menstrual attitudes of Orthodox Jewish, Protestant, and Roman Catholic women.[10] Among the subjects were women who observed the Orthodox Judaism ritual of Mikvah, "cleansing oneself of the uncleanliness and unholiness of menstruation in order that physical contact with one's husband may be reinstated."[11] Ninety-four percent of the Orthodox Jewish women who attended the Mikvah ritual believed that women should not have sex during menstruation, and nearly 44% of the Orthodox Jewish women who did not attend Mikvah agreed. Comparatively, 20% of the Protestants and 13% of the Catholics opposed sex during the menstrual period.

In addition to effects on physical intimacy and other emotional responses, some women believe the menstrual cycle can affect academic performance, with poorer scores on examinations just before or during menstruation.[12] However, when Hartley, Lyons, and Dunne tested the memory and reasoning skills of 30 women according to their menstrual cycles, they found the women were more slowed by sentence complexity in their logical reasoning during ovulation than at other times in their cycles.[13] These researchers also found that the ovulatory phase rather than the menstrual phase was associated with poorer performance on semantically confusing lists.

Whatever the effects may be on women's emotions or cognitive responses, the stage of a woman's menstrual cycle has begun to be considered by some hospitals when scheduling the timing of some nonemergency surgery. According to a study by Honkavaara and associates, the phase of the menstrual cycle was directly associated with the likelihood of nausea and vomiting after gynecological laparoscopy.[14] These researchers reported that, "Women undergoing laparoscopy during the luteal phase experienced nausea and vomiting in 77% of cases which was more than the women anaesthetized during the follicular (32%) or pre-menstrual phases (18%). Of the women in ovulatory phase 54% experienced nausea and vomiting."[15]

Other research indicates that there is some initial evidence that timing breast surgery (biopsy or removal of breast cancer) with ovulation has potential for reducing metastases of cancerous tumors.[16] Though these researchers' results are based on studies of mice, their findings point to the need for clinical research in the human population. In one initial evaluation of women undergoing modified and radical mastectomies during different times in their menstrual cycles, Marques and Franco reported *that women undergoing surgical mastectomies 0-2 or 13-32 days after their last day of menstruation (roughly the luteal phase) had better cancer survival rates and less recurrence than the women who had surgical mastectomies 3-12 days after the last day of their menstrual period (roughly the follicular phases).* Marques and Franco urge researchers to note the last menstrual period for all patients undergoing breast cancer surgery so that further data can be gathered regarding this issue; they suggest that the most advantageous timing of surgery during the menstrual cycle should eventually become a treatment policy.[17]

Obviously, researchers have only just begun to consider the relationship of women's menstrual cycles to their reactions to surgery and other medical treatments. Undoubtedly the process of menstruation is more complicated than the shedding of blood and other material from the lining of the uterus. Though medical research suggests that menstruation is a biological process that may affect other physiological processes, social scientists indicate that women's menstrual health may be linked to other cultural and psychological factors. The next section of this chapter considers the menstrual cycle's biological functions.

THE FUNCTIONS OF MENSTRUATION

Early theories attempting to explain the function of menstruation focused on bleeding as an expulsion of a surplus of blood from a woman's body.[18] Explanations for this surplus included the notion that women had more blood than men and periodically needed to reduce this amount, or that women were hotter than men and the expulsion of blood allowed them to cool down. Scholars even reasoned that blood escaped from the womb because this was the weakest part of the female anatomy.[19] Others, such as Aristotle, suggested that women are colder than men and lack the heat necessary to produce sperm, thereby producing a substandard concoction of menstrual blood instead.[20]

The origin of menstrual blood has been clarified as has the physiology of the monthly menstrual cycle.[21] Still, current theorists maintain a notion of the function of the menstrual blood similar to that of early theorists regarding menstrual blood as an unused or "wasted" substance.[22] Scientists continue to base their hypotheses on the premise that menstrual blood is the worthless remains of the reproductive cycle.[23]

One scientist, conducting an adaptationist analysis in an effort to understand the function of menstruation better, reasoned that the costs of menstruation are too great for it to exist as simply a by-product of reproductive readiness.[24] The scientist, Margie Profet, lists two of the primary costs of menstruation as being nutritional and reproductive. According to Profet, nutritionally, the loss of blood and tissue can lower the body's store of iron; and reproductively, the extended cycle of buildup and release of endometrial tissue limits the period of fertility in humans. Profet also notes that the distinctive odor of menstrual blood could be disadvantageous by attracting predators.

The functional mechanism that Profet presents in her adaptationist analysis is that menstruation functions to protect the uterus and oviducts from pathogens.[25] The premise is that menstrual blood accomplishes this (a) mechanically, by shedding and expelling thick layers of potentially affected tissue; and (b) immunologically, through the delivery of white blood corpuscles to the endometrial tissue. Profet notes that there are more white blood cells in menstrual blood than in normal circulating blood, and that menstrual blood contains several compounds not found in other blood, all of which should be investigated.

The most obvious implication of this perspective for women's health is in how physicians should treat menorrhagia (very heavy menstruation) or metrorrhagia (bleeding between regular menstruation). Proponents of the traditional perspective argue that the menstrual blood can facilitate the spread of infections.[26] Profet notes that infections and other pathogens in the uterus and surrounding tissues may prompt the onset of menstruation, or may increase the duration of menstruation.[27] If Profet's premise is correct, physicians should consider the underlying cause of heavy menses or break-through bleeding, and reconsider the use of birth control pills to suppress menstruation in women with dysmenorrhea (painful menstruation). Furthermore, her hypotheses also imply that barrier methods of contraception are useful to reduce the transmission of pathogens by the sperm into the uterine environment.

The adaptationist analysis of Profet and the implications she draws from her analysis should be subjected to careful consideration and examination prior to wide-spread adoption by the scientific community. Nonetheless, by questioning theories of menstruation that have not changed significantly in centuries, Profet's work deserves our attention.

MENSTRUAL COMPLAINTS

Excessive menstrual bleeding (menorrhagia), painful menstruation (dysmenorrhea), and PMS (premenstrual syndrome) are three familiar complaints associated with menstruation. Both physicians and scientists have expressed some apprehension regarding these complaints, because in large part they are *subjectively experienced* by the woman voicing them.[28] For example, "normal" blood loss during menstruation can range from 10 to 80 milliliters per cycle with an average of 40 milliliters per cycle.[29] Women who perceive themselves to be bleeding excessively, however, may actually be falling within this range of normal menstrual flow. Some researchers have found evidence that 50% of women complaining of excessive blood loss actually have a normally expected loss of blood.[30] This overestimation of blood loss may in part stem from communica-tion with friends and family about what they expect as normal menstrual flow and a lack of information and standardized objective criteria by which women can judge the volume of their own menstrual flows.

Painful menstruation (dysmenorrhea) or severe cramping is associated with reduced blood flow to the uterine smooth muscle and with strong contractions of this muscle.[31] Painful menstruation has been considered the primary cause of absenteeism in school and work environments, with some estimates as high as 2 lost workdays per month per woman in the workforce.[32] In their review of dysmenorrhea research, however, Gruber and Wildman indicate that the impact of menstrual pain on daily activities is overes-timated in the popular press and early research.[33] Only 1% of the employees in their sample missed work because of menstrual pain; only 12.6% of the college students missed classes because of menstrual pain.

According to McDaniel,

> the list of symptoms associated with PMS are numerous, but the most commonly reported are tension, insomnia, anxiety, fatigue, irritability, depression, clumsiness, accident-proneness, decreased intellectual and physical performance, decreased efficiency, headache, backache, nausea, weight gain, tender breasts, bloated feeling, and general aches and pains.[34]

There is no general agreement on a definition of the symptoms that indicate when a women is experiencing PMS.[35] Numerous theories and explanations attempt to explain the phenomena of premenstrual syndrome. Many scholars consider PMS to be created by a combination of biological and psychological factors.[36] Others indicate that culture and interpersonal relationships are important in explaining how women experience premenstrual symptoms.[37]

The perspective that PMS may actually be a natural part of menstruation has spurred investigation of alternative forms of treatment other than drugs, such as progesterone (to regulate bodily hormones) and diuretics (to control water retention), including rest, exercise, and diet.[38]

Taylor and Bledsoe note that supportive communication with family, friends, peers, and others in one's interpersonal networks may also help in coping with menstrual pain and PMS. These researchers indicate that personal relationships can provide women with information and coping strategies to prevent or alleviate psychological and even physical stressors related to their menstrual cycles. For example, in a study of a small group of women experiencing moderate to severe premenstrual symptoms, Taylor and Bledsoe found 8 out of 10 women who attended a PMS support group reported the group experience was "somewhat to very effective," saying it provided "education, emotional support, information that they were not alone with their problem, and people with whom to share problem situations and advice."[39]

Christensen and Oei found that partners or spouses who admit the presence of premenstrual changes demonstrate a greater likelihood of providing both instrumental and emotional support.[40] Interestingly, men may perceive premenstrual symptoms as more psychologically and physically debilitating to women than do women themselves.[41] The American College of Obstetricians and Gynecologists advises women to be aware of the impact of PMS on their personal relationships and to seek help if necessary.[42]

Finally, some researchers note that the concept of premenstrual syndrome is both confusing and flawed, with Bancroft and associates proposing that PMS be composed of three factors:[43] (a) "The Timing Factor" (the cyclical pattern that affects the central nervous system possibly displayed through changes in mood, food craving, or clumsiness, and on general body tissues causing changes such as bloating and breast tenderness); (b) "The Menstruation Factor" (effects that may be caused by the development and destruction of endometrial tissue, such as pain sensitivity and "loss of wellbeing [sic]"); and (c) "The Vulnerability Factor" (characteristics unrelated to menstruation that may make a person more vulnerable to symptoms that are related to the menstrual cycle). Other researchers and physicians seek a psychiatric designation for severe symptoms that cyclicly vary in their female patients. The diagnostic category of Late Luteal Phase Dysphoric Disorder (LLPDD) is used by some clinicians to label severe premenstrual disturbance. The specific symptoms triggering this medical label primarily include unstable moods and dysphoria (a feeling of ill-being and anxiety).[44]

Although several researchers and clinicians have noted that the subjective nature of premenstrual symptoms means that women must negotiate a diagnosis of PMS and its subsequent treatment with their physicians, apparently *many women and their doctors do not possess the communication skills necessary to accomplish this negotiation.*

When Brown and Zimmer surveyed women attending a PMS lecture about their help-seeking experiences, they found that women were primarily dissatisfied with these interactions.[45] Brown and Zimmer found that 77% of the women responding to their survey had sought help from a physician, but 67% of them rated this meeting as a negative encounter. Two thirds of the women surveyed sought help for their premenstrual symptoms with psychiatrists, but 63% rated these experiences negatively. Conversely, 42% had sought help from nurse practitioners, and most of these respondents (67%) rated the experiences positively. The women also reported seeking help from others, including friends, counselors, and clergy. Their lack of information about the root cause of premenstrual tension, irritability, mood swings, and other menstrual complaints leaves many women defenseless as their periods approach each month. Although pain relievers may relieve some complaints, there is much to be learned about how nutrition, lifestyle, and communication may alleviate problems associated with women's menstrual cycles.

One disease relating to menstruation that has received medical attention, leading to better diagnosis and treatment, is endometriosis. This disease is characterized by the growth of small portions of the normal tissue lining the uterus—or endometrium—in locations away from normal sites. These locations include the fallopian tubes and ovaries, as well as the bowels, and even the lungs, thighs, and chest.[46] Symptoms of the disease include dysmenorrhea or painful periods; dyspareunia, or pain during intercourse; and chronic pelvic and low back pain. Moreover, infertility may be viewed as another indicator, for 30% to 40% of women with endometriosis are infertile.[47] The accuracy of diagnosis has been increased through use of laparoscopy, the insertion of a small lighted tube—the laparoscope—through a tiny cut in a woman's navel internally to view sites where such cell growth may be occurring. The treatment of the disease, once diagnosed, also is enhanced by laparoscopy to perform laser surgery.[48] Numerous causal factors have been examined in relation to endometriosis, including a woman's age and family history.[49] Overuse of hysterectomy for treatment is one outcome associated with efforts to treat endometriosis, and the woman who is diagnosed with the disease must often assert her rights to other forms of treatment, such as drug therapies, including birth control pills, before making the decision to undergo radical surgery.

Menopause and Change in Women's Lives

As women experience menopause, the perceptions, attitudes, and any accompanying physical changes they experience may be very different.[50] Menopause can be broadly defined as "the period of time preceding and following upon the last menstrual cycle."[51] Other conditions may cause menstruation to cease prior to a woman's final menstruation, creating the need for a more specific definition, used by some scientists and clinicians: "at least 12 months of amenorrhea not attributable to other causes. The term climacteric or perimenopause refers to that time period, usually encompassing several years, during which cyclic functioning of the ovaries is changing."[52]

The average age at which most women experience menopause in the United States is 51.[53] Some women begin to experience the climacteric or perimenopause at 35, however, and others do not begin to experience symptoms until they reach their late fifties.[54] Obviously, menopause is a phenomenon that affects a substantial number of women at any one time. In 1990, according to Kronenberg, one third of all women in the United States were 50 or older.[55] The next several years should witness a dramatic rise in the number of women who are experiencing menopause as the largest wave of the baby boom reaches 50. With a current life expectancy of approximately 81 years, these women will still have a large share of their lives to live after reaching menopause.[56]

The predominate medical model for the management of menopause was developed in the 1930s and 1940s by U.S. medical professionals.[57] This approach essentially defines menopause as a deficiency disease, a physiological condition in which a woman's body becomes depleted of estrogen.[58] An underlying premise of this definition appears to be that women are living longer than their reproductive systems were designed to last. If one accepts the premise that menopause is a disease comprised of deficiency, the obvious treatment of choice would be the administration of estrogen to ameliorate this deficiency.[59]

The primary menopausal complaints associated with this drop in estrogen are vasomotor instability (hot flashes) and urogenital atrophy, with approximately 75% to 85% of menopausal women in the United States experiencing hot flashes.[60] The scientific community has assumed for years that because these hot flashes are strongly associated with dropping estrogen in menopausal women, the lack of estrogen had caused this physiological reaction.[61] However, more recent research challenges this assumption and finds that noradrenergic instability is more likely to cause the hot flash phenomenon.[62] This instability appears to be caused by the diminishing levels of endogenous opioids that accompanies the reduction of estrogen and progesterone during menopause.[63]

A second menopausal complaint, urogenital atrophy, causes pain during intercourse (dyspareunia) for approximately 8% to 25% of menopausal women.[64] Not all women experience this complaint; however, a change in genital appearance and function does appear to be directly linked to dropping estrogen levels, with some women noticing symptoms after only months of lowered estrogen. This reduction in estrogen lowers the vascular supply to the pelvis, which can facilitate change in the appearance and function of the urogenital area.[65]

Women who present complaints regarding vasomotor instability and symptoms of urogenital atrophy to their physicians will often be prescribed estrogen in order to reduce these complaints. Estrogen replacement therapy appears to be particularly effective in controlling hot flashes and in reducing bone loss due to osteoporosis. Uro-vaginal itching, dryness, and loss of elasticity are also relieved by estrogen therapy.[66] There is also some evidence that an additional benefit of estrogen replacement therapy may be a reduced risk of heart disease through inhibition of plaque formation in the arteries and a lowering of low density lipoprotein and raising of high density lipoproteins in plasma serum levels.[67]

The primary risk of estrogen replacement therapy appears to be a sixfold increase in risk for endometrial cancer (i.e., from 1 in 1,000 to 6 in 1,000).[68] There is also a possible breast cancer risk, although the research is less definitive, with the risk occurring in growth of estrogen dependent breast cancers and not in the actual initiation of breast cancers.[69] Other problems with estrogen replacement therapy in some women are breast tenderness, nausea, and edema. Progestin is sometimes prescribed with estrogen to reduce these problems and to lower the risk for uterine cancer, but may also stimulate a return of menstruation and can reduce the effect of estrogen on lipoprotein levels.[70]

Estrogen replacement therapy is considered to be a preventive treatment for osteoporosis, because the rate of bone loss is significantly reduced with this treatment.[71] Critics suggest that other therapies might be more appropriate to control menopausal complaints. Specific concerns include a lack of research on the effects of long-time exposure to estrogen replacement therapy, cancer risk, and the medicalization of a natural developmental process (menopause).[72] Estrogen is not advised for about 10% of females, or those who have: (a) current breast or endometrial cancer, or a history of these; (b) acute or chronic liver disease; (c) undiagnosed vaginal bleeding; (d) current thrombophlebitis or thromboembolic disorder, or a history of these disorders; (e) endometriosis; (f) heart, pancreatic, or gallbladder disease; (g) fibrocystic breast disease; or (h) hypertension or migraine headaches aggravated by estrogen usage.[73]

Given the large number of women who will soon be affected by menopause, there is surprisingly little research available on this life phase. Locating research that explores methods of controlling menopausal complaints other than through use of estrogen therapy is even more challenging. The estimated number of women who are using estrogen replacement therapy ranges from 10% to 15% of the menopausal female population.[74] There is little information on what the other 85% to 90% of this population are doing to manage their menopause experience. Anecdotal reports suggest that vitamin B complex, vitamins C and E, and zinc supplements may relieve hot flashes. Other suggestions include ginseng tea, bee pollen, or cohosh.[75]

Alternatives to estrogen replacement therapy for reduction of bone loss due to osteoporosis include increasing calcium intake and increasing exercise. Although an increase in calcium intake appears to work in a similar manner as estrogen replacement therapy by reducing the rate of bone loss, an increase in exercise appears to combat osteoporosis by actually increasing bone mineral.[76] As with the control of hot flash phenomena, more research is needed on both the medical and nonmedical control of osteoporosis in aging women.

Though the bulk of scientific study on menopause focuses on those systems that show response to estrogen replacement therapy, other complaints associated with menopause, which do not respond to estrogen replacement therapy, are primarily overlooked in the scientific literature. These complaints (sometimes classified as secondary complaints) include irritability, nervousness, insomnia, depression, and fatigue.[77] As early as the 18th century, disturbances of mood and behavior have been associated with menopause. The existence of a specific affective syndrome associated with menopause remains controversial.[78] Studies of psychological characteristics associated with menopause have been plagued by small sample sizes, samples of self-selecting women, failure to use standardized instruments for measuring complaints, and study of only one or two symptoms at a time without using any standard method of symptom classification or measurement.[79] Until more definitive evidence exists that ties these complaints directly to menopause, treatment and evaluation of women expressing these complaints should be based on a woman's specific life characteristics rather than on her menopausal status.[80]

There is some preliminary evidence that both biological and psychological reactions to menopause may be related to a woman's culture, perceptions, and interpersonal relationships. In an ethnographic study of Mayan Indian women living in Mexico, Beyene stated, "my data from the village women and men, physicians, midwives, and local healers indicate that menopause is not a personally or culturally elaborated stage in the life of Mayan women."[81] Beyene did not find anyone in this culture who experienced hot flashes or any other menopausal complaints. Menopause was recognized only as the cessation of menstruation and the end of childbearing, with women describing more enjoyment from sex with their husbands, freedom from taboos and restrictions, and feeling like young girls again. Women who had not yet experienced menopause looked forward to when their periods would cease.

Matthews reports a somewhat similar reaction to menopause in the United States when premenopausal women looked forward to receiving some benefits with menopause. Women who looked forward to menopause reported higher levels of social support during menopause and fewer menopausal complaints than women who were not looking forward to this time in their lives. Unlike the Mayan women, these women did experience some complaints, suggesting that positive and negative perceptions of menopause may affect how menopause is experienced. It is not clear from this study, however, whether the reported increased social support helped smooth the menopause transition or whether the women experienced increased social support because they perceived menopause as being a positive life event.[82]

Women in several other cultures have also been found to experience minimal or no menopausal complaints.[83] Unfortunately, cross-cultural research on the experience of menopause is limited, making it difficult to determine common factors influencing the experience of menopause across cultures. Also, women's lives are complex, and establishing a factor or combination of factors to identify how menopause may be experienced is a difficult task. In the United States, menopause may happen concurrently with children leaving home and other sources of increased interpersonal and relational stress, events that may contribute to the psychological distress sometimes described as accompanying menopause.[84]

Diet may effect how menopause is experienced. Goodman and associates report that both Japanese and Caucasian women living in Hawaii report minimal menopausal complaints. Because both groups of women living in Hawaii eat large amounts of rice, Goodman concludes that perhaps diet could explain different reactions to menopause.[85] Mayan women in Beyene's study ate very little meat and no milk, relying instead on a diet composed primarily of beans and vegetables.[86] If diet is a contributing factor to how menopause is experienced, this would explain some of the cross-cultural differences.

At this point, there is simply not enough information to know why women in different cultures may experience menopause differently, or even to know if these are actual differences or are spurious results from inadequate research on this topic. Clearly, additional research is necessary if we are to understand how menopause affects women's bodies, emotional well-being, and interpersonal relationships. A better understanding of menopause could empower women, giving them more control in making decisions about treatment possibilities and reassurance that they are going through a natural life cycle.

A network of supportive communication relationships with spouse or partner, family, close friends, and health care providers can also provide empathic understanding, reassurance, and concern for women's well-being to help them maintain healthy emotional attitudes about the changes affecting them. Women need to share information about their experiences with other women to learn new coping strategies for menopausal complaints. Close friendships between older women can provide a basis for emotional support, as women are more likely to confide in those they perceive to be close friends.[87] Women should also seek ways to eliminate myths and stereotypes about menopausal women that devalue those entering midlife. Women should respect and value themselves as cyclical beings, pursuing knowledge about their menstrual lives, sharing it with other women, appreciating those who have gone before them, and preparing their daughters to continue the cycle of life.

Notes

1. D. Taylor, *Red Flower: Rethinking Menstruation* (Freedom, CA: Crossing Press, 1988).

2. P. Weideger, *Menstruation and Menopause: The Physiology and Psychology, the Myth and the Reality* (New York: Knopf, 1976): 158.

3. A. McGrory, "Menarche: Responses of Early Adolescent Females," *Adolescence* 25 (1990): 265-270.

4. K. P. Skandhan, A. K. Pandya, S. Skandhan, & Y. B. Mehta, "Menarche: Prior Knowledge and Experience," *Adolescence* 23 (1988): 149-154.

5. M. Amann-Gainotti, "Sexual Socialization During Early Adolescence: The Menarche," *Adolescence* 21 (1986): 703-710.

6. B. B. Jackson, "Black Women's Responses to Menarche and Menopause," in A. J. Dan & L. L. Lewis (Eds.), *Menstrual Health in Women's Lives* (Urbana: University of Illinois Press, 1992): 178-190.

7. K. H. Ulman, "The Impact of Menarche on Family Relationships," in A. J. Dan & L. L. Lewis (Eds.), *Menstrual Health in Women's Lives* (Urbana: University of Illinois Press, 1992): 236-245.

8. C. A. Graham & W. C. McGrew, "Social Factors and Menstrual Synchrony in a Population of Nurses," in A. J. Dan & L. L. Lewis (Eds.), *Menstrual Health in Women's Lives* (Urbana: University of Illinois Press, 1992): 246-253.

9. J. LeFevre, C. Hedricks, R. B. Church, & M. McClintock, "Psychological and Social Behavior of Couples Over a Menstrual Cycle: 'On-the-Spot' Sampling From Everyday Life," in A. J. Dan & L. L. Lewis (Eds.), *Menstrual Health in Women's Lives* (Urbana: University of Illinois Press, 1992): 75-82.

10. B. O. Rothbaum & J. Jackson, "Religious Influence on Menstrual Attitudes and Symptoms," *Women and Health* 16(1) (1990): 63-78.

11. Rothbaum & Jackson, "Religious Influence," p. 65.

12. Weideger, "Menstruation and Menopause."

13. L. R. Hartley, D. Lyons, & M. Dunne, "Memory and Menstrual Cycles," *Ergonomics* 30 (1987): 111-120.

14. P. Honkavaara, A. Lehtinen, J. Hovorka, & K. Korttila, "Nausea and Vomiting After Gynecological Laparoscopy Depends on the Phase of the Menstrual Cycle," *Canadian Journal of Anesthesiology* 38 (1991): 876-879.

15. Honkavaara et al., "Nausea and Vomiting After Gynecological Laparoscopy," p. 877.

16. S. A. Gruber, K. L. Nichol, R. B. Sothern, M. E. Malone, J. D. Potter, D. Lakatua, & W.J.M. Hrushesky, "Menstrual History and Breast Cancer Surgery," *Breast Cancer Research and Treatment* 13 (1989): 278.

17. L. A. Marques & E. L. Franco, "Association Between Timing of Surgery During Menstrual Cycle and Prognosis in Pre-Menopausal Breast Cancer," *International Journal of Cancer Research* 53 (1993): 707-708.

18. J. Delaney, M. J. Lupton, & E. Toth, *The Curse: A Cultural History of Menstruation* (rev. ed.) (Urbana: University of Illinois Press, 1988).

19. C. F. Fluhmann, *Menstrual Disorders: Pathology, Diagnosis, and Treatment* (Philadelphia: W. B. Saunders, 1939).

20. Aristotle, *De Generatione Animalium I* (D. M. Balme, Trans.) (Oxford, UK: Clarendon, 1972).

21. C. A. Finn, "Why Do Women and Some Other Primates Menstruate?" *Perspectives in Biology and Medicine* 30 (1987): 566-574.

22. Finn, "Why Do Women and Some Other Primates Menstruate?"

23. M. Profet, "Menstruation as a Defense Against Pathogens Transported by Sperm," *The Quarterly Review of Biology* 68 (1993): 335-386.

24. Profet, "Menstruation as a Defense."

25. Profet, "Menstruation as a Defense."

26. W. Plummer & J. DeClaire, "A Curse No More," *People* (October 11, 1993): 75-76.

27. Profet, "Menstruation as a Defense."

28. J. Bancroft, L. Williamson, P. Warner, D. Rennie, & S. K. Smith, "Perimenstrual Complaints in Women Complaining of PMS, Menorrhagia, and Dysmenorrhea: Toward a Dismantling of the Premenstrual Syndrome," *Psychosomatic Medicine* 55 (1993): 133-145.

29. G. Rybo, J. Leman, & E. Tibblin, "Epidemiology of Menstrual Blood Loss," in D. T. Baird & E. A. Michie (Eds.), *Mechanism of Menstrual Bleeding* (New York: Raven, 1985): 181-193.

30. Rybo et al., "Epidemiology of Menstrual Blood Loss."

31. L. Gannon, "The Potential Role of Exercise in the Alleviation of Menstrual Disorders and Menopausal Symptoms: A Theoretical Synthesis of Recent Research," *Women and Health* 14 (1988): 105-127.

32. V. A. Gruber & B. G. Wildman, "The Impact of Dysmenorrhea on Daily Activities," *Behavior Research Therapy* 25 (1987): 123-128.

33. Gruber & Wildman, "The Impact of Dysmenorrhea."

34. S. H. McDaniel, "The Interpersonal Politics of Premenstrual Syndrome," *Family Systems Medicine* 6 (1988): 134-149.

35. Bancroft et al., "Perimenstrual Complaints in Women."

36. D. Taylor & L. Bledsoe, "Peer Support, PMS, and Stress: A Pilot Study," in V. L. Olesen & N. F. Woods (Eds.), *Culture, Society, and Menstruation* (Washington, DC: Hemisphere, 1986): 161.

37. N. F. Woods, M. J. Lentz, E. S. Mitchell, K. Lee, D. Taylor, & N. Allen-Barash, "Perimenstrual Symptoms and the Health-Seeking Process: Models and Methods," in A. J. Dan & L. L. Lewis (Eds.), *Menstrual Health in Women's Lives* (Urbana: University of Illinois Press, 1992): 155; A. Reading, "Cognitive Model of Premenstrual Syndrome," *Clinical Obstetrics and Gynecology* 35 (1992): 693; McDaniel, "The Interpersonal Politics of Premenstrual Syndrome."

38. E. Rome, "Premenstrual Syndrome (PMS) Examined Through a Feminist Lens," in V. L. Olesen & N. F. Woods (Eds.), *Culture, Society, and Menstruation* (Washington, DC: Hemisphere, 1986): 149.

39. Taylor & Bledsoe, "Peer Support, PMS, and Stress," p. 167.

40. A. P. Christensen & T.P.S. Oei, "Men's Perception of Premenstrual Changes on the Premenstrual Assessment Form," *Psychological Reports* 66 (1990): 615-619.

41. D. N. Ruble, A. K. Boggiano, & J. Brooks-Gunn, "Men's and Women's Evaluations of Menstrual Related Excuses," *Sex Roles* 8 (1982): 625-638.

42. *Premenstrual Syndrome* (Washington, DC: American College of Obstetricians and Gynecologists, 1985).

43. Bancroft et al., "Perimenstrual Complaints."

44. S. K. Severino & K. A. Yonkers, "A Literature Review of Psychotic Symptoms Associated With the Premenstruum," *Psychosomatics* 34 (July-August 1993): 229-306.

45. M. A. Brown & P. A. Zimmer, "Help-Seeking for Premenstrual Symptomology: A Description of Women's Experiences," in V. L. Olesen & N. F. Woods (Eds.), *Culture, Society, and Menstruation* (Washington, DC: Hemisphere, 1986): 173-184.

46. C. C. Bird, T. W. McElin, & P. Manalo-Estrella, "The Allusive Adenomyosis of the Uterus—Revisited," *American Journal of Obstetrics and Gynecology* 112(5) (1972): 587.

47. R. Pokras & V. Hufnagel, "Hysterectomy in the United States: 1965-1984," *Vital and Health Statistics* 13(2) (National Center for Health Statistics, Ed.) (Washington, DC: Government Printing Office, 1987): 1-16.

48. H. Reich & F. McGlynn, "Treatment of Ovarian Endometriomas Using Laparoscopic Surgical Techniques," *Journal of Reproductive Medicine* 31 (1986): 583.

49. K. Lamb, R. G. Hoffman, & T. R. Nichols, "Family Trait Analysis: A Case Control Study of 43 Women With Endometriosis and Their Best Friends," *American Journal of Obstetrics and Gynecology* 154 (1986): 596-601.

50. A. M. Voda, "Menopause: A Normal View," *Clinical Obstetrics and Gynecology* 35 (1992): 923.

51. P. A. Kaufert & P. Gilbert, "Women, Menopause, Medicalization, and Culture," *Medicine and Psychiatry* 10 (1986): 8.

52. P. J. Morokoff, "Sexuality in Perimenopausal and Postmenopausal Women," *Psychology of Women Quarterly* 12 (1988): 490.

53. S. M. McKinlay, N. L. Bifano, & J. B. McKinlay, "Smoking and Age at Menopause in Women," *Annals of Internal Medicine* 103 (1985): 350-356.

54. S. R. Leiblum, "Sexuality and the Midlife Woman," *Psychology of Women Quarterly* 14 (1990): 495-508.

55. F. Kronenberg, "Hot Flashes: Epidemiology and Physiology," *Annals of the New York Academy of Sciences* 592 (1990): 52.

56. Morokoff, "Sexuality."

57. S. E. Bell, "Changing Ideas: The Medicalization of Menopause," *Social Science Medicine* 24 (1987): 535-542.

58. Kaufert & Gilbert, "Women, Menopause, Medicalization, and Culture."

59. Kaufert & Gilbert, "Women, Menopause, Medicalization, and Culture."

60. K. L. Miller, "Alternatives to Estrogen for Menopausal Symptoms," *Clinical Obstetrics and Gynecology* 35 (1992): 884-893.

61. L. Gannon, S. Hansel, & J. Goodwin, "Correlates of Menopausal Hot Flashes," *Journal of Behavioral Medicine* 10 (1987): 277-285.

62. Miller, "Alternatives."

63. Gannon, "The Potential Role of Exercise."

64. Miller, "Alternatives."

65. Leiblum, "Sexuality and the Midlife Woman."

66. N. Schmitt, J. Gogate, M. Rothert, D. Rovner, M. Holmes, G. Talarcyzk, B. Given, & J. Kroll, "Capturing and Clustering Women's Judgment Policies: The Case of Hormonal Therapy for Menopause," *Journal of Gerontology* 46 (1991): 92-101.

67. A. A. Skolnick, "At Third Meeting, Menopause Experts Make the Most of Insufficient Data," *Journal of the American Medical Association* 268 (1992): 2483-2485.

68. Schmitt et al., "Capturing and Clustering Women's Judgment Policies."

69. Skolnick, "Menopause Experts."

70. Skolnick, "Menopause Experts."

71. Schmitt et al., "Capturing and Clustering Women's Judgment Policies."

72. Voda, "Menopause."

73. Miller, "Alternatives."

74. Miller, "Alternatives"; Schmitt et al., "Capturing and Clustering Women's Judgment Policies."

75. Miller, "Alternatives."

76. E. L. Smith, W. Reddan, & P. W. Smith, "Physical Activity and Calcium Modalities for Bone Mineral Increase in Aged Women," *Medicine and Science in Sports and Exercise* 13 (1981): 699-702; Gannon, "The Potential Role of Exercise."

77. J. Wilbur, A. Dan, C. Hendricks, & K. Holm, "The Relationship Among Menopausal Status, Menopausal Symptoms, and Physical Activity in Midlife Women," *Family and Community Health* 13 (1990): 67-78.

78. P. J. Schmidt & D. R. Rubinow, "Menopause-Related Affective Disorders: A Justification for Further Study," *American Journal of Psychiatry* 148 (1991): 844-852.

79. M. C. Lennon, "Is Menopause Depressing? An Investigation of Three Perspectives," *Sex Roles* 17 (1987): 1-16; K. A. Matthews, R. R. Wing, L. H. Kuller, E. N. Meilahn, S. F. Kelsey, E. J. Costello, & A. W. Caggiula, "Influences of Natural Menopause on Psychological Characteristics and Symptoms of Middle-Aged Healthy Women," *Journal of Consulting and Clinical Psychology* 58 (1990): 345-351.

80. Matthews et al., "Influences of Natural Menopause."

81. Y. Beyene, "Cultural Significance and Physiological Manifestations of Menopause: A Biocultural Analysis," *Culture, Medicine, and Psychiatry* 10 (1986): 57.

82. K. A. Matthews, "Myths and Realities of the Menopause," *Psychosomatic Medicine* 54 (1992): 1-9.

83. M. Lock, "Introduction," *Culture, Medicine, and Psychiatry* 10 (1986): 1-5.

84. Lennon, "Is Menopause Depressing?"

85. M. J. Goodman, C. J. Stewart, & F. Gilbert, Jr., "Patterns of Menopause: A Study of Certain Medical and Physiological Variables Among Caucasian and Japanese Women Living in Hawaii," *Journal of Gerontology* 32 (1977): 291-298.

86. Beyene, "Cultural Significance."

87. K. A. Roberts & P. J. Kimboko, "Friendships in Later Life: Definitions and Maintenance Patterns," *International Journal of Aging and Human Development* 28 (1989): 9-19; P. J. Kalbfleisch, "Public Portrayals of Enduring Friendships," in P. J. Kalbfleisch (Ed.), *Interpersonal Communication: Evolving Interpersonal Relationships* (Hillsdale, NJ: Lawrence Erlbaum, 1993): 203.

19

Media Portrayals of Women's Menstrual Health Issues

Pamela J. Kalbfleisch
Karen H. Bonnell
Tina M. Harris

Do you have any idea how many women experience vaginal dryness? One in four! And since it's not exactly a topic we sit around and discuss openly, I'll bet every one of us thinks we're alone.

Advertisement[1]

The messages that women receive from television, magazines, and other forms of mass communication can inform them about important health issues, including menstrual health. These messages may, however, also appeal to women's needs for security or their fears of embarrassment in order to persuade them to buy certain products. In living rooms all across the United States, women are being told they can have moister vaginas. They are not whispering about it in intimate settings; this information is broadcast between programs on their television sets. Their daughters learn about feminine protection as they thumb through teen magazines. *Better Homes and Gardens* not only gives women advice about what to plant in their backyards but also the latest hormones that can be implanted in their bodies. If women want information about premenstrual symptoms or other menstrual concerns, they can call an advertised 1-900 telephone number.

Media messages about menstruation may also shape the way girls feel about themselves and their periods. In their book *The Curse: A Cultural History of Menstruation,*

Delaney and her associates note that the common media themes have not changed much over the past generation: "The information about menstruation available to our daughters, compared with what our mothers might have read, shows few changes: deodorize, sanitize, hide your shame, although some companies seem to be groping their way toward a more positive educational message."[2]

Some feminists view media hype about premenstrual syndrome as damaging to women by promoting "stereotypes about menstruating women as sick and hysterical, victims of their hormones."[3] Stereotypes of menopausal women may also be found in various media, including physicians' journals where menopausal women are characterized as "worried, sad, and despairing about ugly aging liver spots, the empty nest, sexual intimacy in relation to atrophic vaginitis, hot flashes, and decaying bones."[4]

In her book *The Change: Women, Aging, and Menopause,* Germaine Greer claims that the messages women receive from mass media propagate the medicalization of menopause. Feminists believe such a view should be rejected because it treats menopause as a disease, not a normal life process. "Certainly the campaign to eliminate menopause has been initiated and is run by men. Since menopause became big business there has been a vast explosion of propaganda disseminating male views of menopause."[5]

Margaret Morganroth Gullette emphasizes that media messages affect women's self-image, attitudes about life, and interpersonal relationships:

> We're all more vulnerable because of the way *menoboom* [italics ours] discussions have been framed. At the moment, the mid-life woman has an enormous amount to lose from listening to scare/pain/embarrassment stories and feeling she has no choice but to take them to heart, repeat them as truth, and rush to find "therapies."[6]

Although media messages can have a powerful effect on women's attitudes, they also offer a means to supply vital information about women's menstrual health. Popular media channels have the potential to provide essential information almost instantaneously to millions of women listening, viewing, or reading. For these reasons, the messages the public receives about menstrual health through popular media are worthy of study as they impact women's perceptions of their menstrual health.

Information for this chapter about media portrayals of women's menstrual health issues comes from a comprehensive review of sources available in most public libraries. Newspaper and magazine articles referenced in databases such as *Magazine Article Summaries, InfoTrack, The Readers' Guide to Periodical Literature, ABI/Inform, Essay and General Literature, Modern Language Association,* and *Books in Print* were searched for the years 1987 through August 1993. In addition, nine popular magazines widely read by women were selected for a page-by-page search for articles and advertisements related to women's menstrual health. Those magazines were *Redbook, Parents, Better Homes and Gardens, Glamour, Seventeen, Young & Modern, Modern Maturity, Prevention,* and *Health.* Issues covering 9 months of publication in 1992-1993 were collected for each of those magazines to provide a consistent base for content analysis. To complement the published information, a review of broadcast programming about menstrual health issues was available through transcripts identified in the *Health and Well Being Index,* prepared by Journal Graphics. This specific index catalogues transcriptions of programs from ABC News, NBC News, CBS News, Cable News Network, Public Broadcasting Service, National Public Radio, and syndicated programs through May 13, 1993.

Messages About Menarche

> I'm almost fourteen and I haven't gotten my period yet. I feel embarrassed that I'm not a true woman, and sometimes I tell my friends (who have gotten it) that I've gotten it, too. My question is, what are the signs that will occur before I begin my first period?[7]

The most discouraging news about menarche is the lack of news about it. In contrast to the number of articles referenced about the ongoing processes of menstruation and menopause, very little has been presented in the media about the onset of menstruation. Of the more than 300 magazines referenced in the *Magazine Article Summaries* database, 256 citations reference menopause in text, 119 articles reference menstruation, but only 12 citations are identified as articles that mention menarche.

While society grapples with ways to protect young people from AIDS and to prevent teenage pregnancies, the media can assist in two ways: It can provide parents with information about what, when, and how to communicate the facts about menstruation to their daughters and sons; and it can provide direct information to young viewers, listeners, or readers. Many girls experience menarche with little or no preparation: "I was nine when I got my period. I hated getting it. I didn't tell my mother or my sister. I just put toilet paper in my underpants and tried to pretend nothing was happening."[8]

Our review of popular teen magazines reveals adolescents have many questions about the onset of menstruation and may consult teen health columns for information. Publishers have a responsibility to provide accurate information and an opportunity to reassure and enlighten the thousands troubled by the same questions. Only a few have taken that opportunity.

Television programs that cultivate audiences of younger viewers have dealt with the topic of menstruation. In 1991, four television series presented episodes about menarche: *Life Goes On, The Cosby Show, Blossom,* and *I'll Fly Away.*[9] But despite this new openness in media portrayals about the onset of menstruation, the topic remains a source of extreme embarrassment to young people. At least half of the 1992-1993 issues of *Young & Modern* reviewed for this chapter presented letters from young readers who considered their most embarrassing experiences related to their periods. They describe the humiliation they felt when others found out they were having their periods.

Messages About the Process of Menstruation

Two important areas where the media can be helpful with information about the process of menstruation are (a) reassuring women about what is normal in the course of their monthly cycles and (b) dispelling myths about limitations created by their cycles. Both adolescent and adult females have questions about their periods for which they need answers. Because menstruation as a process involves physical, psychological, and social responses, not every woman perceives it the same.

Media messages can be responsible for providing factual information about the process of menstruation, or they can be blamed for perpetuating confusion and superstition. Our review of messages presented to viewers and readers from 1987 through 1993 shows the process of menstruation took a back seat to the process of menopause during this time. For example, a search for books published about menstruation listed in the database *Books in Print* revealed 35 publications during that time period; but there were 80 books published on the topic of menopause for those same years. Although some books covered both topics, the emphasis in recent years has been about the cessation of a woman's menstrual cycle, and not about the cycle as an ongoing process.

Messages About the Problems of Menstruation

The public's perception of the media is that it too often dwells on bad news by highlighting the bizarre, negative, or abnormal over the routine, positive, or normal. The perception is not far from the mark when the subject is women's menstrual health. For example, from January 1987 through July 1993, the *Readers' Guide to Periodical Literature* referenced 41 titles under the general topic of menstruation, whereas 42 titles were referenced as dealing specifically with premenstrual syndrome. Under both subject headings, most of the articles leave readers believing menstruation is indeed a curse of cramps, bloating, mood swings, and general suffering that disrupts women's emotional and social lives. The process as presented is something to endure, suffer through, or medicate. Readers learned that menstruation is even associated with oral health problems such as swollen gums and canker sores. One beauty and health article advised against hair waxing or electrolysis prior to menstruation, but told readers it's a good time to get a scalp treatment.[10] Little positive news about the process is presented outside of treatments or preventative measures to alleviate premenstrual symptoms.

> Charlotte had been suffering from various forms of abdominal discomfort and severe pelvic pain. For years, no doctor had been able to help her or tell her what was wrong. Lately, she'd begun to personalize her pain, blaming herself for it.[11]

Although millions of women have endometriosis, they have often failed to be diagnosed, with physicians attributing their pain to menstrual cramps and/or work-related stress. Images of this condition are not frequent in television or movie theaters, although more information about the condition, as well as more physicians specializing in its treatment, may contribute to the availability of books, pamphlets, and newspaper articles about the subject.[12] The condition has been referred to as the "professional woman's disease," perhaps because medical research has demonstrated that once a woman has a child, the cervix is more relaxed, allowing easier exit of menstrual blood. Some women with careers postpone pregnancy until their thirties, and an increased incidence of endometriosis has been observed in these women. A number of physicians, however, rather than communicating the relationship of childbirth to the flow of menstrual blood when talking to professional women about the disease, have been found to refer to the women's work and the reduction of job-related stress, as if being a professional woman was the root cause of the disease.[13] This, of course, leads to women blaming themselves for this condition, as well as media stories that pick up and report the phrase "professional woman's disease," also without conveying the full origins of the meaning of this reference. In turn, *others* who read or hear these stories may also *tend to blame the individual woman* suffering from this disease.[14] As discussed in the previous chapter, effective methods of treating this disease do exist, and physicians trained to recognize and to respond appropriately to the disease are more readily available than a decade ago. The woman suffering, however, may have to conduct her own search and research to empower herself in this regard.

Messages About Coping
With Menstrual Problems

> To ease aches and cramps, try an over-the-counter painkiller like ibuprofen. To reduce moodiness, try exercising, stretching, relaxing to music and getting plenty of sleep. If none of this helps, see your doctor.[15]

The articles analyzed for this chapter did attempt to provide vital information to readers about when to seek treatment for potentially serious menstrual health problems. For example, readers were told that severe abdominal pain may be a symptom of the disease endometriosis; and premenstrual spotting could also signal a tumor or growth. The *Readers' Guide to Periodical Literature* cited 16 articles about endometriosis from 1987 through July 1993. The *FDA Consumer* told readers in early 1993 about a new synthetic hormone called Danocrine, a nasal spray called Syunarel, and an injectable drug called Lupton Depot that offer promise for women suffering from endometriosis.[16]

Over-the-counter medications containing ibuprofen were recommended for relieving menstrual cramps. One article reported chiropractic lower back adjustments relieve cramps;[17] and still another touted the benefits of alternative remedies such as drinking red raspberry leaf tea.[18] Too often, readers are presented with limited or conflicting information about possible treatments or preventative strategies. One brief item promoted the benefits of iron supplements for menstruating girls;[19] another cautioned that women need not worry about high iron levels signaling heart attacks because iron is lost when women menstruate.[20] Cravings for foods high in fat content increase as the menstrual period approaches; but one article linked these cravings exclusively to increases in estrogen,[21] and another linked them to increases in progesterone.[22]

Although many of the articles may be intended to provide helpful information to women about their menstrual processes, they primarily focus on the physical rather than the psychological or sociological concerns associated with menstruation as a process or with menstrual problems.

More information is also needed about how menstrual problems affect couple communication and sexual relationships. Women may need to be encouraged to strengthen communication relationships with their sexual partners, friends, family, or support groups, not only to facilitate sharing information about menstrual concerns but also to develop a network of reassurance and support should problems occur. These kind of communicative networks may also assist them in midlife as they begin to seek information about menopause.

Media Messages About Menopause

The *menoboom* is what many are calling the media hype about menopause. From an economical standpoint, the media stand to profit through product advertising aimed at midlife women, the generation of baby boomers now turning into the generation of "menoboomers." As a large segment of female consumers begins to approach the age of the climacteric, it stands to reason that media managers will seek to draw these consumers as readers or viewers by satisfying informational needs about menopause.

A review of television news and "info-tainment" program transcript titles available from Journal Graphics reveals menopause was a "hot topic" on television in the early 1990s; but little attention was given to specific issues associated with menarche or menstruation. The discussion of menopause is along the major themes of (a) symptoms and treatments, especially estrogen replacement therapy; and (b) societal attitudes toward menopause, including the new openness in discussing it and whether it is being viewed as a normal process or being "medicalized."

The controversy over the "medicalization" of menopause is akin to the consumerization of the menopause generation. Some articles published about menopause are critical of the media hype. Susan Jacoby writing for *Woman's Day* reported, "From tales of menopausal gloom and doom, you'd never guess that research shows only 10 to 15 percent of all women encounter menopausal symptoms severe enough to disrupt their lives. The large majority experience only minor and temporary discomfort."[23] Barbara Ehrenreich reviewed two books about menopause for *Time* magazine and concluded that,

> Outside of affluent, white societies, menopause apparently goes by without much notice— either because women's sufferings are considered unimportant or because the sufferings just don't occur. . . . A book titled *Menopause: No Big Deal* might better describe the experience of a generation of busy high-achieving women. But it probably wouldn't leap off the shelves.[24]

Indeed the controversy over the medicalization or consumerization of menopause provides two opposing perspectives: One that seeks to promote new products, medical treatments, and information to a generation of female consumers interested in seeking and maintaining good health for their later years; and the other viewpoint that seeks to approach menopause as a natural process, rejecting it as a medical condition and adopting a "much ado about nothing" attitude. Readers and viewers of popular mass media have heard and seen both perspectives during the early 1990s; and though both sides present valid arguments in these media portrayals, the debate may have left many midlife women confused about their own health care needs.

Media Portrayals
of Menopause Problems

> The symptoms of menopause are very real: hot flashes, vaginal dryness and night sweats which may cause sleep disturbances. For millions of women, these symptoms are effectively treated with estrogen replacement therapy.[25]

Hot flashes and vaginal dryness may be the two most feared symptoms of menopause, according to a review of popular media. Premenopausal women viewing media talk shows about menopause are likely to be concerned about a future consisting of uncomfortable and potentially embarrassing episodes of hot flashes, cold sweats, and loss of interest in or the capacity to enjoy sex.

Another hot subtopic is "Early Menopause." A talk show in 1992 focused on "Menopause in My 20's," and a *Redbook* article sported a headline, "Menopause—In Your Thirties" with a caption that read, "It's happening to more and more women, doctors say."[26] But only by reading the entire article did readers learn it is not happening to more women, it is a matter of doctors being more successful today in diagnosing premature menopause. Menopause in 20- or 30-year-old women is not normal, but as television producers and writers look for "hot topics" to reach audiences, the novelty of such a topic can hardly be argued. Television producers and writers, however, should consider their responsibility in shaping attitudes and opinions about problems linked to menopause.

Media Messages About
Coping With Menopause

> Experts say that exercise counters the thinning of bones that accelerates after menopause, which helps reduce old-age fractures. Try to exercise during menopause, even if only in moderate amounts.[27]

Perhaps the most controversial topic associated with menopause is hormone replacement therapy. Our review of popular press literature reveals that estrogen replacement is the treatment often recommended by physicians to reduce symptoms such as hot flashes and vaginal dryness with added benefits of protecting against bone loss. Reports about controversy relating to this recommendation occur on two fronts: (a) those opposed to the medicalization of menopause also oppose the widespread prescription of hormones for menopausal women; and (b) estrogen has been linked in some medical studies to increased risk for breast and uterine cancer. On the other hand, some reports indicate that estrogen has also been linked to a decreased risk of heart disease. Beyond the recommendations relating to estrogen replacement therapy, information available to readers and viewers promotes use of over-the-counter lubricants to reduce dryness.

Another topic often presented to popular press audiences, though much less controversial, is the association of menopause with loss of bone density. Many programs and articles mentioned the importance of calcium intake; and readers of the July 1993 issue of *Self* were told researchers are now looking into the effect of magnesium on bone density of postmenopausal women.[28] Some recommended that women take magnesium supplements, though cautioning that they can have a laxative effect.

Another physician, educator, and women's health advocate told readers in a *Mirabella* article that she is concerned about the lack of health awareness of young women. Mary Lake Polan says young women are unaware of how osteoporosis applies to them: "Peak bone mass is reached in your twenties. If you don't put bone down then, it won't be there when you're 50 and going through menopause."[29] Exercise, particularly weight bearing exercise, was also recommended to ward off osteoporosis, as were diets high in natural estrogen foods such as soy products.

CNN's *Morning News* profiled a menopause support group in August 1992 and another support group was highlighted on CNN's *Health Week* in December 1992. On *Health Week,* the Red Hot Mamas menopause support group stated that the group's goals included breaking menopause taboos, shattering stereotypes about menopausal women, and contending with doctors who tend to dismiss women's symptoms. The Red Hot Mamas told television viewers that 15% of women experience no problems with their menopause; and that their support group believes men need to be educated about menopause so couples can support each other. From another perspective, a *Better Homes and Gardens* article highlighted the availability of informational support for readers by suggesting a subscription to *Menopause News,* a bimonthly menopause support newsletter.[30]

In contrast to information presented to viewers and readers about menarche and menstruation, there was much more media attention and controversy presented about menopause. Although the topic of older women's menstrual health was the focus of attention on several news and infotainment programs, the quality of the information was influenced by the debate over menopause as a normal process or a condition requiring treatment. Women who viewed such programs were left with little certainty about what to expect during menopause or what kind of response they should make about any possible treatment decisions.

Product Marketing for Menstruation and Menopause

> You never know when it's coming. First your cycle is 28 days. Then it's 35. O.K. Your body will get it together. Until then, Kotex lightdays pantyliners are the perfect just-in-case protection.[31]

Women who thumb through their favorite magazines about parenting, gardening, fashion and beauty, health, and lifestyles, do not have to read the articles about menstruation or menopause to receive powerful messages about these processes. They only need to look at the advertisements between the articles to receive the media signals about products they should buy in order to protect themselves, feel secure, feel better physically, and promote their good health.

Havens and Swenson[32] selected a random sample of issues of *Seventeen* magazine from 1976 to 1986 to study advertising messages about menstruation-related products targeted for adolescent readers. They identified 135 advertisements for sanitary products and 32 advertisements for products to relieve menstrual discomfort. The researchers identified two central themes in the content of advertisements for sanitary napkins and tampons: the scientific approach (touting the characteristics of the products such as design and absorbency) and the athletic approach (portraying the advantages of using the products during physical activities such as sports or exercise).

Themes in the advertisements for products to relieve menstruation-related discomfort included a description of the discomforts, how the products relieve all of them, and how the products enabled women to perform daily activities without limitations. In discussing their findings, Havens and Swenson refer to conflicting themes portrayed in the advertisements:

> ads depict a "hygienic crisis" that is best managed by an effective "security system," affording protection and peace of mind. This confidence permits the continuation of an active life style . . . a second, consistent subtheme: failure of the protection system or failure to choose the correct one places a woman at risk of soiling, staining, embarrassment, and odor. . . . This theme is especially dominant in the pantyliner ads, where protection every day is advocated.[33]

For this chapter, the authors conducted a page-by-page search for menstruation- and menopause-related advertisements appearing over a 9-month period in several popular magazines read by girls and women, in order to obtain additional and updated information about advertising messages.[34] Each advertisement for a menstruation- or menopause-related product was noted, the number of times it appeared and the location in each publication. Results showed the majority of advertisements were for products to absorb menstrual flow. Other products were pain relievers, hormones, vitamins, and vaginal lubricants and cleansers. The initial results are shown in Table 19.1.

A closer examination of the themes and message content of these advertisements yields findings similar to those of Havens and Swenson in terms of the advertisements targeted toward adolescent girls.[35] In the two teen magazines included in this analysis (*Seventeen, Young & Modern*), manufacturers promoted their products to adolescents as being able to help girls keep their periods secret. This implied menstruation is something that should not be talked about, should be hidden away, and was embarrassing if discovered. For example, in order to promote trust in its product, Tampax features an advertisement showing a teenage girl with tight leggings lying face down on an outdoor deck. The copy tells girls that if they trust Tampax tampons, "you're free to wear anything, go anywhere. And no one will ever know you've got your period."[36]

TABLE 19.1 Percentage Comparison of Menstrual Products Advertised

Product	Percentage of Products Advertised
Tampons	27.0
Sanitary pads	22.0
Vaginal lubricants	14.0
Menstrual pain relievers	11.0
Estrogen replacement hormones	10.0
Douches	10.0
Birth control hormones to regulate periods	2.0
Vitamins to fight osteoporosis	2.0
Bidet	1.0
Vaginal deodorant	0.5
1-900 Information number	0.5

The advertisement informs girls that the tampon protects like a pad, "But it's worn inside your body, so you can trust nothing will show. They're also really comfortable, and there's no odor to worry about . . . all that'll show is your confidence."[37] Another Tampax advertisement shows three girls at the pool squeezed together by two boys with the caption, "Trust. It's knowing no one will ever know you've got your period. Period."[38] This advertisement informs girls that the tampon is worn inside, and even close friends won't know. "And everything flushes away, even the biodegradable applicator. Because some secrets were meant to stay that way. Period."[39]

Adolescents seek factual information about these menstrual products, and they receive some answers in the media. For example, *Sassy* published a letter in an advice column from a reader who wanted to know if she could "finish" her period sooner if she used tampons rather than napkins and if tampons with plastic applicators were more likely to cause toxic shock syndrome than those with cardboard applicators.[40] The advice in the article dispelled both myths. She was told the use of tampons or pads does not affect the life of the flow, and that tampon applicators have no causal affect on toxic shock syndrome. To prevent the risk of the bacteria that cause toxic shock syndrome, the girl was advised to remove tampons, sponges, or diaphragms according to their product instructions and to avoid using tampons that were more absorbent than necessary.

Only a few advertisements in the teen magazines provided instructions for use of menstrual products. The o.b. brand tampons ran two instructional advertisements for its tampon in *Seventeen* and *Young & Modern,* but these two advertisements also combined health and beauty information about sunscreen and facial cleaning.[41] These "other easy tips from o.b." linked use of o.b. tampons with health and beauty, a potentially strong message for young consumers. One additional advertisement by Advil aimed at teen readers provided some menstrual education with their product advertisement and offered a toll-free number to call for more information about menstruation. The Advil ad recommended that girls experiencing painful cramps should get plenty of exercise, use a heating pad, keep their knees or legs elevated when resting or sleeping, and take ibuprofen.[42]

For adult readers, advertisements took a different approach, offering information through telephone numbers readers could call in order to receive medical information about menstruation-related issues. Specifically, The Medical Information Line is a 1-900 number advertised as having "confidential, reliable, up-to-date information on over 300 pre-recorded topics."[43] This number costs callers $1.75 per minute to listen to a recorded message about topics that include endometriosis, hormone replacement, menopause, menstruation, painful periods, and vaginal bleeding. The average topic message is 5 minutes, and the copy urges readers to call because, ". . . you'll feel better knowing."[44]

The advertisements promoting hormones (whether for estrogen replacement for older women or birth control hormones to regulate periods in younger women) used considerable advertising space in promoting these products. In the hormone advertisements, nearly one full page of advertisements was devoted to product information such as indications and usage, contraindications, warnings, precautions, adverse reactions, dosage, and administration. A typical hormone advertisement would devote three consecutive pages to the product (including the product information page). Obviously, these ads presumed a highly literate and medically sophisticated audience, although readers would still need to consult with their physicians prior to making decisions concerning the use of hormone products. However, these advertisements provide a considerable amount of information about these products along with their persuasive appeals.

The hormone advertisements were also directed toward solving the needs of different readers. For example, preventing osteoporosis was the primary selling point for the Estraderm estradiol transdermal "patch" and Premarin conjugated estrogen tablets; however, relief of other menopause symptoms were additionally addressed. Further, although birth control was the primary selling point for Ortho-Novum 777, the advertiser also stated, "They [the birth control pills] could even make your period less of a pain by decreasing menstrual cramps and increasing menstrual cycle regularity."[45] Interestingly, the Ortho-Novum 777 advertisements correspond to birth control manufacturers' efforts to market to the over-35 age group and perimenopausal women (women within 10 years of menopause onset).[46] Since the Food and Drug Administration ruled that the new low dose estrogen pills were safe for nonsmoking women over age 40, these pills are being promoted by advertisers as aids for menstrual regularity and for slowing down age-related bone loss.

Though hormone therapy is reported to relieve vaginal dryness for women experiencing it as part of their menopause, there are a variety of additional products marketed for vaginal lubrication. Fourteen percent of the advertisements for menstruation- and menopause-related products were promoting products that relieve vaginal dryness. KY Jelly, Gyne-Moistrin, and Replens were three brands identified in our content analysis. Gyne-Moistrin and Replens specifically mentioned vaginal moisture in their advertisements; KY Jelly advertisements called their product a "personal lubricant" rather than a vaginal moisturizer. Advertisements for KY Jelly primarily promoted the fact that it does not break down latex condoms, an advantage over petroleum jelly.

A final noteworthy theme in the advertisements for menstrual products is that of environmental sensitivity. Concern for the environment, in the sample of advertisements analyzed for this chapter, was exclusively shown in the tampon advertisements. Specifically, several of the tampons advertised were promoted as being biodegradable and environmentally friendly. The marketing of menstrual products to consumers based on their "ecofriendly" capacity was noted in a test of these products reported in *Ms.* magazine.[47]

It is possible that the emphasis on ecology is a sign of a shift from old to new themes in menstrual advertising that is lurking on the horizons. An article in the February 1993 issue of *Marketing* magazine revealed that Tambrands plans to market Tampax products by presenting menstruation as a natural process, not as a problem.[48] Tampax's advertising campaign, on television in the United Kingdom and in print media in Europe, stresses a global advertising approach to menstruation as a positive life event. This approach may subtly affect women's perception of menstruation.

Conclusion

Menarche, menstruation, and menopause play significant roles in the ongoing course of women's lives. For most women, these wonders are phenomena that they each will experience. Media messages directed to young women, however, portray menstruation as embarrassing and something that should be hidden and kept secret. For maturing adults, menstruation is portrayed by the media as a painful process that is something to endure, suffer through, or medicate—with conflicting information on methods of reducing distressful symptoms. Finally, the media inform women—as perimenopausal and menopausal adults—of the numerous problems they face when menstruation ceases.

Although some alternative media messages are available, the natural, distinctly female cycle of menstrual development is predominantly portrayed by the media as a problem that should be treated by drugs and other products. The same media that feature reports on menstrual issues also sell advertising space and time to the manufactures of drugs and other products designed to help cure or cope with menstrual ills. Ultimately, the twin messages available in both the media reports and the advertisements may be a profitable arrangement. A woman's natural menstruation and cessation of menstruation are very profitably addressed as problems to be treated. In other words, menstruation and menopause as "No Big Deal" is no big money.

In light of these findings, readers and viewers of the media's messages concerning menarche, menstruation, and menopause should not only be discerning consumers of the messages presented in popular talk shows, news programs, magazines, and books, but also should selectively digest the information presented in ads for products to "treat" or "manage" these natural phenomena. Messages that menstruation and menopause are natural events may be lost in the undercurrent of messages to the contrary—selling products, expressing anguish and pain, and describing embarrassment and loss.

Notes

1. Gyne-Moistrin advertisement, *Prevention* (April 1992): 61.

2. J. Delaney, M. J. Lupton, & E. Toth, *The Curse: A Cultural History of Menstruation* (rev. ed.) (Urbana: University of Illinois Press, 1988): 108.

3. A. M. Voda, "Menopause: A Normal View," *Clinical Obstetrics and Gynecology,* 35(4) (1992): 926.

4. Voda, "Menopause: A Normal View," p. 926.

5. G. Greer, *The Change: Women, Aging, and Menopause,* (New York: Knopf, 1992): 17.

6. M. M. Gullette, "What, Menopause Again?" *Ms.* (July/August 1992): 37.

7. D. Kent, "Sex & Body: Periods, Period," *Seventeen* (May 1993): 60.

8. J. Marzollo, *Getting Your Period: A Book About Menstruation* (New York: Dial, 1989): 7.

9. "The Year in Television," *Rolling Stone* (December 12, 1991): 199.

10. "Your Looks: Timing Is Everything," *Glamour* (January 1993): 116-121.

11. N. H. Lauerson & C. Deswaan, *The Endometriosis Answer Book: New Hope, New Help* (New York: Macmillan, 1988): 1.

12. Lauerson & Deswaan, *The Endometriosis Answer,* p. 1.

13. N. H. Lauerson & E. Stukane, *Listen to Your Body* (New York: Fireside, 1982): 133.

14. Lauerson & Stukane, *Listen,* p. 133.

15. K. Keller, "Body Q & A: Help for PMS, Tampon Trouble, and More," *Young & Modern* (August 1993): 80.

16. D. Farley, "Endometriosis Is Painful, But Treatable," *FDA Consumer* (January/February 1993): 24-28.

17. S. Young, "Cramps and Chiropractic," *Glamour* (1992): 34.

18. M. S. Gil, "New Ways to Heal," *Redbook* (July 1993): 63-64.

19. D. Schultz, "Mood Boost," *Parents* (January 1993): 22.

20. "Too Much Iron May Be Harmful to Health," *Glamour* (February 1993): 206.

21. J. Cadoff, "Food Cravings," *Glamour* (July 1993): 184-185, 200-202.

22. E. Kunes, "Period Pig-Outs," *Young & Modern* (October 1992): 88.

23. S. Jacoby, "Menopause Madness," *Woman's Day* (October 1992): 196.

24. B. Ehrenreich, "Chronicling the Change," *Time* (October 26, 1992): 80-82.

25. Premarin advertisement, *Prevention* (June 1993): 26.

26. C. Saline, "Menopause—In Your Thirties," *Redbook* (March 1993): 44.

27. G. Legwold, "Managing Menopause," *Better Homes and Gardens* (June 1993): 80.

28. L. Hilgers, "Why Your Bones May Need More Magnesium," *Self* (July 1993): 46.

29. "A Few Good Minds," *Mirabella* (August 1993): 66.

30. "Menopause Information in Your Mailbox," *Better Homes and Gardens* (June 1993): 56.

31. Kotex advertisement, *Seventeen* (August 1993): 177.

32. B. Havens & I. Swenson, "Imagery Associated With Menstruation in Advertising Targeted to Adolescent Women," *Adolescence,* 23 (1988): 89-97.

33. Havens & Swenson, "Imagery," p. 95.

34. *Better Homes and Gardens, Glamour, Health, Modern Maturity, Parents, Prevention, Redbook, Seventeen,* and *Young & Modern,* 1992-1993, were content analyzed.

35. Havens & Shaver, "Imagery."

36. Tampax advertisement, *Young & Modern* (April 1993): 99.

37. Tampax advertisement, *Young & Modern.*

38. Tampax advertisement, *Seventeen* (August 1993): 155.

39. Tampax advertisement, *Seventeen.*

40. Kate, "Help," *Sassy* (August 1993): 30.

41. o.b [tampon] advertisement, *Seventeen* (July 1993): 41; o.b advertisement, *Young & Modern* (February 1993): 31.

42. Advil advertisement, *Seventeen* (August 1993): 98.

43. Medical Information Line advertisement, *Prevention* (August 1993): 104.

44. Medical Information Line advertisement, *Prevention,* p. 104.

45. Ortho-Novum 777 advertisement, *Health* (November/December 1992): 38-40.

46. J. Weber & A. Cunco, "The War of the Pill," *BusinessWeek* (June 29, 1992): 71, 74.

47. J. Dagnoli, "Tampons Go for Green," *Advertising Age* (July 2, 1990): 1; "Feminist Protection," *Ms.* (August 1993): 38-40.
48. V. Latham, "Tampax Back on TV After Two Year Gap," *Marketing* (February 18, 1993): 9.

20

Social Support and Breast Cancer

Why Do We Talk and to Whom Do We Talk?

Maureen P. Keeley

> *For this is the greatest error of our day, that in treatment of the human body, that physicians separate the soul from the body.*
>
> Plato, "Dialogue"[1]

Breast cancer attacks a woman's body; but perhaps just as importantly, it attacks her body image, her sense of self-identity, and her perception of control over her life and body—including her sexuality, womanhood, and financial resources. When a woman is diagnosed with breast cancer, she experiences fear about possibly dying, anxiety about the pain of treatment, and stigma of perhaps having a mastectomy and being left not a "whole woman." Physicians often treat the cancer and the body of the woman, but not the whole woman. Thus, Plato's plea for physicians to treat the body *and* the soul remains unanswered.

This chapter addresses the issue of ministering to the body *and* the soul of women with breast cancer by highlighting women's greatest concerns about the disease and treatment. At present, more appears to be known about how to assist survivors of breast cancer in efforts to live than is understood about *specific* causes of breast cancer. The reasons for this are many, including political and historical agendas about women's health discussed throughout this volume. These traditions contribute to an underemphasis on research trials focused on alternatives such as low-fat diets, as compared to an overemphasis on research trials focused on the introduction and use of chemicals, such as tamoxifen.

The evolution of research and understanding about breast cancer is itself a case study worthy of volumes rather than the space limits of a single chapter. Thus, after briefly reviewing the incidence, mortality, symptoms, possible risk factors, and treatments for breast cancer, I identify the individuals best equipped to deal with the needs of breast cancer patients and describe a framework through which the "whole woman" may be treated and healed. The framework is a growing body of research called "social support."

The Nature and Impact of Breast Cancer

Diagnosis of and mortality from breast cancer continues to rise with the numbers approaching 200,000 a year for the former and 50,000 for the latter.[2] There seems to be some agreement that black women and white women in the United States have a similar incidence of breast cancer.[3] As Audre Lorde points out, however, "black women have consistently had a twelve to fifteen percent poorer five-year survival rate from breast cancer than white women."[4] This lower survival rate could be attributed to limited access to screening and health care, which contributes to failure to seek screening, and advanced stage of disease upon seeking care.[5] In either case, numbers alone may be misleading when referring to ethnicity and breast care.

Numerous factors may contribute to a woman's risk for breast cancer. Most frequently referred to are age, familial history of cancer, and individual history of breast cancer. Other variables that may affect breast cancer risk include parity; age of woman at first birth; whether the woman was breast fed or not; age at first period; menstrual-cycle characteristics; menopause; oral contraceptive use; hormone replacement; and dietary factors including alcohol use, body mass, and height.[6] There is some concern that women exposed to various forms of radiation are more susceptible to breast cancer, as "the female breast is one of the most radiosensitive human body tissues."[7] Despite some research to implicate each of these variables, too little definitive knowledge exists about breast cancer's causes. Feminist health activists have contributed to an influx of funding for research, and greater understanding is, of course, the hoped-for outcome.

The diagnosis and treatment of breast cancer varies for each woman, but the process usually begins when some change in the woman's breast is noticed, often by the woman, her spouse, or clinician. The woman may notice a lump through the conduct of a breast self-exam (BSE), but 60% to 75% of U.S. women report that they do not practice regular self-exams.[8] A woman may notice breast pain or discharge from the nipple, leading her to seek a clinical exam. This may lead to physician detection through a clinical exam and/or mammography.[9]

If a discrete lump is detected, clinical tests should be used to determine whether the lump is suspicious or is one of the various noncancerous lumps that may develop normally. If these noncancerous possibilities are rejected, more tests will be used to determine the type of lump that is present. When further diagnosis is called for, it is likely that a physician will initially perform a needle aspiration.[10] This procedure consists of inserting a fine needle into the lump in order to remove fluid from the lump. This fluid may indicate a need for further treatment. It should be noted, however, that more than 95% of lumps turn out to be cysts,[11] in which case needle aspiration simply collapses the lump. If the fluid is questionable, or if the lump is hard and does not produce fluid, the diagnostic process continues, as physicians seek to determine the stage of the cancer. The widely used classification for staging is based on three aspects of the lump called TNM—tumor size, number of malignant nodes, and metastases (if the cancer has spread to other parts of the body). Staging ranges from Stage 0 (in situ or noninvasive cancer) to Stage IV (the lump is greater than 2 inches, lymph nodes seem to be involved, smaller tumors are attached to the chest wall, cancer has metastasized).[12]

There are three aspects to this staging procedure: clinical staging (physical exams and tests) with a biopsy to confirm assumptions, local surgical treatment if necessary, and pathological staging (microscopic).[13] Once cancer is diagnosed clinically, the physician must confirm this diagnosis with a biopsy. The most practical biopsy in terms of time, cost, pain, and disfigurement is a needle biopsy. A cutting needle is inserted through the breast into the lump and small pieces of the lump are removed. "There are no false positives using this technique, but a negative result must be ignored and the lump dealt with by open biopsy."[14] In other words, this test can only confirm that the lump is cancerous, but cannot confirm that it is not cancerous (because a cancerous portion may be missed).

There are two types of open biopsy: incisional and excisional. With the incisional biopsy, only a portion of the lump is removed; with the excisional biopsy, the entire lump is removed. The tissue removed is used for histological confirmation that the lump is cancerous. At this time, the physician and woman begin to determine the course of action she should take. For example, there may be no further need for treatment if the biopsy was excisional. Or the woman may need further local treatment and/or systemic treatment.[15]

The most common form of treatment today is the modified radical mastectomy in which the breast and lower axillary lymph nodes are removed but the chest muscles are left in place.[16] The removal of lymph nodes does not aid in curing the cancer, but is used to determine how much the cancer has spread. It is widely accepted that analysis of the lymph nodes can determine the extent of metastases. In a simple mastectomy, the lymph nodes are not removed. Other forms of local treatment include the lumpectomy, which is the removal of the lump with some surrounding tissue, or the quandrantectomy, which removes the quarter of the breast containing the lump. Radiation treatment may be used in conjunction with either of these.[17]

Systemic or adjuvant therapies such as chemotherapy and hormone therapy are used in addition to local treatments. The concept of systemic therapy is based on the perspective that cancer is microscopically present throughout the body. Chemotherapy refers to the use of drugs. Women up to the age of 60 seem to be the only women who respond significantly to chemotherapy, but there is the chance that it may cause early menopause.[18] One way that researchers are trying to increase chemotherapy's effectiveness is through use of high dose consolidation. This treatment would involve high doses of a number of different drugs and could damage the woman's bone marrow, so it involves removal of her bone marrow and replacement of the marrow after the treatment.[19]

In addition to these measures undertaken after cancer has been diagnosed, there are efforts to try to prevent breast cancer from occurring, beyond such screenings as mammography, breast self-exams, and clinical breast exams. These include use of such measures as prophylactic mastectomies (preventative removal of breast) and prophylactic oophorectomies (preventative removal of ovaries).[20] Both procedures are considered controversial, because the preventative benefits have not been proven. Other researchers continue to investigate whether a change in diet, such as lowering fat consumption, can help reduce incidence of breast cancer.[21] Finally, a controversial trial of a drug to prevent cancer is also currently under way. Until more is known about how to prevent breast cancer, women must be proactive in demanding that research on its causes and cures be funded. At the same time, it is important to take seriously the second part of the breast cancer equation—that of psychological support. More efforts should also be made to disseminate information about the importance of supporting the woman with breast cancer and the women who have survived the disease.

Social Support for Breast Cancer Patients

Social support is a communication phenomenon that may be defined in the following manner: "Social support refers to verbal and nonverbal communication between recipients and providers that reduces uncertainty about the situation, the self, the other, or the relationship, and functions to enhance a perception of personal control in one's life experiences."[22] Social support is one means for physicians and others to treat not just the body, but the soul of women with breast cancer.

Twenty years of research on social support have identified three conclusions concerning social support that are pertinent for women living with breast cancer. First, women want and need human contact to help make sense of situations or circumstances of all serious life events, especially traumas like breast cancer. Second, supportive acts that are identified as being supportive reduce uncertainty about ourselves, a situation, and relationships, granting individuals greater control of life circumstances. Third, social support is a reciprocal process whereby individuals both give and receive support within primary (family and friends) and secondary (acquaintances, co-workers, and others) networks.

RISKS IN SEEKING SOCIAL SUPPORT

Seeking social support presents five very real risks to the support seeker, and so women with breast cancer are unlikely to strive to fulfill all of their support wants and needs. The first risk posed to support seekers is loss of "face," as rejection and negative judgments about the message of needing support may occur.[23] To admit that one needs help can make a woman feel that she is weak and may cause her to wonder what others will think. Second, individuals have different expectations about the support that is given and received, and unfulfilled expectations could create a misunderstanding between a woman and her support providers.[24] Support providers may not realize a woman's needs or the degree of support that she wants, and as a result, she may be disappointed at their efforts.

A third risk of seeking social support is that it may create uncertainty about a relationship:[25] A woman may feel that her friends have let her down and were not "true friends." Also, the elicitation of social support may reveal weaknesses in the identity and personality of a support seeker and/or support provider.[26] Requests for help may make support providers (or seekers) look like people who cannot cope with a crisis; may create feelings of mistrust, dislike, or vulnerability; and may eventually lead to a reevaluation of a person's character. Social support may even be associated with helplessness as support providers may realize that they cannot help, and a woman may realize that she is unable to help herself.

In general, supportive acts are a natural and active part of relationships. People expect to feel supported in close friendships[27] and romantic relationships.[28] Giving and receiving support is a method of maintaining relationships.[29] Perhaps not too surprisingly, then, social support has been found to be strongly associated with breast cancer survival.[30]

TYPES OF SUPPORT MESSAGES

Albrecht and Adelman identify five types of messages that are seen as supportive and that reduce specific types of uncertainty, all of which can be examined from the perspective of women with breast cancer. When a woman is diagnosed with breast cancer, she often wants to know how and why breast cancer has happened to her. Supportive messages that give "perspective shifts on cause-effect contingencies" are often needed and constitute instrumental/informational aid.[31] Information brings with it reality, which reduces the desirability or relevance of unattainable goals; information increases the desirability of achievable goals.[32] Without these messages, women may focus on false hopes, or on treatments that are not conducive to survival or to living effectively with the realities of breast cancer and the effects of treatment. Informational support can help women to keep a realistic perspective on the cancer.

Once breast cancer patients come to terms with their affliction, they need to learn specific ways to adapt and to begin rebuilding their lives. This second category of informational support consists of messages that "enhance control through skill acquisition," which is instrumental/informational aid.[33] Affected women need to identify the specific problems that accompany breast cancer and counter them with problem-solving techniques. Some of the most relevant problem-solving techniques that support providers can offer to women with breast cancer are "instruction on the use of a breast prosthesis, arm exercises to increase the strength and movement in the affected arm and chest area, and effective methods of detection concerning the return of cancer."[34]

Support providers might also provide instruction about conflict management techniques. Conflict may occur from feelings that develop from one or a combination of emotions such as anxiety, fatigue, tension, and/or confusion brought on by the breast cancer.[35] Women may also need to develop communication proficiency to ask physicians direct and specific questions to learn more about breast cancer. Albrecht and Adelman stress that, "the process of providing information on problem solving and social skills gives the individual a way to define and reconcile a quagmire of stressors during times when one lacks confidence due to uncertainty over appropriate behavior."[36]

Women with breast cancer often need concrete help as well as informational support. Assistance with chores around the house, prepared meals delivered to the family, and rides to the hospital for chemotherapy provide supportive messages that Albrecht and Adelman specify as "enhanced control through tangible assistance" or tangible aid.[37] Tangible aid incorporates the exchange of time, labor, and resources between the support giver and the support recipient. It is often difficult to ask for this kind of help; therefore, whenever it is offered, especially during critical times of the illness (e.g., following surgery, during chemotherapy), tangible assistance may help to reduce stress. Tangible assistance must also bear a cautionary note: "exchanges can either seed bonds of helpfulness and affection or incur feelings of deep indebtedness and anxiety."[38] Whether women interpret the help as being helpful or as creating more anxiety is dependent upon the messages that come with the assistance.

The fourth type of supportive message described by Albrecht and Adelman focuses on "enhanced control through acceptance or assurance," which is a type of emotional aid.[39] To discover that one has breast cancer is a frightening experience, challenging one's self-concept. These feelings are aggravated by the fact that this society's image of a woman is so closely linked to her breasts; the image of breasts as a symbol of femininity and sexual appeal is reflected in advertising, film, and television. Women face disfigurement that has the potential to destroy their image of body and sexual identity.[40] Messages that communicate acceptance or assurance to women with breast cancer can validate them, confirm their identity as mothers or lovers, and reassure them that their relationships are still valid (e.g., wife, mother, daughter, friend, co-worker). This validation can restore a woman's sense of control over her life. Emotional aid is vital to reinforce a woman's knowledge that she is not alone as she goes through the process of accepting and dealing with breast cancer.

Albrecht and Adelman's final category of supportive messages highlights the need to have sounding boards against which women can articulate uncertainties. "Enhanced control through ventilation," also a type of emotional aid, is described as a way for individuals to release internal pressures and to clarify fears, anger, despair, and frustrations. If women with breast cancer have individuals who will actively listen to them, they may have the opportunity to become more objective after an emotional release. They may also be able to resolve unspoken issues concerning the cancer, the death and pain associated with the cancer treatment, or relational changes that have occurred as a result of the breast cancer. Although "venting" or "whining" or "com-plaining" are not often encouraged in our society, breast cancer survivors need to engage in emotional release or they may experience some alarming repercussions. Women who choose to be stoic, to suppress their anger and frustrations, tend to have higher incidence of depression, irritability, and hostility 6 months after having a mastec-tomy than women who chose to vent their feelings.[41] Further, women who accept their breast cancer silently or who accept cancer with an almost fatalistic attitude have a lower incidence of survival.[42] Women who do *not* accept their illness easily, are more anxious and hostile at diagnosis, and cooperate less, tend to be the long-term survivors.[43]

Providers of Social Support

Not everyone can provide social support. Moreover, different people have been found to have varied strengths in what they have to offer to women with breast cancer.

HUSBANDS AND LIFE PARTNERS

The first, and perhaps most obvious, support provider for those of us with breast cancer is our husband or significant other. Husbands or lovers are expected to be there during the diagnosis and treatment and to stay long after friends and others have grown weary and gone home. To complicate matters, such relationships are fraught with expectations of support provision and opportunities for social conflict. They are also often plagued by undermining behaviors (e.g., criticizing spouse, unpleasant attitude toward spouse, making spouse feel unwanted).[44] The role of a woman's husband or lover as social support provider is complex and warrants closer examination.

Pederson and Valanis identified seven specific problems that husbands face when they are trying to cope with their wives' breast cancer. First, husbands must learn how to cope with and react to their wives' symptoms, needs, and physical and emotional reactions.[45] Treatment such as radiotherapy and chemotherapy can make women violently ill, cause irritability, induce mood swings, or leave women feeling exhausted, to name a few symptoms. Life partners generally have little time to adapt and often feel unsure about how to care for women during their illness.[46]

Husbands and life partners must also deal with their own emotional reactions to breast cancer, which run the gamut from fear to anger, frustration, and rejection.[47] The diagnosis of breast cancer tends to create two conflicting reactions: (a) feelings of fear of and aversion to cancer; and (b) the assumption that the appropriate way to act is to keep an optimistic facade.[48] The conflicting reactions experienced by life partners tend to produce anxiety and ambivalence in women, as reactions are often displayed through positive verbal but negative nonverbal behaviors.[49] When faced with conflicting verbal and nonverbal messages, we tend to believe the nonverbal.[50]

A third problem highlighted by Pederson and Valanis focuses on husbands' ability to cope with the need and desire to obtain information and to secure assurances about patients' conditions from doctors, nurses, or other relevant health care providers.[51] Life partners of women with breast cancer want information about a number of issues, such as the disease itself, projections of life expectancy, and the normalcy of patients' reactions.

The fourth issue addressed by Pederson and Valanis is change that occurs at home during the breast cancer crisis. Women are often the focal point of the home, coordinating the activities of family members. Breast cancer leaves life partners with the

responsibility of managing and reorganizing the home environment, as well as redirect-
ing every family member's energy to keep the family functioning. This may be one
reason that 42% of husbands of women with breast cancer found that their ability to
work outside the home was temporarily impaired.[52]

Communicating interpersonally is a fifth challenge for life partners coping with their
wives' breast cancer.[53] Interpersonal communication requires talk about fears and
concerns about the breast cancer, personal stresses, reaction to women's periodic
withdrawal, or even whether or not to discuss stressful issues concerning the children.
These types of conversations may contradict beliefs that life partners should keep up
a happy facade to support women during their stress.[54]

Breast cancer's impact on relationships depends on the life cycle stages of individual
family members. This is, in part, because the needs of the wife, husband, and children
change for each stage.[55] Research has found that younger couples and couples in
unstable relationships are more adversely affected by the cancer, as the emotional stress
of cancer may cause preexisting marital strife to crystallize.[56] Young marriages may
not have the relational history to sustain them during this difficult period. Research
examining people in advancing age groups and lengthy marriages finds women with
breast cancer giving more social support to husbands than they receive.[57]

In addition to coping with women's emotions, their own emotions, the need for information, a shift in family roles, and a change in communication patterns, life partners
must address financial difficulties that may result from the breast cancer.[58] These
difficulties may focus around the treatment of the breast cancer (e.g., doctor bills,
hospital costs, medicine), the temporary need to pay for child care, or the decline of
income due to the change from a two-income family to a one-income family.[59]

The last, and perhaps most widely discussed, problem facing life partners in relation
to coping with breast cancer is the maintenance of the marital relationship.[60] This
problem concentrates on the intimacy, closeness, and sexual aspect of marriage.
Thirty-three percent of women experience some sexual problem during the first year
after a mastectomy.[61] When a woman has a breast amputated, she may experience a
number of reactions to the sight of her own body. Many women report hiding their
breasts; refusing to undress in front of others; refusing to let their husbands touch their
scars; and refusing to discuss the cancer or their feelings with their husbands.[62] Scott
and Eisendrath found that "husbands who reaffirmed their love and their wives' sexual
attractiveness and refused to allow them to conceal the scar, to withdraw socially, or
to avoid lovemaking positively assisted their wives' recoveries."[63] Women must realize
that life partners and family members provide more empathetic support than any other
group of people.[64] Life partners' support is especially crucial if women are to be
successful in accepting their altered body image and addressing insecurities about
sexuality. A study by Waxler-Morrison and associates emphasized that breast cancer
survivors have reported supportive and helpful responses from husbands.[65] Husbands
perceive the loss of their wives a much more serious consequence than the loss of
a breast.

IMMEDIATE FAMILY

Members of the immediate family are the second most likely group of support providers. Families with strong communication patterns and experiences in dealing with stress are more adept at handling stress and pitching in to help.[66] Unfortunately, support and protective behaviors from family members are often viewed by breast cancer survivors as ambivalent and stressful.[67] Young children whose mothers have breast cancer focus on "bad things happening" and on fears about what will happen to the family unit.[68] Children in their middle years are preoccupied with involvement outside the home[69] and tend to want specific information about their mother's condition.[70]

Young adult children offer the most capabilities for rendering emotional and tangible assistance, but are attempting to become more independent of family.[71] Thus, young adult children are the least supportive, providing the least help to their mothers and staying away during this period.[72]

FRIENDS

A third important group of social support providers are friends. Breast cancer survivors can encourage the friends who offer the most support and discourage friends who are not as useful or helpful.[73] Friendships are also less burdened by past and future obligations that are typical of family relationships.[74] Women also perceive the help of friends as generally sincere and less ambivalent.[75]

Friends provide less support of every kind when compared with family members, yet breast cancer survivors are more satisfied with the support provided by friends.[76] This may be the result of a perception that friends' support is strictly voluntary, whereas family support may be considered "required." Some of the acts include cooking meals, shopping, and child care. A ride to the hospital and knowing that someone is waiting while a woman endures chemotherapy is often seen as incredibly supportive.[77]

Co-workers can provide a different kind of friend network as potential support providers. Women who work have a broader network of friends, and this network is often a valuable resource for gathering useful information regarding the survival of breast cancer.[78] Friends at work have the potential to take women's minds off of illness by focusing on specific tasks.[79] Many women with breast cancer see going back to work as being symbolic of "getting back to living."[80]

SUPPORT GROUPS

In addition to husbands, families, and friends, support group members often become new friends to breast cancer survivors. These friendships develop through contact at weekly support group meetings of fellow breast cancer survivors. Support groups are an important resource for information, social comparison, and empathy. Van den Borne and associates found that regular meetings with other breast cancer patients decreased feelings of uncertainty.[81] This reduction in uncertainty was especially prevalent when women did not get relevant information from a doctor. By becoming involved in self-help groups, women take an active role in helping others like themselves survive breast cancer. This action often leads to an increase in self-esteem, reinforcement of self-identity, and increase in survival rate,[82] a benefit most prevalent during crisis points. Research suggests that "contact with fellow sufferers is only effective when strong negative feelings are being experienced."[83] Thus, participation in self-help groups lessens with time.

HEALTH CARE PROVIDERS

The fifth and final group of potential support providers for women with breast cancer are medical health care providers. Doctors may be the most important resource for informational aid for breast cancer patients. Unfortunately, surgeons face a number of significant obstacles as social support providers. First, breast cancer survivors and families expect surgeons to give informational aid and some emotional support. The expectation to give informational aid is obvious and understandable, but even when doctors give the requested information, patients may not recall the information later. Doctors give a lot of important medical information during very stressful and emotional periods in the patient's life when the levels of listening and understanding are decreased due to emotional distress. Doctors often fail to repeat information or to take time to listen, to understand, or to answer all of their patients' questions and concerns.[84]

The second expectation, that doctors should also give some emotional support, also presents problems for doctors. Most surgeons do not think that talking with patients about their feelings is an integral part of the professional role.[85] Surgeons believe that their primary duty is to diagnose and treat disease; they fail to ascribe the same importance as patients do to reassuring the patient or providing informational and emotional support.[86] Researchers note an awareness by doctors about these expectations, and many doctors are concerned with breast cancer patients' psychological *and* physical well-being.[87]

Doctors are hindered in their ability to give social support by their own expectations as well, as they expect patients to "behave" like good patients and do not know what to do with those who do not "accept" the cancer. However, women with breast cancer who are described as less well-adjusted to the illness, less cooperative with doctors, and more anxious and hostile at the diagnosis have been found to live longer than survivors who were described as stoic, helpless, or fatalistic.[88]

Doctors face other potential problems as support providers. First, most doctors are wary of becoming emotionally involved in their patients' lives. They worry about compromising their professional detachment, which may influence their judgment.[89]

Nurses are a crucial group of potential social support providers.[90] Nurses spend a great deal of time with patients and families during treatment; consequently, nurses can often provide the family with emotional support, as well as help families discover and use community resources, and help breast cancer patients to develop social networks. Nurses, however, face many of the same obstacles that doctors face when it comes to providing social support.

Dilemmas of Support Providers

Support providers face several general risks as a result of providing social support that are likely to affect the support given to women with breast cancer. First, providing support to a woman with breast cancer may lead to the perception of a "contagion effect."[91] Provision of support to someone who is sick may lead support providers to doubt their own health or to feel vulnerable to fears of developing cancer in the future. Second, providing social support to a seriously and/or chronically ill person may sap the provider of energy, time, and even compassion for the cancer survivor over time.[92] Third, providers may feel as if they are intruding on a patient's privacy or the privacy of the cancer survivor's family.[93] And fourth, support providers may invalidate breast cancer survivors' perceptions or expectations, creating conflict between them. All of these dilemmas affect both the likelihood that support will be given and the effectiveness of the support that is offered.

Conclusion

As discussed herein, there are a number of major fears and concerns commonly confronting women with breast cancer that may be addressed through appropriate social support. Perhaps foremost, the diagnosis of breast cancer is often associated with a death sentence and should be accompanied by opportunities for women to vent their concerns. Empathic messages also help women with breast cancer deal with fear of dying. Support by breast cancer survivors can be particularly useful, because others' personal survival gives credibility to their message. Family members can contribute messages of empathy and love in the face of side effects of cancer treatment.

Issues of body image require an ever broader range of social support, including support messages of all five types. The amputation of a breast may threaten a woman's sense of self. The need for messages of empathy, information, control, tangible assistance, and the chance to vent also apply to other self-image issues, including loss of hair and weight. Closely associated with fears about body image are concerns about the ability to engage in a full range of activities with the same intensity as before cancer, especially in relation to sexuality. Mastectomy patients experience a decrease in sexual enjoyment and tend to involve their breast less in the sexual relationship than they did prior to the treatment. Husbands or lovers need to provide direct supportive messages of acceptance and assurance. Professions of love must be joined by strong encouragement to lovemaking and to seeing and touching the scars to provide assurance of desirability.

The course of treatment options calls for a different emphasis, as research has shown that the ability to choose the type of treatment is important for women's mental health.[94] This type of message primarily involves the physician and other health care providers. Women also seek control over tangible assistance, wanting to be able to decide who helps, who provides support, and who provides information. This requires the cooperation of family, friends, and co-workers, for not all supportive messages actually feel supportive, as information about cancer that comes from less well-informed friends or the taking over of household decisions by relatives may be unwanted and unwarranted. Truly supportive messages give control *back* to the recipient, so being asked about the need for assistance is an important component of effective social support.[95]

The last issue of control centers on financial concerns. For lower-income women as well as other women with breast cancer, financial issues may be tied to resentment and concern about whether or not they will receive the best possible medical attention.[96] Taking time to talk with patients might at least partially alleviate this concern, as women may come to understand better what options they have.

Although by no means exhaustive, the research to date suggests that these commonly held fears for women with breast cancer must be directly addressed by specific types of supportive messages to help instill a sense of control back into women's lives. Plato's appeal to physicians was sincere, but it is likely that physicians are not the only ones in a position to "treat" women's bodies and souls when their bodies suffer from breast cancer.

Notes

1. B. Joweth, *Dialogues of Plato* (New York: Appleton & Co., 1898): 9.

2. American Cancer Society, *Cancer Facts and Figures* (New York: Author, 1993).

3. "Breast and Cervical Cancer in Low-Income Patients," *Patient Care* (February 28, 1993): 61-67; A. Lorde, "Living With Cancer," in E. C. White (Ed.), *The Black Women's Health Book: Speaking for Ourselves* (Seattle, WA: Seal Press, 1990): 27-37; C. Mettlin & E. R. Schoenfeld, "Effect of Race, Geography, and Social Class," in B. A. Stoll (Ed.), *Women at High Risk to Breast Cancer* (Boston: Kluwer Academic, 1989): 15-25.

4. Lorde, "Living With Cancer," p. 27.

5. "Breast and Cervical Cancer in Low-Income Patients," p. 61.

6. See, for example, H. Adami, G. Adams, P. Boyle, M. Ewertz, N. Lee, E. Lund, A. Miller, H. Olsson, M. Steel, D. Trichopoulos, & H. Tulinius, "Breast-Cancer Etiology," *International Journal of Cancer* 5 (1990): 22-39, 39.

7. Adami et al., "Breast Cancer Etiology," p. 32.

8. The Boston Women's Health Book Collective, *The New Our Bodies, Ourselves: Updated and Expanded for the 90's* (New York: Simon & Schuster, 1992): 576; B. L. Glenn & L. A. Moore, "Relationship of Self-Concept, Health Locus of Control, and Perceived Cancer Treatment Options to the Practice of Breast Self-Examination," *Cancer Nursing* 13 (1990): 361-365; K. E. Grady, "Cue Enhancement and the Long-Term Practice of Breast Self-Examination," *Journal of Behavioral Medicine* 7 (1984): 191-204.

9. B. J. Hackeloer, V. Duda, & G. Lauth, *Ultrasound Mammography: Methods, Results, Diagnostic Strategies* (New York: Springer, 1989).

10. Hackeloer et al., *Ultrasound Mammography*, p. 2.

11. Boston Women's Health Book Collective, *New Our Bodies*, p. 578.

12. Hackeloer, *Ultrasound Mammography*, p. 50.

13. Hackeloer, *Ultrasound Mammography*, p. 117.

14. M. Baum, *Breast Cancer: The Facts*, 2nd ed. (New York: Oxford University Press, 1988): 55.

15. Hackeloer, *Ultrasound Mammography*, p. 128.

16. Boston Women's Health Book Collective, *New Our Bodies*, p. 621.

17. Hackeloer, *Ultrasound Mammography*, pp. 68-70.

18. Boston Women's Health Book Collective, *New Our Bodies*, p. 624.

19. Boston Women's Health Book Collective, *New Our Bodies*, p. 625.

20. M. King, S. Rowell, & S. Love, "Inherited Breast and Ovarian Cancer: What Are the Risks? What Are the Choices?" *Journal of the American Medical Association* 263 (April 21, 1993).

21. J. Ellerhorst-Ryan & J. Goeldner, "Breast Cancer," *Women's Health* 27 (December 1992): 821-833; C. Travis, *Women and Health Psychology: Biomedical Issues* (Hillsdale, NJ: Lawrence Erlbaum, 1988).

22. T. L. Albrecht & M. B. Adelman, *Communicating Social Support* (Newbury Park, CA: Sage, 1987): 19.

23. Albrecht & Adelman, *Communicating Social Support,* p. 19.

24. Albrecht & Adelman, *Communicating Social Support,* p. 19.

25. Albrecht & Adelman, *Communicating Social Support,* p. 19.

26. Albrecht & Adelman, *Communicating Social Support,* p. 19.

27. B. R. Burleson, "Comforting as Social Support: Relationship Consequences of Supportive Behaviors," in S. Duck (Ed.), with R. C. Silver, *Personal Relationships and Social Support* (London: Sage, 1990): 66-82.

28. C. E. Cutrona, B. B. Cohen, & S. Igram, "Contextual Determinants of the Perceived Supportiveness of Helping Behaviors," *Journal of Social and Personal Relationships* 7 (1992): 553-562.

29. A. P. Barbee, P. B. Druen, M. R. Gulley, P. A. Yankeelov, & M. R. Cunningham, "Social Support as a Mechanism for the Maintenance of Close Relationships" (1992) (unpublished manuscript under editorial review).

30. D. Spiegel, "Effects of Psychosocial Support on Patients With Metastatic Breast Cancer," *Journal of Psychosocial Oncology* 10 (1992): 113-120.

31. Albrecht & Adelman, *Communicating Social Support,* p. 32.

32. Albrecht & Adelman, *Communicating Social Support,* p. 32.

33. Albrecht & Adelman, *Communicating Social Support,* p. 32.

34. H. W. van den Borne, J.F.A. Pruyn, & K. van Dam de Mey, "Self-Help in Cancer Patients: A Review of Studies on the Effects of Contacts Between Fellow-Patients," *Patient Education and Counseling* 8 (1986): 367-385.

35. Van den Borne et al., "Self-Help," pp. 367-385.

36. Albrecht & Adelman, *Communicating Social Support,* p. 32.

37. Albrecht & Adelman, *Communicating Social Support,* p. 32.

38. Albrecht & Adelman, *Communicating Social Support,* p. 32.

39. Albrecht & Adelman, *Communicating Social Support,* p. 32.

40. D. W. Scott & S. J. Eisendrath, "Dynamics of the Recovery Process Following Initial Diagnosis of Breast Cancer," *Journal of Psychosocial Oncology* 3 (1986): 53-66.

41. L. Grassi & S. Molinari, "Pattern of Emotional Control and Psychological Reactions to Breast Cancer: A Preliminary Report," *Psychological Reports* 62 (1988): 727-732.

42. P. A. Rippetoe & R. W. Rogers, "Effects of Components of Protection-Motivation Theory on Adaptive and Maladaptive Coping With a Health Threat," *Journal of Personality and Social Psychology* 52 (1987): 596-604.

43. N. Waxler-Morrison, T. G. Hislop, B. Mears, & L. Kan, "Effects of Social Relationships on Survival for Women: A Prospective Study," *Social Science and Medicine* 33 (1991): 177-183.

44. A. D. Vinokur & D. Vinokur-Kaplan, " 'In Sickness and in Health': Patterns of Social Support and Undermining in Older Married Couples," *Journal of Aging and Health* 2 (1990): 215-241.

45. L. M. Pederson & B. G. Valanis, "The Effects of Breast Cancer on the Family: A Review of the Literature," *Journal of Psychosocial Oncology* 6 (1989): 95-118.

46. M. A. Ingram, "Psycho-Social Aspects of Breast Cancer," *Journal of Applied Rehabilitation Counseling* 20 (1989): 23-27.

47. Pederson & Valanis, "The Effects of Breast Cancer," pp. 95-118.

48. R. R. Lichtman, S. E. Taylor, & J. V. Wood, "Social Support and Marital Adjustment After Breast Cancer," *Journal of Psychosocial Oncology* 5 (1987): 47-74.

49. Lichtman et al., "Social Support," pp. 47-74.

50. J. K. Burgoon, D. B. Buller, & W. G. Woodall, *Nonverbal Communication: The Unspoken Dialogue* (New York: Harper & Row, 1989).

51. Pederson & Valanis, "The Effects of Breast Cancer," pp. 95-118.

52. Pederson & Valanis, "The Effects of Breast Cancer," pp. 95-118.

53. Pederson & Valanis, "The Effects of Breast Cancer," pp. 95-118.

54. Scott & Eisendrath, "Dynamics of the Recovery Process," pp. 53-66.

55. Lichtman et al., "Social Support," pp. 47-74.

56. Pederson & Valanis, "The Effects of Breast Cancer," pp. 95-118.

57. Vinokur & Vinokur-Kaplan, " ' In Sickness and in Health,' " pp. 215-241.

58. Vinokur & Vinokur-Kaplan, " 'In Sickness and in Health,' " pp. 215-241.

59. Vinokur & Vinokur-Kaplan, " 'In Sickness and in Health,' " pp. 215-241.

60. Vinokur & Vinokur-Kaplan, " 'In Sickness and in Health,' " pp. 215-241.

61. G. Bos, "Sexuality of Gynecological Cancer Patients: Quantity and Quality," *Journal of Psychosomatic Obstetrics and Gynecology* 5 (1986): 217-224.

62. Ingram, "Psycho-Social Aspects," pp. 23-27.

63. Scott & Eisendrath, "Dynamics of the Recovery Process," pp. 53-66.

64. S. J. Neuling & H. R. Winefield, "Social Support and Recovery After Surgery for Breast Cancer: Frequency and Correlates of Supportive Behaviors by Family, Friends, and Surgeon," *Social Science Medicine* 27 (1988): 385-392.

65. Waxler-Morrison et al., "Effects of Social Relationships," pp. 177-183.

66. R. Klein, "A Crisis to Grow On," *Cancer* 282 (1971): 1660-1665.

67. Waxler-Morrison et al., "Effects of Social Relationships."

68. Pederson & Valanis, "The Effects of Breast Cancer," pp. 95-118.

69. Pederson & Valanis, "The Effects of Breast Cancer," pp. 95-118.

70. Pederson & Valanis, "The Effects of Breast Cancer," pp. 95-118.

71. Pederson & Valanis, "The Effects of Breast Cancer," pp. 95-118.

72. Pederson & Valanis, "The Effects of Breast Cancer," pp. 95-118.

73. Waxler-Morrison et al., "Effects of Social Relationships," pp. 177-183.

74. Waxler-Morrison et al., "Effects of Social Relationships," pp. 177-183.

75. Waxler-Morrison et al., "Effects of Social Relationships," pp. 177-183.

76. S. J. Neuling & H. R. Winefield, "Social Support and Recovery After Surgery for Breast Cancer: Frequency and Correlates of Supportive Behaviors by Family, Friends, and Surgeon," *Social Science Medicine* 27 (1988): 385-392.

77. Waxler-Morrison et al., "Effects of Social Relationships," pp. 177-183.

78. Waxler-Morrison et al., "Effects of Social Relationships," pp. 177-183.

79. Van den Borne et al., "Self-Help in Cancer Patients," pp. 367-385.

80. Van den Borne et al., "Self-Help in Cancer Patients," pp. 367-385.

81. H. W. van den Borne, J.F.A. Pruyn, & W.J.A. van den Heuvel, "Effects of Contacts Between Cancer Patients on Their Psychosocial Problems," *Patient Education and Counseling* 9 (1987): 33-51.

82. Pederson & Valanis, "The Effects of Breast Cancer," pp. 95-118.

83. Pederson & Valanis, "The Effects of Breast Cancer," pp. 95-118.

84. C. Ray, J. Fisher, T. Wisniewski, "Surgeons' Attitudes Toward Breast Cancer, Its Treatment, and Their Relationships With Patients," *Journal of Psychological Oncology* 4 (1986): 33-43.

85. Ray et al., "Surgeons' Attitudes," pp. 33-43.

86. Pederson & Valanis, "The Effects of Breast Cancer," pp. 95-118.

87. S. S. Epstein, "Mammography Radiates Doubts," *Los Angeles Times,* January 28, 1991, p. B7.

88. Waxler-Morrison et al., "Effects of Social Relationships."

89. Ray et al., "Surgeons' Attitudes," pp. 33-43.

90. Ray et al., "Surgeons' Attitudes," pp. 33-43.

91. Albrecht & Adelman, *Communicating Social Support,* p. 19.

92. Albrecht & Adelman, *Communicating Social Support,* p. 19.

93. Albrecht & Adelman, *Communicating Social Support,* p. 19.

94. J. M. Deadman, M. J. Dewey, R. G. Owens, S. J. Leinster, & P. D. Slade, "Threat and Loss in Breast Cancer," *Psychological Medicine* 19 (1989): 677-681; Scott & Eisendrath, "Dynamics of the Recovery Process," p. 60.

95. Albrecht & Adelman, *Communicating Social Support,* p. 19.

96. R. Zemore, J. Rinholm, L. F. Shepel, & M. Richards, "Some Social and Emotional Consequences of Breast Cancer and Mastectomy: A Content Analysis of 87 Interviews," *Journal of Psychosocial Oncology* 7 (1989): 33-45.

21

An Analysis of Discourse Promoting Mammography

Pain, Promise, and Prevention

Mary L. Kahl
Joan Lawrence-Bauer

The statistics are nothing less than chilling. According to the National Cancer Institute (NCI), the incidence of breast cancer among U.S. women increased in the 5-year period between 1982 and 1987 by 32%.[1] In 1987, a woman's risk of developing breast cancer was 1 in 11.[2] By 1990, that figure jumped to 1 in 10,[3] and in 1993, the rate had increased to 1 in 9.[4] These numbers mean that in excess of 182,000 women were expected to be diagnosed with the disease, with more than 46,000 dying from it—a rate of one woman's death every 12 minutes.[5]

Although medical experts remain puzzled and deeply concerned about the incidence of breast cancer, they agree that the most effective way to alleviate deaths from the

AUTHORS' NOTE: An earlier version of this chapter was presented by the first author at the annual Speech Communication Association Convention, Chicago, November 1992.

disease lies in early detection through the process of breast x ray called *mammography*.[6] Moreover, this method of early detection must be acknowledged as one contributor to the seeming rise in the incidence of breast cancer itself; for a mammogram allows detection of the disease at much earlier stages than clinical or breast self-exams. Thus, the incidence in women may have always been as great as it appears today, but mammography and early detection drive that point home. More important for women, as Roxanne Roberts reports in the *Washington Post,* the survival rate for breast cancer stands at an amazing 93%, if the disease is caught in its earliest stages.[7] In fact, according to Dr. Stephen A. Feig, a prominent breast cancer researcher, mammography is believed to have reduced breast cancer *deaths* by 50%.[8]

Despite the evidence in support of women having a mammogram, many U.S. women do not have mammograms done.[9] Reporting on a 1987 study of 12,252 women, Eugenia Calle and others noted that 60% of the women they interviewed over age 40 had never had a mammogram and that "86% had not had one in the past year."[10] Calle and her colleagues studied eight demographic factors to evaluate their impact on mammography and Pap smear screening. They found that reduced income, Hispanic ethnicity, low educational attainment, and older age all contributed significantly to nonutilization of mammographic testing.[11] Some women do not undergo the test because of fear, some because of financial considerations or test availability, and many because of ignorance.[12] With these factors in mind, this chapter offers an overview of reasons why women do not receive mammograms, a corresponding assessment of health care messages designed to address these issues and to facilitate the use of mammography, and suggestions for the future design of messages to promote mammographic testing.

Barriers to Women's Use of Mammography

Women in the United States do not undergo mammographic screening for a variety of reasons. Four of the leading factors that mitigate against testing are examined here.

THE FEAR FACTOR

Fear often keeps women from undergoing mammography and this trepidation frequently stems from multiple causes. First, anxiety about the discomfort caused by mammography machines is a frequent topic of informal conversation among women. Though it is true that a good mammogram hurts because it compresses the breast, it is also true that the discomfort is of relatively short duration. Breast cancer activists suggest that women should put the issue of pain in perspective. "A mammogram is not as uncomfortable as wearing high-heel shoes all day," remarked a community health professional. Clearly, the long-term benefits of the procedure exceed the momentary discomfort it produces.[13]

Women's health care practitioners now address the "ouch factor" openly in their messages about mammography. A pamphlet distributed by the American College of

Obstetricians and Gynecologists (ACOG) tells prospective patients that the test "may cause the breasts to ache, but this discomfort will disappear shortly, as will any minor bruising." The ACOG pamphlet also observes that "these aftereffects are harmless" and reminds the reader that mammography "is an excellent method to detect cancer at an early—and more curable—stage."[14] Reassurances notwithstanding, many women regard having a mammogram as a painful process and postpone the test much as they would delay a trip to the dentist.

Women also express anxiety about the amount of radiation they will receive from mammographic x rays. These fears are not without merit, but are usually based on reports of high radiation levels in mammographic testing conducted during the 1970s.[15] Although a lack of uniformity still plagues mammography procedures as a whole, Marie Zinninger, Senior Director of the American College of Radiology, the association that accredits testing facilities, argues that fears of overexposure to radiation are no longer warranted.[16] And, as Feig told the 1990 National Conference on Breast Cancer, "the benefit of mammographic screening is hundreds to thousands of times greater than the theoretical risk of developing breast cancer from the very small dose of radiation used in the screening."[17]

Calls for better control of testing processes have resulted in the formulation of federal legislation designed to set national standards for mammography equipment, quality control, and medical personnel.[18] With passage of the Mammography Quality Standards Act in October 1992, many of the fears about overexposure to radiation, though having some prior basis in fact, have been addressed. Pamphlets promoting mammography increasingly counsel women to learn about the certification status of the facility conducting their mammograms, to inquire about the age of the x-ray equipment used for their examinations, and an ACOG press release urges women to recognize that "the equipment and techniques used today . . . are quite safe, exposing [them] to a very low dose of x ray."[19]

Fear of the unknown, or of discovering "bad news," probably represents the single greatest apprehension on the part of women who avoid mammograms, a fear sometimes acknowledged in media reports about breast cancer.[20] The receipt of "bad news" threatens a woman's self-image on a multiplicity of levels. As twin symbols of sexuality and maternity, breasts represent, for many women, fundamental elements of their personhood. The potential for "bad news" that might precipitate the loss of a breast is often more than some women wish to contemplate. Women who avoid mammography screening for this reason often fear a diagnosis of cancer, the potential for death or disfigurement, and negative reactions of men.[21] Thus far, public education campaigns in support of mammography have done little to address these sorts of fears directly.

THE MONEY FACTOR

Due to cost, many U.S. women simply cannot afford to undergo mammographic tests, even on a one-time basis, and significantly more women cannot afford to repeat the screenings as often as recommended. Some insurance companies have increased and extended the coverage they allow for mammograms, as has the federal government, but these efforts fail to address the cost problem in any systematic manner. Since 1991, changes in Medicare coverage mandate payment for routine screening of women over the age of 65, but only on a semi-annual basis.[22] This new coverage falls short of providing for adequate testing of older women. The American Cancer Society (ACS) recommends that women over the age of 50 receive mammographic screenings every year, as opposed to every other year as suggested for younger women.[23]

Some states, such as Maryland and Virginia, require private insurance carriers to pay all or part of the cost for routine mammograms, but this practice is not widespread and is of virtually no assistance to women who are too poor to buy health insurance.[24] Screening services conducted on an ability-to-pay basis may be found in some parts of the country and provide women access to free mammograms if they are willing to admit financial hardship. A county health department brochure from an economically depressed area in Michigan, for instance, encourages women to undergo mammography and cervical cancer screening, promising that, "Depending on your income, services will be at a greatly reduced rate, or in some cases, even FREE!"[25] More programs of this nature are clearly needed and efforts to promote the self-identification of lower-income women are warranted.

Telephone help lines could be a cost-effective way to assist women in locating the resources to make mammography affordable, but these have been too little used. Presently, five major national hot lines offer assistance to callers and four of the five may be reached by dialing a toll free number.[26] These help lines do work to promote testing, as evidenced by a study conducted for the National Cancer Institute. By providing extensive information, including material on insurance coverage, members of the NCI Cancer Information Service encourage women to undergo screening. Yet the problem with these resources lies in the simple fact that few women realize they exist.[27]

THE AVAILABILITY FACTOR

White, middle-class, suburban women may avail themselves of mammographic procedures fairly easily, but this is not the case for women in rural or urban environments. The location of adequate testing facilities provides yet another reason that many women do not get mammograms. In rural areas, women may have to travel significant distances to reach hospitals or clinic facilities that provide mammography screening.

Although it is true that more physicians are now installing mammography equipment in their offices, many doctors recognize that buying their own units is not cost-effective unless they handle a large volume of gynecological work and charge high mammography prices.[28] Because they do neither, rural physicians find the purchase of their own machines to be cost-prohibitive and, in turn, rural women are disadvantaged in terms of mammographic availability. These women frequently travel longer distances to receive attention for pressing health problems, but they are not as likely literally to "go the extra mile" in order to participate in an elective, diagnostic medical procedure. Furthermore, information about the necessity of mammography is often not as readily available in sparsely-populated areas. In rural Kentucky, for example, a visit to a

Planned Parenthood affiliate yielded an American Cancer Society brochure about breast self-examination but no separate information about mammography.[29] The local hospital in this same Appalachian community offers the identical brochure on self-exams in its reception/waiting area, but specific material about mammographic testing is nowhere to be found. Despite sporadic attempts to screen rural women through irregularly scheduled clinics and health fairs, both information about and access to mammography remain highly problematic in many remote areas of the country.

Similar problems of availability confront women in urban environments, with African American, Hispanic, and other minority women, in particular, suffering from the inaccessibility of mammography screening facilities. Media reports sometimes inform the public about the access problem, as did one published interview with Zora Brown, founder of the Washington, D.C.-based Breast Cancer Resource Committee, which focused on her efforts to bridge the gap between women who have information, understanding, and access to treatment versus women who do not.[30] Indeed, a significant number of inner-city women rarely undergo mammography screening, either because of financial constraints or because they cannot reach testing centers, or both. According to a 1990 survey by the District of Columbia Health Commission, for example, 50% of the women over age 40 in the District had not received a mammogram in 2 or more years. Many had never had one.[31] New, high-volume, low-cost screening clinics are attempting to solve the problem of access to mammography for some inner-city residents, but even though these programs demonstrate promise, they have not yet been developed in sufficient numbers materially to affect the urban woman.[32] Street-corner testing, achieved through the use of mobile mammography vans, offers another answer to the availability problems faced by urban women, but questions about quality of care and continuity of service attend these endeavors. Moreover, easier access to mammography alone may not compel inner-city women to avail themselves of the process. Cultural barriers to testing, recognized—but generally unaddressed—by health care professionals, play a large role in the dilemma.[33]

THE AWARENESS FACTOR

Sadly, lack of awareness constitutes a large factor preventing women from seeking mammography testing. Significant numbers of women in the United States do not understand the risks posed by breast cancer nor do they comprehend the advantages that accrue from periodic mammographic screenings. Although women themselves must bear significant responsibility for self-education on the topic, physicians, too, share the burden of culpability for saying nothing or for misinforming their patients. In a survey conducted for the National Cancer Institute, 80% of women who had never gotten a mammogram indicated that they would have done so if their physicians had recommended the procedure.[34]

Misinformation about the benefits of mammography exists among women of every age group and all socioeconomic circumstances, although some women are less likely to have access to adequate advice on the topic than are others. Many postmenopausal women, for example, mistakenly believe that they do not need to receive annual mammograms. A study conducted by the American Medical Association in 1990 revealed that although more than 90% of women over age 50 visited their doctors regularly, just 25% to 41% of those who responded to various surveys had received mammograms during the previous year.[35] A study undertaken by the Center for Health Sciences at UCLA produced similar findings, with the investigation concluding that about 35% of women between the ages of 50 and 64 and 47% of those women 65 and over had never undergone mammographic screening.[36]

Inadequate awareness plays a role in the numbers of minority women who seek mammographic screening, as well. African American and other minority women are often less informed about the benefits of mammography than are their white counterparts. According to the Centers for Disease Control, black women are twice as likely as white women never to have heard about mammograms.[37] Lack of regular access to a physician accounts in part for a decreased level of awareness by some minority women, as does a link between education and income. Women with higher educational and income levels are more likely to undergo screening than are less educated, less affluent women.[38] Addressing the awareness factor constitutes a herculean challenge for public health communicators and, as with the other barriers to mammography, constitutes a significant topic that should be included in the information women receive about the procedure.

Information Women
Receive About Mammography

The messages women currently receive concerning mammography may be classified under two broad categories; material that is considered as *news* and material that constitutes *information,* both of which must be described as extremely confusing and contradictory. News, which includes front-page headline stories, leads on evening news programs, hourly radio updates, and feature reports in magazine health sections or on women's programs, is, by definition, merely reporting; uncoordinated and dramatic. Information, which includes coordinated public health campaigns, paid advertising, and brochures or pamphlets produced with the specific intent of informing women, tends to be scientific and impersonal, as well as lacking comprehensiveness.

NEWS ABOUT MAMMOGRAPHY

Regardless of the media used to disseminate news concerning mammographic screening, the messages are rarely strong and clear, even when fear appeals are employed to generate response. News stories, in particular, garble the messages of public health campaigns and generally discourage mammographic testing by focusing on questionable issues still being debated rather than on facts that have been established. News stories too often leave the impression that women are somehow at fault for the increased incidence of breast cancer.

A *New York Times* story by respected columnist Jane Brody provides a typical example. Brody begins the article by noting that the incidence of breast cancer is increasing and, like most who write about this subject, Brody continues by posing the obvious question in the form of an indictment: "Why don't most women take advantage of breast cancer screening?"[39] Despite its tone, this deceptively simple query should provide an entrée for the columnist to provide understandable, straightforward answers. In response to her own inquiry, however, Brody further mismanages an already negative message by citing all the concerns, fears, and problems associated with mammography. Not until the 10th paragraph does she note that breast cancer death rates have been lowered as a result of the screening process, but she follows this positive segment with two longer paragraphs highlighting imperfections in mammographic procedures and errors in x-ray interpretations.[40] Thus, a feature story intended to educate readers may only perpetuate confusion, fear, and apathy, a tendency present in articles in other major newspapers as well.[41]

Magazines, too, create particular emphases—in lieu of others—with the placement of assertions, arguments, and information in their articles. *Time* magazine, for example, under the banner "A Puzzling Plague," blames the "American way of life" for breast cancer. After detailing the frightening aspects of the disease, it discusses the relationships among breast cancer, dietary fat content, and estrogen levels, all before it reviews "The Mammogram Muddle."[42] The message that women should engage in mammographic testing remains positive, but is followed by routine citations about why women fail to undergo the screening. The stories are high drama without details.

News features in magazines and journals specifically devoted to health care issues function as more generally effective educational tools about the topic of mammography, but are also negative in tone and are less widely circulated. "Overcoming Mammography Phobia" in *Healthweek* argues that hospitals and clinics need to find additional enticements to encourage physicians to recommend and patients to undergo mammographic screening. The article addresses related issues and provides a comprehensive list of sources for additional information, but its focus on technology fails to address the actual process and omits details of the testing experience that might educate and alleviate fear in the target audience.[43]

A generally felicitous exception to such negative reporting may be found in "Breast Cancer Report," published by *Self* magazine.[44] The glossy, 11-page booklet shows real pictures of a breast after lumpectomy, actual x-ray film from mammograms of healthy and of diseased breasts, and diagrams of breast structures and surgical procedures. Articles in the publication are largely upbeat and stress significant advances in the treatment of breast cancer. Yet the ordering of information in the report remains quite curious. Early essays discuss "The Cure" and "Biopsies," detailing the procedures involved in radical mastectomy, lumpectomy, chemotherapy, hormone therapy, needle aspiration, and excisional biopsy. Not until the reader approaches the middle of the booklet does she encounter an article titled "Mammograms Made Easy: You Have to Find the Cancer Before You Can Cure It." By de-emphasizing, through placement, the role of mammography in discovering and treating breast cancer, the *Self* booklet does less than it could to promote education about the greatest weapon in the fight against the disease.

News media messages about availability and money factors associated with mammographic screening are virtually nonexistent. Women who might be inclined to act on these messages must seek additional information provided by public health campaigns and infrequent paid advertising. Women are more prompted to act when employers encourage mammography by providing on-site testing, but little media attention is given to firms such as Adolph Coors Company, which estimated a medical care cost savings of nearly $600,000 with early detection through in-house screening.[45]

INFORMATION ABOUT MAMMOGRAPHY

Public health campaigns, which could function as sources of quality information about mammography, are not as widely seen as are news stories and often fall far short of optimal effectiveness in their approaches to answering the full range of women's concerns about the subject. Like news stories, campaigns tend to target misinformation and fear while offering little substantive advice about availability and money issues.

The American Cancer Society and the National Cancer Institute conduct the most significant health campaigns promoting mammographic screening. Often, however, the impersonality inherent in their scientific approaches makes it easy for audience members to dismiss the messages. A question-and-answer pamphlet by the National Cancer Institute describes what a mammogram is, but does not mention that a mammogram is virtually painless.[46] The American Cancer Society (ACS) does a better job with information in its *Facts on Breast Cancer* pamphlet, discussing the amount of time the procedure takes, the fact that the test might produce slight pain or pressure, and, significantly, including photographs.[47] More detail is available in the ACS *Mammography Can Save Your Life* brochure but here, too, the impersonal, scientific style of the publication fails to address directly women's fears about the process.[48] An older ACS pamphlet available in a popular Florida retirement community moves away from the scientific approach and offers a softer, warmer message. The *Mammography Found My Breast Cancer* flier pictures a smiling, healthy older woman on its cover but fails to explain even what a mammogram is or how it is conducted.[49] Campaign messages such as these function considerably less effectively than they might, largely because they fail to strike a manageable, audience-centered balance between overly scientific and unscientific approaches to mammography, because they are unresponsive to women's fears about the process, and because they uniformly omit mention of cost and availability considerations.

Other, more locally or regionally targeted public health campaigns about breast cancer and mammography arise on infrequent, ad hoc bases, at best. The conduct and results of two such campaigns merit exploration here, because they illustrate additional problems with communicative strategies that mismanage the issues that matter most to women.

An innovative effort to encourage mammographic screening through the use of television was undertaken in 1990 under the auspices of the Florida Division of the

American Cancer Society and a Tampa television station. The project promoted low-cost mammographic screenings in seven Florida counties and consisted of a television program that was shown for a period of 4 days. The program urged viewers to contact a phone bank in order to receive information about scheduling a mammogram.[50] As a lead-in to the television event, 30-second promotional announcements about breast cancer as well as news stories about mammography were telecast for 1 week prior to the program and were also rebroadcast twice daily on each of the 4 days that the television program aired. The television campaign resulted in 13,920 calls on the part of women who sought information about breast cancer and mammography, and 50.2% of the eligible women actually underwent the low-cost mammographic screening.[51]

Although television clearly captured the attention of the target audience, and the messages of the campaign were sufficient for a significant number of those reached, an even higher response rate would have been gratifying. Suzanne Fuller and her colleagues' report on a group of 1,000 women who responded to the Tampa mammography project reveals several inherent problems with the communicative efficacy of the campaign. Not surprisingly, women who did not schedule mammograms, even after contacting the telephone bank, cited reasons for their nonparticipation in the project that parallel the four major factors we have examined here as impediments to screening. These women indicated that, despite the televised campaign, their greatest barriers to seeking mammography included generalized fear of the process, fear of pain associated with the procedure, fear of discovering cancer, fear of radiation from the x ray, embarrassment while undergoing the test, the cost of the screening, difficulty arranging transportation to a testing facility, and the absence of a physician's recommendation to get a mammogram.[52] For some women, the televised messages apparently failed to allay multiple dimensions of the fear factor sufficiently. Moreover, issues of cost, availability, and misinformation also remained as significant barriers to compliance, suggesting that the televised campaign fell short of addressing these concerns adequately.

A very different kind of public health campaign on the subject of breast disease occurred in New York in 1992. Undertaken during "Breast Cancer Awareness Month," the campaign was sponsored by the State of New York Department of Health (DOH). In a memo sent to all state employees with their paychecks, the DOH outlined steps taken to facilitate breast cancer screening. Although the memo briefly addressed education, money, and availability factors, the fear factor remained unexplored. The memo explained breast self-examination in great detail, but offered no information on mammography screening procedures or resources.[53]

The Health Department promoted awareness of the disease and its prevention for a month, but New York State Senator Kemp Hannon devoted but a single day to the subject and incorporated it with other women's issues in a forum called "It's the Year of the Woman!" Designed to "enlighten" women, the forum included breast cancer and mammography among a list of 14 topics that spanned a range from "Girl Scouting" to "S.I.D.S. Support."[54] The American College of Obstetricians and Gynecologists of New York State demonstrated greater awareness of the campaign's communicative responsibilities by producing a series of news releases and pamphlets that outlined facts about breast cancer, risks, breast self-examination, and mammograms.[55] These materials offered not only detailed information on the topic, but provided avenues for obtaining additional advice, as well. Much like many other messages concerning mammography, however, these failed to address fear factors and required women to make exceptional efforts to seek out additional information from impersonal sources. Though poorly coordinated by contrast, the New York campaign, like its Florida counterpart, employed message strategies that left women very distanced from the actual process of walking into a clinic for a screening.

Finally, paid advertising encouraging mammography constitutes a minuscule portion of the information that women receive about this subject and does little more than announce the existence of the screening process. For example, commercials sponsored by manufacturers of imaging machines make no attempt to assimilate the information that advertisers understand about fear appeals or their impact on inducing audience response. Still other sorts of paid commercials attempt to exacerbate fears for political advantage. As part of his 1992 reelection bid, New York Senator Al D'Amato aired radio and television advertisements that led with the sentence, "There's a killer stalking Long Island!" In the 60-second spots, D'Amato revealed breast cancer to be the killer and positioned himself as the state's sole defender against the disease. D'Amato's ads did not mention the importance of mammography nor did they extend any suggestion that women should avail themselves of screening opportunities.

Informing Public Opinion and Action on Mammography

The missing link in the majority of messages that women receive about mammography involves failed attempts to educate about the disease in ways that promote movement from an emphasis on fear and pain to an emphasis on promise and prevention—in women's own terms. Public perceptions about breast cancer and its prevention must be changed and these changes must be facilitated by a heightened understanding of the ways in which fear and ignorance impact women's decisions about pursuing mammography. Too often, fear and misinformation promote silence and inaction.

"The climate of opinion depends on who talks and who keeps quiet," writes Elisabeth Noelle-Neumann in *The Spiral of Silence*.[56] Individual opinions about disease and disease prevention are shaped by public awareness, making Noelle-Neumann's thesis critical to any study of approaches to mammography. To the extent that women keep or are kept quiet about the disease and their fears of it, the barriers to preventing breast cancer through screening will remain.

Dale Spender discusses just such a conspiracy of silence in *Man Made Language,* suggesting that women's meanings, their thoughts and hopes and fears, remain unarticulated and unaddressed in a society that discredits or dismisses views of reality that fall outside the dominant, male-centered paradigm.[57] Spender cites Dana Densmore's claim that nondisclosure functions as a communicative strategy that can preserve existing bases of power and that people who hide their vulnerabilities may employ "strategies such as denying the validity of a topic, refusing to talk on someone else's chosen topic, abstaining from self-revelation and withholding personal information."[58] Because breast cancer primarily affects women, men rarely discuss it, publicly or privately, and women have a tendency to deny it and to abstain from self-revelation.

It is simple to observe the obvious fears women have about mammography and thereby identify the surface causes of silence and inaction. Women fear the process and fear what might result from the process. But these are merely the easily articulated fears and would probably be present even if the disease were more gender neutral. The fact that breast cancer is a disease that predominantly strikes women presents a wide range of underlying concerns that have remained unaddressed. It is this silence that is killing women in the United States.

Noelle-Neumann identifies fear of isolation as an important motivator not just in what people do, but in what they are able and willing to learn. Her research demonstrated that 6 out of 10 people would state "as their own opinion the obviously false judgment made by the majority."[59] Based on these statistics, one must assume that unless the majority of the population advocates mammography, women will be inclined to avoid it. Fear does not just prevent women from having mammograms: It also prevents them from voicing their true anxieties about the process and it further prevents them from learning the facts about mammography or its relationship to breast cancer.

Noelle-Neumann's "spiral of silence" theory suggests that a more thorough examination of the deep-seated fears women harbor about their very existence is warranted if we are fully to understand their reactions to mammography and all that it signifies. Fear of being afraid, fear of being weak, fear of being unfeminine, fear of being rejected—these are the underlying fears of women—the fears that are never articulated and are therefore never resolved.

Some Suggestions for Future
Messages Promoting Mammography

Public health communicators must understand that education about mammography will succeed only to the extent that it acknowledges and addresses women's deepest fears, trepidations that are now largely silenced in popular dialogue on the subject. The first step toward such a woman-centered perspective for campaigns promoting mammography lies in establishing the proper combination of emotional and logical approaches to education about breast cancer and its prevention. To date, information and campaigns on mammography have been presented with the view that education will motivate women sufficiently and that scaring them a little bit in the process cannot hurt. The success of these efforts to educate women about mammography remains dubious, at best. The efficacy of fear appeals as suasory devices fostering compliance on this issue is unproven, despite the existence of studies indicating the general effectiveness of emotional appeals in persuasive endeavors.[60] Messages that attempt to scare women into getting mammograms play on fears that women already harbor and result in an overload of anxiety that often prevents them from either learning or taking action. Conversely, messages that attempt to allay trepidations about mammography fail to address the underlying, unarticulated fears that prompt women to avoid the process. Neither approach meets the needs of the target audience.

Messages promoting mammography must be predicated on an understanding of the ways in which women view themselves in relation to the larger social structure and must account for the hidden fears which that structure perpetuates. Health care communicators should consider, for example, the manner in which women are portrayed in the media and the inherent contradictions between these images and the realities of women's lives. Campaigns about mammography must facilitate a restructuring of the ways women define themselves and reinforce a female image that is more concerned with health than with stereotypically feminine characteristics. To this end, print and electronic media should be encouraged to produce positive messages on the issues of breast cancer and mammography, such as Roxanne Roberts's essay in the *Washington Post*.[61] Coverage of a woman who speaks to the hidden fears associated with the disease, of a woman who is taking decisive action on behalf of all women, establishes a positive model that might be emulated. Establishment of a "buddy system" through physicians' offices, designed to match female counselors with women who should schedule mammographic exams, is yet another promising possibility. Such a system could be modeled on the ACS Reach for Recovery program and train volunteers to encourage discussion about the unarticulated fears that women confront when they contemplate screening.

Another woman-centered method for promoting mammography could include in-home intervention and education. A pilot program testing this approach, conducted in inner-city Atlanta, demonstrated the efficacy of personalized educational efforts through the use of in-home visits from lay health care workers.[62] The project, which employed demonstrations, print and oral educational materials, and referrals, produced a significant increase in mammographic screening among those women who participated in the study.[63] In the comfort and safety of their own homes, women may be more able to discuss their real fears and misunderstandings about mammography and thus be more able to learn or to act on information that can save their lives.

Traditional messages designed to address the four major barriers to mammographic screening would benefit from adopting more woman-centered approaches, as well. With regard to the *fear factor,* public health messages currently address the topics of discomfort and radiation levels associated with mammograms only sporadically. Discourse about these concerns should be included in all brochures and pamphlets on the topic, with publications explaining the actual testing process from the perspective of the patient and showing pictures or drawings of mammography equipment. Publications of this nature should also inform women of the new federal guidelines for mammographic testing and encourage participation in the screening process as informed consumers.

Personalizing the issue of breast cancer and mammography should dramatically increase the assimilation of positive messages. Greater use of the personal experiences of celebrities such as Betty Ford and Nancy Reagan would not only address self-image problems, but would reduce fear by demonstrating success and survival. Promotion of literature featuring women's experiences, such as Joyce Wadler's book, *My Breast,* could provide the type of exceptional detail that even the most comprehensive brochures and advertisements cannot hope to achieve.[64] Men, too, must be drawn more into the picture. For example, in relating the personal experience of his wife's breast cancer and mastectomy, Douglas Dodge presents a model that shows not just triumph over the disease, but survival of the relationship women most fear losing.[65]

The *money* and *availability* factors that often mitigate against broader use of mammography are more difficult problems to solve purely on the basis of communication campaigns. Structural changes in our health care system need to be effected before these obstacles can be overcome with any measure of success. Nonetheless, locally or regionally generated messages targeted to poorer segments of the population and to women in specifically rural and urban settings should provide current, detailed information on the cost and location of mammographic screening.

Overcoming the exigence of the *misinformation* factor requires both a broad-based communication campaign and several corresponding individualized campaigns targeted to particular segments of the population. Individualized sets of messages could, for example, reach older women through placement of the information in social security check mailings and through advertisements run in magazines such as *Modern Maturity*. Minority spokespersons and role models need to be employed to reach marginalized segments of the population for whom white, upper-class survival stories may not have salience. Physicians, in particular, require specialized messages designed to encourage their cooperation in following the mammographic guidelines developed by the American Cancer Society. Efforts to construct messages for use in professional settings, such as medical conventions, need to reach beyond the specialties of OB/GYN and oncology to capture the attention and address the needs of primary care physicians.

Finally, broad-based messages about mammography ought to be placed in media that attract the attention of a majority of U.S. women. The increased use of television for this purpose seems warranted, as does the placement of messages in contexts that are female-specific. An exceptionally good idea, one that has thus far found little support, would require bra manufacturers to insert tags with their products urging regular mammographic screening.[66] Other examples of targeting women "where they live" might include the placement of messages in women's clothing, on fragrances, or on feminine hygiene products. The idea that regular mammograms are a part of what it means to be a woman should be coupled in these messages with reminders that the x rays are both sensible and safe.

Support for breast cancer research and prevention is becoming a broad-based political priority, potentially addressing structural problems that remain unresolved by earlier public health campaigns. Efforts such as these, coupled with improved public health messages, messages designed to end the spiral of silence surrounding mammography and breast cancer, may well accomplish that which so desperately needs doing.

Notes

1. C. Wallis, "A Puzzling Plague: What Is It About the American Way of Life That Causes Breast Cancer?" *Time* (January 14, 1991): 48.

2. R. F. Jones, *Woman's Health: The Facts About Breast Cancer* (Washington, DC: American College of Obstetricians and Gynecologists, October 1992).

3. Wallis, "A Puzzling Plague," p. 49.

4. B. Corbin, "NOW and Coalition Step Up Breast Cancer Fight," *National NOW Times* (November 1993): 5.

5. K. Mattison, "Facing Cancer Fears: Breast Cancer Survivors Urge Early Detection," *New York Teacher* (October 18, 1993): 15.

6. S. A. Feig, "Decreased Breast Cancer Mortality Through Mammographic Screening: Results of Clinical Trials," *Radiology* 167 (1988): 659-665.

7. R. Roberts, "Nancy Brinker's Race to Save the Women," *Washington Post,* June 12, 1991, p. F1.

8. Feig, "Decreased Breast Cancer"; G. Friedman, "Overcoming Mammography Phobia," *Healthweek* (April 9, 1990): 19.

9. M. Cimons, "More Women Are Having Mammograms, Study Shows," *Los Angeles Times,* September 14, 1990, p. A4.

10. E. E. Calle et al., "Demographic Predictors of Mammography and Pap Smear Screening in U.S. Women," *American Journal of Public Health* 83 (1993): 54.

11. Calle et al., "Demographic Predictors," p. 53.

12. J. Stein, S. Fox, & P. Murata, "The Influence of Ethnicity, Socioeconomic Status, and Psychological Barriers on Use of Mammography," *Journal of Health and Social Behavior* 32 (1991): 111.

13. C. Milloy, "Men Must Join Breast Cancer Fight," *Washington Post,* May 31, 1992, p. B1.

14. American College of Obstetricians and Gynecologists, *Mammography* (Washington, DC: Author, May 1989).

15. Friedman, "Overcoming Mammography Phobia," p. 19.

16. Friedman, "Overcoming Mammography Phobia," p. 19.

17. Milloy, "Men Must Join"; Wallis, "A Puzzling Plague," p. 49.

18. J. DeFao, "Strict Standards for Mammograms Urged," *Los Angeles Times,* October 25, 1991, p. A23.

19. Jones, "Woman's Health."

20. "Breast Cancer: Have We Lost Our Way?" *The Lancet* (February 6, 1993): 343.

21. Roberts, "Nancy Brinker's Race."

22. American Cancer Society, *Cancer Information Database* (Atlanta, GA: Author, 1993): View No. 3005.

23. American Cancer Society, "Breast Cancer: Questions and Answers" (Atlanta, GA: Author, 1992): 5009.03.

24. A. Goldstein, "Insurers Must Pay Cost of Screenings," *Washington Post,* July 6, 1991, p. B1.

25. Chippewa County Health Department, *Do the Right Thing . . . Get a Mammogram* (Sault Ste. Marie, MI: Chippewa County Health Department, 1991).

26. Women seeking information about mammography may telephone the following:

• American Cancer Society Cancer Response System, 1-800-ACS-2345, sponsors of Reach for Recovery program.

• Cancer Information Service (National Cancer Institute), 1-800-4-CANCER.

• The National Alliance of Breast Cancer Organizations, 1-212-719-0154.

• Susan G. Komen, Breast Cancer Information Help Line, 1-800-IM-AWARE.

• Y-ME, National Organization for Breast Cancer Information and Support, 1-800-221-2141; breast cancer survivors answer calls to provide emotional support and to refer patients to local cancer centers. No medical advice is offered.

27. D. M. Anderson, K. Duffy, C. D. Hallett, & A. C. Markus, "Cancer Prevention Counseling on Telephone Helplines," *Public Health Reports* 107 (1992): 278-283.

28. Friedman, "Overcoming Mammography Phobia," p. 21.

29. American Cancer Society, *Special Touch: A Personal Plan of Action for Breast Health* (Atlanta, GA: Author, 1987).

30. M. Sherrill, "Selling a Message of Life: Zora Brown's Cancer Crusade Targets Black Women," *Washington Post,* November 15, 1990, p. C1.

31. Sherrill, "Selling a Message."

32. B. Meier, "Effort to Provide Mammograms Raises Questions of Cost and Convenience," *New York Times,* August 19, 1991, p. A1.

33. Milloy, "Men Must Join."

34. Friedman, "Overcoming Mammography Phobia," p. 19.

35. Cimons, "More Women Are Having Mammograms."

36. Friedman, "Overcoming Mammography Phobia," p. 19.

37. Milloy, "Men Must Join"; Sherrill, "Selling a Message."

38. Cimons, "More Women Are Having Mammograms."

39. Jane Brody, "The Value and Limits of the Mammogram and Exams," *New York Times* (Late Edition), June 5, 1991, p. C10.

40. Brody, "The Value and Limits."

41. "Regular Mammograms Aren't Scheduled by Most Women," *Washington Post,* September 25, 1990, p. WH5.

42. Wallis, "A Puzzling Plague."

43. Friedman, "Overcoming Mammography Phobia," p. 19.

44. E. Lauder (Ed.), "Breast Cancer Report" (*Self* booklet).

45. Friedman, "Overcoming Mammography Phobia," p. 22.

46. National Cancer Institute, *Questions and Answers About Breast Lumps* (Washington, DC: U.S. Department of Health and Human Services, Public Health Service, National Institutes of Health, 1992).

47. American Cancer Society, *Facts on Breast Cancer* (Atlanta, GA: Author, 1989).

48. American Cancer Society, Texas Division, Inc., *Mammography Can Save Your Life Through Early Detection of Breast Cancer* (Atlanta, GA: Author, 1992).

49. American Cancer Society, *Mammography Found My Breast Cancer Early* (Atlanta, GA: Author, 1987).

50. S. M. Fuller et al., "Breast Cancer Beliefs of Women Participating in a Television-Promoted Mammography Screening Project," *Public Health Reports* 107 (1992): 683-684.

51. Fuller et al., "Breast Cancer," p. 684.

52. Fuller et al., "Breast Cancer," p. 686.

53. State of New York Department of Health, *Dear State Employee* (Albany: State of New York Department of Health, 1992).

54. K. Hannon, "It's the Year of the Woman!" (Albany, NY: State Senate, forum flyer, 1992).

55. Jones, "Woman's Health."

56. E. Noelle-Neumann, *The Spiral of Silence: Public Opinion—Our Social Skin* (Chicago: University of Chicago Press, 1984): 64.

57. D. Spender, *Man Made Language* (London: Routledge & Kegan Paul, 1985): 55-59.

58. Spender, *Man Made Language,* p. 47.

59. Noelle-Neumann, *The Spiral of Silence,* pp. 37-38.

60. See C. Hovland, I. Janis, & H. Kelly, *Communication and Persuasion: Psychological Studies of Opinion Change* (New Haven, CT: Yale University Press, 1974): 57.

61. Roberts, "Nancy Brinker's Race."

62. J.F.C. Sung et al., "Cancer Screening Intervention Among Black Women in Inner-City Atlanta—Design of a Study," *Public Health Reports* 107 (1992): 381-388.

63. Sung et al., "Cancer Screening," p. 383.

64. J. Wadler, *My Breast: One Woman's Cancer Story* (New York: Addison-Wesley, 1992).

65. D. Dodge, "Our Breast Cancer," *New York Times,* February 20, 1993, p. 19.

66. Roberts, "Nancy Brinker's Race."

PART VI

Contemporary Priorities in Communicating
About Women's Reproductive Health

Women have a harder time getting health coverage than men do . . . are
penalized for pregnancy . . . may be penalized for suffering domestic
violence . . . pay more . . . face more problems with long-term care.
Editorial, *Glamour,* August 1994, pp. 86-87[1]

The final part of this volume is devoted to consideration of contemporary priorities in
communicating about women's reproductive health. Competition between access and
technological advances underlie many of these debates. Perhaps most striking are
these conclusions:

1. Women's relationships—to family, including their own children and their life partners; to
   parents; to community—their own, their country's, and the world-at-large—form the thesis
   of arguments both "for" and "against" support for access and advances in medical technology; and
2. campaigns designed to inform women about access to health care and advances in medical
   technology continue to rely on messages with a maternal and fetal health focus.

In other words, the more things appear to change in relation to women, research
addressing their reproductive health, and communication about women and their reproductive health, the more things stay the same.

C. Condit illustrates the media's maintenance of a narrow focus in the promotion
and use of reproductive technology—a focus aimed at women's relationships, with
particular emphasis given to a couple's desire to conceive their own child, but also to
a woman's relationship with children not even yet conceived. Flores reviews the medical

research relating to women's use of reproductive technology, demonstrating the priority given to conceiving over reviewing women's physical and emotional well-being—with the latter being downplayed in support of the former.

These same themes run through the research and reporting relating to women and hysterectomy. If a woman is past childbearing age or desires no more children, surgical removal of the womb has been, and often still is, recommended as the first response to many women with many varied complaints, as Ross reveals in her review of the medical literature. A woman has to expend considerable effort to achieve a full picture of the physical and emotional effects of hysterectomy, as Sefcovic reveals in her review of the available public literature about the topic.

As but one example of why women need to counsel carefully with trusted providers when considering a hysterectomy, a woman who is premenopausal, has had as many pregnancies as she desires, and seeks a form of birth control may interact with a physician who recommends a hysterectomy. The physician may observe that the surgery provides permanent birth control and—as a bonus—may even reduce the woman's risk for some types of reproductive cancers. As a result of the hysterectomy, however, the woman may experience severe menopausal symptoms for which the physician then prescribes hormone replacement therapy. Due to the woman's hypertension, use of the drug therapy may actually put her at higher risk for some reproductive cancers, as discussed by Kalbfleisch and Bonnell in the previous section of this volume. The failure of women and physicians to communicate about reproductive health from a systems perspective, therefore, may be detrimental to a woman's overall health and well-being.

Research and reporting about women and HIV have also continued the trend of treating women's health as synonymous with maternal and fetal health, while simultaneously perpetuating myths and stereotypes about women. Many of the most significant efforts to study HIV and women have been the result of efforts to understand the effects of a woman's positive HIV status on her fetus, rather than the effects of HIV on women. Cline and McKenzie provide a thorough analysis of both the medical and social science research in this arena, illustrating strengths and weaknesses and offering alternative explanations for some findings, as well as approaches to the design and development of future undertakings. Raheim overviews the media's focus on women and HIV, which has simply reflected much of what the medical and social science literature has had to say about women and HIV in terms of women as carriers of the disease, infecting both their fetuses and the men who come into sexual contact with them. Raheim reveals, however, a slow movement and evolution toward a focus more centrally on the woman in the media reports about HIV and women.

Raheim foreshadows the closing chapter in this book and the proposal to communicate with women about their reproductive health in a more women-centered fashion. Raheim also reinforces one of this volume's core themes: Societal values significantly impact the design of media messages about human reproduction *and* medical research relating to this process. Moreover, there is a symbiotic relationship between research and reporting, as illustrated consistently and persistently throughout this text. At the end of the year 1993, for example, as health care reform occupied much media time and space, the cover of *Time* magazine read, "Cloning Humans," and asked the question,

"Where do we draw the line?"[2] That question might have referenced the risk posed to a woman's health in order to retrieve an egg to be combined with a sperm in the production of a human embryo outside the womb. The question could also have been a reference to the expenditure of societal resources—both financial and human—to achieve such accomplishments as the creation of a human embryo in a laboratory setting. But the picture on the magazine cover suggests a different issue.

There is a single hand on the right side of the *Time* magazine cover, with five replicates of a human hand lining the left side of the cover, all against a canvas backdrop with cracks and crevices similar to the ones that line a person's hand. The single hand has the forefinger outstretched toward the line of replicate hands, although there is no point where the hands actually touch—a computer-altered version of Michelangelo's work titled "Adam." There is no explicit reference to family; no image of a fetus, a woman, a mother and child, or even a whole human being—just the hands. The implicit message, however, is clear: This is *not* the way to create human life; humans should *not* be playing God—summarily illustrating the recursive relationship between media messages and societal values.

Societal values influence the design of media messages. Media messages, however, act to sustain societal values. And so, women, in their efforts to be informed about their reproductive health, and even without expending effort toward that goal, are affected by the agendas that continue to underlie the direction for research and reporting about women's reproductive health.

Notes

1. "Why Every Woman Should Be Fighting Now for Health Care Reform" [editorial], *Glamour* (August 1994): 86-87.

2. *Time* (November 8, 1993): cover.

22

Options and Risks With Reproductive Technologies

Lisa A. Flores

Reproductive technology is often hailed as the way that women and men, eager but unable to have children, can seek help that no one else seems able to provide. Since the well-known breakthrough in 1978 when Louise Brown, the first "test-tube" baby was born, more medical experts, biotechnologists, and infertile couples have explored the possibilities of science for reproduction. Benefits of such technology appear clear. Women and men suffering from infertility can use scientific knowledge to conceive and bear children. The rapid growth of the technology, however, has led to the possibility that couples proceed to use the technology though lacking full understanding of it. This phenomenon may be due to the absence of informational campaigns to educate the public about reproductive technologies. The complexities of the various techniques require not only knowing what new procedures we have to choose from, but what exactly is involved in each of the different techniques. This chapter examines the medical research that has led to these choices and women's place in this research. Moreover, attempts were made to locate systematic efforts to convey this information to women, although none were found. The discussion presented in this chapter affords important insights about both why such campaigns are needed and the important messages to be included.[1]

Who Chooses to Try Reproductive Technology

Studies in the United States, England, and Australia estimate that 10% of the adult population is involuntarily childless.[2] The Office of Technology Assessment estimates that one in six couples in the United States is involuntarily childless. Of that population, 1.2 million seek treatment for infertility each year, resulting in $1 billion dollars spent on infertility treatment each year.[3] In 1990, more than 19,000 women participated in IVF (in vitro fertilization) treatment alone.[4] In an effort to define infertility, medical researchers have established guidelines in terms of the duration and frequency of a couple's intercourse.

The scientific consensus is that infertility is the inability to conceive after 1 year of regular intercourse without the use of contraception.[5] Use of 1 year is based in part on the probability of conceiving during a year of regular intercourse. Women between the ages of 20 and 30 who have intercourse without contraception have an approximately 20% chance of conceiving each menstrual cycle. By age 40, the chance of conception per cycle drops to 5%. Thus, although younger women often conceive in five cycles, older women may go 20 cycles before conceiving.[6] The 1-year time frame as a gauge for chances of becoming pregnant, therefore, has a significantly different meaning for women over 40. This is also a more restrictive standard than that used by the World Health Organization, which specifies a 2-year time frame.

Causes of Infertility

For some women, scarred or blocked fallopian tubes lead to the inability to conceive. A number of factors can lead to tubal blockage, such as abdominal surgery, ectopic pregnancies (in which the embryo is lodged in the fallopian tubes), appendicitis, endometriosis, venereal diseases, scarring from abortions, and pelvic diseases.[7] Approximately 25% to 30% of involuntarily childless women have blockages in their fallopian tubes.

Though the trend in infertility is often to assume that the cause lies with the woman, about one third of the time infertility can be traced to the man. Sperm ducts are often blocked, the testicles may be unable to produce healthy sperm, or the sperm count may be low (known as oligospermia).[8]

Some couples experience problems in which the combination of egg and sperm does not lead to fertilization. A common factor in these situations is the development of antibodies in either the woman or the man that act as allergic reactions to the sperm. The presence of these antibodies may mean that the cervical mucus repels the sperm, keeping the sperm from traveling up to the fallopian tubes and the eggs.[9] Research indicates that 7% to 17% of infertility cases are due to such antisperm antibodies.[10]

Knowing the causes of infertility makes seeking treatment easier; however, from 5% to 15% of women and their partners are seen as having unexplained, or idiopathic, infertility. Most often, the diagnosis of idiopathic infertility is limited to couples who have been trying to conceive for 2 years and for whom no specific cause can be determined.[11]

Diagnosing infertility is an important first step in the cycle of reproductive technology, because different methods used offer different advantages and disadvantages based on the infertility problem.

The Procedures of Assisted Reproduction

Medical procedures that manipulate men's bodies include surgery to remove dilated scrotal vein (varicocele), stimulation of erection and ejaculation (either electrically or chemically), and hormonal therapy to increase sperm count or vigor. Parallel procedures for women use surgery to unblock the fallopian tubes and to remove endometrial tissue or fibroids. Women may also receive hormones to stimulate ovulation (egg production), make the uterus more receptive to the embryo, or deter miscarriage.

The most widely publicized laboratory technique has been in vitro fertilization (IVF). In this procedure, a sperm and an egg are combined in the laboratory and inserted into the woman who will bear the child. IVF requires intensive hormonal stimulation of the egg donor and may be combined with microsurgery on the egg to permit weak sperm to fertilize the egg. There are a growing number of variations on the basic IVF technique (called GIFT, PROST, ZIFT, etc.).

The IVF technique has extended to use of the bodies of human beings other than the would-be parents. Though sperm donation has long been possible through artificial insemination (AI), IVF also makes egg donation possible. These technologies make a wide variety of surrogate parenting possible. A woman may bear a child that combines her own egg with the sperm from someone other than the rearing father, or a child that combines another woman's egg with sperm either from her husband or from another male. A woman may also act as a "host uterus" to bear a child that combines egg and sperm from members of an adoptive couple or anyone else. Most of these surrogacy arrangements entail expanded medical risks and social complications of many sorts.

Genetic selection provides the final type of reproductive technology. There are limited means by which genetic selection can be made. A fetus may be tested for sex or for a variety of inherited diseases while it is still in the womb. If the fetus is genetically diseased, it can be aborted. If it is a male, and at risk for an "x-linked" disease (such as hemophilia), it can be aborted. Moreover, a technique employing artificial insemination exists for selecting the gender of children. Expanded techniques that would test pre-embryos for genetic irregularities before implantation via IVF are being provided experimentally at this time. In addition, the Human Genome Project, which is mapping the human gene structure, will make available a wide range of information about genetic features.

IVF/GIFT

In vitro fertilization was originally designed for women with scarred, blocked, or absent tubes.[12] With in vitro fertilization, the egg is removed from the ovary before it enters the fallopian tubes and combined with the sperm outside of the body; then the fertilized zygote is placed in the uterus, bypassing the fallopian tubes.

Although the IVF procedure seems relatively straightforward, numerous factors affect the likelihood of achieving pregnancy with IVF. The timing of the fertilization of the embryo in vitro must correspond with the timing of the development of the endometrium. If embryos are implanted too early, the endometrium may reject the embryos. Further, if the embryos are underdeveloped or overdeveloped, they may not implant. The location of implantation is also important. To implant in the endometrium lining, the fertilized egg must be placed at the opening of a fallopian tube so it can simulate normal travel to the endometrium. Every stage of the IVF procedure is crucial, and most women undergo IVF only to find they are not pregnant.

The GIFT (gamete intrafallopian transfer) technique is unlike IVF in that at least one unblocked tube is needed.[13] This procedure, which is a spin-off of IVF, allows for fertilization of the egg and sperm in the fallopian tube. Researchers in reproductive technology note that when the egg was fertilized in an artificial environment, it was less likely to embed itself in the uterine lining. Eggs that were fertilized in the fallopian tubes were in their natural environment and so had a better chance of implanting.

The clear difference between IVF and GIFT is the place where fertilization takes place. While IVF was designed to allow fertilization outside of the fallopian tubes, GIFT places the egg and sperm back into the fallopian tubes for fertilization. Therefore, a major factor in the decision to choose either IVF or GIFT is the condition of the woman's fallopian tubes.

Other factors should also be considered before making a decision. Recently, IVF has been made available to couples with other causes of infertility. When infertility is due to oligospermia, IVF may be helpful. Men diagnosed as having oligospermia have low sperm count. Researchers believe that normal sperm concentration is 20 to 100 million sperm per milliliter of semen; with IVF, however, fertilization can occur with as little as 5 million sperm per milliliter of semen.[14] Because fertilization occurs in a petri dish where the egg and sperm can be artificially brought together, fewer sperm are needed for IVF. IVF is emotionally and financially demanding, however; in cases of oligospermia, it may not be necessary to choose IVF without first considering artificial insemination with donated sperm (AID).[15] This alternative provides a high sperm count sample from a usually anonymous donor. AID is a less-invasive technique than IVF and considerably less expensive. The pregnancy rate in the United States from AID ranges from 80% to 85%.[16] This procedure does not require the use of fertility drugs, and it removes such risks as ovarian hyperstimulation syndrome and multiple pregnancies, two major risks with IVF/GIFT.

Medical research has shown that the IVF technique may also be helpful for women whose inability to conceive spontaneously is due to other factors. When endometriosis is the cause of infertility, IVF may be an option, because endometriosis may have left scarring or blockages in the tubes. A study of 108 cycles of IVF due to endometriosis resulted in 23 pregnancies.[17] The severity of the endometriosis will affect the likelihood of success with IVF, however, with severe cases resulting in few pregnancies with IVF. In a study of 124 couples who chose IVF after the women were diagnosed with endometriosis, nine pregnancies, with five live births, resulted from those women diagnosed as having severe endometriosis.[18]

Initially, GIFT was expected to be of most benefit to women and couples with unexplained infertility. It is now being used, however, with women who have endometriosis but whose tubes are not damaged. The GIFT technique can also be used with oligospermia, but pregnancy rates are often low.[19] For women over 40 who do not have blocked tubes, medical research has suggested that GIFT may offer an advantage over IVF. In a comparison of GIFT and IVF with women of various ages, clinical pregnancy rates remain relatively close until women reach age 35. At this point, GIFT seems to lead to significantly more clinical pregnancies than does IVF, with a 35% clinical pregnancy rate with GIFT versus 15.8% with IVF for women aged 35-39. In women aged 40-45, the ratio was 16.7% for GIFT and 0 for IVF.[20]

Although most medical research has focused on females, some studies have looked to male factor infertility and its effects on IVF and GIFT. The general consensus of these studies is that a complete examination of the male is necessary to examine the characteristics of the semen. The probability of success with either IVF or GIFT will depend on the specific semen quality.[21] When male infertility is evident, the crucial stage in either IVF or GIFT is fertilization. Sperm motility, or the sperm's ability to travel to and through the fallopian tubes, is a significant aspect of fertilization, because, even with IVF, the sperm must be able to penetrate the outer shell of the egg. From an analysis of 290 IVF treatment cycles, fertilization rates ranged from less than 10%, when sperm was low in either count or motility, to close to 50%, when sperm was high in both count and motility.[22] The physical makeup of the sperm, or its morphology, will also affect the likelihood of fertilization. Any defects in the sperm head or tail can reduce the possibility of fertilization. In three separate studies of sperm morphology and fertilization rates, poor makeup led to low rates of fertilization.[23] When the sperm quality is questionable, IVF may offer an advantage over GIFT. When fertilization of the egg occurs in vitro, medical teams can monitor the fertilization to ensure that the sperm does penetrate the egg.[24]

Although certain cases of infertility fall clearly within either IVF or GIFT, some situations are less clear. Damage to the fallopian tubes means IVF, but instances of endometriosis, oligospermia, or combined female/male problems can be helped by either IVF or GIFT. Determining which procedure is more likely to succeed is often difficult, especially when multiple reasons affect the ability to conceive naturally.[25]

Many attempts of either IVF or GIFT, or even natural conception, fail because the fertilized egg does not implant in the uterine wall. The specific placement of the zygote in the uterus affects the likelihood of implantation. Medical research has shown that oocytes and zygotes that remain in vitro for extended periods may have a decreased chance of implanting.[26] Further research, including a study of 67 IVF patients, illustrated the importance of timing of implanting. The common time of implanting of 48 hours after oocyte retrieval may be inappropriate in that either embryos or endometria may not yet be ready. Of the 67 subjects, those who waited 96 hours before implanting were twice as likely to become pregnant.[27]

Though the success rates for IVF and GIFT have improved since their beginnings in 1978, most women still go home childless. As of 1990, approximately 5,000 babies had been born from IVF worldwide.[28] The success rate for either IVF or GIFT depends to a large degree on the particular clinic. The estimated average for IVF/GIFT success in the United States is 5% to 10%, but the success of a particular clinic can range from 0 to 30%.[29]

Each clinic has different degrees of success, and many clinics calculate their successes in different ways. Some clinics count the number of "chemical pregnancies," where a woman tested pregnant, but actual pregnancy is unknown. Other clinics base their success rates on the number of eggs fertilized in vitro, rather than on the number of embryos that implanted in the uterine lining. A third method of measuring success is by the number of embryos replaced in the uterus. This measure eliminates from the calculation all women who for whatever reason did not get to the stage where embryos are implanted. In many clinics, only about 50% of the original number of women who begin treatment get to the implantation stage.[30]

Clinics also may fail to note how many of the pregnancies ended in miscarriage. Commonly, 40 of the initial 100 women will be "canceled" for not responding to the hormone treatment. Of the remaining 60, 2 or 3 will not produce usable eggs, 5 more will have eggs that do not fertilize, 10 will actually get pregnant, 1 or 2 will miscarry, and 8 of the original 100 will give birth.[31] Some clinics do note success based on the number of live births, but even this measure can be misleading if the clinic does not distinguish between single and multiple births. Most women find the most helpful measure of success to be *the number of women who have live births out of the total number of women who have begun treatment at the clinic.*

Both IVF and GIFT can be emotionally and psychologically draining, and a clinic that recognizes a woman's emotional needs can make the experience easier. Women who have attempted IVF/GIFT note the disruption to their lives. Goals, such as attending college, may be postponed, and some women find their lives governed by the waiting involved in assisted conception.[32] A family-type environment that is supportive and views a woman as the central person in the process can mean greater chances of pregnancy.[33] In other words, the clinic's success can be measured in part from its ability to provide humane care.[34]

The Debate Over Cryopreservation

The continued interest and research in reproductive technologies has led to variations on the basic techniques of IVF or GIFT. One of the available technologies is cryopreservation, or the freezing of the sperm, egg, or embryo. A number of factors in early cases of artificial insemination (AI), IVF, and GIFT made cryopreservation popular. In some medical research, women relied on sperm from donors other than their partners, and some women were found to be putting themselves at risk for sexually transmitted diseases.[35] As cases of AIDS became more and more prevalent, cryopreservation provided a means of ensuring that sperm used for artificial insemination could be thoroughly tested for AIDS and other sexually transmitted diseases.[36]

In addition to allowing for testing of sperm before insemination, cryopreservation allows women to freeze eggs and/or embryos for future implantation. Before a woman can undergo IVF or GIFT, she usually takes fertility drugs that cause her ovaries to superovulate, or produce a number of mature eggs. Medical teams often fertilize all the eggs she produced even though only a limited number (usually no more than three or four) of embryos can be replaced into her uterus. Superovulation is a physically and emotionally dangerous procedure. Before cryopreservation, women who produced more than four eggs had to discard them; a woman may now choose to freeze excess eggs or embryos.

Cryopreservation also provides the means to plan ahead, as the process allows women to undergo superovulation while young, but postpone having children. Men having vasectomies can freeze their sperm and later have their own biological children. Women and couples can also use cryopreservation to donate their sperm, eggs, and embryos to others. However, there is a concern with ovum donation about how the individual clinics regulate donation. A survey of 292 members of assisted reproduction associations found that 61.3% had ethics boards, but only 31.4% used the boards in decisions regarding ovum donation.[37]

Although cryopreservation gives some women and couples more choices, there is controversy over its use. Doctors and scientists debate whether cryopreservation increases the possibility of birth defects.[38] As of 1992, three documented cases noted chromosomal abnormalities thought to result from cryopreservation.[39] Cryopreservation involves a good deal of manipulation of the egg or embryo and can damage the egg or embryo from the handling involved in freezing.

A second issue of contention in regard to cryopreservation is whether frozen sperm, eggs, and embryos provide a decreased chance of pregnancy compared to fresh ones. Frozen and thawed sperm often have a lower degree of motility than do fresh sperm, which decreases the possibility that the sperm will be able to fertilize an egg. In a study of 77 couples using artificial insemination by donor (AID), frozen-thawed sperm were found to have lower motility rates that led to reduced fertilization rates.[40] In a separate study, transfer of 776 fresh sperm resulted in 279 clinical pregnancies or 36%; transfer of 449 frozen-thawed oocytes resulted in 128 pregnancies or 29%. Fewer pregnancies resulted from the cryopreserved oocytes, but the researchers concluded that the 29% clinical pregnancy rate justified use.[41] A number of sperm, eggs, and embryos simply do not survive the freezing/thawing process. A 5-year study of cryopreserved oocytes found a 68% survival rate.[42]

Although cryopreservation has been used with semen for close to 40 years, it is still seen by many doctors as experimental when it comes to eggs and embryos. Further exploration of cryopreservation of eggs requires women willing to donate their eggs. Thus, women subjects are necessary for this research, and the results can be physically and emotionally exhausting. With human guinea pigs needed for further research on cryopreservation, women considering it should explore the history of each individual clinic's success with cryopreservation.

Finally, cryopreservation may mean that a couple is confined to only one clinic. Many clinics will not transfer frozen sperm, eggs, and embryos to other clinics, even at the request of the donors. Women and couples who are uncertain that their clinic provides the best environment for them may have no choice but to continue treatment at that clinic.[43] Although cryopreservation seems to offer a number of benefits to women considering IVF or GIFT, there are a number of issues to consider that may or may not be brought up by the medical team.

The Impact of Fertility Drugs

The increased use of cryopreservation impacts another aspect of the IVF or GIFT process, the use of fertility drugs to stimulate production of multiple eggs, for doctors must be able to retrieve more than one egg in order to freeze some for later use. An initial stage in the IVF or GIFT process is the taking of hormones or fertility drugs.[44] These drugs not only cause the ovaries to produce more than one mature egg, they also make it easier to predict when ovulation will occur so that the medical team is better able to remove the mature eggs. These drugs can have serious and dramatic effects on women, however, and potentially on embryos. These include hindering the development of the follicles, inhibiting the normal function of enzymes, causing too rapid growth of follicles, causing tenderness and swelling of the ovaries, increasing the risk of miscarriage and of birth defects, and causing breast tenderness and headaches. Use of fertility drugs can cause kidney and liver failure, or stop production of urine, any of which may be fatal. Hyperstimulation of the ovaries, a condition that causes large ovarian cysts, can also occur; incidence is less common than other side effects.[45] In a study of 168 women, 46 or 11.3% suffered from ovarian hyperstimulation syndrome as a result of fertility drugs.[46]

The current approach to both IVF and GIFT sees fertility drugs and superovulation as crucial; however, every woman reacts differently to the various drugs. Clinics and medical teams rely on different fertility drugs, with Clomid and human menopausal gonadotropin being two of the more commonly used ones. The choice of which one to use is dependent upon each individual woman. Many women taking only Clomid do not produce many mature eggs, and older women who are given Clomid are often even less successful.[47] To increase the number of eggs retrieved, a number of doctors are now combining Clomid with another fertility drug, human menopausal gonadotropin (hMG), often called Pergonal. Though a combined treatment of Clomid and hMG often results in larger numbers of mature eggs, it can also lead to spontaneous ovulation before the medical team has attempted to retrieve the eggs.[48] When spontaneous ovulation occurs, the eggs are released into the fallopian tubes, and the medical team is unable to retrieve them. When this happens, hormone treatment may have to begin again. Even though more eggs are often gained from the combination of Clomid and hMG, no significant increase in pregnancy rates has been found; miscarriages occur often.[49] Even the combination of the two hormones does not guarantee that a woman will superovulate.[50] The combination of gonadotropin-releasing hormone agonists (GnRHa) with FSH (follicle stimulating hormone) may be effective, however. Five women, previously taking pure FSH to stimulate superovulation, were given both GnRHa and FSH, resulting in a doubling of the number of oocytes retrieved per cycle.[51]

The disparity in the discussion of the use of fertility drugs is compounded by the different drugs and their advantages and disadvantages in success of IVF or GIFT. The effects of the drugs vary widely depending on the amount taken, the type of drug used, and the timing of the drugs in relation to the procedure.[52] Doctors also agree that all of the treatments may cause physical side effects that range from nausea and headaches to damage to the ovaries to liver and kidney failure; however, these side effects are rare. The development of ovarian cysts after hormone therapy is also a danger, with approximately 25% risk of cysts appearing.[53] There is the possibility for some women that the introduction of synthetic hormones affects the lining of the endometrium, making it less likely that embryos will implant in the lining.[54] Finally, there is conflicting information available about the cancer risks posed by these drugs.[55] The analysis by Whittemore, Harris, Itnyre, and the Collaborative Cancer Group shows an increased risk of ovarian cancer for women using these.[56] Further research is needed to ascertain the long-term effects of these drugs on women.

In addition to the physical side effects that most women experience after taking fertility drugs, many women are also plagued with emotional reactions to the hormone therapy. Extreme mood swings are common when taking fertility drugs, as is fatigue and nervousness.[57] A study of 20 women found that all women taking fertility drugs experienced emotional reactions, such as mood swings, inability to concentrate, and depression, while on the drugs.[58] The emotional strain is increased because women know that if their ovaries fail to respond to the hormone treatment, they may be canceled from the program.[59]

Multiple Pregnancies

A major concern with the effects of fertility drugs is that they play a role in multiple births in IVF and GIFT. A benefit of superovulation is that more eggs are available to fertilize; when more embryos are replaced in the woman's uterus, there is a greater chance that one or more will implant in the uterine wall. Pregnancy rates can increase to 30% with transference of three and jump as high as 55% with transference of four embryos.[60] Whenever more than one embryo is replaced, the woman runs the risk of having a multiple pregnancy. The incidence of twins and triplets is not uncommon with either IVF or GIFT; some women have four, five, or even six fetuses develop in their wombs. Doctors and scientists agree that a woman's likelihood of bringing home a baby increases when more than one embryo is implanted, but the chance of multiple births also rises, a danger to both mother and fetus(es). Perinatal mortality can rise to more than 20% with triplets, and prematurity and congenital malformation are also possible.[61]

Several factors thought to be related to an increased chance of multiple pregnancy are the number and quality of embryos or eggs replaced in the woman, her age, and the quality of the sperm.[62]

A common consequence of multiple pregnancies is prematurity. A study of 1,510 pregnancies with either IVF or GIFT showed that 56.4% of women with multiple pregnancies had premature deliveries.[63] Multiple pregnancies are also likely to result in birth by cesarean section, as is illustrated in a study that reported a c-section rate of 26% for single births and 61% for multiple births.[64] Women will want to maximize their chances for getting pregnant, but most researchers agree that no more than three embryos should be transferred.[65]

Other Risks of IVF/GIFT

Outside of the risks involved in the use of fertility drugs or the possibilities of multiple pregnancies, the different reproductive techniques can lead to other dangers to both the woman and the baby. Both IVF and GIFT, along with the other variations on the reproductive technologies, are still relatively experimental. Although animal experimentation formed the foundation that eventually led to the first IVF baby, and though this experimentation continues, doctors and scientists often find out more about what works and what does not work from the women who come for help. Research done on eggs, embryos, and reproduction requires access to women's bodies.[66] Acceptance of reproductive technologies has led to a less critical attitude toward procedures, but many women experience serious repercussions.[67]

Every woman who chooses to try to conceive with the help of IVF or GIFT puts her health at risk. The standard case of IVF begins with hormone treatment and goes to the pain of egg retrieval through invasive surgery requiring anaesthesia. Cesarean section rates also increase with IVF and GIFT pregnancies, and with cesarean sections come all of their risks to the mother. Although a hospital may have a general c-section rate of 15%, with IVF and GIFT pregnancies, the rate can jump to 26% for single births and up to 61% for multiple births.[68] Women are also at risk from the introduction of foreign objects into the uterus, which can cause severe cramps and possible infections.[69]

The extensive manipulation of the eggs and embryos involved in both IVF and GIFT has caused some researchers to worry about possible birth defects or later problems of children born from IVF and GIFT.[70] Two problems that have already been noted are heart problems and spina bifida, a problem with the spinal cord that may result in paralysis.[71] One fear is that genetic manipulations and reliance on synthetic hormones may result in serious problems that will not manifest themselves until many years later.[72] Pregnancies from IVF lead to low birth weight and congenital deformities more often than do pregnancies from intercourse; premature births may occur as much as 3 times more often with IVF.[73]

Conclusion

A number of women who want children find they are not able to conceive, either due to problems with their reproductive organs, their partners' sperm, or a combination of problems. Various techniques of assisted reproduction may provide the answers to their desires. Medical research on reproductive technologies, however, illustrates the numerous factors that should be considered before making a decision about assisted reproduction, and no public information campaigns exist to help women assess these medical findings.

One danger associated with reproductive technologies is that scientists and medical researchers can only learn more about the various procedures through the women and men who come to their clinics. Although Louise Brown, the first "test-tube" baby, is now about 17 years old, and many other children have been born with the help of either IVF or GIFT, many issues are still being researched and debated. Science has not yet determined which fertility drugs are most effective and cause the fewest side effects, and cryopreservation of embryos is seen by some as experimental. The possibilities of later effects on either mother or child are also still unknown. As research on reproductive technologies continues, the hope is that the needs of the women who turn to assisted reproduction will be at the forefront.

Notes

1. To gather the literature surveyed in this chapter, I did a search of the University of Georgia holdings using the terms *reproductive technology, assisted reproduction, infertility, fertility, artificial insemination, invitro fertilization,* and *GIFT.* I also used these terms as I searched *Social Sciences Index, Medline, Expanded Academic Index,* and *General Science Index.* Because the *Journal of Assisted Reproduction and Genetics* (previously the *Journal of In-Vitro Fertilization and Embryo Transfer*) is devoted primarily to questions of reproductive technology, I did a manual search to locate those studies that may have been missed in the database search.

2. C. E. Miall, "Reproductive Technology vs. the Stigma of Involuntary Childlessness," *Social Casework: The Journal of Contemporary Social Work* 70 (1989): 43-50; P. Singer & D. Wells, *Making Babies: The New Science and Ethics of Conception* (New York: Scribner, 1985): 15; E. P. Volpe, *Test-Tube Conception: A Blend of Love and Science* (Macon, GA: Mercer University Press, 1987): 23.

3. U.S. Congress, Office of Technology Assessment, *Infertility: Medical and Social Choices* (Washington, DC: Government Printing Office, May 1988).

4. L. S. Wilcox, H. B. Peterson, F. P. Haseltine, & M. C. Martin, "Defining and Interpreting Pregnancy Success Rates for in Vitro Fertilization," *Fertility and Sterility* 60 (1993): 18-24.

5. G. Sher, V. A. Marriage, & J. Stoess, *From Infertility to in Vitro Fertilization: A Personal and Practical Guide to Making the Decision That Could Change Your Life* (New York: McGraw-Hill, 1988): 3.

6. C. Wood, I. Calderon, & A. Crombie, "Age and Fertility: Results of Assisted Reproductive Technology in Women Over 40 Years," *Journal of Assisted Reproduction and Genetics* 9 (1993): 482-484.

7. A. L. Bonnicksen, *In Vitro Fertilization: Building Policy From Laboratories to Legislatures* (New York: Columbia University Press, 1989): 23.

8. Sher et al., *From Infertility,* p. 40; Volpe, *Test-Tube Conception,* p. 12.

9. Sher et al., *From Infertility,* p. 39.

10. H.J.G. Janssen, B. A. Bastiaans, H.J.M. Goverde, H.M.G. Hollanders, A.A.M. Wetzels, & L. A. Schellekens, "Antisperm Antibodies and in Vitro Fertilization," *Journal of Assisted Reproduction and Genetics* 9 (1992): 345-349.

11. E. Katz & B. S. Hurst, "Selection of Patients for in Vitro Fertilization-Embryo Transfer," in M. D. Damewood (Ed.), *The Johns Hopkins Handbook of in Vitro Fertilization and Assisted Reproductive Technologies* (Boston: Little, Brown, 1990): 8-9.

12. M. Warnock, *A Question of Life: The Warnock Report on Human Fertilization and Embryology* (New York: Basil Blackwell, 1985): 29; J. F. Leeton, A. O. Trounson, & C. Wood, "IVF and ET: What It Is and How It Works," in W.A.W. Walters & P. Singer (Eds.), *Test-Tube Babies: A Guide to Moral Questions, Present Techniques, and Future Possibilities* (Melbourne: Oxford University Press, 1982): 2; Sher et al., *From Infertility*, p. 37.

13. I. Craft, "A Flexible Approach to Assisted Conception," in P. L. Matson & B. A. Lieberman (Eds.), *Clinical IVF Forum: Current Views in Assisted Reproduction* (New York: Manchester University Press, 1990): 79-92.

14. J. F. Leeton et al., "IVF and ET," pp. 2-10.

15. M. M. Quigley, "Patient Screening and Selection," in D. P. Wolf & M. M. Quigley (Eds.), *Human in Vitro Fertilization and Embryo Transfer* (New York: Plenum, 1984): 37-46.

16. Quigley, "Patient Screening," pp. 37-46; J. Aiman, "Factors Affecting the Success of Donor Insemination," *Fertility and Sterility* 37 (1982): 94; B. H. Albrecht, D. Cramer, & I. Schiff, "Factors Influencing the Success of Artificial Insemination," *Fertility and Sterility* 37 (1982): 792.

17. H. W. Jones, "The Infertile Couple," in S. Fishel & E. M. Symonds (Eds.), *In Vitro Fertilization: Past, Present, Future* (Washington, DC: IRL Press, 1986): 17-26.

18. J. S. Tummon, K. A. Colwell, C. J. MacKinnon, J. A. Nisker, & A. A. Yuzpe, "Abbreviated Endometriosis-Associated Infertility Correlates With in Vitro Fertilization Success," *Journal of in Vitro Fertilization and Embryo Transfer* 8 (1991): 149-153.

19. M. M. Seibel, "A New Era in Reproductive Technology: In Vitro Fertilization, Gamete Intrafallopian Transfer, and Donated Gametes and Embryos," *The New England Journal of Medicine* 318 (1988): 828-834.

20. I. Craft & T. Al-Shawaf, "IVF Versus GIFT," *Journal of Assisted Reproduction and Genetics* 9 (1992): 424-427.

21. P. L. Matson, "The Usefulness of IVF, GIFT, and IUI in the Treatment of Male Infertility," in P. L. Matson & B. A. Lieberman (Eds.), *Clinical IVF Forum: Current Views on Assisted Reproduction* (New York: Manchester University Press, 1990): 112-122.

22. B. Fisch, R. Kaplan-Kraicer, S. Amit, Z. Zukerman, J. Ovadia, & Y. Tadir, "The Relationship Between Sperm Parameters and Fertilizing Capacity in Vitro: A Predictive Role for Swim-Up Migration," *Journal of in Vitro Fertilization and Embryo Transfer* 7 (1990): 38-44.

23. Katz & Hurst, "Selection of Patients," p. 20; N. Carlon, A. Navarro, C. Giorgetti, & R. Roulier, "Quantified Ultrastructural Study of Spermatozoa in Unexplained Failure of in Vitro Fertilization," *Journal of Assisted Reproduction and Genetics* 9 (1992): 475-481; D. W. Fawcett, "The Mammalian Spermatozoon," *Developmental Biology* 44 (1975): 394-436; B. Bacceti, "The Human Spermatozoon," in J. Van Blerkom & P. M. Motta (Eds.), *Ultrastructure of Reproduction* (Boston: Martinus Nijhoff, 1984): 110-126; L. Zamboni, "The Ultrastructural Pathology of the Spermatozoon as a Cause of Infertility: The Role of Electron Microscopy in the Evaluation of Semen Quality," *Fertility and Sterility* 48 (1987): 711-734.

24. Craft & Al-Shawaf, "IVF Versus GIFT."

25. I. Craft, "A Flexible Approach to Assisted Conception," in P. L. Matson & B. A. Lieberman (Eds.), *Clinical IVF Forum: Current Views in Assisted Reproduction* (New York: Manchester University Press, 1990): 79-92.

26. C. Staessen, M. Camus, I. Khan, J. Smitz, L. VanWaesberghe, A. Wisanto, P. DeVroey, & A. C. Van Steirteghem, "An 18-Month Survey of Infertility Treatment by in Vitro Fertilization, Gamete and Zygote Intrafallopian Transfer, and Replacement of Frozen-Thawed Embryos," *Journal of in Vitro Fertilization and Embryo Transfer* 6 (1989): 22-29 (see especially p. 28).

27. A. Lewin, N. Laufer, N. Yanay, A. Simon, E. Zohav, M. Berger, & J. G. Schenker, "Double Transfer of Embryos in in Vitro Fertilization, or Is There a Delayed Receptivity of the Endometrium?" *Journal of in Vitro Fertilization and Embryo Transfer* 6 (1989): 139-141.

28. L. S. Williams, "Motherhood, Ideology, and the Power of Technology," *Women's Studies International Forum* 13 (1990): 543-552.

29. Bonnicksen, *In Vitro*, p. 68; Williams, "Motherhood, Ideology," p. 543; L. S. Williams, "No Relief Until the End: The Physical and Emotional Costs of in Vitro Fertilization," in C. Overall (Ed.), *The Future of Human Reproduction* (Toronto: Women's Press, 1989): 120-138 (see especially p. 120); J. A. Scutt in reviews of *Infertility: Women Speak Out About Their Experiences of Reproductive Medicine* by Renate D. Klein and of

The Exploitation of a Desire: Women's Experiences With in Vitro Fertilization—An Exploratory Survey, by Renate D. Klein, *Women's Studies International Forum* 13 (1990): 605-608.

30. Bonnicksen, *In Vitro,* pp. 68-69; Sher et al., *From Infertility,* pp. 147-152; D. H. Barlow, D. Egan, & C. Ross, "The Outcome of IVF Pregnancy," in P. L. Matson & B. A. Lieberman (Eds.), *Clinical IVF Forum: Current Views in Assisted Reproduction* (New York: Manchester University Press, 1990): 63.

31. Bonnicksen, "*In Vitro,* p. 68.

32. C. Crowe, " 'Women Want It': In-Vitro Fertilization and Women's Motivations for Participation," *Women's Studies International Forum* 8 (1985): 547-552.

33. R. Hubbard, "Personal Courage Is Not Enough: Some Hazards of Childbearing in the 1980s," in R. Arditti, R. Duelli Klein, & S. Minden (Eds.), *Test-Tube Women: What Future for Motherhood* (Boston: Pandora, 1984): 331-355.

34. Bonnicksen, *In Vitro,* p. 64.

35. A.J.C. van den Brule, D. J. Hemrika, J.M.M. Walboomers, P. Raaphorst, N. van Amstel, O. P. Bleker, & C.J.L.M. Meijer, "Detection of Chlamydia Trachomatis in Semen of Artificial Insemination Donors by the Polymerase Chain Reaction," *Fertility and Sterility* 59 (1993): 1098-1103.

36. C. Carver, "The New—and Debatable—Reproductive Technologies," in C. Overall (Ed.), *The Future of Human Reproduction* (Toronto: Woman's Press, 1989): 46-57.

37. A. M. Braverman, "Survey Results on the Current Practice of Ovum Donation," *Fertility and Sterility* 59 (1993): 1216-1220.

38. See Carver, "The New," 55; K. A. Ginsburg, A. G. Sacco, M. F. Rousseau, C. M. Blacker, K. S. Moghissi, & M. P. Johnson, "Tetraploidy Associated With Human Pronuclear Embryo Cryopreservation: A Case Report," *Journal of Assisted Reproduction and Genetics* 9 (1992): 484-488.

39. Ginsburg et al., "Tetraploidy," pp. 484-488.

40. H. Yavetz, J. B. Lessing, Y. Niv, A. Amit, Y. Barak, I. Yovel, M. P. David, M. R. Peyser, L. Yogev, Z. Homonnal, & G. Paz, "The Efficiency of Cryopreserved Semen Versus Fresh Semen for in Vitro Fertilization/Embryo Transfer," *Journal of in Vitro Fertilization and Embryo Transfer* 8 (1991): 145-147; Carver, "The New," p. 55.

41. L. L. Veeck, C. H. Amundson, L. J. Brothman, C. DeScisiolo, M. K. Maloney, S. J. Muasher, & H. W. Jones, "Significantly Enhanced Pregnancy Rates per Cycle Through Cryopreservation and Thaw of Pronuclear Stage Oocytes," *Fertility and Sterility* 59 (1993): 1202-1207.

42. Veeck et al., "Significantly Enhanced," p. 1204; Further discussion of survival of cryopreserved specimens can be found in M. Bustillo, E. F. Fugger, & J. D. Schulman, "New Reproductive Technologies," *The New England Journal of Medicine* 325 (1993): 1043.

43. Bonnicksen, *In Vitro,* p. 35.

44. S. Minden, "Patriarchal Designs: The Genetic Engineering of Human Embryos," *Women's Studies International Forum* 8 (1985): 561-565.

45. P. Spallone, *Beyond Conception: The New Politics of Reproduction* (Granby, MA: Bergin & Garvey, 1989): 59; J. Blankstein, S. Mashiach, & B. Lunenfeld, *Ovulation Induction and in Vitro Fertilization* (Chicago: Year Book Medical, 1986): 126-127, 145-148; Williams, "No Relief," pp. 120-138; and Sher et al., *From Infertility,* pp. 64-71.

46. M. A. Aboulghar, R. T. Mansour, G. I. Serour, I. Ellatar, & Y. Amin, "Follicular Aspiration Does Not Protect Against the Development of Ovarian Hyperstimulation Syndrome," *Journal of Assisted Reproduction and Genetics* 9 (1992): 238-243.

47. R. Fleming, M. E. Jamieson, & J.R.T. Coutts, "The Use of GnRH-Analogs in Assisted Reproduction," in P. L. Matson & B. A. Lieberman (Eds.), *Clinical IVF Forum: Current Views in Assisted Reproduction* (New York: Manchester University Press, 1990): 15.

48. See Sher et al., *From Infertility,* pp. 73-74; and Fleming et al., "The Use of GnRH-Analogs," pp. 5-7.

49. J. H. Segars, G. A. Hill, S. H. Bryan, C. M. Herbert, K. G. Osteen, B. J. Rogers, & A. C. Wentz, "The Use of Gonadotropin Releasing Hormone Agonist (GnRHa) in Good Responders Undergoing Repeat in Vitro Fertilization/Embryo Transfer (IVF/ET)," *Journal of in Vitro Fertilization and Embryo Transfer* 7 (1990): 327-331.

50. Z.H.Z. Ibrahim, P. Buck, P. L. Matson, & B. A. Lieberman, "Inclusion of Human Growth Hormone (hGH) in Stimulation Regimes for Poor Responders," in P. L. Watson & B. A. Lieberman (Eds.), *Clinical IVF Forum: Current Views in Assisted Reproduction* (New York: Manchester University Press, 1990): 20-28.

51. M. C. Edelstein, R. G. Brzyski, G. S. Jones, S. Oehninger, S. M. Sieg, & S. J. Muasher, "Ovarian Stimulation for in Vitro Fertilization Using Pure Follicle-Stimulating Hormone With and Without

Gonadotropin-Releasing Hormone Agonist in High-Responder Patients," *Journal of in Vitro Fertilization and Embryo Transfer* 7 (1990): 172-175.

52. See A. K. Munabi, D. King, S. Bender, M. Bustillo, A. Dorfmann, & J. D. Schulman, "Small Increases in Circulating Luteinizing Hormone (LH) Concentrations Shortly Before Human Chorionic Gonadotropin (hCG) Are Associated With Reduced in Vitro Fertilization (IVF) Pregnancy Rate," *Journal of in Vitro Fertilization and Embryo Transfer* 7 (1990): 310-313; Edelstein et al., "Ovarian Stimulation," 172-175; M. P. Diamond, T. Buchholz, S. P. Boyers, G. Lavy, B. S. Shapiro, & A. H. DeCherney, "Super High Estradiol Response to Gonadotropin Stimulation in Patients Undergoing in Vitro Fertilization," *Journal of in Vitro Fertilization and Embryo Transfer* 6 (1989): 81-84; and Segars et al., "The Use," pp. 327-331.

53. J. Parinaud, K. Cohen, P. Oustry, M. Perineau, X. Monroziès, & J. M. Rème, "Influence of Ovarian Cysts on the Results of in Vitro Fertilization," *Fertility and Sterility* 58 (1992): 1174-1177.

54. Edelstein et al., "Ovarian Stimulation," p. 175; Diamond et al., "Super High Estradiol Response," pp. 81-84; and Sher et al., *From Infertility,* pp. 64-75.

55. B. Weinhouse & F. Feldinger, "The Miracle Baby," *Ladies Home Journal* (April 1987): 104-177.

56. A. S. Whittemore, P. Harris, J. Itnyre, & the Collaborative Ovarian Cancer Group, "Collaborative Analysis of Twelve U.S. Cancer-Control Studies: II. Invasive Epithelial Ovarian Cancers in White Women," *American Journal of Epidemiology* 136 (1993): 1184-1203.

57. Bonnicksen, *In Vitro,* p. 60.

58. Williams, "No Relief," p. 127.

59. Williams, "Motherhood, Ideology," p. 543.

60. M. Nijs, L. Geerts, E. van Roosendaala, G. Segal-Bertin, P. Vanderzwalmen, & R. Schoysman, "Prevention of Multiple Pregnancies in an in Vitro Fertilization Program," *Fertility and Sterility* 59 (1993): 1245-1250; A. Hershlag, J. A. Floch, A. H. DeCherney, & G. Lavy, "Comparison of Singleton and Multiple Pregnancies in in Vitro Fertilization (IVF) and Embryo Transfer (ET)," *Journal of in Vitro Fertilization and Embryo Transfer* 7 (1990): 157-159.

61. Hershlag et al., "Comparison," pp. 157-159.

62. Nijs et al., "Prevention of Multiple," p. 1247; Craft, "A Flexible Approach," pp. 79-92, 83-87.

63. Barlow et al., "The Outcome," pp. 63-69.

64. S. W. D'Souza, E. Rivlin, P. Buck, & B. A. Lieberman, "Children Conceived by in Vitro Fertilization," in P. L. Matson & B. A. Lieberman (Eds.), *Clinical IVF Forum: Current Views on Assisted Reproduction* (New York: Manchester University Press, 1990): 70-78.

65. C. Staessen et al., "An 18-Month Survey," pp. 22-29; H. C. Liu, Y. M. Lai, O. Davis, A. S. Berkeley, M. Graf, J. Grifo, J. Cohen, & Z. Rosenwaks, "Improved Pregnancy Outcome With Gonadotropin Releasing Hormone Agonist (GnRH-a) Stimulation Is Due to the Improvement in Oocyte Quantity Rather Than Quality," *Journal of Assisted Reproduction and Genetics* 9 (1992): 338-343; D. Meldrum, "In Reference to Follicular Aspiration," *Journal of Assisted Reproduction and Genetics* 9 (1992): 190.

66. L. Koch & J. Morgall, "Towards a Feminist Assessment of Reproductive Technology," *Acta Sociologica* 30 (1987): 173-191.

67. R. Rowland, "A Child at Any Price?: An Overview of Issues in the Use of the New Reproductive Technologies and the Threat to Women," *Women's Studies International Forum* 8 (1985): 539-546.

68. D'Souza et al., "Children Conceived," p. 71.

69. Carver, "The New," pp. 51-52; P. L. Matson, "The Usefulness of IVF, GIFT, and IUI in the Treatment of Male Infertility," in P. L. Matson & B. A. Lieberman (Eds.), *Clinical IVF Forum: Current Views on Assisted Reproduction* (New York: Manchester University Press, 1990): 112-122.

70. Carver, "The New," p. 53.

71. Scutt, *Infertility,* p. 607.

72. Koch & Morgall, "Towards a Feminist," pp. 173-191; D'Souza et al., "Children Conceived," p. 73.

73. D'Souza et al., "Children Conceived," pp. 70-78.

23

Media Bias for Reproductive Technologies

Celeste Michelle Condit

Throughout human history, the ability to bear children has not been a problem for most women. For the overwhelming majority, trying to postpone or prevent conception has been the more pressing concern. There have, however, always been some couples who wanted children and who were unable to conceive. Until recently, they either adopted children or remained childless. But beginning in the 1970s, advanced medical technologies bearing impressive names began to be offered to couples who experienced difficulty conceiving naturally. In vitro fertilization, GIFT (gamete intrafallopian transfer), clomide, AID, and other options have been given wide publicity in U.S. newspapers and magazines.

These mass media accounts have featured a bias that hides the risks of the procedures behind glamorized success stories, and the press may therefore have misled infertile persons in important ways. In addition, as this chapter will indicate, the media's slant has also been problematic for fertile women and men.

AUTHOR'S NOTE: The author thanks Lisa Flores for collecting the materials on which this study is based.

IVF as Model

The mass media introduced these powerful and consequential reproductive technologies to our society with substantial coverage in both magazines and newspapers. For example, between 1986 and 1991, there were 37 magazine articles and 308 newspaper articles about these technologies listed in major indexes.[1] These articles acted as a first court of public opinion passing judgment on the acceptability of the new procedures and their proper role in society. Although a small body of articles was intensely critical of these technologies and most articles at least mentioned problems with the procedures, the overwhelming majority of the articles passed a strongly favorable judgment on the use of the technologies. The first feature of this favorable judgment placed IVF as the model technology.

In the overwhelming majority of the press coverage available to the average reader, it was in vitro fertilization (IVF) that was the most visible technology. Twenty-eight articles featured IVF exclusively. The nearest competitors were 13 feature articles on frozen embryos, six articles on surrogacy, and six feature articles on egg donation, but these procedures depend on IVF as well. Another 28 articles featured IVF as the central technology, although discussing other alternatives in brief. Only 17 articles provided a survey of the range of technologies in a relatively balanced manner. Furthermore, only four articles featured the technology most likely to be employed—fertility drugs.

There were, of course, reasons for this fixation with IVF. From the journalist's perspective, IVF was the best attention-getter because it is newest and most representative of the far-reaching imaginative potential of modern medical science and technology. It simply made more exciting copy than mundane treatments such as stress reduction, hormone therapy, and getting men to wear boxer shorts to reduce the heat on their sperm. There were also medical reasons for featuring IVF. The research clinicians interested in reproductive medicine attempted to define themselves as specialists in infertility. IVF was the one technology that they could control without challenge from nonspecialists. IVF was also medically central because it is the key to several different technical procedures.

The impact of the focus on IVF was significant for women. Women readers were bombarded with coverage on the most expensive and difficult procedure, the procedure that the fewest number of infertile women would use; about 20,000 women per year in this period would turn to IVF, whereas 1.8 million were seeking fertility treatments of all kinds.[2] At the same time, readers were given virtually no information about less invasive and less expensive procedures they were likely to use.

The portrayal of IVF as the central miracle did not go completely unchallenged. Most reports disclaimed the centrality of IVF by tucking in a statement that it was a "last resort." These disclaimers, however, were balanced by the statements of doctors who urged that IVF be a first resort. Arguing that it is more likely to be effective than other treatment and that it ultimately wastes less time and money, Dr. Paul Katayama, for example, encouraged couples to try IVF early.[3]

This focus on IVF also had an impact on the fertile majority of the public. The media presented an image in which the natural process of procreation was transferred to a high-tech medical procedure, resting in the hands of specialized physicians and scientists rather than the bodies of human beings. Making this new image an appealing one required substantial revision of the social basis of reproduction.

The Importance of Biological Parenthood

Most people see having children as positive, as one of the most desirable options available to human beings. The news media, however, presented this positive feeling toward child rearing in the most extreme possible terms. The newspaper articles enthusiastically endorsed the belief that bearing children is the single most important element of adult life. In the 133 articles examined, 64 made explicit statements that supported that position, but only 2 articles made explicit statements that countered the view that parenthood was a mandatory part of everyone's life.

In some articles, the necessity of parenthood was conveyed by statements of women who were undergoing the high-tech reproductive procedures. An article titled "Baby Craving" began with the following introduction: "Pamela says she'll never quit trying. Having a baby is the most important goal of her life and she'll try anything."[4] *People* magazine likewise presented the story of Dr. Barbara Strong, who exclaimed that, "I knew people with big families, and they always looked like they were having so much fun. I wanted that more than anything."[5] In the words of another high-tech mother, "If you ask people what they treasure most in life, most will say their children."[6]

The consequences of this emphasis on parenthood were deepened by the fact that many of the articles explicitly ruled out adoptive parenthood as a satisfactory option. A plurality of the articles emphasized the need for *biological* parenthood.[7] In one article, we met Dick, the genetic father of a baby who was born from his sperm and his wife's egg, but gestated in another woman. He argued that, "Adoption gives you a baby, but it doesn't take away the desire to have a biological child."[8] His wife, Cynthia, agreed; she didn't want a baby that was not hers genetically, insisting that, "It would have made me absolutely crazy."[9] Even critics of the procedures often presumed that biological ties were crucial. An opponent of assisted reproduction, Betty Jean Lifton, warned, "I am worried about all these new arrangements because, as an adoptee, I can tell you that being brought up apart from your blood clan can produce a profound sense of alienation."[10]

Gradually, the mass media constructed the assumption that biological parenthood is the only real option. One IVF mother concluded that, "For people like me, its [sic] *the only way* to have our babies [my emphasis]."[11] The reporters generalized this emphasis on genetic linkage to all infertile couples, indicating that for all of the 2.5 million infertile couples, these techniques were the only way to preserve "family" genes and produce their "own" child.[12]

Sterility produces no physical harm to the non-procreator. The creation of the social norm of mandatory procreation allowed the press to justify medical intervention for non-health-related purposes on psychological grounds. Infertility was portrayed as a catastrophic psychological disease worse than divorce or the loss of a family member by death.[13] Other press reports frequently included statements of individuals testifying to their "desperation" and even suggesting that infertility leads to divorce, among other major life stresses. These claims were overstated, if not false. Psychologists Dunkel-Schetter and Lobel conducted a survey of the 25 extant research studies on the psychological state of infertile couples and concluded that "the average infertile individual does not experience severe or clinically significant distress, marital problems, sexual problems, or other psychological difficulties, nor is there evidence for a set sequence of emotional reactions."[14]

These studies reveal that, contrary to the press hype, the majority of women are not driven to frantic desperation when they are unable to become pregnant. This is not to disparage those women for whom the desire for biological parenthood is intense. It is not possible, however, to determine to what extent this desire is biologically grounded (as distinct from the drive for the sex act) and to what extent it is the product of centuries of cultural portrayals that have "normalized" maternity as the sole legitimate identity for women. Further, it is not reasonable to portray such women as the *only* models for dealing with infertility, as the press did. Some women accept the limitation, filling their lives with many of the other rich alternatives available, including adoption, careers, service work for other children, community action, and play.

The press went astray in casting an extreme reaction as normative, in part because it relied on anecdotal accounts of those using the reproductive technologies, as well as on unrepresentative surveys. People have a wide range of responses to infertility, although only the distressed see psychiatric counselors or seek medical intervention.[15] The rigors of infertility treatment may actually exacerbate the negative emotions associated with infertility.[16] It was these unusual individuals whom the reporters interviewed and then cast as if they were a "norm" representing everyone. In addition, reporters relied on the medical experts who were selling the technologies. These experts had both financial gain and prestige as reasons for presenting an unbalanced case that favored the technologies. Infertility was thereby presented in a manner that might increase the clientele for the new procedures. This presentation depended on careful construction of the character of the "infertile couple."

CONSTRUCTING THE "INFERTILE COUPLE"

During the 1960s and 1970s, adoption was widely normalized in the mass media and it was endorsed as "real parenthood." In order to overturn this positive view of non-genetically related families, the media had to change "sterile individuals" into "infertile couples."

Sterility implies a permanent condition. In earlier years, the inability to conceive was described as "sterility" or "barrenness." Those who found themselves "sterile" were sometimes pitied but were expected to learn to cope with the situation. With the coming of new technologies, the medical community replaced these words with the term *infertile;* the newspapers adopted the new vocabulary.

The term *infertility* serves the interests of the medical establishment through its plasticity. As the previous chapter indicates, it was somewhat arbitrarily defined by the U.S. medical community as the failure to conceive after a year of uncontracepted heterosexual intercourse.[17] This definition labels a huge number of couples—2.4 million—as "infertile" and as appropriate consumers or patients needing medical care.

There are two important fallouts of this redefinition. First, it reframes the presumption so that almost everyone is threatened by infertility. In the old days, most women presumed that they were fertile and that unprotected intercourse with men would eventually cause pregnancy. With this new definition, however, women are all tentatively infertile. (Even if they have previously borne children, they may develop "secondary infertility.") With each month that passes without pregnancy, women remain in the "infertile" category, rather than the "normal" category. But this is surely an unreasonable definition. Most people who have no medical complications may not conceive within a year of unprotected heterosexual intercourse. Matters as simple as timing may prevent conception. Moreover, complications that deter pregnancy fall on a wide spectrum, from temporary impediments to permanent obstacles. Yet these people are all classed as subnormal, needing medical care.

For this huge group of people, the treatment regimen may never be completed. "Infertile" persons are never ultimately pronounced sterile, beyond the treatment of medicine. Either physicians locate a treatable cause for infertility, or the patient is diagnosed as "infertility unknown," in which case IVF becomes an acceptable medical regimen. There is no medically acceptable reason for a couple not to bear "their own" children.

One other factor was necessary to build a demand for these new consumer products. The articles had to place the emphasis on "the couple" rather than the individual. Many of the technologies produce a child genetically linked to only one of the parents. Therefore, the treated individual might well end up with a child who is not her or his biological kin. They would be "treated," but their medical problem—infertility— would not be solved. By focusing on the "couple," this problem is avoided. The "couple" always gets a biologically linked child (even if the link is only to one of the parents). Thus, sperm donation, egg donation, or the use of a host uterus could be treated as a medical cure for the "couple's infertility" even though it might not solve the individual's sterility.

This had a special impact on women. In most cases, it is the woman who will be the medical patient.[18] In order to motivate her to undergo the difficult, painful, sensitive, and/or risky medical procedures to produce a child that is not genetically hers, the press focused on "the couple" rather than on the woman. In this case, she is rewarded by producing a child that is "theirs" rather than one that is simply "his."

The image of reproduction that pervaded the press accounts of the new technologies thus did not simply respond to existing cultural norms or experiential needs (which could have either permitted adoption or urged personal fertility). Instead, it subtly altered the ideal reproductive patterns in a way that was tailored to fit what IVF as a consumer product could deliver.

CELEBRATING THE "MIRACLE"

In spite of this vivid construction of a "reproductively handicapped" couple eager for "their own" children, and capable of being cured, individuals might still not seek these technologies. Some groups argue that these technologies are morally undesirable. The Catholic Church especially has taken a firm stand against the use of these technologies on the ground that they violate the close natural bonding of husband, wife, and child.[19] In a different critique, essentialist feminists have argued that these technologies are undesirable because they result in the unhappiness and oppression of women.[20] In addition, there are problems of effectiveness and safety with these technologies. As a whole, the press failed to present a balanced account of the problems and benefits.

Overall, 53% of the articles were slanted toward a positive direction, whereas only 16% were negative and only 17% were balanced.[21] The positive slant was usually portrayed with greater intensity than the negative angles, with one of the most frequent labels applied to the new technology being—"a miracle." In contrast, criticisms were offered in more neutral tones and were also more abstract. To see the contrast, consider some sample headlines. In favorable reportage, we get "Modern Miracles: In Vitro Program Helps Dreams Come True for Childless Couples," or "Baby Begun in Test Tube Is a Happy One-Year-Old," "High-Tech Delivers Them Hope," and "Success Is Born at University as 'In Vitro' Process Matures."[22] In less favorable coverage, the titles tell us merely that in "The New Motherhood: Science Creates Social Issues," or that "High-Tech Reproduction Breeds Ethical Dilemmas," or "Birth Science: Clash of Ethics, Economics."[23] As opposed to the "Miracle Baby" that some received, the losers have suffered only "False Hope."[24]

Having positioned couples as seeking their own biological children, and having portrayed the new reproductive technologies as largely unproblematic "miracles" to answer the demand, all that was needed was "consumer information" about the specific purchase and use of these products.

Information for Consumers

The media coverage of "assisted reproduction" could have focused on many different angles. The press might have reminded us of the eugenic implications of the new technologies. Alternately, they might have featured issues of equity in the distribution of health resources or the impact on women as a class of childbreeders. Each of these topics received some treatment in isolated articles, but the overwhelming majority of articles assumed the guise of providing consumer information.

THE PROCEDURES AND THEIR EFFECTIVENESS

Most people have only the vaguest notions about the subtle mechanisms of natural reproduction, let alone the complexities of medical interventions. Consequently, the majority of the articles that the reporters presented to the public spent the bulk of their space describing, in a relatively nontechnical fashion, the scientific basis and medical process involved in assisted reproduction. Such information constituted the necessary prelude to the second step, making informed judgments about the controversies surrounding the technologies.

The most commonly addressed concern about the use of the technologies was the success rate of the techniques. As in other issues, IVF gained center stage. In 1989, Congressional Representative Ron Wyden released a study of the success rates of IVF clinics that showed that half had never produced a live baby. This temporarily stirred journalists to report on IVF with a great deal of skepticism about the effectiveness of the product.[25] In the period immediately following the report, the plurality of articles were hostile to IVF and warned consumers against being taken in by false claims of unscrupulous clinics. These reports focused on the presumably anomalous "unscrupulous clinics" and implied that the norm was success. All women had to do was shop carefully and the search for a miracle baby would be successful.

Meanwhile, other articles continued to portray the technology favorably, with disparity being evident in the range of success rates reported in different periodicals, including 6%, 11%, 12%, 17%, all the way up to the highly positive estimate of a 50% chance.[26] Over time, the skeptical estimates faded.[27] Little documented improvement in overall success rates backed this shift, and comparison to natural rates depended on a host of questionable assumptions, including a high estimate of success for in vitro and a low estimate for natural conception and questionable calculations with regard to birth defects.[28]

COSTS

About half of the articles accurately portrayed the psychological rigors and demanding physical procedures entailed in IVF. They noted that women would have to undergo intensive hormone therapy requiring daily shots, along with intensive monitoring, including daily trips to a clinic to have blood levels checked and for repeated ultrasound. They would have to undergo one invasive procedure to remove the eggs and another to replace the pre-embryo. Given that failure was statistically likely, they would then have to undergo crushed hopes and the decision whether to repeat the cycle again. In the face of these relatively damaging descriptions, one might have expected IVF to come out as an undesirable choice, but the media were able to avoid that conclusion. Enthusiastic reporters redeemed these costs by repeatedly citing the declarations of successful IVF participants that "it was all worth it."[29] The financial costs of the program were similarly reported and then mitigated.

IVF is an expensive procedure, costing between $4,000 and $10,000 for a single cycle (although experimental or nonprofit companies sometimes provide the service for $1,500). The newspapers routinely noted this price, and they portrayed it as high.[30] They also occasionally lamented that the procedures were not available to all persons on an equitable basis. They offered, however, a solution—a sometimes tacit, sometimes vehement, endorsement of insurance coverage for the procedure. They thereby declared that IVF was not only "worth it" for the individuals involved, but was a cost that the entire society should be willing to bear to provide infertile couples with children who are genetically linked to themselves.

Several articles were able to mitigate the costs in other ways as well. The "it was all worth it" claims implicitly included costs and sometimes did so explicitly. Ed Barlow, an IVF father, responded to questions about the financial expense with the declaration that, "No cost is too much."[31] In addition, the fertility specialists gradually learned to downplay the cost of a round of IVF by pointing out that it was similar to a normal hospital birth.[32] (Ignoring that birth costs would be added on to the IVF procedural costs and that more than one attempt is generally needed; or that the 25% increased chance of multiple births would mean delivery costs many times higher than normal). Thus, although they accurately reported the price tag, the press subtly prepared the consumer and society to be ready to pay dearly for this "medical miracle."

SHOPPING GUIDES

Having established that people should undergo the expensive and relatively ineffective IVF procedure, the newspapers and magazines offered infertile persons "shopping guides" so that they might be wise consumers in selecting which clinic to use for their IVF procedures. Local newspapers provided insets describing local clinics and their success rates or even wrote articles deifying local infertility practitioners.[33] The national media provided addresses for organizations that gave clinic addresses and success rates, or they printed addresses for organizations that provided "support groups." The articles portrayed the infertile as savvy consumers[34] and provided rules for learning to fill that role. For example, they warned the consumer to be sure that the physician was board-certified in reproductive endocrinology, and that in asking about success rates one be sure to get the "take home baby rate" rather than the "chemical pregnancy" rate. The fact that the newspapers had a slant that emphasized the perspectives of the consumer was nowhere more evident than in the treatment of surrogacy. With one exception, the articles on surrogacy generally took the stance of the "purchasing" couple,[35] and surrogate mothers were redefined as providing only a "host uterus" or serving as the "ultimate wet nurse."[36] The legislation that was suggested by the articles was usually consumer-protection style legislation that included regulation such as surrogacy contracts, AIDS testing for sperm banks, or licensing of fertility clinics.

Extensive advice about cost and purchasing was not sufficient to normalize unfamiliar technological regimens for average readers. Therefore, the newspapers provided role models who could help both the infertile and the fertile to imagine what it would feel like to be a consumer of this new technology.

ROLE MODELS

Advertisements for products such as automobiles and perfumes have long employed role models as a form of persuasion. The goal in such efforts is to present a sympathetic figure with whom the audience can identify. By showing the pleasures that representative characters enjoy and the techniques they use to employ the product, the mass media can introduce the audience both to the identity characteristics appropriate for consumption and the procedural information necessary for effective consumption.

The news articles introducing Americans to the new reproductive technologies accomplished this task by employing narratives that told about the experiences of women who had used the technologies; 63 of the 133 articles included such narratives. They often focused on "local firsts"—that is "the first couple" in a region or community to have an IVF baby, or to have a child who had been frozen as an embryo or had been conceived from a donated egg, and so on. Other times, they focused on sensational stories. The most popular of these were the birth of quintuplets and the use of "grandma" as the surrogate for a wombless daughter's egg and the daughter's husband's sperm. These cases were almost uniformly presented to us in a highly positive manner. In the story about the surrogate grandmother, *Time* magazine was obviously defensive, daring the "professional ethicists," at whom they openly sneered, to find anything wrong in this "heartwarming situation" and its "miracle babies."[37]

In building a consumer identity, the most effective stories were those about ordinary people. In these stories, the reading public was often introduced with substantial depth to a likeable married couple and then encouraged to share the shock and grief of the couple as they discovered that they were infertile. Next, the audience was led through the experiences of the couple as they employed the new technologies. The difficulties and costs were often accurately described, but at the end of the story, the audience experienced the couple's joy and celebration at a successful outcome—the birth of a biologically linked baby.

In several respects, these stories provided an effective introduction to the realities of the experiences these new technologies will bring to women's lives. They familiarized women relatively well with the economic costs, psychological roller-coaster, and relational pitfalls that would be experienced. They prepared women in infertile couples for numerous invasions of their bodies and warned them in advance that they would be required to sacrifice job, or at least job performance, in order to meet the exacting demands of the IVF schedule, however, the articles offered a false ending to the story.

In the magazine articles, only two women were portrayed as unsuccessful and ultimately as giving up. The vast majority of stories had happy endings with couples taking babies home. This, of course, is exactly the opposite of the normal experience that the average consumer can expect. With IVF, the majority of consumers will not achieve a baby. With other less invasive procedures, the majority of "infertile" couples will achieve pregnancy, but then, as a Canadian study indicated, the majority of "infertile couples" who use no health-invasive reproductive technology at all may achieve a higher rate of pregnancy on their own.[38] This gross overrepresentation of success stories is particularly important, because scientific studies and common sense both indicate that people's judgments of likely success are more strongly influenced by familiarity with successful and unsuccessful models than by numbing statistics.[39] A person who knows only role models who have experienced success is likely to overestimate the likelihood of conceiving using these technologies, even in the face of statistical evidence to the contrary. By focusing on the success stories, the press thus inflated the hopes of the infertile. The press accounts also failed to include one additional and crucial set of consumer information.

HEALTH CLAIMS

Although the press provided extensive, if somewhat weighted, information on cost and effectiveness, there was an appalling failure to describe the health risks to women. As the previous chapter indicates, these interventions entail health risks that range from the known and serious to the unknown.[40] Pregnancy itself, though far safer than at any other time in U.S. history, carries a risk of death.[41] Some articles mentioned that there were health risks, but only one or two gave these risks more than a line of coverage.[42] In fact, the reporters seemed to have a very strange ability to look straight at the health risks involved and to sublimate them. One article, in reporting on a surrogacy arrangement between friends, included in its narration of the story of the pregnancy the fact that the surrogate's hemorrhaging was so severe as to be potentially fatal. The surrogate lost a third of her total blood volume and was subjected to searing pain as the physician reached into her womb to remove the placenta, without anesthesia. In spite of this incident, the reporters left the issue of health risks unexplored, allowing the surrogate herself to warn in a vague understatement, "things *can* go wrong."[43]

Perhaps this failure to provide detailed coverage of health issues occurred because consumer reporting does not usually have to concern itself with anything more than cost and the effectiveness of the product. Perhaps women are supposed to be willing to die in order to have children. Whatever the cause, the articles seriously failed to engage the crucial issue of the safety of the "medical assistance" offered to women for technologically based reproduction.

Implications for Women's
Control of Reproductive Health

When new technologies are offered to a society, the ways in which they will come to be used and the role they will play in that society will be shaped and regulated by a variety of factors and forces. In a mass-media democracy, one major force in this shaping is the portrayal new technologies are given by the mass media. As the new reproductive technologies were introduced, the mass media chose to highlight the positive elements of these new offerings and downplay the problems. Although these positive stories may have been reassuring for those who sought out and used the technology, they inhibited informed decision making on the part of potential patients and the citizenry. They also had negative impacts on other men and women in two ways.

ANXIETY ABOUT CONCEPTION

The press coverage of the new reproductive technologies was such that it was likely to increase the anxiety that many women (fertile or not) experienced about their ability to conceive. Anxiety about conception was induced in part by the extensive spotlighting of individual women who were in couples where fertility was a problem. This was generalized to large numbers of people in headlines such as "Millions Seeking End to Infertility" and in the false and repeated emphasis on the claim that infertility rates were rising, dramatically.[44]

Anxiety about conception was also encouraged by the statements of doctors, who indicated that pregnancy for all human beings is naturally a difficult process, which, on the whole, rarely occurs successfully. As the Austin (Texas) *American-Statesman* told its readers, "human reproduction is an extremely inefficient process—so inefficient that it is truly cause for rejoicing each time conception occurs."[45] Imagine the response to such claims by a teenaged reader who comes to believe that unprotected intercourse is no problem: She is not very likely to get pregnant anyway. Further, as Kristin Luker's work suggests, introducing such anxiety about conception may make young women more likely to test themselves, to see if they are able to get pregnant.[46] This anxiety is especially significant because the press coverage related fertility to one's fundamental identity.

Fertility was not presented as a simple issue about a functional failure in an important human activity but as a matter of fundamental identity. Women who found themselves unable to bear a biologically linked child were brought forth to testify that they "didn't feel like a woman."[47] These women were portrayed as "desperate" for children because it was "the most important thing in their lives," and they routinely were pictured as giving up their paid employment for this end. In the mass media, therefore, female identity once again became tied, as it had been before the 1960s, to the ability to produce children.

A couple's infertility is male-caused about 40% of the time. Nonetheless, studies show that even when medical evidence indicates that infertility is traceable to the husband's sperm, women still tell friends and family that it is caused by themselves.[48] A woman is, therefore, encouraged to undergo the rigorous and potentially risky new technological treatments to protect her "feminine identity" *even when she herself is fertile*.[49] In this widely disseminated media construction, women's identity was constructed not solely in response to their own biological fertility, but also as a measure of their willingness to "do anything" to overcome the infertility of male partners as well.

CONTROL OVER REPRODUCTION

Although the media constructed the new reproductive technologies in a manner that required women to produce children, they allocated the control over this reproductive process in shares with physicians and husbands. The introduction of physicians occurs in such a way that they gain substantial power in the reproductive process. This control was mythicized when reporters portrayed the physicians as "life givers" or even as the parents to the children. One (female) doctor, for example, was reported as saying about the children conceived in her infertility program that, "I guess you could call me the father of these kids."[50] This grand image of a literal medical paternalism should trouble men and women alike. At stake here is the control over future generations. To the extent that physicians come to be perceived as the creators of children, they are likely to gain increased legal control of these children. Already, some states have allowed legal control over embryos to be retained by clinics. Furthermore, doctors repeatedly asserted authority to decide who would be acceptable customers for them to serve; that is, with whom they would create a baby. The fertility clinic operators routinely emphasized that they screened prospective patients for psychological health, commitment to the procedure and to child rearing, marital status, and other factors, just as they screened sperm donors for selected characteristics.[51] Through this mechanism, they not only screened out single women and men, but also homosexual couples or any other infertile person they did not personally think should be involved in creating a child.[52]

Much ink has been spent in science fiction and nonfiction about governmental control of reproductive decisions. The press's attempt to normalize physician control suggests that ordinary citizens ought perhaps to begin to worry about corporate control of the human race's reproductive future by the medical community as well.

The medical community's control is not, however, unshared. Emphasis on the "couple's infertility" ensured the representation of the husband as a key decision maker. The husband's role was made to eclipse the role of the wife through portrayals that painted husbands as rational decision makers and wives as emotional incompetents. According to one physician, "The wives are usually so motivated by desperation that they'll almost agree to anything that's not ridiculous. . . . But husbands are 'a little more analytical' and usually are the ones who decide the freezing issue."[53]

Even though the woman is usually the "patient" in these procedures, within the public vocabulary created by the media, her medical choices were tightly circumscribed and dependent on the will of others, in this case the team of husband and doctors. Unlike the media's portrayal of the abortion issue, where "women's choice" was a central if contested term, in the media coverage of reproductive technologies, "the couple's decision" and the doctor's "screening" dominated—with virtually no mention of women's rights. This way of talking constituted a stark move away from reproductive freedom for women.

Conclusion

The mass media's campaign to introduce the new reproductive technologies into society cast women as desperate consumers of whatever new procedures the medical community offered. It provided coverage slanted toward physicians and it ignored the interests of ordinary women. It also reframed the delicate, natural, personal process of human procreation as an expert-controlled technological procedure. These portrayals were not necessary for a successful introduction of the new technologies into our society. A more balanced approach might have admitted the positive potentials for those who seriously wanted children without misrepresenting the risks and costs and without reconstructing social values in destructive ways. New portrayals are needed for the future in the interest of our collective well-being and women's health.

Notes

1. This study is based on all of the magazine articles and on a 50% sample of the newspaper articles drawn by use of a random numbers table. The indexes used were *The Readers' Guide to Periodical Literature*, *Newsbank*, and *Infotrac*.

2. A. Dunkin, "In Vitro Fertilization: Delivering That Ray of Hope," *BusinessWeek* (September 3, 1990): 112-113; L. Gubernick, "Easier Than Selling Soap," *Forbes* (February 9, 1987): 112-114.

3. J. Mitchard, "Advanced Fertility Clinic Gives Birth to Hope," *Milwaukee Journal*, May 11, 1987, pp. A1-A2.

4. M. Widger, "Baby Craving," *Middlesex News*, July 12, 1987, p. E13. Quoted material used by permission.

5. M. Rosen & M. Moneysmith, "How Science Can Help Infertile Couples," *People* (November 12, 1990): 115. Quoted material used by permission.

6. B. Weinhouse & F. Feldinger, "The Miracle Baby," *Ladies Home Journal* (April 1987): 177. © 1987, Meredith Corporation. Reprinted from *Ladies Home Journal* magazine with their permission.

7. Edward Panetta, in a personal communication (December 12, 1993), points out that reproductive technology is in direct economic competition with adoption. Both procedures may easily run between $12,000 and $20,000 and even reasonably comfortable upper-middle-class couples are forced to decide which route to take, because pursuing both routes simultaneously is prohibitively expensive even for the highly motivated.

8. N. E. Gupta, "Brave New Baby," *Ladies Home Journal* (October 1989): 214. Quoted material used by permission.

9. Gupta, "Brave New Baby," 214. Even when a married woman carried her husband's sperm and her friend's ovum, and was legally the parent, the gestation experience was apparently not enough to make it "her own child." *Redbook* described one such pregnancy, saying, "The only hitch was that she was pregnant with someone else's child" (J. Liebmann-Smith, "Two Friends With One Dream," *Redbook* [March 1989]: 122).

10. E. Bronner, "Fetal Science: A Dilemma for the Future," *Boca Raton News*, July 26, 1987, p. D6. Quoted material used by permission.

11. L. Spears, "Eastbay's Test-Tube Babies and Parents Gather" (Oakland, CA) *Tribune*, July 26, 1987, p. A13.

12. R. L. Holtz, "Couple, Fearful of Diseased Baby, Hunting 'Genetically Clean' Egg," *Palm Beach Post*, May 11, 1987, p. A3.

13. K. Costigan, "The Pain of Baby Craving," *Savvy Woman* (January 1989): 96.

14. C. Dunkel-Schetter & M. Lobel, "Psychological Reactions to Infertility," in A. L. Stanton & C. Dunkel-Schetter (Eds.), *Infertility: Perspectives From Stress and Coping Research* (New York: Plenum, 1991): 53.

15. Dunkel-Schetter & Lobel, "Psychological Reactions," p. 53.

16. R. D. Klein, *Infertility: Women Speak Out About Their Experiences of Reproductive Medicine* (London: Pandora, 1989); Dunkel-Schetter & Lobel, "Psychological Reactions," 54; C. F. McCartney & C. Y. Wada, "Gender Differences in Counseling Needs During Infertility Treatment," in N. L. Stotland (Ed.), *Psychiatric Aspects of Reproductive Technology* (Washington, DC: American Psychiatric Press, 1990): 142.

17. S. Halpern, "Infertility: A Search for Solutions," *Reader's Digest* (July 1989): 135.

18. The main exceptions are when men take hormones to increase sperm count or vigor, or for varicocele surgery. Even when the problem is weak sperm or sperm count, the woman will be the one who receives AI or GIFT or even IVF, as the most effective techniques that have been developed to overcome male deficiencies still work on the women's bodies.

19. E. D. Pellegrino, J. C. Harvey, & J. P. Langan, *Gift of Life: Catholic Scholars Respond to the Vatican Instruction* (Washington, DC: Georgetown University Press, 1990).

20. R. Arditti, R. D. Klein, & S. Minden (Eds.), *Test-Tube Women: What Future for Motherhood* (London: Pandora, 1989); G. Corea, R. Duelli Klein, J. Hanmer, H. B. Holmes, B. Hoskins, M. Kishwar, J. Raymond, R. Rowland, & R. Steinbacher (Eds.), *Man-Made Women: How New Reproductive Technologies Affect Women* (Bloomington: Indiana University Press, 1987); P. Spallone, *Beyond Conception: The New Politics of Reproduction* (Granby, MA: Bergin & Garvey, 1989).

21. The others were not clearly classifiable. More specifically, 46 articles provided a strongly positive slant toward the technologies, unmitigated by serious critique; 27 articles presented a positive slant but included some critique; 24 articles included a balance between support and critique; only 13 articles provided a negative slant with some support; and 10 articles featured a strong negative slant.

22. See *American-Statesman* [Austin, TX], February 28, 1988, p. A9; *Lexington [KY] Herald-Leader,* July 6, 1987, p. E9; *Register Guard,* September 3, 1989, 116, p. A5; and *Deseret News,* June 15, 1987, p. E7, respectively.

23. See *Philadelphia Inquirer,* June 22, 1986, p. E4; *Plain Dealer,* January 31, 1989, p. F9; and *Chicago Tribune,* October 19, 1987, p. B11, respectively

24. B. Weinhouse & F. Feldinger, "The Miracle Baby," *Ladies Home Journal* (April 1987): 105 ff; A. Alexander, "For Some a Baby; For Many, False Hope," *Asbury Park Press,* December 4, 1988, p. E6.

25. In general, national publications (which tended to be magazines) were slightly more critical of the technologies in all their aspects than were local publications, especially "hometown" newspapers, which heavily relied on "local first" articles that put them in a sort of "booster" position for the local clinic and the technology it supplied.

26. M. King, " 'Test-Tube' Surgery on Eggs Helps Infertile Couples Conceive," *Atlanta Journal,* October 11, 1988, p. A6; R. Baron-Faust, "Infertility Clinics: How Do You Choose?" *McCalls* (January 1990): 60; Dunkin, "In Vitro Fertilization," pp. 112-113; M. D. Lemonick, "Trying to Fool the Infertile," *Time* (March 13, 1989): 53; S. Berlfein, "Searching for Fertility," *Los Angeles Times,* October 6, 1991, pp. 21-31.

27. B. K. Michels, "Pairs Pin Hopes on Test-Tube Baby Clinic Here," *Saginaw News,* March 27, 1987, p. A11; Freyer, "R.I. Couple, Hospital Produce a Pair of Test-Tube Miracles," *Providence Journal,* July 1, 1990, pp. E9-E10, suggested a success rate higher than natural conception. Quoted material used by permission.

28. Most of the articles insisted that there was no higher rate of birth defects. However, this interpretation depended on discounting birth defects on the basis that they were "maternally related"—that is, due to the greater-than-average age of the mothers and to the higher-than-average rate of premature birth and multiple births. But these latter factors were themselves traceable to the IVF procedure.

29. N. Livingston, "The Baby Chase," *St. Paul Pioneer Press-Dispatch,* February 22, 1988, pp. A6-A8. Quoted material used by permission.

30. J. Seligmann, "The Grueling Baby Chase," *Newsweek* (November 30, 1987): 81.

31. Freyer, "R.I. Couple," p. E10.

32. B. Knapp, "Modern Miracles," [Austin, TX] *American-Statesman,* February 28, 1988, p. A10.

33. "At the Beginning," *Oregonian,* January 12, 1986, pp. D17-D19. Quoted material used by permission of Northwest Magazine of The Oregonian.

34. S. Lutz, " 'Test-Tube' Births Get Scrutiny," *Modern Healthcare* (July 21, 1989): 60.

35. D. L. Elbert, "Encouragement for Infertile Couples," *Hackensack Record,* April 1, 1987, p. D3.

36. S. Rovner, "How Science Can Help Infertile Couples," *Washington Post,* August 6, 1986, p. C1. Quoted material used by permission.

37. J. M. Nash, "All in the Family," *Time* (August 19, 1991): 58.

38. A. Boroff Eagan, "The Trouble With High-Tech Pregnancy," *Vogue* (February 1988): 196.

39. N. Adler, S. Keyes, & P. Robertson, "Psychological Issues in New Reproductive Technologies: Pregnancy-Inducing Technology and Diagnostic Screening," in J. Rodin & A. Collins (Eds.), *Women and New Reproductive Technologies: Medical, Psychosocial, Legal, and Ethical Dilemmas* (Hillsdale, NJ: Lawrence Erlbaum, 1991): 113.

40. Most drugs have been tested on men, even though men are not the primary users of the drugs, on the grounds that women's menstrual cycles make scientifically rigorous controls too difficult. Given that women are the target population of the drugs, however, this tacit admission that women's systems are different amounts to a serious failure of ethics and responsibility in the name of a spurious version of "scientific rigor."

41. In 1988, the maternal mortality rate was 8.4 per 100,000 live births, up for the first time in recorded history, from 6.6 in 1987; 330 women died in childbirth that year (see U.S. Department of Health, *Vital Statistics of the United States, 1988: Vol. 2. Mortality A* [Hyattsville, MD: U.S. Department of Health, 1991]: 68-69).

42. R. L. Hotz, "A Risky Fertility Revolution," *Atlanta Journal,* October 27, 1991, pp. A5-A7; G. Zoroya, "Woman, Claiming Infection, Sues Santa Ana Center for Man's Identity," *Orange County Register,* September 21, 1987, pp. C8-C9, reports in detail the risk of contracting disease through artificial insemination; D. Zinman, "Fertility Drug in Question," *Newsday* (January 26, 1988): B9-B10, described the risks of taking fertility drugs to the children of the women who took them.

43. Gupta, "Brave New Baby," pp. 140-216.

44. M. A. Gindhart, "Millions Seeking End to Infertility," *Arizona Republic,* July 17, 1988, pp. F12-F14. On the misleading coverage of fertility rates, see J. L. Stone, "Contextualizing Biogenetic and Reproductive Technologies," *Critical Studies in Mass Communication,* 8 (1991): 321.

45. Knapp, "Modern Miracles," p. A9.

46. K. Luker, *Taking Chances: Abortion and the Decision Not to Contracept* (Berkeley: University of California Press, 1975).

47. Widger, "Baby Craving," p. E13.

48. J. Downey & M. McKinney, "Psychiatric Research and the New Reproductive Technologies," in N. L. Stotland (Ed.), *Psychiatric Aspects of Reproductive Technologies* (Washington, DC: American Psychiatric Press, 1990): 158.

49. Lemonick, "Trying to Fool the Infertile," p. 53.

50. "At the Beginning," p. 6.

51. J. Whitlow, "Never Too Late," *Newark Star-Ledger,* October 26, 1990, p. G9.

52. It also has eugenic implications; see D. Nelkin, "The Social Power of Genetic Information," in D. J. Kevles & L. Hood (Eds.), *The Code of Codes: Scientific and Social Issues in the Human Genome Project* (Cambridge, MA: Howard University Press, 1992): 177-190. It is not clear how much impact this screening has had. Market forces encourage doctors to accept anyone who has the money and/or who is a physiologically good candidate for the procedure (so that success rates can look attractive). Clinicians, however, routinely asserted that they screened carefully so that they could rebut attacks from right-wing critics who asserted what they were doing is immoral. For other means of doctors' control see R. D. Klein, *Infertility: Women Speak Out About Their Experiences of Reproductive Medicine* (London: Pandora, 1989).

53. A. Schrader, "Hopes Linked to Frozen Embryo Use," *Denver Post,* September 11, 1989, p. G12. Quoted material used by permission.

24

Hysterectomies

Don't Ask "Why Not?" . . . Ask "Why?"

Cathey S. Ross

Hysterectomies are the second most frequently performed surgery in the United States, second only to cesarean sections. Between 650,000 and 675,000 hysterectomies are performed each year.[1] A report from The National Center for Health Statistics estimates that without changes in the current rates, the number of hysterectomies performed annually will rise as the baby-boom generation ages.[2] The Bureau of the Census predicts 783,000 such operations will be performed in 1995 and 824,000 in 2005.[3] If these trends continue, experts agree that 1 in 3 women can expect to receive a hysterectomy in her lifetime.[4] By age 60, 37% of women in the United States have had a hysterectomy, according to a report by the Rand Corporation.[5] One half of those hysterectomies were performed on women who are age 40 and younger.[6] This chapter examines the costs of this surgery for women and considers options to communicate to women in order to help inform their choices.

American women are 2 or 3 times as likely to receive a hysterectomy as are women in England.[7] A survey in several European countries found that hysterectomies were performed less often in Sweden than in England,[8] and the hysterectomy rate in England is less than one half of that in the United States. Disparities exist although no medical reasons have been found to account for the discrepancies.[9] Thus, U.S. women show no health gains from more aggressive treatment.[10]

More hysterectomies are performed in the southeastern United States than in any other region.[11] Indeed, a woman who lives in the southeastern part of the United States is more likely to receive a hysterectomy than is a woman who lives in the northeast.[12] The disparities in rates among countries and regions exist even though there is no evidence that uterine disease is significantly more common in one country or area than in another.[13]

A study conducted by the University of Maryland School of Medicine found that women with less education and lower incomes are more likely to receive a hysterectomy than women of higher education and greater incomes.[14] Kjerulff and her colleagues found that a woman with an income of less than $10,000 a year is more than 1½ times more likely to undergo a hysterectomy than is a woman with an annual income of $35,000 or more.[15] One legitimate reason for higher rates of hysterectomies among women of lower socioeconomic class is that these women are less likely to receive regular gynecological checkups, and actual medical problems are not as likely to be caught in early stages when hysterectomies can be avoided.[16] The University of Maryland study found no difference in hysterectomy rates due to race.

Since the 1970s, the rate of hysterectomies has come under attack by women's groups and health care associates. There has been some decline in percentage of procedures performed in the United States since the early 1970s, when a hysterectomy was likely to be performed for contraceptive reasons, though the absolute rates have leveled off.[17] Even so, numerous women *and* physicians are continuing to battle the established medical practice of performing hysterectomies regardless of the financial, physical, psychological, and emotional costs.

Hysterectomy Defined

What exactly is involved in the surgical procedure known as *hysterectomy?* In general terms, a hysterectomy is the removal of a woman's uterus or womb, the pear-shaped organ that contains and nourishes an embryo during pregnancy.[18] A total hysterectomy usually involves cutting away the cervix, which is the mouth of the womb, as well as the uterus, whereas a subtotal or partial hysterectomy leaves the cervix behind.[19] Often, a hysterectomy also involves removal of one of the ovaries, a procedure known as oophorectomy.[20] A bilateral oophorectomy results in the removal of both ovaries.[21] The surgical removal of both ovaries and the fallopian tubes (through which the egg travels on its way to the uterus) is called a bilateral salpingo-oophorectomy.[22] In medical circles, the removal of a woman's ovaries is referred to as female castration.[23]

A hysterectomy can be performed either through the abdomen or through the vagina. The majority of the operations are performed through the abdominal route.[24] This involves a midline incision either running down from the woman's navel or across the abdomen right below the pubic hairline. The operation can also be done through the vagina, however. The latter procedure is done less often, and there is some debate about which route is safest. The vaginal procedure will result in a faster recovery, in general, and there will be no visible scar.[25]

Regardless of whether the hysterectomy is performed through the abdomen or through the vagina, a hospital stay is involved. With vaginal surgery, the patient can expect to stay in the hospital 2 to 3 days, with complete recovery in 3 to 4 weeks.[26] For those women who have an abdominal hysterectomy, the hospital stay is anywhere from 5 to 7 days, with a 6- to 8-week recovery period.[27] Costs for hysterectomies vary across the United States with the average cost being between $4,400 and $4,900.[28]

Hysterectomy is a major surgery and, as such, carries with it the risks of major surgery. A 1981 study of hysterectomy in the United States commissioned by the Office of Technology Assessment, U.S. Congress, states that "anywhere from 62 percent to 81 percent of hysterectomy patients have been reported to develop some degree of morbidity [disease] after the operation."[29] Though the chance of death is small (about 1 in 1,000),[30] the number of hysterectomies performed each year is so large that the number of women who die is substantial. If the number of hysterectomies performed in 1995 reaches the 783,000 estimated by the Bureau of the Census, then 783 women might die as a result of hysterectomy that year.

According to a RAND report published in 1992, the two most frequently reported major complications of hysterectomy are bleeding and reoperation.[31] A review of 12 studies published in the 1970s and 1980s shows that 3% to 13% of patients undergoing hysterectomy receive blood transfusions, and that 1% to 5% of patients will have to have a reoperation to investigate uncontrolled hemorrhage or to repair bladder, bowel, or ureteral injuries.[32] These are just two of the possible immediate postoperative complications that result from hysterectomy. As will be seen in a later section of this chapter, there are other serious and debilitating aftereffects that a woman needs to be informed about as she considers this surgery.

Indications for Hysterectomy

Hysterectomies are performed for a variety of reasons. The three most common reasons for hysterectomies are fibroids, endometriosis, and prolapsed uterus.[33]

FIBROID TUMORS

Fibroids are benign (noncancerous) tumors that develop on the muscle tissue of the uterus. Fibroids are common; some experts believe that up to 50% of women will have fibroids at some time during their reproductive lives.[34] Large or numerous fibroids can cause a number of problems: abdominal extension, heavy menstrual bleeding and pain, pressure on the urinary tract or bowel, or infertility.[35] More than half of women with fibroids suffer no symptoms at all, however.[36] These women may not even be aware of the presence of the fibroid tumors except for their discovery by a gynecologist during a routine annual pelvic exam.[37] Only about 1 fibroid tumor in 1,000 is malignant.[38]

Many doctors believe that the only necessary treatment for fibroids that cause no symptoms is a regular examination to ensure that the fibroids are not growing too rapidly.[39] Fibroids, which grow in response to estrogen and shrink when estrogen levels decrease, shrink as a woman nears menopause, when the production of estrogen declines.[40] For those fibroids that do cause problems, abdominal extension, heavy menstrual bleeding and pain, pressure on the urinary tract or bowel, or infertility, treatment remains quite controversial. Yet at this time, fibroids remain the number one reason for hysterectomies, accounting for about 27% of the hysterectomies performed in the United States yearly.[41]

ENDOMETRIOSIS

Endometriosis, the second most common reason hysterectomies are performed in the United States, is a condition wherein tissue identical to the uterus lining begins forming on other surfaces such as the fallopian tubes, the ovaries, or the surface of the bowels.[42] Because the tissue mimics the tissue of the uterine lining, each month it bleeds in response to hormonal changes just as the uterus does. This tissue also produces the hormones responsible for causing the uterus to contract. In some women, this action results in menstrual pain, which can be experienced at the sites of the misplaced tissue during menstrual periods.[43]

Endometriosis is not malignant, but for many women it is very painful and can cause infertility. Research findings differ, but general estimates are that from 50% to 90% of women with endometriosis will experience some pain.[44] Between 15% and 50% of infertile women have endometriosis.[45] A recent study of women who had endometriosis found no pain occurred in up to 45% of the patients, depending on the stage of the disease.[46] Hysterectomy remains the treatment of choice for some physicians even in women who are presenting no symptoms with endometriosis. Again, there are treatments now recognized by many doctors as effective alternatives to hysterectomies performed to eliminate endometriosis.

PROLAPSED UTERUS

The third most common reason for hysterectomies is a prolapsed uterus or "dropped womb," which may result from damage to supporting muscles and ligaments.[47] Twenty-one percent of hysterectomies performed from 1970 through 1984 were for prolapse.[48] Although heredity is thought to be a factor, prolapse usually comes from damage during pregnancy and childbirth. In many cases, the prolapse is so severe that the uterus actually sags from the vagina and causes discomfort. Up to 50% of women may have some evidence of prolapse, but unless the condition is uncomfortable, treatment may not be necessary.[49] Even when discomfort is a factor, a hysterectomy may not be the best treatment. Once the uterus is removed, other organs can shift, leading to prolapse of the vagina or of the bladder or bowel, conditions that are difficult to correct surgically.[50]

OTHER INDICATIONS FOR HYSTERECTOMY

Other conditions that often lead to hysterectomies are complaints of heavy bleeding and pelvic pain.[51] Heavy bleeding, which can be a result of fibroids or endometriosis, is also associated with hormonal imbalance.[52] Pelvic pain can arise from endometriosis or fibroids, but may be a result of ovarian cysts or of pelvic infection.[53] Pelvic inflammatory disease (PID), which can cause pain and infertility, is a generic term used for infections in the uterus, ovaries, fallopian tubes, or pelvic peritoneum.[54]

Cancer of any reproductive organ is almost always an indication for a hysterectomy, but only about 10% of hysterectomies are performed because of malignant conditions.[55] In addition, a diagnosis of cancer does not necessarily call for radical surgery. Cancer, if caught in its earliest stages, may be responsive to more conservative treatments.[56] Nearly 90% of the hysterectomies performed in the United States are for conditions that are not life-threatening.[57] Hysterectomies, then, are not usually performed to save a woman's life. Thus, physicians offer hysterectomies to women as a means of improving women's "quality" of life.[58] The question becomes whether doctors define quality of life in the same ways women do.

Outcomes of Hysterectomy

Many women and physicians are now speaking out against unnecessary hysterectomies. As indicated, women who have this surgery will suffer immediate financial costs, as well as (work) time lost while in the hospital and at home recovering. They may also suffer immediate complications from the surgery itself. What many physicians do not tell women, and in fact *some physicians do not even acknowledge,* is that there are a number of serious long-term effects that are now known to result when a woman's body enters abrupt menopause as a result of removal of the ovaries. Even when a woman has a hysterectomy where the ovaries are retained, there are potential adverse effects: There is now evidence that the uterus may have functions outside of the obvious reproductive role.[59] Women should be informed about these possibilities when making decisions about hysterectomy, but too often they are not. To date, no public campaigns aim to increase women's understanding and, again, physicians are often the advocates rather than the adversaries of the procedure.

The ovaries produce the hormones estrogen and progesterone, which we now know are important to a woman apart from their roles in the reproductive cycle.[60] The ovaries also produce testosterone, commonly thought of as male hormones. These hormones are thought to be particularly important in a woman's sexual desire.[61] "When the ovaries are removed or slow down hormone production, a woman's testosterone level may drop by a third. Many women, though not all, require the full quotient of testosterone to feel sexy."[62]

In women who do not have a hysterectomy, the process of menopause is a gradual one and thus the hormone production slows down gradually.[63] When the ovaries as well as the uterus are removed during surgery, however, a woman experiences premature menopause, a sudden and dramatic cessation of hormone production. Loss of hormones can lead to hot flashes and mood swings, as well as bone density loss and loss of protection against heart disease.[64] Numerous studies have documented the effects of early menopause (i.e., from surgery) on women. One study found that women who had their ovaries removed and who had not taken replacement sex hormones had lost 20% of their spinal bone mass *within 2 years!*[65] Calcium supplements alone cannot fight the disease, because a woman's body cannot use the calcium to build up the bones unless estrogen is present.[66]

The largest portion of deaths of women in the United States results from cardiovascular disease.[67] The Framingham Study, which looked at a large population of healthy individuals as they matured, found in their investigation of approximately 8,500 premenopausal person-years' experience that no premenopausal women had a heart attack or died as the result of coronary heart disease. Yet such events were common among postmenopausal women.[68] Another study found that women who had undergone surgery to remove both ovaries had *more than twice* the incidence of coronary heart disease as compared to women who had not had both ovaries surgically removed.[69]

> By the late 1980s, an array of cardiovascular health deficits after hysterectomy have been documented. The situation is very much like the one that exists for women's bones after hysterectomy. Ovarian failure and the loss of estrogen secretion triggers most of the changes. With increasing time after a natural menopause, there tends to be an increased incidence of hypertension and other cardiovascular diseases, but after a surgical menopause, the increase is much worse.[70]

In addition to the physical problems that some women experience as a result of a hysterectomy, many women are now talking about the change in their sex drive and in their general sense of well-being after such surgery. Although there are studies that conclude that depression and psychological problems are no greater in hysterectomized women than in women who have not had hysterectomies,[71] other studies conclude otherwise.[72] There may be physiological results from hysterectomy that could lead to sexual dysfunction as well as to depression.

Estrogen, the important hormone produced by the ovaries, is known to play a role in enhancing a woman's sexual desire as well as her mood in general.[73] Loss of libido may come about due to the loss of not only estrogen but also of the androgen hormones, which are found in greater quantities in men but are also present in women. Sherwin and Gelfand found that women who had received both estrogen and androgen after complete hysterectomy reported higher rates of sexual desire, sexual arousal, and number of fantasies than women who had either been given estrogen alone or who were untreated.[74]

Even if a woman has a partial hysterectomy and loses only her uterus, she may be losing more than she bargained for. Scientists are still making discoveries about the functioning of the uterus outside of reproduction. In about 50% of premenopausal women who retain their ovaries after having the uterus removed, the ovaries stop cycling.[75] The uterus, therefore, may play a significant role in keeping the ovaries healthy and functioning. The uterus produces two important groups of chemicals: (a) beta endorphins, which are also produced in the brain and which are the body's natural painkillers, produce a mild euphoria and sense of well-being; and (b) prostaglandins, which serve a variety of functions.[76] The second group of chemicals causes contractions of smooth muscles and may play a protective role against heart disease because of their role in preventing blood clotting.[77] Thus, the physical changes resulting from loss of the uterus and ovaries can impact physical *and* emotional well-being. As Cutler concludes about the interrelated contributions of the various parts of a woman's body, *"it is naive to believe it possible to remove any of them with impunity."*[78]

Although many women immediately begin hormone replacement therapy (HRT) to counteract the body's loss of the hormone(s) estrogen and perhaps progesterone, that route is not trouble free.[79] The replacement hormones are synthetic substitutes. Though they may provide some help in working for the body as the natural hormones did, they are not totally successful. Finding the right combination of hormones is not easy. Hormones are complex, and many women have gone from doctor to doctor trying to find the right combination for themselves. Some women also find that they are unable to take the synthetic substitutes. Moreover, there is some evidence that HRT leads to increases in a woman's chance of having breast cancer, as well as causing some preexisting cancers to grow.[80] The research on the effects of HRT on cancer are contradictory. As I reviewed the research for this chapter, I was struck by the mixed and often confusing findings in this area, which may help to explain why there are so few messages available for women from public or professional sources. We do not yet know what to say. Some studies have shown a strikingly consistent relationship between HRT and breast cancer, but others have found no clear relationship.[81] As Goldfarb and Greif conclude in *The No-Hysterectomy Option* concerning estrogen, "May increase chance of breast cancer; extremely controversial"![82] So women who receive hysterectomies are left with tough choices, including whether to take hormones and the increased chances of some kinds of cancer, or to forgo the hormones and suffer increased risk of osteoporosis and heart disease as well as loss of sexual desire and of general feelings of well-being.

Some Alternatives to Hysterectomy

A number of alternatives to hysterectomy are now available to women, but a woman may have to rely on her own research to uncover this information as no campaigns are available to inform women about alternatives, and physicians seldom select to address these choices. Sophisticated diagnostic procedures now allow physicians to make determinations about the causes of presenting complaints. Hysteroscopy, a low-risk procedure wherein a fiber-optic scope is inserted into the uterus via the cervix, and laparoscopy, where the fiber-optic scope is inserted through the navel to view the internal organs, are now used so that physicians can actually see into the uterus and look for problems.[83] Ultrasound, CAT, and MRI are now available to doctors for help in diagnosis of problems in the female organs. Ultrasound (sonogram) utilizes the emission of intermittent high-frequency sound waves to provide a picture of the size, shape, and any irregularities of the uterus and ovaries.[84] CAT, computerized axial tomography, is a specialized form of x ray, and MRIs are magnetic resonance imaging, which relies on a powerful magnet rather than x rays to examine body tissue.[85] These diagnostic procedures, as well as treatments for a number of the gynecological problems experienced by women, provide alternatives that women may choose rather than undergoing hysterectomy.

For fibroid tumors, a myomectomy, a surgical procedure that results in the removal of the fibroid tumors without removal of the uterus, can be conducted.[86] Depending on the number, size, and location of the fibroids, a myomectomy may be a longer, more complicated, and thus riskier, procedure than hysterectomy.[87] For this reason, some traditional surgeons do not recommend a myomectomy and continue to advocate a hysterectomy, especially for those women for whom childbearing is not a consideration. A hysterectomy does take care of the problem of fibroids, and for some surgeons, a myomectomy is technically more difficult than a hysterectomy. With a myomectomy, there is a slightly higher death rate and greater blood loss.[88] In addition, fibroids can recur, but 60% to 97% of the time patients need no further treatment.[89] Most informed gynecologists now agree that with modern techniques and surgeon training, the problems associated with myomectomy can be averted. Regardless of a woman's childbearing plans, good reasons exist for arguing in favor of retaining the uterus until menopause when fibroids usually go away on their own as their supply of estrogen is depleted.

Laser techniques are also now being used to remove fibroid tumors as well as endometrium tissue.[90] The lining of the uterus can be completely removed using a technique called laser ablation.[91] This results in complete sterilization, so it is not a technique that women who want to have more children should pursue. Its advantages include that it is a bloodless surgery, is an extremely precise way of destruction and cutting of tissue, allows the physician to reach otherwise inaccessible areas, and allows for preservation of more normal tissue than does traditional surgery.[92] It does not affect the ovaries, so it does not induce premature menopause. Some physicians do not recommend laser surgery for women who have suspicious tissue found during a diagnostic hysteroscopy. Theoretically, a woman who has had her blood vessels destroyed through laser surgery and who then develops endometrial cancer will not bleed from the cancer, thus removing an important symptom of cancer.[93] In cases where there is limited endometriosis, the aberrant tissue can be removed by using a laparoscope or a hysteroscope.[94]

Female reconstructive surgery, wherein all of the ligaments and organs in the pelvic cavity are restructured and lifted with complete resuspension and correction of the prolapse, can correct uterine prolapse.[95] A nonsurgical means of treating prolapse is to insert a plastic or metal ring around the cervix to help prop up the uterus. The drawback of such a device is that it is inconvenient, because it must be removed for intercourse and periodic cleaning.[96] For women who want to have children, the device is another means of postponing surgery.

If hormonal imbalance is found to be the cause of heavy bleeding, the use of estrogen and progesterone, either individually or in combination, can help restore hormonal balance.[97] Dilation and curettage (D&C), wherein the cervix is dilated and the lining of the uterus is scraped away, can be useful in diagnosis and sometimes in curing heavy bleeding.[98]

As we have seen, presently there are reliable and effective alternative treatments to most of the problems that have in previous years resulted in hysterectomies, and the evidence is clear; hysterectomy is not a benign surgery for all women. Some women experience slight or even no problems, but thousands of women experience problems that may be life-changing ones.

Despite the repeated warnings against unnecessary hysterectomies and despite the medical advances that now offer effective alternative treatments to women with complaints, the operation is still being performed at rates that are alarming to women's groups as well as physicians.

Why Hysterectomy
Is Still So Prevalent

Cheryl Brown Travis offers four hypotheses as possible explanations for the high incidence of hysterectomies.[99] The fee-for-service hypothesis focuses on the economic impact of surgeries. Some experts suggest there is an economic incentive behind the incidence of hysterectomies.[100] A correlation appears to exist between the number of surgeons in a region and the incidence of surgery, with more surgeons generally resulting in more surgeries.[101] The costs of running a medical practice are immense.[102] Hysterectomies may be seen by some physicians as a means of providing additional income.[103]

Travis's second hypothesis deals with the patterns of training for surgical residents. Physicians are likely to use the procedures they are trained in.[104] Unfortunately, many training institutions still teach hysterectomy as a cure for most women's ailments. The newer techniques that are now available for dealing with most of the problems (laser technology and myomectomy, for example) require specific training and skills. Many physicians are not trained in those procedures and, therefore, do not offer them as options to their patients.[105]

The third hypothesis offered by Travis suggests that sexism and racism may explain the high incidence of hysterectomies.[106] The power struggles and social norms of a culture impact the medical and health care communities. Travis explains,

> The health care women receive is a product of their social status in general. The respect and autonomy accorded to others are denied to women in general and minority women in

particular. These arguments are supported by analyses of the treatment women receive in gynecology textbooks, anecdotal surveys among medical students, and the fact that women have historically been denied admission to medical schools.[107]

The lack of research in the general area of women's health issues is also evidence in support of the social norms hypothesis.[108] Because many of the diseases that cause women problems are not life threatening, they do not hold much fascination for researchers. Without research to investigate diseases specific to women, numerous questions go unanswered.[109]

Travis's final explanation for the number of unnecessary hysterectomies focuses on the elimination of the threat of cancer as a result of the surgery. Even though the performance of hysterectomies for protection against cancer is being repeatedly rejected by experts, Travis concludes that, "The fact that it has been repeatedly questioned in the professional literature suggests that it continues to be a major factor in decision making with respect to elective hysterectomies."[110]

In hysterectomy, physicians have an answer to their patients' complaints. Many of the problems women have with their reproductive organs are complex. Finding the right treatment may often be a matter of trial and error. Meanwhile, the patient continues to experience the pain and discomfort that has initially brought her to her gynecologist. When gynecologists perform a hysterectomy, they have done something. It is a definitive step that is supposed to take care of the presenting complaint. The fact that the surgery may lead to even more complaints, many of which are more serious than the original one, is something that can be dismissed.

Finally, it is important to acknowledge that some women suffer few if any adverse effects as a result of a hysterectomy. Though thousands of women are speaking out now about their negative experiences with hysterectomies, some women say that after hysterectomies they have never felt better. One recent study found a general decrease in a sample of women's scores on the Hamilton Depression Scale and the Zung Self-Rating Depression Scale over the year following a hysterectomy.[111] Women who face the prospect of a hysterectomy must have all of the information if they are to make the best decision for their own bodies.

What Women Can and Should Do

One of the best ways to curb unnecessary surgeries in general is to get a second opinion. One study of 1,698 women insured through a major insurance carrier that required second opinions for elective hysterectomies found that 135 of the women were not confirmed for the surgery.[112] Another study of a second opinion program in New York concluded that not only did second opinions result in savings for such high-volume surgeries as hysterectomy, but patients were more comfortable with their decisions.[113] Patients have reported being grateful for mandatory second opinion insurance programs, because under those programs it does not appear as if the patients do not trust their doctors if they go for a second opinion.[114]

In addition to getting second opinions, women must *be willing to ask questions and be persistent about getting answers.* Many people, especially women, are reluctant to question their doctors or to ask for a second opinion. But information is one of the major weapons women have against needless surgery, and they should demand a doctor who will take the time to explain thoroughly their conditions and the pros and cons of all alternative treatments. Maureen Porter has conducted a number of studies of doctor-client relationships and women's reproductive health care in Great Britain.[115] She has found that in all of the settings she studied, "The amount of information given out by doctors and knowledge of the working of women's bodies shared with them are still minimal."[116] Why?

Porter found that relatively few women ask questions even though they have questions. Doctors often said that patients would not take in or understand what is explained to them. Many doctors also suggested that the majority of patients have no wish to know the details of their medical condition.[117] Porter concludes by contending that the medical domination of women's lives and lifestyles in Great Britain is increasing.

If this is the case in Great Britain where the incidence of hysterectomy is half that of the United States, we can only assume that the state of sharing of information and decision making in the United States is equally meager, if not worse. The best defense against unnecessary hysterectomy remains knowledge and persistence. Part of that persistence must be a woman's willingness to speak out about her own personal experience with hysterectomy.

Notes

1. G. Maleskey & C. B. Inlander, *Take This Book to the Gynecologist With You: A Consumer's Guide to Women's Health* (Reading, MA: Addison-Wesley, 1991): 106.

2. R. Pokras & V. Hufnagel, "Hysterectomies in the United States, 1965-1984," in *Vital and Health Statistics* 13(92) (Washington, DC: Government Printing Office, 1987): 1-16.

3. U.S. Bureau of the Census, "Projections of the Population of the United States, by Age, Sex, and Race: 1983 to 2080," in *Current Population Reports* P-25 (U.S. Bureau of the Census, Ed.) (Washington, DC: Government Printing Office, 1984).

4. R. Pokras, "Hysterectomy: Past, Present and Future," *Statistical Bulletin* 70(4) (1989): 12-21.

5. S. J. Bernstein, E. A. McGlynn, C. J. Kamberg, M. R. Chassin, G. A. Goldberg, A. L. Siu, & R. H. Brook, *Hysterectomy: A Literature Review and Ratings of Appropriateness* (Santa Monica, CA: RAND, 1992): 4.

6. Bernstein et al., *Hysterectomy,* p. 4.

7. A. Coulter, K. McPherson, & M. Vessey, "Do British Women Undergo too Many or too Few Hysterectomies," *Social Science Medicine* 27 (1988): 987-994.

8. Coulter et al., "Do British Women," pp. 987-994.

9. J. P. Bunker, "Surgical Manpower: A Comparison of Operations and Surgeons in the United States and in England and Wales," *The New England Journal of Medicine* 282(3) (1970): 135-144.

10. H. A. Goldfarb & J. Greif, *The No-Hysterectomy Option: Your Body—Your Choice* (New York: John Wiley, 1990): 16.

11. Pokras & Hufnagel, "Hysterectomies in the United States," pp. 1-16.

12. Pokras & Hufnagel, "Hysterectomies in the United States," p. 8.

13. Goldfarb & Greif, *The No-Hysterectomy Option,* p. 16.

14. K. Kjerulff, P. Langenberg, & G. Guzinski, "The Socioeconomic Correlates of Hysterectomies in the United States," *American Journal of Public Health* 83(1) (1993): 106-108.

15. Kjerulff et al., "The Socioeconomic Correlates," pp. 107-108.

16. Kjerulff et al., "The Socioeconomic Correlates," p. 108.

17. Pokras & Hufnagel, "Hysterectomies in the United States," pp. 1-16.

18. Goldfarb & Greif, *The No-Hysterectomy Option,* p. 186.

19. S. M. Wolfe & R. D. Jones, "Hysterectomy: The Myth of Cures by Cutting," in *Women's Health Alert* (Reading, MA: Addison-Wesley, 1991): 46-72.

20. Wolfe & Jones, "Hysterectomy," p. 49.

21. Wolfe & Jones, "Hysterectomy," p. 49.

22. Wolfe & Jones, "Hysterectomy," p. 49.

23. N. M. Stokes, *The Castrated Woman: What Your Doctor Won't Tell You About Hysterectomy* (New York: Franklin Watts, 1986): 85.

24. W. B. Cutler, *Hysterectomy: Before and After, a Comprehensive Guide to Preventing, Preparing for, and Maximizing Health After Hysterectomy* (New York: Harper & Row, 1988): 108.

25. Goldfarb and Greif, *The No-Hysterectomy Option,* p. 188.

26. B. D. Shepherd & C. A. Shepherd, *The Complete Guide to Women's Health* (New York: Plume, 1990): 300-301.

27. V. Hufnagel, *No More Hysterectomies* (New York: New American Library, 1988): 28.

28. "Variations in Hysterectomy Costs by Region," *Statistical Bulletin* 66(3) (1985): 10-17.

29. C. Korenbrot, A. B. Flood, M. Higgins, N. Roos, & J. P. Bunker, "Case Study #15: Elective Hysterectomy: Costs, Risks, and Benefits; Background Paper #2: Case Studies of Medical Technologies," in Office of Technology Assessment (Ed.), *The Implications of Cost-Effectiveness Analysis of Medical Technology* (Washington, DC: Government Printing Office, 1981): 9.

30. Pokras & Hufnagel, "Hysterectomies in the United States," pp. 1-16.

31. Bernstein et al., *Hysterectomy,* p. 38.

32. Bernstein et al., *Hysterectomy,* p. 38.

33. Pokras & Hufnagel, "Hysterectomies in the United States," pp. 1-16.

34. S. S. Entman, "Uterine Leiomyoma and Adenomyosis," in *Novak's Textbook of Gynecology,* 11th ed. (Baltimore, MD: Williams & Wilkins, 1988): 443.

35. Goldfarb & Greif, *The No-Hysterectomy Option,* p. 62.

36. Bernstein et al., *Hysterectomy,* p. 20.

37. Hufnagel, *No More Hysterectomies,* p. 46.

38. A. Ranard, "The "Good" Problem," *Health* 22 (1990): 66-69.

39. T. H. Green, Jr., *Gynecology: Essentials of Clinical Practice,* 2nd ed. (Boston: Little, Brown, 1971).

40. Green, *Gynecology.*

41. Pokras & Hufnagel, "Hysterectomies in the United States," p. 2.

42. Goldfarb & Greif, *The No-Hysterectomy Option,* p. 251.

43. V. R. Tindall, *Jeffcoate's Principles of Gynecology,* 5th ed. (London: Butterworths, 1987).

44. Bernstein et al., *Hysterectomy,* p. 8.

45. Bernstein et al., *Hysterectomy,* p. 7.

46. T. Fukaya, H. Hoshiai, & A. Yajima, "Is Pelvic Endometriosis Always Associated With Chronic Pain? A Retrospective Study of 618 Cases Diagnosed by Laparoscopy," *American Journal of Obstetrics and Gynecology* 169 (1993): 719-722.

47. Pokras & Hufnagel, "Hysterectomies in the United States," p. 11.

48. Pokras & Hufnagel, "Hysterectomies in the United States," p. 11.

49. N. G. Kase & A. B. Weingold (Eds.), *Principles and Practice of Clinical Gynecology* (New York: John Wiley, 1983).

50. Goldfarb & Greif, *The No-Hysterectomy Option,* p. 127.

51. Bernstein et al., *Hysterectomy,* pp. 18, 23.

52. Goldfarb & Greif, *The No-Hysterectomy Option,* pp. 97-103.

53. Bernstein et al., *Hysterectomy,* p. 23.

54. Bernstein et al., *Hysterectomy,* p. 31.

55. Pokras & Hufnagel, "Hysterectomies in the United States," pp. 1-16.

56. M. Coppleson, "Management of Preclinical Carcinoma of the Cervix," in J. A. Jordon & A. Singer (Eds.), *Cervix Uteri* (London: W. B. Saunders, 1976).

57. Wolfe & Jones, "Hysterectomy: The Myth," p. 52.

58. S. I. Sandberg, B. A. Barnes, M. C. Weinstein, & P. Braun, "Elective Hysterectomy: Benefits, Risks, and Costs," *Medical Care* 23 (1985): 1067-1085.

59. L. Zussman, S. Zussman, R. Sunley, & E. Bjornson, "Sexual Response After Hysterectomy-Oophorectomy: Recent Studies and Reconsideration of Psychogenesis," *American Journal of Obstetrics and Gynecology* 140 (1981): 725-729.

60. Maleskey & Inlander, *Take This Book to the Gynecologist,* pp. 121-130.

61. B. B. Sherwin & M. M. Gelfand, "The Role of Androgen in the Maintenance of Sexual Functioning in Oophorectomized Women," *Psychosomatic Medicine* 49 (1987): 397-409.

62. J. Talan, "The Male Hormone Is a Female Hormone, Too," *American Health* 10 (1991): 18.

63. G. Sheehy, *The Silent Passage* (New York: Random House, 1991).

64. Sheehy, *The Silent Passage.*

65. H. K. Genant & C. E. Cann, "Vertebral Mineral Determination Using Quantitative Computed Tomography," in H. F. DeLuca, H. M. Frost, W.S.S. Jee, C. C. Johnston, & A. M. Parfitt (Eds.), *Osteoporosis: Recent Advances in Pathogenesis and Treatment* (Baltimore, MD: University Park Press, 1981): 37-47.

66. Maleskey & Inlander, *Take This Book to the Gynecologist,* p. 125.

67. Cutler, *Hysterectomy: Before and After,* p. 4.

68. T. Gordon, W. Kannel, M. Hjortland, & P. McNamara, "Menopause and Coronary Heart Disease: The Framingham Study," *Annals of Internal Medicine* 89 (1978): 157-161.

69. G. Colditz, W. Willett, M. Stampfer, B. Rosner, F. Speizer, & C. Hennekens, "Menopause and the Risk of Coronary Heart Disease in Women," *The New England Journal of Medicine* 316 (1987): 1105-1110.

70. Cutler, *Hysterectomy: Before and After,* p. 206.

71. M. J. Gitlin & R. O. Pasnau, "Psychiatric Syndromes Linked to Reproductive Function in Women: A Review of Current Knowledge," *American Journal of Psychiatry* 146 (1989): 1413-1422.

72. Zussman et al., "Sexual Response After Hysterectomy-Oophorectomy," pp. 725-729.

73. Cutler, *Hysterectomy: Before and After,* p. 126.

74. Sherwin & Gelfand, "The Role of Androgen," pp. 397-409.

75. Cutler, *Hysterectomy: Before and After,* p. 33.

76. Cutler, *Hysterectomy: Before and After,* pp. 256-259.

77. Goldfarb & Greif, *The No-Hysterectomy Option,* p. 34.

78. Cutler, *Hysterectomy: Before and After,* p. 8.

79. Cutler, *Hysterectomy: Before and After,* pp. 121-144.

80. Wolfe & Jones, "Hormone Replacement Therapy," pp. 198-200.

81. P. A. Wingo, P. M. Layde, N. C. Lee, G. Rubin, & H. W. Ory, "The Risk of Breast Cancer in Postmenopausal Women Who Have Used Estrogen Replacement Therapy," *Journal of the American Medical Association* 257 (1987): 209-215.

82. Goldfarb & Greif, *The No-Hysterectomy Option,* p. 193.

83. I. K. Strausz, *You Don't Need a Hysterectomy: New and Effective Ways of Avoiding Major Surgery* (Reading, MA: Addison-Wesley, 1993): 159-166.

84. R. Andreotti, N. Zusmer, J. Sheldon, & M. Ames, "Ultrasound and Magnetic Resonance Imaging of Pelvic Masses," *Surgery, Gynecology and Obstetrics* 166 (1988): 327-332.

85. Strausz, *You Don't Need a Hysterectomy,* pp. 79-80.

86. Cutler, *Hysterectomy: Before and After,* p. 90.

87. Wolfe & Jones, "Hysterectomy: The Myth," p. 55.

88. Goldfarb & Greif, *The No-Hysterectomy Option,* p. 48.

89. C. R. Garcia & R. W. Tureck, "Submucosal Leiomyomas and Infertility," *Fertility and Sterility* 42 (1984): 16-19.

90. Goldfarb & Greif, *The No-Hysterectomy Option,* p. 58.

91. Goldfarb & Greif, *The No-Hysterectomy Option,* p. 58.

92. A. P. Chong & M. S. Baggish, "Management of Pelvic Endometriosis by Means of Intraabdominal Carbon Dioxide Laser," *Fertility and Sterility* 41(1) (1984): 14-19.

93. Goldfarb & Greif, *The No-Hysterectomy Option,* p. 60.

94. W. B. Norment, "The Hysteroscope," *American Journal of Obstetrics and Gynecology* 71 (1956): 426-432.

95. Hufnagel, *No More Hysterectomies,* p. 152.

96. H. H. Keyser, *Women Under the Knife: A Gynecologist's Report on Hazardous Medicine* (Philadelphia: George F. Stickley, 1984): 43-44.

97. Wolfe & Jones, *Women's Health Alert,* p. 63.

98. Wolfe & Jones, *Women's Health Alert,* p. 63.

99. C. B. Travis, "Medical Decision Making and Elective Surgery: The Case of Hysterectomy," *Risk Analysis* 5 (1985): 241-251.

100. Keyser, *Women Under the Knife,* pp. 50-51.

101. J. Wennberg & A. Gittelsohn, "Variations in Medical Care Among Small Areas," *Scientific American* 246(4) (1982): 120-135.

102. Keyser, *Women Under the Knife,* p. 50.

103. Keyser, *Women Under the Knife,* p. 110.

104. J. E. Wennberg, "Factors Governing Utilization of Hospital Services," *Hospital Practice* 14 (1979): 115-127.

105. Wolfe & Jones, "Hysterectomy: The Myth," p. 55.

106. Travis, "Medical Decision Making," pp. 241-251.

107. Travis, "Medical Decision Making," pp. 248-249.

108. Ranard, "The "Good" Problem," pp. 66-69.

109. Bernstein et al., *Hysterectomy,* p. 4.

110. Travis, "Medical Decision Making," p. 249.

111. M. Lalinec-Michaud, F. Engelsmann, & J. Marino, "Depression After Hysterectomy: A Comparative Study," *Psychosomatics* 29 (1988): 307-314.

112. M. L. Finkel & D. J. Finkel, "The Effect of a Second Opinion Program on Hysterectomy Performance," *Medical Care* 28 (1990): 776-783.

113. J. K. Barr, M. Schachter, S. N. Rosenberg, P. Factor-Litvak, M. R. McGarvey, & L. Leto, "Procedure-Specific Costs and Savings in a Mandatory Program for Second Opinion on Surgery," *Quality Review Bulletin* 16(1) (1990): 25-32.

114. Keyser, *Women Under the Knife,* p. 12.

115. M. Porter, "Professional-Client Relationships and Women's Reproductive Health Care," in S. Cunningham-Burley & N. P. McKeganey (Eds.), *Readings in Medical Sociology* (New York: Tavistock/Routledge, 1990): 182-210.

116. Porter, "Professional-Client Relationships," p. 198.

117. Porter, "Professional-Client Relationships," p. 209.

25

Hysterectomy

What the Popular Press Said (1986-1992)

E.M.I. Sefcovic

The first hysterectomy reportedly was performed by the ancient Greek physician, Archigenes, in the first century A.D., but the procedure was not widely practiced until anesthesia was introduced in 1846. After that, the hysterectomy rate rose wildly. Hysterectomy was touted as a cure for everything from overeating to insanity, and from lustfulness to sour personality. One medical historian estimated that only 100 hysterectomies were performed in all human history up to that time, whereas between 1846 and 1878, a single physician boasted of removing the uterus and ovaries from 400 women.[1]

During the early 1970s, feminist challenges to the high hysterectomy rate made "news" and were reported in the mass media. This outcry of public sentiment may have contributed to a 20% drop in the rate during the mid-1970s.[2] Since then, however, even

AUTHOR'S NOTE: Celeste M. Condit is thanked for providing the framework of questions and focus for this chapter and for her considerable assistance throughout this project.

continued exposure of U.S. women to newspaper and magazine articles, as well as books, that caution conservatism and promote alternatives has done nothing to produce any additional reduction in the hysterectomy rate.

Hysterectomy, as the previous chapter indicates, is implicated in a variety of complications and negative side effects that can adversely affect the individual patient. This chapter will describe the messages that the popular press purveyed between 1986 and 1992 about hysterectomy, alternative treatments, and women's role as consumers of health care and health technologies. Published newspaper and magazine articles were found using *Newspapers Abstracts, NewsBank, Infotrac,* and *The Readers' Guide to Periodical Literature.* Books were located by using the University of Georgia, Athens, library; procuring books mentioned in articles; perusing library and bookstore shelves; and tracking down leads conveyed through personal communications. Almost everything was read (a less daunting task than it sounds), and several questions guide the review: (a) Who is the authority? Physician? Patient? Others? (b) How are the side effects of hysterectomy presented, if at all? (c) How are new procedures presented? (d) What are the woman's responsibilities in making a choice?

Media and Messages

Discussions of hysterectomy by popular media are characterized by two approaches: general discussion of hysterectomy, or the introduction of a new technology. Whether the topic is presented in a newspaper, magazine, or book influences the way information is treated. For example, in newspaper articles, members of the medical establishment are presented as the experts through the extensive use of quotations and paraphrased attribution. This is a style inherent to the nature of news gathering and "reporting." Books are usually written by experts—gynecologists, medical researchers, or other presumably qualified writers—and present much information without attribution to other sources, establishing the author as the expert. Because of these media-constrained presentational choices, this discussion focuses on each medium in turn.

What is generally striking about popularly published information on hysterectomy between 1986 and 1992 is how little there is of it. Here is a procedure that is variously the most performed, or second most performed, surgery in the United States. Yet over 6 years, the major newspaper indexes revealed only 36 articles related to hysterectomy. In addition, there were 13 magazine articles. Six books intended for popular consumption were identified.[3] In some general books about women's health issues, the subject of hysterectomy did not appear at all, or occupied only a page or two. This vast silence about an operation that approximately 1 in every 3 American women is expected to undergo by age 60 says much about the lack of importance of female health care issues in our society. Hysterectomy has been called "female castration," and we may wonder if the mass print media would be so silent if 1 in every 3 men could expect to undergo loss of important sexual organs by retirement age.

NEWSPAPERS

With only three dozen articles relating to hysterectomy appearing in major newspaper indexes over 6 years, it is clear that a woman who relies on her hometown paper for information will remain largely uninformed. This dearth of information is startling because several newsworthy "angles" on the subject were current during this period: (a) new technologies for the treatment of endometriosis and fibroids (traditional indicators for the procedure) were developed, including endometrial ablation and drug therapies; (b) hysterectomy surgery was updated with new technologies using fiber optics and the hysteroscope; (c) insurance companies instigated investigations into the nation's high hysterectomy rate; (d) and California passed a law requiring physicians to fully disclose possible side effects of hysterectomy and possible alternatives. The Oregon legislature, too, considered such a law but scuttled it after medical groups developed educational materials for hysterectomy candidates. Whether other states enjoined the issue is unknown because of the lack of newspaper coverage. The point is, newspaper editors cannot explain away the lack of attention to this topic by saying that the high rate is long-standing and simply not "news."

Of the articles recovered, 11 related to new techniques; 3 discussed hysterectomy and alternative treatments for fibroids; 7, including an article that used insurance carrier investigation as the angle, covered hysterectomy in general and alternatives; 5 were published interview articles (4 with book authors, 1 with the founder of Hysterectomy Educational Resources and Services [HERS]—Nora Coffey); 1 was about a hysterectomy support group; 3 discussed hysterectomy rates; and 5 fall in none of these categories.[4] As previously noted, newspaper articles constructed outside sources as experts. This is their job. Even large newspapers, such as the *New York Times,* the *Los Angeles Times,* and the *Washington Post,* relied on quotations from physicians (typically, in local papers, area practitioners rather than those with national reputations), patients, book authors, and consumer groups as the sources of authority. The interview articles articulated the opinion of the interviewees without critical assessment or opposing testimony; all interviewees took a negative view of hysterectomy. The fact that the interviewees' challenge to hysterectomy was considered newsworthy substantiates the dominance of the view that hysterectomy is "normal" for aging women.

Articles discussing new technologies were the most problematic in their construction of authority, because they usually portrayed these innovations with the guileless welcome that typifies modern society's relation to science. Three techniques achieved this effect: enthusiastic language; glowing testimonials; and "burying" questions about risks, research, and side effects late in the article, often on the jump page, which may very well go unread.

A *San Antonio Express* article is an example of this kind of boosterism.[5] The headline proclaimed, "Surgery for Menstrual Stress," which turned out to be endometrial ablation. Although stress is a pervasive evil in our society, the implication that women's stress is related to female biological processes and curable through medical intervention contextualizes a normal bodily function as an illness. This may affect both the acceptance of the procedure and the widespread social perception of women as diseased and dysfunctional. For example, the article presented a testimonial from an office worker who underwent the procedure even though she was not experiencing any menstrual problems. She explained that she does not want to bother with monthly ovulation any longer and is delighted with the results of the operation. The procedure was briefly explained by two male physicians. A female gynecologist warned that, "Nature knows best, and we have to be careful about tampering with these things." But the warning occurred on the jump page, while the lead paragraph assured that endometrial ablation is "a relatively safe, simple, and less costly technique replacing hysterectomies." The only evidence of the procedure's safety was an allusion that the technique "has been performed since the mid-1980s."

Journalistic techniques that construct new technologies in a positive manner were endemic among large and small newspapers alike. Even a national paper of record, the *Washington Post,* was not immune. It began an article on a new technology with a case history of a patient who, "Two days after she underwent surgery . . . was back at her job . . . with endometrial ablation, a fast, nearly painless alternative that costs an average of $1,500 to $2,000, much less than the $4,000 to $7,000 fee for a hysterectomy."[6] A physician described the potential immediate surgical risks 2 inches later in the article, but one would have to read until nearly the end to learn that "the long-term risks of ablation are unknown." And this statement was "buried,"—that is, followed by additional testimony from a doctor's wife who "has recommended the procedure to all her friends and encouraged them to ask their doctors to perform it." For the reader who skips to the end, those are the last words. Of five articles concerned with endometrial ablation, only the *New York Times* devoted significant space to questioning use of the procedure, especially if it is desired to eliminate "bothersome" menstrual conditions or to reduce the fear of pregnancy.[7]

Similarly, three articles about laparoscopic hysterectomy depicted the procedure enthusiastically. Using this technique, the surgeon makes three smaller incisions, instead of a single, large, abdominal incision. By using fiber optics that function much like a periscope, the physician is able to remove the uterus and related organs. Arizona newspapers hailed the new technique in effusive headlines like this one, "Surgery Here Ushered Into the 'Space Age.' "[8] Only one of these newspapers noted—albeit belatedly on the jump page—that the new technique requires a higher degree of surgical expertise and thus may entail a higher degree of operating room risk. The most conservative position was offered by the *Miami Herald.* Its headline asked, "Belly-Button Procedure Is Less Painful, but Is It Really Necessary?"[9] The reporter sought out Nora Coffey of HERS, a widely quoted critic of hysterectomy, who questioned the circumstances under which *any* hysterectomy technique is necessary. In addition, a representative of the National Women's Health Network warned that the new procedure is still "experimental." Again, however, an enthusiastic testimonial and case history appeared much earlier in the story than the negative comments. The use of positive testimonials for new technologies is a message strategy that a reader should scrutinize closely. Health researchers have found that, in trying to change health behaviors such as cigarette use, positive change is more likely to occur when the messages include depictions of ordinary people modeling new skills and behaviors.[10]

The newspaper articles took quite a different tack when portraying the potential after-effects of hysterectomy. A swelling tide of quotations and evidence indicated that many sources consulted by reporters believe that hysterectomy is performed far too often and with negative results for patients. The negative effects too often highlighted were those of sexual and emotional dysfunction; in short, those that confirm traditional views of women as biologically predisposed to emotional and mental instability. The message strategies that structured this emphasis were the use of case histories and quotations. For example, in no article was there a statement from a hysterectomy patient who believed a heart attack was triggered by hormonal changes induced by premature menopause due to removal of the uterus and ovaries, or that a broken hip may have resulted from bone thinning that occurred after hysterectomy. The following excerpts are typical—and far from inclusive—of portrayals of sexual and emotional side effects:

From a *Washington Post* author interview that mentions only libido problems:

Ultimately Wanda Wigfall-Williams [author of *Hysterectomy: Learning the Facts, Coping With the Feelings, Facing the Future*] had a radical hysterectomy—in which not only the uterus but also the ovaries and fallopian tubes were removed. And she was barely awake from the anesthesia when she knew she had trouble. "Within 24 hours I was having hot flashes and night sweats and was depressed to boot." . . . And that was only the beginning. . . . There was, says Wigfall-Williams, "nothing, just nothing. I'm not aroused. Nothing is going on. It's like that part of me is completely dead."[11]

From a report about hysterectomy and alternatives in the *Allentown [PA] Morning Call:*

Goldfarb [the gynecologist-author] says the complaints of hot flashes, depression, loss of sexual desire, vaginal dryness and other problems are all too real. . . . June . . . is still emotionally distraught three years after her hysterectomy. Although she was 40 at the time she had the operation, [she] says she desperately wanted to have a child.[12]

This appeared on the first jump page of the article. It was not until the second jump that the reader learned that a hysterectomy patient's "chances of developing osteo-porosis, a crippling bone disorder, skyrocket." Interestingly, that information was immediately followed by a revealing non sequitur:

"As soon as they did my ovaries, I bet it was three days later, I was having such terrible heat flashes. I was just a wreck. I threw spaghetti at my husband. I ripped the door off a hinge" [recalled another hysterectomy-ovariectomy patient].[13]

Sometimes the tendency to highlight sexual and emotional side effects above all others was subtle, as in an article in the *Rochester [NY] Democrat and Chronicle* that questioned the current skeptical attitude toward hysterectomy, citing only depression as a negative side effect and presenting testimonials from two cancer patients who successfully learned to cope with their initial feelings of emotional loss after hysterec-tomy.[14] Other times, it was blatant. But the perception that emerged from newspaper information about hysterectomy was that loss of libido is a fate worse than death (from heart attack) or the crippling bone condition, osteoporosis.

Newspapers did *not* make a strong case for a woman's involvement in the process of diagnosis and treatment. A woman's responsibility for informing herself about treatments, advantages, and disadvantages was not often discussed. In articles touting new technologies, women might be advised to ask their doctors about them.[15] At best, indirect reference to such a perspective occurred, as in a *Times* article that presented information from a HERS-sponsored "patient education meeting" and boxed a list of books suggested as additional reading.[16]

Articles that present information about hysterectomy that cause women to question the usefulness of the procedure, or to look more deeply into the topic, perform a useful function. It is, however, a decidedly limited service. Physicians constitute an elite group in our society, and it is not always easy for patients—especially women patients—to get the answers they need and deserve. For women, the entrenched authority of the medical profession is validated by our patriarchal tradition. This makes many women, especially older women, fearful of asking questions or challenging the doctor. Newspaper articles that provide information about hysterectomy rarely suggest what to do to cope with this unequal power relationship, but when providing sound information, they point the way toward empowerment.

When newspapers did advise women to take an active role in the doctor-patient equation, the message inevitably was articulated by a source consulted for the article; it was not a judgment made by the writer. For example, the *Allentown [PA] Morning Call,* using a local consumers' group, The People's Medical Society, as its source, recommended that women get second and even third opinions before choosing to undergo a hysterectomy. In addition, women were urged to ask questions, even if they had to be assertive to get answers.[17] The *Los Angeles Times* quoted author-gynecologist Herbert Goldfarb, who stated his belief that the health care provider ought to present the alternative options to a patient, explain them, and let the patient make the final decision.[18]

Two of the most urgent calls for self-education appeared in articles about fibroids. Although many articles were unclear about a woman's role in questioning her physician or making a decision, articles in the *Dallas Morning News* and the *Philadelphia Inquirer* were explicit. Interestingly, both writers used a case history to make the point, and perhaps—recalling the positive effect that role modeling can have on influencing health-related behaviors—that is why their messages seemed so strong compared with other articles. The *Inquirer* article, for instance, described a young physical education teacher who didn't want to become sterile to treat troublesome fibroids. She therefore read everything she could about fibroids and learned what treatments other than hysterectomy were available to her.[19] Use of the testimonial to promote a health behavior other than purchasing new technology is encouraging because of the powerful persuasive potential of this strategy.

In summary, newspapers constructed the topic of hysterectomy by presenting information from disparate sources: most often local physicians and happy patients, but also authors on tour to promote their books, consumer groups, and hysterectomy support groups. Women in specific markets were able to learn something about the disadvantages of the procedure and about alternative treatments. Unfortunately, depictions of the disadvantages of hysterectomy tended to focus on mental and sexual dysfunctions that perpetuate the widespread perception of women as emotionally unbalanced and bio-logically impaired. News of medical innovations was favorable—even enthusiastic—and relied on the medical establishment as the primary source of information. The overall lack of information questioning high hysterectomy rates means that hundreds of thousands of women have no local source of information. When they go into their physicians' offices, they must rely on their doctors as a primary—if not the sole—source of information, unless they take aggressive steps to educate themselves.

MAGAZINES

If newspapers are stingy in their treatment of hysterectomy, magazines are frugal cousins. *Vogue, McCall's,* and *Ms.* were the only strictly "women's" magazines to cover hysterectomy or related techniques in any depth during the 6 years surveyed. Of 12 magazines referenced, several carried news briefs of only a few paragraphs, such as *Jet*'s announcement of higher hysterectomy rates among black women, unaccompanied by any speculation about why;[20] or the *Consumer Reports* health page tidbit about what to do when post-hysterectomy estrogen treatments don't alleviate menopausal symptoms (Answer: Ask your doctor to increase the dosage);[21] and *Vogue's* announcement of a California law requiring a signed consent form stating the patient has been fully informed of risks, side effects, and alternatives.[22]

Magazines were more likely than newspapers to assume a voice of authority—per-haps because of their status. They are nationally distributed publications rather than "hometown papers" like most (but not all) of the newspapers assayed. Magazines have earned a niche in our perceptions nearer the top of the hierarchy of information sources, along with newspapers "of record" such as the *New York Times,* the *Washington Post,* and the *Los Angeles Times.* There is no doubt, for example, in the *Consumer Reports* articles that the publication is secure in its position as the purveyor of information.[23] The main and the companion pieces carried no bylines and only three brief quotations were counted—one from a New York State publication and two from gynecologists with national reputations. *U.S. News & World Report* similarly stood on the reporter's expertise in distilling and collating information, attributing data to research sources and institutions, rather than quoting people.[24] Though other magazine writers used quotations more liberally, they were usually employed as stylistic devices to sustain reader interest, rather than as the basis of a "report" by a self-effacing journalist.

Magazine articles were more likely to cover hysterectomy as a general topic, rather than presenting a new technique as a basis for the story. Only *U.S. News & World Report* and *Ms.* built articles around news of scientific advances.[25] A *U.S. News & World Report* roundup of new techniques listed their advantages—with nary a word of risks, research, or other cautionary remarks. The *Ms.* article on endometrial ablation was the most thorough, of both newspaper and magazine articles, in recapping exactly what research on the procedure was available. *Health* magazine took a different approach in introducing a new treatment to its readers.[26] In an article inspired by the discovery of the efficacious treatment of fibroids using the drug Leuprolide, the presentation focused on the causes and cure of fibroids themselves. News of the technology comprised only a small portion of the article.

Magazines avoided the excessive boosterism for new technologies of some newspapers, and they were also—with the exception of *New York*—less likely to construct the emotional and sexual effects of hysterectomy as being the most important risks.[27] *Ms.*, for example, implicated hysterectomy in increased risk of heart disease, osteoporosis, and sexual dysfunction, without privileging any of the three. *U.S. News & World Report* cited the long-term effects of "incontinence, chronic pain and diminished sexual response. Among pre-menopausal women, hysterectomy increases the risk of heart disease three times."[28] *Consumer Reports* also presented a more balanced account. It advised readers that medical research indicates hysterectomy puts women at greater risk for coronary disease if the surgery occurs before menopause. In addition, the article noted that sexual pleasure may be reduced, and women who hoped to have children may suffer emotionally. Depression was listed as one side effect experienced by some women, but that other women experience relief because debilitating and painful medical conditions are removed. The article reminds readers that many individual psychological and environmental factors contribute to whether a woman experiences a hysterectomy as beneficial or detrimental.[29]

New York stands out for adopting an almost hysterical tone toward the reputed ills of hysterectomy.[30] This article detailed a lawsuit in which a woman won a million-dollar judgment against a physician for after-effects that ranged from depression to debilitating numbness that forced her to leave her job. A single, extreme example, couched in melodramatic prose, is used to imply that hysterectomy leads to dire results. In an article in *Health,* however, this same writer used a less histrionic approach, listing shocking statistics that indict hysterectomy for surgical complications and the tripled risk of heart attack before mentioning sexual dysfunction.[31]

Magazines were more likely than newspapers to position women as responsible for becoming educated health care consumers and for making the choice of which alternative is right for them. *Consumer Reports,* perhaps fulfilling its mission as a publication for informed shoppers, suggested, "A woman who feels fully informed about the reasons for her surgery and in control of the decisions made about her body stands a better chance of avoiding adverse psychological after-effects." *U.S. News & World Report* also cautioned women not to rely on physicians to steer them toward the newer, less invasive technologies. It urged women to inform themselves about the new options as preferable to the surgical solution of hysterectomy. *Health* magazine also insisted that women take control of their surgical fate, reminding them that in most cases hysterectomy is an elective procedure. Advice included getting a second opinion from a doctor who is not an associate of your physician, finding out the details about why this surgery is necessary, and being aware that the choice is yours, not your physician's, to make.[32]

In other articles, the woman's responsibility remained implicit: The existence of the information itself suggests our modern version of the old adage, that knowledge is empowerment. In no instance—whether magazine or newspaper article—did a writer suggest how women are to cope with the role of inquisitor and decision maker. Magazine articles, on the whole, present a balanced picture of hysterectomy but are still slightly skewed toward admiring, without much substantiation, any medical marvel that comes along. The potential emotional and sexual ill effects of hysterectomy are not foregrounded to the extent that they are in newspapers. Women are more likely to be constructed as knowledgeable health care consumers and decision makers. If only there were more such coverage.

BOOKS

It is probably safe to conclude that the audience for books about hysterectomy is women who are either experiencing some menstrual or menopausal complaint or who have been advised by family, friends, or a physician to have a hysterectomy. Books about hysterectomy published between 1986 and 1992 catered to this need for self-education by publishing informed authorities—sometimes gynecological surgeons—and providing information about the subject that was consistent across sources. Books, because they were presumed to be written by experts, were written in a manner that purveyed the information as authoritative. This does not mean that quotations and case histories were absent, but that they were stylistic strategies, a way of presenting information as storytelling in order to hold the reader's interest. Book writers were likely to assume the woman was ready to take an active role as a health consumer, rather than explicitly telling her to question her doctor.

Of books on the general subject of health care, Apple's historical account of women's health care in the United States was typical in the short shrift it gave to hysterectomy.[33] A scant two paragraphs were all that was devoted to one of the most frequently performed surgeries in the United States. Moreover, this book concluded that the reason for the high U.S. hysterectomy rate is a lack of agreement in the medical community about indicators. This conclusion ignored the examples of medical bias toward the uterus as a "useless" organ that other works attributed to medical textbooks and periodicals.

Two other general books on health care were just as uninformative. Miles devoted two nonconsecutive pages to the topic of hysterectomy, and they were not very educational for a woman considering the procedure or alternatives.[34] Ratcliff, professing to write from a feminist perspective, offered primarily the fact of differences in hysterectomy rates between black and white, and between insured and uninsured, women.[35]

On a more positive note, all of the books that were devoted entirely to the topic of hysterectomy were good sources of information. Gynecologist Vicki Hufnagel (*No More Hysterectomies!*) adopted the most strident tone among the authors.[36] She accused the medical establishment of acting on an outdated, 90-year-old notion that the uterus is useless after childbearing. Her book was loaded with case histories of women who have been "victimized" by the procedure, which she terms "female castration."

Perhaps the best of the lot was *The No-Hysterectomy Option* by gynecological surgeon Herbert Goldfarb.[37] The medical aspects of hysterectomy were covered in depth without being overly technical. He even described what each instrument is and how it is used. He did not conceal the risks and side effects of hysterectomy, but did not rely on scare stories to the extent that Hufnagel did. Alternative treatments, their advantages and disadvantages, were thoroughly discussed. Every woman should consider reading the sections of this book pertaining to the treatment(s) for which she is a candidate before making a decision.

Some books about hysterectomy were not written by physicians. Winnifred Cutler, a reproductive biologist, wrote *Hysterectomy: Before and After* after suffering ill effects from a hysterectomy while in her thirties.[38] Besides covering all the bases concerning hysterectomy and alternatives, she has several chapters on how to cope with the after-effects of hysterectomy. Wanda Wigfall-Williams, a psychologist and another disenchanted hysterectomy patient, is the author of *Hysterectomy: Learning the Facts*.[39]

Three books about women's health that have helpful sections included Sanders's account of endometriosis in *Women's Health: Readings on Social, Economic, and Political Issues*,[40] Stotland's discussion of "Medical Issues in Menopause" in *Social Change in Women's Reproductive Health Care: A Guide for Physicians and Their Patients*,[41] and—most useful of all—"Hysterectomy and Oophorectomy" in *Ourselves, Growing Older*.[42]

The aim of *Ourselves, Growing Older* is to empower women, and it succeeds at this better than any other material I found during this research. Enough information is provided so that a woman contemplating hysterectomy or ovariectomy (or oophorectomy) will understand the procedures, alternatives, advantages, and disadvantages. Alone of the work surveyed, this text advised women on how to cope with the inevitable power configuration inherent in the female patient-physician relationship, recommending that the woman have someone with her when she visits the physician, take time to consider alternative treatments, consider positive and negative aspects of all possible therapies—including drugs—and remember that she has the right to withdraw from either a treatment or surgery, even after being admitted to the hospital.[43] These books illustrate the fact that *no literate woman need enter the operating room uninformed and unprepared about what is going to happen and what to expect.* Reader-friendly books by informed sources offer detailed information. It may take some time and effort to do one's homework, but with so much at stake, surely it is advisable. A word of caution: Because of the burgeoning pace of developments in the field of medicine, how recently the material was published is of vital importance.

Conclusion

Given the preeminent place of hysterectomy in the national health care picture, there is a need for further research into hysterectomy and its effects, as well as the effects of the new technologies that are superseding it. A woman who wants to learn more about hysterectomy will probably have to make a trip to the local library or bookstore. Books provide the most complete information about hysterectomy and alternatives without constructing women as victims of their biology, and best equip a woman for dealing with physicians. Books, given their length, have the scope for providing information about all the side effects, not just the emotional or sexual complications, not only for hysterectomy but for the alternative treatments as well. Not all books, however, are equally useful. Magazines may also do a good job in equipping a woman to make a decision about whether hysterectomy is the right choice for treatment of her symptoms, and are less likely than newspapers to emphasize emotional dysfunction as a possible side effect. The daily newspaper, however, perpetuates perceptions of female hormonal imbalance and of routine biological processes as bothersome and symptomatic. New technologies are presented without much attention to research or potential disadvantages. Women need and deserve more balanced information in popular sources on this important topic.

Notes

1. H. A. Goldfarb & J. Grief, *The No-Hysterectomy Option* (New York: John Wiley, 1990): 7.

2. Interestingly, this figure correlates with a 25% decline in the hysterectomy rate in a Swiss canton following a very limited mass media campaign, as reported by G. Domenighetti, P. Luraschi, A. Casabianca, F. Gutzwiller, A. Spinelli, E. Pedrinis, & F. Repetto, "Effect of Information Campaign by the Mass Media on Hysterectomy Rate," *The Lancet* 2 (1988): 1470-1473.

3. Of newspaper articles, 34 of 36 were located and read. Of magazine articles, 12 of 13 were located and read. Of six books entirely about hysterectomy, four were read. The others were described in newspaper articles, and there is no reason to believe they cover substantially different ground. Women's health books that included some mention of hysterectomy are included only when the work is relevant to the discussion.

4. The eight articles constituting the last two categories plus two articles concerning the discovery of a new drug for the treatment of endometriosis will not be discussed further in this chapter. All are believed neutrally valenced toward hysterectomy, usually because hysterectomy was not sufficiently discussed in the article. In addition, one article enthusiastically introducing a new technique described it so vaguely and briefly that it was not possible to identify the technique as any of the procedures with which this research provided familiarity. Yet the procedure sounded enough like endometrial ablation that it could not be categorized definitely as a new and different technology.

5. D. Finley, "More Women Seek Surgery for Menstrual Stress," *San Antonio News,* June 23, 1991, p. B13.

6. S. Squires, "An Alternative to Hysterectomy [endometrial ablation]," *Washington Post,* March 12, 1991, Sec. 7, p. 1.

7. S. Blakeslee, "Nonsurgical Means Used as Alternative to Hysterectomies," *New York Times,* July 31, 1991, p. C10.

8. C. McClain, "Surgery Here Ushered Into 'Space Age,' " *Tucson Citizen,* March 28, 1990, p. G12.

9. M. Fichtner, "Belly-Button Procedure Is Less Painful, but Is It Really Necessary?" *Miami Herald,* June 5, 1991, p. D4.

10. J. A. Flora, E. W. Maibach, & N. Maccoby, "The Role of Media Across Four Levels of Health Promotion Intervention," *Annual Review of Public Health* 10 (1989): 181-201.

11. S. Rovner, "Hysterectomy: The Sexual Changes," *Washington Post,* February 10, 1987, p. C8.

12. K. Reinhard, "Women Urged to Get Facts Before Undergoing Hysterectomies," *Allentown [PA] Morning Call,* September 16, 1991, p. A2. Copyright © September 16, 1991 The Morning Call, Inc., Allentown, PA. Reprinted with permission of The Morning Call.

13. Reinhard, "Women Urged to Get Facts."

14. D. L. Tomb, "Hysterectomy Debate Challenges Old Ideas," *Rochester [NY] Democrat and Chronicle,* December 11, 1988, p. G3.

15. Blakeslee, "Nonsurgical Means Used as Alternative to Hysterectomies."

16. J. E. Brody, "Hysterectomies, the Second-Most Frequent Operation, Need Not Be So Common, Some Say," *New York Times,* January 3, 1991, p. B5. Copyright © 1991 by The New York Times Company. Reprinted by permission.

17. Reinhard, "Women Urged to Get Facts."

18. S. Roan, "Incidence of Surgeries Questioned" (with sidebars, "Alternatives to Having a Hysterectomy" and "Hysterectomies Do Pose Some Risks"), *Los Angeles Times,* January 1, 1991, pp. E1, E3.

19. V. Williams, "Options for Coping," *Philadelphia Inquirer,* July 29, 1990, p. C12.

20. "Black Women Have More Hysterectomies, *Jet* (July 21, 1987): 30.

21. "Estrogen After Hysterectomy," *Consumer Reports* (May 1992): 335.

22. M. Weber, "Informed Consent for Hysterectomies, *Vogue* (May 1988): 172.

23. "Hysterectomy and Its Alternatives" (with sidebars, "The Operation and Its Effects: What to Expect" and "Are Ovaries Dispensable?: Benefits and Risks"), *Consumer Reports* (September 1990): 603-607.

24. D. Podolsky, "Saved From the Knife: New Treatments Mean Many Women Can Avoid Hysterectomy," *U.S. News & World Report* (November 19, 1990): 76-77.

25. Podolsky, "Saved From the Knife"; M. Napoli, "Medical Breakthrough: Laser Hysterectomy," *Ms.* (March 1986): 31, 33.

26. A. Ranard, "The 'Good' Problem" [fibroids], *Health* (March 1990): 66-69.

27. P. A. Dranov, "Change of Life," *New York* (October 19, 1987): 70-76.

28. Podolsky, "Saved From the Knife."

29. *Consumer Reports,* "Hysterectomy and Its Alternatives," p. 604.

30. Dranov, "Change of Life."

31. P. A. Dranov, "Do You Need These Operations?" [hysterectomy, breast surgery, D & C] *Health* (June 1986): 24-30.

32. Dranov, "Do You Need These Operations?"

33. R. D. Apple (Ed.), *Women, Health, and Medicine in America: A Historical Handbook* (New York: Garland, 1990).

34. A. Miles, *Women, Health, and Medicine* (Philadelphia: Open Press, 1991).

35. K. S. Ratcliff (Ed.), *Healing Technology: Feminist Perspectives* (Ann Arbor: University of Michigan Press, 1989).

36. V. Hufnagel & S. K. Golant, *No More Hysterectomies!* (New York: Plume/Penguin/New American Library, 1989).

37. Goldfarb & Grief, *The No-Hysterectomy Option.*

38. W. B. Cutler, *Hysterectomy: Before and After (A Comprehensive Guide to Preventing, Preparing for, and Maximizing Health After Hysterectomy)* (New York: Oxford University Press, 1988).

39. W. Wigfall-Williams, *Hysterectomy: Learning the Facts, Coping With Feelings, Facing the Future* (n.p.: Michael Kesend Publishing Ltd., 1987). This book was not available for this research. In addition, the interested reader may wish to consult Dennerstein, Wood, and Burrows's slim volume about "*Hysterectomy,*" previously cited. Some women may find its concise physiological information useful. It is based on British health affairs and statistics, however, and takes a misanthropic view of feminine emotions.

40. J. Sanders, "Endometriosis," in N. Worchester & M. H. Whatley (Eds.), *Women's Health: Readings on Social, Economic, and Political Issues* (Dubuque, IA: Hunt, 1988): 148-151.

41. N. L. Stotland, "Medical Issues in Menopause," in *Social Change in Women's Reproductive Health Care: A Guide for Physicians and Their Patients* (New York: Praeger): 52-54, 218.

42. Reider, "Hysterectomy and Oophorectomy," in P. D. Doress, D. L. Siegal, & Older Women Book Project (Eds.), *Ourselves, Growing Older* (New York: Simon & Schuster/Touchstone): 295-312.

43. Reider, "Hysterectomy and Oophorectomy," pp. 309-310.

26

Women and AIDS

The Lost Population

Rebecca J. Welch Cline
Nelya J. McKenzie

Both globally and nationally, AIDS is emerging as a disease of women. Worldwide, AIDS currently is an "equal opportunity" disease with regard to gender. The World Health Organization has acknowledged that since January 1992 women throughout the world have been becoming infected with HIV at a rate approximately equal to that of men.[1] That gender balance will shift by the year 2000, however, when women will account for most new infections.[2] In the United States, the disease has been the leading cause of death among women aged 25 to 34 in New York City since 1986 and nationwide among young black women since 1990.[3] Women comprise approximately 12% of adult/adolescent cases of AIDS in the United States.[4] Although some may argue that this relatively small proportion justifies the dearth of scientific and popular literature— as well as educational interventions—focused on women, the attention remains disproportionately small relative to the growing incidence of AIDS in women.

Beyond the sheer numbers of AIDS cases in women, several other features of the epidemiology of AIDS in women, and the roles women have played socially in this epidemic, argue the need for magnifying attention to this population. Yet the literature on AIDS is characterized by the invisibility of women. Ironically, at the same time, the literature indicates that, in general, women seek health care more often than men and are more likely to take preventive health steps than are men[5]; yet as a result of their invisibility in the literature, women generally have been ignored by AIDS education and prevention campaigns. To target the needs of women, researchers and program planners first need to understand specific groups of women, with an eye to cultural sensitivity, while placing educational efforts in the context of social networks. The meaning of AIDS, personally, socially, and economically, is very different for women than for men,[6] and efficacious prevention efforts demand different interventions. Our review of the literature analyzes the sources of the invisibility of women; the skewed emphasis on women in their reproductive capacities; and implications for blinding women, their health care providers, and educators to the significance of AIDS for women.

Women and AIDS:
The Scientific Literature

In 1981, the first case of AIDS in a woman in the United States was identified. Since then, little attention has been paid to women in the AIDS epidemic in research, clinical practice, or in the media, causing Wiener, who called women "the invisible participants" in the AIDS epidemic, to ask, "Where are the women?"[7] Among other critics, Campbell noted that "despite women's vulnerability to AIDS, there has been a general lack of attention to the seriousness of the problem of AIDS in women."[8] A similar observation led Anastos and Marte to claim women as "the missing persons in the AIDS epidemic."[9]

WHERE ARE THE WOMEN?

In an effort to identify the patterns, gaps, and points of focus in the scientific literature with regard to women, we conducted literature searches using the data bases *PsychLit* and *Medline*. Using combinations of the key terms *women* and *acquired immune deficiency syndrome* and of *women* and *human immunodeficiency virus* we identified a total of 1,953 citations. This represents 244 articles in *PsychLit* (1 for the years 1974-1986 and 243 for the years 1987 through March 1992) and 1,709 articles in *Medline* (127 for the years 1981-1986, 1,259 for the years 1987-1991, and 323 for January-May 1992). We further narrowed and focused the database of scientific literature for our analyses in several ways. First, we limited ourselves to articles published in the English language. Second, we limited ourselves to articles for which abstracts were available. Third, upon reviewing these sources we discovered that the key term *AIDS* yielded some articles inappropriate to our investigation (e.g., hearing aids, educational aids, etc.); we eliminated these articles from our database. Fourth, we eliminated citations duplicated by using the two sets of key terms within two databases. This process yielded 610 articles. Finally, we screened out articles that did not focus on women and AIDS (i.e., articles that included the key words in the abstracts but focused on other topics and/or populations). This screening process yielded a set of 217 articles on women and AIDS that constituted the database for further analyses.

The most striking finding in this cursory attempt to quantify the nature of the literature is the dominant, overshadowing emphasis on women in their reproductive capacities (120 articles, or 55% of our database). The upshot of this emphasis is a concern about women as a population that may transmit the virus perinatally. In fact, less than half of the literature on women and AIDS is rooted in concern for women themselves. Within that remaining small body of literature, we are struck more by what is *not* present (i.e., the issues that are virtually ignored) than by what is present.

HOW DID THE WOMEN "GET LOST"?

The failure of the literature to address the concerns of women is rooted in the larger social construction of AIDS as a disease that has gender (as well as sexual orientation). Although epidemiologists identified AIDS with women since early in the history of the disease, women remained invisible in the literature.

Few researchers have explored the theoretical and pragmatic implications of the social construction of AIDS as a disease that "has gender."[10] Not only has the medical literature virtually ignored the association of women with AIDS, so too has the social scientific literature that provides the knowledge base for AIDS education and prevention programs. The observed result is that "women are frequently omitted from AIDS brochures and media coverage, and eclipsed in medical research."[11] Despite the fact that a variety of literature suggests that gender is a *significant* factor in understanding, predicting, and promoting interpersonal AIDS-preventive actions (e.g., condom use), the issue of gender has remained largely unexplored.

What exploration has occurred was slow in its start. In fact, our *PsychLit* searches for articles on women and AIDS for the period up to December 1986 yielded only one article! Five years into the epidemic, and 5 years after AIDS had been identified in women, only one article in the database recognized women as role players in the epidemic. That first article, like a preponderance to follow, did not focus on women per se; instead it recognized that homophobia is rampant among health professionals, with women being less homophobic than men. The most prominent message conveyed by an analysis of the content of the literature is the absence of awareness and/or concern for women as potential sufferers of AIDS. Several factors contributed to that message.

Gender and the Construction of HIV Disease

Despite global and national epidemiological trends, the social construction of AIDS in the United States remains a disease identified as gay, white, and male. These factors account for the invisibility of women in the AIDS literature and directly relate to defining AIDS as a disease that has both gender and sexual orientation.

Homophobia. As Bell notes, rampant homophobia interfered with both under-standing and responding to what was seen as a "gay disease"; it was "unthinkable that a gay disease should be a public health priority."[12] Shilts suggests that the initial labels ascribed to the disease led to avoiding rather than confronting the problem: "by its very name, Gay-Related Immune Deficiency (GRID) was a homosexual disease, not a disease of babies or their mothers."[13]

Epidemiologic data make clear that AIDS now affects women as often as men worldwide. Further, for women in the United States, AIDS is "almost exclusively a disease of heterosexuals."[14] Homophobia likewise contributed to the slowness in the United States to recognize AIDS as a disease threatening heterosexuals, and therefore women, despite recognition of heterosexual intercourse as the major mode of trans-mission of AIDS worldwide.[15]

Controversy Regarding Heterosexual Transmission. The proportion of AIDS cases in women is increasing both worldwide and nationally.[16] Heterosexual transmission accounts for only 2% of AIDS cases in men in the United States, but 35% of women with AIDS contracted the virus via heterosexual transmission.[17] These increases are attributable to the tendency for heterosexual women to contract HIV via sexual intercourse with HIV-infected men.[18]

Because the disease initially was labeled a gay men's disease, the scientific com-munity, as well as the public at large, was slow in accepting evidence that AIDS can be transmitted through heterosexual intercourse. So disbelieving were researchers that

accounts by women that their only possible source of risk behavior could have come from heterosexual intercourse with a male who had told them he was not HIV-positive were not taken seriously . . . until they were corroborated by a study of *men* who admitted that 35% of them would lie about their HIV status; 20% said they had lied about having been tested.[19]

When AIDS was seen to be transmitted heterosexually, researchers who believed the disease to be dominantly one of males, seemed reluctant to admit what the data appeared to make evident—that the risk of contracting the virus via heterosexual intercourse was greater for women than for men.[20] By 1988, researchers had established that the risk of male to female transmission was far greater than female to male transmission, and that risk was greater among women of color.[21]

A Male-Centered Research Paradigm. As in other health research,[22] in the context of the AIDS epidemic, women may be eliminated systematically from research protocols by several factors. Women often specifically are excluded from drug trials,[23] despite the fact that women may respond differently to drugs than men. The original studies of AZT investigated 282 patients but included only 13 women.[24] Likewise, drug trials conducted by the National Institute for Allergy and Infectious Diseases (NIAID) through August 1989 enrolled almost exclusively men; only 6.8% of participants were women and these likely were not representative of the population of women with AIDS.[25]

Women often are eliminated from drug trials because they are pregnant, *may* be pregnant, or *may become* pregnant.[26] Many poor and minority women are excluded by their inaccessibility to the health care system. In addition, culturally based suspicion of the white health care establishment and its research may cause minority women to decline the opportunities they do encounter to participate in research. As a result, current medical literature "allows only the most rudimentary understanding of AIDS in women."[27]

The Devaluation of Woman Qua Women

Perhaps the most significant contribution to the invisibility of women in the AIDS literature has been the devaluation of women in their own right. The literature on women and AIDS largely views women "in relation to" others, primarily in relation to their sexual partners and their children. Chavkin argues that, "The tensions between concern for woman qua women and for women as fetal vessels or vectors of transmission of disease to others permeates all of the current efforts to target women for AIDS prevention work."[28] The failure to be concerned for women as women is exacerbated by the fact that "undervalued populations of women" have received attention disproportionate to their significance in the epidemic (i.e., as prostitutes, IV drug users, and women of color).

Prostitutes. Relative to the role they have played in the AIDs epidemic in the United States, prostitutes have been *over*-attended to in the scientific literature, an emphasis adopted and disseminated to the public via the media portrayal of prostitution.[29] Despite the fact that there is little evidence of HIV being transmitted from prostitutes to the public,[30] the literature base we analyzed included 15 articles focusing on prostitutes as a factor in the epidemic. This figure may seem small, but it should be contrasted in relative terms. Only 14 articles focused on black and Hispanic women; a mere 12 focused on IV (intravenous) drug use as a factor.

The language surrounding concern for AIDS in prostitutes constructs a reality contradicted by epidemiological data. In the literature, including epidemiological studies, prostitutes are referred to routinely as "reservoirs for transmission" of sexually transmitted disease despite the fact that HIV infection actually is low among non-drug using prostitutes. Identifying prostitutes as "AIDS reservoirs" functions to suggest that women's bodies "are infectious pools of AIDS viruses, storing large quantities of infected liquids, and the source of disease for many."[31] This language also implies that men are the unsuspecting transmitters of virus from one woman to another, a metaphor that indicts women as "the originating cause of the disease."[32] The overemphasis, relative to actual risk (in the United States), on prostitution as a risk factor amounts to a focus on transmission of the virus to others (i.e., the clients of women prostitutes) versus on the manifestation of the disease in women.[33]

Further, the term *prostitute* frames the issue in moral terms (i.e., it highlights the issue that individuals are taking money for sexual favors), rather than in terms of risky behavior (i.e., having a large number of partners). A similar focus on men with multiple partners is not existent in the literature.[34] Thus, both men and women with a large number of partners may not see themselves at risk because their activities do not involve the exchange of money.

Most female prostitutes use condoms with customers (but not with their boyfriends), which may account for why they have the same rate of infection as other women.[35] As a result, "evidence to date suggests that HIV is much more likely to be transmitted to prostitutes than from them."[36] Moreover, nowhere in this literature did we find an ethical concern raised regarding the men procuring prostitutes. Only rarely, and this among critics, did we find concern for risk of HIV infection *of* prostitutes *by* clients.[37]

IV Drug Use. At the same time that female prostitutes are over-attended to, IV drug use as a factor in AIDS among women is ignored relative to the problem's magnitude. Among women, AIDS is a disease largely of heterosexuals, driven by IV drug use, either by themselves or their sexual partners. Yet the literature has paid scant attention to women in connection to IV drug use. Our review found only 12 articles on women and AIDS that focused directly on IV drug use (or sexual intercourse with IV drug users) as a risk factor, despite the fact that IV drug use (49%) and heterosexual intercourse with an IV drug user (20%) together account for more than *two thirds* of AIDS cases among women.[38]

Risk of HIV infection from a sexual partner who is an IV drug user is greater for women than for men, as transmission of the virus is more "efficient" from men to women than vice versa, and there are more male than female IV drug users in the population (a ratio of about 3 to 1).[39] Further, women IV drug users typically are in relationships with male drug users, whereas 80% of men using IV drugs are in primary relationships with women who do not use IV drugs.[40]

Although drug use quickly is overtaking homosexual intercourse as the leading risk factor in HIV infection, there is little evidence of changes in risk-taking behavior, either drug use or sexual, among IV drug users. One study of methadone patients reported that 45% of the men and 50% of the women said they had never used a condom for sexual intercourse in the previous 6 months.[41]

Women who are sexual partners of drug users make up no particular population, share no unifying social structure; they are a diverse group but most are of childbearing age, have children, and are living in poverty.[42] Despite the fact that IV drug users and their partners constitute "a discrete risk group with specific problems and needs,"[43] they are hard to reach for both the purposes of research and interventions. Reaching women who use drugs or are in relationships with drug users requires understanding the social context of drug use (i.e., values, roles, status). For example, sharing "works" (needles and syringes) needs to be understood as an act of social bonding as well as serving an economic function. Sharing works creates a sense of cooperation and friendship as well as a shared savings.[44] Finally, fewer drug treatment programs exist for women than for men, creating additional barriers for women seeking help (see Lemieux, Chapter 4, this volume).[45]

Women of Color. Women of color are particularly devalued in the AIDS literature. They are an "already disenfranchised" group that lacks the means "to command the public's attention to their lot" and are considered "disposable."[46] Women of color constitute a population subject to status double jeopardy. They are devalued by virtue of both gender and ethnicity. The literature on women and AIDS contained only 14 articles that focus on black and Hispanic women despite the fact that three quarters of the AIDS cases among women are accounted for by blacks (53%) and Hispanics (25%).[47] Both Hispanics and blacks are diagnosed with AIDS in numbers disproportionate to their population. For example, Hispanics account for 7% of the general population in the United States[48] but 16.5% of AIDS cases and 25% of cases of women with AIDS.[49] One result of so little attention in the scientific literature to these populations is the "minimal development of prevention efforts" sensitive to the cultural values of black and Hispanic women.[50]

Women as "Vectors"

Anastos and Marte argue that in the literature on women and AIDS, women are treated more often as the vectors of disease than as its victims. They blame "deeply ingrained societal sexism as well as racism and classism" for skewing public perception of AIDS and HIV infection in women in the United States by creating a reality in which women are regarded as "vectors of transmission to their children and male sexual partners rather than as people with AIDS who are themselves frequently victims of transmission from the men in their lives."[51] Campbell argues that "The distinction between women as 'infectors' and women as 'infectees' can be made and it becomes evident that far more attention has been given to women as infectors than to the very real risks that they face as infectees."[52]

The majority of AIDS research involving women concentrates on perinatal transmission rather than on the effects of the disease on women.[53] Anastos and Marte observe that, "Both in clinical practice and public discussion, pregnant women with HIV infection are perceived as incubators of sick babies who are destined to become a burden to society, not as individuals with a life-threatening illness, nor as mothers in struggle and in pain."[54] Thus, women who are HIV infected not only are faced with stigma and the problems of coping with a life-threatening disease, they are required to face complex decisions regarding reproductive issues in a context that often functions to strip them of choice.

"VECTORS" STRIPPED OF CHOICE:
WOMEN, AIDS, AND REPRODUCTIVE FREEDOM

AIDS in women, due to its association with perinatal transmission, has generated political, ethical, and moral debate regarding women's reproductive rights. Historically, women have been accorded reproductive rights as a matter of common law. Nevertheless, states, in general, have tended to demonstrate greater concern for the protection of fetal rights over those of the mother. However, the AIDS epidemic places women's reproductive freedom at risk along with their health, and, at the same time, interest in protecting the fetus tends to waffle when considering the potential of "another AIDS victim" and additional welfare cost for the middle-class.[55]

Women of "Childbearing Age"

The phrases *women of reproductive age* and *women of childbearing age* dominate the scientific rhetoric on women and AIDS, labeling both women at risk for HIV infection and those already infected.[56] The literature is unclear regarding the parameters associated with these terms, with Mantell, Schinke, and Akabas identifying childbearing ages for women as 13 to 39 years,[57] whereas Gayle, Selik, and Chu delimit the age to between 15 and 44 years.[58] Regardless of the parameters, the terms suggest that women and AIDS deserves attention primarily because HIV-infected women are the major source of HIV infection for infants.

HIV can be transmitted from the infected woman to her child either in utero, during labor and delivery, or through breast milk.[59] The probability of HIV transmission from mother to fetus has been estimated to be as low as 20%.[60] Pediatric AIDS cases accounted for only 1.5% of the total AIDS cases in the United States as of December 1993.[61] Thus, although women constituted 12% of the AIDS diagnosed population in the United States as of December 1993, they have received scientific focus primarily because of their relationship with a fetus.

HIV-infected women must make choices regarding whether to become pregnant or, if pregnant, whether to continue the pregnancy. Reproductive decisions are based on many factors including the significance of the mother role for women.

Mother Role, Motherhood Roulette?

According to Carovano, women's sexual identities have long been associated with their ability to reproduce. "Motherhood legitimizes a woman's sexuality—and very often her life."[62] As a result, being HIV infected jeopardizes not only a woman's health but also her very identity when providers and policy makers alike discourage women from enacting their role as a mother. For example, the CDC (Centers for Disease Control) recommends that women who are HIV infected delay pregnancy, with the goal being to prevent vertical transmission of AIDS by having women who are HIV positive forgo pregnancy, ostensibly for *the present*.[63] Seropositive women realize that the risk of infection to an unborn child is not likely to change during their lifetimes,[64] so the imperative "delay pregnancy" actually translates to mean "do not have a child."[65]

The CDC guidelines fail to take into account the profound meaning of childbearing for some women.[66] Black and Hispanic women, who make up the majority of women with HIV disease, come from cultures that place much value on having children.[67] Suggestions to forgo pregnancy may be met with suspicion by minorities who interpret the directive to "forgo pregnancy" as a prelude to genocide.[68] For women who exist on the margins of society because of race or poverty, having a child and becoming a mother can define self-worth and provide a source of love.[69] Even a 50% chance of having a healthy child is preferable to a 100% chance of not having a child at all.[70]

HIV-infected women who become pregnancy by choice or by chance are faced with another set of obstacles and challenges when they seek prenatal care.

Health Care for Pregnant
Women Who Are HIV Positive

Many women who are HIV positive have limited access to quality health care, even without the complications of AIDS. Most of these women live in poverty and have inadequate resources for acquiring sufficient health care.[71] Consequently, women often learn of their HIV status after they become pregnant, if testing is a routine part of prenatal care, or after they give birth to an infected child.[72] As a result of learning their HIV status, women's prenatal care becomes the venue for decisions about whether to continue or to terminate pregnancy.

More than a decade into the AIDS epidemic, it remains unclear whether pregnancy exacerbates HIV/AIDS.[73] Public Health Service guidelines avoid recommendations for therapies in pregnancy as the side effects of some treatments on the fetus are unknown. Unfortunately, these guidelines ignore the health of the woman in favor of concerns for the fetus.[74]

HIV-infected women who elect abortion rather than risk bearing an infected infant face the hurdle of obtaining an abortion, as facilities that provide pregnancy termination services often are reluctant to treat HIV-infected women.[75] Beyond inaccessibility to services, a situation exacerbated during much of the epidemic by restrictions on public funding for abortion,[76] many women of poverty do not qualify for abortions, as they tend to enter prenatal care in the second or third trimester,[77] beyond the point of legal abortions[78]; most facilities do not offer abortions past 12 weeks.[79]

In addition to tensions emanating from external sources, a woman who is HIV positive and who faces the decision about the possible termination of her pregnancy, must wrestle with many internal (personal and interpersonal) tensions. These tensions rise out of issues of morality and religion,[80] attitude of the partner or other family members, desire to replace a child lost to death or foster care,[81] childbearing as a source of self-esteem,[82] suspicions about motives of those recommending abortion, and/or concerns for a child who may be born HIV infected.[83] The conspicuous concern for others (i.e., the health of the unborn child, economic costs to the public), almost to the exclusion of the woman, makes the reproductive decisions of HIV-infected women a wellspring of ethical dilemmas.[84]

ETHICAL ISSUES

Along with the many personal and interpersonal issues faced by the pregnant HIV-infected woman, she faces an array of ethical issues that emanate largely from institutional and policy sources. A primary issue is the right of an HIV-infected woman to become pregnant and to maintain that pregnancy. As the incidence of pediatric AIDS increases, so too does the debate about women with AIDS and their reproductive rights.[85]

Mandatory Testing

Mandatory HIV testing of "at-risk" women of childbearing age has been recommended for controlling *pediatric* AIDS.[86] Some critics fear that mandatory testing actually will exacerbate the problem of pediatric AIDS, as compulsory testing may keep women away from health care facilities,[87] particularly those who may not want to make a decision about abortion.[88] Evidence suggests that a woman's knowledge about AIDS is insufficient motivation to seek testing and that knowledge about her own HIV status is an insufficient basis for making reproductive decisions.[89]

One rationale for testing women of "childbearing age" is that early detection can lead to better medical care.[90] Testing women who are "at risk" for HIV infection, however, often is seen as an effort to prevent AIDS in children rather than a means of providing appropriate health care for women themselves.[91] Logically, women who test positive for HIV when they are not pregnant can be advised to "delay pregnancy" and can begin to receive treatments that might not be available to pregnant women. The rationale for testing women who already are pregnant is less clear.[92] Other arguments in favor of testing pregnant women include the patient's right to know and the need for public health information.[93] One largely unspoken reason for identifying pregnant women who are HIV positive is that these women then can receive counseling about their reproductive options, including abortion.

Counseling to Inform or Direct Choice?

Individuals who elect to be HIV tested should receive both pretest and posttest counseling. For pregnant women who test positive, the most appropriate posttest counseling style is the nondirective model (as is used in genetic counseling) that leaves choice in the woman's hands.[94] In this model, individuals receive objective information regarding their options and risks; the counseling stops far short of making recommendations.

The ideology of a nondirective style typically has not been followed in HIV reproductive counseling.[95] According to Bayer, a more directive approach to reproductive counseling has been emerging that goes beyond providing options by attempting to persuade a patient to pursue a particular course of action.[96] Many health care providers feel that it is their right and responsibility to persuade an HIV-infected woman to abort her pregnancy even in the face of clear statements by the woman that she does not want to choose an abortion.[97] That bias is stronger for women of color and women from lower socioeconomic classes who are advised more strongly to abort.[98]

Defining the Patient: Mother or Fetus?

Much of the medical advice given to pregnant women implies that the fetus, not the mother, is the patient.[99] Legal decisions historically support the import of the fetus over the mother, and women for whom court-ordered intervention has been sought generally are young women of color.[100] Given the fact that the majority of women with HIV disease are young women of color, past legal trends set the stage for criminalizing women for giving birth to HIV-infected babies.[101] The implication of legal intervention in the case of AIDS is that it is more important that a woman protect an unborn child from the potential of HIV infection than that she be allowed to have a child as part of her (and her partner's) reproductive choice (despite the fact that most children born to women with HIV disease are not HIV infected).[102]

Individual Versus Societal Rights

The pregnant woman with HIV disease finds her reproductive rights in competition with those of society at large. For example, Mantell et al. recommend proactive encouragement of delayed pregnancy among infected women and women at high risk "in the best interest of protecting the public's health."[103] The argument in favor of the rights of the many over the rights of the few creates a climate conducive to regulation of reproductive rights among certain groups. Presently, reproductive freedoms are protected by law; as the incidence of pediatric AIDS increases, however, those freedoms may be restricted. As some feminists argue, it is a short leap from "recommending postponement" to prohibiting reproduction.[104] Concerns are that future public policy could include voluntary sterilization of HIV-infected women[105] or imposition of involuntary HIV testing of certain "high-risk" groups.[106]

Chowdbury expresses grave concerns about the continued right of HIV-positive women to become pregnant and to maintain their pregnancy.[107] Levine and Dubler state, "Middle-class, professional concern about poor women of color or mentally disabled women having babies repeats a familiar pattern, but the overlay of HIV is relatively new,"[108] an attitude that reflects a social class structure that seems to value some over others. The majority of women who are HIV infected are among the most politically powerless members of society. They are four times discriminated against: they are predominantly minorities; they are female; they are poor; and they have HIV disease. Their powerlessness makes them especially vulnerable to politics and practices imposed by others.

If the primary public health goal of HIV testing in women is, in fact, prevention of pediatric AIDS rather than appropriate health care for women (as has been suggested here), that goal will not be served by promoting abortions of *possibly* HIV-infected fetuses.[109] Public health officials are shooting at the wrong target. The most effective prevention of pediatric AIDS is prevention of HIV infection in women.[110]

In summary, the devaluation of women in their own right is at the root of the invisibility of women in the social construction of AIDS. The dominant images of women in the AIDS literature are in the roles of vector, prostitute, and mother, with more than half of the literature on women and AIDS actually focusing on perinatal transmission. That trend has jeopardized women by placing them at risk in the context of numerous ethical issues. Further, the very psychosocial factors that likely enhance women's risk and result in their differential response to the epidemic are virtually ignored in the literature (i.e., interpersonal relationships, culture, economic factors).[111] In short, sexism, racism, and classism "have resulted in the ignorance and neglect of the conditions confronting women"[112] relative to the AIDS epidemic.

Implications of the Social Construction of Women and AIDS in the Scientific Literature

AIDS is a socially constructed disease defined by gender, race, and sexual orientation. The language and symbols surrounding the story of women and AIDS are threads in a tapestry that portrays the disease as a gay, white, male disease, thus rendering women invisible. The implications of that construction are far-reaching because the systematic social construction of AIDS as a disease devoid of women has functioned to blind both women themselves and those charged with the responsibility for women's health care and education to the risks of women.

FAILURE OF WOMEN
TO SEE THEMSELVES AT RISK

Defining AIDS as a disease of gay white men focused attention away from women. As a result, many women are unaware of their potential risk for IIIV infection.[113] Nyamathi and Vasquez, for example, studied Hispanic women who were homeless, IV drug users, sexual partners of IV drug users, diagnosed with sexually transmitted diseases, and/or were prostitutes. Despite their own risk-taking behavior, many of the women in this sample considered Hispanic women at little risk for HIV infection.[114]

The image that AIDS is a gay white male disease is perpetrated further into the public as people learn about AIDS via the media. The typical speaker/representative in AIDS-prevention campaign messages is a white male; a not-so-subtle secondary message broadcast by this portrayal is that AIDS is a disease of white males. Not surprisingly then, blacks tend to see themselves at less risk for HIV infection than do whites, and it is likely that some groups of women, by virtue of their gender and ethnicity, doubly fail to perceive their own vulnerability.[115] Without a perception of risk, women are unlikely to be motivated to change behavior or may change their behavior in ineffective ways if the risk is inaccurately seen or misunderstood.[116] Personalization of risk, one of the primary factors associated with activating preventive behavior, has not been developed among women.[117]

DIAGNOSTIC FAILURES

AIDS is a disease likely to be highly underreported in women for several reasons. Due to differences in the manifestation of HIV disease in men and women, we can safely assume that "significant numbers of women remain undiagnosed."[118] Rosser contends that this underreporting is related directly to the social construction of the disease that focused on men.[119]

Although substantial evidence long indicated that AIDS manifests itself differently in women than in men, the Centers for Disease Control's diagnostic criteria were not altered in any way to reflect those differences until 1992.[120] Beginning with its 1993 epidemiological reports, the CDC included invasive cervical cancer as a diagnostic criterion. Yet chronic vaginitis, yeast infections, and pelvic inflammatory diseases that are resistant to treatment, as well as abnormal Pap smears, appear to be common symptoms of HIV disease in women, though they are not included in the diagnostic criteria.[121] The gynecologic manifestations of HIV have not yet been adequately described.[122] Moreover, women tend to become severely ill and die more quickly than men after diagnosis. The latter trend could be due to the disease operating differently in women than in men or could be due to the tendency for women to be diagnosed relatively late in the course of the disease.[123]

Physicians are directly influenced by the social construction of AIDS in the scientific literature. Thus, doctors tend to misdiagnose or make a late diagnosis of AIDS in women as they tend not to see HIV disease as a diagnostic option unless a woman is a prostitute or an IV drug user.[124] The "persistent attitude among many physicians that 'good girls don't get AIDS' "[125] interferes with diagnosis in women.

Finally, underreporting results in part from the fact that many women at risk are poor and do not have access to health care.[126] Among IV drug using women, many do not seek health care until they have had multiple opportunistic infections.[127] Many women are not diagnosed until they seek health care related to pregnancy or a child has been identified as infected.[128] Often, pregnancy conceals or delays an HIV diagnosis.[129]

INTERVENTIONS DESIGNED FOR WOMEN: FLAWED AND FEW AND FAR BETWEEN

One of the clearest implications of the volume and limitations of the scientific literature on women and AIDS is the relative absence of AIDS-prevention interventions designed specifically for women. Without a knowledge base to clarify the need to address women and to adapt to their particular needs, the motivation to address women never developed. As a result, "specific approaches most efficacious for women are not known."[130] Some evidence suggests that relatively few women have been reached by national prevention campaign efforts designed for the general public (e.g., the CDC's America Responds to AIDS campaign).[131] Existing campaigns have made few attempts to adapt to women as an audience.[132]

Kelly and Murphy identify some of the important components necessary to an efficacious prevention intervention for women, yet few of these principles have been put into effect. They include the recognition that: (a) knowledge does not produce behavior change—instead, cognitive and behavioral skills need to be promoted; (b) empowerment, believing one can effect behavior change, is a significant factor; (c) behavior change may require changing social networks and social environments; (d) the type or level of relationship (long-term vs. casual) influences behavior; and (e) in order to be effective, interventions must be consistent with the norms and values of the target audience's peer group.[133]

Limited Audiences

AIDS prevention programs for women are limited not only by their sheer numbers but by the tendency of existing programs to ignore dominant portions of the population of women. Most campaign efforts to date are a direct mirroring of the nature of the scientific literature on women and AIDS that overemphasizes prostitutes and women as mothers relative to the roles that they play epidemiologically. In addition, Ostrow contends, in spite of the few efforts targeted to IV drug using women and the partners of drug users, that there is a "relative paucity" of prevention efforts for women who do not fit into these two categories, as well.[134] As a result "those women—and they are most of us—who do not fall into one of these limited spheres are largely ignored" by prevention programs.[135]

Stereotypic Messages

The failure of the scientific literature to provide an adequate basis for developing prevention campaigns for women has resulted in the development of some major emphases in the few existing prevention messages directed toward women that actually may be counterproductive. In the absence of an adequate knowledge base, these efforts are rooted in a forced reliance on stereotypic views of women.

Women as Mothers. Because the scientific literature functionally stereotypes women primarily as "mothers" it is not surprising that campaign efforts do likewise. More campaign efforts for women are based on concern for perinatal transmission than on any other factor. Thus, the primary messages that *do* reach women emphasize women as mothers, with an associated message that women are valued *most* as mothers. This most often repeated and implied message could have a boomerang effect with regard to AIDS prevention. As indicated earlier, some subpopulations of women already place primary value on women as mothers. The implied message may subtly encourage "motherhood" or the promulgation of additional children, results that are incompatible with both abstention and condom use. In addition, these messages provide no motivation for behavior change for women who do not plan to be mothers.

Impotent Interventions: Talking as Risk Assessment. A second potentially dangerous emphasis in campaign efforts targeted at women is likewise rooted in gender socialization and misguided assumptions about the role of interpersonal communication in AIDS prevention. Women are socialized to place high value, including the foundation for personal identity, on their interpersonal relationships. At the same time, interventions targeted to women tend to build on that value by emphasizing "talk" as a prevention behavior. Early guidelines from the Surgeon General about AIDS prevention included talking with a potential sexual partner about AIDS.[136] Because few alternative models were available and because the Surgeon General is viewed as a highly credible source of health information, those guidelines became the boilerplate for many campaign efforts. As a result, this message has been disseminated widely, and although not targeted to women, may have particularly dangerous implications for women.

The particular danger to women of the message that AIDS can be prevented via talk is rooted in gender socialization. Not only are women socialized to value relationships (with men in particular), they are socialized to value self-disclosure. The advice to "talk" with a partner as a means of AIDS prevention occurs in a social context that encourages women to enjoy intimate disclosure and to be attracted to men who self-disclose.[137] The advice is problematic because it encourages women to use "talk" as a means of risk assessment; no amount of talk can ensure accurate risk assessment. Research indicates that men are unlikely to tell female sexual partners about IV drug use or HIV seropositivity.[138] Beyond just withholding information, evidence suggests that men are more likely than women to lie to have sex, including lying about caring, ejaculatory control, number of partners, and having been HIV tested.[139]

The advice includes two false assumptions: that people do not lie and that one can tell when another person is lying. In the context of this potential danger, Cochran confirms that women increasingly are using "talking to their partners" as a means of reducing HIV infection.[140] This trend persists in spite of the fact that the majority of women seem to recognize the unreliable nature of men's disclosure in this context. One study found that more than 75% of women interviewed recognized that "you can't trust a partner to tell you about any of their sexually transmitted diseases";[141] yet more than half of this group reported having unprotected sex with a primary partner. Thus, "behavior change" may be occurring that actually *promotes* the spread of AIDS.[142]

Conclusion

Extant literature related to gender and interpersonal communication, gender and culture, and gender and economic issues points to the likelihood that men and women themselves construct different realities in these areas with differential implications for AIDS prevention. Because the success of AIDS-prevention campaigns is contingent upon understanding the needs and values of target audiences, research needs to identify relevant gender differences, and campaign strategies and research programs need to be adapted accordingly.[143]

Commitment in the scientific literature to a social construction of AIDS that erases women from the epidemic has resulted in an absence of research regarding gender issues; in minimal targeting of prevention programs to women; and in a lack of understanding by researchers, clinicians, policy makers, the public, and women themselves regarding the significant role that gender issues may play in achieving AIDS prevention.

Among the many implications of this trend are women's diminished access to medical resources, potentially higher rate of incorrect diagnoses, failure to identify themselves with the disease and therefore as being at risk, reduced access to information, and a general failure to meet women's education and prevention needs. Not only has the medical literature virtually ignored the association of women with AIDS, so too has the social scientific literature that is responsible for providing knowledge as a foundation for prevention efforts. Despite all of this, the limited hodgepodge of available literature does make one trend evident: Gender is a *significant* factor in understanding, predicting, and promoting AIDS prevention actions; yet beyond this trend, the issue of gender has remained largely unexplored.

Notes

1. L. K. Altman, "Women Near Men's AIDS Infection Rate," *Gainesville Sun,* July 21, 1992, p. 1A.

2. Altman, "Women Near Men's AIDS Infection Rate."

3. New York City Department of Health, *AIDS Monthly Surveillance Report* (New York: New York City Department of Health, May 1987); S. Chu, J. Buehler, & L. Berkelman, "Impact of the HIV Epidemic on Mortality of Women of Reproductive Age," *Journal of the American Medical Association* 264 (1990): 225-229.

4. Centers for Disease Control (CDC), *HIV/AIDS Surveillance Report* (Atlanta, GA: Centers for Disease Control, 1994).

5. C. A. Campbell, " Women and AIDS," *Social Science and Medicine* 30 (1990): 407-415.

6. J. E. Mantell, S. P. Schinke, & S. H. Akabas, "Women and AIDS Prevention," *Journal of Primary Prevention* 9 (1988): 18-40.

7. L. S. Wiener, "Women and Human Immunodeficiency Virus: A Historical and Personal Psychosocial Perspective," *Social Work* 36 (1991): 375.

8. Campbell, "Women and AIDS," p. 413.

9. K. Anastos & C. Marte, "Women—The Missing Persons in the AIDS Epidemic," *Health/PAC Bulletin* 19 (1989). 6-13.

10. See the following for exceptions: P. A. Treichler, "AIDS, Gender, and Biomedical Discourse: Current Contests for Meaning," in E. Fee & D. Fox (Eds.), *AIDS: The Burdens of History* (Berkeley: University of California Press, 1988): 190-266; J. S. Murphy, "Women With AIDS: Sexual Ethics in an Epidemic," in I. B. Corless & M. Pittman-Lindeman (Eds.), *AIDS: Principles, Practices, and Politics* (New York: Hemisphere, 1988): 65-79; N. K. Bell, "AIDS and Women: Remaining Ethical Issues," *AIDS Education and Prevention* 1 (1989): 22-30.

11. Murphy, "Women With AIDS," p. 65.

12. Bell, "AIDS and Women," p. 23.

13. R. Shilts, *And the Band Played On* (New York: St. Martin's, 1987): 124.

14. Campbell, "Women and AIDS," p. 310.

15. S. V. Rosser, "Perspectives: AIDS and Women," *AIDS Education and Prevention* 3 (1991): 230-240.

16. D. Q. Haney, "Study: AIDS Will Explode in 1990s," *Gainesville Sun* June 4, 1992, pp. 1A, 5A.

17. CDC, *HIV/AIDS Surveillance Report.*

18. Altman, "Women Near Men's AIDS Infection Rate," p. 1A.

19. S. Elkin, *Information on Women and AIDS,* paper presented at the 4th International Interdisciplinary Congress on Women, Hunter College, New York, June 1990.

20. M. J. Rosenberg & J. M. Weiner, "Prostitutes and AIDS: A Health Department Priority?" *American Journal of Public Health* 78 (1988): 418-423.

21. Mantell et al., "Women and AIDS Prevention," pp. 18-40.

22. J. Rodin & J. R. Ickovics, "Women's Health: Review and Research Agenda as We Approach the 21st Century," *American Psychologist* 45 (1990): 1018-1034.

23. Rosser, *AIDS Education and Prevention,* pp. 230-240.

24. M. A. Fischl et al., "The Efficacy of Azidothymidine (AZT) in the Treatment of Patients With AIDS and AIDS Related Complex: A Double-Blind Placebo-Controlled Trial," *The New England Journal of Medicine* 317 (1987): 185-191.

25. C.C.J. Carpenter, K. H. Mayer, A. Fisher, M. B. Desai, & L. Durand, "Natural History of Acquired Immunodeficiency Syndrome in Women in Rhode Island," *American Journal of Medicine* 86 (1989): 771-775.

26. C. Levine, "Women and HIV/AIDS Research," *Evaluation Review* 14 (1990): 447-463.

27. Anastos & Marte, "Women," p. 8.

28. W. Chavkin, "Preventing AIDS, Targeting Women," *Health/PAC Bulletin* 20 (1990): 22.

29. A. Juhasz, "The Contained Threat: Women in Mainstream AIDS Documentary," *The Journal of Sex Research* 27 (1990): 25-46; D. King, "Prostitutes as Pariah in the Age of AIDS: A Content Analysis of Coverage of Women Prostitutes in the *New York Times* and *The Washington Post,* September 1985-April 1988," *Women and Health* 16 (1990): 155-176.

30. J. B. Cohen, P. Alexander, & C. B. Wofsy, "Prostitutes and AIDS: Public Policy Issues," *AIDS & Public Policy Journal* 3 (1988): 16-22; J. B. Cohen, "Why Women Partners of Drug Users Will Continue to Be at Risk for HIV Infection," *Journal of Addictive Diseases* 10 (1991): 99-110.

31. Murphy, "Women With AIDS," p. 72.

32. Murphy, "Women With AIDS," p. 72.

33. Rosser, "Perspectives," pp. 230-240.

34. Anastos & Marte, "Women," pp. 6-13.

35. N. Shaw, "Preventing AIDS Among Women: The Role of Community Organizing," *Socialist Review* 100 (Fall 1988): 77-92.

36. Cohen, Alexander, & Wofsy, "Prostitutes and AIDS," p. 20.

37. Working Group on HIV Testing of Pregnant Women and Newborns, "HIV Infection, Pregnant Women, and Newborns," *Journal of the American Medical Association* 264 (1990): 2416-2420.

38. CDC, *HIV/AIDS Surveillance Report.*

39. J. B. Cohen, L. B. Hauer, & C. B. Wofsy, "Women and IV Drugs: Parenteral and Heterosexual Transmission of Human Immunodeficiency Virus," *The Journal of Drug Issues* 19 (1989): 39-56.

40. D. C. Des Jarlais, M. E. Chamberland, S. R. Yancovitz, P. Weinberg, & S. Friedman, "Heterosexual Partners: A Large Risk Group for AIDS," *The Lancet* 2 (1984): 1346-1347.

41. R. F. Schilling, N. Ei-Bassel, S. P. Schinke, S. Nichols, G. J. Botvin, & M. A. Orlandi, "Sexual Behavior, Attitudes Toward Safer Sex, and Gender Among a Cohort of 244 Recovering IV Users," *The International Journal of the Addictions* 26 (1991): 859-877.

42. Cohen, "Why Women Partners," pp. 99-110.

43. Cohen, Hauer, & Wofsy, "Women and IV Drugs," p. 41.

44. S. R. Friedman, D. C. Des Jarlais, & J. L. Sotheran, "AIDS Health Education for Intravenous Drug Users," *Health Education Quarterly* 13 (1986): 383-393.

45. J. Mondanaro, "Strategies for AIDS Prevention: Motivating Health Behavior in Drug Dependent Women," *Journal of Psychoactive Drugs* 19 (1987): 143-149; B. H. Chaffee, "Prevention and Chemical Dependence Treatment Needs of Special Target Populations," *Journal of Psychoactive Drugs* 21 (1989): 371-379.

46. Bell, "AIDS and Women," p. 24.

47. CDC, *HIV/AIDS Surveillance Report.*

48. H. Amaro, "Considerations for Prevention of HIV Infection Among Hispanic Women," *Psychology of Women Quarterly* 12 (1988): 429-443.

49. CDC, *HIV/AIDS Surveillance Report.*

50. M. T. Fullilove, R. E. Fullilove, K. Haynes, & S. Gross, "Black Women and AIDS Prevention: A View Towards Understanding the Gender Rules," *The Journal of Sex Research* 27 (1990): 47.

51. Anastos & Marte, "Women," p. 10.

52. Campbell, "Women and AIDS," p. 413; see also C. Wofsy, "Human Immunodeficiency Virus Infection in Women," *Journal of the American Medical Association* 257 (1987): 2074, 2076.

53. Wiener, "Women and Human Immunodeficiency Virus," pp. 375-378.

54. Anastos & Marte, "Women," p. 10.

55. A. N. Chowdhury, "Reproductive Rights of Women and AIDS" [letter to the editor], *Journal of the Indian Medical Association* 87 (July 1991): 185-186; C. Levine & N. Dubler, "Uncertain Risks and Bitter Realities: The Reproductive Choices of HIV-Infected Women," *The Milbank Quarterly* 68 (1990): 321-351; Murphy, "Women With AIDS," pp. 65-79.

56. Chu et al., "Impact of the HIV Epidemic," pp. 225-229; J. A. Gayle, R. Selik, & S. Chu, "Surveillance for AIDS and HIV Infection Among Black and Hispanic Children and Women of Childbearing Age, 1981-1989," *MMWR CDC Surveillance Summaries* 39 (July 1990): 23-30.

57. Mantell et al., "Women and AIDS Prevention," pp. 18-40.

58. Gayle et al., "Surveillance for AIDS and HIV Infection," pp. 23-30.

59. Campbell, "Women and AIDS," pp. 407-415; J. Efantis, "The Impact of HIV Infection on Women," in J. Durham & F. Cohen (Eds.), *The Person With AIDS: Nursing Perspectives* (New York: Spring, 1991): 300-315.

60. P. Stratton, L. Mofenson, & A. Willoughby, "Human Immunodeficiency Virus Infection in Pregnant Women Under Care at AIDS Clinical Trials Centers in the United States," *Obstetrics & Gynecology* 79 (1992): 364-368; see also A. B. Williams, "Reproductive Concerns of Women at Risk for HIV Infection," *Journal of Nurse-Midwifery* 35 (1990): 292-298.

61. CDC, *HIV/AIDS Surveillance Report.*

62. K. Carovano, "More Than Mothers and Whores: Redefining the AIDS Prevention Needs of Women," *International Journal of Health Services* 21 (1991): 132.

63. CDC, "Recommendations for Assisting in the Prevention of Perinatal Transmission of Human T-Lymphotropic Virus Type III/Lymphadenopathy-Associated Virus and Acquired Immunodeficiency Syndrome," *Morbidity and Mortality Weekly Report* 34 (July 1985): 721-732.

64. A. Kurth & M. Hutchinson, "A Context for HIV Testing in Pregnancy," *Journal of Nurse-Midwifery* 34 (1989): 259-266.

65. R. Bayer, "AIDS and the Future of Reproductive Freedom," *The Milbank Quarterly* 68 (1990): 179-204.

66. Cohen, "Why Women Partners," pp. 99-110; D. Richardson, "AIDS Education and Women: Sexual and Reproductive Issues," in P. Aggleton, P. Davies, & G. Hart (Eds.), *AIDS: Individual, Cultural, and Policy Dimensions* (London: Falmer, 1990): 169-179.

67. Levine & Dubler, "Uncertain Risks and Bitter Realities," pp. 321-351.

68. Chaffee, "Prevention and Chemical Dependence," pp. 371-379; Working Group on HIV Testing, "HIV Infection," pp. 2416-2420.

69. W. Chavkin, T. Coates, D. Des Jarlais, T. Ehrhardt, T. E. Miller, J. Stryker, & D. Worth, "Prevention: The Continuing Challenge," in H. Miller, C. Turner, & L. Moses (Eds.), *AIDS: The Second Decade* (Washington, DC: National Academy Press, 1990): 81-146; Cohen, "Why Women Partners," pp. 99-110.

70. Levine & Dubler, "Uncertain Risks and Bitter Realities," pp. 321-351; Anastos & Marte, "Women," pp. 6-13.

71. Campbell, "Women and AIDS," 407-415; H. Minkoff & J. DeHovitz, "Care of Women Infected With the Human Immunodeficiency Virus," *Journal of the American Medical Association* 266 (1991): 2253-2258; J. L. Mitchell, "Drug Abuse and AIDS in Women and Their Affected Offspring," *Journal of the National Medical Association* 81 (1989): 841-842.

72. Campbell, "Women and AIDS," pp. 407-415; Carovano, "More Than Mothers and Whores," pp. 131-142; S. Ybarra, "Women and AIDS: Implications for Counseling," *Journal of Counseling and Development* 69 (1991): 285-287.

73. Campbell, "Women and AIDS," pp. 407-415; Mitchell, "Drug Abuse and AIDS," 841-842; C. Wilfert, "HIV Infection in Maternal and Pediatric Patients," *Hospital Practice* 26 (1991): 55-67.

74. R. Sperling & P. Stratton, "Treatment Options for Human Immunodeficiency Virus-Infected Pregnant Women," *Obstetrics and Gynecology* 79 (1992): 443-448; Stratton et al., "Human Immunodeficiency Virus," pp. 364-368.

75. K. M. Franke, *Discrimination Against HIV Positive Women by Abortion Clinics in New York City,* paper presented at the Fifth International Conference on AIDS, Montreal, Canada (June 1989).

76. R. B. Gold, *Abortion and Women's Health: A Turning Point for America?* (New York: Alan Guttmacher Institute, 1990); Levine & Dubler, "Uncertain Risks and Bitter Realities," pp. 321-351.

77. Stratton et al., "Human Immunodeficiency Virus," pp. 364-368.

78. Chavkin et al., "Prevention," pp. 81-146.

79. S. K. Henshaw, "The Accessibility of Abortion Services in the United States," *Family Planning Perspectives* 23 (1991): 246-252, 263.

80. Anastos & Marte, "Women," pp. 6-13.

81. Chavkin et al., "Prevention," pp. 81-146.

82. Kurth & Hutchinson, "A Context for HIV Testing in Pregnancy," pp. 259-266; Carovano, "More Than Mothers and Whores," pp. 131-142.

83. Chavkin, "Preventing AIDS, Targeting Women," pp. 19-23.

84. Rosser, "Perspectives: AIDS and Women," pp. 230-240; Anastos & Marte, "Women," pp. 6-13; A. B. Williams, "Reproductive Concerns of Women at Risk for HIV Infection," *Journal of Nurse-Midwifery* 35 (1990): 292-298.

85. Campbell, "Women and AIDS," pp. 407-415; Chowdhury, "Reproductive Rights of Women and AIDS," pp. 185-186.

86. Campbell, "Women and AIDS," pp. 407-415.

87. Bell, "AIDS and Women," pp. 22-30; Cohen, "Why Women Partners," pp. 99-110.

88. Williams, "Reproductive Concerns," pp. 292-298.

89. A. Sunderland, G. Moroso, M. Bertahud, S. Holman, F. Cancellieri, H. Mendez, S. Landesman, & H. Minkoff, *Influence of HIV Infection on Pregnancy Decisions,* paper presented at the Fourth International Conference on AIDS, Stockholm, Sweden (June 1988); Cohen, "Why Women Partners," pp. 99-110.

90. Kurth & Hutchinson, "A Context for HIV Testing in Pregnancy," pp. 259-266.

91. Kurth & Hutchinson, "A Context for HIV Testing in Pregnancy, pp. 259-266; Campbell, "Women and AIDS," pp. 407-415; Levine & Dubler, "Uncertain Risks and Bitter Realities," pp. 321-351.

92. Chavkin et al., "Prevention," pp. 81-146.

93. Kurth & Hutchinson, "A Context for HIV Testing in Pregnancy," pp. 259-266.

94. Chavkin et al., "Prevention," pp. 81-146; C. Marte & K. Anastos, "Women—The Missing Persons in the AIDS Epidemic: Part II," *Health/PAC Bulletin* 20 (1988): 11-18.

95. Bayer, "AIDS and the Future of Reproductive Freedom," pp. 179-204.

96. Bayer, "AIDS and the Future of Reproductive Freedom," pp. 179-204; Marte & Anastos, "Women—Part II," pp. 11-18.

97. Anastos & Marte, "Women," p. 10.

98. Marte & Anastos, "Women—Part II," pp. 11-18.

99. G. J. Annas, "Protecting the Liberty of Pregnant Patients," *The New England Journal of Medicine* 316 (1987): 1213-1214.

100. V. Kolder, J. Gallagher, & M. T. Parsons, "Court-Ordered Obstetrical Interventions" [letter to the editor], *The New England Journal of Medicine* 316 (1987): 1192-1196.

101. Bayer, "AIDS and the Future of Reproductive Freedom," pp. 179-204.

102. Bayer, "AIDS and the Future of Reproductive Freedom," pp. 179-204.

103. Mantell et al., "Women and AIDS Prevention," p. 36.

104. R. Bayer, "Perinatal Transmission of HIV Infection: The Ethics of Prevention," in L. O. Gostin (Ed.), *AIDS and the Health Care System* (New Haven, CT: Yale University Press, 1990): 62-73.

105. Chowdhury, "Reproductive Rights of Women and AIDS," pp. 185-186.

106. Mantell et al., "Women and AIDS Prevention," pp. 18-40.

107. Chowdhury, "Reproductive Rights of Women and AIDS," pp. 185-186.

108. Levine & Dubler, "Uncertain Risks and Bitter Realities," p. 447.

109. Working Group on HIV Testing, "HIV Infection, Pregnant Women, and Newborns," pp. 2416-2420.

110. Working Group on HIV Testing, "HIV Infection, Pregnant Women, and Newborns," pp. 2416-2420; Kurth & Hutchinson, "A Context for HIV Testing in Pregnancy," pp. 259-266.

111. R.J.W. Cline & N. J. McKenzie, "HIV/AIDS, Women and the Threads of Discrimination: A Tapestry of Disenfranchisement," in E. B. Ray (Ed.), *Communication and Disenfranchisement* (Hillsdale, NJ: Lawrence Erlbaum, in press).

112. D. Stuntzner-Gibson, "Women and HIV Disease: An Emerging Social Crisis," *Social Work* 36 (1991): 22.

113. Mantell et al., "Women and AIDS Prevention," p. 36.

114. A. Nyamathi & R. Vasquez, "Impact of Poverty, Homelessness, and Drugs on Hispanic Women at Risk for HIV Infection," *Hispanic Journal of Behavioral Sciences* 11 (1989): 299-314; see also D. F. Harrison, K. G. Wambach, J. B. Byers, A. W. Imershein, P. Levine, K. Maddox, D. M. Quadagno, M. L. Fordyce, & M. A. Jones, "AIDS Knowledge and Risk Behaviors Among Culturally Diverse Women," *AIDS Education and Prevention* 3 (1991): 79-89.

115. V. M. Mays & S. D. Cochran, "Issues in the Perception of AIDS Risk and Risk Reduction Activities by Black and Hispanic/Latina Women," *American Psychologist* 43 (1988): 949-957.

116. S. D. Cochran, "Women and HIV Infection: Issues in Prevention and Behavior Change," in V. M. Mays, G. W. Albel, & S. F. Schneider (Eds.), *Primary Prevention of AIDS* (Newbury Park, CA: Sage, 1989): 309-327.

117. J. A. Kelly & D. A. Murphy, "Some Lessons Learned About Risk Reduction After Ten Years of the HIV/AIDS Epidemic," *AIDS Care* 3 (1991): 251-257.

118. S. I. Duke & J. Omi, "Development of AIDS Education and Prevention Materials for Women by Health Department Staff and Community Focus Groups," *AIDS Education and Prevention* 3 (1991): 92; see also Anastos & Marte, "Women," pp. 6-13.

119. Rosser, "Perspectives: AIDS and Women," pp. 230-240.

120. CDC, *HIV/AIDS Surveillance Report*.

121. Rosser, "Perspectives: AIDS and Women," pp. 230-240; Stuntzner-Gibson, "Women and HIV Disease," pp. 22-28.

122. A. Feingold, S. Vermund, R. Burk, et al., "Cervical Cytologic Abnormalities and Papillomavirus in Women Infected With Human Immunodeficiency Virus," *Journal of Acquired Immune Deficiency Syndrome* 3 (1990): 896-903; D. Povenchar et al., "HIV Status and Positive Papanicolaou Screening: Identification of a High-Risk Population," *Gynecologic Oncology* 31 (1988): 184-190; J. L. Rhoads et al., "Chronic Vaginal Candidiasis in Women With Human Immunodeficiency Virus Infection," *Journal of the American Medical Association* 257 (1987): 3105-3107; L. K. Schrager et al., "Cervical and Vaginal Squamous Cell Abnormalities in Women Infected With Human Immunodeficiency Virus," *Journal of Acquired Immune Deficiency Syndromes* 2 (1989): 570-575.

123. M. H. Allen, "Primary Care of Women Infected With the Human Immunodeficiency Virus," *Obstetrics and Gynecology Clinics of North America* 17 (1990): 557-569; G. H. Friedland, B. Saltzman, J. Vileno, K. Freeman, L. Schrager, & R. Klein, "Survival Differences in Patients With AIDS," *Journal of*

Acquired Immune Deficiency Syndromes 4 (1991): 144-153; R. Rothenberg, M. Woelfel, R. Stoneburner, et al., "Survival With the Acquired Immunodeficiency Syndrome," *The New England Journal of Medicine* 317 (1987): 1297-1302.

124. G. Kolata, "Women With AIDS Seen Dying Faster," *New York Times,* October 19, 1987, pp. A1, B4.

125. Carovano, "More Than Mothers and Whores," p. 133.

126. Carovano, "More Than Mothers and Whores," pp. 131-142.

127. Stuntzner-Gibson, "Women and HIV Disease," pp. 22-28.

128. V. T. Shayne & B. J. Kaplan, "Double Victims: Poor Women and AIDS," *Women and Health* 17 (1991): 21-37.

129. Cohen, Hauer, & Wofsy, "Women and IV Drugs," pp. 39-56.

130. Kelly & Murphy, "Some Lessons Learned About Risk Reduction," p. 254.

131. D. A. Dawson, "AIDS Knowledge and Attitudes for January-March 1989: Provisional Data From the National Health Interview Survey," *Advance Data From the Vital and Health Statistics of the National Center for Health Statistics,* DHHS Publication No. 89-1250 (Hyattsville, MD: National Center for Health Statistics, 1989): 176.

132. Duke & Omi, "Development of AIDS Education and Prevention," pp. 90-99.

133. Kelly & Murphy, "Some Lessons Learned," pp. 251-257.

134. D. G. Ostrow, "AIDS Education Through Effective Education," *Journal of the American Academy of the Arts and Sciences* 118 (1989): 246.

135. Carovano, "More Than Mothers and Whores," p. 132.

136. *Surgeon General's Report on Acquired Immune Deficiency Syndrome* (Rockville, MD: U.S. Department of Health and Human Services, October 22, 1986).

137. R.J.W. Cline, *Dangerous Liaisons: Challenging the Assumptions of Interpersonal AIDS-Prevention,* paper presented at the International Communication Association Annual Convention, Chicago (May 1991).

138. Des Jarlais et al., "Heterosexual Partners," pp. 1346-1347.

139. S. D. Cochran & V. M. Mays, "Sex, Lies, and HIV, *The New England Journal of Medicine* 322 (1990): 1774-1775.

140. Cochran, "Women and HIV Infection," pp. 309-327.

141. Harrison et al., "AIDS Knowledge and Risk Behaviors," p. 87.

142. J. H. Flaskerud & J. Thompson, "Beliefs About AIDS, Health, and Illness in Low-Income White Women," *Nursing Research* 40 (1991): 266-271; B. A. DeBuono, S. H. Zinner, M. Daamen, & W. H. McCormack, "Sexual Behavior of College Women in 1975, 1986, and 1989," *The New England Journal of Medicine* 322 (1990): 821-825; see also Cline, "Dangerous Liaisons."

143. R. E. Rice & C. K. Atkin (Eds.), "Preface: Trends in Communication Campaign Research," in *Public Communication Campaigns* (Newbury Park, CA: Sage, 1989): 7-11.

27

The Reconstruction of AIDS as a Women's Health Issue

Salome Raheim

What the media tell us about women and HIV/AIDS comes from many sources. Their story is told through the eyes, the thoughts, the words, the anger, and the tears of women with HIV/AIDS. The message comes from social activists who pass out condoms in beauty parlors and on street corners and who demonstrate in front of the National Institutes of Health to increase funding for AIDS research on women. The message comes from public health officials, health care practitioners, and medical researchers. And the message is fairly consistent. We do not know enough. We have not done enough. We did not anticipate the potential impact of AIDS on women early enough, and we have not been effective in stopping the epidemic.

For individuals, media constructions of HIV infection and AIDS can influence (a) perceived risk of infection, (b) knowledge of effective preventive measures and perceptions of responsibility for employing them, and (c) attitudes toward infected persons. Together, the potential influence of media messages on individual and collective responses to the AIDS epidemic and the increasing threat of AIDS to the lives and health of women demand a critical analysis of media messages about HIV infection and AIDS. The following analysis evaluates the television and radio public service announcements (PSAs) in the most extensive mass media, public health campaign in U.S. history, the Centers for Disease Control's "America Responds to AIDS" campaign. Next, it analyzes a sample of the print media coverage of women and HIV/AIDS during the *second* decade of the epidemic.

The Centers for Disease Control's Media Campaign: "America Responds to AIDS" (ARTA)

In 1987, the newly established National AIDS Information and Education Program (NAIEP) of the Centers for Disease Control (CDC) launched the most extensive mass media, public health campaign in U.S. history to disseminate information about AIDS. The centerpiece of this public education and information system was the "America Responds to AIDS" (ARTA) campaign. The ARTA campaign materials include brochures, posters, displays, public service announcements for broadcast and print media, and some non-English language materials.[1] As new materials were introduced, they were intended to supplement rather than to replace existing materials.

The CDC used a media marketing strategy for the ARTA campaign in an effort to set and sustain a national media agenda for AIDS education and prevention. The strategy was intended to enlist the media as partners in establishing a clear national public health agenda on AIDS.[2] To generate media coverage of AIDS-related information, the CDC held news conferences and satellite interviews, designed press kits, and developed video and audio news releases and public service announcements for each phase of the campaign. Clearly, analysis of the CDC's "America Responds to AIDS" campaign is fundamental to understanding mainstream media messages generated about AIDS in general, and about women and AIDS specifically. The campaign attempts to accomplish behavioral change in target audiences by (a) altering attitudes toward specific behaviors and (b) altering perceptions of the social norms regarding those behaviors. The CDC's express goal is to encourage and reinforce social norms supportive of healthful behaviors among specifically targeted audiences.

"America Responds to AIDS" evolved in six distinct phases. Phase III featured efforts targeted specifically at women.

What Does "America Responds to AIDS" Tell Women?

The CDC first emphasized the vulnerability of women to HIV infection in Phase III of its ARTA campaign, launched in the fall of 1988. Although Phase III was intended to begin in June 1988 as a stand-alone release, it was implemented later than planned along with a set of PSAs targeting sexually active adults with multiple partners. Consequently, Phase III became "Women at Risk, Multiple-Partner Sexually Active Adults."

PUBLIC SERVICE ANNOUNCEMENTS

In Phase III of the ARTA campaign, there were 13 different public service announcements (PSAs) released. Six of these targeted women, and all were available in a 60-second format. Each of these PSAs contained one or more of three basic themes: (a) the importance of being informed about AIDS; (b) reasons why women are at risk; and (c) the necessity for women to take action to (i) become informed or (ii) protect themselves and their unborn children.

Three questions guide this analysis: (a) What specific behaviors of women do these messages target? (b) How do these messages attempt to alter women's attitudes toward these behaviors? (c) How do these messages attempt to alter women's perceptions of the social norms regarding these behaviors?

TARGET BEHAVIORS

The six ARTA PSAs that target women specifically can be classified in two ways. The first category will be referred to as the "Talk About AIDS" messages. These attempt to encourage women to talk with friends and those they are dating about AIDS. The second category will be referred to as the "Don't Let It Happen to You" messages. These attempt to encourage women to take action to protect themselves from contracting HIV.

The "Talk About AIDs" PSAs strive to reach women who are at different levels of comfort when talking about AIDS. In one PSA, titled "Heard Much," an interviewer initiates a conversation about AIDS with a middle-aged woman saying, "Heard much 'bout AIDS lately?" Initially, the woman responds that she has heard a great deal about AIDS from the media, but that "no one" talks about it. As the conversation progresses, the woman admits that, although AIDS is important, she and her friends do not talk about AIDS because "they're embarrassed" and because of feeling uncertain about how to discuss the subject.

In another PSA, "Dinner, a Movie, & Talk," a woman reveals to an interviewer that the thought of AIDS is depressing and "not exactly my idea of a great date," but that she is beginning to broach the subject with men. In a third PSA, "Best Friend," an interviewer talks to a young woman whose "best friend has AIDS." She talks about the hardship, emotional difficulty, and sadness involved because "[t]his person I love is falling to pieces." The interviewer empathizes with how tired the woman must be and encourages her to tell others about AIDS. She responds, "every day, I do." All three of these PSAs end with an announcer's voice saying, "Talk about AIDS because talking will help you understand." The announcer also provides the telephone number to the National AIDS Hot Line.

Each PSA attempts to appeal to women at different levels of comfort and experience in talking about AIDS, and therefore each message attempts to alter attitudes toward talking about AIDS in different ways. Together, these three PSAs attempt to alter women's attitudes toward talking about AIDS by addressing concerns about fear, embarrassment, sadness, and hardships related to AIDS. They also attempt to construct talking about AIDS as a social norm by providing examples of two women who say they are talking about AIDS, one who is starting to talk about AIDS with others, and one who talks about AIDS "every day."

Unlike the "Talk About AIDS" PSAs, the "Don't Let It Happen to You" group of PSAs advocates that women take more assertive action to protect themselves against AIDS. These PSAs aim (a) to increase women's perceptions of risk of contracting AIDS from male partners who may be engaging in high-risk behaviors (e.g., unprotected sex with men or other women or sharing needles); and (b) to encourage them to protect themselves by terminating relationships with men whose behavior puts the women at risk.

One of the most direct of these messages is "Guess Who I Saw Today." Presented as a monologue, a woman reads a letter to her partner, Les. She explains to him that she saw him with another woman in the park on a day that he told her he was out of town on a business trip:

> I been walking around thinkin' there was no way I was gettin' AIDS. I knew my man wasn't foolin' around. But you lied to me. And you've put me at risk. . . . I'm going to find a man who wants to be with me—just me. And that's not you!

"Guess Who I Saw Today" targets women who believe they are in monogamous relationships and attempts to increase their awareness that they may be at risk for contracting the AIDS virus because of their partner's infidelity. The message seeks to increase women's negative attitudes toward unfaithful male partners and increase their positive attitudes toward terminating relationships with such men. No other prevention strategies (e.g., condom use) are proposed.

"Women at Risk" conveys the same message using a different strategy. In this PSA, three women are engaged in conversation. The interaction begins with the first woman, Marsella, explaining that she ended a relationship with her male partner when she learned of his high-risk behavior. She says, "Listen, let me tell you. When I found out, I just told mine to take a long walk." A second woman, Iona, responds that her economic dependence upon her male partner makes such a course of action difficult: "Easy for you, you've got a job. What about me? I've never even had one. With him gone, it's just me and the kids, another on the way."

The first woman who spoke, Marsella, and a third woman, Hattie, do not empathize with Iona's concerns, nor do they address them. Marsella reinforces her position about male high-risk behavior, saying, "I didn't play that stuff before this AIDS thing started up, and I'm not about to start." Hattie interjects, "That's the main problem we've got to face. Men. I mean, I didn't know what my man was up to out there." Marsella is unrelenting in her stance. "Like I said, if you can't trust 'em, dump 'em." Iona introduces another objection, but is interrupted by Marsella:

> But nothin', Sis. We've got to look out for ourselves. I've been readin' about women gettin' the AIDS virus from their husbands, their boyfriends, and then wind up havin' their babies born with it. Do you want that to happen to you?

"Women at Risk" identifies terminating relationships with male partners with high-risk behaviors as a desirable and necessary behavior, no matter what the woman's circumstances. The message attempts to create a positive attitude toward this behavior by overcoming the objections women might have to leaving partners with high-risk behaviors. The message also seeks to present this course of action as a social norm. The women advocating for this course of action are more forceful and outnumber the woman who voices objections.

A third PSA, "Baby," is the monologue of a woman against a background of the street noises of an urban setting. She explains to an unidentified audience that "her man" died of AIDS and that she did not know she had been infected with the virus until her baby was born with it. She explains that her partner was "shootin' up and sharin' needles," but that she did not know. She ends her monologue saying, "Don't let it happen to you." The central message is that women are at risk of AIDS infection because of the behavior of their male partners and that women must take action to protect themselves and their unborn children. In this case, a specific behavior is not identified. Women are told to take responsibility for protecting themselves, but *how* to accomplish this is not stated. The message only admonishes women, "don't let it happen to you."

The "Don't Let It Happen to You" messages effectively convey that women are at risk of HIV infection because of their male partners' high-risk behavior (e.g., having multiple partners or sharing needles) of which women are unaware. One of these PSAs, however, leaves women with no recommended prevention strategy. The others advocate leaving partners who engage in high-risk behavior. For many women, this strategy is not a viable alternative. One of the PSAs, "Women at Risk," even articulates the dilemma that employing this strategy presents for many women: "Easy for you, you've got a job? What about me? I've never even had one. With him gone, it's just me and the kids, another [child] on the way."

In the PSA, this woman's statement is ignored. Her conversational partners neither empathize with her predicament nor offer her alternatives for resolving her dilemma. For women who are neither economically, socially, nor emotionally prepared to separate from a partner whose behavior may be putting them at risk of HIV infection, this message is more likely to be disempowering than empowering. Presenting them with a message that asserts they are responsible for protecting themselves and their unborn children from infection in conjunction with a prevention strategy they perceive as impossible to implement can create feelings of powerlessness instead of a sense of self-efficacy and of personal responsibility for their own health. If a woman perceives her choices as risking infection versus risking homelessness, poverty, and isolation from a love relationship, a woman may choose to risk infection, a more abstract and distant threat to her and her children's survival.

The "Women at Risk" PSA is especially problematic because it acknowledges the dilemma that women face but renders it insignificant. Trivializing the critical survival issues that some women encounter discounts the reality of many women's lives, rendering the women insignificant as well. The net result is disempowerment.

Print Media Coverage
of Women and AIDS/HIV

Although important, the CDC campaign was not the only source of messages about AIDS that women would receive. The following analysis focuses on newspaper articles published during the first 3 years of the decade, 1990 through 1992. Unlike other studies in this volume, articles for this chapter were selected from a single, major newspaper published in a city that is an AIDS "epicenter." The goal is to examine in depth (rather than breadth) an elite paper that represents the "best" coverage available. The *New York Times* was selected because in 1990 (a) New York City had the highest incidence of AIDS of any city in the United States, and (b) AIDS was the leading cause of death for women in New York City during the period being studied.

To identify relevant articles, a key word search was conducted using the database *ProQuest,* which contains the written text of *New York Times* articles published during the period of interest. The key words used were *women* and *acquired immune deficiency syndrome* or *human immunodeficiency virus.* The search yielded 387 *New York Times* articles. From these, articles were eliminated that did not discuss women and AIDS/HIV in at least a minor way, leaving 207 published over the 3-year period, 1990 through 1992.

The 207 selected articles were categorized according to the relative amount of content about women and AIDS or HIV that they contained. Three categories were identified: (a) women or an issue of central importance to women was the main topic; (b) women or an issue of central importance to women was of major significance but not the main topic; and (c) information relevant to women was mentioned but was not prominent. (An example of an article classified as an issue of central importance to women and AIDS/HIV is "Abortion Clinics Often Reject Patients With the AIDS Virus.")[3]

Of the 207 articles, 52 (25%) were classified in the first category, 59 (29%) in the second, and 96 (46%) in the third. This selection of articles indicates that the *New York Times* published an average of 6 articles per month that had some content relating to women and AIDS/HIV. Articles that focused on women and AIDS/HIV as the main topic and those with significant content on women were published on an average of three times per month. It cannot be assumed, however, that these findings are representative of the amount of coverage on women and AIDS/HIV in newspapers nationwide. As a leader in the field, it is expected that the *New York Times* would provide more responsible and thorough coverage of this issue than might be expected of a local newspaper. It represents, therefore, the best potential outlet with newspapers, rather than a norm.

If categorized by topic, these articles fall into four types of AIDS news stories: (a) business stories that focus on production of new drugs; (b) policy stories that discuss AIDS-related legislation and regulations; (c) legal stories about AIDS-related litigation; and (d) public health and science stories that report the incidence, rate, and impact of the epidemic, as well as findings of recent studies, treatment, and prevention efforts. Of course, some news articles contained several of these topics.

AIDS: A Contested Definition

Prior to its revision in 1992, the CDC's AIDS definition contributed to the under-recognition of HIV infection in women. As women with AIDS, AIDS activists, and women's health organizations began to recognize the impact on women of the CDC's AIDS definition, the struggle around redefining AIDS began. The media reflected this emerging struggle, bringing the debate to broader public awareness. Three *New York Times* articles published in late 1990 exposed the debate. The first of these articles was a legal story, in which the article begins:

> Hundreds of women, children, drugs addicts and homeless people disabled by the AIDS virus are being improperly denied Federal benefits because the Government is using a flawed and outdated definition of the disease, a lawsuit filed yesterday in Federal court in Manhattan charged.[4]

The article explains that the suit charges that people are being denied benefits in spite of repeated hospitalizations for disabling conditions, including gynecological disorders, because those symptoms are not included in the CDC's AIDS definition used by the Social Security Administration. This article brings to public attention that the definition of AIDS is a contested issue and cannot be taken for granted. It also offers a convincing argument that the definition may be fundamentally discriminatory.

Two other articles further challenged the definition, including an article with a photograph and one editorial. The editorial, by David Barr, the Assistant Director of Policy at Gay Men's Health Crisis, provides a compelling and cogent critique of the CDC's AIDS definition. Barr discusses the deficiencies in the official definition and its consequences for women and calls for a new definition:

> What the CDC definition fails to acknowledge is that HIV manifests itself differently in different populations. Women, for whom AIDS is now the leading cause of death in certain age groups in New York City, often develop serious gynecological problems that are HIV-related. . . . Yet, because they do not fit into the CDC definition, [they] are ineligible for AIDS benefits and services. When these illnesses result in death, they are rarely recorded as AIDS-related, significantly skewing the statistics on AIDS. Because of this, we do not really know how many people have died of AIDS.[5]

This article convincingly argues that the CDC's AIDS definition negatively impacts women regarding AIDS diagnosis, treatment, and qualification for disability benefits.

Together, these three articles provide some evidence that media reports about AIDS served to highlight the debate about AIDS as a women's health issue. It is not being suggested here that the issue of women and AIDS has been given the attention that it deserves based on the serious and critical nature of the disease. Yet it cannot be ignored that as media articles brought to public awareness divergent opinions about issues regarding women and AIDS, such as the issue of the definition of AIDS, the media were playing a significant role in the reconstruction of AIDS as a women's health issue.

Position of Women in the Spread of the Epidemic

Another issue emerging from *New York Times* coverage of women and AIDS is the position of women in the spread of the epidemic; women as vectors versus women as victims. Certainly, the media in the 1990s have identified women as prostitutes spreading AIDS to various male clients and have also identified children as innocent victims who contract AIDS from mothers who are drug addicted or who have had sex with IVDUs (IV drug users). This analysis suggests, however, that in the elite media during the period of 1990-1992, women were constructed as victims who had contracted AIDS from men who are gay or bisexual, who are IVDUs, or who have had unprotected heterosexual contact with multiple partners.

Women as Victims

In news stories about HIV positive women, numerous messages appear about monogamous women contracting the AIDS virus from men partners. In contrast, public health policy has been directed toward preventing HIV positive women from infecting other people in their lives.[6] As the previous chapter, by Welch Cline and McKenzie, indicates, emphasis in the scientific media on early detection of HIV in infants and the study of AIDS transmission by prostitutes positions "women as vectors" or "vessels of infection" and ignores their health care needs.[7] News stories that focus on HIV positive women and how they became infected offer a competing construction of women as victims, vulnerable to infection due to male high-risk behavior.

In spite of the media construction of women as victims in the AIDS epidemic, there are significant instances of the media's propensity to emphasize the construction of women as vectors.[8] Of the findings reported, two mention women, and of those two, one focuses on women as prostitutes and the effectiveness of the use of condoms. The other mentions the impact of HIV infected mothers on the mental development of their children. It is significant to note that of the findings from 3,000 research papers, this article does not identify a single paper that reports findings regarding AIDS diagnosis, treatment, or prevention issues relevant to women.

Humanizing HIV Positive Persons

In the *New York Times* articles in which women were central or in which there was equal focus on women as on men or children, there appeared to be an effort made to humanize HIV positive people. Many of the stories identified provide detailed examples of women with AIDS and what their lives are like. The stories that are told represent a diverse group of women. Women who are current and former IVDUs who have been infected through needle sharing or unprotected sex in exchange for drugs or money; women who are African American, Latino, and white; women who contracted

HIV from sex with partners who are IVDUs; poor and middle-class women who contracted the virus, sometimes from a partner in a casual sexual encounter, sometimes from a steady partner, sometimes from a husband as a result of his current or previous high-risk behavior. Some of these women have children and some do not.

The message that comes through clearly as a result of presenting a diverse group of HIV positive women is that any woman can be infected with HIV. That is a consistent message. Ceasing to use language like "high-risk group," these news articles convey the message that any woman who is sexually active is at risk. AIDS is not restricted to specific populations. One article notes, "AIDS has become an equal opportunity disease."

These news stories depict the inaccurate assumptions about HIV infection that women who had contracted the disease had held: (a) that they could not contract the virus from heterosexual sex; (b) that their male partners had been honest about their sexual or drug histories; and (c) that their male partners were not currently sharing needles or sexually active with other men or women. Although some women in these stories had knowingly engaged in high-risk behavior (particularly drug addicted women and those who exchanged sex for drugs or money), most of the HIV positive women were not aware that they were at risk of infection. Through these stories, women's vulnerability is made clear; and the pain and despair caused by the disease, compounded by inadequate health care, discrimination in housing, the social welfare system, employment, and the health care system become apparent. Several cases illustrate these points. A woman with AIDS was fired from her job.[9] Many HIV positive women have been denied federal disability benefits.[10] Women are denied health care because they are HIV positive,[11] and many clinics routinely deny abortions to HIV positive women, although such discrimination is illegal.[12]

Discrimination Against Women With HIV

The articles reporting on denial of abortion to HIV positive women highlight discrimination against women with AIDS in the health care system, as well as efforts to end that discrimination. These articles indicate that some health care providers have been resistant to complying with New York laws and the American Disabilities Act of 1988, which prohibit discrimination against persons with disabilities, including AIDS. A news story on the subpoena of records of abortion clinics that refused to treat HIV positive women is an example.[13]

Articles about AIDS activist protests and legal actions help to highlight other types of discrimination against women. The *New York Times* article titled "18 Arrested in Washington AIDS Protest" focused attention on the concern regarding women's underrepresentation in clinical drug trials.[14] Another article focusing on legal action highlighted the concern about the timely release of findings regarding 300 women who had been included in clinical drug trials but whose test information had not been released.[15] Under the Freedom of Information Act, AIDS activists were petitioning for the release of these records so that the results of this study could be made available to women in a timely way. The article revealed that there is often a delay in the release of significant research findings because of researchers' needs to publish and journals' reluctance to publish findings that have been previously released to the public. The question raised here is how much of a priority is given to helping the people about whom the studies are being conducted—in this case, women.

AIDS Activists and Activities

News reports of AIDS activists' activities and positions have increased public awareness of contested issues and have helped to begin to reconstruct AIDS as a women's health issue. A *New York Times* article on ACT-UP's policies and positions discusses the organization's accusations that women were underrepresented in the National Institute of Allergy and Infection Diseases (NIAID) AIDS research.[16] The article reports that Dr. Anthony Fauci, director of NIAID, "credits the group with playing a constructive role."[17] By reporting both AIDS activists' and government officials' positions, contested issues are brought to public attention.

Another important aspect of AIDS as a women's health issue that becomes apparent from analysis of news media is who the participants are in the dialogue that is reconstructing AIDS as a women's health issue. The leading actors are women with AIDS; AIDS activists such as ACT-UP; education and prevention workers with private nonprofit organizations, such as Marion Banzhaf with the New Jersey Women and AIDS Network; state and federal public health officials; and AIDS researchers. Analysis of news reports makes it evident that although there are common concerns, there are different agendas, different understandings of what needs to be done and by whom, and different priorities about how funds should be spent and on whom. There are several articles that illustrate these differing perspectives.

This discussion is not intended to suggest that the media actively seek to air all minority opinions. The social movement literature, however, tells us clearly that social movement organizations can effectively stage media events and manipulate the media in a way that their views gain media attention. This is evident through protests and other activities that AIDS activists have devised to force attention to the issues these organizations thought were important, as well as to gain attention to the perspective on issues that these organizations were advocating.

Another significant area in which the media are participating in the reconstruction of AIDS as a women's health issue is through news stories on prevention efforts. In the case of AIDS, prevention is of particular importance because there is no cure in sight for the disease. Consistent with the medical scientific literature, media articles have made clear that prevention is a complex issue, the success of which is dependent upon addressing other social problems, including drugs, poverty, sexism, and racism. Consistent with the social scientific literature, news articles have highlighted reasons why prevention efforts to date have not been successful. These reasons include the lack of knowledge about sexual mores, sexual behaviors, and cultural practices of specific populations and what types of education and prevention approaches are likely to be successful with them. News stories have also made clear that successful prevention efforts and successful implementation of prevention behaviors depend upon gender roles, cultural issues, and social conditions that women face, especially poor women and women of color.

Social Vulnerability and Social Change

Discussions about AIDS education and prevention for women bring to the fore "women's social vulnerability" to HIV infection, due to various oppressive factors such as unequal distribution of social, economic, and political power among men and women. Media articles have recognized that it is in part women's social vulnerability that fuels the epidemic and perpetuates and accelerates the spread of AIDS among women. The absence of preventive methods that women can control is an example of women's continuing vulnerability to infection.

Media articles about specific prevention efforts also publicize what is being done and the debates that accompany these prevention efforts. Clean needle programs and condom distribution programs in high schools are among the most hotly debated prevention issues. Most prevention articles focus, however, on the efforts of individuals within organizations who work "in the trenches." These prevention workers are usually women, including HIV positive women, former prison inmates, ex-prostitutes, and former drug addicts. These women conduct AIDS education discussions in private homes, distribute condoms and AIDS information at beauty parlors, and distribute clean needles on the streets. The stories of their efforts emphasize the overwhelming magnitude of this epidemic, highlight the dedication of these women, and point to the necessity for innovative strategies to educate women and empower them to protect themselves from HIV infection.

Conclusion

Turning the spotlight on women and on media such as the *New York Times* may play a role in bringing about a shift in our understanding of AIDS. By including more voices through responsible reporting, the medical and social welfare establishment may be encouraged finally to treat the issue of women and AIDS with the seriousness it deserves.

Notes

1. U.S. Department of Health and Human Services, *Catalog of HIV and AIDS Education and Prevention Materials,* prepared by CDC National AIDS Clearinghouse (Rockville, MD: Government Printing Office, 1993).

2. N. Hutton Keiser, "Strategies of Media Marketing for 'America Responds to AIDS' and Applying Lessons Learned," *Public Health Reports* 106 (1991): 623-627.

3. E. Rosenthal, "Abortion Clinics Often Reject Patients With the AIDS Virus," *New York Times,* October 23, 1990, p. A1.

4. J. Barbanel, "U.S. Is Sued Over AIDS Benefits," *New York Times,* October 2, 1990, p. B3. Copyright © 1990 by The New York Times Company. Reprinted by permission.

5. D. Barr, "Who Has AIDS? Think Again," *New York Times,* December 1, 1990, p. 25. Copyright © 1990 by The New York Times Company. Reprinted by permission.

6. National Lawyers Guild AIDS Network, "Women and AIDS: Epidemic of Societal Denial, Blame, and Poverty," *The Exchange* 14 (1991): 2-7.

7. "AIDS: Women vs. Their Infants in HIV Testing Debate," *AIDSLINE* (1992): 1-4.

8. For a good example, see J. P. Hilts, "3,000 Papers at AIDS Gathering Point to Gains and Frustration," *New York Times,* June 26, 1990, p. C11.

9. B. Lambert, "New York Area Tour Shows Panel Havoc of AIDS," *New York Times,* February 28, 1990, p. B3.

10. Barbanel, "U.S. Is Sued," p. B3; Hilts, "3,000 Papers," p. C11.

11. C. P. Weinstock, "Public and Private Toll of Living With AIDS," *New York Times,* October 21, 1990, pp. 1-3.

12. Rosenthal, "Abortion Clinics," p. A1.

13. Rosenthal, "Abortion Records Subpoenaed," *New York Times,* November 6, 1990, p. B2.

14. "18 Arrested in Washington AIDS Protest," *New York Times,* October 3, 1990, p. A22. Copyright © 1990 by The New York Times Company. Reprinted by permission.

15. G. Kolata, "The Nation: Patients and Scientists Fight for Control of Medical Information," *New York Times,* December 2, 1990, sec. 4, p. 3.

16. J. DeParle, "Rude, Rash, Effective, Act-Up Shifts AIDS Policy," *New York Times,* January 3, 1990, p. B1. Copyright © 1990 by The New York Times Company. Reprinted by permission.

17. DeParle, "Rude, Rash," p. B1.

28

Conclusion

A Woman-Centered "Sense-Making" Approach
to Communicating About Women's Reproductive Health

Roxanne Louiselle Parrott

> *The problem is not only to conceptualize communication-as-dialogue, but
> also to practice it as dialogue.*
>
> Brenda Dervin, "Audience as Listener
> and Learner, Teacher and Confidant"[1]

There is a *constant* tension between serving the social versus the economic health and
well-being of human beings. Because resources are finite, decisions must be made
about what research questions to fund in order to increase medical knowledge and
understanding, and to communicate what has been learned. We conclude this volume
by arguing for a different criterion in making these decisions in relation to women's
reproductive health. Our approach would be woman-centered foremost, relying upon
the building of both environmental and social support for women's health behaviors.

Sense-Making and Women's Reproductive Health

To advance a woman-centered approach to communicating about women's reproductive health, it is proposed that a *sense-making* framework be adopted. A woman-centered sense-making approach to communicating about women's reproductive health gives prominence to situation in constructing women's behavior, acknowledging the inherently systemic nature of the "place" in which a woman resides—both temporally and culturally—in ordaining, maintaining, and sustaining her day-to-day thoughts, emotions, and actions.[2] The sense-making campaigner does not ask, "Why aren't women doing what we want them to do?" but rather, "How could women be expected to do other than what they are doing?" Whereas the second question may motivate institutions to reassess their priorities and agendas, the former question too frequently lays blame at the feet of those intended to be helped by the institutions.[3]

In this volume, we explore communicating about women's reproductive health research, practices, and policies in order to expand the purview of audiences, including institutions, with direct responsibilities for setting the agendas in relation to women's reproductive health. The enlargement of audience to include the individuals, groups, and institutions with direct responsibility for communicating with women about their reproductive health constitutes a critical step in the process of operationalizing a sense-making approach. It also fulfills an ethical obligation to refrain from health promotion in an environment not equipped to support recommended practices.[4] As part of the efforts to enlarge the meaning of *audience,* a sense-making approach depends upon the identification of discontinuities.

IDENTIFYING DISCONTINUITIES AS SENSE-MAKING

The foundational assumption of a sense-making approach, the discontinuity premise, acknowledges that gaps exist between what one group may view as real or possible versus what another group experiences or observes. Gaps are "always cognitive [i.e., constructed in the head] and sometimes are overbearingly physical as well [i.e., coping with illness]."[5] In relation to women's reproductive health, a sense-making approach demands the identification of the potential realities based both on what actually exists and is possible in a woman's environment; and, perhaps more importantly, on which of these potential realities are known to exist by the women.

A number of overarching discontinuities are identified in this volume that might be addressed through the adoption of a sense-making approach to communicating with women about their reproductive health:

1. *There is a gap between what is known about communicating social support and the inclusion of this knowledge and information in health care policies and programs designed for women.*
2. *There is a gap between what is known about pregnancy and disease control, and promotion efforts to increase women's confidence in their ability to exercise control in these areas.*

3. *There is a gap between the rhetoric that espouses women's choice and the legal status of women's choices relating to reproductive health.*

4. *There is a gap between the campaign communication that promotes prenatal care and mammography to women and the availability of such care for women.*

5. *There is a gap between the design and implementation of reproductive health programs for women and women's religiosity and/or altruism.*

6. *There is a gap between what is medically known about women and menopause and the definition of menopause as deficiency.*

7. *There is a gap between what is medically known about women and abortion, and definitions of health risks for women from abortion, especially for teens.*

8. *There is a gap between policy and practice in the delivery of reproductive health care to women, especially women of color.*

9. *There is a gap between the importance ascribed to physical versus psychological effects in women's reproductive health, with the latter assuming prominence primarily when the former fails to support political or historical agendas.*

10. *There is a gap between a marketing agenda to sell products to women for their reproductive health and a health agenda to promote understanding to women about their reproductive health.*

These gaps may be the result of legislative or community structural barriers to access to health care and information, as well as cognitive limits to women's involvement and knowledge about their own reproductive health.[6] To identify discontinuities, a sense-making approach begins with systematic formative evaluation of an environment. The activities involved in this process help to guide planners' efforts in building environmental and social support in advance of promoting individual health behavior.

The "Place" Where Women Reside: Building Environmental Support

An examination of the environment in which health behavior is promoted acknowledges the importance of structural facilitators and barriers to women's reproductive health behavior. This issue, in particular, vitally assists in the expansion of audiences to enlarge the purview for communicating about women's reproductive health.

Structural Characteristics of Communities: Evaluating Availability

Structural characteristics of communities explain the gap that occurs between the effects of information diffused into a system on women's knowledge about reproductive health as compared with women's reproductive health behavior in terms of the societal resources necessary for a woman to act in a recommended fashion. To identify gaps in relation to structural characteristics of communities and women's reproductive health, the following questions should be considered:

1. what societal conditions *must* be present in order for women to behave in a recommended fashion,
2. what conditions could function to *motivate* women's behavior, *and*
3. what conditions could function to *inhibit* women's behavior?

A cursory examination of the broad discontinuities previously identified in relation to the discussions in this volume points to the gap between campaigns to promote prenatal care and mammography, and women's compliance, as an example of the failure of community structural characteristics to support behavior being recommended to women. Prenatal care and mammography require the presence of an adequate number of qualified facilities and providers in order for women to act. In the absence of either, women's behavior simply is not possible.

The identification of a structural barrier to health behavior in a community provides a different focus for efforts to communicate to women about their reproductive health than the usual emphasis on the women. If an environment lacks sufficient qualified providers to screen women, for example, high school graduates looking for employment opportunities could become one audience for communication efforts designed to increase the availability of technicians to provide mammograms. Technical schools aiming to increase student enrollment might become one audience to whom to communicate the need for such training; they, in turn, communicate the need to their students. Investors looking for opportunities in the medical field might provide another audience, with efforts being aimed at gaining their support in the development of additional screening centers.

Each of the above audiences and the goals of communicating with them provide a focus for campaign communication, as well as the impetus for newspaper and television stories. The story of one woman who seeks prenatal care but can find no one to provide the care may be seen by voters and legislators alike, prompting action. One high school graduate or welfare recipient who trains to become a qualified technician and successfully gains satisfying employment may provide a story that motivates others to do the same.

The discontinuity identified between the rhetoric of women's choice and the legal status of women's choice relating to reproductive health provides another example of a community structural gap. The availability of reproductive health services is integrally related to legislative activities that—although they may not guarantee a woman access—can clearly *deny* access through both inaction *and* action. For example, the 102nd Congress passed a law in 1992 titled the "Cancer Registries Amendment Act"[7] that finds that "cancer control efforts, including prevention and early detection, are best addressed locally by State health departments that can identify unique needs."[8] Thus, cancer control activities within states determine whether or not women will have access to Pap tests or mammograms.

As one example of how a state may support such activities, Georgia's Cancer Control Program was legislated in 1937 through the recommendation of Georgia physicians that the state pay the hospital costs for cancer treatment for the medically indigent. The state agreed to pay the hospital costs, physicians agreed to provide their services

without charge, and the *Cancer State Aid program* came into being. Georgia also has
a Governor's Cancer Advisory Committee that provides overall guidance in program
planning and policies, and serves as the state *advocacy* group for expanding and improving
the Cancer Program. By law, the Committee includes one member from each of the
four area medical schools, two members who represent hospitals and cancer clinics,
two members who represent the American Cancer Society, one member who represents
the Health Insurance Association of America, one member who represents the Division
of Rehabilitative Services of the Department of Human Resources, one member who
represents the Georgia Nurses Association, one member who represents the Georgia
Association of Pathologists, one member who represents the Georgia State Medical
Association, one member who represents the Georgia Pharmaceutical Association, and
two members who represent the general public. This is noteworthy, as the majority of
the Committee's members are medical professionals, and their advocacy efforts may
well differ in direction and tone from what a group of Georgia women seeking services
would advocate.

Georgia's Division of Public Health of the Department of Human Resources functions through a network of 19 district health units and 159 county health departments.
Recall that the federal law leaves the responsibility for cancer control, prevention, and
detection efforts within the sphere of influence of state health departments. In Georgia,
funding for the system is provided by county, state, and federal governments. By
Georgia law, the county board of health has authority over the county health department, with the district medical director and staff providing programmatic guidance to
county health department staff. Georgia provides cancer screening services through its
local county health departments, including Pap smear screening, breast examinations,
and instruction in breast self-examination. The state functions as a planning body,
seeking to guide the activities of health districts in a programmatic fashion, contracting
with units to perform particular interventions and demonstrations, and evaluating both
the means and the needs of the state in relation to cancer control and the interventions
contracted with the state as demonstration projects.

In Georgia, requests for additional funding to provide cancer control services must
come up from the local health districts, through the Division of Public Health, the
Department of Human Resources, and the Board of Human Resources, to the Governor's
Office. The governor presents a budget to the legislature, and health-related and
appropriations committees of both House and Senate must include these requests in
the state budget package that is submitted to state House and Senate for approval.
Clearly, these activities will impact the design and delivery of cancer control activities
to women living in Georgia.

In sum, women's reproductive health behaviors occur in an *organizational and
legislative environment;* both should be assessed in efforts to understand what a woman
will experience when she attempts to act on advice to behave in a particular fashion.
The presence of an adequate number of centers and clinicians, however, or of other
structural characteristics to support women's reproductive health behavior, does not
guarantee the performance of recommended practices. A woman-centered sense-making

approach must also consider what structural characteristics of the women are necessary prerequisites in order for action to occur.

Structural Characteristics of
the Women: Evaluating Eligibility

Beyond the structural constraints imposed on behavior by the community in which a woman lives, an examination of structural characteristics of individual women is a necessary step toward adopting a sense-making approach to health promotion. This focuses attention on the tangible personal resources that a woman needs in order to turn knowledge into behavior. To identify gaps in relation to structural characteristics of women, the following questions should be considered:

1. What resources *must* women have in order to behave in a recommended fashion;
2. what personal resources increase the likelihood that women will act; *and*
3. what personal resources decrease the likelihood that women will act?

The identification of discontinuities in terms of gaps in women's resources enlarges the meaning of access, suggesting that the construct has at least two dimensions, one related to availability—an issue associated with the structural characteristics of community—and another related to eligibility, which more closely approximates the issue of structural characteristics of the individual. In terms of the broad discontinuities emerging from the analyses and reviews in this text, the gap between policy and practice in the delivery of reproductive health care to women, especially women of color, suggests a neglect of considering structural characteristics of the women. The women may not have health care insurance to cover the cost of care, even if the opportunities to receive care exist in their environment. Women may lack transportation, the ability to take time off from work (which may also be a structural characteristic, for clinics with more flexible hours may be better able to serve women), or child care in order to follow through with practices recommended in relation to their reproductive health.

The identification of individual structural barriers provides yet another focus for communicating about women's reproductive health in a more woman-centered fashion. If the resources women need relate to the operating hours of a clinic, the availability of transportation, or even child care, the audiences to address to bridge these gaps need to include more than the women. Again, clever entrepreneurs, including home day care providers or day care centers, might be the appropriate target of messages aimed at building partnerships to provide women with child care. Individuals who already run vans to provide transportation to groups in and around particular areas might be solicited to provide transportation for women to receive prenatal care, mammograms, or other screenings promoted to groups of women. In rural areas, pilot programs to assess the outcomes of providing transportation to women have demonstrated the value of using mobile mammography units to deliver screening services to women. More innovations such as these may provide avenues to promote women's reproductive health by continuing to build environmental support for behavior.

The focus on the structural characteristics of an audience, such as women in relation to their reproductive health, harnesses yet another avenue for communicating, at the campaign level as well as in print or visual media. The presence of an adequate number of centers and clinicians, and findings that women have sufficient personal resources to support recommended practices, does not diminish the importance of other discontinuities that may block a woman's action. As suggested throughout this volume, garnering support for women's health behaviors must encompass efforts to address the members of a woman's social network.

Social Influences: Building Social Network
Support for Women's Reproductive Health Behaviors

A third explanation for the gap that occurs between individuals' knowledge and their behavior, social network support, rounds out the meaning of environment. Social network support directly examines the effects of groups and individuals with whom one affiliates on behavior. An examination of this issue acknowledges that behavior belongs to groups rather than individuals.[9] To identify gaps in relation to women's social networks, the following questions should be considered:

1. who *must* support the recommended practice in order for women to act;
2. whose support increases the likelihood that women will act; *and*
3. whose support decreases the likelihood that women will act?

An entire section of this volume is devoted to the overwhelming neglect of social support in communicating about women's reproductive health. One of the broad gaps identified as a constant theme throughout the chapters in this book is the failure to utilize all that we know about communicating social support in order to aid women in their decision making about reproductive health.

The members of a woman's social network are likely to be the beneficiaries of her love, concern, and care, which serve the interests of their own health and well-being. Yet these actions may too seldom be reciprocated. This provides a new arena for campaigners and reporters to use in the design of health messages and media stories. In an effort to promote awareness about the role that partners may play in a woman's reproductive health and well-being, her survival of cancer, and her experience of pregnancy, the inclusion of an appropriate role model in the storyline of a situation comedy or movie provides an entertaining way to reach mass audiences that may not at present have a reason to use such information. Such stories can contribute to the process of building new norms and traditions among women's social network members.

One of the problems associated with enlarging the promotion and use of social support and network members to communicate with women about reproductive health relates to the same reason that such an approach is likely to be so effective. This method does not involve the use of medical technology, although the support of a woman's friend may make following through with a test that requires such use more likely. Social support also does not depend upon drug therapy; in fact, it may reduce the need for medication. The promotion of social support, in other words, appears to have no likely benefactors in the environment. It is difficult to imagine how even a clever entrepreneur could reap financial rewards from promoting understanding about the benefits of social support to women in their decision making about reproductive health. Thus, one of the areas that offers the greatest promise also appears likely to face the most formidable obstacles in adopting a woman-centered sense-making approach to communicating with women about reproductive health.

Having examined the environment in which women reside, and/or in conjunction with these undertakings, formative evaluation activities should carefully consider the women.

LEARNED CHARACTERISTICS OF THE WOMEN: OVERCOMING LESSONS OF THE PAST

An assessment of the learned characteristics that a woman must or should personally possess in order to behave in a prescribed fashion offers a broad arena for identifying discontinuities. Many variables may be thought to facilitate or inhibit behavior. The significant issue is which of these is *critical* to the performance of an act. Identification of these grants the greatest likelihood of an efficient balance between effort expended and return on investment—*both* the audience's *and* the campaigner's. To identify gaps in relation to women's learned characteristics, the following questions should be considered:

1. what learned characteristics *must* be present in order for a woman to behave in the recommended fashion;
2. what learned characteristics facilitate a woman's behavior; *and*
3. what learned characteristics inhibit a woman's behavior?

Many of the overarching gaps identified in this volume in relation to women's reproductive health have to do with what women have learned: that menopause is a deficiency and abortion is life-threatening are but two examples of such lessons. One potential learned characteristic is knowledge itself. Gaps in understanding of *both* facts *and* procedures produce less likelihood of behavior.[10]

Another learned characteristic likely to affect women's decision making in relation to their reproductive health is their perception of self-efficacy, beliefs that they can exert control over their motivation and behavior, as well as their social environment.[11] Extensive evidence from divergent domains supports the claim that self-efficacy strongly influences the attainment and maintenance of preventive health behaviors.[12] When people lack a sense of self-efficacy, they are more likely to fail to use the knowledge and skills they already have in their possession.[13] This is likely to be the case in situations relating to women's confidence in their ability to exercise control in pregnancy and disease prevention.

Behavioral scientists may utilize the theories and research from communication to guide the selection of variables to consider in this regard. In combination with environmental and social network support, a focus on the individual woman and her present and past reproductive health decision making and behavior is vital to understanding her needs in the future.

ENDURING CHARACTERISTICS OF THE WOMEN: WORKING IN CONCERT WITH LESSONS OF THE PAST

One final consideration in the design of formative research undertaken to operationalize a woman-centered sense-making approach to communicating about women's reproductive health is the characteristics of women that may be beyond the reach of influence—such enduring traits as personality, for example, but also an audience's use of language and emotional expression. To identify gaps in relation to women's enduring characteristics, the following questions should be considered:

1. what enduring characteristics *may* facilitate the likelihood that a woman will behave in the recommended fashion; and
2. what enduring characteristics *may* inhibit the likelihood that a woman will behave in the recommended fashion?

Collecting sense-making data has as its primary objective the identification of discontinuities among what may be known to be possible, what is presently in existence, and how individuals reconcile these differences. Sense-makers should look for consistent patterns in discontinuities as a means to understand how women's actual experiences might be broadened. Critical to the success or failure of communicating with women about their reproductive health is the identification of "linguistic discontinuities"—gaps in communication of meaning between campaigners' and the audience's experience, as conveyed through the use of language. An example of vital information about language use that may be gleaned from this analysis includes such findings as the fact that many groups think that reference to "health care providers" has to do with insurance agents rather than doctors and nurses.[14]

Beyond the language and emotional expression used by particular women, the prominence of religion or the importance of altruism in their lives as displayed through volunteer activities, for example, may offer an important insight. Women making decisions about their reproductive health will certainly cast those decisions within the boundaries of their definitions of *self* and personal identity.

The individual characteristics of women, both those that are learned and those that are more enduring, have captured the focus of some storylines on television and in movies. Many of these are reviewed in this volume and afford insights about the ways that media act to sustain a traditional focus in women's health on maternal and fetal health. Different ways to approach the same discussions are considered by the contributors to this volume. Adopting some of their ideas—such as the one advanced in regard to offering a newspaper column as a forum for women to ask questions about pregnancy and prenatal care—within an environment that supports women's abilities to make the best decisions for themselves provides one way to redirect the focus of communicating about women's reproductive health.

Conclusion

Identifying discontinuities as part of a woman-centered sense-making approach to communicating about women's reproductive health provides a strategy to compensate for and, perhaps, even to evolve the political and historical agendas relating to women's reproductive health. Messages that women receive about their reproductive health may contribute to this evolution, but only through the vigilance of women, health care providers, and the media asking for and seeking answers to the questions that women have about their reproductive health.

A sense-making approach constitutes an underutilized framework; for a hard-to-reach audience, it may arguably afford the most valid way to develop a campaign. The goals of this analysis may be summarized as constructing a discontinuity map to identify structural (community and individual), cognitive (perceived social network support, knowledge, outcome expectations, and self efficacy), and linguistic gaps between the ideal and the real world as experienced by an audience. The identification of discontinuities serves three functions.

Enlarge Audience to Bridge
Structural Discontinuities

One purpose for identifying discontinuities is to enrich a campaigner's understanding of the meaning of *audience* in reference to increasing the involvement of a specific group with a particular campaign topic. One reason that campaigners may find themselves back in the mold of treating audience as monolithic rather than pluralistic, however, even in the face of their own best intentions, is failure to forecast at the outset just how much time it takes to conduct formative evaluation, particularly if undertaken from a sense-making approach. As in so many domains, the pressures to satisfy short-term outcomes may often lead to a narrowing of vision that ultimately leads to the failure to attain any of the original goals. We support the admonition to self and agencies to construct formative evaluation plans that resemble rolling stones that gather no moss; a significant function of a sense-making approach to conducting formative research might best be captured by the oxymoron "rigid flexibility."

Design Messages to Address
Cognitive Discontinuities

Yet another purpose for conducting formative research using a sense-making approach is to enhance a campaigner's ability to design messages that an audience wants and perceives itself to be in need of obtaining. Audience, in this regard, must include all of the component parts identified through the process of enlarging the meaning of *audience.*

The failure to link what is learned during the formative research to the actual design of campaigns reduces the likelihood that bridges will be built that make meaningful connections among parts of the larger audience. If attempts are made to bridge the gaps without links to formative research findings, the likelihood that they will have meaning for the lives of women will be less.

Construct Evaluation Instruments
to Accommodate Linguistic Discontinuities

At a pragmatic level, campaigners and policy makers must provide some evidence of the effectiveness of particular programs. Too often, it appears from a review of the methods evaluators use to operationalize their judgments about impact that items for measurement instruments are general and relate only vaguely to the specific behavior being advocated in a particular program. The development and use of instruments to assess audiences must reflect not only their educational level, but the manner and fashion in which they use language.

In sum, the use of a woman-centered "sense-making" approach to identify structural, cognitive, and linguistic discontinuities provides an opportunity to better understand women's reproductive health decision making and behavior. As a result of a sense-making approach, efforts to bridge organizational and legislative discontinuities in support of women's reproductive health decision making and behavior increases. The likelihood of designing more appropriate messages and programs that address structural, cognitive, and linguistic discontinuities will be enhanced. And as a result, there is a greater likelihood that women will receive the health care and information that they want and need.

Notes

1. B. Dervin, "Audience as Listener and Learner, Teacher and Confidante: The Sense-Making Approach," in R. E. Rice & C. K. Atkin (Eds.), *Public Communication Campaigns,* 2nd ed. (Newbury Park, CA: Sage, 1989): 75.

2. Dervin, "Audience as Listener and Learner," pp. 67-86.

3. C. T. Salmon, *Information Campaigns: Balancing Social Values and Social Change* (Newbury Park, CA: Sage, 1989).

4. R. L. Parrott, M. Kahl, & E. Maibach, "Enabling Health: Policy and Administrative Practices at a Crossroads," in E. Maibach & R. Parrott (Eds.), *Designing Health Messages: Approaches From Communication Theory and Public Health Practice* (Newbury Park, CA: Sage, 1995): 270-283.

5. Dervin, "Audience as Listener and Learner," p. 77.

6. R. Hornik, "The Knowledge-Behavior Gap in Public Information Campaigns: A Development Communication View," in C. T. Salmon (Ed.), *Information Campaigns: Balancing Social Values and Social Change* (Newbury Park, CA: Sage, 1989): 133-138. Hornik provides alternative hypotheses to explain the knowledge-behavior gap, findings that mass media information diffused into a social system may actually increase the distance in understanding between those who understood less versus those who understood more before the information diffusion. Hornik's discussion is intended as a way to explain communication campaign outcomes in developing countries. My thesis is that these explanations afford the means to construct

appropriate formative research undertakings in order to identify gaps that need to be bridged in order to build environmental and social support in a health care environment before promoting health behavior.

7. Public Law 102-515, 102nd Congress, "Cancer Registries Amendment Act," *Congressional Record* 138 (1992): 69-139.

8. P.L. 102-515, "Cancer Registries Amendment Act," p. 69.

9. J. G. Bruhn & B. U. Phillips, "Measuring Social Support: A Synthesis of Current Approaches," *Journal of Behavioral Medicine* 7 (1984): 151-169.

10. A. Bandura, "A Social Cognitive Approach to the Exercise of Control Over AIDS Infection," in R. DiClemente (Ed.), *Adolescents and AIDS: A Generation in Jeopardy* (Newbury Park, CA: Sage, 1991).

11. Bandura, "A Social Cognitive Approach."

12. A. Bandura, "Self-Efficacy Mechanism in Physiological Activation and Health-Promoting Behavior," in J. Madden, S. Matthysse, & J. Barchas (Eds.), *Adaptation, Learning, and Affect* (New York: Raven, 1991).

13. Bandura, "Self-Efficacy Mechanism."

14. Ongoing research addressing cancer control among agricultural families in Georgia included the collection of formative research such as that being promoted in this chapter. One of our findings included the fact that farmers and their wives thought that our reference to "health care providers" was a reference to their insurance agents.

Index

About the Contributors

Karen H. Bonnell (Ph.D., University of Kentucky) is Assistant Professor of Communications at the University of Southern Indiana at Evansville, Indiana. A former TV news producer, she now manages the University of Southern Indiana Television Center and teaches broadcast production and management at the university.

Sally A. Caudill is a doctoral candidate in speech communication at the University of Georgia. Her areas of interest include feminist theory, rhetoric, communication education, and multicultural education. Her work in these areas has been presented at several national and regional Speech and Women's Studies conferences. She is currently beginning work on her dissertation, which will focus on rhetoric in multicultural education. She received her M.A. in Speech Communication from the University of South Florida. She has received teaching awards during her tenure at both universities.

Rebecca J. Welch Cline is Associate Professor of Communication Studies in the Department of Communication Processes and Disorders at University of Florida. She received her Ph.D. from The Pennsylvania State University. Her general research interests are interpersonal communication and health communication. Her recent research focuses on interpersonal communication issues and HIV/AIDS, including interpersonal communication for the prevention of HIV infection, interpersonal communication with people with HIV disease, and gender issues associated with communicating about HIV/AIDS. She has published research in the *Journal of Applied Communication Research, Human Communication Research, Communication Monographs, Communication Research,* and the *Communication Yearbook.*

Celeste Michelle Condit is Professor of Speech Communication at the University of Georgia in Athens. She is the author of *Decoding Abortion Rhetoric: The Communication of Social Change* (1990) and coauthor of *Crafting Equality: America's Anglo-African Word* (1993; winner of the Marie Hocmuth Nichols Award). She has served as a Visiting Investigator at the National Institutes of Health in the National Center for Human Genome Research. She has authored several essays on abortion, reproductive technologies, and the discourse of genetics in academic journals, as well as methodological and theoretical essays on the processes of public and technical discourses and social change processes. She has served as chair of the Women's Caucus of the Speech Communication Association and published essays on the meaning of feminism.

Deirdre M. Condit (Ph.D., Rutgers University, 1996) is Assistant Professor of Political Science and Women's Studies at Virginia Commonwealth University. Her research interests include reproductive rights and technology, the social construction of the reproductive body, and theoretical issues concerning the sex/gender distinction in feminist theory. At present, she is working on a manuscript-length piece on the conflict between fetal rights and the political identity of the pregnant woman.

Margaret J. Daniels (M.A., Speech Communication, University of Georgia, 1993) is an instructor at Trident Technical College in Charleston, South Carolina. Her research interests include women and health, and health campaigns.

Lisa A. Flores (Ph.D., University of Georgia, 1994) is Assistant Professor at Arizona State University. She specializes in critical rhetorical studies, feminist criticism, communication and culture, and Chicano/Chicana discourse. She is currently working on a book on Mexican American women in mass media.

C. Jay Frasier (A.B.D., Southern Illinois University at Carbondale) is Assistant Professor at Lane Community College in Eugene, Oregon. His research interests include general semantics, dramatic forms of educational discourse, the use of magic as an educational tool, and interpersonal conflict. His research has appeared in ERIC and *The Looking Glass.*

Theresa D. Frasier (M.A., Southern Illinois University at Carbondale) is Adjunct Professor at Linn-Benton Community College in Lebanon, Oregon. Her research interests include family communication, health communication, and communication satisfaction.

Kathryn J. French (Ph.D., University of Southern California, 1989) is Assistant Professor at Southern Illinois University at Carbondale. Her primary research interests include the study of resistance to persuasion, giving bad news, and health communication. Her research has appeared in *Psychology of Tactical Communication* and *American Communication Administrators Bulletin.*

Tina M. Harris (Ph.D., University of Kentucky, 1995) is Assistant Professor in the Department of Communication at Bowling Green State University. Her areas of interest include intercultural and interpersonal communication.

Mary L. Kahl (Ph.D., Indiana University, 1994) is Assistant Professor in the Department of Communication and Media and a member of the Women's Studies Faculty at the State University of New York at New Paltz. She holds a B.A. in Communication and in English from the University of Michigan, and earned her advanced degrees in speech communication from Indiana University. During her 15-year academic career she has taught at the University of California—Davis, Stonehill College, and Boston College. She has written and published in the areas of political communication, women and communication, health communication, and rhetorical theory. An officer in national and regional communication associations, she also volunteers as a communication consultant and speech writer for local and national political campaigns.

Pamela J. Kalbfleisch (Ph.D., Michigan State University, 1985) is Associate Professor in the Department of Communication and Mass Media at the University of Wyoming in Laramie, Wyoming. Her research focuses on the elements of trust and distrust in interpersonal relationships. She is the editor of *Interpersonal Communication: Evolving Interpersonal Relationships* (1993); coeditor of *Gender, Power and Communication in Human Relationships* with Michael J. Cody (1995); and is the author of a persuasion text, *The Persuasion Handbook* (1989). She is on the board of directors for the IMPACT foundation in New York City, and works with this foundation and several groups in her local community to help foster the development of mentoring relationships. She is especially concerned with helping women and members of disadvantaged groups find mentors and other sources of social support.

Maureen P. Keeley (Ph.D., University of Iowa, 1994) is Assistant Professor in Speech Communication at Southwest Texas State University. She has published research in national communication journals such as *Human Communication Research* on nonverbal communication and issues focusing on relational communication. The NVPS acknowledges and uses this expertise; it also provides a method with which to explore the communication process of second guessing as well as the consequences of the functions of nonverbal behaviors. Future research will continue to examine women, communication, and their relationships in a variety of situations.

Michele Kilgore is a doctoral candidate in the Department of Speech Communication at the University of Georgia, with interests in intercultural communication in health care, critical discourse analysis, and teaching English for medical purposes. She received an M.S. in Applied Linguistics from Georgia State University, was an Apprentice

Teacher in the Harvard Summer School ESL Program, and completed coursework in Teaching English for Specific Purposes at the Institute for Applied Language Studies at the University of Edinburgh. She has published contributions to TESOL's *New Ways in Teaching* series. Prior to graduate study, she spent 10 years working in hospitals in respiratory therapy.

Cynthia P. King is a doctoral candidate in the Department of Speech Communication at the University of Maryland. With a B.A. and M.A. from Auburn University, she has focused her research on the rhetoric of African Americans. Her dissertation is a study of history texts about and written by African Americans in the 19th century.

Kimberly N. Kline (doctoral candidate at the University of Georgia in Athens) is Assistant Professor in the Department of Communication at Purdue University. Her research incorporates rhetorical theory and method to explore the construction of illness and identity (especially in regard to women's health) as well as to discuss the persuasiveness of various health messages and/or campaigns. She received the top student paper award in the Health Communication Division for the 1995 Speech Communication Association convention.

Joan Marie Kraft (Ph.D., Northwestern University, 1989) taught at Wittenberg University for 2 years before receiving a post-doctoral fellowship (funded by the National Institute on Alcohol Abuse and Alcoholism) at the Center for Research on Deviance and Behavioral Health, Institute for Behavioral Research at the University of Georgia. In general, her research investigates links between young women's experiences in the labor market and their premarital sexual behavior. She also analyzes connections between work roles, family roles, and alcohol consumption among women and men. Several papers and presentations based on this research concentrate on whether drinking practices (i.e., frequency of drinking, escapist reasons for drinking, and binge drinking) are associated with work-family conflict. She currently works at A&C Enercom where she conducts research for utility companies.

Joan Lawrence-Bauer is the Interim Executive Director of the Kingston (New York) YWCA. She received her B.A. in Communication from the State University of New York at New Paltz in 1993. She has worked in the field of business administration and communication for more than 20 years, is a member of the Catskill Women's Network, and serves on the Board of Directors of the M-ARK Project and of the Belleayre Conservatory.

Robert Lemieux (M.A., Michigan State University, 1988) is a doctoral candidate in speech communication at the University of Georgia. His research interests in health communication focus on the creation and dissemination of health campaigns—specifically, the use of fear appeals in the message, the emotions the message evokes, and cognitive channels to deliver the message. His other primary research interest is in relational communication, with a focus on the development and maintenance of romantic relationships. Current research is testing the triangular theory of love and exploring the use of routine behaviors as relational maintenance strategies. Aside from his chapter in this book, other research has appeared in *Communication Research*. He is also a past recipient of an Excellence in Teaching Award from the International Communication Association.

Nelya J. McKenzie (Ph.D., University of Florida, 1994) is Assistant Professor in the Department of Communication, Auburn University at Montgomery. Her research interests include gender and communication and intergenerational communication.

Diane Helene Miller (M.A., University of California—Berkeley, 1989) is a doctoral candidate in speech communication at the University of Georgia, where she has also completed a Graduate Certificate in women's studies. She is a recipient of the Berkeley Fellowship, the University of Georgia University-Wide Assistantship, and the AAUW Athenian Award for Outstanding Scholarship. Her research interests include feminist rhetorical theory and criticism, media criticism, lesbian studies, and queer theory. She is currently writing a dissertation that examines recent representations of lesbians and the discursive construction of "lesbianism" in public discourse.

Mary Moster, Ph.D., is Assistant Professor of Psychology at Martin University, Indianapolis. Her overall research interest is in the area of health promotion and disease prevention, focusing especially on low-income, minority, and other underserved populations. Past research (unpublished) was on psychosocial factors influential in mediating the impact of stressful life events. She is currently planning a research project to investigate the availability of health information and evaluating the impact of increased health information on current health practices, especially in low-income or minority populations.

Elizabeth Jean Nelson (Ph.D., University of Iowa) is Associate Professor in the Department of Communication at the University of Minnesota, Duluth, where since 1988 she has taught courses in rhetorical theory, public address, and popular culture. Her research interests include Western mass media and the presentation of woman's body, media and diet messages that target women, the language women use as they talk about their bodies, as well as a host of campaigns (health care and social campaigns) that pertain directly to women. Her published work includes "Living With the Fat of the Land: A Mythic Analysis" in *Feminist Forum;* "Who's Looking Out for the Boys? Public Reaction to 'Take Our Daughters To Work Day' " in *Understanding Language and Gender;* "The Lessons of History" in the *Women's Review of Books;* and "Public Purge, Private Excess: *The Weight* in Western Popular Culture," under revision for publication in *Women and Language*.

Margot L. Nelson, R.N., Ph.D., C.S., is Associate Professor of Nursing at Augustana College, Sioux Falls, South Dakota. Her research has primarily involved the lived experiences of individuals infected with the human immunodeficiency virus and psychoneuroimmune responses in life-threatening health conditions. She has published articles related to advocacy in nursing as well as collaborative nursing education and the lived experience of HIV infection in books and nursing journals, including *Nursing Outlook, Nursing & Health Care,* and *Research in Nursing & Health.*

Susan A. Owen (Ph.D., University of Iowa, 1989) is Associate Professor in the Department of Speech Communication at the University of Puget Sound.

Roxanne Louiselle Parrott, Ph.D., is Associate Professor in the Department of Speech Communication and a Fellow in the Institute of Behavioral Research at the University of Georgia. She also has an adjunct appointment in the Department of Medicine at the Medical College of Georgia. She is coauthor (with Michael Pfau) of *Persuasive Communication Campaigns* and coeditor of *Designing Health Messages.* Her research interests include an examination of how mediated and interpersonal communication interface, affecting individuals' involvement with message content.

Michael Pfau, Ph.D., is Professor in the School of Journalism and Mass Communication at the University of Wisconsin—Madison. His overarching research interest is social influence, particularly campaign influence. He has authored more than 50 articles and book chapters, many dealing with influence strategies in health campaigns, appearing in *Communication Monographs, Communication Research, Human Communication Research,* and elsewhere. He is a past recipient of the SCA Golden Anniversary Monographs Award. He has coauthored four books, the most recent being *Persuasive Communication Campaigns* (with Roxanne Parrott) published in 1993.

Salome Raheim (Ph.D., University of Iowa, 1990) is Assistant Professor in the School of Social Work at the University of Iowa. Her research interests include the discourse of social movements and ideology and their relationship to the empowerment of oppressed social groups. Her work appears in a variety of journals such as *Affilia: Journal of Women and Social Work, Journal of Gay and Lesbian Social Services,* and the *International Journal of Social Work.*

Cathey S. Ross is Assistant Professor in the Communication Department at the University of North Carolina at Greensboro. She received her doctorate in Speech Communication from the University of Georgia. Her main research interest is interpersonal influence. She has investigated influence in health, family, and educational contexts. She is currently working on a project investigating the communication behaviors of adult children and their still active, healthy parents. In addition to her research and teaching, she conducts seminars and workshops on family communication for local groups and organizations.

E.M.I. Sefcovic (M.A., University of Georgia, 1991) is a doctoral candidate in the Department of Speech Communication, University of Georgia, Athens. Her current areas of research interest are rhetorical theory and criticism, qualitative methods, and labor discourse. She is a past winner of and runner-up for the Southern Speech Communication Association's Bostrom Award for competitive student papers. Her work has been published in the *Journal of Communication Inquiry*. Before becoming a member of the academic community, she was a reporter and editor for more than 20 years for Hearst and Cox newspapers. She has also served as community relations director for Glens Falls Hospital, a regional acute-care facility in New York State.

Helen M. Sterk (Ph.D., University of Iowa, 1986) is Associate Professor at Marquette University, in Milwaukee, Wisconsin. She coauthored *After Eden: Facing the Challenge of Gender Reconciliation* (1993), a book analyzing feminist and religious resources for community. With Lynn Turner, she edited *Differences That Make a Difference* (1994), an anthology of essays devoted to discussion of the utility of "difference" as a concept in gender communication research. With Linda A. M. Perry and Lynn Turner, she edited *Constructing and Reconstructing Gender* (1992). In addition, she has authored numerous articles on the interactions among variables such as narrative, gender, religion, and popular culture. She won the Cheris Kramararae dissertation award in 1987 from the Organization for the Study of Communication and Gender. Her current work is a two-book project presenting women's narratives on birthing and a coauthored interpretation of those narratives from the points of view of anthropology, history, English, rhetoric, and midwifery.

Mary Anne Trasciatti is a doctoral candidate in the Department of Speech Communication at the University of Maryland. She received her B.A. from Providence College and her M.A. from Emerson College. Her research interest focuses on women's rhetoric. Her dissertation is a study of the process of Americanization of Italian women immigrants in the early 20th century.

Martha Solomon Watson (Ph.D., University of Texas at Austin) is Professor and Chair in the Department of Speech Communication at the University of Maryland, College Park. A former editor of the *Southern States Communication Journal* and the *Quarterly Journal of Speech,* she has also served as Chair of the Publications Board for the Speech Communication Association. Her research interests include women's rhetoric, social movements, and autobiography. She is the author of critical biographies of Emma Goldman and Anna Howard Shaw (with Wil Linkugel), the editor of *A Voice of Their Own: The Woman Suffrage Press, 1848-1915,* and a forthcoming book on the autobiographies of women activists: *Lives of Their Own: The Rhetorical Dimensions of the Autobiographies of Women Activists*.

Melanie Ayn Williams is a doctoral candidate in the Department of Speech Communication at the University of Georgia. She received her M.A. from the University of North Texas in 1993. Her primary research interests are in the areas of social influence and health campaigns, research methods, interpersonal theory, and women's and Mexican American's health communication. She has presented her scholarship at both national and regional conferences. While at the University of Georgia, she has twice been honored with a competitive university-wide research appointment.